A HISTORY OF COLOMI

CW00544065

In recent decades, the international recognition of Nobel Laureate Gabriel García Márquez has placed Colombian writing on the global literary map. *A History of Colombian Literature* explores the genealogy of Colombian poetry and prose from the colonial period to the present day. Beginning with a comprehensive introduction that charts the development of a national literary tradition, this History includes extensive essays that illuminate the cultural and political intricacies of Colombian literature. Organized thematically, these essays survey the multilayered verse and fiction of such diverse writers as José Eustacio Rivera, Tomás Carrasquilla, Alvaro Mutis, and Darío Jaramillo Agudelo. Written by a host of leading scholars, this History also devotes special attention to the lasting significance of colonialism and multiculturalism in Colombian literature. This book is of pivotal importance to the development of Colombian writing and will serve as an invaluable reference for specialists and students alike.

RAYMOND LESLIE WILLIAMS is Distinguished Professor of Spanish at the University of California, Riverside. His scholarly work has been recognized in Colombia with the Order of San Carlos. His books include *The Twentieth-Century Spanish American Novel, The Modern Latin American Novel,* and *The Colombian Novel, 1844–1987.*

A HISTORY OF COLOMBIAN LITERATURE

RAYMOND LESLIE WILLIAMS

University of California, Riverside

CAMBRIDGE
UNIVERSITY PRESS

Shaftesbury Road, Cambridge CB2 8EA, United Kingdom

One Liberty Plaza, 20th Floor, New York, NY 10006, USA

477 Williamstown Road, Port Melbourne, VIC 3207, Australia

314–321, 3rd Floor, Plot 3, Splendor Forum, Jasola District Centre, New Delhi – 110025, India

103 Penang Road, #05–06/07, Visioncrest Commercial, Singapore 238467

Cambridge University Press is part of Cambridge University Press & Assessment,
a department of the University of Cambridge.

We share the University's mission to contribute to society through the pursuit of
education, learning and research at the highest international levels of excellence.

www.cambridge.org
Information on this title: www.cambridge.org/9781107441453

First published 2016
First paperback edition 2023

A catalogue record for this publication is available from the British Library

Library of Congress Cataloging-in-Publication data
Names: Williams, Raymond, editor.
Title: A history of Colombian literature / Raymond Williams [editor].
Description: Cambridge ; New York : Cambridge University Press, 2016. |
Includes bibliographical references and index.
Identifiers: LCCN 2015039557 | ISBN 9781107081352 (Hardback : alk. paper)
Subjects: lcsh: Colombian literature–History and criticism.
Classification: LCC PQ8161 .H48 2016 | DDC 860.9/9861–dc23 LC record available
at http://lccn.loc.gov/2015039557

ISBN   978-1-107-08135-2   Hardback
ISBN   978-1-107-44145-3   Paperback

Contents

Contributors

JAMES J. ALSTRUM is a professor emeritus at Illinois State University. A former Fulbright scholar in Colombia, he is an authority on Colombian poetry, about which he has numerous publications, including several books.

MARK D. ANDERSON is an associate professor of Latin American Literature at the University of Georgia. He has published eco-critical studies on Latin American fiction and on the topic of the total novel in Latin America. His collaborator Marcela Reales is a doctoral student in Latin American literature at the University of Georgia.

GENE H. BELL-VILLADA is a professor of Latin American literature at Williams College. An internationally recognized authority on Gabriel García Márquez, he has also published books on Borges and other topics, as well as his own fiction.

LUCÍA GARAVITO is a professor of Latin American Literature at Kansas State University. A Colombian national, she has published on Colombian and Latin American theater, as well as gender topics.

VALENTÍN GONZÁLEZ-BOHÓRQUEZ teaches Latin American Literature at Biola University. A Colombian national, he has published on Roberto Bolaño and modern Latin American literature.

JUAN CARLOS GONZÁLEZ ESPITIA is an associate professor of Latin American Literature at the University of North Carolina. A Colombian national, he specializes in nineteenth-century Spanish-American literature, twentieth-century Spanish-American literature, and discourses of crime and sickness in nineteenth-century literary theory.

KEVIN GUERRIERI is the departmental chair and an associate professor at the University of San Diego. A former Fulbright scholar in Colombia, he has published on Colombian literature and modern Latin American fiction.

HÉCTOR HOYOS is an assistant professor of Latin American Literature at Stanford University. A Colombian national, he has published on the contemporary Latin American novel, Colombian literature, visual culture, and critical theory.

DARÍO JARAMILLO AGUDELO is a Colombian writer from Antioquia who currently resides in Bogotá. He has published numerous volumes of poetry and books of fiction, as well as essays on cultural and literary topics.

DIANA DODSON LEE is an assistant professor of Hispanic Studies at Pepperdine University. Her work focuses on ecocriticism and violence in Latin America.

MERCEDES LÓPEZ RODRÍGUEZ is an assistant professor of Colonial Spanish American Literature at the University of South Carolina. A Colombian national, her research focus stems from a long-term interest in the representation of difference and the emergence of new cultural practices amid contexts of conflict in Latin America.

JUAN LUIS MEJÍA ARANGO is a Colombian academic who is currently serving as Chancellor of the Universidad EAFIT in Medellín, Colombia. He has published a book on the Antioquian writer Tomás Carrasquilla, as well as essays on a broad range of Colombian cultural topics.

ANA MARÍA MUTIS holds a PhD in Latin American literature from the University of Virginia. A Colombian national, she has published on eco-criticism and Colombian literature.

RORY O'BRYEN is a university senior lecturer of Latin American literature at the University of Cambridge. He has published on Post-Boom Latin American fiction, as well as nineteenth- and twentieth-century Colombian culture and history. He is one of the editors of the *Journal of Latin American Cultural Studies*.

MICHAEL PALENCIA-ROTH is a professor of Comparative Literature and Spanish at the University of Illinois, Urbana. A Colombian national, he has published on the work of Gabriel García Márquez, Colonial Latin American literature, and Colombian literature.

ELIZABETH M. PETTINAROLI is an assistant professor of Spanish at Rhodes College, where she teaches and researches Colonial Latin American literature, eco-criticism, and Colombian literature. Her work focuses on the early modern Hispanic world in a comparative context.

GINA PONCE DE LEÓN is an associate professor of Latin American Literature at Fresno Pacific University. She has published articles and books on Colombian fiction, postmodernism, and gender issues.

ENRIQUE SALAS-DURAZO is an assistant professor of Latin American literature at Westminister College. He has published on the poetry and fiction of Roberto Bolaño as well as poet-novelists in Colombia and Mexico. His research interrogates the interactions between fiction and poetry.

ELZBIETA SKLODOWSKA holds the title of Randolph Family Professor of Latin American Literature at Washington University in St. Louis. She has published on Latin American fiction, *testimonio,* and nineteenth- and twentieth-century Caribbean narrative, as well as poetics and politics of memory.

CLAIRE TAYLOR is a senior lecturer in Hispanic Studies, Culture, Languages and Area Studies at the University of Liverpool. Her research and publications have been in the areas of women's writing in Latin America, digital culture, and Latina(o) culture.

RAYMOND LESLIE WILLIAMS holds the title of Distinguished Professor of Latin American Literature at the University of California, Riverside. A former Fulbright scholar in Colombia, he has published on Latin American fiction and Colombian literature. His collaborator, Marina Nájera, is an advanced doctoral student at the University of California, Riverside.

Preface

A century before Nobel Laureate Gabriel García Márquez published his landmark novel *Cien años de soledad* (1967, One Hundred Years of Solitude), the first history of Colombian literature, written by José María Vergara y Vergara, appeared in print under the title *Historia de la literatura en Nueva Granada* (1867, History of literature in New Granada). This first history of the literature of "New Granada," a keystone in the nation-building process in Colombia, was mostly about the Colonial literary tradition in the region called New Granada at the time, and not truly about the literature of the new nation per se. In a newly founded nation without a clear sense of exactly what its national culture might be considered to be, Vergara y Vergara's book was as much a proposal for a national literary tradition as it was a literary history.

By the end of the century, during a period identified in Colombia as the Regeneration ("La Regeneración," 1886–1909), an insistence on the key place of national literature and national culture led Colombians to refer to their capital, Bogotá, as the "Athens of South America." The efforts to consolidate the literature of this region into a national "Colombian" literature was highlighted by Daniel Samper Ortega's massive project to anthologize and historicize all Colombian writing in his *Selección Samper Ortega de Literatura Colombiana* (1935–7). These multiple volumes of Colombian literature, consisting mostly of poetry and essays and which included many political speeches, were mostly a collection of writings from the Colonial period. Thus, the actual literature representing the new nation was minimal. The efforts in Colombia to construct a national literature were accompanied in Latin America in general by attempts to write the first histories of Latin American literature, as has been outlined by Roberto González Echevarría and Enrique Pupo-Walker in *The Cambridge History of Latin American Literature*. They point out that the first history of Latin American literature was published in 1893 in the form of an anthology by Marcelino Menéndez y Pelayo.

During the period of Ortega's anthology of national Colombian literature – the first three decades of the twentieth century – several histories of Colombian literature did appear in print. Thus, José Joaquín Ortega Torres published his *Historia de la literatura colombiana* in 1935, and later Antonio Gómez Restrepo came forth with his own authoritative *Historia de la literatura colombiana* in 1945. In the context of the genre of the novel, the most monumental of these histories was Antonio Curcio Altamar's encyclopedic study *Evolución de la novela en Colombia*, first published in 1957. Curcio Altamar was not versed in the skills of the New Criticism in vogue in the 1950s in the United States, nor had he learned how to carry out the French *analyse de texte;* he was not familiar with close reading. Nevertheless, he was a highly informed scholar, and this book was, by far, the most exhaustively researched and complete history of the Colombian novel yet to be seen. Since then, several histories of the Colombian novel have appeared in print, including Sebastián Pineda Buitrago's recent volume.

International reading of Colombian literature and the academic study of it had been focused, for more than a century, almost exclusively on the three canonical novels: Jorge Isaacs's *María* (1867, Maria, A South American Romance), José Eustacio Rivera's *La vorágine* (1924, The Vortex), and García Márquez's *Cien años de soledad*. A considerable amount of scholarly work on these three works has been published by scholars in Colombia, Latin America in general, Europe, and the United States. As Latin American literature became increasingly a subject of academic study after World War II, broader studies on Colombia began to appear in print. Two pioneer foreign scholars during the 1940s and 1950s were Gerald Wade ("An Introduction to the Colombian Novel," 1947) and Kurt Levy (with an early 1950s study offering new light on Tomás Carrasquilla in the prestigious and high-circulation *Publications of the Modern Language Association*). Several articles and a book on the Colombian novel written by Seymour Menton have also been foundational work on the Colombian novel. Since then, scholars such as Donald McGrady, Michael Palencia-Roth, David William Foster, Roberto González Echevarría, Héctor Orjuela, Juan Gustavo Cobo Borda, Pablo Montoya, Malcom Deas, Rafael Gutiérrez Girardot, Juan José Hoyos, Betty Osorio, Karl Kahut, Alvaro Pineda Botero, Huberto Poppel, Fernando Ayala Poveda, Jaime Alejandro Rodríguez, Gerald Martin, Héctor Hoyos, James Alstrum, Raymond Souza, Jonathan Tittler, Luz Mery Giraldo, Isaias Peña, Gene Bell-Villada, and Ramón Illán Baca have contributed significantly to the study of different aspects of Colombian literature. Noteworthy recent books on Colombian literature per se are Héctor H. Orjuela's *Historia crítica de la literatura colombiana: literatura colonial* (three volumes, 1992, Critical History of Colombian Literature), María Mercedes Jaramillo, Angela Inés Robledo, and Flor María Rodríguez Arenas's *?Y las mujeres? Ensayos sobre literatura colombiana* (2001, And the women? Essays on Colombian Literature), and Sebastián Pineda Buitrago's *Breve historia de la narrativa colombiana: Siglos XVI–XX* (2012, Brief History of Colombian Narrative). In terms of more postcolonial approaches to culture and society in Colombia, recent important contributions have been Joana Rappaport's exploration of indigenous Colombian intellectuals, *Intercultural Utopias: Public Intellectuals, Cultural Experimentation, and Ethnic Pluralism in Colombia* (2005), and Lesley Wylie's ground-breaking work *Forgotten Frontier: A Literary Geography of the Putumayo* (2013).

The region covered in this history, identified today as the Republic of Colombia, has undergone several name changes over the centuries. During the Colonial period it was identified as the Nuevo Reino de Granada (thus, "New Granada"), and in the republican period it was called Colombia (including Ecuador and Venezuela, 1819–30), Nueva Granada (1832–57), the Confederación Granadina (1857–63), Estados Unidos de Colombia (1863–86), and República de Colombia (1886 to present). For the sake of simplicity, in this volume we will tend to use "New Granada" for the Colonial period and "Colombia" since 1810. As one contemporary social scientist, Harvey Kline, has affirmed, perhaps more than any other country in Latin America, Colombia has frustrated outsiders who try to understand and explain it. In some ways, he notes, Colombia does not exist except in popular myth, academic reification, and the assemblies of international organizations.

I would like to extend a special thanks to the Fulbright Commission in Colombia, whose grants over the early years of my research on Colombian literature were key to my learning this field and about this nation, as well as my initial publications on the Colombian novel. More recently, the Faculty Senate from the University of California, Riverside, has provided supporting funds for my research in Colombia.

I would also like to thank individuals who, over the years, have contributed directly or indirectly to my understanding of Colombia. The list of individuals who have contributed to my understanding of Colombian literature would be too long to attempt to make here and would lead to inevitable oversights. A short version of this list would include John S. Brushwood (who introduced me to the Colombian novel in 1973),

Germán Vargas, Juan Luis Mejía, Darío Jaramillo, Otto Morales Benitez, Belisario Betancur, Néstor Madrid-Malo, David William Foster, R. H. Moreno-Durán, and Gabriel García Márquez. More recently, Kevin Guerrieri provided valuable insights in the formulation of this book plan. In graduate seminars, several former graduate students (all faculty today) have contributed to my knowledge of the Colombian novel over the years, including Elzbieta Sklodowska, Guillermo García Corales, Gina Ponce de León, Amarilis Hidalgo de Jesús, Sandra Garabano, Mark Anderson, Enrique Salas-Durazo, and Diana Dodson-Lee.

Several graduate student research assistants provided efficient and valuable research for this project, including Diana Dodson-Lee, Judith Cervantes, Juan Pablo Bustos, Stefanie Márquez, and Melissa Barragán. Editorial assistants Marina Nájera and Brigitte Flores provided efficient and always good-willed support for this project, and their work was significant. Last but not least, I thank mentors Chris Kostman, Alfredo Mirandé, and Walt Lamp for their ongoing support, as well as the sage advice that kept me more than healthy enough to keep reading and writing. I have greatly appreciated Ray Ryan's interest, support, and patience.

Introduction

Raymond Leslie Williams

Colombia's literature is one of its most revered national treasures, yet, paradoxically, it is generally less known outside of its national boundaries than are its internationally recognized visual artists, performance artists, soccer players, and even drug traffickers. Since the 1970s, this international ignorance with respect to Colombian literature has gradually changed, primarily because of the enormous international impact of the writing of Gabriel García Márquez. Since the meteoric rise in the international scenario of García Márquez, particularly since his Nobel Prize in Literature in 1982, today international readers have become aware of translations of writers such as Alvaro Mutis, Fernando Vallejo, Jorge Franco, and Laura Restrepo. At the same time, scholars from around the world have become increasingly regular readers of Colombian literature published in the original Spanish.

In the early sixteenth century, when the Spanish conquistador Gonzalo Jiménez de Quesada explored and conquered the region we now call Colombia, he was motivated by a fiction—the legend of El Dorado. Venturing up the Magdalena River with his soldiers, he found neither gold mines nor the fountain of eternal youth but some emeralds, a mountain full of salt, and butterflies. When he returned to Spain, he filled the ears of the Spanish Crown with more fictions and was sent back to the New World to pursue his dream. The experience of Jiménez de Quesada was but an early example of the complex, often confounding interaction between a literary and a more scientific understanding of Colombia over the centuries. Jiménez de Quesada was the quintessential man of letters, for he was the author of several tomes on a variety of political and literary topics. His *Antijovio*, written in approximately 1567 and published centuries later, is the earliest literary or historical text to which the contemporary reader has access.

The formative period of the new nation, from 1810 to 1862, was dominated intellectually by Julio Arboleda (1817–62) and José Eusebio Caro (1817–53). Writers of this period were typically young large landowners and aristocrats, most of whom were either actual participants or sons of those who had fought in the battles of independence. Arboleda and Caro, men of letters who thought of themselves primarily as poets, belonged to the landed gentry. Two of the most noteworthy novelists of the period were Eugenio Díaz and Juan José Nieto. During their lifetimes, however, they were viewed as social and intellectual novices whose work was relatively unimportant as literature, since their novels in particular and the genre in general rendered an insignificant contribution to the ideo-logical enterprises of the upper class political and literary elite. Political essays, for example, had much more immediate impact; Díaz and Nieto today remain relatively unrecognized as novelists.

During the second half of the nineteenth century, José María Vergara y Vergara had a major role in authenticating the novelists into the "national" literature he was promulgating. He admitted new intellectuals into this essentially male and Conservative national literary group – El Mosaico – with the proper class and literary credentials, as in the case of Jorge Isaacs, a young aristocratic. After serving his early literary apprenticeship with El Mosaico, Isaacs returned to the Greater Cauca to write his only novel, María, which appeared in 1867.

The major intellectual figures of the 1886 to 1909 period were Rafael Núñez (1825–94), Miguel Antonio Caro (1843–1909), Rufino José Cuervo (1844–1911), and José Asunción Silva (1865–96). Núñez was president, and Caro was his vice president and later became president. Many Colombian scholars have also considered them to be the "official" poets of the period. Núñez composed the "himno nacional," the present-day national anthem. This song is a text parallel to the constitution of 1886, which, in turn, became the instrument for the political legitimization of the Regeneration. These four leading intellectual figures of the Regneration were poets and scholars of the language. An exception was Silva's one novel of "moder-nista" aesthetic, De sobremesa (1886).

The rise and the fall of the concept of Bogotá as the "Athens of South America" took place from 1910 to 1929, a period of Conservative domin-ation. Following the Regeneration model, and despite such irreverent writers as José María Vargas Vila and Clímaco Soto Borda, literature in Colombia continued to function to a considerable extent in its role as moral ideology. The writer and Conservative president Marco Fidel Suárez was perhaps the most prominent example of the socially beneficial effects of writing, as his essayistic production contributed to his own social acceptance by the elite. Suárez was the last Colombian president to embody the ideal of the capital as the Athens of South America. At the same time, Suárez was the last representative of the nineteenth-century pastoral ideal as nation.

A period of unprecedented peace, never achieved before or after in Colombia, transpired from 1910 to 1929. No conflicts of national importance took place until the roots of La Violencia began to appear in certain rural areas in the 1930s. Signs of modernity were the establishment of the national airline in 1919 and the first radio transmission in 1925. With respect to culture, several regional publishing houses began to publish novels and to distribute them regionally. An important contribution to national culture involved the national newspaper *El Tiempo* initiating a literary supplement in 1923 and *El Espectador* making its debut with a weekly literary supplement in the following year.

The two generations of writers and intellectuals are often placed in this period are the Generación del Centenario and the Generación de los Nuevos. Following the Spanish idea of a national literature developed by successive generations since the Generation of '98 and Colombian intellectuals have assigned to these generations of task of producing an organic national literature.

José Eustacio Rivera was considered the major novelist of the period. In the cultural debates, nationalistic attitudes prevailed and lengthy debates on the existence of a national cultural tradition, such as music, were carried out in the 1920s. Emilio Murillo, Pedro Morales Pino, Guillermo Quevedo, and Luis A. Calvo participated in the debates; Osorio and Rafael Burgos founded a national theater, and in 1927 a national film company was established. A lacuna for a "national culture" was the novel. Rivera's *La vorágine* was the timely answer to this lacuna, and the nationalistic positive reaction to it has often eliminated any question in Colombia about its authentic value.

Tomás Carrasquilla proclaimed a national literary independence in 1906, calling for what he considered a "modern," national literature. Despite the allusions to modernity and newness, Carrasquilla's literary practice itself, was, paradoxically, quite traditional – basically an ideal of nineteenth-century rural Antioquian values and its oral and popular culture. His novel *Grandeza* (1910) concerns Medellín's turn-of-the-century new rich and relates the eventual ruin of the female protagonist who negates the elitist aestheticism of the Highland writers and intellectuals. Carrasquilla states in his preface that *Grandeza* is a book of few aesthetic concerns – only some notes on his milieu.

A series of Liberal governments promoted modernization from 1930 to 1946, with progressive social and economic reform being particularly dramatic under Alfonso López Pumarejo's government. The most widely recognized national literature, however, continued to be the elitist poetry. The novel, often written by Liberals, functioned as a relatively minor genre, for Colombian literature was viewed primarily as a generational succession of poets. After the national frenzy generated by *La vorágine*, some writers attempted to imitate it; it was a novel that lauded the sensitive poet figure.

By following literary history chronologically as it is frequently projected in Colombia, the reader of Colombian letters can conclude that the literature of this period was continued by the generation of Piedra y Cielo and soon thereafter by the generation of Cántico. The poet Jorge Rojas founded the Piedra y Cielo group in 1939 by publishing an ongoing collection of poetry using this name. The poets Rojas, Eduardo Carranza, Arturo Camacho Ramírez, Carlos Martín, Tomás Vargas Osorio, and Gerardo Valencia were the main poets of this generation of writers, who espoused inspiration from the poetry the Spaniards Juan Ramón Jiménez, Rafael Alberti, and Gerardo Diego. The Cántico group (an homage to Spanish poet Jorge Guillén) was established in 1944 by the Colombian poet Jaime Ibáñez. Polemics around the Piedra y Cielo poets, such as the debate fomented by Juan Lozano y Lozano in 1940, contributed to the group's authenticity. In the big picture of national culture, they were a relatively small group of poets based in Bogotá.

Along with these poets, a group of scholars and critics, mostly employing very conservative criteria, came forth during this period with a body of work, most of which promoted the idea of a national literary tradition in a country historically fragmented by region. This series of national literary histories included José Joaquín Torres's *Historia de la literature colombiana* (1935), Antonio Gómez Restrepo's *Historia de la literatura colombiana* (1938–45), Javier Arango Ferrer's *La literatura colombiana* (1940), Baldomero Sanín Cano's *Letras colombianas* (1944), Rafael Maya's *Consideraciones críticas sobre la literatura colombiana* (1944), and Gustavo Otero Núñez's *Historia de la literatura colombiana* (1945). The most informational of these books of traditional and essentially conservative literary history was Antionio Gómez Restrepo's history of Colombian literature.

Given the traditional and conservative overtones of Guillermo Valencia's poetry, which was still much lauded in the 1940s and 1950s, the strong presence of several generations of poets, and the central place of the novel *La vorágine*, the Colombian novel did not play a major role in the cultural scenario. Colombia was not the kind of setting that promoted the kind of modern novel that was arising throughout most of Latin America as Jorge Luis Borges, Miguel Angel Asturias, Alejo Carpentier, and a host of others were actively involved in creating a new, modern fiction closely aligned to the European avant-gardes and Anglo-American Modernism. Colombia would not host the modern novel until the rise of Gabriel García Márquez in the 1950 and the publication of *La hojarasca* (1955, *Leafstorm*), followed by the fiction of Alvaro Cepeda Samudio and Héctor Rojas Herazo.

Three decades before being awarded the Nobel Prize for Literature, García Márquez claimed in 1960 that Colombian literature was a fraud to the nation. This was both a political statement and aesthetic judgment about an elite literary establishment that had supported its mediocre poets – such as Guillermo Valencia – as canonical Colombian writers. This was also an attack against a weak corpus of critical work by scholars and journalistic critics who were unwilling or unable to recognize legitimate literary value. For García Márquez, the Colombian novel had reached a point of nothingness and the supposedly great poetic voices were mediocre.

In this volume, we review and discuss Literature and society in Colombia in essays that have been organized into three parts. In Part I, "Colombian literature, culture, and society" we provide an overview of Colombian literature over the centuries, from the Colonial period into the twenty-first century. The first three chapters deal primarily with the complexities of the Colonial period. In the first of these chapters, Michael Palencia-Roth discusses the diversity of literatures of Colonial period, focusing on Spanish-language authors primarily, but also taking into account "colonial discourse." He makes the case that the Colonial period had much to offer in terms of intellectual history. In Chapter 2, "Cosmography, ethnography, and the literary imagination of the New Kingdom of Granada," Elizabeth Pettinaroli interrogates issues related to the 1538 publication of Alonso de Santa Cruz's *Epítome de las conquistas del Nuevo Reino de Granada*. James Alstrum begins in the Colonial period and the epic poetry of Juan de Castellanos in "Colombian poetry from the Colonial period to *Modernismo* (1500–1920) in Chapter 3. Chapter 4 consists of Kevin Guerrieri's presentation of more than a century of the Colombian novel in "The Colombian novel: 1844–1970." Guerrieri's approach, however, is less a chronological overview than a reflection on the literary historiography of the novel in relation to the novel during this long century. He identifies and discusses four "tensions" or "vectors" for his discussion. In Chapter 5, James Alstrum reviews the major and minor movements in modern Colombian poetry since 1920. Chapter 6 is an overview of the Colombian novel of the late twentieth century by Juan Pablo Bustos and Raymond L. Williams. We cover from the novel of "La Violencia" of the 1970s to the new urban violence of the 1980s and 1990s. In "Twenty-first century fiction," Claire Taylor and I review recent trends in twenty-first-century fiction in Chapter 7, from the new urban violence and the "sicaresque" to fiction written using recent digital technology. In Chapter 8, Lucía Garavito addresses issues related to transgenerational violence and the sociopolitical body in theater in her contribution "Colombian theater: staging the sociopolitical body." In the closing chapter of Part I, Chapter 9, Héctor Hoyos provides a thorough and insightful overview of the Colombian essay from the Colonial period to the twenty-first century, thus providing much of the intellectual background to many of the previous essays of this first part of the volume.

In Part II, "Colombian culture and society in regional contexts," we recognize that Colombia was really a grouping of relatively autonomous regions during the first century of its existence as a nation of sorts. Thus, we provide a closer look at some specific regional scenarios in Colombia, with no intention of exhaustive completeness with respect to the regions. In this second part, we are more interested in depth than breadth, with more in-depth consideration of society and culture per se. In Chapter 10, "Literature, culture, and society of the Magdalena River," Rory O'Bryen considers a broad range of cultural and socioeconomic issues related to the economic consequences of capitalistic enterprise in the Caribbean coastal region of the Magdalena River. Juan Carlos González Espitia's "The Highland region as seen by an outsider from the inside and an insider from the outside" in Chapter 11 offers an analysis of how foreigners to Colombian society viewed the Highland region, as well as how Colombians living abroad viewed Colombia from afar. Thus, much of this discussion deals with how the German scientist and explorer Alexander Von Humboldt viewed the Highland region compared to how the iconoclastic Colombian José María Vargas Vila viewed it from abroad. In Chapter 12, Mercedes López Rodríguez analyzes racialized discourse in the Andean highland region of Colombia. Studying a variety of nineteenth-century texts, she reveals how lettered elites defined and limited "whiteness" in literature. She includes such canonical texts in Colombia as *María* and *Manuela*. Chapter 13 is an analysis of society and culture in Antioquia, written by a lifetime intellectual and resident of Antioquia, Juan Luis Mejía. In Chapter 14, to conclude Part II, González-Bohórquez and Dodson Lee provide an overview of regions that have been historically marginalized by mainline Colombian culture. In regions such as La Guajira, indigenous peoples were recognized for the first time in the Colombian constitution of 1991 as true citizens of Colombia. This constitution recognized Colombia as a multiethnic nation. Since then, an increasing number of indigenous writers have begun publishing in their indigenous languages and in Spanish. Writers in the Caribbean islands of San Andrés, known as *raizales*, have also become increasingly active in the past two decades. In addition, some writers in Colombia who are recognized writers in Spanish have begun recounting the traditional stories of San Andrés.

In Part III, "Beyond the boundaries," we consider Colombian culture and literature from a wide variety of perspectives not offered in Parts I and II. In our consideration of García Márquez (in Chapter 15), we did not consider it necessary, at this point in the second decade of the twenty-first century, to construct yet another overview of García Márquez's fiction in itself. Our alternative approach is Gene H. Bell-Villada's discussion of the figure of García Márquez as a public intellectual. Bell-Villada provides an historical perspective on the figure of the public intellectual in the West, introduces some of the major public intellectuals in Latin America, and then provides informed insight into the role García Márquez had as a public intellectual until his untimely death in 2014. Claire Taylor's Chapter 16 "Women writers in Colombia" offers an in-depth perspective on exclusively women writers in Colombia, from the nation's independence until well into the twenty-first century. She includes *crónicas* of the nineteenth century and journalism in the twenty-first century, as well as the traditional short story and the novel. In Chapter 17, Gina Ponce de León discusses queer narrative in contemporary Colombia. She goes back to the renowned early twentieth-century poet Barba Jacob and covers up to the twenty-first century with writers such as Fernando Vallejo and Jaime Manrique, particularly in the context of their queer topics. Chapter 18 consists of Mark Anderson and Marcela Reales's "Extracting nature: toward an ecology of Colombian narrative," a detailed proposal for rereading nature in Colombian fiction. In Chapter 19, Ana María Mutis and Elizabeth Pettinaroli, "Visions of nature: Colombian literature and environment from the Colonial period to the nineteenth century," the two authors analyze visions of nature in major texts written by Colombian writers of the Colonial period and the nineteenth century. Enrique Salas Durazo's "The intersections between poetry and fiction in two Colombian Writers of the Twentieth Century: Alvaro Mutis and Darío Jaramillo Agudelo" (Chapter 20), is the author's exploration the subtle ways in which the respective authors' poetry informs their fiction, and vice versa.

In the "Afterwords," we offer two chapters of reflection on the entirety of Colombian literature, one reflection by a Colombian writer, another by a scholar of Latin American literature who generally works outside the borders of Colombia. In Chapter 21, a writer and reader of Colombia literature, Darío Jaramillo Agudelo, writes "Colombian literature: national treasure or fraud?" He offers an in-depth overview of how Colombian and foreign critics have viewed and judged Colombian literature since the early nineteenth century. He delves into how foreign critics, such as the Argentine Miguel Cané, praised Colombian literature to such a degree in the late nineteenth century that it became a widely accepted assumption, in Colombia, that Colombian literature was widely recognized in the international scenario as a literary leader. It is not until García Márquez's oft-cited essay in 1960, "La literatura colombiana: un fraude a la nación," (Colombian literature: a fraud to the nation) that the virtuosity of Colombian letters had ever been seriously placed into doubt. Jaramillo Agudelo's chapter thoroughly rethinks how Colombian literature has been perceived and evaluated before and after this seminal 1960 essay by the Nobel Laureate. In Chapter 22, Elzbieta Sklodowska, offer some well-informed and thorough final reflections on the state of culture, literature, and criticism in Colombia. She reviews the study of Colombian literature and culture in the context of recent developments in postcolonial studies, signaling the important recent contributions of scholars such as Joana Rappaport and Lesley Wylie.

BIBLIOGRAPHY

Brushwood, John S. *The Spanish American Novel: A Twentieth-Century Survey.* Austin: University of Texas Press, 1975.
Foster, David William. *Gay and Lesbian Themes in Latin American Writing.* Austin: University of Texas Press, 1991.
    Sexual Textualities: Essays on Queering Latin American Writing. Austin: University of Texas Press, 1997.
Gómez Ocampo, Gilberto. *Entre "María" y "La vorágine": la literatura colombiana finisecular (1886–1903).* Bogotá: Fondo Cultural Cafetero, 1988.
González Echevarría, *Roberto and Enrique Pupo-Walker. The Cambridge History of Latin American Literature.* 3 vols. Cambridge: University of Cambridge Press, 1996
Kline, Harvey. *Colombia: A Portrait of Unity and Diversity.* Boulder: Westview Press, 1983.

Levy, Kurt. *Tomas Carrasquilla*. Medellín: Institución de Integración Integral, 1985.

McGrady, Donald. *María*. Boston: G. K. Hall, 1972.

McGreevey, William Paul. *An Economic History of Colombia*. Cambridge: Cambridge University Press, 1971.

Menton, Seymour. *La novela colombiana: planetas y satélites*. Bogotá: Plaza y Janés, 1977.

Rappaport, Joana. *Intercultural Utopias: Public Intellectuals, Cultural Experimentation and Ethnic Pluralism in Colombia*. Durham: Duke University Press, 2005.

Wade, Gerald. "An Introduction to the Colombian Novel," *Hispania* 30, No. 4 (November 1947): 467–83.

Wylie, Lesley. *Forgotten Frontier: A Literary Geography of the Putumayo*. Liverpool: Liverpool University Press, 2013.

PART I

Literature and society in Colombia

CHAPTER I

Colonial realities and colonial literature in "Colombia"

Michael Palencia-Roth

Introduction

"Colombia" did not exist as a country until the nineteenth century. Therefore, the field "Colonial Literature of Colombia" is a designation for the convenience of those who wish to construct a nation-centric literary history. "The New Kingdom of Granada" (*El Nuevo Reino de Granada*), so named by Gonzalo Jiménez de Quesada to honor Granada, where he had lived before going to the New World (Ruíz Rivera xxi; Ramos 306–7), was an administrative region created in the sixteenth century larger than present-day Colombia. In 1717 the Crown established the "Vice-royalty of New Granada" (*El Virreino de Nueva Granada*), which included modern Colombia, Ecuador, Panama, and Venezuela, as well as parts of the Guyanas, Brazil, Peru, Costa Rica, and Nicaragua. Santa Fe de Bogotá was its capital. Around the middle of the eighteenth century, Nueva Granada began a fundamental transformation that ended with the declaration of independence on July 20, 1810, or in 1819, when the Vice-royalty of New Granada was dissolved. "La Gran Colombia" succeeded the vice-royalty and was at first roughly contiguous with it. However, Simón Bolívar's dream of an enduring Gran Colombia, with a centralized administration, failed by 1831. Its territories were lopped off bit by bit until the last one, Panama, seceded in 1903, "encouraged" by the United States.

An argument could be made for including in the present essay the major texts, whatever their genres, produced between 1492 and 1819 in the New Kingdom of Granada and the Vice-royalty of New Granada because those regions were a single administrative colonial domain.[1] However, this essay is limited to Spanish-language authors and literary texts – and occasionally to the more inclusively designated "colonial discourse" – produced during the colonial era up to the early eighteenth century in the region demarcated by the boundary lines of present-day Colombia.

Marcelino Menéndez y Pelayo (Spain, 1856–1912) is generally credited with establishing the literary history of Spanish America as a "field," with his *Historia de la poesía hispano-americana*. Three scholars dominate the field of Colombian literary history and are considered pioneering and indispensable. José María Vergara y Vergara (d. 1872) wrote *Historia de la literatura en Nueva Granada*, which has been available in several editions since its first publication in 1867. Antonio Gómez Restrepo (d. 1946) published *Historia de la literatura colombiana* in 1938 and 1945. In the 1980s and continuing well into the twenty-first century, Héctor H. Orjuela has published (as author and as editor) a series of volumes dealing with colonial literature and culture, most of them under the general title *Historia crítica de la literatura colombiana*. Some volumes deal with poetry, others with fiction, theater, the *crónica*, and indigenous literature. He has also published anthologies of the same. Besides the work of single authors or editors, important collections of individual essays are under the sponsorship of the Ministry of Culture or a university (see, for example, essays by Cristina, Arciniegas, Moreno-Durán, and Vélez de Piedrahita).

Until the middle and later twentieth century, relatively few creative writers seem to have had an interest in the colonial period in Colombia.[2] Then postcolonial studies became fashionable, along with the history of both colonization and decolonization. A number of nations, from areas as disparate as the Caribbean, Africa, South Asia, and East Asia, acquired their independence. Quincentenary celebrations focused attention on the conquest and its aftermath.[3] Throughout Latin America, writers like Alejo Carpentier (*El arpa y la sombra*), Augusto Roa Bastos (*La vigilia del Almirante*), Carlos Fuentes (*El naranjo; Terra Nostra*), Miguel Otero Silva (*Lope de Aguirre*), Abel Posse (*Los perros del paraíso*), and Laura Esquivel (*Malinche*), among many others, treated colonial subjects. In Colombia itself, Gabriel García Márquez, in works like *El otoño del patriarca, El amor y otros demonios*, and his Nobel Prize acceptance speech, reminded the world of the colonial period as he creatively reconsidered the sources of Colombian and Latin American identity. So did Colombian writers who came before him, like Augusto Morales Pino (*En el tiempo del ruido*); those who were his contemporaries, like Manuel Zapata Olivella (*Changó el gran putas*) and Álvaro Mutis ("El último rostro"); and those who followed him, like Germán Espinosa (*Los cortejos del diablo; La tejedora de coronas*), William Ospina (*El país de la canela; Ursúa; Las auroras de sangre*), Fernando Cruz Kronfly (*La ceniza del libertador*), Próspero Morales Pradilla (*Los pecados de Inés de Hinojosa*), Roberto Burgos Cantor (*La ceiba de la memoria*), Álvaro Pineda Botero (*El esposado:*

Memorial de la Inquisición), and many others. Major Colombian men of letters like Germán Arciniegas wrote extensively on the colonial period in works like *Los comuneros, Jiménez de Quesada, Los alemanes en la conquista de América,* and *América en Europa.*

"Siempre la lengua fue compañera del imperio," Antonio de Nebrija famously wrote in the prologue to his Spanish grammar in 1492, addressing Queen Isabella. The first texts in the New World are not strictly "literary." They are "companions of empire": reports, petitions, laws, letters, commentaries, observations, and official instructions. These texts are official and bureaucratic communiqués designed to consolidate the territories of discovery and conquest and then to transform them into a peaceful and profitable colony reflecting the cultural and religious values of Spain. While the history of the colonial literature of "Colombia" does not include these texts, it must consider some nearby genres that are not always thought of as "literature," like the *crónica* and the autobiography.

An additional issue has complicated the study of the literature of Nueva Granada. In establishing the field of colonial literature in "Colombia," some of the most respected scholars have been determined, even obsessed, to establish "firsts." Who was the first "author" of "Colombian" literature? To be designated "the first one," did the author have to be born in "Colombia" or could he have been born in Spain and have lived in "Colombia" for many years? Which was the first work written on "Colombian" soil? If written in "Colombia," is it still "Colombian" if it treats a European subject like medieval chivalry? Does a work about "Colombia" but written in Spain count as "Colombian"? Which was the first Native American work, and could it be said to precede the arrival of the Spaniards, even if it was not written down and published until centuries later? How does one assess Colombia's oral tradition in relation to its "literary" history? Many of the indigenous languages, though they were studied and taught for a while by priests and friars, disappeared. Few, if any, written transcriptions survived. In this respect, the native American legacy in Colombia differed from that of the Aztec, the Mayan, and the Incan cultures (Gómez Restrepo 11).[4] Which was the first poem, the first drama, the first prose work, and the first novel? Literary historians of Colombia have not only wrestled with these questions. They have sometimes in effect also altered texts and thus revised literary history to champion this or that author or work.

During the first half century after Columbus's voyages, little in the way of literature was produced in "Colombia." There was too much hardship and uncertainty everywhere, too much impermanence, even as conquest and colonization progressed successfully. Germán Arciniegas highlights the "impermanence" as he describes the foundation and fortunes of the first modern city on the continent and first city in present-day Colombia, Santa María la Antigua del Darién. Founded in 1510, the city saw the first cathedral constructed on the continent, as well as the first two-story house. In this city, says Arciniegas, Gonzalo Fernández de Oviedo wrote the first novel in Spanish America, *Claribalte*, a chivalric romance published in Spain in 1519.[5] Martín Fernández de Enciso passed through Santa María la Antigua del Darién; on his return to Spain he wrote the first geography text of the New World, the *Suma de geographia*, in 1519. The city figures in the work of Oviedo, Gómara, and Las Casas. But nothing of it remains (Arciniegas 34). Destroyed by Indians in 1524, Santa María la Antigua del Darién has been wiped out without a trace, devoured by the jungle.

The literary history of the colonial period in "Colombia" is not a diachronic history of authors in dialogue with one another. Most authors wrote in isolation, had no "influence," and belonged to no "school" or "literary movement." Most authors looked to Spain or other parts of Latin America for literary stimulation rather than to Nueva Granada itself. Literary censorship was pervasive, though not as pervasive as was once thought (Leonard 75; Cristina 514–16). Authors could not publish their work in Nueva Granada, for no printing press existed until well into the eighteenth century.[6] Yet colonial authors shared certain broad commonalities of experience. The Catholic Church and the Spanish bureaucracy controlled everything. This dual reality is what most writers responded to either as lay persons or as members of one or another order of the Catholic Church. The Church itself came to dominate all aspects of colonial life, whether for individuals, for the family, or for society at large. From about the middle of the sixteenth century, no colonial author can be read apart from his or her relationship to the Church as an institution and to Catholicism as a worldview. And no one escaped the sometimes long reach of the bureaucracy, either in Nueva Granada or in Spain. Consequently, colonial literature cannot be understood or appreciated apart from the lives – the difficult, contentious, nomadic, controversial, adventurous, and sometimes dangerous lives – of the authors themselves.

Gonzalo Jiménez de Quesada

It was primarily the Spanish bureaucracy, rather than the Church, that dominated the life of Gonzalo Jiménez de Quesada (1509–79). In 1536, Quesada traveled from Santa Marta up the Magdalena River and, eventually, defeated the Indian tribes on the high plateau which became the site of Santa Fe de Bogotá, capital of El Nuevo Reino de Granada and of today's Colombia. At about the same time, the conquistador Sebastián de Belalcázar, coming north from today's Ecuador, conquered regions that became the sites of cities like Pasto, Popayán, and Cali. Nicolás de Federman came south to the interior from Cabo de la Vela and Venezuela. Though Quesada had arrived first at the high plateau, the other two conquistadors laid claim to primacy concerning El Nuevo Reino de Granada. Not being able to come to an agreement, the trio traveled together to Spain to argue their cases. After prolonged litigation, Quesada eventually won that particular argument. But his legal victories turned out to be incomplete and the source of bitterness in later life. Returning to Santa Fe de Bogotá in 1551, he remained restless and drawn to further adventures; he convinced creditors to fund an expedition in search of El Dorado, which he thought to be in the "llanos orientales" of today's Colombia. After that expedition failed, his creditors embargoed his possessions, despite the fierce legal defense he mounted. Even in retirement, sick and dying, he continued to litigate. During these years he wrote *Relación de la conquista del Nuevo Reino de Granada, Ratos de Suesca*, and *Compendio historial de las conquistas del Nuevo Reino*. All of these works, and others besides, have been lost.

Colombian literature is born, says Antonio Gómez Restrepo, with the discovery of the Nuevo Reino de Granada, and the first name that exalts it is that of the discoverer and founder of Santa Fe de Bogotá, Gonzalo Jiménez de Quesada.[7] Moreover, Gómez Restrepo continues, Colombia was fortunate to have been conquered not by an ignorant and brutal adventurer but by a cultured man of letters (Gómez Restrepo 15).[8] Quesada belongs alongside Hernán Cortés and Francisco Pizarro, and the fact that he is not generally mentioned with them is due only to the lesser importance of Nueva Granada to the Crown, in comparison to Mexico or Peru (Gómez Restrepo 15). Gómez Restrepo is not the only one to consider Quesada the first "author" of Colombian literature, as skilled with the pen as he was with the sword. His opinion is shared by José María Vergara y Vergara (54), Marcelino Menéndez y Pelayo (vol. 2: 17), José J. Ortega (6–7), Gustavo Otero Muñoz (79), and María Teresa Cristina (498), among others. Ortega (7) and Otero Muñoz (25–6) cite Juan de Castellanos, who in chapter 13 of the fourth part of his *Elegías de varones ilustres* mentions the debates he had with Quesada about the relative virtues of Spanish versus Italianate versification. Quesada, says Castellanos, is not ignorant in matters of poetic taste and practice ("de quien puedo decir no ser ayuno/del poético gusto y ejercicio"). But where are the poetic works? Juan Friede does not include a single one among the writings of Quesada in the documents volume of his two-volume biography of Quesada. Quesada's two brief surviving *crónicas* are printed elsewhere and rarely studied; they will be briefly characterized here in the section on the *crónica*. It is as if all we really knew of Homer as an author were the comments and extracts found in Plato and Aristotle. The lack of authenticated creative work by Quesada has been too tempting for some. In 1919, the *Revista del Colegio Mayor de Nuestra Señora del Rosario* published a hitherto "unknown" work, supposedly written in 1538 by Antón de Lezcámez, chaplain for the troops following Jiménez de Quesada as he traveled from Santa Marta toward what would become Santa Fe de Bogotá. The work is entitled *Romance de Ximénez de Quesada*. From the moment of its publication, its authenticity has been questioned. It has been both praised as genuine and condemned as a fraud (see Pacheco Quintero, vol. 1: xxii–xxiv) In sum, until incontrovertible evidence proves otherwise, Jiménez de Quesada can only be "reputed" to be Colombia's first "creative author."

Juan de Castellanos

In 1562, Juan de Castellanos arrived in the city of Tunja, located to the northeast of Bogotá in the "Cordillera Oriental" at an altitude of 9,250 feet. The city had been founded less than twenty-five years earlier.[9] By the time he died in 1607, Tunja had become the cultural center of Nueva Granada, superior to Santa Fe de Bogotá (Cristina 499). Today Tunja is known as a university town and tourist attraction famous for its convents and its colonial architecture. Founded as a model of the "humanist city" transposed from Spain, in which the classical world of Greece and Rome would achieve a rebirth through the Catholic Church, Tunja was twice designated the capital city of Nueva Granada (Morales Folgera 21–2). It came to be known as "New Athens" (*La Nueva Atenas*) and was celebrated as such by Castellanos. A number of the major figures of the colonial literature of Nueva Granada lived in Tunja at widely separated intervals: Juan de Castellanos, Juan Rodríguez Freyle, Hernando Domínguez Camargo, and "La Madre Castillo" (Francisca Josefa de Castillo y Guevara), as well as more minor writers like Alberto Pedrero, Pedro Verdugo, Sebastián García, Gaspar de Villarroel y Coruña, Jerónimo Gálvez, Francisco Soler, Diego de Buitrago, and Alonso de Carvajal.[10] Not far from Tunja, the desert of "La Candelaria" was the setting for what has been called the first Spanish-American novel set in the New World, *El desierto prodigioso y prodigio del desierto* by Pedro Solís y Valenzuela.[11] Two cities – Tunja and Santa Fe de Bogotá – are responsible for virtually all the literary texts of Nueva Granada that are studied today.

Born in Spain in 1522, Juan de Castellanos came to the New World as a young man in search of adventure. He tried his hand at soldiering, mining, business, even fishing for pearls. Eventually tiring of this nomadic life, he took holy orders in 1554 or 1555, either in Cartagena or in Santafé de Bogotá. In 1562, the probable year of his arrival in Tunja, he was subjected to an inquisitorial inquiry, from which he emerged "absolved." In 1568, after a vetting process that took four years, he received a generous benefice from the Church that, in return for some unspecified pastoral duties, enabled him to lead a comfortable life. He died a wealthy man (Alvar xi–xiii). It is not known exactly when he began to write his magnum opus, the *Elegías de varones ilustres de Indias*, but we know that he first wrote it, or much of it, in prose. Later he turned the prose into verse. In time he became the center of the first literary circle in Nueva Granada.[12] His was therefore not a hermetic life in a barely literate frontier village high in the Andes Mountains. The prefaces to each of the four books of the *Elegías* contain multiple *laudatios*, or poems of praise, in both Latin and Spanish, authored by members of his literary circle.

Inspired by Ercilla's *La araucana*, Castellanos wrote the longest poem in the Spanish language, at more than 113,000 verses. Only the first of its four parts was published during his lifetime. Assessments of the *Elegías* have varied widely. Marcelino Menéndez y Pelayo, in his influential *Historia de la poesía hispano-americana*, fulminated that the most unfortunate aspect of the poem is that it is written in verse (Menéndez y Pelayo, vol. 2: 16; cited by Alvar 3).[13] Others have been more generous. William Ospina was so taken by the *Elegías* that he wrote a large and enthusiastic study of it (*Las auroras de sangre*, 1999) that brings Castellanos and his times to life. Even the genre of the *Elegías* has been debated. Is it an "epic," an "elegy," or just a very long and metrically varied "poem"?[14] Castellanos conceived of his work first of all as "history," as a reliable – and elegiac – record of what happened in the New World and in Nueva Granada. He wanted to disinter from the tomb of oblivion (*a sacar del sepulcro del olvido*) all those who deserve fame, the *varones ilustres* of the title. Moreover, since so much of what he has to relate is sad, he promises to tell the truth without embellishment; he will refuse to invent stories or create fictions.[15] If his polished verses should fall a bit short, he writes also in the first canto, they will be uplifted by the material itself, which is grand. For Manuel

Alvar, the enduring interest of the *Elegías* lies in how it documents the evolution of the Spanish language as it came in contact with American realities: it is a treasure trove of terminology, of the names for plants, places, animals, and things. Castellanos is no Homer, to be sure, but Alvar's statement is reminiscent of those classicists for whom the *Iliad* seems to be primarily a linguistic archeological dig.

Whatever one may think of the literary quality of Castellanos's epic, one cannot deny the extraordinary persistence that moved him to labor by candlelight for so long ("en cuya narración he consumido/Noches en cuantidad y alguna vela)."[16] The "elegy" of the title is the organizing principle behind the work. After the first elegy on "Columbus and the Discovery" of the New World, he entitled each of the next several elegies "On the death of . . ." They are, in sequence, Rodrigo de Arana, Francisco Bobadilla, Cristóbal Colón, Diego Colón, Juan Ponce de León, Diego Velásquez de Cuéllar, Francisco de Garay, and Diego de Ordás. The tenth elegy treats the conquest of the island of Trinidad. The eleventh and twelfth return to "On the death of . . ."; the thirteenth praises (Castellanos uses the term "elogio") the island of Cubagua; the fourteenth praises the island of Margarita. Having lived on both islands, Castellanos nostalgically evokes them through language taken from the pastoral tradition.

The second part of *Elegías* moves to events in Venezuela and Santa Marta. The third gives a history of Cartagena and Popayán. The fourth, on the Nuevo Reino de Granada, narrates the internecine wars among the Muisca Indians, the expedition of Gonzalo Jiménez de Quesada up the Magdalena River, the founding of Santa Fe de Bogotá, and events toward the end of the sixteenth century. At the beginning of the fourth part, he states that he himself has finally found refuge in Tunja where, thanks to the benefice he has received from the Church, he has lived for many years and where he has been able to devote himself to describing events in the history of Nueva Granada. He declares that he personally witnessed many of these events, or had them described to him by participants. In addition, he writes, many men had begged him to write of their deeds and what they themselves had seen and heard.

Curcio Altamar insists that, because of the "complete absence" of the novel as a genre in Nueva Granada (3–14), the origins of "fiction" in Colombia are to be found in narratives embedded in other works, for instance, in Juan de Castellanos's *Elegías de varones ilustres de Indias* (15–32) or in Juan Rodríguez Freyle's *El carnero* (33–43).

Juan Rodríguez Freyle

After losing a long legal battle that left him penniless, Juan Rodríguez Freyle (or Freile) died in 1640 or 1642 at the approximate age of seventy-five. Like Bernal Díaz del Castillo and many other colonial authors, Freyle felt the creative impulse late in life. At seventy, he began to write what has come to be known as *El carnero*. The book circulated in manuscript for many years before it was published in 1859.[17] *El carnero* is sometimes called the first work of Colombian literature. Héctor Orjuela rejects this status and in one of his edited publications claims it for *Alteraciones del Dariel* by Juan Francisco de Páramo y Cepeda, a seventeenth-century epic poem set in Nueva Granada in what is now Panama and Urabá (which is still part of Colombia). *Alteraciones* is considered part of Panamanian literary history by others. Yet it belongs to both countries.[18] This sort of debate about primacy illustrates one of the many difficulties facing the historian of Colombian literature in the colonial era.

By any measure, *El carnero* is an odd work. Ostensibly it is a historical account of the early years of discovery and conquest of what would become Nueva Granada, and much of it is just that. What separates it from almost all other historical accounts is the inclusion of a number of gossipy stories (in Spanish, *chismes*), mostly of people in and around Santa Fe de Bogotá or in Tunja. These *chismes* are accompanied by homilies on life, greed, jealousy, vengeance, power, and the corrupting influence of a beautiful woman. Behind all the stories is the presence of Freyle himself, almost as a character in his tale. He often interrupts the narration, much as Cervantes interrupted the duel between Don Quixote and the Biscayan. For example, in chapter 4 of *El carnero*, Freyle asks the reader to mark the page with his finger and wait until he (Freyle) finishes telling the story of a particular war.[19] Returning to his story about ten pages later, Freyle asks the reader to remove his finger from the page (Rodríguez Freyle 85).

El carnero consists of twenty-one chapters introduced by a "prólogo al lector" that gives the main motive for writing the book: to see that the events of Nueva Granada are not forgotten.[20] He promises to write in plain style ("en tosco estilo"), without rhetorical flourishes and to adhere always to the truth, as well as to complement the writings of Fray Pedro Simón and Juan de Castellanos. Though the "Nuevo Reino" is his focus, Freyle comments that he must lead up to it with a consideration of what happened earlier in Santa Marta, Cartagena, and their environs (Rodríguez Freyle 50).

The best way to appreciate the eccentric delights of *El carnero* is to summarize a famous episode, told in Freye's inimical manner, perhaps modeled after *La Celestina*: the story of Inés de Hinojosa and her lovers, a story that has been expanded to novel length by the twentieth-century Colombian writer Próspero Morales Pradilla in *Los pecados de Inés de Hinojosa* (1986).

In the city of Carora in the governmental district of Venezuela, there lived a rich and extraordinarily beautiful woman, Inés de Hinojosa, wife of a wealthy landowner, Pedro de Avila. His two great faults made her unhappy: he was unfaithful and he gambled. One day, a musician and dance teacher named Jorge Voto came to town. Doña Inés asked her husband to permit Jorge Voto to give dance lessons to her niece, Juana, in the house. Immediately an affair began between Doña Inés and Jorge Voto, and both soon decided to assassinate Pedro de Avila and then to live together. Making sure to be publicly seen, Voto left town. In three days, he secretly returned. That night, he waylaid Avila and killed him. No one saw Voto return to town; no one saw him leave again. Doña Inés lamented loudly the death of her husband, and the crime remained unsolved. After a year of secret correspondence, the two lovers reunited and moved to Tunja, where Freyle just happens to be living as he writes *El carnero*. In Tunja, another Pedro, named Pedro Bravo de Rivera, pretended to court Doña Inés's niece in order to seduce the beautiful Doña Inés. Or perhaps it was Inés's ruse to seduce him. As their affair deepened, Pedro de Rivera bought the house next door and arranged his bedroom so that its wall was next to Doña Inés's bedroom. He cut a passageway between the two bedrooms so that the two lovers could come and go as they pleased. Somehow, Jorge Voto never noticed. Suddenly the moralist, Doña Inés decided that Voto must be punished for his crime of killing Pedro de Avila. Pedro Bravo de Rivera agreed. He solicited the help of his half-brother and a verger named Pedro de Hungría. One night, they lured Voto to a nearby river by saying that two women had asked to meet him. At the riverbank, Pedro de Rivera, his brother, and Pedro de Hungría, disguised as women, fell upon Voto, killed him, and threw his body into the river. The next morning, the townspeople, who drew their drinking water from the river, came upon the bloodied corpse.

As before, Doña Inés again loudly lamented the death of her husband and demanded justice. But this time things turned out differently. The magistrate put her in jail and put Pedro Bravo de Rivera in handcuffs. Then the magistrate went to the church and, seeing the bloodied sleeve of the verger, tried to arrest him. But Pedro de Hungría evaded the magistrate and escaped on the horse meant for Pedro Bravo de Rivera. He exchanged horses in a ranch near Ibagué and was never heard from again. Pedro Bravo de Rivera's horse, however, went on to sire a number of horses that, says Freyle, can be seen to this day. Pedro Bravo de Rivera was condemned to death and had his throat slashed. His brother was hanged from a tree near Voto's house. And Doña Inés was hanged from a different tree, next to her front door. That tree lives to this day, though it is a bit dry by now, since seventy years have passed since these events took place.

So ends the story of the three Pedros, Jorge Voto, and Doña Inés de Hinojosa. At the beginning of the story, Freyle exclaims that such beauty is so dangerous that it should be placed before a court of law (Rodríguez Freyle 151). At the end, this Colombian Polonius asserts that a woman's beauty is quite an unfortunate thing if wrongly directed and not governed by reason. (Rodríguez Freyle 159). Like other stories of venality, adultery, murder, passion, vengeance, or even witchcraft in *El carnero*, it is embedded within supposedly objective historical accounts. It is women who have caused the most problems, and it all began, says Freyle (chapter 5), with Eve. But as far as Freyle himself is concerned, well, he says, he is too old to be seduced by a beautiful woman.

Hernando Domínguez Camargo

Hernando Domínguez Camargo (1606–59), a poet of the "Barroco de Indias" influenced by the Spanish poet Luis de Góngora, is the quintessential representative of *gongorismo* in the New World. In general, critics praise or condemn Domínguez Camargo according to whether they like or dislike Góngora and his poetics. The negative assessments are scathing. Marcelino Menéndez y Pelayo, repeating the opinion of Vergara y Vergara, famously stated that Domínguez Camargo's long versified biography of Ignatius Loyola is, "without a doubt one of the most dismal miscarriages of *gongorismo*, without a trace of creativeness to make tolerable its aberrations." Menéndez y Pelayo is in turn cited by Gómez Restrepo (117).[21] This negative assessment of Domínguez Camargo represented the standard view of him and his work for many years. However, just as Luis de Góngora and John Donne were rehabilitated by twentieth-century critics and poets, Domínguez Camargo has been rehabilitated and even celebrated. Gerardo Diego called him a poet among poets in Spanish America (Mendoza Varela, 133). Pacheco Quintero called him the greatest poet of Latin America (Pacheco Quintero, vol. 1: xxxv), greater even than Sor Juana Inés de la Cruz (Pacheco Quintero, vol. 1: 127).

Domínguez Camargo entered the Jesuit order as a boy, receiving holy orders in 1623. Educated in Colombia and in Ecuador (Quito), he spent considerable time in the Jesuit college of Cartagena before being forced to renounce the Jesuit Order in 1636. The reasons for that forced renunciation are not known. He did not relinquish his sacerdotal calling, however, and he worked as a curate in several towns in the interior of the country before spending the last years of his relatively short life in Tunja, supported, as was Juan de Castellanos, by a benefice. He had an apparently well-deserved reputation for indulging in expensive wines, elaborate dinners, and fine clothing (Mendoza Varela 12–13). Like Castellanos, he died a wealthy man. Unlike Castellanos, he was forgotten for centuries.

Domínguez Camargo's reputation rests primarily on a series of poems in *Ramillete de varias flores poéticas* and on his long "heroic poem," the biography of Ignatius Loyola. The *Ramillete*, a collection of poems by various hands, was published in Spain in 1676. It contains Domínguez Camargo's first poem, written while he was a student in Quito, entitled "A un salto por donde se despeña el arroyo de Chillo" (To a waterfall from which the stream of the Chillo hurls itself). This poem in eleven quatrains is constructed as an extended metaphor. The stream is a crystal pony (*un potro cristalino*), rearing and falling through the rocks and boulders, its mane glistening and nostrils snorting; the pony neighs as the pearl-like waves of its skin strike at the precipice and as it unseats its riders. At last, at the bottom, boulders tame (or kill) the crystal pony; that is, they tame or kill the crystalline waters. The elaboration of the extended metaphor is as consistent as Rimbaud's drunken boat (*le bateau ivre*). It is obviously a rhetorical exercise, for in another poem, apparently celebrating the same waterfall, the metaphor is of a "crystal bull." There, too, the metaphor operates throughout the poem (see Gómez Restrepo 126–7).

Such *gongorista* versification is intensified in the poem of his maturity, *San Ignacio de Loyola Poema Heróico*, a work of more than a thousand *octavas reales* (eight-line stanzas of eleven syllables per line) and published as "obra póstuma" in Spain in 1666.[22] This poetic biography of Ignatius Loyola takes Ignatius from his birth, early life, and military campaign against France (and being seriously wounded and then miraculously healed by St. Peter) in book 1, to his conversion and trials in book 2, to his journeys to Rome, Geneva, the Holy Land, and back to Spain in book 3, to his studies and tribulations in book 4. The fifth book finds him on the way to Rome, about to found the Jesuit Order. There the work breaks off and remains incomplete. Domínguez Camargo does not limit himself to the details of the life of Ignatius but creates many descriptive scenes filled with classical allusions and extended metaphors. Some scenes praise the Eucharist; others praise elaborate banquets or glorious landscapes. Figures alluded to, in extended similes, include Orpheus, Polyphemus, Trojan soldiers, and Mars. This is not poetry to be read quickly and easily; it is, like Góngora's work, poetry to be deciphered. Consider the opening stanza of the entire work:

> Si al de tu lira néctar armonioso,
> dulces metros le debo, heroica ahora,
> en número me inspira más nervoso,
> los que Euterpe le bebes a la aurora:
> al clarín ya de acero numeroso,
> plumas le den del cisne, voz sonora;
> que el vizcaíno Marte es tan guerrero,
> que aún melodías las querrá de acero.

A line-by-line translation of these verses is well-nigh impossible. However, Eduardo Mendoza Varela has recast them in prose to make their meaning more accessible. A translation of the rendition by Mendoza Varela, with his parenthetical explanations, is as follows: "If I owe the composition of sweet lyric poems to the harmonious nectar of your lyre, o Euterpe my muse, inspire me now to heroic, more vivid and sinewy verses, to the melodies that you drink at dawn (that, in turn inspire you). May the feathers of the swan give to the musical steel of the trumpet its sonorous voice; for the Biscayan Mars (Ignatius Loyola, the brave warrior of Pamplona and the great captain of the armies of God) is such a warrior that he would prefer that even the melodies that sing of him be of steel" (Mendoza Varela 193).

For Gómez Restrepo, Castellanos is the Colombian Homer, but Domínguez Camargo is the Colombian Lycophron (fl. 260 BCE), the Hellenistic grammarian and minor poet of the decadent period of Greek literature (Gómez Restrepo 120). A more generous critic might say that Domínguez Camargo is Colombia's Góngora and leave it at that.

Francisco Álvarez de Velasco y Zorrilla

Francisco Álvarez de Velasco y Zorrilla (1647–1708) despised Góngora, admired Quevedo, and, from an unbridgeable distance, fell in love with Sor Juana Inés de la Cruz. Unlike most of the writers treated in this essay, Álvarez de Velasco y Zorrilla neither lived from a benefice nor became a recluse in a monastery. He was a highly placed bureaucrat in Nueva Granada, a one-time mayor of Santa Fe de Bogotá, and even governor and captain general of a province (Tello xxii). These positions were not honorary; they required a great deal of work and brought with them many headaches (Tello lxii–lxxi). In 1669, he married Teresa de Pastrana y Pretel, whose wealth enlarged his own (Tello xxiii). In the year after her death in 1694, he composed an elegy to her entitled "Vuelve a su quinta Anfriso solo, y viudo" (see *Rhythmica sacra, moral y laudatoria* 394–8), a lamentation with only faint echoes of the *gongorismos* preferred by Domínguez Camargo and, perhaps for that reason, praised by Gómez Restrepo as a love poem of graceful lyricism and freshness of expression (Gómez Restrepo 162). What a terrible thing death is (the poet begins), that it should take away my life without killing me, and in this death-in-life to leave me in a state of sad calmness that makes its wound even more cruel. The rest of the poem is in a verse form called "endecha real," which is used for laments, and consists of four-line stanzas, with three lines usually of seven syllables and a fourth line of eleven syllables that ends in an assonant rhyme with the second line. The varying length of the lines contributes to the poem's lyricism.

The "Anfriso" in the title of the poem is a reference to Amphryssos, who, as a river god in Ovid's *Metamorphoses* (book 1, ll. 550ff.), laments the transformation of Daphne into a laurel. Chased by Apollo, she flees and, before he can capture her, is turned into a tree. The episode takes place in Thessaly, in a region famous for its pastoral characteristics. As one might expect, pastoral references to sheep and sweet melodies abound in Álvarez de Velasco y Zorrilla's lamentation for his dead wife Teresa (Daphne in the poem).

After his wife's death, Álvarez de Velasco y Zorrilla made out his will, leaving most of his estate to the church, named legal representatives to take care of his remaining properties, and in 1700 left the Indies for Spain. There, he officially represented the "Nuevo Reino de Granada" before the Crown and the "Supremo Consejo de las Indias." He spent his remaining years and much of what was left of his fortune attempting to secure the publication of the eclectic compilation that is the "strange and curious" *Rhythmica sacra, moral y laudatoria,* published in 1703 and described by Rafael Torres Quintero as a kind of encyclopedia of the "barroco colonial granadino" (xvi). The title page of the 1703 edition gives a flavor of the work. The title is followed by the name of the author and his many offices, and that is followed by the proclamation that inside are various poems in different metrical schemes, an epistle in prose and two more in verse, followed by poems in celebration of Sor Juana Inés de la Cruz (identified here as "Soror Inès Juana de la Cruz") and prose apologias on the angelic choir and on the silken sash of the tunic of St. Thomas.

The "poem" in honor of the Virgin Mary that opens the collection is actually a group of poems: a sonnet, followed by eighty-one quatrains, a madrigal, a "romance eneámetro,"[23] another sonnet, and a final madrigal (*Rhythmica* 21–63). This opening set of poems is dedicated to the Virgin Mary's suffering. Each of the quatrains treats a religious theme that is connected to her directly or indirectly. Each quatrain is followed by a two- or three-line quotation, in the original Latin (sometimes misremembered), usually from the works of Virgil: *Georgics*, the *Eclogues*, and the *Aeneid*. Some lines in the quatrains adapt or loosely translate phrases from the four Gospels, in the Vulgate.

A recent book-length study entitled *El enamorado de Sor Juana* describes and analyzes the "strange and curious" love of Francisco Álvarez de Velasco y Zorrilla for Sor Juana Inés de la Cruz (see José Pascual Buxó, passim). He never met Sor Juana, but he so admired her that in 1698 he addressed a "love letter" to her, a *carta laudatoria*, not knowing that she had died several years earlier. The *carta*'s elaborately allusive and elegant baroque prose is accompanied by a series of poems, in various verse forms, in which he declares his love and admiration for Sor Juana, called, anagrammatically, "Nise" (Inés). The opening lines of the first poem are as follows:

> A vos divina Nise (¡mas qué susto!)
> tiritando la pluma entre los dedos,
> toda anegada en miedos,
> descolorido el gusto,
> amarillo el papel, la tinta roja,
> muerta la mano y viva la congoja
> de pensar que es a Nise (¡oh qué vergüenza!)
> a quien quiere escribir un poeta raso;
> ¿Yo a vos? Que ciego amor me lo dispensa.
> (*Rhythmica Sacra* 528)

"It is to you, divine Nise, (and what a fright!), the quill trembling between the fingers, silenced by fear, the pleasure made pale, the paper yellowed, the ink red, the hand dead and the anguish alive from the thought that it is to Nise (oh what shame!) that this simple poet wishes to write. Me to you? It is blind love that urges me on."

Not all poems in the collection are so abjectly devotional, timid, and adoring. Some are even familiar, daring to address Sor Juana Inés de la Cruz first in the diminutive as "paysanita querida" and then to move from that intimate familiarity into regions of ever more comprehensive allegorical significance and praise. Though Álvarez de Velasco y Zorrilla's verse can be as intricate and complex as that by Domínguez Camargo, his poetry is more engaging and heartfelt. It is less of a rhetorical exercise.

Pedro de Solís y Valenzuela

In and about 1650, Pedro de Solís y Valenzuela (1624–1711) composed *El desierto prodigioso y prodigio del desierto*. Before the three-volume edition by Caro y Cuervo was published in 1977, 1984, and 1985, the existence of this work was known through an article published in *Yerma* in 1963, which identified the author as Bruno de Solís y Valenzuela (Pomareda 1977 xii–xiii). The true author is his younger brother Pedro.[24] Héctor Orjuela and others have called *El desierto prodigioso y prodigio del desierto* the first Spanish-American novel. There are problems with this designation. It might be more accurate to describe the work, as it was originally written, as an *omnium gatherum* containing a variety of forms besides narrative fiction: travel narrative, *crónica*, biography, drama, poetry of various kinds by different authors, religious meditation, and homiletic writing.

There are two published versions of this work: a relatively complete version of more than 1,600 pages and a radically reduced version. In the more complete edition, the chapters are extensive and varied. Chapter V (or "mansión" as the chapters are called in the Spanish) consists of fifty-three pages mostly in verse. *Mansiones* IX through XI consists of 214 pages, the majority of which are in verse. *Mansión* XXI consists of 277 pages of prose, verse, and more than one dramatic piece in several acts. Héctor Orjuela condensed this enormous corpus to fewer than 190 pages and called the result a "novel." He reduced the *mansiones* and changed their literary profiles. Thus, *mansión* V is reduced from 53 to 5 pages, *mansiones* IX through XI from 214 pages to 22 pages, *mansión* XXI from 277 pages to 25 pages.

It may be argued that Orjuela, by so drastically editing *El desierto*, has misrepresented it. But it may also be said that his editorial zeal has saved the work from obscurity, made it more readable, and thus "preserved" it for future readers and scholars. Whatever side of the argument one defends, it is undeniable that the editorial manipulations by Orjuela have complicated the debate about the true nature of the work and its place in the history of Colombian and Spanish-American literature. Even the narrative portions of the work raise questions about genre. Those sections appear to have been inspired by a variety of earlier prose genres: historical narrative, the *crónica*, biography, autobiography, hagiography, Greek romance and adventure narrative, religious parable, and monastic history. Of greatest interest here are the work's autobiographical dimensions and its most prominent "narrative," which Orjuela has "reconstructed" by taking the story from different *mansiones* and arranging it.

In the autobiographical portion, the author has inserted himself "as Pedro" in the main narrative of four friends. These four (Andrés, Antonio, Fernando, and Pedro, the last two being brothers) have decided to travel to the "desierto de la Candelaria" during their long Christmas vacation. This part of the work follows their "adventures" in the desert and after. Their adventures are frequently interrupted by other narratives, poems, and dramas in the work, but Pedro de Solís y Valenzuela always returns to the story of the four friends, thus forming the principal *Rahmenerzählung* or frame narrative for the entire work. At the beginning, Andrés, who has been pursuing a deer while on a hunt, comes upon a mysterious cave.[25] In it, he finds a notebook containing spiritual meditations and poetry. He takes the notebook back to his friends and tells them about the cave. They are so enthralled by this discovery and so taken by the quality of the writing that they insist on meeting the author. The next day they all go to the cave and come upon Arsenio, a hermit of many years who has dedicated himself to the anchoritic life. He is cordial to his uninvited guests. "Who, oh gallant young men, has brought you to this rude place in the flower of your youth?"[26] There is nothing here of value, he continues, and asks that they return the notebook to him. They do so, beg the anchorite's pardon, introduce themselves, and ask for his story.

The hermit Arsenio obliges with a tale, also often interrupted, that owes much to the Greek adventure novel, to the "confessional" mode in the manner of St. Augustine, and to the *imitatio vitae* tradition that generally has served to inspire possible followers of the religious life. No sooner has Arsenio begun his tale than Andrés decides to visit a nearby monastery, where he is so moved by what he experiences that he professes, becoming a monk. In this way, Solís y Valenzuela weaves the lives of the four friends into the other embedded and interrupted narratives in the work.

Parts of Arsenio's story might well have been written by an epigone of Chariton (fl. probably in the first century BCE), author of *Chaereas and Callirhoe*, classified by B. P. Reardon as "the first extant work of Greek prose fiction" (Reardon 17), of Longus (fl. second century CE), or of Heliodorus (third or fourth century CE). Arsenio's tale begins with a side story of his good friend Leoncio, who marries Roselinda, is unfaithful to her, and, fearing her anger, murders her. First, he proclaims his innocence. Later, however, her ghost appears to him and frightens him into confessing. Remorseful, he asks to be punished (all this in *mansión* IV). That sets up the story of Arsenio's own dissolute behavior, as a youth in his native Spain, in *mansión* VI. As a young man, Arsenio squandered his inheritance and married a beautiful woman who died in childbirth, leaving him with a daughter whom he entrusted to an aunt in a convent. He fell in love with his cousin, Casimira, who spurned him. Determined to have her, he kidnapped her from her convent to take her to the New World where he intended to force her to yield to him. He and his friends disguised her as a man for the ocean voyage to the New World. During it, they encountered terrible storms as well as pirates. After arriving in the New World, she fled from him and became a recluse in a hermit's cave. Arsenio tracked her down, begged her forgiveness, and also became a recluse, taking on the name of the eremite who had protected Casimira. This second Arsenio, who is the narrator of this episode, withdrew further from society to the desert of Candelaria and to the cave where the four friends have now come upon him.

Solís y Valenzuela then turns to stories concerning the four friends, each of whom leads a pious life. At the end of the entire work, the four friends come together at the convent of Candelaria; there, they learn of the saintly Arsenio's death. At this point, the manuscript breaks off, and a promised sequel is never written.

Bit by bit, throughout this long work, sometimes within Arsenio's narratives, sometimes within the stories concerning one or more of the four friends, other tales unfold. The most elaborate one is also told by Arsenio and utilizes the stock motif of the voyage to the underworld, prominent in western literature since Homer's *Odyssey*, Virgil's *Aeneid*, and Dante's *Divine Comedy*. In Arsenio's telling, the devil himself becomes a guide to the underworld for the main character (a man named Pedro Porter) and plays a major role in a tale about money, theft, the problems of bureaucracy, the long reach of the law, the consequences of sin, and the power of piety. Like the previous story, this one begins in the secular world but is soon transformed through a Christian framework of piety, faith, and wondrous events ("prodigios"). All of *El desierto prodigioso y prodigio del desierto* is like this. Even the four friends, at first just four young men on vacation, eventually lead lives intimately connected to the Church. This narrative pattern is typical of literature in the colonial period and reflects the hegemonic reach of the Church in Nueva Granada.

Pedro de Solís y Valenzuela's older brother Fernando (1616–77) emigrated from Colombia to Spain and became a Carthusian monk in the monastery of El Paular, taking the name "Bruno." Under this name, the hermit Bruno became a prolific author, almost all of it lost. Some of it may have been lost through neglect and some may have been destroyed in a fire of 1676 in the monastery of the Grande Chartreuse. One work sent by Bruno to the mother house survived: *El cisne de los desiertos poema heróico*, an epic poem on the life of Saint Bruno of Cologne, who founded the order in 1084. Somewhat reminiscent, because of its hagiographic subject, of Domínguez Camargo's *San Ignacio Loyola poema heróico*, Bruno de Solís y Valenzuela's work is, like that of Domínguez Camargo, baroque in its aesthetic sensibility, though certainly not as indebted to Góngora. Since *El cisne de los desiertos* has just been published (in 2013), there is no criticism on it apart from Dom G. Thalmann's extensive introduction in which, in addition to describing the history of the manuscript and contents of the work, he identifies Bruno, rather than Pedro, as the "true" author of *El desierto prodigioso y prodigio del desierto*.

Francisca Josefa de Castillo y Guevara

Some of the best writing in the colonial period occurred in convents. There were long stretches of time, and writing as a form of spiritual self-exploration was not only encouraged, it was sometimes demanded. Drawing their inspiration largely but not exclusively from a trio of Spanish mystics of the sixteenth century, Juan de la Cruz, Luis de Granada, and Teresa de Ávila, as well as from the Mexican nun Sor Juana Inés de la Cruz, three nuns from Nueva Granada have enriched Colombian literature: Francisca Josefa de Castillo y Guevara (1671–1742), Jerónima Nava y Saavedra (1669–1727), and María de Jesús (who professed in 1714).[27] Each followed a different "camino de perfección," in the phrase of Saint Teresa, in search of ultimate mystical experiences. Sor Francisca followed the path of suffering and the mortification of the flesh; Jerónima Nava y Saavedra the path of ecstatic love; María de Jesús that of good works and prayer.[28] Urged by her confessor to do so, each wrote an autobiography: *Su vida* (by Sor Francisca), *Autobiografía de una monja venerable* (by Jerónima Nava y Saavedra), and *Escritos de la Hermana María de Jesús*. The autobiography of Jerónima Nava y Saavedra was mistakenly identified for years in the National Library of Colombia as authored by Juan de Olmos, her confessor.

Francisca Josefa de Castillo y Guevara, known to posterity also as "Sor Francisca" or "La Madre Castillo," is of greatest interest here. Her autobiography (*Su vida*) and her devotional magnum opus (*Afectos espirituales*) are commonly acknowledged to be the most important spiritual works of Nueva Granada. Despite her admiration for Sor Juana Inés de la Cruz (she copied some of her poems in her commonplace book known to scholars as the "Cuaderno de Enciso"), she was neither primarily a poet nor a *gongorista* influenced by "Barroco de Indias" writers. An obsessively self-referential writer, she owed the most stylistically to Teresa de Ávila, Luis de Granada, Juan de la Cruz, and the Bible.

Sor Francisca was born in Tunja in 1671 and died there in 1742, having spent all of her adult life in the Convent of Santa Clara. Three times she was elected abbess. Tunja was no longer the cultural center that it had been during Juan de Castellanos's residence. For some scholars of Colombian literature, Tunja by this time was a cultural backwater of some 4,000 inhabitants, dull and uninspiring.[29] But Darío Achury Valenzuela, perhaps the most devoted critic of Sor Francisca's work, imagines the Tunja of her times as a town in which daily life was ordered by the tolling of the bells from its six convents. Incense burned in its many cloisters, its patios were silent, and convent windows opened out onto herb and flower gardens (Achury Valenzuela, *Obras* xi).[30] This idyllic picture is belied by La Madre Castillo's own words in *Su vida*. There she describes a life filled with suffering and pain. On the very first pages of *Su vida*, Sor Francisca states that she intends to meditate on and consider before the Lord all the misused years of her life in the bitterness of her soul (chapter 1).[31] Any moments of happiness in her childhood are followed by guilt or regret. At age nine, she thought of hanging herself because she had received a marriage proposal from another child. At age fourteen she so punished herself physically with a hair shirt and chains that her flesh began to grow into them. She slept fully clothed on plain wooden boards and mortified her flesh whenever and however she could (chapter 3). She knew of St. Teresa as well as other mystics. She tried to meditate in the manner of St. Ignatius of Loyola, whose *Spiritual Exercises* she read with devotion (chapter 4). She experienced nightmares and visions.

She entered the convent at age eighteen, a place characterized by Rocío Vélez de Piedrahita as a "casa de locos" or madhouse (1988: 106). Nightmares and visions intensified and continued all of her cloistered life.[32] For instance, Satan, generally called "el enemigo," appeared to her frequently, sometimes as a ferocious figure dressed all in black (chapter 33), sometimes disguised as a monk (chapter 25), sometimes as a thin dark man with a fierce face (chapter 39), sometimes as a snake (chapter 43). She punished herself with self-flagellation and once asked a servant to beat her (chapter 19). Some nuns bullied her. One night, a nun entered her cell and hurled insults at her. Other nuns joined in, as did some of her own servants (chapter 25). In the same chapter, Sor Francisca quotes her own Mother Superior's reactions: "I have been sharpening a knife in order to send it to her [Sor Francisca], and a rope so that she can hang herself" (chapter 24, 90).[33] Her companions mocked her ascetic practices and devotional intensity, calling her a fake. A servant of one of the other nuns tried to suffocate her (chapter 25). Often, especially after beatings or visions, she fell ill and spent time in the convent infirmary; these illnesses lasted for days, weeks, or even months (chapters 43 and 53). Once, all of her teeth became loose and began to move about in her mouth. Sor Francisca herself pulled them all out. Other nuns then fled from her when she came near, toothless, to pray (chapter 51). In an extensive hundred-page analysis that is otherwise penetrating and sympathetic, Rocío Vélez de Piedrahita calls Sor Francisca mentally unbalanced ("desequilibrada"; 1995: 161–2). Through it all, Sor Francisca never wavered in her hunger to know God and to achieve the *unio mystica* of the Christian mystics who were her models.

This hunger for the divine runs through the *Afectos espirituales*. She begins as *Su vida* began, with pain and suffering: "I forgot to eat my bread of pain, and my talent dried up like a tile; my tongue stuck to the roof of my mouth and I was reduced to the dust of death" (*Afecto* 1).[34] But she does not remain trapped, as she seemed to be in *Su vida*, by litanies of pain and suffering. For example, the word "amargura" (bitterness) appears in the *Afectos* on its first page, just as it did in *Su vida*, but her relationship to bitterness is different. "In bitterness most bitter I will find peace, and in bitterness I shall dwell; I will make of it a restful nest."[35]

Darío Achury Valenzuela ascribes the difference between *Su vida* and the *Afectos espirituales* to the distinction between a "physical" autobiography and a "spiritual" one. There is more to it than that. Though the same person wrote both works, the *Afectos espirituales* is astonishingly different. Religious passion is at its core, its lyricism both extended and intense. Many of the 196 *afectos* are prayers directly addressed to God as "Señor," "Dios," "mi padre," "mi amado."

> Sor Francisca's prose is saturated with the Bible, its rhythms, phrases, words, and images. Consider some of the biblical echoes – especially from the Psalms and Song of Solomon – in *Afecto* no. 20 (*Obras completas*, vol. 2, edited by Achury Valenzuela). She begins by having God address the poor, tormented soul: be not afraid; I am the Lord your God who brought you out of Egypt. You shall dwell in his protection. [Then the point of view abruptly shifts, and it is the soul, or Sor Francisca, who speaks]: The Lord is my protection and my refuge, my God: In Him I will have hope, until the

day should decline and the shadows abate, the entire day of a mortal life encircled by shadows, until [the day] should call the soul to crown it on the heights from which the lions and the leopards fell. . . . Be comforted and have courage . . . for the Lord is your shield and your protection. He will guide your hands in battle. . . . He will free you from the snares of the hunters and from the words of the evildoers. The shield of his truth will surround you so that you need not fear the terrors of the night. He will send angels to guide you. He will vanquish your enemies and they will flee from your presence. My God, you will capture them like small foxes that try to ruin the vineyards. Oh, my soul, how joyfully will you sing of the victories of your beloved.[36]

Any alert reader of the Bible will hear in the earlier paraphrased translation the allusions to *Exodus* and to *Nehemiah* 9:18 ("This is your God who brought you out of Egypt"), to the Psalms, and to the Song of Solomon. What is clear to the native Spanish reader is not only how beautiful the biblical prose is but also how undisciplined it is syntactically, even logically. In this *afecto*, as in many others, the reader occasionally cannot tell who the subject is, for the possessive pronoun "su" seems at times to refer to her own soul, to the soul in general, or to God (in the third person). The shifts from second to third and to first person are abrupt. It is the intertextual mingling of Sor Francisca's own words with those of the Bible that gives her prose here and elsewhere, as Sister María Teresa Morales Borrero has pointed out (25–6), its music, rhythms, and spiritual depth. For Sor Francisca, the Bible and Church liturgy are the kaleidoscopic prism through which she saw the world; in effect, she did not think or speak in any other language. Sor Francisca lived in her convent as if suspended in time, as if the conquest and colonization of Nueva Granada had not happened, and as if the "Barroco de Indias," elsewhere a literary hurricane from which no colonial author escaped, had somehow turned into a gentle breeze, barely registered by her, if at all.

Where there were nightmares in *Su vida*, there are mystical visions of joy and love in the *Afectos*. If *Su vida* is like Dante's *Inferno*, then the *Afectos* is like *Paradiso*. For instance, in *Afecto* no. 90 she imagines the Holy Spirit inside her, her soul encircled by its divine flame, filled by it and delighted by it, as if it were an immense sea or sphere of life and love, greater than all the spheres of the earth.[37] She also thinks of mystical love in sensual terms, as in the Song of Solomon. In *Afecto* no. 32, she addresses God as most beloved love, beloved, greatest friend of the soul.[38]

There is suffering in the *Afectos*, just as there is in *Su vida*, but more often than not the suffering is countered by joy and love. Words like *dicha*, *dichoso, amor, clemencia, benignidad,* and *virtudes* fill its pages. The final words of *Afecto* no. 196 sum up, for Sor Francisca, her life and her struggles: "In God you will find all things to be good. Away from God, you will find all things to be bitter."[39] It is this conflict, between good things and bitter ones, between joy and suffering, between salvation and damnation, between love and hate, that animates both the life and the work of Colombia's greatest spiritual writer.

Sor Francisca wrote poetry also, though not often and, some critics have said, not well. Her poetry does not have the dense and complex lyricism of Sor Juana Inés de la Cruz, but it is sincere devotional poetry. Achury Valenzuela praises her poetic skill and devotes thirty-four detailed pages to an analysis of *Afecto* no. 46 (elsewhere, numbered 45), which is written entirely in verse (Achury Valenzuela 1962: 383–417). In the introduction to his selection of poems by Sor Francisca in his anthology of Colombian poetry (volume 1), Jorge Pacheco Quintero writes that, after Domínguez Camargo, hers is the best lyrical voice of the colonial period in Colombia. Her poems are few but first rate (Pacheco Quintero, vol. 1: 413).[40] María Teresa Cristina finds this praise to be excessive, especially when her poetry is compared to that of the great Spanish mystics (Cristina 566). Readers of Sor Francisca seem eager either to praise or to criticize her. She was, and remains, a polarizing figure.

The *crónica*

The *crónica* is the most common form of writing during the early colonial period in the New World. The English term "chronicle," though from the same Latin root, conveys little of the flexibility implied by the Spanish term. Derived from the Latin, which is in turn derived from the Greek *khronika* (annals) and *khronikos* (of time), the term *crónica* refers to a narrative or an account in which the temporal order, or chronology, is paramount. In Spanish and in Portuguese, the term has also come later to identify a particular kind of article in a newspaper that combines observation, event, and plot into a small gracefully rounded narrative. For the colonial period, it is not useful to insist that the *crónica* be one kind of writing only. It has already been noted that genres in Nueva Granada literature may blend into one another, often within a single work, as if the realities of the New World cannot be contained within the conventional and traditional European literary forms. That is true of the *crónica* as well. It is generally more than just a narrative account of an event or events. It often combines official accounts and historical research with oral accounts and human interest stories. In one prominent case, Juan de Castellanos even transformed his own *crónica* into poetry.

In *Crónicas y cronistas de la Nueva Granada*, Héctor Orjuela tries to bring some order into this disordered field. He groups the *cronistas* into four historically distinct groupings: the conquistadors, the colonizers, the Baroque, and the Enlightenment. Each grouping is further divided into secular and religious kinds. For Orjuela, Gonzalo Jiménez de Quesada (25-33) and Pedro Cieza de León (33-43) are conquistador *cronistas*. Juan de Castellanos (49-58), Pedro de Aguado (60-9), and fray Pedro Simón (71-89) are colonizer *cronistas*. Juan Rodríguez Freyle is a baroque *cronista* (891-9), as is Lucas Fernández de Piedrahita (109-15). Except for Castellanos and Freyle, these writers are not often studied by literary historians. Orjuela's classifications and discussion present certain difficulties. One is that some writers fit better in categories other than the *crónica*. Juan de Castellanos might be better discussed as a writer of epic or heroic poetry, and Juan Rodríguez Freyle as composer of narrative short fiction. Another is that the surviving texts sometimes have been altered by their colonial editors.

As an author, Quesada is sometimes called a poet; he is more usually considered a *cronista*. The difficulty here is that few of his *cronista* writings have survived, and then in sometimes heavily altered versions. Two brief *crónicas* by Quesada are extant: *Gran cuaderno* and *Epítome de la conquista del Nuevo Reino de Granada*. The provenance of these texts and their subsequent fortunes in the works of historians like López de Gómara and Fernández de Oviedo have been discussed – words like "alteration" and "mutilation" are used – in the authoritative study on Quesada by Demetrio Ramos Pérez (passim). For instance, in his *Historia natural y moral de las Indias*, Gonzalo Fernández de Oviedo writes that, in Madrid and in Valladolid (in 1548, according to Ramos 219), he had long conversations with Quesada and learned about the conquest of Nueva Granada. Quesada even showed him a "Gran cuaderno" and allowed him to keep it for many days (179-80). Chapters 18 through 31 of this section of the *Historia natural y moral de las Indias* consist of detailed paraphrases and extended excerpts from the *Gran cuaderno* (179-238), but, according to Demetrio Ramos (passim), it is difficult to determine which words originally belonged to Quesada and which to Oviedo, and what passages have been excised. Similar problems exist with the *Epítome*, first published in 1889 by Marcos Jiménez de la Espada (see Ramos Pérez xvii–xx). Editorial difficulties aside, Quesada's *Gran cuaderno*, written in the third person as if Quesada were discussing someone else's actions, is of interest for its informative details on the march from Santa Marta to Santa Fe de Bogotá, the battles against the Indians and their pacification, and its descriptions of Indian customs. Other writings of Quesada that have survived cannot be considered *crónicas*.

Born in Spain, Pedro de Aguado (1538–1609) arrived in the New World when he was twenty-two. Not much else is known about his life. The title page of his *Historia de la provincial de Sancta Marta y Nuevo Reino de Granada* identifies him as a Franciscan. In his introduction, "Proemio al lector," Aguado places the work in a cosmogonic context, recounting the creation of the world by God and proceeding from there through Adam's act of naming things, down through stories of the Greeks and the Romans, ending with the foundation of the cities of "Sancta Fee, Tunja, Vélez" (Aguado, vol. 1: 15). Chapter 1 narrates the foundation of the city of Santa Marta by Rodrigo de Bastidas. Other chapters narrate the actions of Quesada, Belalcázar, Federman (spelled Fredemán), the campaigns against the Indians, and the establishment of monasteries. Aguado's prose is plain, and the narrative unfolds without rhetorical flourishes or self-reflection. He describes Indians as they are often described in the historical writing of the period: "barbarians," idol worshippers, great drunkards, and even "butchers" of human flesh willing to sell their own family members to other Indians for cannibal feasts (Aguado, vol. 1: 414–18).

Aguado's work was one of the sources for fray Pedro Simón's *Noticias historiales de las conquistas de Tierra Firme en las Indias occidentales*, the first part of which was published in 1627, the rest not being published until 1882–92, when the complete edition appeared for the first time. Like Aguado, Simón (1574–1628) was born in Spain. He arrived in Nueva Granada at age thirty. He begins *Noticias historiales* by citing, in its entirety, a "cédula real" or royal license of 1572 that orders any and all persons to give to historians of the *Nuevo Reino de Granada* assistance and information not only on the Indians and their culture but also on the discoveries, conquests, and such wars that have been necessary (Simón, vol. 1: 1). *Noticias historiales* is written in a plain but engaging style. Usually Simón confines himself to describing events of the conquest and colonization. Sometimes, however, he mixes into his narrative the amusing and seemingly irrelevant detail. For example, in the middle of narrating Quesada's expedition, Simón stops and asks himself why Indians have no beards (*Segunda noticia historial*, chapter 3, vol. 2: 124–5). That is because, he says, Indians pulled out their facial hair, and, after several generations, the hair stopped growing. The same thing happens with dogs, he says: if their tails are cut off, those, too, will eventually stop growing. Some of his descriptions are entirely fanciful and lifted from the teratological tradition of finding (and classifying) monsters – and especially cannibals – which are to be found in far-away places or newly discovered lands.[41] He begins his work by depicting a tribe of men whose ears are so large that they reach to the ground and can shelter five or six men. In another province, men sleep under water. Elsewhere, people subsist on the scent of flowers and fruit and quickly die if the scent is unpleasant. There are giants in the kingdom of Peru, and pigmies in other places. Many of the Indians in the New World are habitual drunkards, cruel and vengeful, completely without religion and eaters of human flesh (*Primera noticia historial*, chapters 2, 3, and 4, in vol. 1: 5–8). All of this is related without irony or skepticism, without differentiating the fanciful from the real, the impossible from the possible, or the improbable from the probable.

The "noticias historiales" in the title announces that at least part of this historical work, this *crónica*, will be devoted to "stories" writ small rather than "history" writ large. Héctor Orjuela excerpted one such story for his *Antología de la narrativa breve de ficción en la Nueva Granada* (57–60). He gave the story a title, which it did not have in its original incarnation as chapter 2 and part of chapter 3 of the *Tercera noticia historial* (Simón, vol. 2: 244–7). "La cacica de Guatavita"[42] tells of the wife of a chieftain who was so beautiful that the demon of the lake (in the form of a "dragoncillo" or snake) convinced her to be unfaithful with one of the "gentlemen" who was part of the chief's entourage. Hearing of the betrayal, the chief had the young man impaled and then forced his wife to eat the man's penis in a specially prepared dish. Humiliated by her treatment, the wife secretly left the chief's house and, with her daughter, went to Lake Guatavita. Throwing her daughter in, she jumped in after. The priests who lived around the lake heard the splashes and tried to save them but could not. Both mother and daughter drowned. The chief repented of his vengeful actions and tried to get the priests to bring the mother and daughter back to life through sorcery. Nothing worked. Finally, a priest dove into the depths of the lake and, coming back to the surface, reported that the woman and her daughter were alive and living in underwater houses better than the ones they had left. The mother wanted to be left there. Eventually the chief became resigned to having lost his family. Ever after, according to legend, the chief's wife and daughter, together with their servants and other Indians, have lived at the bottom of Lake Guatavita. This story is the origin, Simón says, of the practice of sending the dead down to the lake's bottom with many of their valuables.

Lucas Fernández de Piedrahita (1624–88), like El Inca Garcilaso de la Vega, was the son of a woman descended from Indian royalty and a Spanish conquistador. Unlike El Inca, he did not emigrate to Spain but spent most of his life in Nueva Granada. He is reputed to have written plays and poetry, but none of that work has survived. Like so many intellectually ambitious *criollos*, he entered the Church and was ordained. He eventually became Bishop of Santa Marta and later Panamá, where he died in 1688. He did spend more than five years in Spain in the 1660s as a defendant in a case before the Council of the Indies, from which he emerged absolved. During his enforced leisure in Spain, he wrote his best-known work, *Historia general de las conquistas del Nuevo Reino de Granada*, which was published in Antwerp in 1688; the *Historia general* was based on two manuscripts that he was able to consult while in Spain, the *Compendio historial* of Jiménez de Quesada and the fourth part of the *Elegías de varones ilustres* of Juan de Castellanos. Quesada's manuscript has been lost; therefore, Fernández de Piedrahita's work is as close as one can come to the *Compendio historial*. The *Historia general* is very much a historian's work. He does not usually insert gossip or carry tales, as Juan Rodríguez Freyle was wont to do. But he does sometimes moralize in the manner of Freyle. Sometimes, he places conversations in the mouths of his protagonists, and the source of those spoken words remains unclear. Thus, in chapter I of book V, which narrates a battle of Captain Céspedes against Indians in the province of "Los Panches," Céspedes encourages his troops in the grand manner of Henry IV in Shakespeare's *Henry IV, Part I* (Fernández de Piedrahita 98–105). Despite these dramatic moments, Fernández de Piedrahita is one of the more objective historians of the colonial period. Unlike El Inca, he is severely critical of the Indian half of his heritage, calling the Spanish conquistadors and colonizers heroic and the Indians barbarian idol worshippers who deserve to be conquered. The harsh view of Indians becomes more pronounced as he progresses through the work, as Rocío Vélez de Piedrahita has noted in her chapter on Fernández de Piedrahita in her book on colonial literature (1995: 133–58).

Theater

Antonio Gómez Restrepo states that that he would have liked to discuss preconquest literatures of Nueva Granada. Unfortunately they don't exist (*desgraciadamente*, not existent; 11). The Chibchas may have been good artists in jewelry and pottery, but they did not have a writing system. Even after being instructed in their own grammar and given a writing system by missionaries, they abandoned that knowledge. As a result, there is no pre-Colombian literature to discuss. In a somewhat similar vein, historians of colonial literature in Nueva Granada lament the nearly nonexistent genre of colonial theater.[43] In 1970, when Leon Lyday published his important, largely descriptive survey of "The Colombian Theatre before 1800," he could identify only a few plays for the entire colonial period: *Los Alarcos* (1580), *Láurea crítica* (1629), *La competencia en los nobles y discordia concordada* (1659), and *Paráphrasis panegírica* (1662). The possible existence of other plays is hazarded: *Comedia de la guerra de los Pijaos* (1610? listed as lost by José María Vergara y Vergara) and *Vida de hidalgos* and *En Dios está la vida*, both "attributed to one Bruno de Valenzuela by Ortega Ricaurte" (Lyday 36).

Since 1970, scholars have expended considerable effort in the search for indigenous texts and hitherto undiscovered examples of colonial theater. Thus, for instance, *Yuruparí*, a foundational myth from the Vaupés region of Colombia, was transcribed from the late-nineteenth-century oral version of Maximiliano José Roberto and translated into Italian; the Italian was then translated into Spanish and published in an annotated edition by Héctor Orjuela in 1983 (see Osorio de Negret, passim). Departing from general work on colonial theater in Spanish America by José Juan Arrom and Pedro Henríquez Ureña, Fernando González Cajiao (*Historia del teatro en Colombia*, 1986), Héctor H. Orjuela (*El teatro en la Nueva Granada*, 2000), and Carlos José Reyes Posada (*El teatro en el Nuevo Reino de Granada*, 2008), among others, have expanded the corpus of colonial theater in Nueva Granada.

When the Spaniards arrived in the New World, they came upon evidence of "theater" that was usually religious in content. Native practices included dances, parades, and ceremonial skits like the *areito* (in the Caribbean) and the *mitote* (in New Spain). In his history of Colombian theater, Fernando González Cajiao writes that "one of the cronistas" (alguno de los cronistas) reports that early on some Indians to the southeast of Santa Fe de Bogotá asked for permission to perform a ceremony in the precontact manner. Permission was given, and observers were sent to control the "legality" of the performance. "Legality" means the degree to which the performance is subversive, idolatrous, or blasphemous. The observers returned full of wonder for the dances, the costumes, the jewels, and elaborate plumage (González Cajiao 39).[44]

Throughout the New World, Dominicans, Franciscans, and, later, Jesuits soon saw that drama could be a powerful instrument in the evangelizing process, and "missionary theater" was born. These early dramas tended to be short allegorical pieces, biblical in subject matter, like the *auto sacramental,* the *loa,* the *coloquio,* and the *entremés,* all derived from Spanish models. They were often performed in bilingual versions (Spanish and the indigenous language) and used pantomime. While examples of missionary theater have survived in New Spain, none has survived in Nueva Granada. In Mexico, the best known later *auto sacramental* of the colonial period is by Sor Juana Inés de la Cruz. Her play *El divino Narciso* (1689) and its *loa* present the conquest and colonization of Mexico, in part through such allegorical characters as Narcissus representing Christ, and Echo representing Satan, and in part through explicitly symbolic characters like America, Occident, Music, Religion, and Zeal. While Nueva Granada cannot claim to have a dramatist of Sor Juana's stature, it can claim a theatrical canon more extensive than that identified by Leon Lyday.

Knowledge of colonial theater continues to be rather fragmentary and incomplete, however. A number of plays were not preserved as separate playbooks and no longer exist. Others are a part of longer works. Some "exist" by reputation only. The text of the first play performed in Santa Fe de Bogotá, *Los Alarcos,* does not exist. We have only a description of the performance in either 1580 or 1583 (see Reyes Posada 23–8). The plot of this *loa* treats the battle of "Los Alarcos," in which the Moors defeated the Spanish army of Alfonso VIII on July 19, 1195. The play was performed in the patio of one of the prominent men of the city. Nothing else is known about it, not even the name of the author. But a mere ten years later, according to Héctor Orjuela (*Teatro* 17) and González Cajiao (45), a theater company was established, and by 1618 there is evidence of written contracts between impresarios and actors (Orjuela, *Teatro* 19).

The first dramatist to be known by name is Hernando de Ospina. His play *Comedia de la guerra contra los pijaos* has been lost (Reyes Posada 29). Its significance is that it treats local and contemporary history, not a subject set in Europe's medieval past. An important early historian of Nueva Granada, Lucas Fernández de Piedrahita (1624–88), discussed earlier as a *cronista,* is reputed to have written plays, but none has survived. His best known work, *Noticia historial de las conquistas del Nuevo Reino de Granada,* devotes some attention to Indian ceremonies and dances (book I, chapter III). He finds them to be inspired by the devil and examples of the barbarism which the civilizing process of evangelization is meant to eradicate.

The first play to have survived into the present is by Bruno de Solís y Valenzuela, written when he was but thirteen years old and included in his *Thesaurus Linguae Latinae*. The play's title is *Láurea crítica* (1629). The fact that a play by a thirteen-year-old has received serious critical attention (Lyday 37–9; González Cajiao 46–8; Reyes Posada 58–69) is indication enough of the meagre corpus of dramatical production in Nueva Granada. This short play, the length of an *entremés*, adds to the literary history of the "Barroco de Indias" insofar as it attacks the style of Góngora and defends the style of Quevedo. According to Lyday (39), the precocious Bruno de Solís y Valenzuela is attacking not Góngora himself but his epigones, the most prominent of them being Hernando Domínguez Camargo. Domínguez Camargo was ten years older than Bruno and known to him (Reyes Posada 61–3). Two other plays attributed to Bruno de Solís y Valenzuela, *En Dios está la vida* and *Vida de hidalgos*, have been lost.[45]

If the dramas contained in longer prose works were extracted and anthologized, the corpus of theatrical work in colonial Nueva Granada would be expanded and better known. Consider the case of *El desierto prodigioso y prodigio del desierto*, studied earlier for its contribution to the history of narrative fiction. This work contains several dramas presented as autonomous and free-standing plays. The plays in question are (1) a short play on the prodigal son (*mansión* vi, 241–51), in which a series of dialoguing sonnets are placed in the mouths of characters like the father, the son, and the servant; (2) a play on the baptism of Jesus by John the Baptist (*mansión* xxi, 466–503) attributed to Joan del Rossario; and (3) an "auto sacramental" in five acts (*mansión* xxi, 535–683), with allegorical characters like Husband and Wife (the dialogues echo the Song of Solomon), Gentlemen, Demons, and Lucifer. This *auto* is also attributed to Joan del Rossario (535), and the main characters – Fernando, Antonio, Pedro, with some guests – watched it during a theater evening (535). A poem entitled "El hostal" (*mansión* x, 521–33) follows a play of the same name which the main characters have also watched. The play itself, however, was dropped from the manuscript, and the editors have noted a lacuna of some sixty-five pages. This dropped play has never been found. In his introduction to his edition of *El cisne de los desiertos*, Dom S. Thalmann refers to the "Yerbabuena" manuscript of *El desierto prodigioso y prodigio del desierto* and, apparently following remarks by the editors of the "Yerbabuena" manuscript, states that the manuscript contains two dramatic works (*comedias*) by an unknown hand (Thalmann xxx). However, these two dramatic works either do not exist, for they did not make it into the printed version of the Yerbabuena manuscript, or Thalmann has misidentified them.[46]

Rhythmica sacra, moral y laudatoria by Franciso Álvarez de Velasco y Zorrilla, whose sensibility is poetic rather than dramatic, contains a number of works with dramatic touches. Several of the *villancicos* are in dialogue form. A short work entitled "Mysterios del Rosario" (340–6) is printed as a series of choral responses. One poem is entitled "Letras para la comedia, y loa de Santa Bárbara" (441–2). But no *comedia* follows. Very little actual drama is included in *Rhythmica sacra, moral y laudatoria.*

Juan de Cueto y Mena (b. 1604–69?) was a Spaniard who lived most of his life in Cartagena. Unlike most of the authors of the colonial period, he was not a man of the Church but a pharmacist. Famous in Cartagena for his erudition (he had a library of more than two hundred books), he was well off financially until he became embroiled in a legal process which led to him be jailed for debt (a charge that he contested, unsuccessfully) and resulted in his impoverishment (see Rivas Sacconi, "Prólogo," passim). Héctor Orjuela (*Teatro*, 31) calls him a baroque dramatist whose work is superior to that of Pedro de Solís y Valenzuela. Cueto y Mena wrote two works that have survived, *La competencia en los nobles y discordia concordada* (1659) and *Paráphrasis panegírica* (1660). Both plays are discussed briefly by Reyes Posada (107–11) and Orjuela (*Teatro*, 31–40). In *La competencia en los nobles y discordia concordada*, allegorical characters called (Telus) Earth, (Aeolo) Air, (Pireo) Fire, and (Doris) Water converse, criticize one another, and extoll their own virtues. The sky (Cielo) asks why this "competencia" or conflict should be permitted to disturb the universe. Order needs to be restored ("discordia" needs to be "concordada"). *La competencia en los nobles y discordia concordada* is a dramatic presentation of the worldview of seventeenth-century Nueva Granada's authors. Allegorically, any disorder will be dealt with and harmony will be restored. Central to the colonial mind-set is the notion of the feudal harmony and hierarchy that reflect the "great chain of being," a Ptolemaic conception of the world, and an Aristotelian understanding of "science." Uncertainty and tragedy may hound a man in his life, as it did Cueto y Mena, but the universe that surrounds him is permanently harmonious and ordered. This is not the worldview of a seventeenth-century savant of early modern Europe wrestling with the implications of the Copernican revolution. *Paráphrasis panegírica*, also by Cueto y Mena, is a hagiographic play that celebrates the life and death of the archbishop of the Spanish city of Valencia, Tomás de Villanueva, and his canonization. Here, too, allegory is central, for Time (El Tiempo) is the main character.

Of all the literature in colonial Nueva Granada, theater is the least studied and about which the discovery of new or forgotten material is the most likely.

Conclusions

In Nueva Granada, there was little sense of a developing national literary tradition among the writers themselves. It is not only that they looked to Spain and elsewhere in the New World for their literary models nor that, on the secular side, most of the writing was bureaucratic in nature and on the religious side, most had to do with missionary reports and evangelization. It is also that, in 1531, 1536, and 1543, royal decrees were issued prohibiting the dissemination of books from Spain that were not religious (Leonard 81–2). Those decrees and the lack of a printing press had a dampening effect on creative writing in Nueva Granada. Little evidence exists of writers being in communication with one another, of reading and commenting on each other's works. They were isolated by geography, by circumstance, by the hardships of daily life. Most of the literary works from Nueva Granada that are now studied and analyzed were not published during the writers' lifetime. Quesada's *Gran cuaderno* did not appear until the latter parts of Oviedo's *Historia natural y moral de las Indias* were published in 1851 55. His *Epítome de la conquista del Nuevo Reino de Granada* appeared in 1889. Only the first part of *Elegías de varones ilustres* by Castellanos was published during his lifetime. Three other parts were published in 1837. *El carnero* first appeared in print in 1859. Domínguez Camargo's two principal works, *San Ignacio Loyola* and the poems in *Ramillete*, were published shortly after his death in 1666 and 1676, respectively, and he was then forgotten. The *Rhythmica sacra moral y laudatoria* by Francisco Álvarez de Velasco y Zorrilla was published five years before he died in 1708. The very existence of *El desierto prodigioso y prodigio del desierto* was not known until 1963, and the text itself was not published until 1977, 1984, and 1985. *El cisne de los desiertos* was published in 2013. Sor Francisca's work was published by her nephew many years after she died. *Su vida* was published in the United States in Philadelphia in 1817; *Afectos espirituales* was published in 1843 in Bogotá. The performance history of the theater is not recoverable. Historiography was probably the genre most available to writers of Nueva Granada.

In the eighteenth century, the influence of Spain began to decline and that of France (and later the United States, with its revolution in both thought and deed) began to rise. The "Enlightenment" – in Spanish, *el siglo de las luces* – entered first through a traditionalist Spanish version and later through the more radical and revolutionary rationalism of the French *philosophes*. Much of the change took place beneath the surface of society and probably was not that evident in social life. But in Santa Fe de Bogotá *tertulias* or literary salons came into being (Cristina 582–6). Scientific, political, and social writings were debated, along with literature. Not much "literature" per se was produced in later eighteenth-century Nueva Granada. Menéndez y Pelayo calls the period sterile in terms of poetry ("estéril para la poesía"; vol. 2: 31). Rather, "genres" like the essay, the scholarly paper, and journalist stories became more prevalent. The rise of rationalism and scientific thought culminated in the scientific work of José Celestino Mutis (1732–1808), leader of the Royal Botanical Expeditions of the 1780s. Though ordained as a priest, he thought as a rationalist and even delivered university lectures on Copernicus and the scientific method, activities which his alarmed colleagues denounced to the Inquisition, unaware that the Church no longer prohibited the teaching of Copernicus (Cristina 568–9). His fame was such that Alexander von Humboldt visited him in Santa Fe de Bogotá in 1801.

As the hold of religion on colonial society weakened somewhat, more secular writing and thought came to the fore. The arc of Mutis's career is paradigmatic in this regard. The increase in secularism led to the establishment of those great institutions that facilitate the progress of knowledge and thought: the secular university, the printing press, the newspaper, the public library. Though the Jesuits were expelled from Colombia in 1768, it would be almost a century before the first national public university was founded. The printing press was established definitively in 1778.[47] Besides publishing religious tracts, it published scientific research and journalistic pieces (Cristina 574). The first important newspaper was a weekly, which began publication in 1791: *Papel periódico de la ciudad de Santafé de Bogotá*. In 1777, the first public library in the New World was established; this library became the national library of Colombia, the Biblioteca Nacional (Cristina 573).

Eighteenth-century Nueva Granada may have less to offer literary critics than earlier centuries of the colonial era. However, it offers more in terms of intellectual history, for the intellectual ferment in the society resulted in the great transformation of Nueva Granada into Colombia. After all, both Antonio Nariño and Simón Bolívar were formed in colonial Nueva Granada and through contacts with the wider world.

REFERENCES

Achury Valenzuela, Darío. See Castillo y Guevara, *Obras completas*.

Achury Valenzuela, Darío. "Tunja en tiempos de Sor Francisca Josefa de la Concepción de Castillo." *Boletín Cultural y Bibliográfico del Banco de la República* 10, no. 6 (1967): 1276–82.

Achury Valenzuela, Darío. *Análisis crítico de los 'Afectos espirituales' de Sor Francisca Josefa de la Concepción de Castillo*. Bogotá: Biblioteca de Cultura Colombiana, 1962.

Aguado, Pedro de. *Historia de la provincia de Sancta Marta y Nuevo Reino de Granada (finished about 1581)*. 3 vols. Madrid: Espasa-Calpe, 1930–31.

Alvar, Manuel. *Juan de Castellanos: Tradición española y realidad americana*. Bogotá: Instituto Caro y Cuervo, 1972.

Álvarez de Velasco y Zorrilla, Francisco. *Rhythmica sacra, moral y laudatoria. Edited, with a critical study, by Ernesto Porras Collantes*. Presentation by Rafael Torres Quintero. Preliminary study and notes by Jaime Tello. Bogotá: Instituto Caro y Cuervo, 1989.

Arciniegas, Germán. "Los cronistas," in *Manual de literatura colombiana*, 27–51. Bogotá: Planeta Colombiana Editorial, S.A., 1988.

Aventuras de Arsenio, El Ermitaño. *Novela*. Collated and edited by Héctor H. Orjuela. Bogotá: Editorial Guadalupe, 2003.

Briceño Jáuregui, Manuel. *Estudio histórico-crítico de 'El desierto prodigioso y prodigio del desierto' de Don Pedro de Solís y Valenzuela*. Bogotá: Instituto Caro y Cuervo, 1983.

Castellanos, Juan de. Elegías de varones ilustres de Indias. *Madrid: Imprenta de la Publicidad, á cargo de M. Rivadeneyra, 1874*. Series: Biblioteca de Autores Españoles (Tomo 4).

Castillo y Guevara, Madre Francisca Josefa de la Concepción de. Obras completas. 2 vols. *Introduction, Notes, and Indices by Darío Achury Valenzuela*. Bogotá: Banco de la República, 1968.

Cristina, María Teresa. "La literatura en la conquista y la colonia," in *Manual de historia de Colombia*, 493–592. Vol. 1. Bogotá: Procultura, 1982.

Curcio Altamar, Antonio. *Evolución de la novela en Colombia*. Bogotá: Instituto Caro y Cuervo, 1957.

Domínguez Camargo, Hernando. *San Ignacio de Loyola. Fundador de la Compañía de Jesús. Poema Heróico*. Bogotá: Editorial ABC, 1956.

Fajardo Valenzuela, Diógenes. "Anotaciones sobre literatura colonial y su historia," in *Leer la historia: Caminos a la historia de la literatura colombiana*, 23–59. Ed. Carmen Elisa Acosta Peñalosa, Diógenes Fajardo Valenzuela, Iván Vicente Padilla Chasing, and Patricia Trujillo Montón. Bogotá: Universidad Nacional de Colombia, 2007.

Fernández de Piedrahita, Lucas. *Historia general de las conquistas del Nuevo Reino de Granada. Edición basada en la de Amberes de 1688*. Bogotá: Imprenta de Medardo Rivas, 1881.

Gómez Restrepo, Antonio. *Historia de la literatura colombiana. Época colonial.* Bogotá: Imprenta Nacional, 1945.

González Cajiao, Fernando. *Historia del teatro en Colombia.* Bogotá: Instituto Colombiano de Cultura, 1986.

Herrera, Clara E. *Las místicas de la Nueva Granada: Tres casos de búsqueda de la perfección y construcción de la santidad.* Barcelona: Paso de la Barca, 2013.

Jara, René and Nicholas Spadaccini (eds.). *1492–1992: Re/Discovering Colonial Writing.* Minneapolis: University of Minnesota Press, 1991.

Jiménez de Quesada, Gonzalo. See Oviedo y Valdés, *Historia general y natural de las Indias,* vol. 6, and Ramos, *Ximénez de Quesada y su relación con los cronistas y el Epítome de la conquista del Nuevo Reino de Granada.*

Leonard, Irving A. *Books of the Brave, Being an Account of Books and of Men in the Spanish Conquest and Settlement of the Sixteenth-Century New World.* Cambridge, MA: Harvard University Press, 1949.

Lyday, Leon, "The Colombian Theatre before 1800," *Latin American Theatre Review* 4:1 (1970): 35–50.

McKnight, Kathryn Joy. *The Mystic of Tunja: The Writings of Madre Castillo 1671–1742.* Amherst: University of Massachusetts Press, 1997.

Maya, Rafael. *Estampas de ayer y retratos de hoy.* Bogotá: Editorial Kelly, 1954.

Mendoza Varela, Eduardo. *"Prólogo"* to Hernando Domínguez Camargo. *Antología poética,* 7–21. Medellín: Editorial Bedout, 1969.

Menéndez y Pelayo, Marcelino. *Historia de la poesía hispano-americana.* 2 vols. Madrid: Victoriano Suárez, 1911, 1913.

Morales Borrero, María Teresa. *La Madre Castillo. Su espiritualidad y su estilo.* Bogotá: Instituto Caro y Cuervo, 1968.

Morales Folguera, José Miguel. *Tunja. Atenas del Renacimiento en el Nuevo Reino de Granada Málaga.* La Universidad de Málaga, 1998.

Moreno Durán, Rafael Humberto. *"Poesía en la colonia,"* in *Gran Enciclopedia de Colombia. Tomo 4. Literatura, 39–54.* Bogotá: Printer Latinoamericana, 1992.

Nava y Saavedra, Jerónima. *Autobiografía de una monja venerable.* Edited, with a preliminary study by Ángela Inés Robledo, 7–28. Cali: Centro Editorial de la Universidad del Valle, 1994.

Orjuela, Héctor H. *Antología de la narrativa breve de ficción en la Nueva Granada.* Bogotá: Editora Guadalupe, 2003.

Orjuela, Héctor H. *Crónicas y cronistas de la Nueva Granada.* Bogotá: Editora Guadalupe, 2004.

Orjuela, Héctor H. *El teatro en la Nueva Granada. Siglos XVI–XVIII.* Santafé de Bogotá: Quebecor Impreandes, 2000.

Orjuela, Héctor H. "Introducción" to *'El desierto prodigioso y prodigio del desierto' de Pedro de Solís y Valenzuela. Primera novela hispanoamericana,* 19–83. Bogotá: Instituto Caro y Cuervo, 1984.

Ortega, José J. *Historia de la literatura colombiana.* 2nd ed. Bogotá: Editorial Cromos, 1935.

Osorio de Negret, Betty. "Literatura indígena en Colombia," in *Gran Enciclopedia de Colombia*, 15–20. Tomo 4. Literatura. Bogotá: Printer Latinoamericana, 1992.

Otero Muñoz, Gustavo. *La literatura colonial de Colombia*. La Paz, Bolivia, 1928.

Oviedo, Gonzalo Fernández de. *Libro del muy esforzado e invencible caballero Don Claribalte*. *(Facsimile edition of 1519)*. Madrid: Real Académica Española, 1956.

Oviedo y Valdés, Gonzalo Fernández de. *Historia general y natural de las Indias*. Vol. 6 (Asunción del Paraguay: Editorial Guaranía, 1944): 179–239. [These pages excerpt Quesada's *Gran cuaderno* and contain chapters 18–31 of the second book of the seventh part of the *Historia*, which is also known as the 26th part of the work.]

Pacheco Quintero, Jorge. *Antología de la poesía en Colombia*. 2 vols. Bogotá: Instituto Caro y Cuervo, 1970.

Padilla Chasing, Iván Vicente. "Del olvido a la memoria histórica: problemas de la historia del teatro en Colombia," in *Leer la historia: Caminos a la historia de la literatura colombiana*, 109–62. Ed. Carmen Elisa Acosta Peñalosa, Diógenes Fajardo Valenzuela, Iván Vicente Padilla Chasing, and Patricia Trujillo Montón. Bogotá: Universidad Nacional de Colombia, 2007.

Palencia-Roth, Michael. "The Cannibal Law of 1503," in *Early Images of the New World: Transfer and Creation*, 21–64. Ed. Jerry M. Williams and Robert E. Lewis. Tucson: University of Arizona Press, 1993.

Palencia-Roth, Michael. "Enemies of God: Monsters and the Theology of Conquest," in *Monsters, Tricksters and Sacred Cows: Animal Tales and American Identities*, 23–50. Ed. A. James Arnold, with an afterword by Derek Walcott. Charlottesville: University Press of Virginia, 1996.

Palencia-Roth, Michael. "Mapping the Caribbean: Cartography and the Cannibalization of Culture," in *A History of Literature in the Caribbean, Vol. 3: Cross-Cultural Studies*, 3–27. Ed. James Arnold. Amsterdam: John Benjamins, 1997.

Páramo y Cepeda, Juan Francisco de. *Alteraciones del Dariel. Poema Épico*. Ed. Héctor H. Orjuela. Santafé de Bogotá: Editorial Kelly, 1994.

Pascual Buxó, José. *El enamorado de Sor Juana: Francisco Álvarez de Velasco Zorrilla y su 'Carta laudatoria (1698)' a Sor Juana Inés de la Cruz*. México: UNAM, 1993.

Picón Salas, Mariano. *De la conquista a la Independencia*. México: Fondo de Cultura Económica, 1967.

Pomareda, Jorge Páramo. "Introducción" to *Pedro de Solís y Valenzuela, El desierto prodigioso y prodigio del desierto*, xi–lxxxix. Vol. 1. Bogotá: Instituto Caro y Cuervo, 1977.

Porras Collantes, Ernesto. "La prosaica vida del poeta neogranadino don Francisco Álvarez de Velasco y Zorrilla," in *'Rhythmica Sacra, Moral y Laudatoria' de Francisco Álvarez de Velasco y Zorrilla*, xlv–ciii. Bogotá: Instituto Caro y Cuervo, 1989.

Ramos, Demetrio. *Ximénez de Quesada en su relación con los cronistas y el 'Epítome de la conquista del Nuevo Reino de Granada'*. Sevilla: Consejo Superior de Investigaciones Científicas, 1972.

Reardon, B. P. (ed.). *Collected Ancient Greek Novels*. Berkeley: University of California Press, 1989.

Reyes Posada, Carlos José. *El teatro en el Nuevo Reino de Granada*. Medellín: Fondo Editorial EAFIT, 2008.

Rivas Sacconi, José Manuel. *"Prólogo" to Obras de Juan de Cueto y Mena*, ix–xxix. Ed. Archer Woodford. Bogotá: Instituto Caro y Cuervo, 1952.

Ruíz Rivera, Julián B. *Encomienda y mita en Nueva Granada en el siglo XVII*. Sevilla: Escuela de Estudios Hispano-Americanos de Sevilla, 1975.

Simón, Fray Pedro. *Noticias historiales de las conquistas de Tierra Firme en las Indias Occidentales*. 5 vols. Bogotá: Editorial Medardo Rivas, 1882–1892.

Solís y Valenzuela, Pedro. *El desierto prodigioso y prodigio del desierto*. 3 vols. Bogotá: Instituto Caro y Cuervo, 1977; 1984; 1985). [Volumes 1 and 2 (*mansiones* i–xxii) are edited from the Madrid manuscript; volume 3 (*mansiones* i–iii) is edited from the Yerbabuena manuscript.]

Tello, Jaime. *"Estudio Preliminar" to Rhythmica Sacra, Moral y Laudatoria de Francisco Álvarez de Velasco y Zorrilla*, xix–xliii. Bogotá: Instituto Caro y Cuervo, 1989.

Thalmann G., Dom S. *"Introducción general" to Bruno de Solís y Valenzuela, El Cisne de los desiertos. Poema heróico*, ix–xcvii. Salzburg: FB Anglistik und Amerikanistik, Universität Salzburg, 2013.

Torre Revelo, José. *El libro, la imprenta y el periodismo en América durante la dominación española*. México: UNAM, 1991.

Torres Quintero, Rafael. *"Presentación" to Rhythmica Sacra, Moral y Laudatoria de Francisco Álvarez de Velasco y Zorrilla*, xv–xvii. Bogotá: Instituto Caro y Cuervo, 1989.

Vélez de Piedrahita, Rocío. "La madre Castillo (1671–1742)," in *Manual de literatura colombiana*, 101–41. Bogotá: Planeta Colombiana, 1988.

Vélez de Piedrahita, Rocío. *Literatura en la colonia – de Rodríguez Freile a Francisco José de Caldas*. Medellín: Biblioteca Pública Piloto, 1995.

Vergara y Vergara, José María. *Historia de la literatura en la Nueva Granada*. 3 vols. Bogotá: Presidencia de la República, 1968 (1867).

Yurupary. *Mito, leyenda y epopeya del Vaupés*. Ed. Héctor Orjuela. Bogotá: Instituto Caro y Cuervo, 1983.

Notes

1 Antonio Curcio Altamar in *Evolución de la novela en Colombia*, an important but seldom consulted work, makes this argument. What mattered in the colonial period was an administrative region, not what would become a modern country (3–5).

2 Diógenes Fajardo Valenzuela has discussed this situation concerning the historiography of the colonial period, mostly but not exclusively in Nueva Granada.

3 All through the Americas, from the Dominican Republic to Mexico to Colombia to Argentina, celebrations of the five hundred years since the European discovery of the New World gave rise to conferences and then to publications on the colonial period. In the United States, for example, we may point to the edited volume by René Jara and Nicholas Spadaccini.

4 Quesada, cited by Gómez Restrepo (12), spoke of the "songs" that the Chibchas would chant to the gods as they requested guidance before going to war, praying that the war would be "just" and that the victory would be theirs. No record of those songs exists.

5 In the prologue to his work, Oviedo writes that, being in the Indies, on order of the Catholic King Ferdinand V, as inspector (*veedor*) overseeing the establishments for smelting gold (*fundiciones de oro*, in Santa María la Antigua del Darién), he dedicated considerable time to writing this work (*aquesta crónica*). See Fernández de Oviedo, *Claribalte*, fol. ii, alphabetized in the bibliography under Oviedo.

6 The history of the book and of printing, together with an overview of censorship and the circulation of printed matter, has been thoroughly studied by José Torre Revelo in *El libro, la imprenta y el periodismo en América durante la dominación española*.

7 "La literatura colombiana nace con el descubrimiento del Nuevo Reino de Granada; y el primer nombre que la enaltece es el del descubridor y fundador de Santafé de Bogotá, el licenciado don Gonzalo Jiménez de Quesada" (Gómez Restrepo 15).

8 "Para este país constituye una fortuna el haber sido conquistado, no por un aventurero ignorante y brutal, sino por un hombre culto y letrado."

9 Rafael Maya, in *Estampas de ayer y retratos de hoy*, characterized Castellanos and Tunja thus: [Castellanos buscó] la oscuridad y silencio de la vida sacerdotal en la ciudad más gris y recóndita del Nuevo Reino de Granada, su Tunja, que es solar de apacibles latinistas, de conventos sombríos y de brisa helada" (13).

10 These writers are all identified by Pacheco Quintero as inhabitants of Tunja. See the headnotes to the selections from their poetry in Pacheco Quintero, *Antología de la poesía en Colombia*, vol. 1.

11 The argument for Tunja's importance as the center of literary culture in Nueva Granada is persuasively, if briefly, presented by Rafael Humberto Moreno Durán, who is also a native of Tunja (see Moreno Durán 51–2).

12 "En torno a la figura de Castellanos se formó el que puede ser considerado el primer cenáculo literario del Nuevo Reino" (Cristina 499).

13 "La gran desdicha de este libro es estar en verso" (vol. 2: 16).

14 Mariano Picón Salas, in his history of colonial Latin American literature, remarks that during this time the "epic" suffered an "internal decadence" as it evolved from the heroic and dramatic portraits in *La araucana* to work that is

lyrical rather than martial in *El arauco domado* (Picón Salas 117–18). The *Elegías* may be characterized as more lyrical than martial, more elegiac than heroic.

15 At the beginning of Part II of the *Elegías*, there is a curious approval from a "censor" who is none other than Alonso de Ercilla, author of *La Araucana*. Ercilla states: "Yo he visto este libro, y en él no hallo cosa mal sonante ni contra buenas costumbres; y en lo que toca a la historia, la tengo por verdadera, por ser fielmente escritas muchas cosas y particularidades que yo vi y entendí en aquella tierra, al tiempo que pasé y estuve en ella: por donde infiero que va el autor muy arrimado a la verdad, y son guerras y acaecimientos que hasta ahora no las he visto escritas por otro autor, y que algunos holgarán de saberlas" (*Elegías*, 180).

16 Castellanos, *Elegías*, Part II, Elegía 3, canto 4 (249).

17 The first edition of 1859 of *El carnero* had a different and much longer title, of which a portion is reproduced here: *Conquista i descubrimiento del Nuevo Reino de Granada, de las Indias Occidentales del Mar Océano y fundación de la ciudad de Santa Fe de Bogotá, primera de este reino donde se fundó la real audiencia i cancillería, siendo la cabeza se hizo arzobispado Cuéntase en ella su descubrimiento, algunas guerras civiles [etc.].* Rodríguez Freyle's name is given on the title pages as "Rodríguez Fresle." The title *El carnero* came later. Its meaning is obscure and much debated.

18 See Juan Francisco de Páramo y Cepeda, *Alteraciones del Dariel*.

19 "Ponga aquí el dedo el lector y espéreme adelante, porque quiero acabar esta guerra" (Rodríguez Freyle 74).

20 "[para que] no quede sepultado en las tinieblas del olvido lo que en este Nuevo Reino aconteció" (Rodríguez Freyle 49).

21 See also Eduardo Mendoza Varela, "Prólogo" to *Hernando Domínguez Camargo, Antología poética* (16). Menéndez y Pelayo wrote: "Su Poema Heróico, de San Ignacio de Loyola, es, sin duda, uno de los más tenebrosos abortos del gongorismo, sin ningún rasgo de ingenio que haga tolerables sus aberraciones" (vol. 2: 22).

22 See Domínguez Camargo, *San Ignacio de Loyola*, passim.

23 "Romance eneámetro" is a verse form which, as described by the editors of the *Rhythmica*, requires that each eleven–syllable line begin and end with an "esdrújula", that is, a word with the accent on the antepenultimate syllable: thus, "Ánimo . . . tímido" or "Prófugo . . . pávidas."

24 The question of authorship has been resurrected by Dom S. Thalmann G. in a text published in 2013 entitled *El cisne de los desiertos* by Bruno de Solís y Valenzuela. Thalmann argues for Bruno as the true author of *El desierto prodigioso y prodigio del desierto*, on the grounds that lists in Carthusian monasteries, of which Bruno was a member, include both works in catalogues of works authored by the extraordinarily prolific Bruno (xcviii).

25 The cave, called "la Cueva del Emitaño," does exist, as do the desert of Candelaria and the convent of that name. All of these places can be visited. The Andrés of the story also existed and a portrait of him in his monk's robes hangs in the convent of Candelaria. Fernando became a Carthusian monk,

taking the name of Bruno; his portrait hangs in the basilica of Monserrate in Bogotá. Photographic plates of these places and people are reproduced in Manuel Briceño Jáuregui's critical study of *El desierto prodigioso y prodigio del desierto.*

26 "¿Quién, oh jóvenes gallardos, os trae a esta aspereza en la flor de vuestros años?" (*mansión* iv).

27 The "autobiographies" of nuns were sometimes authored not by them but by their male confessors, so it sometimes remains unclear who wrote what, thus making the question of authorship at times deeply problematic. In her preliminary study to Jerónima Nava y Saavedra's autobiography, Ángela Inés Robledo has outlined some of the problems (Nava y Saavedra 9–11). The true authorship of a number of other nuns' lives has yet to be determined conclusively.

28 This is how Clara E. Herrera, in her excellent study of the three nuns, characterizes the differences in the paths they chose to follow, basing her characterizations especially on their autobiographical writings. See Herrera, passim.

29 See Vélez de Piedrahita (1988: 103–5).

30 In an essay published in 1967 in *Boletín Cultural y Bibliográfico del Banco de la República,* entitled "Tunja en tiempos de Sor Francisca Josefa de la Concepción de Castillo," Darío Achury Valenzuela tries valiantly to make Tunja relevant to Sor Francisca's work by taking his readers on a "walking tour" of Tunja as if she herself were to take a long stroll around the town. He has so little social and sociological information at his disposal that he can do little more than point out houses where certain people or important families lived, or had lived. (See Achury Valenzuela, 1967, passim.)

31 "Pensar y considerar ante el Señor todos los años de mi vida en amargura de mi alma, pues todos los hallo gastado mal."

32 A more tempered and generous view of convent life, and in particular the kind of life that theoretically was likely in the "Convento Real de Santa Clara" in Tunja, is offered by Kathryn Joy McKnight in her excellent book on Sor Francisca (see McKnight 79–100).

33 "Ya he estado amolando muy bien un cuchillo para enviárselo que se lo meta, y le enviaré una soga para que se ahorque."

34 "Olvidéme de comer mi pan de dolor, y mi virtud se secó como teja; a las fauces se pegó mi lengua, y fui reducida a polvo de muerte."

35 "En la amargura amarguísima tendré paz, y en la amargura moraré; haré de ella un nido de descanso." The word "moraré" is an allusion to one of the works of Teresa de Ávila: *El Castillo interior, o las moradas.*

36 "Pobrecilla, combatida de la tempestad, sin ninguna consolación, no temas; yo soy el Señor Dios tuyo, que te saqué de Egipto. ... Morarás con Él en su protección. El Señor es mi amparo, y mi refugio, mi Dios; en Él he de esperar hasta que decline el día, y se abatan las sombras, todo el día de la vida mortal cercado de sombras, hasta que llame al alma a coronarla en las alturas, de donde cayeron los leones y leopardos. ... Confórtese tu corazón y haz

varonilmente . . . que el Altísimo . . . es tu ayudador; el Señor es tu escudo y tu fortaleza, . . . el que enseñará tus manos a la batalla. . . . Él te librará de los lazos de los cazadores, y de las palabras de los malos; el escudo de su verdad te cercará . . . para que no temas los temores nocturnos. Enviará sus ángeles . . . disparará a sus enemigos y huirán de su presencia . . . tú, Dios mío, los cogerás como a zorrillas pequeñas que pretenden demoler tu viña. . . . ¡Oh alma mía, cuán contenta cantarás las victorias de tu amado!" (*Afecto* 20, 65–6).

37 "Habiendo comulgado, y pensando cómo en el Santísimo Sacramento, junto con la persona de Nuestro Señor Jesucristo, por la unión inseparable de la divinidad en las tres divinas personas, está allí el Espíritu Santo, me parecía hallarse cercada mi alma de aquel fuego divino, llena y embebecida en él, como un inmenso mar o globo de luz y de amor, más grande que todos los orbes de la tierra" (*Afecto* 90, 207).

38 "Amantísimo amor, amado, amabilísimo del alma" (*Afecto* 32, 91).

39 "En Dios hallarás buenas todas las cosas. Fuera de Él, todas las hallarás amargas" (*Obras completas*, vol. 2: 489).

40 "Como poetisa es sor Francisca, después de Domínguez Camargo, la más alta voz lírica conocida durante el período colonial colombiano. Sus poesías son pocas, pero de primera calidad."

41 See the relevant essays by Palencia-Roth on the history of fantastical beings, teratology, monstrosity, and cannibalism in relation to the discovery, conquest, and colonization of the New World.

42 Guatavita is a remote, high altitude lake not far from today's Bogotá famous for having gold ornaments thrown into it during religious ceremonies that included human sacrifice. Many of these ornaments are now in the Gold Museum – El Museo del Oro – in Bogotá.

43 This is the general thesis of Iván Vicente Padilla Chasing's historiographical survey (passim). He devotes relatively little space to colonial theater, or its absence.

44 Unfortunately, González Cajiao does not specify either the identity of the *cronista* or the source of this description.

45 These plays were supposedly written in 1618 and performed shortly thereafter. If that is the case, then Bruno de Solís y Valenzuela could not have written the plays, for he was born in 1616 (Pacheco Quintero, vol. 1: 171–3).

46 The editor of the Yerbabuena manuscript, Rubén Paez Patiño, writes in his "advertencia editorial" (vol. 3, ix) that the manuscript contains not two *comedias* but one, copied by two different hands. The editorial history of *El desierto prodigioso y prodigio del desierto* is both complex and confusing.

47 Compare this date with the dates of the first printing presses in Mexico (1535) and Peru (1585).

CHAPTER 2

Cosmography, ethnography, and the literary imagination of the New Kingdom of Granada

Elizabeth M. Pettinaroli

The *Epítome de las conquistas del Nuevo Reino de Granada* (1538) is the earliest text to present the region of the New Kingdom of Granada to the imagination of the European world. The work has offered scholars the first characterization of the peoples of the region alongside with the description of its landscape. It was penned by Alonso de Santa Cruz, a most influential chronicler, astronomer, and cartographer to Charles V and Philip II, who dedicated his life to crafting a coherent notion of the *orbis terrarum* by incorporating the discoveries brought by trans-Atlantic and trans-Pacific exploration. The *Epítome* has puzzled scholars for its apparently incomplete, fragmentary nature and its coverage of myriad topics, which imbue it with a sensibility not shared in later works informed by Santa Cruz's description, such as Juan López de Velasco's *Geografía y Descripción Universal de las Indias* (1574) and Antonio de Herrera's *Historia general de los hechos de los castellanos* (1601) among others. In particular, the treatment accorded the indigenous Moxca and Panche peoples in this foundational work bewilders readers, subverting their expectation of a presumably instructive account of exotic alterity among the inhabitants of the Equinox. A report on the abuses committed by conquerors in the region and the frustrations endured by missions of discovery led by Gonzalo Jiménez de Quesada, founder of Santafé de Bogotá, breaks with generic conventions that dictated praise of the heroic deeds of explorers and the utopian landscapes they traversed. It was slighted as little more than a scientific and ethnographic reference source and relegated to literary oblivion.

Perhaps the absence of topical focus in the manuscript can be viewed differently, less as a failing than as a literary strategy. Santa Cruz's treatment of the material can be seen as an exercise of creative fragmentation in which the author inscribes the region through the mobile point of view of an itinerary along the Magdalena River, interposing abstract representations of New Granada, and invites readers to join him in a fluidity of inquiry through the deployment of multiple viewpoints. His mode of description rearranges inherited taxonomies of knowledge, crafting "ethnographic fictions" that venture new answers to the paradox of the Amerindian through an entanglement of the literary, cosmographic, chorographic, and historical realms. Tom Conley coins the term to characterize the articulation of myth and observation that André Thevet deploys in his cosmographic work; at this intersection, Conley locates the early unfolding of ethnography (190). From a network of allusions to Homer's *Iliad* and Thucydides's *History of the Peloponnesian War* spring allusive panoramas that yield a new theorization of the Amerindian, and in particular of the Moxca peoples, from a local perspective. This novel alignment between literary interpretation and geographical observation illuminates the production of new knowledge brought about by the assimilation of the Indies to European worldview. Santa Cruz's text engages a sixteenth-century debate of paramount importance, in which intellectuals attempted to reconcile old cosmographies and cosmologies with new worlds and peoples. As Nicolás Wey-Gómez has signaled, this debate was instrumental in reconceptualizing the ancient Antipodes as the early-modern Tropics and influenced the politics of empire. The *Epítome* is a constitutive text in the dialogic process of what Edmundo O'Gorman understood as the "invention of America." The struggle that later authors have faced in locating the Moxca on the region's historical and political landscape lays bare the political and moral consequences of the colonial enterprise and exposes the continued challenges in grounding foundational narratives of the region in these ethnographic fictions.

Thus the *Epítome* has confounded scholars for its generic transgressions, its seemingly unfinished quality, and the astounding variety of subject matter that it encompasses. During the sixteenth century, authors progressively abandoned the inherited rhetorical models that had constrained the writing of epitomes, privileging abridgement of the sources and their restriction to only the most essential matter. Refashioning the parameters that their predecessors had established in previous centuries, they offered wider critical possibilities that allowed wide latitude to the contrasting and combining of materials in these works. Deliberate in his attempt to refashion the parameters of the genre, Juan Antonio de Vera y Figueroa warns his readers in the *Epitome de la vida y hechos del emperador Carlos V* that departures from inherited models are not due to ignorance, but rather to his license to critique the events he relates in chronological order. This shift gave their works an apparent fragmented texture and disjointed character that is present in Santa Cruz's *Epítome*. The process of epitomizing (*epitomar*) according to the 1732 *Tesoro* dictionary renders the action as "compendiar, abreviar y resumir una obra dilatada, reduciendola a términos mui breves, y sacando de ella lo mas substancial" (to compile, abridge, and summarize an extended work, reducing it to briefer terms, and extracting from it what is most substantive). The process of critical abridgement in the selection of its "substance," alluded to in the definition – with its challenges of inclusion, exclusion, and hierarchies of preference – reveals the interpretive agency of the compiler who organizes the avalanche of simultaneous information encountered into a narrative that masters the world's historical and geographical complexity.

Where the genre as a whole, though, used to introduce readers to the chronology of great events and a roster of heroes and prodigious historical deeds derived from earlier models, the *Epítome*'s opening surprises readers with the most dramatic depiction imaginable of the Magdalena River. Through the foregrounding and unconventional treatment of waters, and a later shift to more abstract modes of representation, Santa Cruz imposes the description of the river as guiding perceptual framework that transforms the topography of the river into an embodied experience. Through an ontological metaphor, the description emplaces the river as a natural agent that divides lands and imposes order in the natural realm by arranging it into geopolitical entities. In lieu of a detailed topographic description, the author provides a list of obstacles set in space — force and fury of waters, unexpected currents, overwhelming floods – offered as surrogate for a surveyor's report. The list elides the array of aquatic topographies along the Magadalena's course (a combination of shallow, deep, slow, or rough currents in flat or mountainous terrain throughout its length). Instead, the verbal list of obstacles in the *Epítome* shapes fragments of the trajectory into discrete spaces, and through the narrator's point of view transforms them into places. The relations implied among these spatial sequences render the river a landscape of hopelessness and impossibility.

This projection of a list of selected, particular elements emplaced along a coastline follows the mode of representation of spaces typical of itineraries. Common in medieval maps such as the Peutinger Tabula, and in Early Modern nautical charts, the perspective offered by these types of maps requires a mapmaker's decision on what to include, exclude, and, as P. D. A. Harvey notes, entails a projection of the material chosen. Santa Cruz adopts the model of a classical itinerary to describe the islands in his *Islario* (1530–40). Our cosmographer possessed both practical and theoretical knowledge of this type of projection, given his experience as ship's captain during Sebastian Cabot's expedition to the Moluccas in 1526 and his own scholarly studies on navigation evidenced in his *Libro de las Longitudes*, his "Instructions for discoverers" to the Marquis of Mondéjar, and his overall cartographic production. In his *Islario*, he followed Pomponius Mela's *Cosmographia* (1498) and Benedetto Bordone's *Isolario* (1528). In these works, the portrayal of the coastline determines the text's narrative sequence. This mode privileges a linear imagining of space through a sequential plotting of places visited and experienced by travelers. Like itineraries and nautical charts, the description of the Magdalena introducing the *Epítome* disregards fixed scales, weaving a sequence of spaces that dramatizes the territory in a particular manner. Santa Cruz's itinerary narrative renders a space where torrents of water, vast aquatic expanses, and salt blur into a virtual seascape. Enveloping the readers on the journey, the narrative moves from one ordeal to the other and imbues abiding disquiet.

Through powerful literary and mytho-poetic evocations of Augustan landscapes, Santa Cruz transforms the Magdalena into a maritime itinerary of torrential force and destruction, disregarding the praxis of chorographic description (the depiction of particular places, as Peter Apian reminds his readers of the Ptolemaic definition), and engaging in a "kaleidoscope of imitation" to borrow Nicolopulos's phrase to describe Ercilla's integration of remote and central spheres of the imperial enterprise through a tapestry of variegated imitation (65–117). Santa Cruz's selective point of view focuses on floods that effect transformations of the fluvial landscape and frustrate the mission of discovery led by the founder of Santafé de Bogotá, Gonzalo Jiménez de Quesada. The surfeit of waters acquires new agency, this time by swallowing the coastline that surveyors were to plot in their topographic report (106). Direct observation replaces the embodiment of the river, transforming the depiction from a kinetic to a static experience, and imposing a new viewpoint from which readers can imagine the riverscape as a massive, quasi-maritime space. In the absence of saline waters in the Magdalena, Santa Cruz plots glimpses of the salt trade in soldiers' reports that recur throughout the description, functioning as a virtual poetic motif. The new maritime perspective allows the author to introduce an omniscient view into the description, in which he aligns the suffering of his itinerary with its source. With providential overtones, the source of the relentless battering of the river and constant flooding is revealed to readers: "entrava en el rio grande y paresçía venir de unas sierras y montañas grandes questaban a mano yzquierda las cuales montañas segund supimos después de descubiertas se llamaban las sierras de oppon" (106) (it entered the great river and seemed to come from some ranges and high mountains to the left, which mountains, we later learned after their discovery, were called the Sierras de Oppon).

This particular sequence of rivers, transformed into maritime spaces connected to mountains, is evocative of landscapes far from New Granada and the New World. The suggestive references establish a synecdoche with rivers of classical epic, in particular those in the *Iliad*. Amid episodes of warfare, Homer pauses to reflect on impiety and foolishness in human action in the city of Troy and emplaces the power of rivers at the center of the judgment and restoration of balance brought by the gods: "[T]hen it was that Poseidon and Apollo take counsel to sweep away the wall, bringing against it the might of all the rivers that flow forth from the mountains of Ida to the sea" (12.13–30). Poseidon's wrath redirects mountain rivers and transforms their once idyllic courses into torrential forces of destruction that execute an ethical cleansing of the city. Wyman H. Herendeen notes the formulaic pattern in which rivers appear to mark the juxtaposition of good and evil, buttressing the strict symmetry of the epic (47). The allusive transformation of the Magdalena into a quasi-maritime landscape fed by violent torrents descending from the mountains echoes repeatedly the representation of waters in epic, evoking the well-established classical motif. Its imitation emplaces an analogic association between the river of New Granada and imperial landscapes of past and present, thus projecting the region onto larger narratives of universal expansion. Those waters from epic were eventually traversed by the valiant Trojans after they were cast out onto the maritime journey that led them to found Rome. Through an analogy with the torrential waters of the *Iliad*, Santa Cruz transcends space and time, emplacing the region in wider contexts – indeed, within the framework of the Spanish imperial enterprise writ large.

This alignment of the literary, chorographic, and cosmographic realms yields the often used passage in the *Epítome*, particularly by early modern chroniclers: a novel portrayal of the Moxca and Panche peoples. Moreover, this intersection begets an ethnographic fiction that builds upon the intersection of itinerary and synoptic perspectives, the description of local inhabitants, and further Augustan allusions. A section that has informed the work of later authors like Juan de Castellanos, Gonzalo Fernandez de Oviedo, and Antonio de Herrera among others, the composition follows the rhetorical parameters of description present in the "Cuestionarios de Indias." Juan de Ovando y Godoy drafted the "Cuestionarios" following Santa Cruz's early recommendations – as noted by Mundy, Portuondo,

Cuesta, and Millán de Benavides. Santa Cruz overlooks the multilingual confederacies of power that, as Carl Langebaek notes, populated the region (34–8). Instead, he advances a binary taxonomy that divides the mountains surrounding Bogota and Tunja between two very different peoples: the Panches who practiced cannibalism and the Moxcas who did not. He traces the customs of the locals directly to characteristics of the climate, ascribing the differences to the fact that the land of the Panches is torrid, whereas that of the New Kingdom is cold, or at least temperate. Furthermore, a first reference to the range of latitude in the region frames the ethnographic account in cartographic terms, detailing the New Kingdom's extension and configuration. Breaking with the former itinerary projection, here our cosmographer engages notions of planar representation: insisting on extension and on orientation with respect to the reference point of "la línea" (latitude), he employs this projection to advance an abstract emplacement of the region in multiple ways. Mapping the region entailed establishing a framework within which to plot distant localities on the grid of abstract space and permitted situating the region within that cartographic grid. The planar projection invites readers to imagine blank spaces that can be traversed and to establish relationships between locations not previously linked. This quasi-Apollonian view removes the point of view from the coastline, elevating it from the surface to a remote vantage point of abstraction above the globe.

This complex projection inaugurates Santa Cruz's engagement with a key philosophical and cosmographic debate on the nature of places and their ostensible influence on the nature of peoples – specifically, in the Indies, on Amerindians. This debate heralded a broad shift in geographical thought by which the ancient Antipodes were transformed into the modern Torrid Zone. In both his *Historia de las Indias* and the accompanying *Apologética,* Bartolomé de Las Casas leads a full challenge to the spatial principles that undergirded the geopolitical model of expansion. In Ptolemaic tradition, latitude determined the constitution of all matter in the cosmos. This included the nature of a people, which could be determined by its location within a tripartite division of the world into one torrid belt in the Equinox region surrounded by two temperate regions that extended to the poles. The position of the line separated uninhabitable hot climes from milder fringes where *polis* and civility were possible. Columbus's strategy of southing challenged theories of insularity and the tripartite scheme of the Ptolemaic inheritance. The admiral's venture onto the newly discovered lands confirmed an open geography that conceived of further territories and the possibility of human habitation of the Torrid

Zone. As Nicolás Wey Gomez has shown, this ideological innovation led to a complex, gradual process by which the former torrid, desert, unpopulated Antipodes were reconceptualized as the early modern hot-temperate, inhabited Tropics. Yet, while advancing the geographic possibilities for new territories in the tropics, supporters of this model did not extend to the Amerindians the new ontological status of civility and policy implicit in the cosmographic breakthrough. Within this paradox, retention of the old categorization of peoples according to zones continued to furnish critical legitimization of territorial expansion. On this view, their place in the world (confirmed by their ostensible nature – dark and without the ability to control their passions) made the indigenous peoples of the Indies natural slaves.

Santa Cruz's discursive abstraction does not seem to suffice for a full ontological reconsideration of the relationship between peoples and climatic belts. The reimagining of the Amerindian entails further reemplacement of the Moxca within planar projections that challenge the old correlation between lands and peoples. According to the premodern cosmographic model, latitude positioned New Granada within the Torrid Zone, given its short distance from the equinoctial line. Yet Santa Cruz confirms the existence of temperate climes even at such latitudes, locates the Moxca within such a climatic belt, and reshuffles the taxonomy of the tropico. In his *Islario*, he demanded reconsideration of old views of the Torrid Zone by asserting visual evidence acquired through exploration. Mariano Cuesta notes that he limited the implications of these findings solely to climate. Indeed, Santa Cruz's rendering of the region's Amerindians remains notably asymmetrical and inconsistent. While the *Epítome* breaks with spatial determinism for the Moxca, it denies such consideration to the Panche, whose latitude was farther from the Equinox. This partial application of the cosmographic findings toward a new ontology for the Panche survives until century's end in the cartography of the region in the *Carta Corográphica* of the Kingdom of New Granada (c. 1570) compiled in Eduardo Acevedo Latorre's *Atlas*; there, the Panches appear literally engulfed in fire (pl. XIII).

Once more by appeal to the literary and reintroducing observation of the region's singularities (chorography), Santa Cruz fashions a productive fragmentation that unveils various shapes of difference in the constitution of the Amerindian. A further cosmo-mythographic representation in the *Epítome* buttresses new emplacements of Augustan landscapes in the region and offers a response to the paradox within the new cosmographic model. Insistent on discussing "la línea," Santa Cruz infuses the region

with powerful epic resonance, transforming New Granada into a Mediterranean landscape by characterizing the *cacique's* dwellings as fortresses
surrounded by many walls, in the manner of the Labyrinth of Troy
(112). While scientific knowledge is built on experimentation and exploration, the spatial analogies in the text remind us that interpretation rests on
the literary. Santa Cruz combines the ethnographic and the literary to
translate New Granada from unknown to known imaginations. The spatial
displacement effected through the simile between Trojan and Moxca
cityscapes emplaces the region in one of the most famous landscapes of
epic expansion in all of history: that of the Roman civil war. As Anthony
Pagden and David Lupher remind us, the metonymic relationship between
campaigns of imperial expansion in the Mediterranean and in the New
World was deeply appealing to the Hapsburgs, with their ideological and
propagandistic appropriation of the Roman legacy.

Moreover, the simile suggests a meta-literary gesture that connects the
beginning and end of the *Epítome* by calling to mind the metaphoric use of
Troy and labyrinths. Sixteenth-century writers appealed to these particular
references to denounce the perils of endless wars, as with the Trojan
precedent, and drew on the labyrinthine quality of the maze to remind
readers that there was no easy way out of military struggle. Santa Cruz
opens the text condemning the decimation of nature brought by conquest
and closes it relating the squabbles among conquerors over the control of
the New Kingdom. Reference to these antecedents of the Augustan world
entailed an exercise of cognition that engaged the alterity of the past to
explore the foreignness of new geographies and open a space in which to
critique the manner in which conquest was conducted in the region.
Antiquity, as Sabine MacCormack reminds us in her *On the Wings of
Time*, introduced a measure of disruption and discontinuity into the
dynamics of power both by offering models for the Spanish and by
exposing their failures and limitations (14).

The refashioning of inherited taxonomies of civility entailed in the
Epítome changes the projection of the terrain along with the Augustan
undertones and affords readers an Apollonian perspective on New Granada
that connects distinct world spaces into a universal place. The simile
between Troy and New Granada suggests parallels between the ancient
heroes of Mediterranean expansion and New World Amerindians, elevating the ontological capacity of the latter, and contributing a new theorization of the Amerindian. Following the Early Modern European notion of
stages of world civilization, non-Christian societies held the potential to
reach full humanity by progressing from idolatry and barbarism, finally

attaining Christianity, the highest stage. European domination could bring Christianity and civilization to indigenous nations either by persuasion or by force. Yet in the *Epítome*, the author appeals neither to the arguments of anthropologic asymmetry upheld by Ginés de Sepúlveda to differentiate between civilized and barbarous peoples, nor to the explicative power of Christian universalism upheld by José de Acosta and Bartolomé de Las Casas to vindicate the cultural and spiritual value of natives. It is, rather, the very local characteristics of the Moxca that complete the moral and political life presumably consistent with civilized habitation in the temperate zone. Proof of Moxca morality is their display of modesty, reverence for authority, and extraordinary devotion to their religion (114). Customary punishment of nefarious sins, murder, and robbery, among others, in turn confirm their political capacity, showing the praxis of polity common to civilized communities. Possession of "mediana razón" (halfway rationality) rounds out the picture of a people with an inclination to prudence, temperance, intelligence, humanity, and religion (113). For Ginés de Sepulveda, these traits among others manifested in peoples that possessed reason and followed natural law. Though cautiously incomplete, Santa Cruz's ascription of reason to local peoples was remarkable in no longer restricting this capacity to Christians. Their adherence to natural law challenges inherited taxonomies, and the resulting ontological paradox, within a new cosmographic model.

Through the literary imagining of the New Kingdom of Granada, Santa Cruz's portrayal of the Moxca reenvisions the notion of *ius gentium* advocated by Francisco de Vitoria in the context of the polemic over possession of the Indies. The debate in which Vitoria took part placed in question the validity of the Roman model as legitimate precedent for territorial expansion in the New World. Our cosmographer refashioned the theologian's arguments, transcending the latter's limited geographic reach in order to advance his own vision of a global *oikoumene*. Domingo de Soto, Vitoria's pupil at Salamanca, challenged the Roman model invoked by imperial propagandists to support their New World claims in his *Relectio de dominio* (1535). Mounting a historical argument, he dismissed claims of seizure by disputing that ancient Romans could have known of the existence of the "islanders" of the Indies, much less conquered them. Furthermore, he questioned the morality of conquest by rejecting Augustus's tyrannical rule as a legitimate precedent for the rightful possession of new territories. As Lupher points out, de Soto's objections confirmed that neither divine nor natural law lent legitimate support to Spanish claims of global dominion embracing the Indies (61–8).

Four years later, Vitoria downplayed de Soto's arguments of geographic limitation and exercise of just rule, reaffirming the legitimacy of the Roman model on grounds of human justice and the virtues of an ancient imperial model divinely ordained as a precursor of Spanish Hapsburg expansion.

The positive application that Vitoria made of the notion of *ius gentium* in his *Relectio de Indis* (1539) traced a body of practices in Roman law, identified a group of customs shared by all societies, and extended the Roman imperial model to Spanish dominion in the Indies. In his pledge, these common traditions ostensibly aligned interests between Europe and New World (347). Following this logic, Spaniards could enter the new territories not only to spread the Gospel but also to lend solidarity to those oppressed by their neighbors. Santa Cruz's analogy delineates a plot that accords legitimacy to European intervention in putative defense of subjugated groups.

In one last analogy with the Augustan past, Santa Cruz calls forth a kaleidoscopic dynamic akin to those deployed earlier in the text and makes a final appeal to the principle of *ius gentium*, conceding to Amerindians the will to territorial expansion and lordship over subjects and things. This turn begets a paradoxical, familiar otherness to the readers' imagination. He reports that in Moxca worldview the soldier who dies in battle, or the woman in childbirth, though depraved in their earlier conduct, deserves honor "por solo aquella Voluntad que an tenido de *ensanchar y acrecentar la republica*" (117; my emphasis) (for the simple fact of their resolve to *extend and enlarge the republic*). His projection abandons the charting of insular empires spearheaded by Francisco Lopez de Gómara and Gonzalo Fernández de Oviedo, insisting instead on a depiction of New Granada that capitalizes his interconnected global cosmography through the appropriation of *ius gentium*. Echoing Pericles's funeral oration, that most celebrated praise of imperial ethics as it appears in Thucydides, Santa Cruz transfers the notion of imperial aspiration from Mediterranean to New World settings, establishing it as a universal custom that emplaces identity between Moxca and Athenian *Weltanschauungs*. In this praise of the ideals of Athenian democracy before the crushing campaign in the Peloponnese, Pericles reminds the audience that the good that ancestors brought to the Republic outweighs their faults. Their highest virtues were the prudence, industry, arts, and manner by which Empire and dominion were established and enlarged (83). Nevertheless, the intertextual allusion cannot escape the powerful context in which Thucydides imbricates Pericles's eulogy – an anti-imperial critique of Athenian expansion, a denunciation of the ravages wrought on Attica by the Peloponnesian campaign, and the plague that leaves the region abject. As in Homer's Troy, an allusion emplaced by Santa Cruz in his description of the Magdalena, unethical human excess begets a purifying force of judgment and destruction. The meta-historical allusion calls up the same kaleidoscopic, abstracted projection that connects discrete spaces into a unified literary place – one that furnishes a vantage point from which to contemplate the domestic discontent that the imperial enterprise can bring. For Thucydides, the juxtaposition originated in restless innovation and ended in blind hunger for dominion – a merciless ambition that Santa Cruz identifies and denounces repeatedly in European conquerors in the New Kingdom of Granada.

Through the literary transformation of the region and its peoples, Santa Cruz's ethnographic fiction problematizes the dialectic process by which imperialist ideology acquires coherence, explicative power, and authority. In Santa Cruz's interpretation of the new cosmographic model, theology plays no part. It is in epic and meta-historical commentary, instead, that he finds the resources to expose the insoluble paradox that, like the impossible and labyrinthine itinerary of the Magdalena, led European expansion down unethical paths. His reconsideration of inherited taxonomies through literary means addresses the paradox of the nature of the Amerindian and overcomes the limitations inherent in the cosmographic model, reminding readers of the dangers such frameworks entail.

Prophecy borrowed from epic is encoded in a literary and geographic, rather than a purely historical, projection. In the end, Santa Cruz's proposed response to the paradox did not prevail. However, it lays bare the oscillating nature of interpretation through literary and geographic abstraction and the unfolding of the ethnographic fantasies of the era. Despite his attempt to avoid essentials by problematizing the mendacious and overwrought binaries, the text remained a founding document for European science and informed later imaginings of the region and its peoples. Luis Fernando Restrepo warns us in *El estado impostor: apropiaciones literarias y culturales de la memoria de los muiscas y la América indígena* about the ways in which later authors arrogated, borrowed, and erased the memory of the Moxca in the service of their own intellectual projects. By the evocative power of myth, the other comes to be the identity of the self, and, as Conley reminds us, their myths are mobilized as presumptive accounts of the future arrival of Europeans. The epic landscapes that Juan de Castellanos paints in his *Elegías de varones ilustres de Indias* (Part I, 1588) contribute to the historiographical effort to exalt the project of conquest, advanced by the curate of Tunja in his "Historia del

Reino de Nueva Granada" (Part IV of *Elegías*), profiting from ambiguity in the treatment of the indigenous warriors – a gesture that Alonso de Ercilia displays in *La araucana* (1569). The later suppression of the sections dedicated to the customs and religion of the indigenous of modern-day Colombia and Venezuela in Fr. Pedro de Aguado's *Recopilación historial* (c. 1570) contribute to furthering the obliteration of the Moxca and mark the path for the historiography of the seventeenth century. Gaps in Pedro de Simón's *Noticias historiales de las conquistas de Tierra Firme en las Indias occidentales* (1628) and reticence and ambivalence in the treatment of the indigenous past in Juan Rodríguez Freyle's *El carnero* (1639) reveal tensions in inserting local confederacies into a patriotic narrative of origins for the region. Lucas Fernández de Piedrahita appropriates the Moxca past to locate the indigenous within creole consciousness in his *Historia general de las conquistas del Nuevo Reino de Granada* (1688), yet not without encountering the challenges inherent in reconciling Neo-Granadan criollismo with the colonial oppression. The debates over the nature and legitimacy of the colonial order addressed by Vitoria and present in the *Epítome* are addressed by Fernando de Orbea in his *Comedia nueva: la conquista de Santa Fe de Bogotá*; as Restrepo reminds us, those debates unfolded within the aesthetic and political sensibilities of Baroque modernity.

In epitomizing the New Kingdom of Granada, Alonso de Santa Cruz ventures far beyond the synthesizing of human realities and geographic observation into scientific knowledge. That his vision did not carry the day should not blind us to the continuing value of his work. The literary achievement is considerable: Drawing on ancient epic and on what was then an emerging corpus of new geographical knowledge, Santa Cruz's narrative innovations created new ways of bringing landscapes and peoples to life on the page to harness mytho-historic analogy in the service of new fictions of meaning. Out of the landscapes of that prodigious New Kingdom of Granada, and with a force undiminished across half a millennium, Santa Cruz's ethnography of the Moxca contains within its folds nothing less than an admonition against the perils of empire.

An earlier version of this essay was published in *Troubled Waters: Rivers in Latin American Imagination*, ed. Elizabeth Pettinaroli and Ana María Mutis, Hispanic Issues Online, 12, University of Minnesota Press, 2013, http://hispanicissues.umn.edu/assets/doc/01_PETTINAROLI.pdf. I would like to thank Pablo J. Davis for his help with translations. All citations of the *Epítome* follow Millán de Benavides's edition.

BIBLIOGRAPHY

Acevedo Latorre, Eduardo. *Atlas de mapas antiguos de Colombia: Siglos XVI a XIX*. Bogotá: Litografía Arco, 1971.

Aguado, Pedro de. *Recopilación historial*. Ed. Juan Friede. Bogotá: Empresa Nacional de Publicaciones, 1956–7.

Apiano, Pedro. *La cosmographia de Pedro Apiano, corregida y añadida por Gemma Frisio, médico y matemático*. Anveres: Juan Bellero, 1575.

Casas, Bartolomé de las. *Apologética historia sumaria*. Ed. Edmundo O'Gorman. México: Universidad Nacional Autónoma de México, Instituto de investigaciones históricas. 1967.

Historia de las Indias. Caracas: Biblioteca Ayacucho, 1986.

Castellanos, Juan de. *Elegías de Varones Ilustres de Indias*. Madrid: Imprenta de los Sucesores de Hernando, 1914.

Conley, Tom. *The Self-Made Map: Cartographic Writing in Early Modern France*. Minnesota: University of Minnesota Press, 1996.

Cuesta Domingo, Mariano, ed. *Alonso de Santa Cruz y su obra cosmográfica*. Madrid: Consejo Superior de Investigaciones Científicas, Instituto "Gonzalo Fernández de Oviedo," 1983.

Ercilla y Zúñiga, Alonso de. *La Araucana*. Ed. Isaías Lerner. Madrid: Cátedra, 2002.

Fernández de Oviedo y Valdés, Gonzalo. *Historia general y natural de las Indias*. Madrid: Ediciones Atlas, 1959.

Harvey, P. D. A. *The History of Topographical Maps: Symbols, Pictures and Surveys*. London. Thames and Hudson, 1980

Herendeen, Wyman H. *From Landscape to Literature: The River and the Myth of Geography*. Pittsburg: Duquesne University Press, 1986.

Herrera y Tordesillas, Antonio. *Historia general de los hechos de los castellanos*. Santo Domingo: Museo de las Casas Reales, 1975.

Homer. *Iliad*. Ed. William F. Wyatt. Cambridge, Mass.: Harvard University Press, 1999.

Langebaek, Karl Henrik. *Mercados, poblamiento e integración étnica entre los Muiscas, siglo XVI*. Bogotá: Banco de la República, 1987.

López de Gómara, Francisco. *Historia general de las Indias y vida de Hernán Cortés*. Caracas: Biblioteca Ayacucho, 1979.

López de Velasco, J. *Geografía y descripción universal de las Indias*. Madrid: Ediciones Atlas, 1971.

Lupher, David A. *Romans in a New World: Classical Models in Sixteenth-Century Spanish America*. Ann Arbor: University of Michigan Press, 2003.

MacCormack, Sabine. *Religion in the Andes: Vision and Imagination in Early Colonial Peru*. Princeton: Princeton University Press, 1993.

Mela, P. *Cosmographia, sive de situ orbis. Cum figuris necnon cum annotationibus Francisci Nunnis de la Yerva*. Salamanca: Nebrissensis, 1498.

Millán de Benavides, Carmen. *Epítome de la conquista del Nuevo Reino de Granada: La cosmogonía española del siglo XVI y el conocimiento por cuestionario.* Bogotá: Pontificia Universidad Javeriana, Instituto de Estudios Sociales y Culturales Pensar, 2001.

Mundy, Barbara. *The Mapping of New Spain: Indigenous Cartography and the Maps of the Relaciones Geográficas.* Chicago: University of Chicago Press, 1996.

Nicolopulos, James. *The Poetics of Empire in the Indies: Prophecy and Imitation in La Araucana and Os Lusíadas.* State College: Penn State University Press, 2000.

Nuevo Tesoro Lexicográfico de la lengua española. Real Academia Española. www.rae.es/recursos/diccionarios/diccionarios-anteriores-1726-1992/nuevo-tesoro-lexicografico.

O'Gorman, Edmundo. *La invención de América: Investigación acerca de la estructura histórica del Nuevo Mundo y del sentido de su devenir.* México: Fondo de Cultura Económica, 1986.

Orbea, Fernando de. *Comedia nueva: la conquista de Santa Fe de Bogotá.* Ed. Héctor Orjuela. Bogotá: Editora Guadalupe, 2002.

Pagden, Anthony. *Lords of All the World: Ideologies of Empire in Spain, Britain and France c. 1500–c. 1800.* New Haven: Yale University Press, 1995.

Piedrahita, Lucas Fernández de. *Historia general de las conquistas del Nuevo Reino de Granada.* Bogotá: Imprenta de Medardo Rivas, 1881.

Portuondo, María M. *Secret Science: Spanish Cosmography and the New World.* Chicago: University of Chicago Press, 2009.

Restrepo, Luis Fernando. *El estado impostor: apropiaciones literarias y culturales de la memoria de los muiscas y la América indígena.* Medellín: Editorial Universidad de Antioquía, 2013.

Santa Cruz, Alonso de. *Islario general de todas las islas del mundo.* Madrid: Imprenta del Patronato de huérfanos de intendencis é intervención militares, 1918.

Sepúlveda, Juan Ginés de. *Tratado sobre las justas causas de la guerra contra los indios.* México: Fondo de Cultura Económica, 1941.

Demócrates segundo; o, de las justas causas de la guerra contra los indios. Ed. Angel Losada. Madrid: Consejo Superior de Investigaciones Científicas, Instituto Francisco de Vitoria, 1951.

Solano, Francisco de, ed. *Cuestionarios para la formación de las relaciones geográficas de Indias: Siglos XVI/XIX.* Madrid: Consejo Superior de Investigaciones Científicas, 1988.

Thucydides. *Historia de la guerra del Peloponeso.* México: Editorial Porrúa, 1985.

Vitoria, Francisco de. "On the Evangelization of the Unbelievers." In *Political Writings.* Ed. Anthony Pagden and Jeremy Lawrence. Cambridge: Cambridge University Press, 1991.

Vera y Figueroa, Juan Antonio de. *Epitome de la vida y hechos del invicto emperador Carlos V.* Milan: Phelipe Ghisolsi, 1645.

Wey-Gómez, Nicolás. *The Tropics of Empire: Why Columbus Sailed South to the Indies.* Cambridge, Mass.: MIT Press, 2008.

CHAPTER 3

Colombian poetry from the colonial period to Modernismo (1500-1920)

James J. Alstrum

Traditionally, Colombians have believed that their nation has always been a land of poets. Undoubtedly, such a belief stems in part from the beginning of the country's lyrical tradition with the lengthiest epic poem ever written in Spanish by Juan de Castellanos (1522–1606) entitled *Elegías de los varones ilustres de las Indias* (Elegies of the Illustrious Men of the Indies). This extensive poem consisted of 113,609 hendecasyllable verses, some of which were rhymed while others were not. It is thought that Castellanos originally began writing a prose chronicle about the conquests in which he had participated or was told about by others. However, he later was convinced that he should express his account in verse to rival Alonso de Ercilla's (1533–94) epic poem *La Araucana* (1569; The Araucan) and thereby give equal glory to the heroism of the conquerors of the Caribbean islands and Nueva Granada (present-day Colombia and Venezuela). After his youthful career as a soldier, Castellanos was ordained a priest and assigned to Tunja. There, he began writing his epic poem mostly from memory. The poem comprises four parts, of which only the first was published in Madrid (1589) during the author's lifetime and the rest did not appear until 1879. The elegies of each part are divided into cantos. The first part covers Columbus's four voyages, the conquest of Puerto Rico, Cuba, and Jamaica, the conquests of the islands closest to the South American continent (Trinidad, Margarita, and Cubaguas), the entrance into the Orinoco River, and the ill-fated misadventures of Pedro de Ursúa (1526–61) and the legendary tyrant Lope de Aguirre (1518–61) in pursuit of El Dorado. The second part deals with Venezuela and Santa Marta, and the third part presents historical events associated with Cartagena, Popayán, and Antioquia. The last part is entitled *The History of the New Kingdom of Granada* and relates events occurring in Tunja, Santa Fe, Guane and other places in the area until 1592. Although Castellanos's work is not as highly regarded as Ercilla's by most literary critics, nevertheless, it is significant for its incorporation of words from indigenous languages into

Spanish and its vivid depiction of historical events and detailed descriptions of natural landscapes.

Another clergyman who also resided in Tunja and held the same ecclesiastical office as Castellanos, Hernando Domínguez Camargo (1606–59), was Colombia's most important Baroque poet of the seventeenth century. Together with the Mexican Sor Juana Inés de la Cruz (1651–95), he is considered to be the most prominent disciple of the Gongorist style of the Spanish poet Luis de Góngora (1561–1627) in Spanish America. All of Domínguez Camargo's poetry was published posthumously and includes the following: his unfinished masterpiece *San Ignacio de Loyola, Poema Heróico* (1666; Saint Ignatius of Loyola, Heroic Poem) and seven other poems found in a section of a book published in Madrid ten years later by the Jesuit Jacinto de Evia entitled *Ramillete de varias flores poéticas* (Bouquet of Several Poetic Flowers) containing "A don Martín Saavedra y Guzmán" (To Sir Martin Saavedra y Guzmán), "A un salto por donde se despeña el arroyo de Chillo" (To a Waterfall through Which the Chillo Stream Plunges), "A la muerte de Adonis" (On the Death of Adonis), "Al agasajo con que Cartagena recibe a los que vienen de España" (To the Party with Which Cartagena Receives Those Who Come from Spain), "A la pasión de Cristo" (To Christ's Passion), and the sonnet "A Guatavita" (To Guatavita). Domínguez reveals in these works that he is a poet's poet primarily interested in displaying a vast array of tropes and rhetorical figures emphasizing language for language's sake rather than mimetic descriptions recreating the world or persons around him. Therefore, his long unfinished epic poem of admiration for St. Ignatius Loyola, the founder of the religious order to which he himself belonged but from which he was expelled, presents an allegorical depiction of the life of the saint based on metaphor, classical allusions, and conceptual wordplay rather than the straightforward narration of biographical events. Although written in the typical form of royal octaves for epic poetry, this poem is not easily read and places demands on even the most erudite readers. Nevertheless, its original metaphors and innovative use of language have impressed modern critics and poets alike. Domínguez Camargo's poetics, like much of the poetry in the Gongorist style, were ignored for almost 300 years in large measure because of the harsh criticism by the Spanish critic and philologist Marcelino Menéndez Pelayo (1856–1912) whose views were echoed by Colombian critics who had not analyzed Domínguez Camargo's work. Domínguez Camargo's poetry was rediscovered in the twentieth century and highly acclaimed by the Spanish poets of the "Generation of 1927," especially Gerardo Diego (1896–1987). Throughout his brief poems, Domínguez Camargo's original use of metaphor stands out, especially, for example, in the poem about the stream of Chillo in which this river's descent from a waterfall is metaphorically described as a wild crystal colt. The sonnet devoted to Guatavita is an ironic satire reminiscent of the conceptual poetry of Francisco de Quevedo (1580–1645).

Throughout the rest of the seventeenth century, although the baroque style prevailed, no other outstanding poets were comparable to Domínguez Camargo. However, several prose works also contained sections of poetry such as the extensive baroque verse found in Colombia's first novel *El desierto prodigioso y prodigio del desiertro* (The Prodigious Desert and Prodigy of the Desert) written by Pedro Solís y Valenzuela (1624–1711) around 1650 but not published until 1984 by the Colombian Caro y Cuervo Institute. The novel contains an immense variety of verses including 45 tercets, 1,279 quatrains, 70 sestinas, 159 octaves, 146 ten-line stanzas, 107 sonnets, 93 lyric poems, and 20 ballads.

The work entitled *Afectos espirituales* (Spiritual Affections) written by Sister Francisca Josefa del Castillo y Guevara (1671–1742) and published posthumously in 1843 includes both prose and poetry. All her writing relates her mystical quest for union with God similar to the spiritual writings of St. Teresa de Ávila (1515–82), whose works she had read prior to entering the convent of St. Clare in Tunja at the age of seventeen. She spent the rest of her life there. Mother Castillo, as she is also known, was Colombia's first important women writer, and one of her poems "Afecto 45" (Affection 45), popularly titled "Deliquios del divino amor" (Swoons of Divine Love), frequently appears in historical anthologies of Colombian poetry. The language and imagery employed are much clearer and simpler than in baroque poetry and resemble the musical style found in St. Teresa's verse. The book also includes prose and lyrical poems heavily influenced by the biblical psalms and the writing of medieval theologians and other mystics like St. Thomas Aquinas (1225–74).

During most of the eighteenth century leading up to the independence of Colombia from Spain, very few outstanding poets left important books. However, a few names of poets and poems are worthy of mention. Friar Blas de Umaña (1720–?) is considered to be the author of an epic poem called "Descripción del sitio de Cartagena" (Description of the Siege of Cartagena) written in 1744 three years after the historical event took place when the city heroically and successfully resisted the attack led by British Admiral Edward Vernon. Francisco Antonio Vélez Ladrón de Guevara (1721–81) wrote some memorable occasional verses, usually devoted to feminine beauty, as well as a vivid description of the Tequendama waterfall outside of Bogotá.

Colombia's first poet of independence was José Fernández de Madrid (1789–1830), although he is better known as a dramatist for his plays *Atala* (1822) and *Guatimocín* (1824), which were written and performed in Cuba while he was in exile there for his political activism in the struggle to free Colombia from Spain. His poetry can be divided into both patriotic and personal verse. His patriotic poetry includes mainly odes and elegies such as the poems "Canción nacional" (National Song), "Himno a Bolívar" (Hymn to Bolívar), "Mi bandera" (My Flag), "A los libertadores" (To the Liberators), and "A la muerte del coronel Antanasio Girardot" (On the Death of Colonel Antanasio Girardot). His personal poetry deals with themes like love, the family, and local customs. He was one of the most popular poets of his time although his verse is little read today. He was a lawyer and physician and therefore also wrote about law and medicine.

Another poet of Colombian independence worthy of mention was Luis Vargas Tejada (1802–29). Unlike Fernández de Madrid, Vargas Tejada was mainly self-taught yet could speak English, Italian, French, and German and also knew Latin, Greek, and Hebrew. Also like Fernández de Madrid, Vargas Tejada is best known for a short humorous play *Las convulsiones* (1828), which was performed before his tragic death in which he drowned while attempting to flee to Venezuela because of his involvement in the failed assassination of Simón Bolívar (1783–1830). His most famous poem was entitled "El anochecer" (The Twilight) and was published during his short lifetime. Other poems such as "A mi lira" (To My Lyre) circulated only in manuscript and were not published until many years after his death in 1857.

Romanticism was introduced in Colombia through the sentimental and very personal verses of José Eusebio Caro (1817–53), who initially wrote in a neoclassic style. Caro was at his best when dealing with personal themes like erotic love and individual liberty, but many of his poems suffer from an orthodox allegiance to conservative ideology that makes them almost unreadable today. In typical romantic fashion, much of his lyricism is tied to a search for national identity through glorification of the past and unique facets of the country's cultural customs and geography. Although in some poems Caro took liberties with traditional metrical forms, his neoclassic formation did not permit him to deviate from established poetic norms as the modernists did a half century later. Two of Caro's most characteristically romantic poems were "La hamaca del destierro" (The Hammock of Exile) and "Buenas noches, patria mía" (Good Night,

My Homeland). Most other poems by Caro do not frequently appear in poetic anthologies today except "La boca del último inca" (The Mouth of the Last Inca), "Héctor" (Hector), "En alta mar" (On the High Seas), "El hacha del proscrito" (The Outlaw's Ax), and "Estar contigo" (Being with You).

Undoubtedly, Rafael Pombo (1833–1912) was the most important Colombian romantic poet and one of the major poets of the entire Colombian lyrical tradition as well as all of Spanish American Romanticism. His rhymed short stories for children called "Cuentos pintados" (Painted Stories) are still widely read and enjoyed by Colombian children today. Although trained as a civil engineer and mathematician, Pombo never practiced those professions and devoted his entire adult life to poetry, which he began writing at an early age. He was a very prolific poet, and consequently his poetry is of uneven quality. At the end of his life, Pombo was crowned as national poet (1905) and was also highly regarded as a literary critic and advisor to younger poets such as José Asunción Silva (1865–96).

Pombo's poetic works correspond to three different cycles in his life. The first cycle was that of his early youthful poetry. His early poetry was profoundly religious and philosophical in theme, including poems such as "La copa de vino" (The Cup of Wine), "Mi amor" (My Love), and "La hora de las tinieblas" (The Hour of Darkness). This last poem written in 1855 deals with a deep spiritual crisis and tension felt amidst skepticism, religious faith, and despair.

Pombo's mature poetry was written while he served as a diplomat and translator in the United States, where he became the Spanish American romantic poet most influenced by North American poets such as Henry Wadsworth Longfellow (1807–82) and William Cullen Bryant (1794–1878). He befriended both of these poets and carried on a continuous correspondence with them. Most critics consider the poetry written during Pombo's residence in the United States to be of the highest lyrical quality. Two poems – "Al Niágara" (To Niagara) and "Elvira Tracy" – especially stand out. The first poem reflects the typical importance given to nature by the romantics as a mirror of inner emotional turmoil as well as the conflict between natural goodness and corrupting civilization. The second poem deals with erotic love, lost innocence, death, and beauty. Among other recurring romantic themes found throughout Pombo's poetry, we encounter history and the search for national identity together with the glorification of local customs and unique national characteristics found in dance and music.

Pombo's later poetry was written after his definitive return to Bogotá, where he spent the rest of his life. Two other famous poems by Pombo were "Noche de diciembre" (December Night) and "Decíamos ayer" (We Were Saying Yesterday) in which human and divine love converge. The main rhetorical figure employed in both poems, as throughout most of his poetry, was apostrophe, reflecting an emotional outpouring and invocation typically present in most romantic verse.

Two contemporaries of Pombo were Gregorio Gutiérrez González (1826–72) from Antioquia and Candelario Obeso (1849–84), who was the first published Afro-Colombian poet and the originator of Afro-Colombian literature. These two were significant romantic poets of lesser universal appeal than Pombo because they emphasized the regions they were from as characteristic of national identity. Both poets wrote in a style that featured their local dialects. Gutiérrez González even claimed in one poem that he wrote in Antioquian instead of Spanish. He is most famous for his poem entitled "Memoria del cultivo del maíz" (Remembrance of Corn Cultivation), which provides a lyrical description of how corn is grown and harvested. Obeso is best known for his book of poetry *Cantos de mi tierra* (1877; Songs of My Land), which contains sixteen poems and one prose piece written phonetically to reproduce the oral speech of Afro-Colombian speakers of Spanish like the oarsmen who rowed boats from the coast inland down the Magdalena River, Colombia's main fluvial artery. Obeso's poetry, like his life, was an attempt to dignify and call attention to the importance of the black experience and contribution to Colombian society and culture. His use of authentic popular speech was often denigrated by critics from the interior of the country who had an ethnic and cultural bias and thought that Obeso's verse undermined their vision of national identity based on linguistic purity and correctness.

Romanticism in Colombian poetry, unlike many other Spanish American countries, perdured through three generations well into the first two decades of the twentieth century, especially in the poetry of Julio Flórez (1867–1923), who remains one of the nation's most controversial yet popular lyric voices of all time. Even today, many Colombians can quote from memory some of Flórez's most famous verses such as "todo nos llega tarde, hasta la muerte" (Everything arrives late for us, even death), although most critics cannot cite a single outstanding poem or book by this very prolific author. Nevertheless some critics still consider a few of Florez's poems such as "Mis flores negras" (My Black Flowers), "La araña" (The Spider), "Resurecciones" (Resurrectons), "Altas ternuras" (High Tenderness), and "Oh poetas" (Oh Poets), to be veritable classics of

Colombian literature. Indeed, some of Flórez's poems were later adapted as popular songs by famous Spanish American singers such as Carlos Gardel (1890–1935), known as the "King of the Tango." At the turn of the century, Flórez led a literary coterie in Bogotá known as *La Gruta Simbólica* (The Symbolic Grotto), which included many writers like him who were Liberal dissidents opposed to the Conservatives during the bloody Thousand Days' War, a civil war between the two political parties. Shortly before his death and despite his lifelong devotion to Liberal causes, the Conservative government of Pedro Nel Ospina (1858–1927) cosponsored Flórez's coronation as a national poet. In any event, the poetry of Julio Flórez seemed to capture the maudlin and gloomy national mood of Colombia at the beginning of the twentieth century.

Unlike Flórez, José Asunción Silva (1865–96) never published a complete book of poetry during his short life, which tragically ended in suicide. Most critics consider Silva to be Colombia's greatest poet of all time despite the sparse quantity of his complete works. Silva's "Nocturno III" (1894), one of the few poems published during his life, is now thought of by many critics as the beginning of modern Spanish American verse because of its innovative polymetric musicality, employment of chromatic symbolism, and use of a tripartite structure to convey an emotional intensity leading up to a dramatic climax. Also, the alternation of long and short lines anticipates the avant-garde by giving the poem a spatial dimension that reflects the varying sizes of the shadows cast by the lyric voice and the woman in the composition as they walk at night through the savannah of Bogotá. In addition, most critics believe Silva was one of the first originators of Spanish American *Modernismo* together with Cuban José Martí (1853–95) and Mexican Manuel Gutiérrez Nájera (1859–95).

The eight poems published by Silva in an 1886 anthology entitled *Lira nueva* (New Lyrics) constitute the only new kind of poetry found in that tome, which consists mainly of romantic and rigidly formal neoclassic verse. The Silva poems found there include "Estrofas" (Stanzas) later retitled "Ars," "La voz de marcha" (The March's Voice), "El recluta" (The Recruit), "Resurrecciones" (Resurrections), "Obra humana" (Human Work), "La calavera" (The Skull), and "A Diego Fallón" (To Diego Fallón). Unlike the other poems in this anthology, Silva's poetry does not contain traditional rhetoric and formal correctness but rather evokes suggestive imagery while expressing an original modernist aesthetic. Throughout most of Silva's verse there is generally a nostalgic tone and expression of mystery, expectation, and uncertainty about the future. Many of the poems contrast light and shadow and present a variety of themes including the lost innocence of childhood, dreams, disillusionment, nature, and the supernatural evoked in a nocturnal setting. Critics have collected Silva's dispersed poetry and organized it into the following books: *El libro de versos* (The Book of Verses), *Gotas amargas* (Bitter Drops – satirical poems that Silva refused to publish but were reproduced from memory by his friends), *Poesías varias* (Various Poetry), and *Intimidades* (Intimacies). Unlike many other modernists such as Rubén Darío (1867–1916), no allusions are made to classical mythology or exotic scenarios in Silva's work. Indeed, Silva wrote a poetic parody of extremely decorative and exotic Modernism that mocked the Parnassian notion of "art for art's sake" in a poem called "Sinfonía color fresa con leche" (A Strawberry and Milk Colored Symphony). However, like all modernists, Silva's poetry strives to harmonize form and theme. Silva is considered to be the most innovative of all modernists in regard to metrics. Silva also made a major contribution to modernist poetic prose in his novel *De sobremesa* (After Dinner), which was not published until 1925. It tells the story of the artist José Fernández, considered by some to be Silva's alter ego, who vainly searches throughout Europe for a lost lover and artistic purity.

In stark contrast to Silva's willingness to experiment with new forms to express theme, Guillermo Valencia (1873–1943) was Colombia's other most important modernist poet, who in his single published book, *Ritos* (1899; Rites), preferred a definitive Parnassian emphasis on "art for art's sake." For Valencia, form mattered much more than theme, and hardly any heartfelt connection was made with the poet's personal circumstances. For example, in Valencia's poem "Cigüeñas blancas" (White Storks), the poetic voice exclaims "¡Quiero el soneto cual león de Nubia:/de ancha cabeza y resonante cola!" (I want the sonnet like a Nubian lion:/with a wide head and resonant tail!). Most of Valencia's poems are unlike Silva's; for example, "Los camellos" (The Camels) are descriptive and contain exotic locales or plants and animals. In reality, Valencia was much more dedicated to politics than poetics, having run three times unsuccessfully as the Conservative Party candidate for president. Nevertheless, his poetry would cast a heavy shadow over much of Colombian verse during the first three decades of the twentieth century because it was considered to be the ideal modernist paradigm.

Eduardo Castillo (1889–1937) was another modernist poet, and he was Valencia's personal secretary. He followed his mentor's Parnassian model of formal perfection and published only one book of poetry, *El árbol que canta* (1928; The Tree Which Sings). Despite his attempt to emulate

Valencia's commitment to formal correctness, now most critics esteem his sonnets more than those of his master because of their poignant emotional content and innovative use of musicality.

Another modernist poet, José Eustacio Rivera is much better known for his novel *La vorágine* (1924; The Vortex). He wrote a book of sonnets entitled *Tierra de promisión* (1921; Land of Promise) devoted to the flora and fauna of Colombia. In his only book of poetry, one finds vivid pictorial imagery and outstanding musicality together with frequent use of personification. His sonnets have a dramatic although often illogical ending that appear to apply Valencia's admonition found in "Cigüeñas blancas" (White Storks) about the structure of this kind of poem.

Porfirio Barba Jacob (1883–1942), the pseudonym under which Miguel Antonio Osorio Benítez wrote his best known poetry, is considered by some critics to be one of Colombia's greatest poets; he incorporated modernist techniques to express an intensely personal lyricism characterized by contradictory imagery, free from exotic evocations and Parnassian emphasis on form over theme. Certainly, his most popular poems "Futuro" (Future) and "Canción de la vida profunda" (Song of Profound Life) regularly appear in anthologies of both Colombian and Spanish American poetry. Most of his poetry, written under several pseudonyms such as Ricardo Arenas and Main Ximénez in addition to Barba Jacob, reflect different egocentric perspectives on his own identity and bohemian, homosexual lifestyle, which led him to live outside Colombia in several Caribbean and Central American nations until his death in Mexico. Barba Jacob wrote 150 poems but did little to promote his own work, although three collections of his verse were published during his lifetime in three different countries: *Canciones y elegías* (1932, Mexico; Songs and Elegies), *Rosas negras* (1933, Guatemala; Black Roses), and *La canción de la vida profunda y otros poemas* (1937, Colombia; The Song of Profound Life and Other Poems). The most reliable edition of 120 of his poems edited by his biographer Fernando Vallejo (b. 1942) entitled *Poemas* (Poems) appeared in 1985. Throughout most of his poetry an internal tension is present between his quest for a refined and elevated language typical of most modernist verse and the authentic expression of a turbulent and troubled life filled with vices like alcoholism and drug addiction, misery, and the socioeconomic instability of a pilgrim in search of a place in which to reside and still remain true to his homosexual identity. Other outstanding poems by Barba Jacob include "Parábola del retorno" (Parable of the Return), "La estrella de la tarde" (Afternoon Star), "Elegía de septiembre"

(September Elegy), "Lamentación de octubre" (October Lamentation), "Los desposados de la muerte" (The Newlyweds of Death), and "Balada de la loca alegría" (Ballad of Crazy Joy). Finally, the poem that perhaps best attains the modernist ideal of harmonizing form and theme while resolving the inner conflict between sordid experience and refined language is "Futuro" (Future) in which the poet concludes in the last stanza:

> *Y supo cosas lúgubres, tan hondas y letales,*
> *que nunca humana lira jamás esclareció,*
> *y nadie ha comprendido su trágico lamento ...*
> *Era una llama al viento y el viento la apagó.*
> *(And he found out about mournful things, so deep and lethal,*
> *that never a human lyric ever clarified,*
> *and nobody has understood his tragic lament ...*
> *He was a flame in the wind and the wind extinguished him.)*

Luis Carlos López (1879–1950) from Cartagena wrote poetry unlike that of his modernist and postmodernist contemporaries because it was essentially satirical and parodic, reminiscent of Silva's *Gotas amargas;* his work anticipated by a half century the antipoetry of the Chilean Nicanor Parra (b. 1914). Luis Carlos López published three books of poetry and coauthored another. His three books were entitled *De mi villorio* (1908; Of My Village), *Posturas difíciles* (1909; Hard Postures), and two editions of *Por el atajo* (1920, 1928; Through the Shortcut). He also coauthored a book *Varios a varios* (1910; Several to Several), while the rest of his poems appeared dispersed in magazines and newspapers including his poetic sketches of prominent citizens of Cartagena and descriptions of the main streets of the colonial sector of the city.

López was the most important Colombian poetic satirist of all time. He was the antipoet of the mawkish late romantic verse of Flórez and the decorative Parnassian modernism of Valencia, or as the critic Federico de Onís (1886–1966) expressed, his work was modernism "al revés" (reverse modernism). López often wrote poetic caricatures of people and places like landscapes. He mainly subverted the modernist sonnet with an irreverent and ironic tone by juxtaposing lyrical and prosaic language within the same poem. He also employed the epigram, which he disparagingly called "despilfarros" (wasteful extravagances), to make fun of the provincial ambience of his beloved native city of Cartagena and its bourgeois inhabitants while mocking all poets and poetic writing in general. He was the first Colombian poet to regularly use local phrases and colloquial language (*colombianismos*) with humorous effect to criticize politicians of both political parties and ridicule sacred customs and established institutions like the Roman Catholic Church and its clergy. Besides the romanticism of Flórez, the other main target of López's poetic parodies was the verse of Valencia. A clear example that contrasts the poetry of both poets is their vision of their native cities of Cartagena and Popayán, which were important urban centers in colonial times. In his famous sonnet "A mi ciudad nativa" (To My Native City), López presents a nostalgic but realistic vision of a once great and heroic city fallen into ruins and misery, yet still evoking the affection one has for a comfortable pair of old shoes: "Mas hoy, plena de rancio desaliño,/bien puedes inspirar ese cariño/que uno les tiene a sus zapatos viejos" (But today, full of rancid neglect,/you can well inspire that affection/which one has for his old shoes"). On the other hand, in his ode to Popayán, Valencia employs grandiloquent and idyllic imagery to describe his native city in a way similar to the oratorical rhetoric of a politician on the campaign trail: "Tú vives del silencio … de tus glorias … de tus dones … de imposibles … del martirio … del orgullo … y vives con tu cielo, lbélula errante" (You live from silence … from your glories … from your gifts … from the impossible … from martyrdom … and you live with your heaven, wandering dragonfly). Although the importance of Luis Carlos López's iconoclastic antipoetry and satire with its ironic tone and colloquial language was often belittled as crude humor and unappreciated during his time, today critics have come to realize that his verse left a legacy for poets of the second half of the twentieth century like the *Nadaístas* and many belonging to the "Generación desencantada de *Golpe de Dados*" (the Disillusioned Generation of *Throw of the Dice*).

REFERENCES

Alstrum, James J. *La sátira y la antipoesía de Luis Carlos López*. Bogotá: El Banco de la República, 1986.

Barba Jacob, Porfirio. *Poemas*. Recopilación y notas, Fernando Vallejo. Bogotá: Procultura, 1985.

Cobo Borda, Juan Gustavo. *Historia de la poesía colombiana siglo XX: De José Asunción Silva a Raúl Gómez Jattin*. Bogotá: Villegas editores, 2003.

Domínguez Camargo, Hernando. *Obras*. Editado por Rafael Torres Quintero. Bogotá: Instituto Caro y Cuervo, 1960.

Historia de la poesía colombiana. Bogotá: Fundación Casa de Poesía Silva, 1991.

Holguín, Andrés. *Antología crítica de la poesía colombiana 1874-1974*. Tomo I, Bogotá: Biblioteca del Centenario del Banco de la República, 1974.

Luque Muñoz, Henry, ed. *Domínguez Camargo, la rebelión barroca.* Bogotá: Instituto Colombiano de Cultura, 1976.

Mendoza Varela, Eduardo, ed. *Hernando Domínguez Camargo: Antología poética.* Medellín: Editorial Bedout, 1969.

Onís, Federico de. *Antología de la poesía española e hispanoamericana (1882–1932).* New York: Las Américas Publishing, 1961.

CHAPTER 4

Reflections on the historiography of the Colombian novel: 1844–1953 and beyond

Kevin Guerrieri

The first notions of a Colombian literature as such, as well as concepts of a national culture and identity in general, were nineteenth-century inventions authored primarily by a minority of intellectuals. In the wake of their struggle for independence from colonial rule during the first three decades of the nineteenth century, the urgent task at hand for the Creole elites of the former Spanish colonies was the consolidation of their respective republics and the creation of nations. This was a tumultuous endeavor characterized by internal conflict that predominated the nineteenth century and, for some states, reached well into the twentieth century. As territorial boundaries were (re)defined and institutions were constructed, national cultures were being articulated. While the novel and print capitalism did play an instrumental role in fostering national consciousness in the Americas, as suggested in Benedict Anderson's classic book on "imagined communities," subsequent studies have emphasized that it is much more accurate to speak of multiple contested meanings of national identity and of very disparate projects of national formation throughout the first century of post-Colonial existence in Spanish America (see Castro-Klarén and Chasteen). In the Colombian context this was very much the case, and the official institutionalization of a national literature in general and a national novel in particular can be understood as a century-long project whose trajectory is inscribed on the backdrop of the fragmented realities of the nation-state.

The Republic of Colombia – commonly referred to as Gran Colombia – was established in 1819 and included a region currently comprising Colombia, Ecuador, Panama, Venezuela, and parts of northwestern Brazil, western Guyana, and northern Peru. Following the disintegration of Gran Colombia and the subsequent civil war fought between 1830 and 1831, the formation of the Republic of New Granada in 1832 marks the beginning of the juridical – political entity that would become present-day Colombia. The actual name of the state, however, underwent additional transformations in the nineteenth century: In 1858 it became the Grenadine Confederation, in 1863 the United States of Colombia, and in 1886, once again, the Republic of Colombia. These name changes, as well as the numerous disputes, constitutions, and wars that marked the period, all reflect the conflictive nature of Colombia's nineteenth century, which, it should be pointed out, was not unlike that of other nascent republics in the Americas. The century came to a close under the centralist constitution of 1886 and the rule of the ultra-Conservative regime known as the Regeneration. Colombia subsequently entered the twentieth century in the midst of the War of a Thousand Days, a civil war between Liberals and Conservatives that devastated the country and did not end until 1902. Further territorial dismemberment then followed with the separation of the province of Panama, which was executed with the support of United States intervention. Thereafter, during the first three decades of the twentieth century, Colombia's political model was predominated by Conservative tendencies that were met with growing opposition from multiple sectors including a strengthening labor movement. Accelerated modernization, industrialization, and significant advances in the communications and transportation infrastructure of the country accompanied the shift to Liberal governments in the 1930s and 1940s. Finally, four key events mark the Colombian mid–twentieth century: the period of intense conflict and bloodshed known as La Violencia, whose roots trace back to the 1930s; the assassination of the populist leader Jorge Eliécer Gaitán on April 9, 1948, and the subsequent destruction during the Bogotazo; the dictatorship of general Gustavo Rojas Pinilla from 1953 to 1957; and, the following year, the implementation of the National Front, an agreement between the leaders of the Liberal and Conservative Parties to alternate their control of the government.

It was during this long century from the 1830s to the 1950s – summarized here in broad brushstrokes – that the national novel was constructed. In this essay, far from any pretension of rewriting the history of the Colombian novel, I propose neither an exhaustive bibliography of critical studies on the genre nor a chronological accounting of individual works and movements from the period, but rather a brief reflection on the historiography of novel and nation as reflected in three general paradigms. Within the first paradigm, the Colombian novel is reified from a teleological perspective as an organic national literary tradition whose autochthonous development is framed within European models. The next paradigm makes two fundamental gestures: on the one hand, the former construction of the national novel is questioned and reconfigured according to different parameters, and, on the other, notions of the

Colombian modern (and postmodern) novel are institutionalized. Finally, in the third paradigm the pluralization of interpretations is promoted, and the leveling of novelistic hierarchies is postulated. While these paradigms are presented as emerging during three consecutive periods – the long century culminating in the 1950s, the 1950s–1980s, and post-1991 – they are not envisioned necessarily as being anchored historically but rather as continuing to function in different articulations, overlapping to different degrees, and still operational in recent studies. In this essay, I also identify some underlying tensions or vectors that run through the aforementioned paradigms and that serve, collectively, as a methodological lens through which to approach the relationship between novel and nation from the twenty-first century.

Among the numerous histories of the Colombian novel published since the early 1950s – referring here to those written with an evident purpose of providing a comprehensive survey of the national novel – the first most significant study is *Evolución de la novela en Colombia* by Antonio Curcio Altamar, published posthumously in 1957. Establishing the roots of the Colombian novel in its colonial past, Curcio Altamar suggests in the first part of his book that *El Carnero*, written by Juan Rodríguez Freyle between 1636 and 1638 but not published until the mid–nineteenth century, possesses certain novelistic elements and serves as a starting point for the national literary tradition. He perceives in this seventeenth-century text the intersection of Medieval and Renaissance tendencies as inscribed in the Colonial setting and classifies it as "celestinesco" alluding to its traces of Fernando de Rojas's *La Celestina*. In the second part of the study, which shifts to the nineteenth century, the author organizes the works analyzed into a series of categories, including Romanticism, Post-Romanticism, *Costumbrismo*, Realism, *Modernismo*, the *Novela Terrígena*, and the contemporary novel. As evident throughout this classification of texts, Curcio Altamar examines the Colombian novel through the lens of European models while simultaneously seeking autochthonous singularities, those works that offer distinctly Colombian or American realities. Rather than focusing on sketches of individual works and authors, the author explicitly seeks to establish the Colombian novel within "universal" trends.

Curcio Altamar considers Juan José Nieto the first national novelist based on *Yngermina o la hija de Calamar: novela histórica, o recuerdos de la conquista, 1533 a 1537, con una breve noticia de los usos, costumbres i religión del pueblo de Calamar*, a historical novel published in 1844 during the author's exile in Jamaica, which narrates the union of the indigenous princess Ingermina and the conquistador Alonso de Heredia, brother of

Pedro de Heredia, founder of Cartagena. Among the *costumbrista* writers, Curcio Altamar gives special recognition to José María Vergara y Vergara, José María Samper, and Eugenio Díaz, and he designates *Tránsito* (1886), by Luis Segundo de Silvestre, one of the most accomplished *costumbrista* novels. An entire chapter is dedicated to Jorge Isaac's *María*, a "novela poemática" praised by the author as a masterpiece of sentimental Romanticism. By the time of Curcio Altamar's study, *María* had already been consecrated as the most widely read – both nationally and internationally – Colombian novel of the nineteenth century. Some fifty editions of the work had been published by the end of the century, and by 1967 the number of editions reached 150 (McGrady, *María*, 13–14). Indeed, literary criticism on the nineteenth century in Latin America for a long time tended to focus on the triad formed by *María*, along with Sarmiento's *Facundo* and Mármol's *Amalia* (Corral, 316).

In the transition from the *costumbrista* to the realist novel, Curcio Altamar highlights the works of José Manuel Marroquín and Tomás Carrasquilla, among others. Carrasquilla produced an expansive body of work from 1885 to 1935, comprising eleven novels, numerous short stories, chronicles, and articles. His most salient works are *Frutos de mi tierra* (1896), *Grandeza* (1910), and *La marquesa de Yolombó* (1926). Curcio Altamar praises the modern impulse in Carrasquilla and indicates that the Colombian novel reaches universal interest in his novels (155). Shifting to the *Modernista* novel, the author emphasizes the influence of the French literary tendencies of the epoch on José Asunción Silva's *De sobremesa*, written in 1896 and identifies other modernista writers, such as Daniel Samper Ortega, José María Vargas Vila, and Emilio Cuervo Márquez, among others. The prolific and scandalous Vargas Vila, who published more than a hundred books and was one of the most widely read authors in the Spanish language during the period, is portrayed by Curcio Altamar as a forgotten figure with no literary legacy in Colombia. This is attributed in *Evolución*, as least implicitly, to Vargas Vila's iconoclastic fury, which was aimed at all religious and patriotic sentiment, and against love, marriage, and procreation (172).

In José Eustasio Rivera's *La vorágine* (1924), Curcio Altamar discovers a transformative moment in the development of the Colombian novel in particular and the Spanish American novel in general: With this work – and others such as *Doña Bárbara* by the Venezuelan Rómulo Gallegos, for example – a new era is initiated in which exquisite idealisms and exotic academic salons are replaced by the "true" American natural world. Curcio Altamar's evaluation of *La vorágine* is marked by expressions of authenticity, veracity, and the autochthonous, and he regards Rivera's novel as one of the great works of the national literature; in his estimation, *La vorágine* is on equal standing with *María*. Among the contemporary novelists in the following chapter, Curcio Altamar names Luis López de Mesa, Antonio Álvarez Lleras, José Restrepo Jaramillo, Isabel de Monserrate, Jaime Ardila, César Uribe Piedrahita, Eduardo Zalamea Borda, Bernardo Arias Trujillo, Arnoldo Palacios, and others. One of Eduardo Caballero Calderón's three novels focused on the period of La Violencia, *El Cristo de espaldas* (1952), is the final work included in the study.

Curcio Altamar's *Evolución de la novela colombiana* can be seen as the culmination of a century-long project of "constructing" the national novel. For Colombia's intellectual and cultural elites, going back as early as the founding of the republic, the novel was a minor genre, and Curcio Altamar laments the fact that poetry was still granted a privileged position in educational textbooks on the national literary tradition, even in the mid–twentieth century. His study is motivated by an explicit intention to legitimize the genre of the novel in the history of Colombian literature, and he suggests – albeit with slight hesitancy – that the quality of the novel is, perhaps, comparable to that of poetry. The historian's efforts to establish the roots of the Colombian novel in the Hispanic cultural traditions of the colonial period, to trace its gradual development through the lens of European literary tendencies and movements during the nineteenth and early twentieth centuries, and to identify what he considers to be salient autochthonous and singular works all demonstrate both a desire to legitimize the novelistic genre within the national context and to contribute to the consolidation of the national literature beyond the borders of the nation-state. It is symbolically quite significant that Curcio Altamar gained national recognition – in fact, international recognition, evidenced by the reviews of his book – and his efforts would be crowned by receiving the Premio Nacional de Literatura José María Vergara y Vergara in 1953.

In *The Colombian Novel, 1844–1987* (1991), Raymond L. Williams affirms that "Colombia would not have a truly modern novel until García Márquez, following the lead of European and North American moderns, published *La hojarasca* in 1955" (44–5). In many ways this statement encapsulates the next historiographical paradigm of novel and nation, and it can be understood as a product of the literary phenomena, which took place between the 1960s and mid-1980s, that tend to be grouped under notions such as the boom of the Spanish American novel, the post-boom novel, and the postmodern novel, which are studied elsewhere in this volume. The principal organizing element of Williams's study consists of the marked regionalism that historically characterized the country, and he groups the novelistic production into four broad territories, with a chapter dedicated to the panoramic survey of each region: the Interior Highland (*altiplano cundi-boyacense*), from *Manuela* (1858) to *El buen salvaje* (1966); the Costa (Caribbean Coastal Region), from *Ingermina* (1844) to *Cien años de soledad* (1967); Greater Antioquia, from *Frutos de mi tierra* (1896) to *El día señalado* (1964); and Greater Cauca (*El Gran Cauca*), from *María* (1867) to *El bazar de los idiotas* (1974). The final part of this study, "After Regionalism," shifts to an overview of the novelistic production organized around the "modern impulse," embodied by García Márquez, and the "postmodern gesture," represented by R. H. Moreno-Durán.

While the regional focus predominates his study as an organizing principle, Williams identifies two additional premises that inform his approach: the role of ideology and politics in relation to literature, and the noetics of orality and writing, based on Walter Ong's study *Orality and Literacy* (1982); the latter premise addresses the question of the different relationships with oral culture and/or writing culture that a given novel may reflect. Williams attributes the commonly accepted belief that the novel has always been considered a minor genre in Colombia to the preferences of the dominant elite, and he indicates that the literary critics and scholarly establishment have always been linked to the nation's oligarchy. This has resulted, according to the author, in the marginalization of novelists in the construction of the national literature. In addition, he traces the distinction between the literary critics and the novelists along political party lines: The former have tended to be Conservatives, and the latter have been mostly Liberals. For the aforementioned reasons, Williams questions any approach that proposes an organic Colombian novelistic tradition – such as Curcio Altamar's *Evolución* – and he postulates a regionalist perspective, attuned to different manifestations of the interplay between oral and writing culture, with an emphasis on the exploration of the ideological dimensions within novelistic production. García Márquez can be seen as the pivotal figure in this historiographical paradigm, both in his role as a key figure of the boom and the internationalization of the Spanish American novel, and in the *costeño*'s explicit deconstruction of the institutionalized national literature.

The third historiographical paradigm of novel and nation is represented here by a series of studies written by Álvaro Pineda Botero, who is also a novelist himself. Pineda Botero begins the first book in the series, *La fábula y el desastre. Estudios críticos sobre la novela colombiana, 1650–1931* (1999), with an in-depth analysis of the Colonial work *El desierto prodigioso y prodigio del desierto*, which was written in the mid–seventeenth century by the *bogotano* Pedro de Solís y Valenzuela (1624–1711) and remained unpublished for some 300 years. Although the text does contain pronounced medieval roots and is predominated by an overarching monologic Catholic doctrine cloaked in mysticism, Pineda Botero regards *El desierto* a "modern" novel in the same sense that *El Quijote* is considered as such: It is a self-aware and metafictional work rich in intertextuality with a plurality of genres and patent skepticism (29–93). From *El desierto*, the author shifts to the nineteenth century and identifies *María Dolores o la historia de mi casamiento*, written in 1836 by José Joaquín Ortiz and published in installments in *El Cóndor* in 1841, as the first novel of the republican era; Curcio Altamar deemed this work a short story rather than a true novel, and Williams considered it an incomplete novelistic sketch. What follows is a series of close readings of fifty Colombian novels. Among the nineteenth-century works, *Manuela* (1856), *María* (1867), and *De sobremesa* (1896) are highlighted. As the study enters the twentieth century, Pineda Botero indicates that those Colombian novelists who were swept up by the spirit of innovation from Spanish-American *modernismo* and the European avant-garde tendencies during the first few decades were still, in many ways, anchored in the nineteenth century. Nonetheless, he does reveal a handful of exceptions that he considers examples of writers who break with the past and offer new literature: Clímaco Soto Borda in *Diana Cazadora* (1915), José Eustasio Rivera in *La vorágine* (1924), and José Félix Fuenmayor in *Cosme* (1927). The author states that an expanding range of worldviews expressed through the themes, structures, language, and characterization began to emerge and aligned with new awareness among readers following *La vorágine*; he then ends this volume somewhat arbitrarily with his analysis of José Restrepo Jaramillo's *David, hijo de Palestina* (1931). The second volume in this series, *Juicios de residencia, 1934–1985* (2001), starts with Eduardo Zalamea Borda's *4 años a bordo de mí mismo* (1934); of the following thirty novels analyzed, four more were published in the 1930s, five in the 1940s, and four in the 1950s.

The characteristics of this historiographical paradigm, which is exemplified by Pineda Botero's series of studies, are not immediately visible in the preceding summary. Structurally, the analysis of each novel constitutes a chapter, and the chapters are organized chronologically; *Juicios de residencia* concludes with García Márquez's *El amor en los tiempos de cólera* (1985). Finally, it should be noted that Pineda Botero's series continues with a third volume that reaches the twenty-first century, *Estudios críticos sobre la novela colombiana, 1990–2004*. Instead of using any type of predetermined system of classifications or implementing a specific theoretical framework to guide the selection and organization of novels, the author postulates the notion of flexible canons and transitory maps of navigation elaborated by the reader and based on individual interpretations, pleasure, and aesthetics as well as on cultural diversity and respect for the other. This paradigm harbors a tacit resistance to the teleological conception of an organic Colombian novel but also to the subsequent institutionalization of the boom. Moreover, Pineda Botero links this approach to the Colombian novel, at least in part, to new configurations of Colombian rights as manifested in the constitution of 1991, which provides for citizenship based on cultural or ethnic distinction and heterogeneity. A clear anticanonical impulse in this paradigm seeks to level all hierarchies, from the aesthetic to the political.

As mentioned previously, in spite of having emerged in three consecutive periods, the historiographical paradigms presented here should not be conceived of as static; on the contrary, they are oftentimes superimposed, and different aspects become visible in different approaches. They serve as multiple lenses through which to examine and question the changing facets of the relationship novel and nation, and, similarly, they evoke diverse concepts of the literary critic and historian. This presentation of the three paradigms parallels Juan Carlos González Espitia's idea of the interaction between the open archive and the *carnero*, the public area of the archive and the section of discarded documents, which the author uses to replace the typical distinction between canonical and marginal. Parting from Derrida's notion of the supplement and entering into dialogue with González Echevarría's *Myth and Archive* (1990) and Doris Sommer's *Foundational Fictions* (1991), in *On the Dark Side of the Archive* (2010) González Espitia reconceptualizes the archive so that all works – one could say all texts and documents in general – are, in fact, included and essential parts of the archive: "no narrative can be created beyond the Archive" (26). Accordingly, what matters is the continual reorganization of the (national) Archive, not with the purpose of establishing new canons and discarding old ones, but rather to continue exploring the heterogeneous histories and narratives of the "barred Nation *It/Self*," thinking here of Homi Bhabha's "DissemiNation." Within this framework, I propose three general inter-woven tensions as a methodological lens for exploring the complexity of novel and nation (seeking to avoid reductionist classifications) while serving to navigate across different historical periods in a meaningful manner – the first of which could be called "ways of belonging" or modes of inclusion and exclusion; the second consists of the "temporal poetics" of discourses within, between, and about novel and nation; and the third consists of the "spatial contours and flows" that constitute the body of national and novelistic text(s).

At the most fundamental level, ways of belonging are manifested in the articulation of citizenship and citizens' rights, as well as the state institutions – legislative, juridical, and so on – that implement, interpret, and protect them. Although most current understandings of the discourse of human rights in the twenty-first century are framed within the direct legacy of the 1948 United Nations Universal Declaration of Human Rights, the independence movements and eventual formation of constitutional republics in the early nineteenth century represent a key moment in the history of the idea of human rights in Latin America. The role of European Enlightenment ideologies and the revolutionary movements of both France and North America were key influences in the intellectual and political elites of the region. In 1794 the *bogotano* Antonio Nariño, for example, translated and circulated the French *Déclaration des droits de l'Homme et du Citoyen*, a crime for which he was imprisoned and exiled. In the independence movements and early republican constitutions, Carozza identifies a Latin American singularity in the convergence within the region's prevailing scholastic tradition of two separate strands of Western legal thought, the French Declaration and the United States discourse of rights (300). On the matter of Simón Bolívar's political thought, the author emphasizes the influence of Rousseau, especially with regard to the notions of basic individual liberty, equality, and material security, all firmly inscribed "within a Rousseauian understanding of political life" (302).

That being said, the independence moment in Colombian and Latin American history is characterized by a Janus discourse of rights: On the one hand, the mostly white Creole elites were looking to universal principles of natural rights and individual liberty as they sought to distance themselves from their Colonial rulers; accordingly, to achieve independence, it was necessary to unite the native-born majorities by employing nativist rhetoric that affirmed "American" or regional identities as a basis of affiliation. On the other hand, once the imperial yoke was lifted, the Creole elites looked to mechanisms of differentiation – in many cases adopting or (re)implementing Colonial models based on a pigmentocracy or caste system – to maintain their privileged position in the political realm and in society in general. A defining feature of their nation-building projects was an overarching "will to civilization," as Cristina Rojas indicates in reference specifically to the Colombian context, in which "the political economy was organized around the process of production, exchange, and circulation of 'civilizing' capital. The market or field of this capital was characterized by the distribution of those civilizing qualities that were accumulated by male creole literati: law, grammar, and morality" (50). Likewise, the systems of differentiation were gendered, racialized, and ethnologized as part and parcel of the multifaceted processes of naturalization of marginalization. In the nascent republic, "history becomes imprinted in the body," as Rojas indicates in reference to *Ensayo sobre las revoluciones políticas* (1861), written by the prominent intellectual José María Samper, "and intelligence, beauty, and knowledge are attributes of the white race, whereas ugliness, stupidity, and malevolence are attributes of races of darker colors" (30). The Creole elites on both sides of the political spectrum proposed miscegenation – understood by them as the whitening of the national populace – as part of their civilizing projects. Clearly, these are not uniquely Colombian or Latin American phenomena of the era. Lynn Hunt points out, for example, similar tendencies in European and North American contexts: "In short, if rights were to be less than universal, equal, and natural, then reasons had to be given. As a consequence, the nineteenth century witnessed an explosion in biological explanations of difference" (186).

The notion of "temporal poetics" in the historiography of novel and nation speaks to the convergence of multiple times in a given juncture and (con)text; for example, it probes the merging of the successive projects of salvation, civilization, modernization, and development – as part of the processes of occidentalization (see Mignolo) – with the physical transformation of the nation's infrastructure, and in relation to the aesthetics of modernity. The notion of "spatial contours and flows," in turn, seeks to deconstruct and engage with various classifications that have been utilized throughout the history of the nation and the novel to define the relationships between the human being and the natural world, between the individual and urban space, between city and country, etc. The trajectory of novel and nation, ultimately, is manifested through the past, present, and future articulations of these three tensions.

BIBLIOGRAPHY

Anderson, Benedict. *Imagined Communities*. New York: Verso, 1996.

Andrade, María Mercedes. *La ciudad fragmentada: una lectura de las novelas del Bogotazo*. Cranston, R.I.: Ediciones INTI, 2002.

Bhabha, Homi K. "DissemiNation: Time, Narrative, and the Margins of the Modern Nation." In *Nation and Narration*. New York: Routledge, 1990. 291–322.

Bushnell, David, and Lester D. Langley, eds. *Simón Bolívar: Essays on the Life and Legacy of the Liberator*. Lanham, Md.: Rowman and Littlefield, 2008.

Carozza, Paolo. "From Conquest to Constitutions: Retrieving a Latin American Tradition of the Idea of Human Rights." *Human Rights Quarterly* 25 2 (2003): 281–313.

Castro-Klarén, Sara, and John Charles Chasteen. *Beyond Imagined Communities: Reading and Writing the Nation in Nineteenth-Century Latin America*. Baltimore: Johns Hopkins University Press, 2003.

Corral, Wilfrido. "Hacia una poética hispanoamericana de la novela decimonónico (I): el texto." In González Stephan et al., 307–30.

Curcio Altamar, Antonio. *Evolución de la novela en Colombia*. Bogotá: Instituto Colombiano de Cultura, 1975.

González Echevarría, Roberto. *Myth and Archive: A Theory of Latin American Narrative*. Cambridge: Cambridge University Press, 1990.

González Ortega, Nelson. *Colombia: Una nación en formación en su historia y literatura (siglo XVI–XXI)*. Madrid: Iberoamericana/Vervuert, 2013.

González Stephan, Beatriz. *Esplendores y miserias del siglo XIX: cultura y sociedad en América Latina*. Caracas: Monte Ávila Editores Latinoamericana, 1995.

Guerrieri, Kevin. *Palabra, poder y nación: la novela moderna en Colombia de 1896 a 1927*. Ciudad Juárez, México: Universidad Autónoma de Ciudad Juárez, 2004.

Hunt, Lynn. *Inventing Human Rights: A History*. New York: W. W. Norton, 2007.

LaRosa, Michael, and Germán Mejía. *Colombia: A Concise Contemporary History*. Lanham, Md.: Rowman & Littlefield, 2013.

McGrady, Donald. Introducción. In *María de Jorge Isaacs*. Madrid: Cátedra, 1998.

La novela histórica en Colombia 1844–1959. Bloomington: Indiana University Press, 1962.

Menton, Seymour. *La novela colombiana: planetas y satélites*. Barcelona: Plaza y Janés, 1978.

Mignolo, Walter. *The Darker Side of the Renaissance: Literacy, Territoriality, and Colonization*. Ann Arbor: University of Michigan Press, 1995.

Ordóñez Vila, Montserrat, comp. *La vorágine: textos críticos*. Bogotá: Alianza Editorial Colombiana, 1987.

"Cien años de escritura oculta: Soledad Acosta de Samper. Elisa Mújica y Marvel Moreno." In Luz Mary Giraldo (comp.) *Fin de siglo: narrativa colombiana*. Edit. Facultad de Humanidades. Bogotá: CEJA, 1995, pp. 323–38.

Pineda Botero, Álvaro. *La fábula y el desastre. Estudios críticos sobre la novela colombiana, 1650-1931*. Medellín: Fondo Editorial Universidad EAFIT, 1999.

Juicios de residencia. La novela colombiana, 1934–1985. Medellín: Fondo Editorial Universidad EAFIT, 2001.

Estudios críticos sobre la novela colombiana, 1990–2004. Medellín: Fondo Editorial Universidad EAFIT, 2005.

Pineda Buitrago, Sebastián. *Breve historia de la narrativa colombiana.* Bogotá: Siglo del Hombre Ediciones, 2012.

Porras Collantes, Ernesto. *Bibliografía de la novela en Colombia.* 1976.

Rama, Ángel. *La ciudad letrada.* Hanover, N.H.: Ediciones del Norte, 1984.

Ramos, Julio. *Desencuentros de la modernidad en América Latina. Literatura y política en el siglo XIX.* México: Fondo de Cultura Económica, 1989.

Rojas, Cristina. *Civilization and Violence: Regimes of Representation in Nineteenth-Century Colombia.* Minneapolis: University of Minnesota Press, 2002.

Sommer, Doris. *Foundational Fictions: The National Romances of Latin America.* Berkeley: University of California Press, 1991.

Viviescas, Fernando and Fabio Giraldo Isaza, eds. *Colombia: el despertar de la modernidad.* Bogotá: Foro Nacional por Colombia, 1991.

Von der Walde, Erna. "El 'cuadro de costumbres' y el proyecto hispano-católico de unificación nacional en Colombia." *ARBOR Ciencia, Pensamiento y Cultura* 183 724 (2007): 243–53.

Williams, Raymond L. *The Colombian Novel, 1844–1987.* Austin: University of Texas Press, 1991.

CHAPTER 5

Modern Colombian poetry: from modernismo to the twenty-first century

James J. Alstrum

During the first two decades of the twentieth century, two lingering poetic movements from the previous century – the late sentimental Romanticism of Julio Flórez (1867–1923) and the Parnassian modernismo modeled on the poetry of Guillermo Valencia (1873–1943) – overlapped and still dominated Colombian verse. The poets belonging to the group of Los Nuevos (The New Ones) were new in name only since they were still writing essentially in the modernista style and prevented Colombia from having any significant participation in the avant-garde-isms flourishing in Europe and the rest of Latin America after World War I. The major poets of the group of Los Nuevos included Rafael Maya (1897–1980), León de Greiff (1895–1976), Luis Vidales (1900–1990), and Jorge Zalamea (1905–69). Of the abovementioned poets, only Luis Vidales in his first book of poetry, *Suenan timbres* (1926, Bells Sound), and León de Greiff in *Tergiversaciones* (1925, Distortions) wrote verse similar in many ways to the European avant-garde without having any direct influence.

Although León de Greiff cannot be considered a true vanguard poet, he undoubtedly was one of the most important Colombian poets of all time. Like the avant-garde poets, he used neologisms but mixed them with colloquial and archaic language to create a very musical verse based on rhyme that made some critics call it symphonic and made him an *ultra-modernista* within the gamut of post-modernista Latin American poetry. Especially in his early poetry, like Luis Carlos López (1879–1950), he mocked his own poetry with an irreverent and ironic tone about the genre that he wrote in calling his extensive books of poems *mamotretos* (bulky books of junk). Like the great Portuguese poet Fernando de Pessoa (1888–1935), León de Greiff wrote under various heteronyms that were projections of different aspects of his personality and also alluded to his Scandinavian family background, such as Erik Fjordson, Sergio Stepansky, Matías Aldecoa, Guillaume de Lorges, Gunnar Fromhold, Ramón Antigua, Leo LeGris, and Diego de Estuñiga among others. In one of

De Greiff's most famous poems, "El relato de Sergio Stepansky" (The Story of Sergio Stepansky), the main character described and the person to whom the epigraph of the work is attributed (Erik Fjordson) are both heteronyms. The epigraph is paraphrased and used as a refrain at the beginning and end of this poem to provide it with a circular structure as it reiterates the theme that life is an absurd game in which all men are destined to lose: "Juego mi vida, cambio mi vida./De todos modos/la llevo perdida" (I play with my life, I change my life./At any rate/I go on losing) Repetition is one of the techniques used to underscore the musicality of almost all of De Greiff's verse together with alliteration, onomatopoeia, and rhyme. Indeed, De Greiff's poetry is a continuous attempt to fuse sound and sense in perfect harmony with the typical *modernista* employment of conceptual symbolism and double entendres. Also, the poet's work is filled with intertextual allusions to all of the Western literary tradition and history. For example, in another stanza of the already cited poem we read:

> *Cambio mi vida . . .*
> *por las perlas que se bebió la cetrina Cleopatra –*
> *o por su naricilla que está en algún Museo;*
> *cambio mi vida por lámparas viejas,*
> *o por la escala de Jacob, o por su plato de lentejas*
> *(I exchange my life . . .*
> *for the pearls which melancholy Cleopatra drank up –*
> *or for her little nose which is in some Museum;*
> *I exchange my life for old lamps,*
> *or for Jacob's ladder, or for his plate of lentils)*

The titles and subtitles of León de Greiff's books reflect his lifelong obsessions with music, irony, and humor and include *Tergiversaciones de Leo Legris, Matias Aldecoa y Gaspar* (1925, Distortions of Leo Legris, Matias Aldecoa and Gaspar) with sections entitled *Libro de las baladas* (Book of the Ballads), *Rondeles* (Rondels), *Arietas, Ritornelos y otros Ritmos* (Short Airs, Ritornellos and Other Rhythms), and *Estampas* (Engravings); *Libro de signos* (1935, The Book of Signs) with sections entitled *Segundo libro de baladas. Otras canciones* (The Second Book of Ballads. Other Songs), *Música de cámara y al aire libre – Primer ciclo. Bogotá 1921–1925* (Chamber Music and in the Open Air – First Cycle. Bogotá 1921–1925), and *Fantasías de nubes al viento (Primera ronda. – Esquema)* (Fantasies of Clouds in the Wind [First Round – Outline]); *Prosas de Gaspar* (1937, Proses of Gaspar); *Variaciones alrededor de nada* (1936, Variations around Nothing) with sections entitled *Fantasías de nubes al viento (Segunda Ronda)* (Fantasies of Clouds in the Wind [Second Round]), *Musurgia* (Musings), *Mitos de la noche* (Myths of the Night), and *Libro de relatos* (The Book of Stories); *Farrago* (1954, Hodgepodge) with sections entitled *Secuencias (Primer tranco)* (Sequences [First Big Step]), *Baladas in modo antico para me diverter* (Ballads in an Antimode to Amuse Me), *Poemillas* (Little Poems), *Fantasías de nubes al viento (Tercera ronda)* (Fantasies of Clouds in the Wind [Third Round]), and *Dos relatos (Del segundo libro dellos)* (Two Stories [From the Second Book of Them]); *Bárbara Charanga bajo el signo de Leo* (1957, Barbara Charanga under Leo's Sign); *Velero paradójico* (1957, Paradoxical Sailmaker) with sections entitled *Secuencia de secuencias* (Sequence of Sequences), *Sonatina* (Short Sonata), *Canciones, cancioncillas y otros sones* (Songs, Little Songs and Other Sounds), and *Poemilla de Bogislao (Relato de relatos derelictos)* (Bogislao's Little Poem [Story of Derelict Stories]); *Otras tergiversaciones de Leo, Matías y Gaspar* (Other Distortions from Leo, Matias and Gaspar); *Laberinto lunario* (Lunar Labyrinth); and *Nova et vetera* (1973, Nova and Vetera).

Luis Vidales's book of poems *Suenan timbres* most intuitively approximates vanguard poetry among Los Nuevos although the poet never had any direct contact with the European and Latin American avant-garde. The poems in this book were meant to scandalize and surprise through irony, humor, and colloquial language the kind of verse being written in Colombia at the time of its publication (1926) and to mock the resistance of the most conservative society in Latin America to outside pressures for modernization. Some critics consider this book to initiate an urban focus in Colombian poetry and to be a precursor of both conversational and antipoetry through its use of irony and colloquial language. After his first book and as one of the founders of the Colombian Communist party, Vidales's subsequent poetry and books were mostly political and of questionable aesthetic value. The singular importance of the contribution of *Suenan timbres* to the evolution of Colombian poetry was overlooked for several decades and not rediscovered by critics and literary historians until the 1970s or early 1980s, resulting in Vidales's being awarded the national poetry prize in 1985 by the University of Antioquia.

Most Colombian critics consider Rafael Maya's poetry to be a classic example of excellent modernista verse. Although he wrote many of his poems in a traditional metric form, he probably was the most innovative of the group in creating poems written in free verse. He also was an outstanding critic of poetry and teacher of literature. He is credited with first discovering and publishing the early poems of Aurelio Arturo (1906–74). Beginning with his first book of poems, *La vida en la sombra* (1925, Life in the Shadows), and ending with his last, *El tiempo recobrado* (1974, Recovered Time), Maya published nine books of verse. In addition, he also published many books of literary criticism, among which the most important was his *Los orígenes del Modernismo en Colombia* (1961, The Origins of Modernism in Colombia). Maya shunned the label of classic poet that many Colombian critics assigned him and like a true modernist considered himself to essentially be a romantic.

Jorge Zalamea's best poetry was his translations of the verse of Saint-John Perse (1887–1975) although he always aspired to be a great lyrical poet. Nevertheless, he stood out more as both an essayist devoted to literary criticism and for his use of poetic prose in his trilogy about the Latin American dictator, including *La metamorfosis de Su Excelencia* (1949, The Metamorphosis of His Excellency), *El Gran Burundún-Burundá* (1942, The Great Burundún-Burundá), and *El sueño de las escalinatas* (1964, The Dream of the Flight of Steps). Like his friend Luis Vidales, Zalamea became more and more influenced by Marxist ideology as he grew older, and probably for that reason his posthumous complete works are entitled *Literatura, política y arte* (1978, Literature, Politics and Art).

Emerging between the group of Los Nuevos and the poets belonging to Piedra y Cielo (Stone and Sky) were two poets who made singularly important contributions to the evolution of Colombian poetry: Aurelio Arturo (1906–74) and Jorge Artel (1909–94). Although Arturo only published a single book, *Morada al sur* (1963, Abode in the South), and a mere thirty-two poems (two posthumously) during a forty-three-year literary career, despite the brevity of his entire poetic works, his poetry has exercised an enormous influence over younger poets who began writing after *nadaísmo* (Nothingness), not only because they admired his rigorous self-criticism but also due to his innovative mythification of nature and his geographic region (Nariño) and the nostalgic tone with which he evoked the memory of his youth and infancy. Arturo's earliest poems were first published in 1931 in the literary supplement *La Crónica Literaria* edited by the poet and critic Rafael Maya. Fourteen years went by until thirteen more poems were published in 1945, of which nine would later form part of *Morada al sur* in 1963. When *Morada al sur* was finally published by the Ministry of Education and won the national poetry prize, the well-kept secret of Arturo's important poetry was exposed to a much wider reading public. The rhetoric and imagery of Arturo's poetry are unlike that of his contemporaries from the Piedra y Cielo group or anything else written before in Colombian poetry and appear to contain influences of the English poetry of T. S. Eliot (1888–1965), Jorge Guillén (1893–1984) from the Spanish poets of the Generation of 1927, and Vicente Huidobro's (1893–1948) *Creacionismo* (Creationism). The poet's language is lucid, apparently simple, and unadorned, yet especially in *Morada al sur*, an intimate and complex dialogue occurs between the poet's voice and his natural surroundings as he searches for a lost paradise from his innocent childhood and an ever-changing environment that defies his understanding.

Jorge Artel was the pseudonym of Agapito de Arcos, who was born in Cartagena and received a law degree from the University of Cartagena in 1945 although he never practiced law and devoted most of his life to poetry and journalism while also writing one novel (*No es la muerte . . . es el morir* [It's Not the Death . . . It's the Dying]) and a play (*De rigurosa etiqueta* [Of Rigorous Etiquette]), Artel is considered by most critics to be the major Afro-Colombian poet of the twentieth century continuing the verse begun in the previous century by Candelario Obeso (1849–84) with his first book, *Tambores en la noche* (1940, Drums in the Night). This poetry was expressed in the popular oral language and colloquial speech of the poor black laborers such as the oarsmen who rowed boats down the Magdalena River and was similar in many respects to the Afro-Cuban poetry written by Nicolás Guillén (1902–89). In two subsequent editions of the book (1955 and 1986), Artel added new poems that reflected a broader more universal perspective and greater influence from the avant-garde, especially surrealism. After the assassination of Jorge Eliécer Gaitán in 1948 with whose leftist political ideology Artel was closely associated, the poet left Colombia for twenty-four years in self-imposed exile during which time he lived in several different Latin American countries (Costa Rica, Mexico, Guatemala, and mostly Panama where he had relatives) and the United States until his return in 1972. During his exile he continued writing while working as a translator, literary critic, and university professor. He also met the North American poet Langston Hughes (1902–67) whom he admired and who influenced somewhat his later poetry. Throughout his poetry and writings about his own verse, Artel strove, like his predecessor Candelario Obeso, to emphasize the African contribution to his nation's culture and literature while distinguishing his poems from those by other Afro-Caribbean writers such as Guillén. His other books of poetry included *Poemas con botas y banderas* (1972, Poems with Boots and Banners), *Sinú, riberas de asombro jubiloso* (1972, Sinú, Banks of Jubilant Wonder), *Cantos y poemas* (1983, Songs and Poems), and *Antología poética* (1979 and 1986, Poetic Anthology).

After Los Nuevos the next important group of Colombian poets was Piedra y Cielo ("Stone and Sky") which was led by Jorge Rojas (1911–95) and Eduardo Carranza (1913–85) and took its name from a book by the Spanish Nobel laureate and poet Juan Ramón Jiménez (1881–1958). They also admired the post-modernista verse of the Chilean Nobel Prize-winning poet Pablo Neruda (1904–73) and the imagery of the Spanish Generation of 1927 and Spanish Golden Age poetry but sought renovation in tradition. Impelled by Rojas, seven short books of poems by the group were published between September of 1939 and March of 1940 and appeared in the following order, including other poets as well as Carranza and Rojas: *La ciudad sumergida* (The Submerged City) by Rojas, *Territorio amoroso* (Loving Territory) by Carlos Martín (1914–2008), *Presagio del amor* (Foreshadowing of Love) by Arturo Camacho Ramírez (1910–82), *Seis elegías y un himno* (Six Elegies and a Hymn) by Carranza, *Regreso a la muerte* (Return to Death) by Tomás Vargas Osorio (1908–41), *El ángel desolado* (The Desolated Angel) by Gerardo Valencia (1911–94), and *Habitante de su imagen* (Inhabitant of His Image) by Darío Samper (1909–84). Although as the abovementioned poets matured and their poetics became more diverse, at the beginning all were united in their concept of a poetry that avoided the extremes of the avant-garde-isms but also rejected rationalism with an emphasis on the sentimental metaphor and simpler clarity in the expression of their personal poetic visions that found paradigms in the classics of Spanish peninsular verse.

Eduardo Carranza was the indisputable leader of the Piedra y Cielo movement and the best known poet of the group outside of Colombia. He published his first book of poetry, *Canciones para iniciar una fiesta* (Songs for Starting a Party), in 1936. In this tome and throughout his entire work, there is a pursuit of beauty, musicality, and feeling together with the idealization of pure feminine beauty based on the classical lyrical traditions of both Spain and Colombia. He devoted his life to poetry as both a teacher of literature and a diplomat who represented his country as a cultural attaché in Chile and Spain. One of Carranza's high school students of literature was the poet Alvaro Mutis (1923–2013) in whom he inspired a particular love of the verse of the Spanish poet Antonio Machado (1875–1939). In a famous but polemical essay, "Bardolatría," written in 1941, Carranza criticized the unquestioned veneration of the Parnassian modernismo of Guillermo Valencia as the ideal model for Colombian poetry, which he denounced for emphasizing form and technique over personal experience and sentiment. Carranza believed that the best poetry needed to have a transcendental and unstated suggestive significance based on personal circumstances. He remained true to this belief as his poetry evolved and reflected changes in his personal life. Carranza's poetry can be divided into three stages, consisting of his youthful verse, his mature verse, and the verse of his old age. His youthful poetry included the already aforementioned books as well as the following titles: *Sombra de las muchachas* (1941, Shadow of the Girls), *Azul de ti* (1936–1944, Blue of You), *Canto en voz alta* (1942, Out Loud Song), *Este era un rey* (1945, This One Was a King), and *Los días que ahora son sueños* (1946, The Days Which Now Are Dreams). His mature verse was made up of *El olvidado y Alhambra* (1957, The Forgotten and Alhambra) and *Los pasos contados* (1973, The Counted Steps). The poetry of his old age consisted of *Hablar soñando y otras alucinaciones* (1974, To Speak Dreaming and Other Hallucinations), *El insomne* (1974, The Insomniac), and *Epístola mortal y otras soledades* (1975, Mortal Epistle and Other Lonelinesses). The predominant theme of his youthful poetry is young love and the tone of this stage, and his mature poetry is optimistic with love triumphing over death. In Carranza's mature poetry the influence of Antonio Machado is more evident. Loneliness and death are the major themes of his poetry of old age, and a somber and pessimistic tone prevails. Nevertheless, in all of Carranza's poetry a melodious musical quality and a heartfelt sentimentality in the poetic word approximate the pure poetry that Juan Ramon Jiménez sought for lyrical expression.

Jorge Rojas and Arturo Camacho Ramirez were the two other major poets of the Piedra y Cielo movement. Rojas's first book of poems appeared early in 1939 and took its title – *La forma de tu huida* (The Form of Your Flight) – from a verse by Juan Ramón Jiménez. This volume was heavily influenced by the love poetry of Pedro Salinas (1891–1951) from the Spanish Generation of 1927. In 1941, Rojas's third book, *Rosa de agua* (Rose of Water), contained a set of well-crafted, beautifully perfect sonnets. Rojas published three collections with the same title: *Soledades* (1936–40, Lonelinesses), *Soledades II* (1950–64, Lonelinesses II), and *Soledades III* (1979–85, Lonelinesses III). In all three of these collections a theme of idealized eroticism and the evocation of Latin American geography reflects the influence of Neruda and Andrés Bello's (1789–1865) early nineteenth-century neoclassicism. Rojas was awarded the Guillermo Valencia National Poetry Prize by the Colombian Academy of Language for *Soledades II*. He returned to the theme of love in *Cárcel de amor* (1976, Jail of Love). Most of Rojas's poetry was contained in *Suma poética* (1977, Poetic Sum) and *Obra poética. 1939–1986* (Poetic Work. 1939–1986). Rojas's last book, *Huella* (1993,

Footprint), lyrically reiterates his admiration for the classics of Spanish peninsular verse, especially the poetry of the Spanish romantic Gustavo Adolfo Bécquer (1836–70). Ironically, Rojas himself considered that his best poetry was found in his only play written in verse, *La doncella de agua* (1948, The Maiden of Water).

Arturo Camacho Ramírez was probably the most open and receptive of all the poets of Piedra y Cielo to avant-garde influences, especially by Neruda and the Spanish poet Federico García Lorca (1898–1936) of the Generation of 1927 although he also admired French poetry and the verse of Jorge Manrique (1440–79), Luis de Góngora (1561–1627), and Francisco de Quevedo (1580–1645) from Spain. In contrast to Carranza, Camacho Ramírez was much more influenced by Neruda than Juan Ramón Jiménez; where the language of the former was much clearer and luminous, the imagery of the latter was more nocturnal and hermetic. The influence of Lorca's *Romancero Gitano* (1928, Gypsy Romances) and *Poema del cante jondo* (1931, The Poem of Cante Jondo) is most evident in Camacho Ramírez's first book, *Espejo de naufragios* (1935, Mirror of Shipwrecks). The irrational stands out more in the poems of Camacho Ramírez than in the poetry of the other members of Piedra y Cielo, and in particular this comes from the influence of Lorca's book *Poeta en Nueva York* (1929, Poet in New York) and Neruda's *Residencia en la tierra* (1925–31, 1931–35, Residence on Earth) especially in the Colombian's *Límites del hombre* (1964, Limits of Man). His book *La vida pública* (1962, Public Life) presents a nocturnal and urban world. *Carrera de la vida* (1976, The Career of Life) was the last book of poetry published by Camacho Ramírez during his lifetime.

Undoubtedly the poets associated with the cultural magazine *Mito* edited by the poet Jorge Gaitán Durán (1925–62) in the mid–twentieth century constituted some of the most important Colombian lyrical poets of all time and can be credited with bringing the national verse into the mainstream of Latin American poetry – surprisingly, at a time of national crisis when the country was mired in a bloody undeclared civil war known as La Violencia (The Violence) between the main political parties, the Liberals and Conservatives. The forty-two numbers of the magazine published between 1955 and 1962 opened up Colombian culture and literature to the rest of the western world since each number included both original writing by national poets, narrators, and essayists together with the voices of internationally known writers in Spanish and in translation such as Octavio Paz, T. S. Eliot, Gabriel García Márquez, and Jean Paul Sartre, just to mention the Nobel laureates whose writing could be found on the pages of *Mito* during its existence. Besides Gaitán Durán, the other major poets associated with *Mito* were Fernando Charry Lara (1920–2004), Alvaro Mutis, Héctor Rojas Herazo (1920–2002), Eduardo Cote Lamus (1928–64), and Rogelio Echavarría (b. 1926).

Although Gaitán Durán published five books of poetry during his life, his last two, *Amantes* (1958 published originally in *Mito*) and *Si mañana despierto* (1961, If Tomorrow I Awake), which appeared just six months before his tragic death in a plane crash, are his most critically acclaimed tomes. Throughout all his poetry a constant counterpoising of opposed images emphasizes the themes of death and eroticism or violence and beauty along with reflections upon the nature of poetry itself. Indeed, in one poem Gaitán Durán remarked "El poema es un acto erótico" (The poem is an erotic act). As his poetry evolved, traditional rhetoric was abandoned in favor of a simpler laconic language in which eroticism loomed as a momentary participation in what is eternal even as with the passage of time the lyrical voice becomes more conscious of its inevitable mortality. One of the poems from *Si mañana despierto* that best reflects the heightened tension between erotic love and death found in the entire book is the sonnet "Sé que estoy vivo," where we read:

> *Sé que estoy vivo en este bello día*
> *Acostado contigo. Es el verano.*
> *Acaloradas frutas en tu mano.*
> *Vierten su espeso olor al mediodía.*
>
> *Antes de aquí tendernos no existía*
> *Este mundo radiante. ¡Nunca en vano*
> *Al deseo arrancarnos el humano*
> *Amor que a las estrellas desafía!*
>
> *Hacia el azul del mar corro desnudo.*
> *Vuelvo a ti como al sol y en ti me anudo,*
> *Nazco en el splendor de conocerte.*
>
> *Siento el sudor ligero de la siesta.*
> *Bebemos vino rojo. Esta es la fiesta*
> *En que más recordamos a la muerte.*
> (I know that I'm alive on this beautiful day
>
> Lying in bed with you. It's summer.
> Warm fruits in your hand
> Shed their thick smell at noon.

Before we laid down here this radiant world
Did not exist. Never in vain
Did we pull away the human love
Which challenges the stars!

I run naked toward the blue of the sea.
I go back to you like to the sun and in you I'm joined.
I'm born in the splendor of knowing you.

I feel the light sweat of the siesta.
We drink red wine. This is the celebration
In which we most remember death.)

Because of the poets of *Mito* who wrote verse in this vein, the expression of erotic imagery in Colombian poetry was freed from prudish sociocultural constraints.

Among the outstanding poets of *Mito*, Fernando Charry Lara was the most self-conscious and the best critic of all of Colombian and Hispanic poetry and most especially of the verse written by the poets of his generation. As a critic, he was renowned for his book *Lector de poesía* (1975, Reader of Poetry). Charry was a most demanding and critical poet of his own work and therefore only published three books of his verse: *Nocturno y otros sueños* (1949, Nocturne and Other Dreams), *Los adioses* (1963, The Goodbyes) and *Pensamientos del amante* (1981, Thoughts of the Lover). His complete poetic works were later published during his lifetime in a book *Llama de amor viva* (1986, Living Flame of Love). He was greatly influenced by the Spanish poets of the Generation of 1927 and the verse of Luis Cernuda (1902–63). Indeed, his first book contained a prologue written by the Nobel laureate Vicente Aleixandre (1898–1984) of the Generation of 1927. Charry was a nocturnal poet in the tradition established by José Asunción Silva (1865–96), and most of his poems had an urban setting, although a few dealt with La Violencia such as "Llanura de Tuluá" (Tuluá Plain) where images of violent death and tender love are coupled in the fragments cited here:

Al borde del camino, los dos cuerpos
uno junto al otro,
desde lejos parecen amarse.

Un hombre y una muchacha, delgadas
formas cálidas
tendidas en la hierba, devorándose.

. . .

De su suerte ignorantes, de su muerte,

y ahora, ya de cerca contemplados,
ocasión de voraces negras aves.
(At the edge of the road, both bodies
one next to the other,
from afar they seem to love each other.

A man and a girl, slender
warm forms
laying in the grass, devouring each other.
                       . . .
Not knowing their fate, of their death,
and now, already contemplating nearby,
an opportunity for voracious blackbirds.

Recurring themes in Charry's brief poetry were erotic love, the night, poetry itself, and death. Besides his presence in *Mito*, Charry was also one of the founders and major contributors to the perduring poetic journal *Golpe de Dados* directed by the poet Mario Rivero (1935–2009).

Undoubtedly, Alvaro Mutis was the most outstanding poet associated with *Mito* even though the success of his novellas during the last two decades of his life tended to overshadow the importance of his verse. The central character he created – Maqroll El Gaviero (Maqroll the Look-out) – was present in both his poetry and prose. This antihero sought fulfillment but constantly was thwarted in each enterprise he attempted and thus was directly tied to Mutis's main themes of corruption, decomposition, frustration, desperation, and despair. Like Maqroll, Mutis himself lived and travelled throughout the world, especially Europe, Latin America, and Asia Minor but, unlike his wandering character, found great success and renown in Latin America and Europe, which led him to receive every major literary prize in both prose and poetry given in the Hispanic world, such as the Cervantes Prize and the Queen Sophia Prize for poetry and awards for his novellas in translation in France and Italy. Indeed, his close friend for more than half a century García Márquez called him one of the greatest writers of our time. His third book of poetry, *Memoria de los hospitales de ultramar* (1959, Memory of the Overseas Hospitals), which first appeared in *Mito,* was highly praised and admired by the Octavio Paz even before Mutis left Colombia and went to live in Mexico. As the child of a Colombian diplomat in Belgium, he became fluent in French, and he discovered the tropics when his family would travel each summer by ship back to Colombia and his grandfather's coffee plantation in Tolima. Thus, Mutis had easy access to

French literature and was influenced by Proust and the surrealists as well as being inspired to read and write poetry by his high school teacher, the poet Eduardo Carranza. Because of his experiences and love of the sea, it is not surprising that Maqroll was a sailor, and Mutis's work has been compared to that of Joseph Conrad (1857–1924). Because he was accused of embezzlement by the Esso Company for which he had worked as a director of public relations in Colombia, after fleeing to Mexico, he was imprisoned in the Lecumberri prison. This also influenced the creation of his character Maqroll, who was never judgmental. Mutis wrote about this experience in the prose memoir *Diario de Lecumberri* (1960) after charges against him were dropped.

Mutis probably was the most prolific writer of the *Mito* group and published short stories and essays as well as novels and verse even though he was not devoted to full-time literary pursuits until after his retirement when he was sixty years old. Like Charry, Mutis also wrote nocturnal poems but also included lyrical descriptions of sumptuous tropical landscapes in which eloquent words evoked misery with vivid, splendid imagery. This can be seen in the opening verses from Mutis' poem "Nocturno" (Nocturne):

> *Esta noche ha vuelto la lluvia sobre los cafetales.*
> *Sobre las hojas de plátano,*
> *Sobre las altas ramas de los cámbulos,*
> *ha vuelto a llover esta noche en un agua persistente y vastísima*
> *que crece las acequias y comienza a henchir los ríos*
> *que gimen con su nocturna carga de lodos vegetales.*
> *(Tonight the rain has come back over the coffee plantations.*
> *Over the plantain leaves*
>
> *Over the high branches of the cámbulos,*
>
> *a persistent and very vast rain water has come back tonight*
> *which makes the irrigation ditches grow and begins to fill up the rivers*
> *which groan with their nocturnal load of vegetal mud.)*

Maqroll is a dominant presence in Mutis's first books of poetry, which began with a coauthored volume, *La balanza* (1948), which had a limited edition of only 200 copies and were lost in the Bogotazo (urban violence in Bogotá in 1948) following Gaitán's assassination. His second book was *Los elementos del desastre* (1953, The Elements of Disaster) and received critical acclaim both in Colombia and abroad; it showed the influence of

Neruda's *Residencia en la tierra* (Residence on Earth). His fourth book, *Los trabajos perdidos* (1965, The Lost Works), was the first to be published in Mexico. The poems from these aforementioned books were collected in a tome appropriately entitled *Summa de Maqroll el Gaviero. Poesía 1948–1970* (Summa of Maqroll the Lookout. Poetry 1948–1970) and published in Spain in 1973. After publishing his first novella, *La mansion de Araucaíma* (The Mansion), in the same year, his poetry moved toward a new variety of verse forms including foreign free forms and prose poems, some of which were later incorporated into his first novella featuring Maqroll called *La nieve del almirante* (1986, The Admiral's Snow). His poetic work *Caravansary* (1981, Caravan Inn) reflects Mutis's interest in the aura of the Arab world and mainly included prose poems later interpolated into his first Maqroll novella. His next book of verse, *Los emisarios* (1984, The Emissaries), consisted mainly of lyrical poems about different historical events and various geographical sites in Spain and Europe but also included two prose poems that reappeared in *La nieve del almirante*. In *Crónica regia y alabanza del reino* (1985, Regal Chronicle and Praise of the Kingdom), Mutis, always a monarchist and reactionary, presents a favorable but realistic poetic portrait of the Spanish king Ferdinand II and his reign. Mutis last book of poetry, *Un homenaje y siete nocturnos* (1987, A Homage and Seven Nocturnes), was probably his most personal volume of lyrical poems, reflecting his lifelong love of classical music in the first poem devoted to the composer and then his interest in the nocturne and certain historic human icons and Mario Lavista sacred places including the saintly King Louis IX of France and St. James of Campostela, for whom his father and son were named. Finally, throughout the poetry of Mutis, which is truly inseparable from his prose, continuous intertextual allusions are made to his own work and the classics of western civilization and culture and a questioning pursuit of the meaning of poetry, which is best summed up in the chain of metaphors in "Cada poema" (Each Poem) from *Los trabajos perdidos*, where we read:

> *Agua de sueño, fuente de ceniza,*
> *piedra porosa de mataderos,*
> *madera en sombra de las siemprevivas,*
> *metal que dobla por los condenados,*
> *aceite funeral de doble filo,*
> *cotidiano sudario del poeta,*
>
> *cada poema esparce sobre el mundo*
> *el agrio cereal de la agonía.*

(Dreamlike water, ash fountain,
porous stone of slaughterhouses,
wood in the shadow of evergreens,
metal bent by the condemned,
double-edged funeral oil,
daily shroud of the poet,
each poem spreads over the world
the sour cereal of agony.)

Like his fellow North Santanderean Gaitán Durán, Eduardo Cote Lamus had just begun to reach his full poetic potential when his life was cut short in a tragic car accident while he was serving as the governor of his native department. Most critics agree that in his first two poetic tomes – *Preparación para la muerte* (1950, Preparation for Death) and *Salvación del recuerdo* (1953, Salvation of Memory) – the young poet was struggling to find a voice in which to express two of his main themes: suffering and death. In his third book, *Los sueños* (1956, The Dreams), the poet has finally discovered what he wants to say and how to say it, although his very serious and profound conceptual verse marks Cote as the most hermetic of the poets of *Mito*. The personal anecdote becomes the point of departure for the expression of his ideas, although tension is present between the depth of his thought and an attempt to express it in more colloquial language and imagery. The lyrical voice confesses that he is a condemned captive of his own language and thought but feels compelled and challenged nevertheless to continue expressing himself as best he can. In his next book called *La vida cotidiana* (1959, Daily Life), the parallel themes of communication issuesincommunication and isolation emerge as consequences of a consciousness that being and its expression are essentially commingled, reflected in the poem "El acto y la palabra que lo nombra" (The Act and the Word Which Names It). In Cote's last book and extensive poem, *Estoraques* (1963, Gum Trees), the eroded sand dunes resulting from the wind and drought deforming the landscapes of his native North Santander serve as a metaphor for dehumanization and the passage of time toward mortality.

In contrast with the profound hermeticism of Cote was the laconic, colloquial verse of Rogelio Echavarría, who has devoted his life to journalism and never has considered himself to be a "professional poet" but rather a witness who gives testimony to the apparently insignificant happenings of daily life. Before the appearance of the multiple and enlarged editions of his best known book, *El transeúnte* (1964, 1977, 1984, The Passerby),

Echavarría published his first verses in *Edad sin tiempo* (1948, Age without Time). Echavarría's verse has demonstrated that often deep thoughts can be expressed with utmost simplicity, and his poems also reflect the collective wisdom and voice of the man on the street. Intimacy is coupled with objective testimonial observation as we can see in the verses of the poem that gives the book its title:

> *Todas las calles que conozco*
>
> *son un largo monólogo mío.*
> *(All the streets I know*
> *are my long monologue.)*

The last poet from *Mito* who deserves mention was Héctor Rojas Herazo, although like Mutis his poetry may have been overshadowed by his novels and by the fact that he was a most accomplished artist as a painter. Rojas Herazo wrote five books of poetry, including *Rostro de la soledad* (1952, Face of Solitude), *Tránsito de Caín* (1953, Passage of Cain), *Desde la luz preguntan por nosotros* (1956, From the Light They Ask about Us), *Agresión de las formas contra el ángel* (1961, Aggression of the Forms against the Angel), and *Las úlceras de Adán* (1995, Adam's Ulcers). Of all these books, the most notable is his third book, in which stand out the extreme emotions of joy and pain expressed more as epic rather than lyrical outpourings.

Meira Delmar (1922–2009), the pseudonym for Olga Chams, the daughter of Lebanese immigrants to Colombia's Caribbean coast, was the most outstanding woman poet contemporary of *Mito,* whose verse was highly admired and praised by García Márquez. As her pseudonym might suggest, sea imagery is an important part of her verse, which has a continuous nostalgic tone going back to her Middle Eastern cultural heritage but also reflecting the landscapes and environment of Cartagena and Barranquilla, where she lived most of her life. Musicality is one of the most important components of her verse, which presents most of the traditional themes of lyrical poetry such as love, death, loneliness, personal loss, and the attempt to define the nature of poetry itself employing conventional verse forms inspired by models from Spanish peninsular poetry. Her eight books of poetry included the following: *Alba de olvido* (1942, Dawn of Forgetfulness), *Sitio del amor* (Site of Love), *Verdad del sueño* (1946, Truth of the Dream), *Secreta isla* (1951, Secret Island), *Huésped sin sombra* (1971, Guest without Shade), *Reencuentro* (1981, Collision), *Laúd memorioso* (1995, Retentive Lute), and the poetic anthology of most of her verse, *Pasa el viento 1942–1998* (2000, The Wind Passes 1942–1998).

The last number of *Mito* (1962) was devoted to the scandalous nihilistic verse of *Nadaísmo* (Nothingness), which signified the long overdue arrival of the plenitude of the avant-garde to Colombian poetry but with an essentially parodic expression first proclaimed in the 1958 manifesto of its founder Gonzalo Arango (1931–76). Although *nadaísmo* was mainly expressed in poetry, it also encompassed short stories, polemical essays, and a few novels to launch an all-out assault against not only literature but all the sacred cows of Colombian culture and society, including the Church, politicians, customs, and traditional sociocultural values. It was influenced by surrealism and the philosophy of the Antioquian Fernando González (1895–1964) as well as existentialism and the ideas of Nietzsche. Although Arango wrote poetry, the most critically acclaimed poetry by any *nadaísta* first appeared in the book *Los poemas de la ofensa* (1968, Offensive Poems) by Jaime Jaramillo Escobar (b. 1932) under the pseudonym X-504, which underscored his repudiation of the heroic characterization of the poet as a "pequeño Dios" (small god, by the creationist Chilean poet Vicente Huidobro (1893–1948). Jaramillo Escobar ridiculed such a depiction of the poet in his poem "Conversación con Walt Whitman" (Conversation with Walt Whitman) from his first book. There the poetic voice concludes with sarcasm and irreverence that

> *¿Conque la rana es una obra maestro de Dios, no?*
> *¡Entonces yo también!*
> *Y si yo soy una obra maestro de Dios entonces*
> *Dios tiene que ser muy pequeño,*
> *un artista muy malo, francamente.*
> *(So that the toad is a masterpiece of God, right?*
> *Then I am too!*
> *And if I am a masterpiece of God then*
> *frankly, God must be a very bad artist.)*

The poetry of Jaramillo Escobar is iconoclastic and written with the poet assuming the role of an antipoetic minstrel. Most of Jaramillo Escobar's poems are written in free verse in the form of a dialogue or monologue like the poem cited earlier. His language is colloquial with an ironic tone and humor characteristic of satirical antipoetry that continues to stand out in two other prize-winning books: *Sombrero de ahogado* (1984, The Hat of a Drowned Man) and *Poemas de tierra caliente* (1985, Poems from the Hot Lands). These two books contain poetic parody and sociopolitical satire, which extends beyond Colombia and include among their themes denunciations of imperialism and the threat to the world economy from multinational corporations in poems like "Atraco" (Holdup) from *Sombrero de ahogado* and "Zarpa mercante" (Merchant Claw) from *Poemas de tierra caliente*. His poems also provide a revisionist and critical perspective of "official history" and expose the nefarious long-term consequences of La Violencia in the poems "Las hijas del muerto" (The Daughters of the Dead Man) and "San Lorenzo" (St. Lawrence). After nearly thirty years, a new book by Jaramillo Escobar called *Poesía de uso* (Useful Poetry) was published in 2014.

J. Mario Arbeláez (b. 1940) is another important prize-winning *nadaísta* poet who came to the movement from Cali in 1959. His first book, *El profeta en su casa* (1966, The Prophet in His Home), and his other books of poetry are similar to Jaramillo Escobar's work because they also have an ironic and irreverent tone filled with black humor in which surrealist verse is parodied and the sociocultural icons of Colombia are mocked. His second book, *Mi reino por este mundo* (1981, My Kingdom throughout This World), was awarded two prizes: the National Poetry Prize of the Oveja Negra publishing house and the prize given in the same year by *Golpe de Dados* poetry magazine. His third book of verse, *La casa de la memoria* (1985, The House of Memory), won the national prize given by Colcultura. His last two books, *El cuerpo de ella* (1999, Her Body) and *Paños menores* (2008, Underclothing), dedicated to his father who was a tailor, have also won awards. The last work won the International Valera Mora Poetry Prize in Caracas, Venezuela. Erotic themes have especially stood out in his later poetry. He uses feigned narcissism in many poems to make fun of himself and often employs plays on words to underscore his verses' irony. In the poem "Culo" (Behind) eroticism is combined with ironic mockery and irreverence, alliteration, and the characteristic play on words found in most of J. Mario's poetry. Here we read:

> *Complemento genial.*
>
> *Urano reducido al ojo erótico.*
> *Lujoso lulo para la lujuria.*
> *Oscura inclinación.*
> *Territorio extensísimo:*
> *moneda*
> *de a centavo de cobre,*
> *paraíso,*
> *sumersión de gaviotas extraviadas.*
> *En ella se dilata y está vivo,*
> *Violento y vivo y dúctil y agresivo.*
> *(Brilliant complement.*
> *Uranium reduced to an erotic eye.*

Luxurious bundle for lust.
Dark inclination.
Very extensive territory:
coin
of a copper cent.

paradise,
submersion of stray seagulls.

In her it expands and is alive,
violent and alive and pliable and aggressive.)

Two very important transitional poets who emerged between nand the Generación de *Golpe de Dados* were Mario Rivero and Giovanni Quessep (b. 1939). Each poet represented a recurring tendency in twentieth-century Colombian poetry, with Quessep in the classical lyrical tradition of musicality and symbolism beginning with Silva and continuing in Barba Jacob, Eduardo Carranza, and Charry Lara while Rivero was linked to a more narrative and colloquial style typical of Luis Carlos López, León de Greiff, and Echevarría. Although he was identified by some critics with the *nadaístas,* Rivero repudiated any association with them even though they highly admired and praised his verse. Beginning with his first book entitled *Poemas urbanos* (1966, Urban Poems), which many critics consider to be one of the most important books of Colombian poetry of the twentieth century because it marks a break with traditional rhetoric and imagery, Rivero wrote in a direct and simple language about the urban landscape inhabited by the marginalized working class of the city who seldom had appeared before in Colombian verse. He also incorporated the musicality of popular song and dance like the tango and the ballad into his poetry. His poems constitute conversational testimonies of the daily life of the city, especially Bogotá, where he lived most of his life after emigrating to the capital from Envigado, a suburb of Medellín. His poetry continued to evolve throughout the fifteen volumes of verse he published before his death, including antipoetry, conversational testimony, collages, and increasingly intimate and very personal reflections about daily urban life. Among his books besides the aforementioned initial tome the following especially stand out: *Baladas sobre ciertas cosas que no se deben nombrar* (1973, Ballads about Certain Things Which Ought Not to Be Named, which merited the Eduardo Cote Lamus Poetry Prize), *Los poemas del invierno* (1985, Winter Poems), *Mis asuntos* (1995, My Business – collected works), *Vuelvo a las calles* (1989, I Return to the Streets), *V Salmos penitenciales* (1999, Five Penitential Psalms), and *Viaje nocturno* (2008,

Nocturnal Voyage). Colombian poetry will also be indebted to Rivero for keeping alive through his editorship the longest running poetry journal in the history of the national literature, *Golpe de Dados*, which began in 1973 and lasted until his death. This poetic outlet also gave a name to a generation of poets who began publishing their works first in it during the 1970s before they appeared in book form.

Giovanni Quessep is considered both within and outside of Colombia to be one of the nation's most outstanding living poets beginning with the publication of his second book, *El ser no es una fábula* (1968, Being Is Not a Fable), despite the fact that he prefers to employ traditional metric forms and seeks inspiration in Dante's *Divine Comedy*, his Middle Eastern and Lebanese cultural heritage, and the classics of Spanish Peninsular verse while crafting poems with excellent musicality and symbolism based on mythical archetypes and even fairy tales such as "Sleeping Beauty." A recurring theme is that poetry captures and preserves the perduring lessons from the past that otherwise would be lost forever. His lifetime poetic achievements have been recognized by being awarded the National José Asunción Silva Prize (2004) and the National Prize for Poetry given by the University of Antioquia (2007). Perhaps the poem that best synthesizes the characteristic harmony between sound and sense through musicality and the fusion of song and story with a magical aura found in most of Quessep's verse is "Tejido" (Woven Web), where we read:

> *Si tuviese tus ojos, hilandera,*
> *podría ver lo que jamás he visto:*
> *hilos de plata, hilos de oro, hilos de seda*
> *moviéndose en mis manos*
> *para tejer las cuatro estaciones,*
> *especialmente la primavera*
> *o el otoño que todo lo acaba;*
> *vería el agua correr por la madeja*
> *y torres en el fondo de las barcas,*
> *o miraría en la rueca*
> *las bellas formas que ya son el hilo*
> *en que siempre la muerte nos espera.*
> *el hilo de plata, el hilo de oro, el hilo de seda.*
> *(If I had your eyes, spinner,*
> *I could see what I never have seen:*
>
> *threads of silver, threads of gold, threads of silk*
> *moving around in my hands*
> *to weave the four seasons,*
> *especially the Spring*

or the Fall which completes everything;
I would see the water run through the skein of wool
and towers in the back of the boats,
or I would look at the beautiful forms
in the spinning wheel which already are the thread
on which death always awaits us,
the thread of silver, the thread of gold, the thread of silk.

Among Quessep's thirteen books of poetry the most notable were *Duración y leyenda* (1972, Duration and Legend), *Canto del extranjero* (1976, Song of the Foreigner), *Madrigales de vida y muerte* (1978, Madrigals of Life and Death), *Muerte de Merlín* (1985, Death of Merlin), *Un jardín y un desierto* (1993, A Garden and a Desert), *Brasa lunar* (2004, Lunar Ember), and *Metamórfosis del jardín* (2006, Metamorphosis of the Garden).

Most of the poets of the Generation of *Golpe de Dados* published their first poems in an anthology that identified them as a "generación sin nombre" (nameless generation) and included verses written by Elkin Restrepo (b. 1942), Henry Luque Muñoz (1944–2005), Alvaro Miranda (b. 1945), Augusto Pinilla (b. 1946), Darío Jaramillo Agudelo (b. 1947), and Juan Gustavo Cobo Borda (b. 1948). To the aforementioned list of poets can be added the diverse lyrical voices of José Manuel Arango (1937–2002), Miguel Méndez Camacho (b. 1942), Jaime García Maffla (b. 1944), Harold Alvarado Tenorio (b. 1945), María Mercedes Carranza (1945–2003), Juan Manuel Roca (b. 1946), Anabel Torres (b. 1948), Renata Durán (b. 1948), and Alvaro Rodríguez Torres (b. 1948). Almost all of these poets have either published poems in or have been associated with *Golpe de Dados* since its beginnings. Furthermore, their collective works seem to be a synthesis of the intertextual cosmopolitanism of *Mito* and the often irreverent and disillusioned tone of *nadaísmo* concerning the sociocultural realities and values of their country or the nature of the literary genres in which they write. They also have expressed in various ways a thematic obsession with *eros* and *logos*. Several, especially Cobo Borda, Roca, and Jaramillo Agudelo, have garnered international rewards for their poetry or prose writings for the novel and short story as well as the essay. Like most postvanguard Spanish American poets, the paradigms for the Generation of *Golpe de Dados* have been Octavio Paz and the Chilean antipoet Nicanor Parra (b. 1914). From Paz they received a tendency toward a metalinguistic, self-referential, and existentialist poem, and from Parra they gotten ironic and humorous satire and parody of the lyrical genre itself.

At times, the poetry of Elkin Restrepo has alternated and incorporated the abovementioned tendencies found in the models left by Parra and Paz. Restrepo's first published book of verse, *Bla, bla, bla* (1967), was written in a colloquial language and centered in urban scenarios like Rivero's poetry to capture the absurdities of daily life. Much more important in his evolution was the book *Retrato de artistas* (1983), in which he used verbal portraits of famous artists and celebrities principally from motion pictures to express his perspective on both poetry and contemporary life. Although Restrepo has also published some collections of short stories, most of his books are devoted to poetry and now total ten. His later books of poetry like *La dádiva* (1991, The Gift) and *La vista que no pasó del jardín* (2002, The View Which Didn't Pass the Garden) have as a common theme the surprising transcendental epiphanies discovered in daily living. He also has continued to reflect on the meaning of poetry and the role of the poet in today's society. For example, in poem 6 from *La dádiva* we read a series of metaphors to define what today's poet is:

> *El poeta es el rey del camuflaje*
> *. . .*
> *un cameleón*
> *que como la vida misma*
> *adopta mil formas*
> *ninguna mejor que otra*
>
> (*The poet is the king of camouflage*
> *. . .*
> *a cameleon*
>
> *who like life itself*
> *adopts a thousand forms*
> *none better than the other*)

Throughout its evolution, Restrepo's poetry has assumed multiple forms including the prose poem.

Restrepo's colleague at the University of Antioquia and coeditor of the thirty-three numbers of the poetry magazine *Acuarimántima*, José Manuel Arango wrote several early tomes of poetry characterized by their laconic language and use of litote, ellipsis, and the blank space to engage the reader as an accomplice in completing the meaning of the poem. This trait especially stands out in his books *Este lugar de la noche* (1973, This Place of Night), *Signos* (1978, Signs), and *Cantiga* (1987, Song) which also have a profound, aphoristic quality like the *Pensées* of the French philosopher and mathematician Blaise Pascal (1623–62). Arango was an excellent translator of American poets like Dickinson, Merton, and Levertov while employed, not surprisingly, as a professor of philosophy at his university. The poem "Escritura" (Writing) from his first book typifies his early poetry. Here the poetic voice ponders the perennial dilemma of all poets in a very original manner upon declaring "en el empañado cristal/con el índice, escribe/esta efímera palabra" (on the steamy glass/with the index finger, he writes/this ephemeral word." In Arango's later poetry, especially in the volume *Montañas* (1995), the poet wrote longer poems celebrating the beauty of nature, which was personified and associated with transcendent divinity. He also introduced many poems with epigraphs attributed to other Colombian and international poets while employing more intertextual allusions.

María Mercedes Carranza, the daughter of Eduardo Carranza, was the most outstanding woman poet associated with the generation of *Golpe de Dados*. Her first book of poetry, *Vainas y otros poemas* (1973, Nuisances and Other Poems), presented a unique feminist antipoetry with satirical humor, irreverence, and a sardonic tone that mocked the maudlin sentimentality of traditional feminine verse while questioning the inferior role of women in Colombian literature, history, and society. The book's title is based on a colloquial vulgarism denoting frustration and irritation, which is derived from the word vagina and also has phallic connotations since the word *vaina* is the sheath in which the sword is kept. Some critics compared this work to the poetry of Luis Carlos López because of its comic playfulness, although it presented a profound criticism of social mores and conventional Colombian poetic rhetoric, while some considered it to be an ironic contrast to her father's poetry or anti-Carranza just like some critics think the Chilean Parra's verse is anti-Neruda. Her poetic stance became less feminist and more universal because of its intertextuality and the use of the poetic portrait and caricature in the two major poetic tomes that followed: *Tengo miedo* (1983, I'm Scared) and *Hola, Soledad* (1987, Hello, Solitude). She captured the collective *Zeitgeist* of insecurity and fear in her poem "Bogotá 1982" from the first of these two books, and her evocation of the meaning of the life and verse of two other famous poets (e.g., "Una rosa para Dylan Thomas" [A Rose for Dylan Thomas] and "Borgiana") masked her own personal preoccupations and social concerns. Her poem "Miré los muros de la patria mía" (I Looked at the Walls of My Homeland) parodies a famous sonnet by the Spanish Baroque poet Francisco de Quevedo (1580–1645) as the poetic voice censures injustice and depravity in Colombia, concluding "los muros de la patria mía/¿Cuándo los van a limpiar?" (the walls of my homeland/When are they going to clean them?). In *Hola, Soledad*, her poems contrast communication and loneliness and reflect the increased pessimistic tone devoid of humor of all her poetry as it evolved. Typical of this intensified pessimistic tone and disillusioned despair before increased violence and poverty in Colombia is her poem "La patria" (The Homeland) in which synecdoche is used to compare the entire nation to an old colonial home falling down in ruins. Here the frustrated lyrical voice sadly concludes "En esta casa todos estamos enterrados vivos" (In this home we all are buried alive). Carranza's last book of poetry, *El canto de las moscas* (1998, The Song of the Flies), represents an anti-epic series of brief poems called cantos patterned on the Japanese haiku form in which there are no heroes but only innocent victims of irrational political violence or narcotics terrorism. Each poem is a toponymic evocation of the site of a massacre or atrocity in rural Colombia. The book was dedicated to her friend and assassinated Liberal presidential candidate Luis Carlos Galán (1943–89). An example of one of these poems is "Canto 6 – Barrancabermeja" in which the poet plays with chromatic symbolism of the place name to evoke the bloody horror of a massacre that occurred there:

> *Entre el cielo y el suelo*
> *yace*
> *pálida Barrancabermeja.*
> *Diríase*
> *la sangre desangrada*
> *(Between the sky and the ground*
>
> *lies*
> *pale Scarlet Gorge.*
> *One would say*
> *shed blood)*

María Mercedes Carranza also encouraged the study and writing of poetry as the founding director of La Casa de Poesía Silva (The Silva Poetry Home), which published a scholarly journal devoted to the study of Colombian poetry as well as a history of the nation's poetry and also awarded a national poetry prize. She was the director of this important cultural institution until her death by suicide in 2003.

No other Colombian poet of his generation has received more national and international prizes for his poetry than Juan Manuel Roca due in large measure to his original creation of images derived from the influence of Expressionism and Surrealism. Roca Vidales is the nephew of Luis Vidales, and his uncle's influence is also reflected in the social perspective of underdogs in this poet's often gloomy and disillusioned vision of Colombian realities of violence and injustice. Also, Roca has confessed that he had a great admiration for the poetry of the Peruvian César Vallejo (1893–1939). Roca has also been influenced by his love of modern art, which has made him chiefly a visual and nocturnal poet in the tradition of Silva and Charry Lara.

Among the most important poetry prizes awarded to Roca were the Eduardo Cote Lamus National Prize (1975) for *Luna de ciegos* (1976, Moon of the Blind), the National Prize for Poetry of the University of Antioquia (1979) for *Señal de cuervos* (1980, Crows' Signal), the National Poetry Prize of the Ministry of Culture (2004) for *La hipótesis de nadie* (2004, Nobody's Hypothesis), and the Casa de América Poetry Prize (2009) for *Biblia de pobres* (2009, Poors' Bible). In all, Roca has been quite prolific, publishing twenty books of poetry not counting anthologies of his own work and that of other poets. He has also published a few prize-winning collections of short stories, some essays, and one novel. Other important books of verse published by Roca include *Los ladrones nocturnos* (1977, The Nocturnal Thieves), *Ciudadano de la noche* (1989, Citizen of the Night), *Pavana con el diablo* (1990, Pavane with the Devil), and *Un violin para Chagall* (2003, A Violin for Chagall).

His prize-winning tome *Señal de cuervos* seemed to capture the national ethos of collective insecurity at the time of its publication through his skillful employment of macabre images of violence and terror like the following verses: "La señal de lo cuervos/Anuncia la nueva hora del terror/ Los cuerpos otra vez bajando por el río" (The crows' signal/Announces the new hour of terror/The bodies once again going down the river). Indeed, the abovementioned verses and the title of the entire book sound an ominous note as they allude to the traditional, proverbial saying "if you raise crows they will pluck out your eyes." In his metapoem simply entitled "La poesía" ("Poetry"), Roca seems to best characterize his entire lyric poetry. There we read "Riesgosa y vagabunda,/Territorio libre del sueño,/Cultiva las flores prohibidas" (Risky and vagrant,/Free territory of sleep,/It cultivates forbidden flowers).

Nearly as prolific in his early years as Roca has been Jaime García Maffla whose verse usually written in traditional metric forms has been a continuous anguished search for self-identity and transcendence in the poetic word, which seeks to touch on what is ineffable. Along with Quessep, Charry Lara, and Rivero, García Maffla was one of the cofounders of *Golpe de Dados* and usually has published poems in this publication before their inclusion in his eleven books of poetry. Many critics have also noted some affinity between the poetry of García Maffla and that of his former colleague at the Javeriana University of Bogotá Quessep and also Charry Lara. Besides receiving recognition as an outstanding poet, García Maffla has taught literature and been a highly respected critic of Colombian literature with nine books of literary criticism including two studies devoted to the study of the poetry of Charry Lara and Cote Lamus. Although he received the national poetry prize from the University of Antioquia for his book of verse *Vive si puedes* (Live if You Can) in 1997, his most important work to date has been *La caza* (1984, The Hunt), whose title best reflects the evolving trajectory of García Maffla's entire poetic work as an ontological search for the transcendent poetic word. Many of his best verses are metapoems such as the following taken from the poem "Los cantos, las palabras tejidas" (The Songs, the Interwoven Words): "don que no sabe en fin lo que se dice/don misterioso que lo que engendra ignora/y alienta sin embargo en lo que engendra" (a gift which doesn't know in short what is said/a mysterious gift which is unaware of what it engenders/and gives birth however in what it begets). For Maffla in later books the magical poetic word paradoxically leads to what is ineffable or unspoken as reading and writing together engender poetic creation. Thus in the poem "Escritura" the lyrical voice declares "Cuando sin escribirse se escribe ... /Entonces las palabras/serán la compañía toda y sola,/seran esa palabra/que hemos de oir de labios de silencio" (When without writing one writes/Then the words/will be all the company and alone/they will be that word/which we ought to hear from silent lips). Maffla has experimented with self-referential intertextuality by restructuring and reordering poems taken from previous works to create new poems while also employing traditional forms like the canticle in *Cantigas castellanas* (1990, Castillian Songs) or the epic poem in *Caballero en la orden de la desesperanza* (2001, Knight in the Order of Despair).

Although Darío Jaramillo Agudelo has been more devoted to prose narrative in novels during the last decade, his seven books of verse must be considered major contributions to recent Colombian poetry produced by the Generation of *Golpe de Dados*. Jaramillo Agudelo was born in Santa Rosa de Osos, Antioquia, the birthplace of the poets Barba Jacob and Echavarría. In his first book of poems with the prosaic title *Historias* (1974, Histories), Jaramillo Agudelo employed narrativity and intertextuality with a skeptical attitude about the efficacy of the poetic word inspired in part by Parra's antipoetry. Like his contemporaries, he also included lyrical portraits of other writers and poets and in some poems incorporated colloquial language from different communicative modes like popular music in the poem "Arte poética otra" (Another Poetic Art), where the poetic voice declares "Es dura esta vaina de ser poeta; . . . aunque era más difícil antes/ cuando los versos tenían rima/y no había estado Lucy in the Sky with Diamonds" (This nuisance of being a poet is tough /. . . although it used to be harder before/when verses had rhyme/and Lucy hadn't been in the Sky with Diamonds). Jaramillo Agudelo was awarded the Eduardo Cote Lamus National Poetry Prize for his second book, *Tratado de retórica* (1978, Treatise on Rhetoric), and again questioned the validity of poetry in today's world despite the book's subtitle *o la necesidad de la poesía* (Or the Need for Poetry). However, Jaramillo Agudelo's third book, *Poemas de amor* (1986, Love Poems), is his masterpiece and has received unprecedented popular and critical acclaim because it presents the theme of erotic love with beautifully clear and simple imagery. Many critics consider it to be one of the best lyrical expressions of erotic love in recent Colombian poetry, unmatched since Gaitan Durán's erotic verse. The love poems presented in this tome engage all five senses and rely on synesthesia together with repetition and musicality to structure the poem and move the reader's sensitivity. Not only does the poem employ the abovementioned techniques, but at times it also includes contrasts in perspective and distance to lead to a poignant climax, such as when the lyrical voice proclaims "Tu voz por el teléfono tan cerca y nosotros/tan distantes" (Your voice so near on the telephone and us/so far away). This book marked a turning point toward greater intimacy in the evolution of Jaramillo Agudelo's verse while maintaining a nostalgic tone that has been present in almost all his poetry. Besides its erotic verse, the book contained more lyrical sketches similar to what was present also in the works of María Mercedes Carranza, Restrepo, and Cobo Borda as well as the continued use of intertextuality with allusions and epigraphs. The poet's later volumes of poetry emphasized the importance of both classical and popular music and include *Del ojo a la lengua* (1995, From the Eye to the Tongue), *Cantar por cantar* (2001, Singing for Singing's Sake), *Gatos* (2005, Cats), and *Cuadernos de música* (2008, Notebooks of Music).

Juan Gustavo Cobo Borda has earned an international reputation as both a poet and essayist while alternating the publication of books in both genres. Although the poet has published eleven books of verse, he contends that he has continually written the same book under different titles. Nevertheless, most of his poetic tomes stand out for the ironic tone and climax found in many poems with the recurring theme of the search for the poetic *logos* or the relationship between the word and *eros* similar to what his many contemporaries from the Generation of *Golpe de Dados*, especially Roca, have reiterated in their own poetry. The poem "Poética" from his first prize-winning book, *Consejos para sobrevivir* (1974, Advice for Surviving), questions the relevance of poetry in the modern world with antipoetic skepticism in prosaic, colloquial language: "¿Cómo escribir ahora poesía,/por qué no callarnos definitivamente/y dedicarnosa a cosas mucho más útiles?" (How to write poetry now, why not finally shut up/ and devote ourselves to much more useful things?). His often satirical and iconoclastic vision of history, culture, and the absurdities of daily life is in the tradition of Luis Carlos López and the *nadaístas* like Jaime Jaramillo Escobar and J. Mario Arbeláez. No sacred cows were spared from his ironic wit, and his satire was directed toward worldwide targets such as the xenophobia of the Germans and other Europeans fearful of emigration from third world countries to their lands although they were forgetful of their own history of barbarous violence. For example, in the poem "El retorno de las carabelas" (The Return of the Caravels), we read:

> *Y ellos, los rudos visigodos,*
> *los malolientes bávaros,*
> *contemplan como la nueva tribu atrabilaria*
> *devora museos, consume paisajes,*
> *hurta los souvenirs infames.*
> *Se esconden entonces*
>
> *en los cuidados bosques*
>
> *. . .*
>
> *pero no de su propia historia*
> *implacable.*
> *(And they, the rude Visigoths,*
> *the ill-smelling Bavarians,*
> *contemplate as the new acrimonious tribe*
> *devours museums, consumes landscapes,*
> *steals the infamous souvenirs.*
> *They then hide*
> *in the cared for forests*
>
> *. . .*
>
> *But not from their own implacable*
> *history.)*

Cobo Borda also has mocked the traditional poetic themes of love and death, but his recent poetry has become more lyrical and sentimental and less prosaic and ironic while including more classical allusions since his stay in Greece as Colombian ambassador. Like many of his contemporaries from the generation of *Golpe de Dados* he has reaffirmed his identity as a true poet.

Although she never published any of her poems in *Golpe de Dados*, Anabel Torres was the most important female contemporary of María Mercedes Carranza. Since she spent her childhood and most of her adolescence in New York City she became bilingual (Spanish and English) and has won awards for her translations of Colombian poetry into English such as José Manuel Arango's first book *Este lugar de la noche* (This Place of Night) and the poetry of Meira del Mar. Like Carranza her poetry shuns the conventional lyrical rhetoric and sentimentality of traditional feminine poetry and presents her themes from a militant feminist perspective expressed in colloquial language and the use of irony to question and reject the inferior status accorded to women in Colombian society. For example, in one of the poems from her third book, *Las bocas del amor* (1982, The Mouths of Love), the lyrical voice expresses resentment and indignation upon declaring "quiero las bocas del amor/No quiero este cielo frío" (I want mouths of love/I don't want this cold sky). In another poem from the same tome she ironically alludes to the Grimms' fairy tale "Hansel and Gretel" to expose the hypocrisy of a male-dominated society, which demands external beauty from the woman while condemning her to a life of perpetual domestic imprisonment. Her first two books, *Casi poesía* (1975, Almost Poetry) and *La mujer del esquimal* (1980, The Eskimo's Woman) were both awarded prizes from the University of Nariño and the University of Antioquia, respectively.

In the first, Torres offers laconic confessional verses mixed with ironic humor to demythify romantic symbols like the rose, representing ephemeral, fragile beauty, which clash with the harsh realities faced by women in daily life. Thus in one of her poems, the lyrical voice brusquely declares "Cínico/aquel que sabe/que la rosa marchita/A mí no me vengan a hablarme de flores" (A cynic/is the one who knows/that the rose withers/Don't come to me to talk about flowers). In her second book, Torres censures cruel masculine insensitivity with grotesque metaphors and references to patriarchal archetypes. Her more recent books include *Medias nonas* (1992, Odd Stockings), *Poemas de la Guerra* (2000, War Poems), *En un abrir y cerrar de hojas* (2003, In an Opening and Closing of Pages), and the bilingual poetry of *Wounded Water/Agua herida* (2004). In *Poemas de la guerra*, she assumes a pacifist denunciation of all wars and forms of violence since in her personal life as a child and later since 1987 in Holland and Spain she has been forced into exile as a consequence of such strife. Indeed, in her bilingual book *Wounded Water/Agua herida*, the central theme of the volume is the personal trauma and hurt occasioned by violence leading to exile from her country.

Like Anabel Torres, Jaime Manrique Ardila (b. 1949) has spent most of his adult life outside of Colombia in self-imposed exile since he recognized that as a homosexual he could not live in the *machista* and homophobic environment of Colombia. As an illegitimate child, he was rejected by his father and raised by his mother. He established residence in Miami and became a U.S. citizen in 1986. After graduating from the University of South Florida with a degree in English he studied creative writing at Columbia University under the Argentine homosexual writer Manuel Puig (1932–90) whom he greatly admired, and he also befriended the Cuban homosexual novelist Reinaldo Arenas (1943–90). Also, like Torres he has published his work in both Spanish and English, although his prose novels, short stories, and essays have overshadowed his poetry. Nevertheless, his first published book of poetry, *Los adoradores de la luna* (1976, The Adorers of the Moon), was awarded the Eduardo Cote Lamus National Prize for poetry in 1975. Altogether he has published five books of poetry including two bilingual editions, *Mi noche con Federico García Lorca* (1995, My Night with Federico García Lorca) and *Tarzán, Mi cuerpo, Cristobal Colón* (2000, Tarzan, My Body, Christopher Columbus). His works in both prose and verse have emphasized gay themes, erotic love, and death.

After the death of María Mercedes Carranza and the prolonged exile of Anabel Torres, Piedad Bonnett (b. 1951) has been considered the most outstanding living woman poet in Colombia. She also has taught literature at the University of the Andes and written several books of literary criticism, plays, and novels. Bonnett has published ten books of poetry including *El hilo de los días* (1995, The Drift of Days), which was awarded the National Prize for Poetry by Colcultura in 1994, and *Explicaciones no pedidas* (2011, Not Asked for Explanations), which won the Casa de las Américas Prize for Poetry in the year of its publication. Throughout her verse Bonnett has presented the harsh realities of daily life for women in Colombia with an ironic twist. Her verse is mostly autobiographical and deals with the effects of violence, inequality, and conflict in her personal life. Among her themes are love in all its forms both healthy and unhealthy, and her tone has varied between enchantment and disillusionment before life's challenges, trials, and tribulations. An outstanding feature of her poetry is her original use of metaphor and simile. The title poem from her prize-winning book of poetry *El hilo de los días* (The Drift of Days) typifies most of her poetry. There we read the following in the beginning verses of the poem:

Han amarrado trapos rojos en los bombillos,
y el mundo todo ardido está de fiebre púrpura,
de paños en la frente, de pesadillas
que rechinan sus dientes,

en el silencio ciego de la una.
(They have tied red rags on the bulbs,
and everybody is burnt with purple fever,
with clothes on the forehead, from nightmares
which gnash their teeth,
in the blind silence of one o'clock.)

No cohesive poetic groups or movements have formed as yet in Colombia at the onset of the twenty-first century, but nevertheless many diverse voices of outstanding poets have again emerged, and the genre has maintained a vigorous vitality greater than that found in other Latin American countries due to numerous journals and festivals dedicated exclusively to verse. Among the most important poets of the new century the following must be taken into account for enriching the genre: Ramón Cote Baraibar (b. 1963), the son of Eduardo Cote Lamus, Santiago Mutis (b. 1951), the son of Alvaro Mutis, Rómulo Bustos Aguirre (b. 1954), and Juan Felipe Robledo (b. 1968). Cote Baraibar, who earned a degree in the History of Art from the Universidad Complutense, has published seven books of poetry, and he has been awarded two international prizes for his verse, including the Casa de las Américas Prize for *Colección privada* (2003, Private Collection) and the Unicaja Prize from Spain for *Fuegos obligados* (2009, Grateful Fires). Santiago Mutis has written six books of poetry in which his visual poetry is closely tied to modern painting. Several of his more important books were *Tú también eres de lluvia* (1982, You're Also of Rain), *Afuera pasa el siglo* (1999, Outside the Century Goes By), and *Dicen de ti* (2003, They Say about You). Rómulo Bustos Aguirre's poetry has also received national and international recognition, with two of his seven books having been awarded prizes including *En el traspatio del cielo* (1993, In the Back Porch of Heaven), which received the National Prize for Poetry from Colcultura, and *Muerte y levitación de la ballena* (2010), which was awarded the Blas Otero Prize for Poetry from the Universidad Complutense. Throughout his work, which began with *El oscuro sello de Dios* (1988, The Dark Seal of God), there has been a recurring theme of search for the transcendent through poetry with images of angels, birds, and flora and fauna symbolizing the links between heaven and earth. In his more recent books he has presented this serious theme with touches of humor through references to repulsive insects like flies. Juan Felipe Robledo, who teaches classical Spanish poetry at the Javeriana University of Bogotá, has already been honored internationally and in Colombia for his first two tomes of verse: *De mañana* (2000), which received the Jaime Sabines International Prize for Poetry in Mexico, and *La música de las horas* (2002), which was awarded the National Prize for Poetry from the Colombian Ministry of Culture in 2001. Robledo mostly cultivates traditional verse forms inspired by poems from the Spanish Golden Age. These aforementioned poets and many others attest to the continued excellence and vitality of the poetic genre in the twenty-first century.

BIBLIOGRAPHY

Alstrum, James J. *La generación desencantada de Golpe de Dados: Los poetas colombianos de los años 70*. Bogotá: Universidad Central, 2000.

Charry Lara, Fernando. *Lector de poesía y otros ensayos inéditos*. Bogotá: Editorial Random House Mondadori Ltda, 2005.

Cobo Borda, Juan Gustavo. *Historia de la poesía colombiana siglo XX: De José Asunción Silva a Raúl Gómez Jattin*. 3rd ed. Bogotá: Villegas Editores, 2003.

Historia de la poesía colombiana. Bogotá: Fundación Casa de Poesía Silva, 1991

Holguín, Andrés. *Antología crítica de la poesía colombiana 1874–1974*. Tomo II. Bogotá: Biblioteca del Centenario del Banco de la República, 1974.

Romero, Armando. *Las palabras están en situación*. Bogotá: Editorial Procultura, 1985.

El nadaísmo colombiano o la búsqueda de una vanguardia perdida. Bogotá: Tercer Mundo, 1988.

CHAPTER 6

The late twentieth-century Colombian novel
(1970-1999)

Raymond L. Williams and Marina Nájera

The late twentieth century was one of the most productive, heterogeneous, and interesting periods in the history of the Colombian novel. Gabriel García Márquez, Alvaro Mutis, Fernando Vallejo, Darío Jaramillo, and others published some of their most compelling works, and the readership of the Colombian novel, for the first time in the nation's history, became truly international. The centerpiece of this public recognition was the awarding of the Nobel Prize for Literature to García Márquez in 1982. Alvaro Mutis, on the other hand, was prominent as both a novelist and a poet, and much of his fiction appeared in English translation.

Colombian society, culture, and literature had been exceptionally regionalist until the mid-1950s, and the Colombian novel tended to follow this pattern. In the mid-1950s, however, Colombia's modernization and breakdown of a regional nation was transforming the country. By the mid-1950s, television broadcasts began in all major cities, and during that same period Antonio Curcio Altamar published his now-classic study *Evolución de la novela en Colombia* (Evolution of the Novel in Colombia), a book that assumed a national vision for the novel. Similarly, the magazine *Mito*, rather than regional, was modern in conception and national and international in vision. It published writers from all regions, including the then young and relatively unknown *costeño* Gabriel García Márquez, and a then young poet named Alvaro Mutis, who later gained international recognition as both a poet and novelist.

In the 1960s, the irreverent *nadaístas*, primarily poets, successfully scandalized the still predominantly conservative and conventional cultural establishment. Whether or not the poetry and proclamations of Gonzalo Arango and his *nadaísta* cohorts will be judged of permanent value remains to be seen. Nevertheless, their rebellious textual and extratextual postures had a profound impact on literary tastes and paved the way for ongoing modern and postmodern literary activity in Colombia. The *nadaísta* novel prize provided an outlet for the publication and distribution of the most experimental fiction of the time, even though the national concern for understanding and evaluating La Violencia (the civil war of the 1940s and 1950s) meant that the novel of La Violencia was deemed much more important than novels of technical experimentation. The young poets among the *nadaístas,* besides Arango, were Jotamario Arbeláez, Eduardo Escobar, Amilcar Osorio, Jaime Jaramillo Escobar, and Dukardo Hinestrosa.

The literary establishment also provided a heretofore unknown infrastructure for the creation and publication of a national novel of international impact. The magazine *Eco,* published in Bogota from the early 1960s to the mid-1980s, was essentially European in content, with occasional contributions on Latin America and Colombia. It included pieces about Colombian poetry and fiction. The publishing house Tercer Mundo Editores, which began in the early 1960s, became the first truly national publisher to operate with professional criteria for the publication and national distribution of literature. By the mid-1970s the Editorial Plaza y Janés, a multinational commercial operation based in Spain, was successfully publishing and distributing several Colombian novelists, including Gabriel García Márquez and Gustavo Alvarez Gardeazábal. In the 1980s a publishing boom in Colombia resulted in the publication of Colombia's novelists with Plaza y Janés, Tercer Mundo, Planeta, and other firms.

Unquestionably, the novel of major impact during this period was García Márquez's *Cien años de soledad* (1967, *One Hundred Years of Solitude*), and the most resonant literary event of the 1960s was the international heralding of this novel, which appeared in English in 1970. A second round of the García Márquez phenomenon took place in 1982 when he received the Nobel Prize. During the late 1960s and early 1970s aspiring writers in Colombia often spoke of the "shadow" that García Márquez cast upon them. The general crisis of literary modernism experienced in the West had a double edge in Colombia: García Márquez produced in 1967 one of the most celebrated texts of the supposedly exhausted modern tradition of the West; on the other hand, this modern product enjoyed such an enormous success that it made fiction writing afterward a formidable task in Colombia. By the mid-1970s the shadow of García Márquez's Macondo proved less burdensome in Colombia as several writers, such as Fernando Vallejo, Darío Jaramillo, Fanny Buitrago, Marvel Moreno, R. H. Moreno-Durán, Albalucía Angel, Gustavo Alvarez Gardeazábal, and Marco Tulio Aguilera Garramuño, found new, non-Macondian directions for the Colombian novel. Previously marginal and repressed discourses surfaced in the 1970s and 1980s as part of a new, postmodern attitude. They were discourses not necessarily related to the novel of La Violencia or the much heralded "magic realism" of Macondo.

The Colombian poets of this period, belonging to the Generación Desencantada, began to publish poetry in the early 1970s and distinguished themselves from the *nadaístas* of the 1960s. This generation is constituted by a broad an ambiguous group of poets that many critics would consider to be Giovanni Quessep, Harold Alvardo Tenorio, Juan Gustavo Cobo Borda, Elkin Restrepo, José Manuel Arango, Darío Jaramillo Agudelo, Augusto Pinilla, María Mercedes Carranza, and Juan Manuel Roca.

With the increased novelistic production of the 1970s and 1980s and other international factors in play, these directions for the Colombian novel were more heterogeneous than they had ever been before. In the broadest of terms, it is possible to identify an essentially modern novelistic tradition and another fundamentally postmodern tendency over the approximately two-decade period under consideration (1965–87). The modern novel entered Colombia with the publication of three seminal works; García Márquez's *La hojarasca* (1955, Leafstorm), Alvaro Cepeda Samudio's *La casa grande* (1962, The Large House), and Héctor Rojas Herazo's *Respirando el verano* (1962, Breathing the Summer). With respect to politics, the modern texts tend to exhibit their social agenda more explicitly by portraying an identifiable Colombian empirical reality. The modern novel has been cultivated in Colombia by García Márquez, Fernando Vallejo, Fanny Buitrago, Rojas Herazo, Manuel Zapata Olivella, and others. A more innovative and experimental postmodern fiction, best understood within a context of theory and other literary forms, has been published by Darío Jaramillo, R. H. Moreno-Durán, Albalucía Angel, Marco Tulio Aguilera Garramuño, Andrés Caicedo, Rodrigo Parra Sandoval, and Alberto Duque López.

The modern novel

García Márquez's may well be the most significant enterprise of modern fiction by a single author in Colombia. Since the publication of *Cien años de soledad* in 1967, a pinnacle of the modern novel in Colombia and in Latin America, García Márquez has written *El otoño del patriarca* (1975, The Autumn of the Patriarch), *Crónica de una muerte anunciada* (1981, Chronicle of a Death Foretold), *El amor en los tiempos del cólera* (1985, Love in the Time of Cholera), *El general en su laberinto* (1989, The General in His Labyrinth), the documentary work *Noticia de un secuestro* (1995, News of a Kidnapping), and *Memorias de mis putas tristes* (2004, Memories of My Melancholy Whores).

After his initial experiments in his early stories with the techniques of modernism, learned primarily from Kafka and Faulkner, he attained his first truly mature and successful modern writing with *La hojarasca*. In his total fiction, García Márquez appropriated some of the narrative techniques of modernism (fragmentation, collage, multiple points of view, etc.) and used these techniques in what is an identifiable modernist project – the seeking of order and the expression of the ineffable in a world lacking order and waiting to be named. García Márquez, like certain other contemporary Latin American writers, is rooted in the moderns, began as a modern, and basically remained a modern, but not consistently so. He had also read the postmoderns and in his later work participates in some of their subversive and self-conscious exercises. As scholars of contemporary culture have pointed out, the postmodern is not necessarily a temporal concept in the sense of "after the modern."[1]

In many ways, García Márquez's *El otoño del patriarca, Crónica de una muerte anunciada,* and *El amor en los tiempos del cólera* represent a rupture from the fiction of Macondo. *El otoño del patriarca* is located in an unidentified region of the Caribbean, and its subject is a dictator. Conceiving this work in an international rather than regional or national context, García Márquez published this dictator novel in conjunction with an international series of novels of this type, including Alejo Carpentier's *El recurso del método* (1974, Reasons of State) and Augusto Roa Bastos's *Yo, el supremo* (1974, I the Supreme). *El otoño del patriarca* functions as a literary synthesis of numerous Latin American historical dictators, above all of Juan Vicente Gómez. One indicator of the change in García Márquez's fiction is the fact that he does not locate the novel in Colombia. The exact location of the dictator's realm remains impossible to establish, although it is a vaguely Caribbean nation, with images from different countries in the region.

The basic anecdote of *El otoño del patriarca* functions as the point of departure and frame for the storytelling. The transformation of this anecdote into the actual story of this modern text can be described by considering the novel's six chapters as a system of progressive apertures:[2] That is, the narrator develops the first chapter on the basis of an aperture, the second on another aperture, and so on. The qualifier "progressive" underlines the fact that the apertures occur at successively earlier points in each of the six chapters. These apertures occur on four levels. In the novel's experience these levels occur simultaneously. The four levels of aperture are (1) the opening of the original situation, (2) the opening of the sentence length, (3) the opening of narrative focus, and (4) the opening of a "seen" reality. The structure of progressive apertures provides for the dynamic reading experience typical of reader-engaging modern fiction.

The four levels of the structure function in the elaboration of the work's themes and of the text as a modern novel. The opening of the original situation into the general's story yields a broad characterization of the general but is not limited by traditional subordination of the narration to the requirements of space and time. The latter are subordinate, in this modern text, to the act of narrating itself. The opening sentence supports this first opening technically and is a specific device that provides for a progressively more elaborate textual presentation of the story. The opening of the narrative focus creates a multiplicity of views of the general, and this is significant not only in the complexity and completeness of his characterization but also in establishing the overall tone – the humor so fundamental to the novel's experience. On the final level, the opening of a seen reality into a confluence of the visible and invisible, the experience of the novel becomes similar to the principal theme it develops: the illusion of reality and power.

Crónica de una muerte anunciada and *El amor en los tiempos del cólera*, far less complex in structure than *El otoño del patriarca*, nevertheless represent a continuation of García Márquez's modern writing, even though the act of writing in itself is noteworthy, a characteristic these two novels share with many postmodern texts. *Crónica de una muerte anunciada* is comparable to the detective novel. The reader knows the outcome from the first line and continues reading – with interests similar to those aroused in the detective novel – to see the death consummated. The circumstances surrounding the protagonist Santiago Nasar's death become increasingly more incredible: Everyone in his small town seems to know that he is going to die except Santiago himself. As in most of García Márquez's work, life is determined by inexplicable forces and irrational acts. The narrator explains that attempts at rational explanation fall short, although the judge assigned to Nasar's case approaches it with the intention of finding a logical interpretation. The language and boundaries of the predominant mind-set are anchored in medieval tradition – a matter of honor. The bride is rejected; the murder is conceived and then allowed to be executed because of the entire town's tacit acceptance of a medieval concept of human relationships. The novel's structure (the development of the predetermined action) as well as the process in the town (the events that the town's citizenry witness) correspond to a world in which the development of events is determined by a hierarchical and static vision of reality.

El amor en los tiempos del cólera is a story of love and aging in an equally hierarchical and static society. Set in Cartagena colored by some elements of the other Caribbean cities (such as the Café de la Parroquia in Veracruz, Mexico), it tells of Florentino Ariza's wait of more than fifty years for his beloved Fermina Daza, to whom he declares his love at the funeral of her husband, Dr. Juvenal Urbino. The novel is imbued with elements of late nineteenth– and early twentieth-century Colombia, elements notable in the context of this study for two reasons. On the one hand, this is the Colombia of the Regeneration as the Athens of South America. The narrator mentions Regeneration president Rafael Núñez and later president Marco Fidel Suárez, with Dr. Urbino as the Regeneration gentleman-scholar. On the other hand, García Márquez returns to the kind of incorporation of the Caribbean oral culture that formed part of *Cien años de soledad*. Whereas Dr. Urbino is the educated man of science, Florentino Ariza and Fermina Daza frequently see things as an oral-culture person would, even though they are literate. For Florentino Ariza one of the new hydro-planes is like a flying coffin. Fermina Daza, with rural roots, makes similar observations. Like *Cien años de soledad*, *El amor en los tiempos del cólera* is a novel of hyperbole and of prodigious people and events.

Several other writers have assimilated the stratagems of modern fiction, among them Alvaro Mutis, Fernando Vallejo, Fanny Buitrago, Manuel Zapata Olivella, and Héctor Rojas Herazo. After a noteworthy career in itself as a poet, Mutis published seven books of fiction in the late twentieth century, including the documentary work *Diario de Lecumberri* (1956, Diary of Lecumberri), concerning his prison experience in Mexico. His fiction includes *La mansión de Aracaíma* (1973, The Mansion, 2003), *La nieve del Almirante* (1973, The Snow of the Almirante), *Maqroll el gaviero* (1973, Maqroll the Mariner), *The Adventures and Misadventures of Maqroll: Four Novellas* (translation, Edith Grossman, 1995), *Ilona llega con la lluvia* (1988, Ilona Arrives with the Train), *La úlitma escala del Tramp Steamer* (1989, The Last Stop of the Tramp Steamer), *Amirbar* (1990, Amirbar), *Abdul Bashur, soñador de navíos* (1991, Abdul Bashur, Dreamer of Ships), and *Tríptico de mar y tierra* (1993, Three Books on the Sea and the Land). In these novels (and in the poetry that preceded them), Mutis constructs a lifetime character, Maqroll, who travels around the world.

Mutis follows the spiritual search and adventures of this world traveler. He received all the major prizes available in the Hispanic world for a writer in the Spanish language; his poetry was recognized as early as the 1950s by the Mexican critic and poet Octavio Paz.

Still actively writing in the twenty-first century, Fernando Vallejo published an accomplished set of novels during the last two decades of the twentieth century, including *Los días azules* (1985, The Blue Days) and *El fuego secreto* (1986, The Secret Fire), and his widely read and recognized *La virgen de los sicarios* (1994, Our Lady of Assassins), the story of drug violence in Medellín that was successfully adapted for a film version. In this novel, the protagonist returns to Medellín after an extended absence and confronts the violence of the cartels in his daily life and interactions. The first two books form part of a collection of autobiograph-ical novels (*Los días azules, El fuego secreto, Los caminos a roma, Años de indulgencia y Entre fantasmas*) known as *El río del tiempo* (The River of Time) where the author talks about the different stages of his life. However, the first two are the most important because they are the first explicitly gay Colombian novels of this modern period.

In addition to her short fiction, Buitrago has published the novels *El hostigante verano de los dioses* (1963, The Tiring Summer of the Gods), *Cola de zorro* (1970, Fox Tail), *Los pañamanes* (1979, The "Panya" Men), *Los amores de Afodita* (1983, Aphrodite's Love), *Señora de la miel* (1993, Mrs. Honeycomb, 1996), and *Bello animal* (2002, Beautiful Animal). Much of her fiction emanates from Caribbean culture. Several voices narrate *El hostigante verano de los dioses*, the totality of which communi-cates the state of boredom endured by a spiritually exhausted generation of young people. *Cola de zorro* is Buitrago's most complex work and shares some of the generational attitudes found in her first novel: The characters lack clear direction, and their existence tends to be boring. It deals with human relations within the context of a large, extended family. The novel's three parts, which take place in the Interior Highland and the Costa, tell the story of three generations. The characters' identities, a central theme, are in a constant state of fluidity but are defined primarily by family tradition. *Los pañamanes,* set on Caribbean island, portrays the conflicts between, on the one hand, the legends and traditions in a disappearing oral culture on the island and, on the other hand, modernization and its "beautiful people" that are taking over. In *Los amores de Afodita* Buitrago recurs to popular culture in a manner reminiscent of both Manuel Puig's fiction and of Mario Vargas Llosa's *La tía Julia y el escribidor.* In this novel she relates five love stories of different women, using sources similar to

Puig's and Vargas Llosa's, Buitrago cites in her epigraphs the popular women's magazine *Vanidades* and lines from the popular music of *boleros*.

Zapata Olivella has published six novels, including two works during the period at hand, *Changó, el gran putas* (1983, Changó, the Biggest Baddass, 2010) and *El fusilamiento del diablo* (1986, The Shooting of the Devil*)*. His most ambitious novel, the massive (more than five hundred pages) *Changó, el gran putas,* is broad in scope. The Changó in the title refers to the Yoruba deity of war, fecundity, and dance. The novel spans three continents and six centuries of African and Afro-American history. It begins in Africa and then moves to Colombia and other regions of the Americas, ending in the United States. Zapata Olivella incorporates cultural heroes such as Benkos Bioho, Francois Mackandal, and Nat Turner and ends with the death of Malcolm X. The author synthesizes a variety of voices and oral cultures in this saga of peoples striving for liberation, a constant in his entire work. In *El fusilamiento del diablo* Zapata Olivella reelaborates the story of Manuel Saturion Valencia, which had been recounted by Rogerio Velásquez in *Las memorias del odio* (Memories of Hatred). In Zapata Olivella´s version, numerous voices tell the story of this Afro-Colombian who was executed in Quibdó in 1907. The sum of these voices and the novel's numerous narrative segments elevate the protagonist to the level of myth

Héctor Rojas Herazo uses the narrative strategies of a Faulknerian modernity in his trilogy, *Respirando el verano* (1962, Breathing the Summer), *En noviembre llega el arzobispo* (1967, In November the Archbishop Arrives), and *Celia se pudre* (1986, Celia Rots). These novels also evoke the premodern, oral world of Celia, the central character of this trilogy, and her family. *Respirando el verano* focuses on the aging matriarch and her grandson Anselmo. Celia is a minor character in *En noviembre llega el arzobizbo*, a denunciation of the local oligarchy's absolute domination of all sectors of society in the town of Cedrón. It carries with it, in addition, a consistent subtext of terror and violence. *En noviembre llega el arzobizpo* characterizes a broader spectrum of society than did the first novel, its social critique being more strident that that of *Respirando el verano*. Just as *Cien años de soledad* synthetized García Márquez's Macondo, the massive (811 pages) *Celia se pudre* is the summa of the world of Cedrón. Although this hermetic work has multiple narrative voices, the decadence of Cedrón is filtered primarily through Celia´s memory. As in *Respirando el verano*, the central image of *Celia se pudre* is the home – *la casa* – and the predominant tone accentuates the hatred that permeates Cedrón as well as Celia's life.

Writers of the generation before García Márquez who have produced modern fiction since the appearance in 1967 of *Cien años de soledad* include Gustavo Alvarez Gardeazábal, Héctor Sánchez, Jorge Eliécer Pardo, Germán Espinosa, David Sánchez Juliao, and Oscar Collazos. In addition to *Cóndores no entierran todos los días* (1972, Condors Do Not Bury Every Day) and *El bazar de los idiotas* (1974, The Idiots' Bazaar) Alvarez Gardeazábal's work includes *Dabeiba* (1972, Dabeiba), *El titiritero* (1977, The Puppeteer), *Los míos* (1981, My People), *Pepe Botellas* (1984, Pepe Botellas), *El divino* (1986, The Divine One), *El último gamonal* (1987, The Last Boss), *Los sordos ya no hablan* (1991, The Deaf No Longer Speak), and *Las cicratices de Don Antonio* (1997) Since *El titiritero,* the central matter of Alvarez Gardeázabal's fiction has been unequivocal: It is dedicated primarily to questioning and denouncing the Greater Cauca's oligarchy. Héctor Sánchez published *Las maniobras* (1986, The Maneuvers), *Las causas supremas* (1969, The Supreme Causes), *Los desheredados* (1974 The Disinherited), *Sin nada entre las manos* (1976, With Nothing between the Hands), *El tejemaneje* (1979, The Operator), and *Entre ruinas* (1984, Among Ruins). In its totality this fiction expresses the frustration over the seemingly useless life of its characters, who play out repetitive variations of their tedious daily activity. Jorge Eliécer Pardo's two novels, *El jardín de las Weismann* (1978, The Garden of the Weismann) and *Irene* (1986, Irene), are examples of perhaps the most carefully conceived and structured modern fiction of the generation. *El jardín de las Weismann* (titled *El jardín de las Hartmann* in the first edition) deals with La Violencia in an abstract fashion, delineating parallels between the Colombian conflict and anti-Nazi resistance in Germany.

Germán Espinosa, who never received the recognition that he deserved, published several historical novels, including *Los cortejos del diablo* (1970, The Devil's Procession), *El magnicidio* (1979, The Assassination), *La tejedora de coronas* (1982 The Weaver of Crowns), *El signo del pez* (1987, The Sign of the Fish), *Sinfonía del nuevo mundo* (1990, Symphony of the New World), *La tragedia de Belinda Elsner* (1991, The Tragedy of Belinda Elsner), *Los ojos del basilisco* (1992, The Eyes of the Obelisk), and *La lluvia en el rastrajo* (1994, The Rain in the Weeds). *Los cortejos del diablo,* set in Cartagena during the Colonial period, is an account of one of the major perpetrators of the Inquisition in Colombia and a denunciation of this Spanish institution. One of the most technically complex and engaging modern novels of the 1980s, *La tejedora de coronas* also takes place during the Colonial period. It consists of an interior monologue, a life story related by Genoveva Alcocer, a one-hundred-year-old woman accused of witchcraft.

David Sánchez Juliao, from the Costa, has explored the possibilities of secondary orality, writing a popular fiction using the technology of records and cassettes. Sánchez Juliao embellishes *Pero sigo siendo el rey* (1983, But I Am Still the King) with Mexican *rancheras* and other forms of popular music to narrate his melodramatic story of romance and conflict, an anecdote worthy of a soap opera. Oscar Collazos published a politically aggressive set of novels, testimonial in impulse, questioning the authority of the Colombian oligarchy and its values: *Crónica de tiempo muerto* (1975, Chronicle of dead time), *Los días de la paciencia* (1976, Days of Patience), *Todo o nada* (1982, Everything or Nothing), *Jóvenes, pobres amantes (*1983, Young, Poor Lovers), and *Tal como el fuego fatuo* (1986, As in Fatuous Fire). In its totality, Collazos's fiction could be seen as the testimony of a generation of intellectuals who experienced La Violencia in their childhood, the Cuban Revolution in their adolescence, and Colombia's National Front in their maturity. Other writers who pursued a fundamentally modern fiction in the twentieth century were Roberto Burgos Cantor, Marvel Moreno, Eduardo García Aguilar, Fernando Cruz Kronfly, Umberto Valverde, Alonso Aristizábal, Luis Fayad, Tomás González, Julio Olaciregui, José Luis Garcés, José Stevenson, Darío Ruiz Gómez, Evelio Rosero Diago, José Cardona López, Alvaro Pineda Botero, José Luis Díaz Granados, Juan José Hoyos, Humberto Tafur, Antonio Caballero, and Gustavo González Zafra.

Several writers of the García Márquez generation, born in the 1920s, published modern novels during the 1970s and 1980s, including Manuel Mejía Vallejo, Alvaro Mutis, Pedro Gómez Valderrama, Plinio Apuleyo Mendoza, and Mario Escobar Velásquez. After *El día señalado,* Mejía Vallejo wrote *Aire de tango* (1973, Air of Tango), *Las muertes ajenas* (1979, The Distant Deaths), *Tarde de verano* (1980, A Summer Afternoon), *Y el mundo sigue andando* (1984, And the World Moves Along), and *La sombra de tu paso* (1987, The Shadow of Your Step). In *Aire de tango* Mejía Vallejo mythifies the Argentine hero of the tango, Carlos Gardel. Mejía Vallejo's later novels are nostalgic evocations of rural Antioquia. Gómez Valderrama, Apuleyo Mendoza, and Escobar Velásquez also published novels of adventures: *La otra raya del tigre* (1977, The Other Stripe of the Tiger) by Gómez Valderrama relates the nineteenth-century adventures of colonizer Geo von Lengerke in Colombia; Apuleyo Mendoza's *Años de fuga* (1979, Years of Fleeing) is an account of the protagonist's experiences in Paris during the 1960s; *Cuando pase el anima sola* (1979,

When the Soul Is Alone) and *Un hombre llamado Todero* (1980, A Man Named Todero) by Mario Escobar Velásquez are rural adventure stories.

Women writers of this generation engaged in the creation of modern fiction included Marvel Moreno, Flor Romero de Nohra, Rocío Vélez de Piedrahita, and María Helena Uribe de Estrada. This generation of women writers, who have not been engaged in the self-conscious and theoretically based feminist discourse of postmodern feminists such as Albalucía Angel, have been relatively conventional in their approach to storytelling. Romero de Nohra began with *3 kilates, 8 puntos* (Three Kilos and Eight Points) a story of human relationships and conflicts associated with the emerald trade. *Mi capitán Fabián Sicachá* (1968, My Captain Fabián Sicachá) deals with the rural guerrilla movement of the 1960s, as does *Triquitraques de trópico* (1972, Tropical Noise), which is imbued with the language and magic of García Márquez's early Macondo fiction. *Los sueños del poder* (1978), a feminine version of the dictator novel, is an account of a female dictator in an unnamed Latin American country, described in great detail as the stereotypical tropical paradise.

Experimental fiction and postmodern novel

García Márquez's accomplishments with his fiction, his international critical acclaim, and his 1982 Nobel Prize in literature gained unprecedented visibility for the Colombia of the 1980s and 1990s. On the other hand, writers such as Darío Jaramillo Agudelo and R. H. Moreno-Durán exhibited a more experimental or postmodern series of interests. Their public representation of themselves as the writer's writers, as well as their hermetic fictional exercises, gained them the attention of a smaller group of readers, writers, and critics interested in innovative fiction. Solipsistic experiments do not usually become bestsellers, either in the original version or in translation. Nevertheless, Jaramillo Agudelo and Moreno-Durán as well as writers such as Albalucía Angel, Marco Tulio Aguilera Garramuño, Andrés Caicedo, Rodrigo Parra Sandoval, and Alberto Duque López pursued an experimental, fundamentally postmodern project in the last three decades of the century.

Dario Jaramillo Agudelo's early novel, *La muerte de Alec* (1983, The Death of Alec), is also a metafiction – in this case, a self-conscious meditation on the function of literature. It is an epistolary work directed to an unidentified "you" who is one of the characters involved with Alec. This "you" and the letter writer are friends of Alec, who dies during an excursion. The characters are Colombian, but the novel is set in the

United States, where the letter writer is a novelist in the University of Iowa Writers' Program. Jaramillo Agudelo inverts the commonly accepted relationship between empirical reality and fiction: According to the narrator, it is not literature but life that is artificial, baroque, and twisted. Similarly, the acts of storytelling (placing order to a story) and interpretation (giving meaning to a story) become the predominant forces, taking precedence over other forms of understanding reality. As in Aguilera Garramuño's *Paraísos hostiles* (Hostile Paradises) the novel also alludes to the very mechanisms used in telling the story.

Urban and cosmopolitan in interests, many of these experimental writers have preferred to write abroad; Moreno-Durán and Angel have lived for most of their writing careers in Europe and have been as intellectually attuned to contemporary European writing and theory as to Colombia. Similarly, Duque López has been indelibly influenced by such diverse texts as Julio Cortázar's *Rayuela* (Hopscotch) and American film. Aguilera Garramuño has written postmodern texts in the sense that they present no privileged narrator upon whom the reader can rely, nor is there an authoritative discourse or figure to whom the reader can turn for something like an objective, final truth regarding its fiction. The reading difficulties with such experimental texts are created by this absence of an organizing, potentially omniscient mediator who could filter and interpret all the discursive performances in the text. Having immersed themselves in writing culture's recent theory and having assimilated the fiction of the moderns, these experimental postmodern writers are the most distant from oral cultural of any group of Colombian writers to date.

Moreno-Durán's *Los felinos del Canciller* (1985, The Chancellor's Felines) lacks some of the hermetic qualities in many typical postmodern texts; it represents a break from his more hermetic *Fémina Suite* trilogy. In this connection one might speak of an early postmodern attitude that produced hermetic and relatively inaccessible works (found in Moreno-Durán's trilogy, early Sarduy, and the Argentine Néstor Sánchez) and a later more accessible postmodern fiction (found in Latin American novels of the 1980s, among these *Los felinos del Canciller*). The difficulties and the inaccessibility of many postmodern texts are replaced in *Los felinos del Canciller* by wit: Rather than functioning as a hermetic barrier, Moreno-Durán's subtle manipulation of language is frequently the material of humor. A review of the plot suggests another family romance – the modern Latin American family story – as seen in García Márquez, Fuentes, or Carpentier. *Los felinos del Canciller* chronicles three generations of the aristocratic Barahona's family of diplomats, from the patriarch Gonzalo Barahona to his son Santiago and his grandson Félix Barahohna.

Only a superficial reading of *Los felinos del Canciller*, however, would emphasize the family history; the most important referents and the main subject of this novel are language and writing. The verb that synthesizes the novel's action is "to manipulate." The superficial reading would thus render the nuclear sentence "The Barahona family manipulates others," underscoring three generations of political manipulation. Indeed, the art of diplomacy, as practiced by the Barahona family, is the art of manipulation. More significant to the experience of this novel, however, is the manipulation of language, for if diplomacy is Gonzalo's profession, philology is his passion. In this sense, a more accurate synthesis of the novel's action is "The Barahona family manipulates language." Gonzalo, Santiago, and Félix all control the art of manipulation and, above all, the manipulation of language.

As a novel written against the Hispanic and Highland tradition, *Los felinos del Canciller* contains numerous intertexts from Spanish and Colombian literature. Gonzalo is a grand connoisseur of this tradition, from Cervantes to the last of the *presidentes gramáticos*, Marco Fidel Suárez. Other texts are absorbed into this novel in an intertextual relationship that becomes the basis of Moreno-Durán's humorous writing against the Highland tradition. When speaking of the *presidents gramáticos*, the narrator refers to Luciano Mancipe satirically. This type of sentence is an exercise in intertextuality, for the name Luciano Mancipe evokes *Los sueños de Luciano Pulgar*, a book by Marco Fidel Suárez.

Los felinos del Canciller is parody of Colombian institutions, above all, the institutionalized concept of Bogotá as the Athens of South America. The novel also questions the cultural superiority claimed by Colombian intellectuals who were rooted in this classical tradition. To carry out his parody of Bogotá as Athens, the narrator presents Colombia as a distant *ese país* (that country). On those rare occasions when the narrator admits identity with this nation, using the first-person plural ("our"), the vision is of a citizen abroad, observing this philological paradise with spatial and temporal distance.

Los felinos del Canciller is a significant expression of the postmodern. For both the reader and the narrator, it is a novel of surfaces: All actions are superficial in the sense that the very act of manipulation is always more significant than any content or product of this manipulation. Having language as its subject and only absences and indeterminacy as its constants, *Los felinos del Canciller* emerges as the postmodern text par excellence. Like the narrator and the Barahonas, all etymologists who seek truth in origins, Moreno-Duran investigates his own origins in the language of the Hispanic and Highland traditions, synthesized in the phrase "the Athens of South America."

Moreno-Duran's experimental, postmodern writing is best understood by considering the three novels of his *Fémina Suite* as an integral part of his project. The trilogy explores several of his concerns observed in *Los felinos del Canciller*, beginning with his parody of Bogotá as the Athens of South America, a concept also ridiculed in *Juego de Damas*. The ironic distance necessary for the humorous effects in *Los felinos del Canciller* as well as the pervasive and subversive wordplay are experienced throughout the fiction of *Fémina Suite*. The roots of the *Fémina Suite* are not found in the empirical reality of Colombia but rather, as in the case of postmodern fiction, in modernist literature. Moreno-Durán has explained how poems by T. S. Eliot and Paul Valéry generated the first novel of the trilogy, *Juego de damas*.

The reader's most immediate literary association with *Juego de damas* is the work that announced the postmodern project in Latin America, Cortázar's *Rayuela:* Both elements of the form (such as the split columns on a single page) and the content (such as youths listening to jazz) recall Cortazar's proposal for a new, open novel, as articulated in *Rayuela*. *Juego de damas* deals with Colombian female intellectuals, beginning with their radicalized student life of the 1960s and passing through three stages of social climbing and power acquisition, stages in which the narrator identifies them as *Meninas* (young intellectuals), *Mandarinas* (middle-aged social climbers), and *Matriarcas* (aged women in power). As in *Los felinos del Canciller*, Moreno-Durán develops elaborate relationships between language and power: He employs a series of strategies, including parody and euphemism, to subvert language once again. This subversive activity is supported in the text by Monsalve, a character who serves as an author figure. The two main characters of *Toque de Diana*. Augusto Jota and Catalina Arévalo, are also intellectuals who engage in the linguistic and sexual exercises of power noted in *Los felinos del Canciller* and *Juego de damas*. Augusto is a military man who fails both in the military and in his sexual relationship with Catalina, for in the lovemaking of these two devotees of Latin, she "conjugated" while he literally "declined." In the third and most hermetic novel of the trilogy, *Finale capriccioso con Madonna*, Moreno-Durán exploits to the utmost both the eroticism of language and the language of eroticism. He poses the question, for example, of the relationship between "semantics" and "semen" and in the process creates a lengthy, playful, and dense passage of a *ménage à trios*. From the introduction to Laura, the main character, who finds herself caught between two men, this novel develops a series of triangular relationships. It is a playful novel of erotic and linguistic excesses with intertextual allusions ranging from Proust to the Mexican postmodern novelist Salvador Elizondo, subject of all three books.

Other postmodern novelists – Albalucía Angel, Marco Tulio Aguilera Garramuño, Alberto Duque López, Rodrigo Parra Sandoval, and Andrés Caicedo – are generally as demanding of their readers as Jaramillo and Moreno-Durán. Albalucía Angel's experimental fiction, particularly *Misiá Señora* (1982, Mrs. Misiá) and *Las andariegas* (1984, The Ravelers), is part of a feminist project that emanates directly from feminist theory and fiction. She had already published two early experimental novels, *Los girasoles en invierno* (1970, Sunflowers in the Winter) and *Dos veces Alicia* (1972, Alice Twice Over), in addition to a work on La Violencia titled *Estaba la pájara pinta sentada en el verde limón* (1975, The Painted Bird Was Sitting on the Lemon Tree). In the late twentieth century, Angel was the most prominent feminist writer among Colombian novelists. *Los girasoles en invierno* consists of brief narrative segments narrated by a female voice who reacts to her surroundings in Paris and relates memories of an immediate past while traveling around Europe. An indication of Angel's experimentation is evident in her handling of plot: There is no consistently developed plot and only a sketchy story line tracing the narrator's relationship with a novice painter. *Dos veces Alicia*, set in Great Britain, relates the female protagonist's relationship with a series of real and imagined friends. The only consistent element in the novel's disperse associations is the presence of the narrator. She openly invites the reader to imagine with her, making *Dos veces Alicia* yet another product of that postmodern novel proposed by Cortázar in which the reader takes an active role in the creative process. *Estaba la pájara pinta sentada en el verde limón* begins with a quotation from a politician who refers to a labyrinth of facts, men, and opinions. This "labyrinth" indeed serves as an appropriate description of the reader's experience. The early sections of the novel communicate the images of La Violencia as perceived by an innocent young girl who later in the novel will experience La Violencia at the side of the revolutionary Lorenzo. Angel's use of historical documents makes *Estaba la pájara pinta sentada en el verde limón* a documentary novel as well.

The two novels of Angel's self-conscious feminist discourse, *Misiá Señora* and *Las andariegas*, are also her most hermetic. The protagonist of *Misiá Señora*, Mariana, is reared by a family of the landed aristocracy in a coffee-growing region of Colombia. She eventually finds herself caught

between the expectations a traditional society holds for young women –
marriage and motherhood – and a less conventional but potentially more
meaningful existence. The nontraditional lifestyle is stimulated through
her friendships with two women. The structure of *Misiá Señora,* which is
divided into three parts, relates three chronological stages of Mariana's life.
These three parts are formally identified as *Imágenes,* the first of which is
entitled "I have a doll dressed in blue" and deals with Mariana's childhood
and adolescence. The second, "Ancient without shadow," tells of her
courtship, her marriage, her two children's births, and her degenerating
psychological state. The third *Imagen* relates a series of dreamlike visions
often concerning her mother and grandmother. Gender differences are the
paramount issues of *Misiá Señora:* Much of the first *Imagen* deals with
different aspects of female sexuality; Mariana's childhood involves sexual
harassment, initial experiences with *machismo,* and the gradual discovery of
her own sexuality. Gender issues are also associated with class structure and
Christianity. The fictional world of *Misiá Señora* creates a tenuous line
between empirical reality and pure imagination. An important aspect of
this richly imaginative experience is the creation of a new feminist discourse as part of Angel's feminist project.

Las andariegas is Angel's most radical experiment in fiction. It can be
read as a double search: on the one hand, a search for a female language; on
the other, an evocation of a feminine identity. It begins with two epigraphs, followed by a statement by the author that proposes a feminist
program, and then a third epigraph. The first epigraph is from *Les
Guérrilléres* by Monique Wittig, referring to females breaking the existing
order and needing, above all, strength and courage. The second epigraph is
from *Las nuevas cartas portuguesas* by María Isabel Barreno, María Terda
Horta, and María Velho da Costa and refers to women as firm and
committed warriors. Setting forth her feminist program, the author
explains these two epigraphs in a page-long statement, the third prefatory
section to appear before the narrative itself. Angel states that she once
found Wittig's *Les Guérrilléres* illuminating, and, consequently, she
decided to undertake this project with female warriors who advance "from
nowhere toward history." She used as a guide images from stories from her
childhood, transformed into fables and cryptic visions. The third epigraph
is from the mythologies of the Kogui (a Colombian indigenous group) and
emphasizes the role of the female figure in creation. Rather than a traditional plot line, the sixty-two brief anecdotes of this novel present a vision
of women who have been censored from history.

As in much of the experimental writing of Darío Jaramillo Agudelo and Moreno Durán, language is the principal subject in *Las andariegas*. Much of the narrative consists of brief phrases with unconventional punctuation that often function on the basis of an image. The use of verbal imagery is supported by visual images – a set of twelve drawings of a female body in the novel. Angel also experiments with the physical space of language in the text, often in a manner similar to concrete poetry. The four pages of this type offer a variety of circular and semicircular arrangements with the names of famous women. The total effect of this visual imagery is to associate the body of the text with the female body. *Las andariegas* ends with a type of epilogue – another quotation from Monique Witting – consisting of four brief sentences calling precisely for the project that is the radical essence of these two novels: a new language, a new beginning, and a new history for women.

The postmodern writing of Darío Jaramillo Agudelo, Moreno-Durán, and Angel is distant from the modernity of Garcia Márquez's cycle of Macondo. Marco Tulio Aguilera Garramuño, on the other hand, began his writing career with a self-conscious reaction to the Macondo fiction in his parodic *Breve historia de todas las cosas* (1975, A Brief History of Everything). The narrator, Mateo Albán, playfully narrates from prison the story of a small town in Costa Rica. In addition to the town's development (similar in many ways to Macondo), Mateo Albán describes the problems he confronts as creator and as narrator. The metafictional mode reaches its most extreme situation in the sixth chapter when Albán discusses his problems with his fictional readers. Like Moreno-Durán and Angel, Aguilera Garramuño playfully subverts some of Colombia's most sacred institutions: in this case, the Catholic Church, *machismo*, and the fiction of García Márquez. In *Paraísos hostiles* (1985, Hostile Paradises), a dialogue on fiction and philosophy, Aguilera Garramuño moves away from the context of Colombia and García Márquez, but he continues in the metafictional mode. He creates a perverse and hellish fictional world located in a sordid hotel. Several of its economically impoverished but intellectually rich inhabitants write novels, and one of them proposes a novelistic aesthetic that is quite similar – though not coincidentally – to the readers experience in *Paraísos hostiles*.

Andrés Caicedo, Rodrigo Parra Sandoval, and Alberto Duque López conceived different kinds of postmodern projects. Caicedo's *¡Qué viva la música!* (1977, Long Live Music!), like the fiction of the *Onda* writers in Mexico, involves a fictional world of 1960s rock music and drugs. Beyond this superficial comparison, however, Caicedo has little in common with the young Mexican writers, for *¡Qué viva la música!* is an experimental confrontation with a particular generation's cultural crisis in 1960s Colombia. Caicedo deals with this crisis with sobriety rather than with the humor and playfulness of the Mexican writers of the *Onda*. Rodrigo Parra Sandoval's *El álbum secreto del Sagrado Corazón* (1978, The Secret Album of the Sacred Heart) is a collage of textsbooks, newspapers, letters, documents, voices – representing an assault on the novel as a genre. The implied author suggests that the genre suffers limitations similar to those experienced by the protagonist in a very limiting and repressive religious seminary. Colombia's cultural crisis, as seen in Caicedo, is depicted in Parra Sandoval's novel as a questioning of the nation's official, institutional images. *El álbum secreto del Sagrado Corazón* contains two main characters so ambiguously portrayed that they could well be the same person. Alberto Duque López proceeds similarly in *Mateo el flautista* (1968, Mateo the flute player), which in two parts offers two different versions of the protagonist, Mateo. There is no authoritative voice in this narrative nor any authoritative version of Mateo's life. Consequently, *Mateo el flautista* is a quintessential postmodern text that clearly emanates from *Rayuela*, as indicated by the novel's dedication to one of its characters, Rocamadour.

The poets that published in the latter part of the twentieth century and share some commonalities with these postmodern novelists with respect to attitudes are Antonieta Villamil, Andrea Cote, Lucía Estrada, and Felipe García Quintero. Indeed, the very genre of poetry lends itself aptly to most of the discussions of experimental and postmodern fiction; the emphasis on language per se, for example, is prominent in the poetry of this period.

Conclusion

The Colombian novel published in the late twentieth century was a heterogeneous, multivoiced genre that far surpassed the political and aesthetic limits previously set for this genre in Colombia. Until the1960s and the rise of García Márquez, the conservative dominant elite in Bogotá had controlled most aspects of the production of novels, from publication to literary history and criticism. The Garcia Márquez phenomenon in the late 1960s, in addition to factors such as the rise of international Latin Americanism and the expansion of multinational publishing houses, opened the Colombian novel to a heterogeneity of voices heretofore impossible in Colombia's regional and often provincial literary scene. Many of the most successful writers, such as García Márquez, Alvaro Mutis, Fernando Vallejo, Darío Jaramillo Agudelo, Moreno-Durán, and Angel, established their careers abroad – beyond the control of the local literary establishment in

Bogotá. All published a substantive portion of their work abroad, and international Latin Americanism carried out the vast majority of the critical and scholarly activity on these four writers. Given the writers' new independence and the multiple directions found in the novel by the 1980s and 1990s, it was no longer necessary or even appropriate to speak of a "shadow" of García Márquez.

The modern and postmodern tendencies of the Colombian novel in the late twentieth century offer some general differences in these novelists' approaches to institutions. The moderns such as García Márquez, Rojas Herazo, and Fernando Vallejo tend to be more overtly political in the sense that they fictionalize elements generally associated with Colombian and Latin American empirical reality. They criticize or denounce specific institutions and at times specific individuals. The postmoderns, such as Darío Jaramillo Agudelo, Moreno-Durán, Angel, and Aguilera Garramuño, create novels more related to other texts and often more directed specifically to issues of language. All conventions, including those of the traditional and modern novel, are potentially questioned by these irreverent postmodern writers. More specific comparisons between García Márquez's modern impulse and Dario Jaramillo Agudelo's postmodern gesture can help illuminate the differences between the modem and postmodern in Colombia. *El otoño del patriarca* functions on the basis of a structure of progressive apertures, whereas *Los felinos del Canciller* functions on the basis of language play. Both authors use humor for subversive ends, but García Márquez's is anecdotally based, while Jaramillo Agudelo and Moreno-Durán depends more specifically on language to achieve their goals. Generally speaking, García Márquez, Buitrago, and Rojas Herazo create myths out of history and story, while Jaramillo Agudelo, Moreno-Durán, and Angel destroy myths by means of questioning language and theory. García Márquez, Buitrago, and Rojas Herazo often employ a controlling, omniscient narrator, whereas the reader of Jaramillo Agudelo, Moreno-Durán, and Angel encounters no consistent authority figure in the text. Although writers such as García Márquez and Darío Jaramillo Agudelo do share some characteristics, as do many modern and postmodern novelists, their total projects also differ considerably.

In Colombia, the modern writing of García Márquez and his generation, as well as the modern work of Fernando Vallejo, were widely read, accepted, and acclaimed by the end of the century. On the other hand, the more experimental and postmodern fiction of Darío Jaramillo Agudelo, R. H. Moreno-Durán, and Albalucía Angel spoke to the importance of a "minor" literature in Colombia where, as in other nations, the place of "minor" and "marginal" was revised and often considered uniquely central.

BIBLIOGRAPHY

Curcio Altamar, Antonio. *Evolución de la novela en Colombia* (1957, first edition) Bogotá: Instituto Colombiano de Cultura, 1975.

Gómez Restrepo, Antonio. *Historia de la literatura colombiana*. Bogotá: Imprenta Nacional, 1945.

Gutiérrez Girardo, Rafael. "La literatura colombiana en el siglo XX," in *Manuel de historia de Colombia*, ed Helena Araujo, pp. 437–536. Instituto Colombiano de Cultura, 1982.

Kadir, Djelal. *Questing Fiction: Latin America's Family Romance*. Minneapolis: University of Minnesota Press, 1986.

Levy Kurt. *Tomás Carrasquilla*. Medellín: Instituto de integración cultural, 1985.

Lewis Marvin A. *Treading the Ebony Path: Ideology and Violence in Contemporary Afro-Colombian Prose Fiction*. Columbia: University of Missouri Press, 1987.

Lyotard, Jean-Francoise. *The Postmodern Condition: A Report on Knowledge*. Minneapolis: University of Minnesota Press, 1984.

Menton Seymour. *La novela colombiana: planetas y satélites*. Bogotá: Plaza y Janés Editores, 1978.

Peña Gutiérrez Isaías. *La narrativa del frente nacional*. Bogotá: Universidad Central, 1982.

Ponce de Leon, Gina. *Mujer, erotismo, mito, utopia y héroe contemporáneo en Ávaro Mutis*. Bogotá: Universidad Javeriana, 2002.

Roma Ángel. *La ciudad letrada*. Hanover, N.H: Ediciones del Norte, 1984.

Shaw, Donald. *The Post-boom in Spanish-American Fiction*. Albany: State University of New York Press, 1998.

Vargas Germán. *Sobre literatura colombiana*. Bogotá: Fundación Simón y Lola Guberek, 1985.

Williams Raymond Leslie. *The Colombian Novel 1844–1987*. Austin: University of Texas Press, 1991.

"The Dynamic Structure of García Márquez's *El otoño del patriarca*," *Symposium* 32, No. 1 (Spring 1978): 56–75.

Notes

1 In *Questing Fictions*, Djelal Kadir points out that Lytotard had discussed a postmodern that was not "after the modern." See *Questing Fictions* and Lyotard, *The Postmodern Condition*.

2 The author of this chapter has delineated the dynamic structure and the apertures in more detail in "The Dynamic Structure of García Márquez's *El otoño del patriarcia*."

CHAPTER 7

Twenty-first century fiction

Claire Taylor and Raymond L. Williams

Introduction

The Colombian novel of the twenty-first century is a heterogeneous genre of multiple tendencies published by three generations of writers. In addition, with the rise of the new technologies since the early 1990s, the new digital genre offers a different concept of what a novel might be. In the twenty-first century, the most visible generation consisted of the writers known in Latin America as the "McOndo" generation, also identified as the "Crack" generation in Mexico and the Generation of the 1990s in Brazil. This generation was born in the 1960s, began publishing in the 1990s, and includes most prominently Mario Mendoza (b. 1964), Jorge Franco (b. 1962) Santiago Gamboa (b. 1965), Efraim Medina Reyes (b. 1967), Juan Carlos Botero (b. 1960), Octavio Escobar Giraldo (b. 1962), Pablo Montoya (b. 1963), and Enrique Serrano (b. 1960). The generation that preceded it began publishing earlier (in the 1970s and 1980s), and these writers, such as Fernando Vallejo (b. 1942), Darío Jaramillo (b. 1947), Laura Restrepo (b. 1950), Albalucía Angel (b. 1939), Fanny Buitrago (b. 1945), Ramón Illán Baca (b. 1942), Héctor Abad Facciolince (b. 1958), Evelio Rosero (b. 1958), Roberto Burgos (b. 1948), Oscar Collazos (b. 1942), Piedad Bonnet (b. 1951), William Ospina (b. 1954), Azriel Bibliowicz (b. 1949), Gustavo Alvarez Gardeazábal (b. 1945), José Gabriel Baena (b. 1952), and Tomás González (b. 1952), have all published a significant body of work that began appearing in the 1970s and 1980s. With respect to the youngest generation that followed the Generation of the 1990s, born since 1970 are Juan Gabriel Vásquez, Ricardo Silva Romero (1970 b.), Juan Manuel Ruiz, and Juan B. Gutiérrez.[1] In this chapter, we will provide a brief overview of these three generations and then discuss some major topics of twenty-first century writing: the new urban violence, *sicaresque* and urban neorealism, exile and new experience of urban space, and new digital genres.

Three generations of writers

Of the three generations of writers, a Generation of the 1990s has been widely discussed since the mid-1990s, but there is little agreement about exactly what they represent. In general, these writers have rejected some aspects of the 1960s Boom, particularly the magical realism that in Colombia they associate with García Márquez but also, to some degree, with the popular commercial writer Isabel Allende. As was the case of writers in the 1970s, they continue to speak of the "shadow" of the Nobel Laureate for all fiction that has followed into the 1980s and 1990s. The Generation of the 1990s is not generally considered to be as utopian and optimistic as were many writers of the Boom during the 1960s, but not as antiutopian and pessimistic as some writers of the Postboom era.[2] Some critics, writers, and scholars have suggested that this "in between" status of neither consistent optimism nor consistent pessimism places this generation in the sphere of nihilism, as has been pointed out in particular with writers in Mexico such as David Toscana. Indeed, in the fiction of Mendoza and Franco, as well as some other writers of this generation in Colombia, nihilist moments are found. Most of these writers have also been more aligned with the cultural precedent of television more than the grand narrative of European and North American Modernist novel that had been the model for the writers of all previous generations in Colombia since the 1950s.[3] Thus, for these writers, American television of the 1980s and 1990s, as well as the writing of Paul Auster, have been more important than Joyce, Dos Passos, and Faulkner. The Colombian Jorge Franco has embraced the literary past, stating "Aunque suene contradictorio, tengo la percepción de que la literatura de los últimos años también ha tomado los ingredientes de las generaciones anteriores para construir algo que no se parece en nada a la obra de sus antecesores" (Although it may sound contradictory, I have the perception that the literature of recent years has used some of the ingredients of previous generations to construct something that has nothing to do with the work of previous generations).[4]

The most productive of this generation, and perhaps of most resonance, have been Mario Mendoza, Jorge Franco, and Santiago Gamboa. Mendoza is the author of *Relato de un asesino* (2001, Story of an Assassin), *Satanás* (2002, Satan), *Cobro de sangre* (2004, Collection of Blood), *Los hombres invisibles* (2007, The Invisible Men), *Buda blues* (2009, Buddha Blues), *Apocalipsis* (2011, Apocalypsis), and other writings. *Satanás* was the 2002 winner of a very prestigious international prize in Spanish, the Seix Barral Premio Biblioteca Breve, offered by the Spanish publishing house of the same name. His *Cobro de sangre* novelizes an important context for Colombian writers of this generation: the complex web of urban violence perpetrated by forces often closely allied with the military, the drug traffickers, or political dissidents at the same time that the exact connections among these three groups and the perpetrators were often vague and ambiguous. More specifically, paramilitary groups whose alliances with the state were undefined were responsible for a considerable number of deaths and kidnappings. At the same time, connections and collaborations between drug cartels and armed political groups were part of a scenario with a weak and fragile state. *Satanás* is a horror-inspiring historic fiction set in contemporary Bogotá of the late twentieth century. The pervasive vision of evil triumphing over good throughout Colombian society reveals a deep malaise in the country. Mendoza's deep pessimism leaves many victims, and many are also executioners. García Márquez documented some portions of this horrific Colombian urban experience of the 1980s in his documentary novel *Noticia de un secuestro* (1996, News of a Kidnapping). In *Cobro de sangre*, the protagonist loses his parents in the midst of military/political violence in a home invasion and spends the rest of his life living the consequences of this traumatic experience. His fragmented life leads him to political activism and his own reenactment of the traumatic experience, as he leads a group of political dissidents to seek revenge on the military leaders who killed his parents. He spends fifteen years in prison to emerge in 2001 into a new urban setting in Bogotá. *Cobro de sangre* could well be read as an emblem for this generation of the 1990s and a metaphor for the urban experience in Bogotá in the 1980s.

Jorge Franco (b. 1962) is the author of the volume of short stories *Maldito amor* (1996, Bad Love), followed by the novels *Mala noche* (1997, Bad Night), *Rosario Tijeras* (1999, Rosario Tijeras), *Paraíso Travel* (2006, Paradise Travel), *Melodrama* (2006), and *Amar es más difícil que matar* (2010, Loving Is More Difficult than Killing). Franco achieved considerable commercial success with *Rosario Tijeras*, which was made into a successful film version. Identified in Colombia as *sicaresque* (a combination of the paid assassin called a *sicario* and the picaresque of the Spanish literary tradition), this novel tells the story of a paid assassin who works as a prostitute, one kind of perverse manifestation of a drug-cartel culture and its related violence. Franco's *Paraíso Travel* is the story of a Colombian's experience immigrating to the United States illegally; the protagonist ends up alone in New York after crossing into the United States. In this novel, as elsewhere, Franco writes on that ambiguous line often used by Vargas Llosa that blurs the boundary between the literary and commercial literature. Similarly, in

Melodrama Franco blurs the boundary between literary and television melodramas, for the author uses both *telenovelas* (soap operas) and popular news shows as the sources for his parody. To the extent that this is comparable to some of Vargas Llosa's fiction, Franco is part of a generation, as mentioned earlier, that has embraced Vargas Llosa after previous generations had rejected him. In the specific case of *Melodrama*, Franco also writes a self-conscious anti-version of García Márquez's *Cien años de soledad*, for this is not only an anti-Macondo story, but a particularly anti-Buendía family story.[5]

Santiago Gamboa, like Franco, has had his fiction made into films, beginning with one of his most successful novels, *Perder es cuestión de método* (1997, Losing Is a Matter of Method). With this work, Gamboa also takes part in the increasingly popular genre of the thriller (*novela negra*) in Colombia. With a failed journalist as the protagonist, this novel fictionalizes a Colombia of political corruption and violence with respect to Mario Mendoza. The extreme violence of Bogotá as well as everyday urban life are also the subjects of the thriller *Necrópolis* (2009, Necropolis).

If *Paraíso Travel* was Franco's exploration of his generation's concern with exile and the lives of immigrants, Gamboa is even more part of this general trend in *El síndrome de Ulisis* (2009, The Ulysses Syndrome) and *Plegarias nocturnas* (2012, Night Prayers). He had published a novel about the crisis of the youth of his generation, *Páginas de vuelta*, in 1995 and *El cerco de Bogotá* in 2003. In the latter, he imagines a scenario in which Bogotá is taken over by guerrillas and thousands of Colombians flee to the Caribbean coastal town of Cartagena. Mendoza explored the migrant experience in New York, and Gamboa sets his fiction in Paris, China, Israel, and Thailand. In Gamboa's *Hotel Pekín*, the protagonist renounces his Colombian identity. The author has also published *Los impostores* (2001, The Impostors) and *Octubre en Pekín* (2002, October in Beijing).

Gamboa's work, like that of much his generation's foray into the twenty-first century, was written under the presidency of Alvaro Uribe from 2002 to 2010. As Rory O'Bryen has pointed out, Gamboa, like Franco and Mendoza in *Scorpio City*, sees these foreign capitals as increasingly like Bogotá.[6] He has also published *Don Quijote de la Mancha en Medellín* (2012, Don Quixote in Medellín). In novels of political dissidents and social misfits, Gamboa, Franco, and Mendoza reveal a deep dissatisfaction with the social, cultural, and literary world they have inherited from the twentieth century and that they reveal in the twenty-first.

Efraím Medina Reyes is a wide-ranging artist and author who recalls Diamela Eltit's group of heterogeneous writers and intellectuals in Chile in the late 1980s. His novels are *Erase una vez el amor pero tuve que matarlo* (2003, Once upon a time there was love but I had to kill it), *Técnicas de masturbación entre Batman y Robin* (2002, Masturbation Techniques between Batman and Robin), *Sexualidad de la Pantera Rosa* (2004, Sexuality of the Pink Panther), and *Lo que todavía no sabes del pez hielo* (2013, What You Still Don't Know about the Ice Fish). In *Erase una vez el amor pero tuve que matarlo*, the protagonist's intense life in the world of drugs, sex, and music recalls the work's Colombian predecessor by Andrés Caicedo, *Qué viva la música!* (1977, May the Music Live!), as well as Caicedo's predecessors in Mexico, Gustavo Sainz, José Agustín, and the entire group of La Onda. Medina Reyes, however, writes in a constant present and does not limit his urban environments to one city in Colombia, with narratives taking place in the music worlds of Seattle and London. Caicedo's urban fiction was set strictly in Cali. In *Erase una vez*, however, the urban poverty of Bogotá is paralleled with the 1990s grunge of Seattle. Medina Reyes's *Sexualidad de la Pantera Rosa* questions traditional ideas of gender in Colombia and addresses one of the least addressed types of extreme urban violence of the nation in the 1980s and 1990s: urban violence against gays on the streets of the major cities carried out by paramilitary groups that claimed to be carrying out a *limpieza* (cleansing) of the urban areas. This novel also deals with the sexual desperation of the protagonist, who constantly seeks women in a world populated by women and writers. Pablo Montoya, who has received considerable international recognition in recent years, has published *Cuadernos de París* (2006, Notebooks from Paris), *La sed del ojo* (2004, The Silk of the Eye), and *Lejos de Roma* (2008, Far from Rome). Enrique Serrano's fiction includes his collection of short stories *La marca de España* (1997, The Brand of Spain) and a set of linear novels: *Tamerlán* (2003), *Donde no te conozcan* (2007, Where They Don't Know You), and *El hombre de diamante* (2008, The Man of the Diamond). Juan Carlos Botero began with the volume of short stories *Las ventanas y las voces* (1998, The Windows and the Voices) and followed with the novel *La sentencia* (2002, The Sentence).

Among twentieth-century writers of the previous generation, Fernando Vallejo, Laura Restrepo, Héctor Abad Facciolince, and Darío Jaramillo, like the celebrated Chilean writer Roberto Bolaño, have published in several genres. Starting to publish most of his work later, William Ospina has been active as a novelist of the twenty-first century. Fernando Vallejo was a pioneer in gender issues by evoking the topic of being gay in Colombia as a subject of novels such as *Los días azules* (1985, The Blue

Days) (Alvarez Gardeazábal became openly gay in the 1970s, but did not deal with these issues in his fiction). From his early fiction in the 1980s through the twenty-first century, his body of work has become one of the most significant to bridge both centuries. His widely read novel *La virgen de los sicarios* (1994, Our Lady of Assassins) set the tone for much ensuing narco-fiction to be published by Laura Restrepo, Santiago Gamboa, and other writers of the 1990s. He followed with *El desbarrancadero* (2001, The Precipice), *Los días azules* (1985, The Blue Days), *El fuego secreto* (1987, The Secret Fire), *Los caminos a Roma* (1988, The Roads to Rome), *Años de indulgencia* (1989, The Years of indulgence), *El desbarrancadero* (2001), *Entre fantasmas* (1993, Among Ghosts), *La Rambla paralela* (2002, The Parallel Rambla), *Mi hermano el alcalde* (2003, My Brother the Mayor), and *El don de la vida* (2010, The Gift of Life). Vallejo's fiction of the twenty-first century includes, most recently, his eleventh novel, *Casablanca la bella* (2013, Beautiful Casablanca), his nostalgic reflection on returning home to a large family home structure in Medellín and, more specifically, to the upper-middle-class neighborhood of Laureles. Both his house and his neighborhood are points of lengthy novelistic reflection. As he has done consistently in his fiction, he presents Medellín as the setting for an intolerable society in a city he describes at one point as defecation floating on water, drawing a parallel with the ancient floating Mexican city of Tenochtitlán. It is also a homophobic setting in which gays have suffered the consequences of the *sicaresque* culture of the 1980s and 1990s.

Laura Restrepo has been an important chronicler of Colombia's recent political history, in both her journalism and her novels. Like Mario Mendoza and Santiago Gamboa, she has been an acute observer of the nation's complex web of sociopolitical events of the 1980s and 1990s. Her journalistic account of the political scenario was published first in newspaper articles and then appeared as a book under the title *Historia de una traición* (1986, History of a Betrayal) and eventually, as a revised edition, under the new title *Historia de un entusiasmo* (1999, History of an Enthusiasm). Her novel *Leopardo al sol* (1999, Leopard in the Sun) deals with the underworld of kidnapping that had been publicized by García Márquez in *News of a Kidnapping*; it explores the ugly connections between the political world and the world of drug trafficking. Her novel *Dulce compañía* (1998, The Angel of Galilea [note that this novel has been published in translation]) broaches a rarely discussed topic in Colombia's literary and political establishment – the abuse and exploitation of women by the institution of the Catholic Church. Her celebrated novel *Delirio* (2004, Delirium) is a thriller that offers a more international context for the narco-novel, with the crime and drug trafficking set in a more international setting of the "war on drugs" from the United States. Her novel *Demasiados heroes* (2009, No Place for Heroes) is her autobiographical account of her experience as a militant activist in Argentina. Restrepo's career as a novelist, journalist, and public intellectual have given her a place in Colombian intellectual life of the twenty-first century in many ways similar to the role of García Márquez in the twentieth century.

Héctor Abad Facciolince has written a broad range of texts, from short fiction, novels, and poetry to essays, although most of his work has been self-reflective novels. His novel *Basura* (2000, Garbage) is one of his in-depth classic explorations of metafiction. His use of the classic motif of the found manuscript is unique: He rewrites the trash he finds belonging to a neighbor, Bernardo Davenzati. Thus, the narrator is publishing the work of one of those writers who systematically discards his creation. In *Asuntos de un hidalgo disoluto* (1994, The Joy of Being Alive [note that this novel has been published in translation]), Abad Facciolince pursues the form of the memoir to tell the story of a retired Colombian millionaire in Italy. It is also a reflection on writing, language, and the blank page. With a career that began with the publication of the short stories *Malos pensamientos* (1991, Bad Thoughts), followed by numerous translations of his work, Abad Facciolince has also published *El olvido que seremos* (2006, Oblivion: A Memoir), *Tratado de culinaria para mujeres tristes* (1996, Culinary Treatise for Sad Women), and *Fragmentos de un amor furtivo* (1998, Fragments of a Furtive Love). These works are comparable in many ways to the work of this writer's peers of the generation of the 1990s, with its presentation of Colombia's violence and disintegration in the second half of the twentieth century.

Darío Jaramillo has also been a broad-ranging writer of both fiction and poetry and is one of those rare creators, like Chile's Roberto Bolaño and Colombia's Alvaro Mutis, who is actually quite accomplished in both genres. Jaramillo had published a substantive body of work in the twentieth century and has continued writing well into the twenty-first century. A writer associated with experimental postmodern fiction in works such as *La muerte de Alec* (1983, The Death of Alec), a novel of considerable innovation at the time of its publication, but with more emphasis on storytelling in his twenty-first century novels *Memorias de un hombre feliz* (1999, Memories of a Happy Man), *El juego del alfiler* (2002, The Game of the Pin), *Novela con fantasma* (2004, Novel with a Ghost), and *La voz interior* (2006, The Interior Voice). *Cartas cruzadas* (1993, Crossed Letters) is a substantive contribution to an understanding of urban life in Colombia of the 1970s and 1980s as well an ambitious fictionalization of an individual's search for meaning in his life. Jaramillo's synthesis of a wide range of interests related to literature in general, as well as writing novels and poetry in specific, is his totalizing novel *La voz interior*. In this work, Jaramillo offers insights into his entire life as a writer, as well as a compendium of sorts of constant themes and aesthetic interests (see Enrique Salas-Durazo in this volume). Albalucía Angel, like Jaramillo, began as a postmodern-type experimentalist in the twentieth century and wrote a more accessible story-based novel in the twenty-first century, *Tierra de nadie* (2002, Nobody's Land). In his writing career as a poet, he has become a major voice in the Generación Desencantada.

Roberto Burgos, Tomás González, Eduardo García Aguilar, and Oscar Collazos, on the other hand, are writers more closely aligned with what was the twentieth-century novel in a body of work that bridges the twentieth and twenty-first century. With little in common with late twentieth-century postmodern experimentation or the interests of the generation of the 1990s, they write with a nostalgia for a sense of space and time that were the fleeting and unattainable utopias of what was modernity, the modern novel and, in Latin America, the 1960s Boom. Burgos gained a reputation in Colombia early in his career as being one of the nation's most talented short-fiction writers, winning several national prizes, and his volume of short stories *Lo Amador* (1981, On Amador) was highly praised by the critics in Colombia. His major novel of the twentieth-century, *Patio de los vientos perdidos* (1984, The Patio of the Lost Winds) evokes the writer's past in the region of the Caribbean coast of García Márquez's novels. Burgos's novels of the twenty-first century are *La ceiba de la memoria* (2007, The Tree of Memory), *Una siempre es la misma* (2009, One Is Always the Same), *Ese silencio* (2010, That Silence), and *El secreto de Alicia* (2013, Alice's Secret). Tomás González published two novels in the twentieth century and then followed with *La historia de Horacio* (2000, The Story of Horacio), *Abraham entre bandidos* (2010, Abraham among Criminals), *La luz difícil* (2011, The Difficult Light), and *Temporal* (2013, Storm), Eduardo García Aguilar published novels and short fiction in the late twentieth century, but his twenty-first century work has been in several genres other than the novel.

William Ospina and Ramón Illán Baca has been active in the twenty-first century, and the former was awarded the prestigious Rómulo Gallegos novel prize in 2012. Ospina has published the novels *Ursúa* (2005, Ursua), *El país de la canela* (2008, The Cinnamon Nation), and *La serpiente sin ojos*

(2012, The Snake without Eyes). Escobar Giraldo was born in 1958 and initiated his writing career with his volume of short fiction *El color del agua* (The Color of Water) in 1993. Soon after, in the mid-1990s, he began articulating an unofficial generational statement that anticipated some of the statement of the generation of the 1990s: He claimed that the modern classics were less important to him and his generation than television, self-consciously speaking as the first generation of Colombian writers to grow up with access to television. Baca's recent *La mujer barbuda* (2011, The Bearded Woman) is a satire of Colombia's hierarchical society and parody of García Márquez, as well as a questioning traditional understandings of gender in Colombia.

Juan Gabriel Vásquez and Ricardo Silva Romero, although often included with Santiago Gamboa and the writers of the Generation of the 1990s, are actually part of something different. Born in the 1970s, Vásquez and Silva Romero have had access to the internet and digital media from their twenties and have never really had to view themselves as intellectuals writing in the same geographical and temporal space as the writers of the Boom or any other of their Latin American predecessors. Thus, novelists of this generation write with an unprecedented indifference to the writers of the Boom, as well as the need to belong to their national literary tradition in Colombia. They write with a full awareness of the new kind of extreme urban violence and *sicaresque* fiction of the generation of the 1990s. Nevertheless, this extreme urban violence is not a new condition to be discovered and revealed, but a mere everyday reality for Vásquez, Silva Romero, and some of their peers. Both have been highly productive: Silva Romero has published the novels *Sobre la tela de una araña* (1999, The Spider's Web), *Tic* (2003, Tick), *Fin* (2003, End), *Parece que va a llover* (2005, It Seems That It Is Going to Rain), and the lengthy work *El libro de la envidia* (2013, The Book of Jealousy), among other works. Vásquez has published the widely recognized recent novel *El ruido de las cosas al caer* (2011, The Sound of Things Falling), as well as *Persona* (1997, Persona), the short stories *Los amantes de todos los santos* (2004, All the Saints' Lovers), the lengthy novel *Los informantes* (2004, The Informants), and the historical novel *Historia secreta de Costaguana* (2007, The Secret History of Costaguana). *El ruido de las cosas al caer* describes the events connected to the assassination of the Minister of Justice (Rodrigo Lara Bonilla), the director of the newspaper *El Espectador* (Guillermo Cano), and the presidential candidate of the Liberal Party (Luis Carlos Galán). According to Paola Fernández Luna, the characters who deal with these national tragedies are Yammara (who incarnates the national memory) and

Maya Fritts (who represents mourning).[7] It also contains some of the melodramatic elements of other recent Colombian novels.[8]

Extreme urban violence, the *sicaresque*, and urban neorealism

The violent conflict in Colombian society of the 1980s and 1990s left a mark on all three of the generations covered in this introductory overview. The nation's civil war of the 1950s had produced an entire body of fiction identified as *La novela de la Violencia*, a body of work called the "novel of *La Violencia*" that included such canonical novels as Gabriel García Márquez's *La mala hora* (1961), *In Evil Hour*In Evil Hour), Manuel Mejía Vallejo's *El día señalado* (1964, The Assigned Day), and Gustavo Alvarez Gardeazábal's *Cóndores no entierran todos los días* (1972, Condors Do Not Bury Every Day). These twenty-first century novels of violence, however, are significantly different from the 1960s and 1970s *novelas de la violencia*, the latter of which generally dealt with rural violence between the two traditional parties, the Liberals and the Conservatives. The twenty-first-century novels of violence deal with a more comprehensive and complex urban experience that often includes an extreme urban violence. Drug trafficking, urban guerrillas, and political interests other than those of the two traditional parties made the novel a vehicle for communicating a complex set of experiences. Important early books addressing this new urban violence and the sicaresque were Jorge Franco's *Rosario Tijeras* (1999, Rosario Tijeras, and Fernando Vallejo's *La virgen de los sicarios* (2001, Our Lady of Assassins). These were followed by Laura Restrepo's *La multitude errante* (2001, A Tale of Dispossessed, 2004), Mario Mendoza's *Satanás* (2002, Satan), Evelio Rosero's *Los ejércitos* (2007, The Armies, 2008), *En el lejero* (2013, In the Abyss), and Juan Gabriel Vásquez's *El ruido de las cosas al caer* (2011, The Sound of Things Falling). In *En el lejero*, Rosero portrays an extreme urban violence that explores the most intimate spheres of individual lives; the violence is more psychological than in many urban novels of this period. The novels of Santiago Gamboa have dealt with the violence of political conflict and drug trafficking, and his novel *Necrópolis* (2009, Necropolis, 2012) opens with the grotesque image of an impaled corpse. From there, this novel leads the reader into an equally ugly world of counterfeits and false dealings of a society in decadence and lacking a grand narrative worthy of belief.

The *sicaresque* novel in Colombia has its historical roots in a defining act of political violence: the 1984 assassination of Rodrigo Lara Bonilla by two adolescents (*sicarios*) on motorcycles. From this moment forward, the paid assassin that is the *sicario* is a broadly recognized figure in Colombian society, laying the groundwork for the novels mentioned earlier, as well as *Morir con papa* (1997, Dying with Father) by Oscar Collazos and *Sangre ajena* (2000, Foreign Blood) by Arturo Alape, who had already engaged documentary writing on the previous period of national violence, *La Violencia*. A common thread in most of these novels is the presence of a young protagonist with an impoverished background of not only economic deprivation, but also psychological abuse and abandonment. In these novels, as in the historical record, these vulnerable adolescents are the paid assassins of drug cartels, paramilitary groups, political dissidents, and private entities. Detailed visual descriptions of their work has been identified as a new urban neorealism.

Yet another angle on the extreme urban violence of twenty-first century fiction written by the Generation of the 1990s can be appreciated in works such as Efraim Medina Reyes's *Sexualidad de la Pantera Rosa*, a novel in which the homophobia is manifested in violence as it was experienced in the major cities of Colombia in the 1980s and 1990s: the violent "cleansing" (*limpieza*) is part of this novel's content. All in all, the extremity and detail of this urban violence sets these novels apart from their 1950s and 1960s predecessors as novels of violence or *novelas de la violencia*.

Exile, citizenship, and the new experience of globalized space

In Jorge Franco's novel *Paraíso Travel*, the protagonist remembers, near the end of the novel, a series of anecdotes related to his exile from Colombia with some Colombian friends, their immigration to Guatemala, and their crossing the borders into Mexico and the United States. Writing in the present, he recalls his *malos recuerdos* (bad memories) of the trip from the Guatemalan border to Mexico City. This crisis experience was the only moment in the entire trip that he told his partner, Reina, that he wanted to return to Colombia. When he makes this claim to her, she answers with a one-line response that is, in effect, a synthesis of the exile scenario: It is cheaper for a ticket to Monterrey than one to Colombia. This statement underlines, on the one hand, that the group's exile adventure has reached a point of economic no return. On the other hand, it suggests the newness of the numerous anxieties and ambiguities that the group of exiles will begin to face as they are soon to become exile immigrants in New York. In the United States, they each face the numerous crises related to exile, and for the protagonist, Marlon, this crisis seems to be traumatic in nature. His way of dealing with this traumatic experience is a form of avoidance: He speaks, writes, and thinks constantly about his girlfriend Reina, an obsession that helps him to avoid addressing the real trauma of the Colombian immigrant living in exile in New York. Franco continued his exploration of foreign urban spaces in the novel *Melodrama*, which takes place in Paris. Writing from a state of death, the protagonist addresses his narrative to his dead mother. This family drama does not take place exclusively in Paris: It connects back to an entire backdrop of Colombia including the violence of the 1950s civil war of *La Violencia* and the drug violence of the 1980s, as well as the death of drug kingpin Pablo Escobar in 1999.

Paraiso Travel is but one telling example of how writers of the Generation of the 1990s experienced different kinds of exile, and this experience plays an important role in their fiction of the twenty-first century. The fiction of Santiago Gamboa explores the exile experience more amply than does Franco's. Gamboa's novel *Plegarias nocturnas* (2012, Night Prayers), with numerous resonances of Bolaño, explores the exile experience. Franco, Gamboa, and others of this generation present foreign cities in the process of becoming like Bogotá, encountering the violence and chaos of the Colombian capital slowly encroaching on major cities in the West and the East.

Virginia Mayer's first book, *Polaroids* (2013, Polaroids) is an ambitious example of exploring globalized space, for it has scenes in Montevideo, Manhattan, Miami, and Madrid. Her anecdotal interests are as far-ranging as the Holocaust, drug-trafficking in Colombia, the trauma of the military dictatorship in Uruguay, and prostitution in Spain. This novel, as well as Franco's *El mundo de afuera* (2014, The World Outside), are recent examples of the obvious fact that the Colombian novel of the twenty-first century remains interested in exploring the experience of exile in the context of Colombian violence and globalized violence. Both of these novels, then, are written with approaches comparable to that of their Chilean role model, Roberto Bolaño.

The fiction of Jorge Franco has been important for rethinking the role of exile and globalized space is important for the generation of the 1990s, but also the generation of Fernando Vallejo. In Vallejos's recent *Casablanca la bella* (2013, Casablanca the Beautiful), the protagonist faces the globalized space of an old former home before exile. Paradoxically, Vallejo also writes with an awareness of the traditional home in Antioquia as evoked by the previous generation's Manuel Mejía Vallejo in *La casa de dos palmas* and by the earlier generation of Tomás Carrasquilla. For all three, writing about the home is an act of nostalgia – the nostalgia of a literary tradition in Antioquia.

New digital genres and hypertext fiction

Beyond the rise of a new generation of novelists who publish in print, one of most exciting developments in fiction in the late twentieth century and into the twenty-first has been the development of new digital genres within the literary field. Colombia has been at the forefront of these developments, with two authors in particular – Juan B. Gutiérrez and Jaime Alejandro Rodríguez – seen as leading the way in hypertext fiction.

Juan B. Gutiérrez (b. 1973) is one of the leading authors of early hypertext fiction in Colombia. In 1996 he was awarded a grant by the Ministerio de Cultura to fund his work on the hypertext novel *El primer vuelo de los hermanos Wright* (The Wright Brothers' First Flight) and was subsequently awarded two further grants to write his next hypertext novel, *Condiciones extremas*. Gutiérrez's first hypertext novel, *El primer vuelo de los hermanos Wright*, was published in 1997. Visually, the interface to the work is presented in jigsaw format, with pieces of the jigsaw colored yellow and green, or left black, and each jigsaw piece carrying a short phrase. Clicking on a piece of the jigsaw launches a lexia in the main screen, with further rows of jigsaw pieces, each themselves containing new phrases and linking to further lexia, appearing across the top of the screen. The color coding of the pieces relates to two narrative levels within the work: The yellow take us to short chapters within the novel, while the green take us to metanarrative extracts from the work of a fictional author, Solín Deunamor, a Cortazaresque device through which Gutiérrez, much in the manner of Cortázar's Morelli, provides an additional narrative layer to the text.

The jigsaw format immediately figures this work within a wider context of ludic play and again demonstrates similarities with Cortázar's *Rayuela*, as well as with a wider tradition of literary experimentation. In terms of its structure, the work requires the reader to select and move through lexia; as readers, we can choose to piece together our novel through the selection at random and so create our own causal chains. As Sasson-Henry notes, such a structure forces the reader into a more active position in which he or she must work to establish the relationship between the various characters and narrative levels.[9]

Gutiérrez's subsequent hypertext novel, *Condiciones extremas*, has had three main editions, with the first version in 1998, an updated version in 2000 with changes to the user interface, and the third and final version in

2005, using Gutiérrez's own hypertext authoring platform, *Literatrónica*. The novel is set in Bogotá and encompasses three particular timeframes: 1998 (the date of writing of the original version), 2050, and 2090. Through this science fiction narrative, Gutiérrez tells of the appearance of a mutant race and the pollution of Earth, through the perspective of three main characters: businessman Índigo Cavalera, scientist Miranda Macedonia, and mutant Equinoccio Deunamor.

This second hypertext novel is more visual than Gutiérrez's first, and it combines text with comic book images. Made up of approximately 400 possible links, each short lexia and its accompanying images link to two or more possible links. Structurally, the novel allows the reader to follow various pathways and has been described as a "multiform story" (Pajares Tosca 2001:271) and as *arborescente* (García Linares 2014:8). That said, this does not make the novel into a completely dispersed set of lexia; as García Linares notes, the novel throughout maintains narrative continuity (García Linares: 2014:8), and, as Pajares Tosca sums up, "the reader cannot opt for different story lines; she can only choose the order of the same text spaces" (Pajares Tosca 2001:275).

Another notable pioneer in electronic literature has been Jaime Alejandro Rodríguez. In addition to his print texts, including the collections of short stories *Album de cuentos* (1995, Album of Stories) and *Ficción y olvido* (2007, Fiction and Forgetting) and the novels *Debido proceso* (2000, Due Process) and *El infierno de Amaury* (2006, Amaury's Hell), Rodríguez has been one of the leading figures in hypertext literature in Colombia. His first hypertext novel, *Gabriella infinita*, started out as a print text (1995) and was subsequently adapted by Rodríguez into a hypertext novel (1998) and finally a hypermedia narrative in 2005. The resulting work is a complex hypertext narrative, involving a combination of text, images, and audio files that the reader must negotiate to assemble the narrative. The story is located in Bogota, with both the lexia and the visuals making reference to easily identifiable landmarks of that city but is set in a dystopian future in which the city lies in partial ruins and warring gangs wreak havoc across the city. The story is told through the perspective of the protagonist, Gabriella, and focuses on her quest to find her partner, Federico, who has disappeared from her life.

Access to the story is not provided in linear fashion, but instead through three main sections, entitled "Ruinas," "Mudanza," and "Revelaciones," respectively, within which the reader-user must navigate through a rich mixture of text, image, sound, and video files that are presented to us with no immediately obvious teleological structure. Yet at the same time as conveying Gabriella's story, what we see unfold before us, as we navigate through the files and links, is the story of hypertext itself. The story that we navigate is the story of Gabriella's quest to find Federico and at the same time a commentary on the processes of hypertext narrative itself. Thus Gabriella becomes a proxy for the experiences of the reader of hypertext narrative, and her attempts to piece together a story, and to create a logical meaning from the various clues she encounters, mirror the experiences of the reader of hypertext, as he or she pieces together the narrative from the dispersed elements (see Taylor 2010 and chapter 3 of Taylor and Pitman 2012).

Rodríguez's subsequent hypermedia narrative, *Golpe de gracia* (2006, Mercy Blow), again makes use of multiple media formats in the telling of the story. This time, the story takes the format of a whodunit, with the central character, Amaury Gutíerrez, lying dying in a hospital bed. Our role as readers is to navigate the various components of the narrative and piece together the various fragments and clues to work out who has attempted to kill him. The various formats in which these fragments appear include sound files, still images, video files, text, and video games, creating a rich multimedia experience for the reader-user.

From the introductory page, depicting the dying main in a hospital bed, we can then navigate to three sections or "worlds," entitled "Cadáver exquisito" (Exquisite Cadaver) "Línea mortal" (Mortal Line), and "Muerte digital" (Digital Death). "Cadáver exquisito," whose title clearly references the surrealist game of creating unusual and illuminating connections between lexia, presents us with several sound files representing the various visitors to Amaury's deathbed. "Línea mortal" is the most ludic of the three sections and presents us with three computer games through which we have to piece together Amaury's earlier life. In the third section, "Muerte digital," the reader-user is explicitly figured in the role of journalist investigating the death of Amaury and has the task of discovering information, finding suspects, and interviewing them.

Although Rodríguez is undoubtedly a pioneering author in his own right, it is worth mentioning also his initiatives such as *Narratopedia*, a platform for creating and sharing digital narratives, that has given rise to further digital fiction. Works that have been facilitated on the *Narratopedia* platform include *Desencuentros: la vida en clave hipertextual* (Failed Meetings: Life in Hypertextual Codes), which is a collective novel, starting from a base story and generated by multiple authors. Although the mode of production – the bringing together of multiple authors through a wiki format – is perhaps more experimental than Rodríguez's sole-authored works, in terms of the end result itself, *Desencuentros* is predominantly text-based, allowing the reader to click on sections of lexia that are numbered sequentially, but not offering the same richness of multimedia experience as Rodríguez's sole-authored works.

Although Gutíerrez and Rodríguez are unquestionably the leading figures in hypertext narrative within the Colombian literary sphere, other figures who work within different arenas have nevertheless ventured into the literary. Such is the case of Santiago Ortiz (1975), who is more properly a digital artist but who has created some crossover works that engage with the literary. This is the case with Ortiz's *Rayuela* (2013, Hopscotch), which is an online visualization of Cortázar's famous novel (a novel that has itself oft been cited as prefiguring hypertext *avant la lettre*). Here, Ortiz re-presents the text of *Rayuela* in visual format. Presented on a black background, each of the chapters of *Rayuela* appears as a node within a visualization; clicking on each node brings up the text of the chapter, while the multiple links between chapters are illustrated by colored lines criss-crossing the screen.

In a similar fashion, Ortiz's *El cerebro de Edgardo (el inventor de historias)* (Edgardo's Brain [Inventor of Stories]) is a work that generates a narrative via an aleatory algorithm that recombines words and yet maintains grammatical correctness. The work is, as with most of Ortiz's, presented as a visualization, with specific words appearing as nodes that are connected by multiple lines in a constantly shifting diagram. When we click on one of the nodes in the visualization (one of the words) a new phrase or sentence is generated, relating that word to the others around it, and creating new potential phrases each time.

While the above are examples of authors who, for the most part, have created and authored the platforms as well as the content of their work, other authors in the twenty-first century have made use of existing digital platforms for literary purposes. Such is the case of María Paz Ruiz Gil (1978), who has made use of the blog for the purpose of writing microrrelatos in her *Diario de una cronopia* (2009, Diary of a Cronopia), described by the author as a "blog de microrrelatos pop (a blog of pop micro-fictions).

Conclusion

The much-discussed "shadow" of Garcia Marquez – a pervasive factor since the 1970s – is no longer a factor in twenty-first century. García Márquez published his last novel, *Memorias de mis putas tristes* (Memories of My Melancholy Whores), in 2004, a novel already of relatively little importance in the twenty-first century. Journalistic critics and literary scholars continue making references to the magic realism of García Márquez, but primarily in the context of how these twenty-first-century writers have surpassed magic realism. Similarly, the legacy of the Boom is little more than a footnote in these novels of the twenty-first century. Nevertheless, the occasional claims by both critics and the writers themselves about totally rejecting literary tradition in favor of television and the internet as primary sources of formation are sometimes exaggerated in the Colombian case: Franco, Mendoza, and others often refer indirectly to previous texts and occasionally refer directly to the literary tradition. For example, *Paraíso Travel* can be read as a rewriting of Colombia's classic *La vorágine* (1924, The Vortex), and *Cobro de sangre* has resonances of *María* (1867, Maria). Novels such as *La mujer barbuda* by Ramón Illán Baca were written with a playful, parodic awareness of García Márquez. As mentioned earlier, Fernando Vallejo's *Casablanca la bella* is a rewriting of Manuel Mejía Vallejo and Tomás Carrasquilla – a rewriting on the subject of the home in Antioquia. Even the most recent generation of writers born since 1970 (after the Generation of the 1990s), such as Ricardo Silva Romero, refers to the literary play of *Alice in Wonderland*, as in his *Parece que va a llover* (2014, It Seems like It Is Going to Rain), and his novel *Fin* revisits recognizable literary spaces. Even hypertext fictions make references to the literary precedent of Cortázar's *Rayuela* (1963, Hopscotch)

The assassination of Rodrigo Lara Bonilla and the widespread extreme urban violence of the 1980s and 1990s transformed Colombian society and the novel. The legacy of violent 1980s and 1990s has remained, well into the twenty-first century, an important part of trauma and memory being treated in fiction. In the twenty-first century, writers of all three generations are still processing extreme urban violence in their fiction. In the Colombian case, this extreme urban violence deals with a variety of experiences associated with drug trafficking, violent conflict related to drug wars, and political dissidents operating as armed urban and rural guerrillas. The novel of the *sicario* was also the novel of sexual violence identified with the euphemism of the *limpieza*, as seen in Medina Reyes's *Sexualidad de la Pantera Rosa*. This novel of the *sicario* is a major trend for twenty-first century writers in Colombia.

For the Generation of the 1990s – those writers born in 1960s –consisted of a special combination of the totalizing interests of the writing of the Boom and what was postmodern experimentation. For example, Gamboa has totalizing interests, and several of these writers blur the boundaries between popular, commercial literature and more elite literary forms. Efraím Medina Reyes has been the quintessential representative of these multiplicity of interests, for he is a product of popular culture, the experimentalism of the likes of Cortázar, and the writing of Mexico's La Onda, to name the most obvious. *Cobro de sangre* makes several winks at the popular culture of the telenovela at the same time that it interrogates narratives of trauma.

The experience of exile and immigration is a major topic in the writing of the generation of 1990s, as seen in novels such as *Erase una vez el amor pero tuve que matarlo* and *Paraíso Travel*. For writers of this generation, exile and immigration have been associated with traumatic memory. Writers of the previous generations also write about the experience of exile, but usually in a context of an experience less than traumatic. For example, Fernando Vallejo spent much of his writing career in exile in Mexico, but exile and immigration are not central to his writing.[10]

Those authors in Colombia who have ventured into electronic literature tend to do so as not to disengage from contemporary Colombian reality and lose themselves in a globalized hypertextual realm, but, in fact, their work demonstrate concerns for representing contemporary Colombian sociopolitical issues, albeit often filtered through a sci-fi future. Juan B. Gutiérrez's *Condiciones extremas* and its tale of poverty, social injustice, environmental pollution, and corrupt businessmen in a futuristic Bogotá can easily be read as an indictment of contemporary injustices in Colombia of the late 1990s and early 2000s. Similarly, Jaime Alejandro Rodríguez's futuristic Bogotá of *Gabriella infinita* is a dystopian reflection of Colombia under the structural inequalities of late capitalism, while in his *Golpe de gracia* each main character-suspect represents the vested interests and privileges of a certain group within the Colombian establishment.

As with the authors of print texts mentioned above, the shadow of García Márquez is, for these writers, also waning. The most recent reminder of Colombian novelists far surpassing the shadow of García Márquez is the international recognition of the writing of Pablo Montoya. This is not to say that these later writers, along with Montoya, attempt to invent themselves in a literary vacuum or deny the rich literary heritage that informs their writing. Rather, their approach to their literary forebears – García Márquez included – is more of a tongue-in-cheek or knowing one, often including intertextual nods or references to previous generations of writers. What is perhaps most interesting is the way in which these writers negotiate existing literary genres or forebears, both high and low brow – such as the *novela negra* format or Cortazarian literary experimentation – both to embed themselves within a longer trajectory of literary innovation of which their technological innovation is but one chapter and also to question the limitations and possibilities of the technologies themselves.

BIBLIOGRAPHY

Acuna-Zumbado, Eduardo. 2011. "Gabriella infinita: un hipermedio narrativo metafórico y multiforme." *Hispania*, 94, no. 1, 25–34.

Castro, Juan de, Will H. Corral, and Nicholas Birns. *The Contemporary Spanish-American Novel: Bolaño and After.* London, 2013.

Franco, Jorge. *Revista de Crítica Literaria*, Año XXXV, No. 69, Lima-Hanover, First Semester 2009; 207–26.

García Linares, José María. 2014. "Literatrónica: un análisis hypertextual de Condiciones extremas, de Juan B. Gutiérrez." *Álabe: Revista de la Red de Universidades Lectoras*, 9, 1–22. www.revistaalabe.com.

Gutiérrez, Juan B. 1997. *El primer vuelo de los hermanos Wright.* www.literatronica .com/wright/el_primer_vuelo.htm.

    2007. *Condiciones extremas.* www.literatronica.net/src/Pagina.aspx?lng= HISPANIA&opus=1&pagina=1.

Hoyos, Héctor. *Beyond Bolaño: The Global Latin American Novel.* New York: Columbia University Press, 2015.

O'Bryen, Rory. "McOndo, Magical Neoliberalism and Latin American Identity," *Bulletin of Latin American Research* 30, no. 1 (2011): 158–74.

Ortiz, Santiago. 2013. *Rayuela.* http://moebio.com/research/rayuela/.

Pajares Tosca, Susana. 2001. "Condiciones extremas: Digital Science Fiction from Colombia." In *Latin American Literature and Mass Media* , ed. Debra A. Castillo and Edmundo Paz-Soldán, pp. 270–87. New York: Garland.

Pineda Buitrago, Sebastián. *Breve historia de la narrativa colombiana.* Bogotá: Siglo del Hombre Editores, 2012.

Porras, María del Carmen. "La familia Buendía en los tiempos de la globalización: 'Melodrama' de Jorge Franco." *Revista de Crítica Literaria Latinoamericana* Año 35, no. 69 (2009): 207–26.

Rodríguez, Jaime Alejandro. 2005. *Gabriella infinita.* www.javeriana.edu.co/ gabriella_infinita/principal.htm.

    2006. *Golpe de gracia.* http://collection.eliterature.org/2/works/rodriguez_ golpe_de_gracia/.

Ruiz Gil, María Paz. 2009. *Diario de una cronopia.* http://lacomunidad.elpais .com/historias-de-una-cronopia/posts.

Sassón-Henry, Perla. 2007. "Metamorfosis literaria en la era digital: el primer vuelo de los hermanos Wright." *Cuadernos de Literatura*, 12, 142–52.

Shaw, Donald. *The Postboom in Spanish-American Fiction.* Albany: SUNY Press, 1998.

2010. "Golpe de gracia (Coupe de Grâce): a Search for Justice and Independence." In *MACLAS: Latin American Essays* (Foster City: MACLAS), pp. 65–71.

Taylor, Claire. 2010. "De Macondo a Macon.doc: Ficción hipermedia hispanoamericana contemporánea." *Arizona Journal of Hispanic Cultural Studies*, 14, 197–215.

Taylor, Claire, and Thea Pitman. 2012. *Latin American Identity in Online Cultural Production*. New York: Routledge.

Notes

1 See the work of Claire Taylor and Héctor Hoyos in the Bibliography.

2 See Shaw, *The Postboom in Spanish-American Fiction*.

3 This generation in Colombia has proclaimed its identification with television over the canonical modern novels of the West; see Raymond L. Williams's discussion in *The Twentieth-Century Spanish-American Novel*, chapter 13, 206–19.

4 See Franco (2009).

5 For a more elaborate discussion on *Melodrama* as an anti-Buendía family story, see Porras (2009).

6 See Juan de Castro et al. (2013:245).

7 See Paola Fernández Luna, *La palabra*, No. 22, Jan.–June 2013, 29–39.

8 See Camila Segura, "Violencia y melodrama en la novela colombiana contemporánea," 2007, *Revista América Latina Hoy* 55–76.

9 See Sassón-Henry (2007:146).

10 For some of these observations on the Colombian novel of the twenty-first century, Raymond L. Williams is indebted to a dialogue with Marina Nájera, José Medrano, Juan Pablo Bustos, and a group of eight other graduate students in a graduate seminar on the Colombian novel, winter 2015, at the University of California, Riverside, as well as Claire Taylor.

CHAPTER 8

Colombian theater: staging the sociopolitical body

Lucía Garavito

Your body must be heard.

Helene Cixous

The body is the most visible form of the unconscious.

Carl Jung

The symbolic reconfiguration of the sociopolitical body of a displaced, fragmented, dismembered, dispossessed, and invisible nation is a demanding task that Colombian citizens who have faced the devastation caused by various modalities of violence for several generations have begun to undertake.[1] Taking into consideration only the last sixty years, the traditional parties (Liberal and Conservative), the guerrillas (FARC, ELN),[2] the paramilitary (AUC),[3] some sectors of the State Forces (Army and National Police), and the criminal organizations associated with narcotrafficking and *sicariato*[4] have engaged in an ongoing power struggle to control territories, appropriate resources, gain national and international political and social status, and intimidate and assassinate the Colombian citizenry populace to make it comply with their respective agendas.

Various extended periods of intense confrontations throughout the national territory account for much of the devastation afflicting Colombia today. In the first half of the twentieth century, two major events, instigated by the political leadership of both parties in their struggle for power, marked the period known as *La Violencia* (1946–58): the assassination of the charismatic Liberal leader Jorge Eliécer Gaitán on April 9, 1948, and the sectarian rule of Laureano Gómez (Conservative president 1950–3). During the years of *La Violencia*, mounting tensions, competition, and divisiveness between the two parties finally erupted, with the Armed Forces and the Catholic Church taking sides in favor of the Conservative Party. Conservatives actively engaged in rural and urban violence against agrarian movements and workers. Bipartisan brutality against individuals or towns identified with a given political affiliation also took place. The terrorized population experienced displacement as well as loss of property, brewing resentment and a thirst for vengeance. The legacy? Likely more than 200,000 lives lost, a devastated countryside, and deep national wounds.[5]

Statistics provided by the Centro Nacional de Memoria Histórica (CNMH/National Center for Collective Memory) tell a more recent but equally chilling story regarding the so-called armed conflict. Researchers at the CNMH divided the armed conflict into four different stages (1958–82, 1982–96, 1996–2005, 2005–12) characterized, among other factors, by complex changes in the type of violence (from bipartisan to subversive violence), by the increasing political, economic, and territorial power of the guerrillas and paramilitary groups, and by the narcotrafficking boom, all within the context of polarized public opinion and a partially failed state attempting to create a more democratic profile after the constitution of 1991.[6] Between 1958 and 2012, 218,094 people died in Colombia as a result of the armed conflict (81 percent of them civilians). From 1985 to 2012, 150,000 victims were selectively killed by paramilitary forces, guerrillas, the armed forces, and nonidentified armed groups; during the same years, 13,733 people were massacred by these same agents, 25,000 were forcefully disappeared, 5,712,506 were displaced, 10,189 were victims of landmines, and 5,156 were recruited illegally.[7] The documentary *No hubo tiempo para la tristeza* (There Was No Time for Sadness) by the CNMH, dedicated to the memory of the victims, assigns individual stories and faces to the brutal modalities of violence developed during 1995–2005, precisely after the constitutional reform of 1991, which was supposed to open new democratic spaces.[8]

This transgenerational violence invites questions about how human rights violations of this magnitude translate into dramaturgical experience in Colombia. How has Colombian theater responded over the years to the social and political struggles of the country's volatile history? How has it contributed to the exploration and understanding of the relationship between the perpetrators and the victims of violence? How do national events and theater combine to address such pervasive violence in a polarized country now on the verge of either a negotiated peace or a militarized solution to the armed conflict?

There is no doubt that theater has always been a prolific field in which to expose, explore, and question the confluence of forces shaping the nation's inner conflicts. As the forthcoming extensive research by Carlos José Reyes in *Teatro y violencia en dos siglos de historia en Colombia* indicates, theater in Colombia has developed in tandem with the country's violent sociohistorical context. The 200 years of dramaturgy that Reyes examines in his three 900-page volumes cover more than 500 years of history as Colombian playwrights reach as far back as the encounter between indigenous groups and Europeans when selecting topics for their works. By means of an encyclopedic approach to the development of national theater, Reyes provides unparalleled insights into the correlation between the historical event itself and its artistic interpretation, while identifying patterns affecting both history and playwriting.[9] Within this context, it is not surprising that dramaturgy of recent years sustains the focus on history-in-the-making, a trend that has led some to comment tongue-in-cheek that the armed conflict "is the best thing that could have ever happened to theater practitioners in Colombia." This could well be the case.

In 2012 the Ministerio de Cultura (Ministry of Culture), in collaboration with the CNMH, took the unprecedented initiative to research and catalog theatrical activity in Colombia that focused on the country's intense confrontations from 1980 to the present. The resulting report, *Luchando contra el olvido: investigación sobre la dramaturgia del conflicto* (Fighting against Oblivion: Research about the Dramaturgy of Conflict), under the direction of Manuel José Álvarez, is the first systematic academic effort to account for theatrical development connected to the recent decades of violence.[10] In the introduction to this study Marina Lemus Obregón defines the goal of this groundbreaking work: to compile a corpus of dramatic works focused directly or indirectly on the armed conflict and to recognize their contribution to the configuration of *una memoria histórica* (national historical memory) in order to bring forth the experience of the many voiceless victims.[11] Such a task proved to be formidable given the sheer number of works and forms of theatricality developed in Colombia in the last thirty-five years as well as the increasing number of performances presently in progress throughout the nation.[12]

This chapter focuses on a representative slice of both the extensive play production researched by Reyes and the more narrowly defined corpus prefaced by Lemus Obregón and annotated by Pulecio Mariño in order to propose a different angle from which to view the connection between national events and dramaturgy. It expands on their critical framework to suggest that cultural trauma theory provides a useful frame of reference in which to analyze plays focused on events that have marked Colombia's violent history. As defined and explored by Jeffrey C. Alexander, Ron Eyerman, Neil Smelser, and Elizabeth Butler Breese, cultural trauma theory establishes distinctions between individual and collective physical and psychological trauma, on the one hand, and cultural trauma on the other; between devastating individual, group, or national historical events and their subsequent representation:

> As opposed to psychological or physical trauma, which involves a wound and the experience of great emotional anguish by an individual, cultural trauma refers to a dramatic loss of identity and meaning, a tear in the social fabric, affecting a group of people that has achieved some degree of cohesion. In this sense, the trauma need not necessarily be felt by everyone in a community or experienced directly by any or all. While some event may be necessary to establish as the significant cause, its meaning as traumatic must be established and accepted, and this requires time to occur, as well as mediation and representation. Arthur Neal (1998) defines a 'national trauma' according to its 'enduring effects,' and as relating to events 'which cannot be easily dismissed, which will be played over again and again in individual consciousness' and which then become 'ingrained in collective memory.' In this respect, a national trauma must be understood, explained, and made coherent through public reflection and discourse.[13]

It is precisely this "public reflection and discourse" that shapes cultural trauma. For Alexander, "No discrete historical event or situation automatically or necessarily qualifies in itself as a cultural trauma."[14] His observation that "Events are one thing, representations of these events quite another" leads him to foreground the role of carrier groups in the cultural trauma process.[15] These "collective agents," embedded in the social system, have the task of formulating, assigning meaning, and propagating "[collective] symbolic representations – characterizations – of ongoing social events, past, present, and future."[16] Steps associated with the process of "articulation, representation, construction and counter-construction" of significant events that disrupt the social fabric of a given community mark precisely the difference between collective trauma and cultural trauma.[17] In the realm of art, Breese expands, "Through expressive and artistic performance, social actors represent elements of their experience and construct them as traumatic. Painting, dance, song, film, and drama do not accuse in the political or juridical realm; social actors use artistic productions to represent, to speak for, and to construct trauma."[18]

Within this theoretical framework, Colombian theater plays a significant role as an agent or carrier of cultural trauma. It encompasses performative social acts that address topics related to the causes, effects, and circumstances defining the ongoing armed conflict in connection to "the nature of the pain," "the nature of the victim," "the relation of the trauma victim to the wider audience," "and the attribution of responsibility," all crucial elements in the construction of cultural trauma.[19] How do specific individual or collective traumatic experiences configure cultural trauma on the Colombian stage? Are there any specific strategies associated with this process? What kind of stage language has been developed to embody traumatic experiences? How is the body dramaturgically conceived to communicate those experiences? How is the body "seen" and/or "heard" on the stage? What is the connection between body and voice on the (national) stage? How effective are plays in engaging audiences and raising consciousness about violence and its legacy?

A selective corpus of works belonging to different time periods, spanning more than forty-five years of Colombian history, serves as the basis from which to explore these questions: *La maestra* (1968) (The Schoolteacher) by Enrique Buenaventura, *Guadalupe años sin cuenta* (1975) (Guadalupe Countless Years), by La Candelaria, *El sol subterráneo* (1976) (The Sun Underneath) by Jairo Aníbal Niño, *Eart* (1991) by Beatriz Camargo, *El deber de Fenster* (2008) (Fenster's Duty) by Humberto Dorado and Matías Maldonado, and Patricia Ariza's performances.[20] Each of these works focuses on a specific figure associated with a particular kind of sociopolitical stage body: the victim's postmortem body, the reinterpreted/betrayed body, the hidden body, the mourner/healer's intertextual body, and the haunting/haunted bodies of victims and witnesses. The body is the site where individual experience, psychological disruption, memory, national history, armed conflict, and theater intersect to make visible the symbolic map of a wounded and unhealed community reflecting on its own challenges through dramatic reenactment. These works should not be viewed as a simple reconstruction of past or present events but rather as integral to "a [cultural trauma] process that aims to reconstitute or reconfigure a collective identity, as in repairing a tear in the social fabric."[21]

In her work on theater from 1959 to 1975, Claudia Montilla correctly argues that "the true modernization of Colombian theatre begins with the generation of *La Violencia*, around the 1950s," thus circumscribing the so-called *Nuevo Teatro* (New Theater) (post-1975) to one of the stages involved in the development of the *Teatro Moderno* (Modern Theater).[22] Two men stand out as pioneers in the process of configuring a national modern theater, both belonging to the generation of *La Violencia* and both key players in the experimental stage and in the *Nuevo Teatro* phase of theater development in Colombia: Enrique Buenaventura, founder and director of the Teatro Escuela de Cali (1955), later Teatro Experimental de Cali (TEC, 1966),[23] and Santiago García, cofounder of the Casa de la

Cultura in Bogotá (1966), and director and cofounder with Patricia Ariza of the Teatro La Candelaria, also in Bogotá (1968). Their contributions as playwrights, directors, actors, theoreticians, researchers, lecturers, and essayists and the unfolding of their own praxis of *creación colectiva* (collective creation) led them to build a national dramaturgy and turned them into nationally and internationally respected pillars of the theater world.[24] A third theater scholar – the already mentioned Carlos José Reyes, playwright, actor, director, and member of the Colombian Academies of Language and History – also played a pivotal role in the development of modern theater in Colombia and continues to do so as its most renowned researcher.

Buenaventura's and García's commitment to have their work speak for and speak to Colombia's sociopolitical reality led them and their respective groups to develop a corpus of politicized master narratives focused on exposing the ongoing systemic exclusion, marginalization, power struggles, manipulation, betrayal, and victimization of disadvantaged citizens (peasants, workers) by the ruling classes and institutions and by foreign governments. Their *creación colectiva* embodied a dramaturgical response to these concerns through an inclusive, participatory, nonhierarchical approach to making theater, based on improvisation, the cultivation of each actor's creative potential, the use of teamwork, the configuration of an evolving performance text, dialogue with other disciplines and professionals, and a reformulated connection with the public. It is within this context that Buenaventura and the TEC and García and La Candelaria emerged as social agents oriented to the selective construction and articulation of the country's cultural trauma.

Buenaventura's widely acclaimed *Los papeles del infierno* (Papers from Hell), recipient of the Best Play Award at the National Theater Festival in Bogotá in 1968, consists of a collection of one-act plays well known in Colombia but also translated and successfully performed abroad. Diana Taylor quotes the playwright's comment that the collection "is a testimony of twenty years of violence and undeclared civil war" corresponding to *La Violencia*, a historical circumstance that correlates to the fragmented structure of the volume.[25] *La maestra*, considered by many as the first brief play of the set, foregrounds the response of the victim at the core of the encounter between vulnerable, marginalized citizens and repressive state representatives.[26]

According to Nicolás Buenaventura, his father found inspiration to write *La maestra* from Pablo Neruda's poem "Margarita Naranjo (Salitrera 'María Elena'-Antofagasta)" from *Canto general*.[27] There is an intertextual connection between the poem and the play based on the speaking subject, her personal circumstances, and the violence that erupts in her life. The so-called four "W's" of cultural trauma scripts are incorporated into both stories: "What happened? Who were the victims? Who were its perpetrators? And what can be done?"[28] In both cases, the speaker identifies herself from the beginning as a dead woman, an honest, hard-working individual, who starved herself to death and tells her story from the grave. Also, in both cases, her refusal to eat and drink is a psychological and physical response to human rights violations committed by the state and/or its representatives: the forceful and arbitrary detention and disappearance of her husband in the poem, and the equally unjustifiable cruel killing of her father and her subsequent group rape in Buenaventura's play. In both instances, the women's traumatic experiences, voiced through their postmortem bodies, shape narratives of deep individual and social suffering within specific historical contexts: the alliance between a military government and a mining company to oppress workers in the case of Chile, and the climate of repression, dispossession, and abuse by the military in rural areas in Colombia. While in Neruda's poem Margarita Naranjo's experience is inscribed in cultural trauma by the "power of telling," Buenaventura's play offers in addition, through the immediacy of stage representation, the "power of looking . . . the capacity to see and the possibility to make visible" the victim's wounded world.[29]

The play's most striking feature is the Schoolteacher's postmortem status – her opening line is "Estoy muerta" (I am dead) – which confers to her the capacity to look back at her life from her now everlasting present.[30] The two basic scenes of the play, one of her funeral and the other focused on the crimes perpetrated by the Sergeant and his soldiers, take place behind her or to the side and, as indicated in the stage directions, "No debe haber ninguna relación directa entre ella y los personajes de esas escenas. Ella no los ve y ellos no la ven." (There should be no direct interaction between her and the characters in those scenes. She doesn't see them, and they don't see her).[31] Her remoteness places her beyond anyone's reach, reinforced by the presence of the fourth stage wall. The audience – a silent witness who receives her testimony – obtains insight into the perpetrators' political abuses that have dismantled both the teacher's sense of identity and belonging and the life and value system she held dear. Her final journey takes her from fear, shock, self-exclusion from life, silence, depression, and suicide (all symptoms associated with posttraumatic stress disorder) to the recovery of her voice, to her willingness to recall her memories to set the record straight about her father's death and her own passing. She has crossed the boundary between the living and the dead, positioning herself in a liminal, safe (stage) space, "sembrado de hortensias, geranios, lirios y espeso pasto. Es un sitio tranquilo y perfumado" (seeded with hydrangeas, geraniums, lilies and thick grass. It's a quiet and fragrant place). This space is a combination of *locus amoenus* and *temenos*, that is holy, inviolate, allowing her to access her untold inner story.[32]

The presence of a postmortem body, ghost, or spectral figure on the stage is arguably a recurrent feature in cultural trauma theater in Colombia.[33] It seems to address the urgency to re-member marginalized victims in a central position as speaking subjects who bear witness to atrocities they themselves experienced and that have not yet been registered or acknowledged collectively. As Katherine Verdery observes, "Dead bodies have political lives" and become "symbolic vehicles," actively engaged in reconfiguring history.[34] Governments exhume renowned bodies to verify the political accuracy of claims associated with their deaths (Pablo Neruda and Simón Bolívar being the most recent examples). Disappeared bodies found in mass graves in the Southern Cone are submitted as evidence against state crimes and, if possible, contribute to the reconnection of the social fabric through DNA testing. Those in power manipulate dead bodies to control or gain political capital, as in the cases of Eva Perón in Argentina and Hugo Chávez in Venezuela. What do writers do? "Writers retrieve and reanimate bodies through narrative acts of memory," oftentimes to rewrite history, seeking to open for victims the place they have been denied in the context of collective memory and official history.[35]

Buenaventura's Schoolteacher reclaims her presence on the national stage in postmortem status through an act of memory, giving her political agency while foregrounding the metonymic significance of her experience in light of the country's human rights abuses. Since "to remember is to make a body complete,"[36] the play entails both a symbolic exhumation and a dignified ritual of closure, aiming to speak for the thousands of nameless and forgotten victims of the ongoing armed conflict whose stories are not told and whose bodies do not rest in peace in the national territory.

The setting of the play contributes to inscribing the teacher's individual body in the body of the collective. When describing the town in some detail, she emphasizes the pervasive presence of red (in clay, dust, dirt, mud, on people's sandals, on people's and animals' bodies).[37] This visual impression is enhanced by its synesthetic association with the sense of touch and smell to create an ominous atmosphere of violence that reinforces her account of the events. The color red encapsulates the symbolic life cycle of the inhabitants of the town, named "La Esperanza" (Hope) when founded by the Schoolteacher's father. The red soil in which they all are born, live, and are buried may connote both a transgenerational political affiliation (red is the official color of the Liberal political party) and also a collective life defined by the aggression, assassinations, repression, and destruction caused by political violence. Liberals were brutally killed by the *chulavitas* (Conservative Police) in the rural areas during *La Violencia*. In this context, individual confrontations and human rights violations taking place on a stage carry a wider range of resonance for an audience. No wonder that in the area of cultural trauma the relevant question no longer is "Who did this to her?" but instead "What group did this to us?"[38]

Buenaventura's play raises the question of what it means to die in a community devastated by violence. To examine the circumstances surrounding someone's death and the corresponding burial (or lack thereof) opens a significant field of inquiry within cultural trauma studies. In his examination of mourning in Post-Apartheid literature, Sam Durrant observes that crimes against humanity like those that took place in South Africa (and, it should be added, Colombia) have led anthropologists to establish a clear distinction between a "good" death and a "bad" death. While the first one is associated with the natural life cycle and takes place in a familiar and social context that allows preparation and participation in the appropriate rituals, the second one is unexpected, accidental, or brutal and may imply a mutilated body, or a disappeared, irretrievable, or absent body.[39] Durrant's article poses questions that should be addressed by communities particularly affected by this kind of violence. How can those involved respond individually and collectively to these "bad" forms of dying? What kind of literary forms can be developed in a national context to process these type of losses? What cultural expressions may be developed, recovered, or transformed to open new spaces and times for mourning? How can these practices contribute to reestablishing balance in a society or encouraging a feeling of community?

La Candelaria's *Guadalupe años sin cuenta* (*GASC*), the third collective creation of the group, first performed in 1975 and selected as winner of the Casa de las Américas Award for best play in 1976, formulates its own question in this regard. The making of the play involved extensive research on Guadalupe Salcedo – Liberal leader of the *Llanos* – on the guerrillas of this region, and on the music of the area (*corridos*); this also entailed in-depth consultation with historians, sociologists, and other experts on agrarian struggles.[40] The play consists of a prologue and thirteen episodes, with the prologue and the last episode confronting the official and unofficial versions of Salcedo's death. According to the official version, the authorities were forced to kill Salcedo in self-defense when he refused to surrender as requested and fired against them instead. The unofficial account maintains that Salcedo was betrayed by the authorities, who shot him as he was surrendering peacefully under the armistice granted by the government. With humor and irony, *GASC* shows how witnesses and facts are manipulated during the investigation to obstruct justice in favor of the official version of events.

Salcedo himself, however, is an absent character in the play: "Si Guadalupe Salcedo/no aparece en mi cantar/su sombra nombra mi canto/del moriche hasta el palmar" (If Guadalupe Salcedo/is not present in my singing/his shadow names my song/from the moriche tree to the palm-covered area.)[41] Yet this *llanero* leader haunts characters and actions on the stage, just as he has haunted Colombian historiography on the national scene given the questionable circumstances surrounding his death. Was he a victim of State repression, or was he a *guerrillero*? The play answers that question for the audience.

Salcedo is present metonymically in the play through a collective protagonist, the *llaneros* (like Jerónimo Zambrano) who share his fight against the wave of violence sponsored by the Conservative government in power, and who naively believe that the urban leaders of the Liberal Party are willing to support their struggle. The structure of the play, a *contrapunteo* of scenes and songs with Brechtian influence, juxtaposes rural and urban events focused on the fighters' challenges in the *Llanos* that contrast with the individual and institutional political power games and secret negotiations that take place in the city.

According to the record, *GASC* has been performed more than 1,500 times in the most diverse settings of Colombia. What is the secret behind its success? For Carlos José Reyes, the effective articulation of historical events and stage language, together with the play's carefully wrought structure, offer a partial explanation. He adds, however, that its continuous relevance may also respond to the ongoing conflict between the State forces and the guerrillas, a conflict resistant (so far) to being resolved through any lasting peace agreement.[42] For Patricia Ariza, the play keeps alive the memory of the many times in Colombian history when, after an armistice or surrendering of weapons by insurgents, the elite have responded with betrayal and death to those who trusted their word.[43]

Expanding on these comments from the perspective of cultural trauma, the wide acclaim *GASC* has received in the context of Colombian theater may be due to the fact that it has effectively created and enacted drama-turgically a master narrative that exposes the divided sociopolitical body of a nation repeatedly engaged in a traumatic pattern of trust and betrayal. Carlo Tognato discusses the underlying pattern that is at stake in social relations in the country. For Tognato, the discourse of the *hacienda* – still operating in Colombia – implies

> a system of binary oppositions that define what is legitimate in social life and what instead must be resisted. The attributes on the positive side make up the *patrón/peón* code, whereas those on the negative side identify the *bandit* code. . . . If the *patrón* is the head of the social body, the *peón* is its hand and can claim dignity until he fulfills his own function. On the other hand, the bandit is the *peón* who decided to rebel against social, and therefore, natural harmony.[44]

GASC focuses on a moment of rupture of this paternalistic model when the *patrón* (be it the Conservative government in power, the Liberal Party, the bourgeoisie, and/or the Church) betrays the code of support, protection, and respect toward the *peón*, who awakens to his own agency to question the established "natural" order and to defend his life and rights. It is at this point in the construction of the sociopolitical body that the *peón*'s identity is reinterpreted by the *patrón* and he becomes an outlaw (*guerrillero*).

The play articulates a series of binary oppositions derived from the *patrón/peón* relationship: written language/oral language, deceit/betrayal, repression/subversion, historical amnesia/collective memory, partisan mind-set/collective mind-set, power from above/power from below, urban context/rural context. *GASC* undermines the authority of the ruling powers, of the written word (legal documents and letters), and of the official versions of history while empowering social movements, oral discourse, and the reappropriation of history by the communities shaping it.

The *corridos llaneros* play multiple roles as subversive, mnemonic devices in the construction of cultural trauma and consequently should not be viewed simply as entertaining folkloric expressions. The musicians announce that the main objective of the play is precisely "les vamos a interpretar/ historias que nadie cuenta/que ocurrieron de verdad" (We will interpret for you/Stories nobody tells/And that truly happened).[45] In the tradition of the genre, the *corridos* in *GASC* reinstate thematically the theme of surrender and betrayal. Some give specific information about time, place, facts, and protagonists ("Corrido de los años sin cuenta," Corrido of the countless years; "Corrido de las razones diferentes," Corrido of the different reasons). Others serve as narrative devices to provide links in an otherwise episodic story line ("Corrido de las ilusiones," Corrido of the illusions; "Corrido de la reunión llanera," Corrido of the meeting at the *Llanos*). There are those that comment on the action, interpret it or give some kind of warning ("Corrido de la esperanza que no llega," Corrido of hope that never arrives; "Canción de los recuerdos," Song of memories; "Corrido 'El papel aguanta todo,'" Corrido 'paper can take anything'). And some are addressed to the public to invite it to reflect on the stage events, in a clear Brechtian fashion ("Corrido del intermedio," Corrido for the intermission; "Corrido final," Final corrido). All contribute to dismantling the political metadrama set up by the State to discredit the *llaneros'* political struggle and to reinterpret the identity of their leader and the nature of their revolt.

GASC moves backward and forward temporally in mapping the collective wounds of Colombia's sociopolitical body by developing a narrative that makes it possible to represent and locate symbolically recurrent traumatic events taking place nationwide. For Ron Eyerman, an event may be traumatic in retrospection, "mediated through recollection and reflection."[46] But it is also true that recurrent struggles reflecting a sociopolitical rupture within a community may come to configure cumulatively a national trauma that becomes "ingrained in collective memory."[47] Salcedo's haunting figure in terms of his political struggle and "bad" death hovers over the past, the present, and the future of Colombia's landscape, with La Candelaria's play establishing a connection between the past and the present by means of stage representation. As Santiago García has been heard to remark playfully before the performances of *GASC*, "¿Qué podemos hacer si el país se nos ajusta a la obra una vez tras otra?" (What can we do if the country keeps acting out our plots in real life?) Deaths like Salcedo's keep making the news.

In the construction of cultural trauma as it relates to the relationship between the State and oppositional forces in Colombia, *GASC* is an obligatory point of reference. As indicated in the pun of the play's title, *The 50s*, in Spanish *los años cincuenta*, is a play on words with the phrase *años sin cuenta*, the "countless years." In this time frame, Salcedo's metonymic body gains a collective dimension in an increasingly complex, multivocal, and changing political context where old and new social actors and State forces (FARC, ELN, Army, Police, paramilitary, narcotraffickers) reinterpret and redefine their identities. The trust/betrayal pattern that sustains the narrative continues to be played out on all sides in front of an exhausted audience of citizens.[48]

Salcedo was a well-known figure in Colombia at the time of his "bad" death; vested parties conveniently have ignored many nameless others, both at the time of their demise and afterwards. The Banana Massacre is a brutal episode that has haunted official historiography in Colombia since its occurrence on December 6, 1928. What are the facts? All sources pinpoint the detonating factor as the workers strike on November 12th in Ciénaga (Magdalena) against the United Fruit Company (known as La Frutera de Sevilla). The workers' petition to increase salaries, to change hiring practices, to receive paid Sundays off, to have indemnization for accidents, and to improve the condition of their living quarters went unheard and unresolved by the American company. United Fruit considered the workers' requests subversive and even illegal according to Law 69 (*Ley heroica*) deliberately designed on October 30, 1928, to limit the activity and power of unions. The workers' demands for fair labor conditions met the opposition of the company and of the Conservative government of the time. President Miguel Abadía Méndez ordered General Carlos Cortés Vargas to protect American lives and the property of United Fruit and to restore public order in Ciénaga. Cortés Vargas succeeded in doing so by firing against unarmed women, children, and workers who had gathered peacefully in the area to make their concerns visible.[49]

At this point, fact and fiction intertwine to shape the narrative of the massacre, reflecting the biased concerns of the official parties involved in investigating and analyzing the events. Motivations, justifications, circumstances, and the number of people killed have all been highly debated.[50] How many people were actually killed? Dozens? Hundreds? Thousands? Which version of the truth merits belief? As Gonzalo Sánchez, director of the CNMH commented to a reporter eighty years later, "No se afane con la cifra, créale a lo que esta masacre simboliza para la violencia en Colombia" (Don't worry about the numbers, just give credence to what this massacre symbolizes for the violence in Colombia).[51]

For many years, political interests led to excluding the Banana Massacre from the official history of the country and from the collective memory of generations. Jairo Aníbal Niño's *El sol subterráneo* moves in the opposite direction.[52] Niño, a poet, short-story writer, director of numerous theater schools in several major cities in Colombia, and playwright, does not focus on the reconstruction of the Banana Massacre itself; rather, he zooms in on its transgenerational value as cultural trauma. Within the realist tradition, this one-act play first performed at the Teatro Libre in Bogotá in 1976 under the direction of Ricardo Camacho centers on the arrival of a teacher (Tulia Romero) and her handicapped sister (Amalia) to her new post in a small town, later identified (implicitly) as Ciénaga. The local government has assigned them a house. As they arrange their few pieces of furniture and belongings, they receive two visitors that catalyze the action: one, Encarnación de Caldera, a feisty neighbor familiar with the town's collective memory; the other, the *Teniente* (Lieutenant), a brutal, dictatorial, threatening, and repressive force who exerts total control over the town. These four characters set in motion a second-generation trauma narrative since, many decades later, they are experiencing the effects of the infamous massacre physically and psychically.

Gabriele Schwab observes that "In violent stories, the personal is inseparable from the collective and the political."[53] The house is the space in which these dimensions converge in *El sol subterráneo*. Although no stage directions describe it, Amalia's opening words capture its unsettling atmosphere. She finds the house "*rara*" (strange), "*sin una seña*" (without a trace) of ever having been inhabited, as if it had "envejecido sola" (aged by itself).[54] Her intuition takes her a step further to comment on the town where "algo debe estar pasando" (something must be happening) due to the omnipresence of the Army in the region.[55] The final step in this expanding space is the world itself through a reference to a "globo" (globe),[56] one of Tulia's teaching aids. The macrocosmic symbolic significance of the house, the characters, and the events to come is thus spelled out, with the house standing for the sociopolitical body of the nation.

The house is the point where two mutually exclusive histories intersect. Through Encarnación, the newcomers Tulia and Amalia receive a quick and terrifying lesson on the town's political history. It is a history that has been transmitted orally from parents to children, to the extent that when a child is born, he or she is born already knowing it, "como si llegara al mundo con esa conciencia pegada en las tripas" (as if he came into the world with that knowledge inscribed in his DNA).[57] At the other extreme, government forces (the Teniente as a representative member of the army) back a highly selective and opposing configuration of history that responds to their interests; this is evidenced by the Teniente's warning to Tulia: "No se puede salir ni un milímetro del programa oficial" (You cannot deviate even a millimeter from the official program).[58] His order carries the implicit threat that surveillance, persecution, imprisonment, and death await those who oppose the State's rulings.

Encarnación points toward the symbolic role of the house in this second-generation trauma narrative when she explains to the two sisters that as a result of the Army's firing upon the banana workers, hundreds of dead bodies were left on the plaza the day of the massacre. Although some were taken in a train to an unknown destination, those who did not fit into the cars were placed in a big hole and buried. "Debajo de esta casa están enterrados muchos de los trabajadores asesinados el seis de diciembre de 1928" (Underneath this house are buried many of the workers assassinated on December 6, 1928) she says.[59] Terrified, Tulia "Empieza a caminar como si lo hiciera sobre frágiles flores de cristal o como si sus pies tuvieran heridas abiertas que apenas soportaran el contacto con la tierra" (starts walking as if on fragile crystal flowers or as if her feet had open wounds that could barely handle contact with the ground).[60]

Encarnación's revelation exposes not just a historical fact but the psychological dimension of the house as the body of the nation. It opens the door to the crypt that hides the government's criminal actions. Building on Nicolas Abraham and Maria Torok's work, Schwab develops a connection between secret spaces in the psyche, unresolved trauma, and their effect on the next generation. The crypt – defined as a "psychic tomb" for "undead ghosts," as a "psychic space fashioned to wall in unbearable experiences, memories or secrets" – has "'phantom effects' that haunt the children of parents who have lived through a traumatic history."[61] The secrets enclosed in such a crypt may be conscious or even shared, but what is important is that they have been silenced or considered taboo.[62] For Schwab, "this theoretical work is well suited to include larger communities and peoples with collective traumatic histories."[63] *El sol subterráneo* stages this process metaphorically in connection with the Banana Massacre as a cultural trauma. By excluding (repressing) this national event from official history and by disappearing its victims and/or burying them in an inaccessible space of the nation's sociopolitical body (areas under the floor as symbols for the unconscious), the State has relegated one of the most violent episodes of Colombian history to the unreachable chambers of the nation's psyche, and while doing so, has passed the unacknowledged and unresolved conflict to future generations.

What does the next generation do with the nation's buried secrets and oppressive sociopolitical tensions it has inherited? Finding a voice is supposed to be the most effective means to "work through" repressed traumatic histories for individuals and nations.[64] The intrinsic dynamic of the play moves in this direction. Encarnación identifies Facundo Aguilar, a witness to the tragedy, as the voice haunted by the experience of the Banana Massacre. He embodies the living memory of this event that must be taken out of the crypt, passed on transgenerationally and made public. It is true that memory brings empowerment, but it is also true that "perpetrators silence history."[65] As the confrontation between the Teniente and the three women escalates, with language as the only weapon Amalia, Encarnación, and Tulia can use to oppose him, the Teniente repeats Cortés Vargas's action and kills Amalia. She has the same inner strength of the banana workers who challenged the government and United Fruit, but she is also just as vulnerable and powerless. The cycle of violence continues when Encarnación kills the Teniente.[66]

Theater also enables such transgenerational trauma to be addressed, inspiring people to grieve and heal in the process. In the case of the play *Eart*, a natural disaster serves as the historical referent underlying the trauma. *Eart* was written by Beatriz Camargo, actress, playwright, founder, and director of the Teatro Itinerante del Sol (Itinerant Theater of the Sun) and of the Escuela de Biodrama (Biodrama School) in Villa de Leyva (Boyacá).[67] The volcano Nevado del Ruiz (5,321 meters, 17,457 feet, tall) erupted on November 13, 1985, burying the town of Armero (Tolima). That night, shortly after 9:00 P.M., it exploded unexpectedly, sending first ashes and then an unstoppable, swiftly moving combination of water, rocks, mud, and debris down the slopes of the mountain. This covered the town like a blanket, killing 85 percent of the population (about 28,000 of its inhabitants). As described by *Time* writer George Russell,

> Most horrifying of all was the plight of those who were trapped, still living, in the mud. Many were buried up to their necks; some had their mouths stopped with filth, so that they could not cry for help. Sometimes the buried survivors were still locked in gruesome embrace with the dead. One was Omaira Sánchez, 13, who remained up to her neck in ooze two days following the disaster. When the mudslide struck, Omaira was washed up against her aunt, who grabbed hold of her. The aunt died, but kept her grip, even after rigor mortis had set in. Finally, after rescuers worked fruitlessly for 60 hours, Omaira died of a heart attack. In the days after the disaster, one doctor estimated that there were at least 1,000 living victims still trapped in the morass.[68]

This catastrophe was televised as national and international organizations made efforts to rescue victims and provide humanitarian assistance. Many denounced the carelessness of local authorities, their total disregard for scientific studies warning of the impending tragedy, their refusal to give orders to evacuate the town on a timely basis, and the delay in receiving and distributing the aid offered. Paraphrasing García Márquez's famous title, Armero is considered "a chronicle of a death foretold" in the national scene.

Since as Alexander observes, "To transform individual suffering into collective trauma is cultural work,"[69] cultural trauma narratives must carry out a symbolic reconstruction of events, a reconstruction that does not aim at factual accuracy but at exposing, redefining, recontextualizing, and assigning group significance to the original wounds. Camargo has looked to the language of ritual that integrates classical mythology in general, and American indigenous mythologies in particular, to explore the role of the feminine in connection with past and present cultural wounds in her dramaturgy. In *Eart*, the transition from individual and collective trauma to cultural trauma takes place through the intertextual body of Eart, a symbolic figure in whom mythical, historical, indigenous, and folkloric allusions coalesce to foreground women's relationship with memory, their resilience through time, and their role in mourning and healing "bad" deaths.

The protagonist's name is an anagram of the Spanish word for art (*arte*) as well as a reference to the English word *earth*. Eart is an old woman who wanders from place to place looking for her disappeared daughter (Omaira) while selling herbs to cure all kinds of illnesses: "¡Roomerooo! ¡Rooomeroo! ¡Jarilla! ¡Jarilla! ¡La savia, el saúco, el romero! Ajenjo, hinojo, toronjil y perejil ... Sumo de hojas de yerbabuena para la sarna, tiña y culebrilla. Calabacito amargo con ron para arrojar los tumores" (Rooosemary! Rooosemary! Jarilla! Jarilla! Sap, elder, rosemary! Wormwood, fennel, lemon balm ... Juice of spearmint leaves for scabies, ringworm, and shingles).[70] Her monologue frames, with total disregard for chronology, a series of scenes that seem to respond to a psychological inner rhythm, with displacements in time and space. Although Eart's language is poetic and oniric, with touches from old Spanish *romances* and lullabies, it is also ruptured, fragmented, and even cryptic, but it helps her to articulate her traumatic loss: "¿Hay alguien por ventura que está despierto?/¿Llegaron o estaban?/Oculto es, oculto es./Solo lo saben las almas de los muertos/¿Soy alguien yo?/¿Soy esta que soy?/¿Soy solo acaso la sombra inmensa de mis lágrimas?" (Is anybody awake by any chance?/Have they arrived or were they here?/It's hidden. It's hidden./Only the souls of the dead know./Am I someone?/Am I who I am?/Am I only the immense shadow of my tears?)[71]

Camargo counts on the audience's symbolic competence to read the intertextual body of Eart, an insight that should lead to appreciating the wider resonance of her plight. Udo J. Hebel suggests a new way to approach allusions as "evocative manifestation[s] of intertextual relationships" and "metonymic fragments of the intertextual déjà."[72] For Hebel, "a successful allusion ... always evokes theoretically unlimited and unpredictable associations and connotations. ... Each allusion becomes 'the apex of an associative paradigm.'"[73] In order to do so, cotextualization (inserting the allusion into the intertextual dimension) and contextualization (inscribing the text in the corresponding social, historical, political, and cultural framework) work together.[74]

In Camargo's monologue, the first process reveals the interweaving of mythical and folkloric dimensions in Eart while the second leads to a recognition of the significance of this conflated figure in the field of cultural trauma in Colombia and Latin America. Cotextualization evokes the Greek myth of Demeter-Proserpina/Kore as intertext, with the goddess of the harvest, grain, and fertility, searching for her daughter, inquiring as to her whereabouts, and mourning her loss. In Latin American indigenous and folk culture, Eart triggers an additional association with a palimpsestic *La Llorona* (The Weeping Woman). Although usually understood as a woman condemned to wander close to rivers and other waters' edges searching for her drowned children, she has also been associated with Chicomecoatl, the corn goddess who "held power over the people through her ability to provide a renewed source of sustenance and nourishment necessary for life."[75] The layered complexity of this symbol allows Camargo to appropriate *La Llorona* in a sui generis way, discarding her destructive traits (selfishness, madness, and criminal intent, depending upon which version is selected) but maintaining Chicomecoatl's maternal features as a life-giving goddess, like Demeter.

Contextualization, on the other hand, foregrounds and combines both Eart's healing dimension and her historical significance. Her knowledge of the natural world and of the medicinal properties of plants reveals her association with ancient indigenous healing practices in the Andean world.[76] Since antiquity, cultures have interpreted disease as a loss of soul, as the interference of a harming agent, or as a transgression (such as breaking an individual or collective taboo).[77] According to Irene Silverblatt, this was also the case in the Andean region in which an ideal society was described in terms of balance, equilibrium, and reciprocity between the individual and his or her world. A disease (or "sin" in the language of the *cronistas*) meant a rupture of this universal balance, a breaking of the code of social interaction with the ancestors, the community, or the natural world:

> this notion of disease was applied not only to the condition of the individ-
> ual, but to the condition of society as a whole ... the same sins that caused
> personal sickness also produced natural disasters-floods, ice, hail-storms –
> which affected the entire community. By disturbing the harmony of the
> universe, individuals not only harmed themselves, but could bring about
> calamities that damaged the collectivity of which they were part.[78]

Within this context, the connection between the body of the individual and the body of the community links the natural disaster of Armero to an indigenous worldview where healers are called upon to restore harmony. In this plays historical allusions to remote and recent events of Latin America's collective memory identify the region's open wounds in need of healing and point to Eart as the depositary of these memories and of the suffering they have inflicted on communities and on women, in particular. Kidnappings, disappearances, "bad" deaths, and political repression, as exemplified in Argentina's dirty war (1976–82), the encounter between Spain and America in 1492, the Thousand Days War in Colombia in 1903, the conquest of Mexico in the sixteenth century, and the bloody takeover of the Palace of Justice in Bogotá in 1986 – all translate into a sick sociopolitical body in need of healing.[79]

Camargo's play foregrounds the transformative role of the feminine within the context of national trauma. Through the intertextual body of Eart, the play seems to propose an urgency to activate ancestral multicultural wisdom and collective memory to recover the connection between the mythic, the poetic, and the ordinary to heal a world in conflict. As healer, she transmutes personal, individual, and collective pain into poetic performance to bring equilibrium to a world in crisis. Her on-stage rituals evoke communion and bring out the participatory atmosphere of the mise-en-scéne. The closing scene of the play integrates life-generating symbols (boy, stone, bread, doves, and dawn) while changes in light and music contribute to evoke a sacred space where the audience perceives the healer's poetic chanting with a changed perspective. Camargo represents just one of the multiple paths envisioned by Colombian women committed to the peaceful reconstruction of the country's social fabric.

While *Eart* approaches cultural trauma from a diachronic perspective, *El deber de Fenster* focuses on a specific place and time in history: the municipalities of Trujillo, Riofrío, and Bolívar from 1989 to 1992. Written by Humberto Dorado and Matías Maldonado, winner of the Fanny Mikey Award in 2009, and first performed in Bogotá in 2010 at the Teatro Nacional Fanny Mikey[80] under the direction of Nicolás Montero and Laura Villegas, this play focuses on the massacre of Trujillo (Valle) where 342 people were killed.[81] Documents made available by the Grupo de Memoria Histórica de la Comisión Nacional de Reparación y Reconciliación (National Commission for Reparation and Reconciliation's Group for Historical Memory) under the coordination of Gonzalo Sánchez, archival material from various sources, a book written by the people of Trujillo, national newspaper and magazine articles, photographs, interviews with direct and indirect participants in the incident, and images from televised news and other programs provide the material for structuring the play. Together, they tell the story of how officers from the armed forces (Army and Police) worked together with the paramilitary and narcotraffickers in counterinsurgency operations against the guerrillas (ELN) in the area of Trujillo, Riofrío, and Bolívar by bribing informants, displacing families and communities, torturing suspects with unspeakable atrocities, and brutally killing civilians wrongly accused of being accomplices of the ELN. One of the victims, Father Tiberio Fernández, was a beloved local Jesuit priest actively involved in community work, in denouncing the systematic killings, and in pacifying the region.

Why focus on this specific massacre to write a play? In addition to the enormity of the crimes and their humanitarian and sociopolitical reverberations, Dorado and Montero considered the topic to be current: The wounds remained open after almost twenty years, the perpetrators were still fugitives, and justice still needed to be served. They deemed it essential for the government and the whole nation to face an episode of this magnitude with growing indignation instead of impunity and indifference, as had been the case.[82] In the words of a reporter, "Fenster se parece a muchos colombianos que ven la masacre de Trujillo como algo lejano, prácticamente inexistente" (Fenster resembles many Colombians who see the massacre of Trujillo as something very far away, practically non-existent).[83] According to Alexander, crimes of this nature may fail to maintain resonance in a wider context because of the lack of social actors to integrate them into a cultural trauma process through their "resources, authority and interpretive competence."[84]

In *El deber de Fenster* Dorado and Maldonado reconstruct metaphorically the tortured, mutilated disappeared body of a haunted nation through the work of Edel Fenster, a German editor who – from the viewpoint of the future – must work on a documentary based on disquieting material he receives by mail (a metal trunk) visibly marked "11.007," corresponding to the case number of the massacre of Trujillo in the Comisión Interamericana de Derechos Humanos (Inter-American Commission for Human Rights). This material belongs to or is related to the key witness in the case, Daniel Arcila Cardona, an Army informer, who was extremely familiar with the perpetrators, the victims, and the sociopolitical and economic dynamics of the region. Fenster's duty is to reconstruct as faithfully as possible the events of the Trujillo massacre and Arcila's role in it by weighing critically the information contained in a collection of documents in conjunction with the accompanying evidence included in the trunk (blood-stained tools and clothes, a hammer, nail clippers, pliers, a blowtorch, a pound of salt, and a cello case). His studio has three screens: a big one (center stage) and a smaller one to either side. In addition to sparse furniture, the room includes all the necessary high-tech video and audio equipment to display on these screens photographs, texts of various kinds, newsreels, and reports or comments made by the victims' relatives and friends, witnesses, officials, or researchers in the case. This studio setup allows Fenster to read aloud, record, trace names and incidents, and compare and contrast the heterogeneous corpus of evidence submitted to him. He has flexibility to introduce changes in chronology and location as required for his understanding of the events. The result? The audience is engulfed in a thorough account of the systematic killings affecting the region.

The play develops around the veracity (or lack thereof) of Arcila's manuscript, comments, and official testimony concerning the protagonists, incidents, and circumstances surrounding the massacre he witnessed. Arcila is the "ghost writer" behind the play in more senses than one. Dorado comments that the unexpected finding of Arcila's manuscript, shocking in all its details, incited his team to proceed with their dramaturgical project, with the informer's text being the golden document that would clarify the events. Montero observes that the play follows this manuscript in its trajectory to be either discredited or officially recognized as the key evidence in the case to indict the corresponding perpetrators, Urueña (Army) and Berrío (Police).[85] Dorado and Maldonado's handling of the documentary theater format with its use of authentic material and real-life characters (with the exception of Fenster) or actors who represent them, plus the integration of updated technological innovations that appeal directly to the audience's role as witness, convincingly validate the authenticity of Arcila's claims while revealing the identity of the perpetrators.[86] In addition, the playwrights' fragmented approach to the narrative through a puzzle-like structure that juxtaposes images and aural texts serves well the metaphoric mirroring of the victims' broken bodies and the broken body of the nation.

The powerful impact of screen images and oral material is enhanced on stage by various "innocent" props that reveal their sinister nature in the process of deconstructing everyday life as we know it. The tools included in the trunk are all legal evidence of the torture instruments used during the massacre, even the nail clippers. The cello case holds a chainsaw that mutilated the victims and/or cut their bodies in pieces before throwing them into the Cauca River. The *moras* (berries) that Fenster enjoys as an exotic delicacy evoke blood spilled over the studio when accidentally cut with the chainsaw. The water hose Fenster uses to fix himself drinks recalls associations with the hose used to drown victims. Violence implies a resemantization of everyday reality with objects, disclosing their unsuspected lethal potential when placed in criminal hands.

The deconstruction and reconstruction of bodies and identities lie at the heart of the play with Arcila being the haunted informer whose story haunts the nation. Since the play revolves and evolves around him, his dramaturgical body status should be qualified. In addition to his synecdochic presence through his manuscript, belongings, screen images, and voice-over, Arcila is diegetically present through the other characters' discourses. However, Arcila also "speaks" through Fenster when Fenster quotes from his manuscript, which could be considered a type of channeling. To add to the complexity, as the play unfolds, the audience learns that Arcila has been brutally tortured and killed, and yet he materializes on the stage although he does not interact with Fenster. He disappears just as mysteriously as he had appeared. In all these instances Arcila seems to be one dimension away – a ghost.

Arcila's status as ghost on the stage responds appropriately to his sociopolitical standing. The experiences of the Southern Cone have shown that in a military context, state forces are responsible for escalating a process of ghost formation in such a way that they "replace one set of ghosts with another."[87] Avery Gordon explains that such a government may tend to see ghosts everywhere when assigning suspicious roles and activities to ordinary citizens who consequently become their target to haunt. Going a step further, "Disappearance is a state-sponsored procedure for producing ghosts to harrowingly haunt a population into submission."[88] The massacre of Trujillo fits this pattern. The counterinsurgency operation devised and executed by Urueña and Berrío with the support of the paramilitary and narcotraffickers "saw" members of the community as accomplices to the guerrillas and disappeared them (and others) as befitted their own private agendas. "Bad" deaths account for 342 bodies turned into ghosts on the national stage and are symbolically presented through hangers and empty chairs on the theatrical space.

Ghosts have roles to play in unresolved mysteries or untold stories. Kathleen Brogan observes that "Through the agency of ghosts, histories that have in some way been threatened, erased, or fragmented are recuperated and revised."[89] In these cases, a socially marginal character becomes an agent whose discourse challenges official accounts of history by recovering episodes that have been conveniently ignored, distorted, or repressed.[90]

Arcila's ghost in *El deber de Fenster* answers this call of history. By writing the account of the events he witnessed, the supposed liar, an uneducated sociopath with a paranoid, aggressive, and dependent personality, succeeds in reconstructing his own body and identity, along with the bodies and identities of the individuals massacred.[91] Through his narrative, those who have been disposed of, overlooked, and/or discredited by officials and professionals in charge of the investigation recover their standing, dignity, and humanity as social subjects. As Arcila's story gains credibility, the opposition's claims are deconstructed. As perpetrators like Urueña, Berrío, the paramilitary, and narcotraffickers literally dismember the community with their chainsaws (*motosierras*), Arcila remembers that very same community, including himself. As the ghost story behind the judicial system's officially accepted story surfaces, cultural trauma is embodied on the stage.

The *"Mano Poderosa"* (Powerful Hand) image and ritual that opens and closes the play, one that stays in the background throughout the performance, points to Fenster as a figure who consecrates his work on cultural trauma to a transcendental vision. Conjuring up the victims of the massacre through the reconstruction of the events means providing a holy ground on which they can be respected, listened to, and acknowledged. Metaphorically speaking, such practices in the literary context are viewed as "secondary burials."[92] In cases of "bad" deaths when circumstances have not allowed for a proper funeral to take place, "'laying to rest' can take the form of a narrative reconstruction of the past that creates of its readership a haunted community."[93]

In fact, "the modus operandi of a ghost is haunting," understood as a "sociopolitical-psychological state" that establishes a connection between the past and the present.[94] In an ironic and subversive twist, Arcila's story now haunts the perpetrators, their accomplices, and the institutions associated with them. But the victims' account of the massacre of Trujillo should also haunt a nation that must face the task of integrating its untold stories in order to reweave its torn social fabric. For many decades, in spite of the ongoing violence, the pervading feeling in Colombia was "Aquí no ha pasado nada" (Nothing has happened here), an expression of denial famously picked up in dramas like *Golpe de suerte* (Lucky Strike) and *El Paso* (The El Paso Bar) by La Candelaria.[95] Although more research is needed in this field, Carlo Tognato points out that solidarity in Colombia was a slow process that has only accelerated since 2008.[96] Research by Myriam Jimeno complements this view by questioning assumptions about Colombians' indifference and amnesia regarding violence, proposing instead that what has been taking place is the configuration of "emotional communities," groups where ethics and political action coalesce as victims share their stories with others.[97] *El deber de Fenster* embodies a step in this direction through a ghost story that turns out to be history.[98]

Patricia Ariza, founder and Director of the Corporación Colombiana de Teatro (National Corporation of Theater), co-founder of La Candelaria, playwright, actress, poet, and organizer of the Festival Alternativo de Teatro (Alternative Theater Festival) in Bogotá and of the Festival de Mujeres en Escena (Festival of Women on the Stage), creates the type of emotional community identified by Jimeno through the fusion of sociopolitical activism and performance work. Her initiatives address the fourth question of cultural trauma. To the extent that the violent events, victims, and perpetrators may have been identified, "What can be done now?" Ariza envisions the need to reconfigure a different narrative of the country's violence, one built by victims and theater practitioners who in close collaboration repair the country through symbolic work involving the arts. By working with marginalized and displaced populations, with survivors and victims of the armed conflict, in conjunction with actors, singers, dancers, and musicians from various regions of the national territory, Ariza has generated what she calls "an aesthetics of resistance" that has opened a public stage for the wounded body of the nation.

Although Ariza's concern with human rights and the role of women vis-à-vis the violence of a politically oppressive state are integral to her life's work, her numerous performances and various projects oriented to raise public awareness about political violence, to engage and empower the victims themselves, and to clear a space for peace have given particular visibility to her initiatives and have made her deserving of special recognition.[99] Most recently (October 2014), she was selected as the recipient of the prestigious Gilder/Coigney International Theatre Award by the League of Theater Women for her commitment to use theater as a vehicle for raising sociopolitical consciousness in connection to women and the peace process.[100]

Performances such as *Huellas, mi cuerpo es mi casa* (Footprints, My Body Is My House), *Paz haré la* (Peace I Will Make It), *Mujeres en la Plaza. Memoria de la ausencia, ¿Dónde están?"* (Women in the Plaza. Memory of Absence. Where Are They?), *Soma Mnemosine 2013* (Body of Memory2013), *¡No dispare! No soy un falso positivo* (Don't Shoot, I Am Not a False Positive), and *Cien Manuelas por la Paz* (A Hundred Manuelas for Peace)" include collaborative work between professional artists and people who are grieving the loss of their loved ones, of their homes, of a way of life due to the armed conflict. As some of the titles indicate, specific references to the genocide of the *Unión Patriótica* members and to the so-called *falsos positivos* (false positives) demand straightforward answers from State agencies.[101] The occupation of well-known central public spaces such as the Plaza de Bolívar and the Parque Nacional in Bogotá for these performances gives visibility to human rights issues that the Government would prefer to ignore. Now marginalized citizens take center stage.

Thanks to the support of Magdalena Norway and the sponsorship of Fokus from Norway, Proyecto Mujeres de Arte y Parte en la Paz de Colombia (Women of Art and Part of the Peace of Colombia) has allowed Ariza to consolidate twelve groups of women (widows, single mothers, community leaders, and young women) who work on conflicts affecting the nation through acting, song, dance, and story telling. Finding their voice and making their bodies participate in the articulation of their life experience gives them agency in the transformation of their pain and challenges.[102]

Ariza's work is representative of Colombian theater practitioners who are experimenting with new forms of expression that leave behind conventional dramatic configurations to foreground ethical, social, and political issues requiring action by the citizenry.[103] In this new context, theatrical works can no longer be approached according to the usual notions of plot, character development, or well-structured play. Ileana Diéguez explores the liminality and transgression inherent in such performative practices in Latin America conceived "como actos éticos, como gestos políticos de micro-resistencia" (as ethical acts or as political gestures of micro-resistance).[104] Such deconstruction of traditional dramaturgical categories in a sociopolitical context of human rights violations leads to a synecdochic representation of the disappeared body as the trace of an absence, be it a name, a photograph, an article of clothing, a relationship. Lost ones and survivors often fuse in the figure of Antígona, whose public stage presence has come to be ubiquitous in the theatrical realm in Colombia to stand for the body of a nation in mourning that denounces the responsibility of the State in investigating its own criminal activity.[105]

The plays focused on the armed conflict included in the present study are the proverbial tip of the iceberg in connection to the so-called "Theater of the Catastrophe," "Dramaturgies of Resistance," "Dramaturgies of Memory," or even the "Poetics of Horror" developed in Colombia over the last six decades.[106] What is the significance of this extensive corpus in term of victims, victimizers, witnesses, the general population, and future generations? Based on research by Cathy Caruth, Dominick La Capra, Carolyn Yoder, and others, Kate Schick asserts that societies that have experienced ongoing trauma must develop meaning-making narratives to work through their individual and collective experiences.[107] This entails the public retelling of their stories to facilitate mourning and to encourage social and political reengagement through the recovery of their political voice. Creative verbal and nonverbal activities have proven to be helpful in this process by providing a safe space for self-expression and an attentive community of witnesses.[108] Consequently, theater as a carrier of cultural trauma in Colombia can be conducive to the healing of the wounded body of the nation within a transgenerational perspective.

It can also contribute to bridging the gap between the visible and the invisible Colombia. Cities have not experienced the human tragedy of the armed conflict to the extent that rural areas have. Many urban dwellers report not being affected by it or only marginally so, as documented in interviews by the CNMH.[109] This duality of experiences and perceptions may foster what Kai Erikson calls a "gathering of the wounded," resulting in a country divided between those who have suffered this violence and those who have not.[110] The renewed dynamism in current theatrical activity in Colombia with the inner conflict as the backdrop contributes to dismantling that wall by imagining a community with shared memories, responsibilities, and hopes for the future across the national territory. As reported by Lamus Obrdegón and explored by Enrique Pulecio Mariño, numerous initiatives and dramaturgical approaches are in place to meet this challenge. The proliferation of cultural centers that take the risk of fostering a sense of community by embracing new ways of making theater, the exploration of new languages for the stage "to name the unnameable," the dismantling of theater conventions to embody the disintegration of society, the challenges inherent in the characterization of victims and victimizers, the fragmentation of spoken language, the foregrounding of *testimonio*, the holding of performances in nontraditional spaces to incorporate marginalized audiences, and the importance of bearing witness speak of a commonality of features and goals in an otherwise highly heterogeneous corpus of theatrical works.[111]

Although it is yet to be seen which plays and performances stand the test of time, Colombian theater is not alone among the arts and academic disciplines in constructing cultural trauma. In addition to the monumental work and far-reaching interdisciplinary initiatives of the CNMH, *artistas plásticos*, writers, film directors, photographers, journalists, scholars, and ordinary citizens have all heard the call to delve into the physical and psychological pain endured by communities and individuals as violence bursts into their lives, thus becoming cultural trauma vehicles.[112] Their work attests to the democratic nature of a shared awareness by a citizenry deeply committed to making its plight visible in the hope of working toward a lasting peaceful and productive future for the country. Eyerman observes, that "memory is located not inside the heads of individual [social] actors but rather [as Radley says] 'within the discourse of people talking together about the past."[113] Cultural trauma is a *lieu de mémoire* where Colombian collective memory has engaged in a dialogue with its violent history. This is a promising step toward a healed sociopolitical body.

Notes

1 This chapter is part of a book-length study under preparation about cultural trauma in Colombian theater. Special words of gratitude to Dr. Mary Copple for lending her keen sense of language to the careful editing of this chapter. Many thanks to Donna Schenck-Hamlin for her bibliographical expertise at just the right time. Their generous support in the final stage of this project is warmly appreciated.

2 The acronyms correspond to Fuerzas Armadas Revolucionarias Colombianas (Revolutionary Colombian Armed Forces) and Ejército de Liberación Nacional (National Liberation Army) respectively.

3 Autodefensas Unidas de Colombia (United Self-Defense Forces of Colombia).

4 Name given to the criminal activity, organization, and institution of hired assassins, initially associated with the drug cartels.

5 Grupo de Memoria Histórica, *¡BASTA YA! Colombia: Memorias de guerra y dignidad* (Bogotá: Imprenta Nacional, 2013), chapter 2, 111–13, http://centro dememoriahistorica.gov.co/descargas/informes2013/bastaYa/capitulos/basta-ya-cap2_110-195.pdf.

6 Ibid., 111.

7 Grupo de Memoria Histórica, *Estadísticas del conflicto armado en Colombia*, www.centrodememoriahistorica.gov.co/micrositios/informeGeneral/estadisticas .html.

8 Grupo de Memoria Histórica, Documental "No hubo tiempo para la tristeza," www.centrodememoriahistorica.gov.co/micrositios/informeGeneral/documental .html.

9 Gloria Luz Angel Echeverri, "Carlos José Reyes un investigador acucioso," *La Patria, October 27, 2014, Cultura*, www.lapatria.com/cultural/carlos-jose-reyes-un-investigador-acucioso-140431. Additional information about Reyes's forthcoming volumes on Colombian theater and history can be found at http://escenariocultural.jimdo.com/libros/.

10 I would like to thank Juan Carlos Posada for his gracious help in facilitating access to this report for me with information on the affiliated researchers. Manuel José Álvarez, present Director of the Teatro Colón, conceived this project and took the initiative to implement it. The report can be accessed through the following link: Manuel José Álvarez et al., *Luchando contra el olvido: Investigación sobre la dramaturgia del conflicto* (Bogotá: Ministerio de Cultura, 2012), www.mincultura.gov.co/areas/artes/grupos/teatro-y-circo/doc umentos/Documents/Luchando%20contra%20el%20olvido.pdf.

11 Marina Lemus Obregón, "Teatro que se resiste a olvidar," in *Luchando contra el olvido: Investigación sobre la dramaturgia del conflicto*, ed. Manuel José Álvarez et al. (Bogotá: Ministerio de Cultura, 2012), 15–16, www.mincultura.gov.co/areas/artes/grupos/teatro-y-circo/documentos/Documents/Luchando%20contra%20el%20olvido.pdf.

12 "Libro que sintetiza 35 años de horror se entregará este lunes," *El País*, October 8, 2012, *Cultura*, www.elpais.com.co/elpais/cultura/noticias/libro-sintetiza-35-anos-horror-entregara-este-lunes. Out of more than 300 plays identified as relating to the Colombian armed conflict, seventy were initially selected. Critical comments and additional material on thirty-two of them were included in this first report. The remaining thirty-eight plays will be part of a forthcoming publication.

13 Ron Eyerman, "Slavery and the Formation of African American Identity," in *Cultural Trauma and Collective Identity*, ed. Jeffrey C. Alexander et al. (Berkeley: University of California Press, 2004), 61 (boldface added).

14 Jeffrey C. Alexander, "Toward a Theory of Cultural Trauma," in *Cultural Trauma and Collective Identity*, 35.

15 Ibid., 10.

16 Ibid., 11.

17 Elizabeth Butler Breese, "Claiming Trauma through Social Performance: The Case of Waiting for Godot," in *Cultural Trauma and Collective Identity*, 219.

18 Ibid., 214.

19 Alexander, "Toward a Theory," 13–15.

20 This selection is only a limited sample of the vast production of Colombian dramaturgy that focuses on the armed conflict. The present study has been conceived as a point of departure in the exploration of one line of development in the area of Colombian theater, not as an all-inclusive view of theater activity in the country. Although highly representative and recognized, the handful of playwrights included in this study certainly cannot account for the many and complex facets of theater activity nationwide. This chapter discusses a limited selection of work; space constraints do not allow for a review of the multiplicity of established theater groups, playwrights, and directors that could also be discussed.

21 Eyerman, "Slavery," 63.

22 Claudia Montilla, "Del teatro experimental al nuevo teatro, 1959–1975," *Revista de Estudios Sociales/ Universidad de los Andes*, no. 17 (2004): 86–97. By doing so, Montilla debunks the long-held notion that vanguard theater in Colombia unfolded as a result of the *Nuevo Teatro*. She supports the argument that even before *Nuevo Teatro*, experimental approaches were introduced that renovated theatrical activity in Colombia in the fifties, moving the theater of the time away from realism, naturalism, and *costumbrismo*. From Montilla's perspective, the critical, reflective, and selective assimilation of Classical and Golden Age theater and of European and American influences, the commitment to experimentation with new languages and themes for the stage, the awareness of the need for professionalization in the field, and the urgency to

create an audience – all preceded and had a significant impact on *Nuevo Teatro*.

23 Lucy Lorena Libreros, "Jaqueline Vidal: la mujer que salvó al Teatro Experimental de Cali del olvido," *El País*, April 9, 2013, *Cultura*. www.elpais.com.co/elpais/cultura/noticias/jaqueline-vidal-mujer-salvo-teatro-experimental-cali-olvido. After Buenaventura's death in 2003, his wife, Jaqueline Vidal, became the TEC's director to preserve his dramaturgical legacy of an independent theater committed to making the public reflect on issues relevant to national life.

24 Since a study of Buenaventura's and Garcia's dramaturgy is beyond the scope of the present chapter, see Beatriz J. Rizk, "Enrique Buenaventura," in *Latin American Dramatists, First Series*, ed. Adam Versény, *Dictionary of Literary Biography*, vol. 305 (New York: Thomson Gale, 2005), 60–76; Lucia Garavito, "Santiago García," in *Latin American Dramatists, First Series*, ed. Adam Versényi, *Dictionary of Literary Biography*, Vol. 305 (New York: Thomson Gale, 2005), 167–83.

25 Diana Taylor, *Theatre of Crisis: Drama and Politics in Latin America* (Lexington: University Press of Kentucky, 1991), 182–7.

26 Enrique Buenaventura, "La maestra," in *Los papeles del infierno y otros textos* (Bogotá: Siglo XXI Editores, 1990), 16.

27 www.colombianistas.org/portals/o/congresos/documentos/congresoxviii/gardea zabal_bravo_carlos.pdf. Carlos Gardeazábal Bravo includes this information in footnote 5 of his paper "Violencia estructural y mujer en *Los papeles de infierno* de Enrique Buenaventura."

28 Jeffrey C. Alexander and Elizabeth Butler Breese, "Introduction: On Social Suffering and Its Cultural Construction," in *Narrating Trauma: On the Impact of Collective Suffering*, ed. Ron Eyerman et al. (Boulder: Paradigm Publishers, 2013), xxvii.

29 Eyerman, "Formation," 69.

30 Buenaventura, "La maestra," 16.

31 Ibid.

32 Ibid.

33 Miguel Torres, *La siempreviva* (Medellín: Tragaluz Editores, 2011). Enrique Pulecio Mariño in "La dramaturgia del conflicto armado en Colombia" (see note 10) mentions unpublished works where ghosts or spectral forms play a role (27–214). See chart given by subject (211).

34 Katherine Verdery, *The Political Lives of Dead Bodies: Reburial and Postsocialist Change* (New York: Columbia University Press, 1999), 1, 24.

35 Kelli Lyon-Johnson, "Acts of War, Acts of Memory: 'Dead Body-Politics' in US Latina Novels of the Salvadoran Civil War," *Latino Studies*, no. 3 (2005): 207.

36 Marita Sturken, *Tangled Memories: The Vietnam War, the AIDS Epidemic, and the Politics of Remembering* (Berkeley: University of California Press, 1997), 72.

37 Buenavenura, "Maestra," 16.

38 Alexander and Breese, "Introduction," xii.

39 Sam Durrant, "The Invention of Mourning in Post-Apartheid Literature," *Third World Quarterly* 26, no. 3 (2005): 442.

40 http://centromemoria.gov.co/multimedia/cartografia/. Guadalupe Salcedo became a guerrilla leader in the *Llanos* (1949) to defend the region against the violence promoted by the official Conservative government after the assassination of Jorge Eliécer Gaitán. His concern for the rights of the people led him to take up arms. Four years later, when General Rojas Pinilla was in power, Salcedo accepted the armistice he offered to the guerrilla fighters and peace was negotiated. However, many of the peasants who laid down their weapons at this time were then killed by the government, including Salcedo (1953).

41 Teatro La Candelaria, "Guadalupe años sin cuenta" in *5 Obras de Creación Colectiva* (Bogotá: Editorial Colombia Nueva, 1986), 139. Arturo Alape, historian and researcher, collaborated with La Candelaria in the making of *GASC*, as did other individuals who had participated in the original events.

42 Carlos José Reyes, "Guadalupe años sin cuenta," *Revista Arcadia*, January 24, 2014, www.revistaarcadia.com/impresa/especial-arcadia-100/articulo/guada lupe-anos-sin-cuenta-teatro-la-candelaria/35071. Carlos José Reyes cites as sources for the play documents and articles from newspapers of the 1950s and books by Eduardo Franco Isaza and by Coronel Sierra Ochoa on the guerrillas in the *Llanos*. Reyes also observes that the absent figure of Salcedo, who is present through the peasants who joined him, resonates with the style of the film *Salvatore Giuliano* by Francesco Rosi (1962).

43 Patricia Ariza, "Siembra y canto en la plaza (Colombia)" in *Ciudadanías en escena: Performance y derechos culturales en Colombia*, ed. Paolo Vignolo (Bogotá: Universidad Nacional de Colombia, Facultad de Artes y Facultad de Ciencias Humanas, 2008), 152.

44 Carlo Tognato, "Extending Trauma across Cultural Divides: On Kidnapping and Solidarity in Colombia," in *Narrating Trauma*, 200–201.

45 Teatro La Candelaria, "Guadalupe," 139.

46 Eyerman, "Cultural Trauma," 61.

47 Ibid.

48 www.cidh.oas.org/annualrep/96span/Colombia11227.htm. The genocide of the Unión Patriótica (Patriotic Union) political movement is the most egregious example of this trust/betrayal pattern. A negotiated agreement in 1985 between the Colombian government and the FARC opened the way for members of the opposition to participate legally in political life in the country. However, shortly afterwards, Unión Patriótica leaders, members, followers, and sympathizers began to be systematically assassinated. The case was taken to the Corte Internacional de Derechos Humanos (International Court of Human Rights) two decades ago and is still unresolved. The number of individuals affected by the systematic state repression was estimated at 3,000 by the government and at more than 6,500 by the Unión Patriótica.

49 Nicolás Pernett, "La recurrente masacre de las bananeras," *Razón pública*, December 2, 2013, www.razonpublica.com/index.php/econom-y-sociedad-temas-29/7218-la-recurrente-masacre-de-las-bananeras.html.

50 Centro de memoria, paz y reconciliación, http://centromemoria.gov.co/con
   memoracion-masacre-de-las-bananeras/. The reports of the government, of
   Cortés Vargas, and of the United Fruit Company ascribe different lawful
   justifications for the "*sucesos,*" minimize or distort the incidents, and offer
   wildly fluctuating figures for the number of people killed (ranging from 9 to
   1,000). Jorge Eliécer Gaitán, the rising political leader of the Liberal Party,
   carried out an extensive investigation in the 1930s that he submitted to
   Congress, denouncing Abadía Méndez's Conservative administration and
   the Army's abuse of power; in his investigations he even makes mention of
   train loads of cadavers that were subsequently thrown into the sea. Although
   Gaitán's possible political gain in this portrayal has been questioned, many
   others have set the figure of victims at 3,000.
51 Nelson Fredy Padilla, "El mito de las bananeras por dentro," *El Espectador*,
   November 29, 2008, www.elespectador.com/impreso/nacional/articuloim
   preso94669-el-mito-de-bananeras-dentro.
52 Jairo Aníbal Niño, "El sol subterráneo," in *Teatro Colombiano Contemporáneo*
   (Bogotá: Tres Culturas Editores, 1985), 157–82.
53 Gabriele Schwab, *Haunting Legacies: Violent Histories and Transgenerational
   Trauma* (New York: Columbia University Press, 2010), 78.
54 Niño, "El sol," 159.
55 Ibid., 160–1.
56 Ibid.
57 Ibid., 168.
58 Ibid., 177.
59 Ibid., 169.
60 Ibid., 170.
61 Schwab, *Haunting Legacies*, 1, 78.
62 Ibid., 79.
63 Ibid., 78.
64 Ibid., 81.
65 Ibid., 53.
66 Mauricio Archila Neira, "Masacre de las bananeras: diciembre 6 de 1928,"
   Credencial Historia 117 (1999), www.banrepcultural.org/node/32968. After the
   initial exclusion of the Banana Massacre from national cultural trauma due to
   politically motivated interests, the event has gained its place in collective
   memory thanks to the work of several social agents. Gabriel García Márquez
   (*Cien años de soledad*), Álvaro Cepeda Zamudio (*La casa grande*), Ricardo
   Rendón (cartoonist), Ricardo Arenas Betancourt (sculptor, *Prometeo de la
   libertad*), and Enrique Buenaventura (*La denuncia*) have brought it back to
   national awareness.
67 Beatriz Camargo, *Teatro Itinerante del Sol*, www.teatroitinerantedelsol.org/
   index.html.
68 George Russell et al. "Colombia's Mortal Agony," *Time* magazine, http://
   content.time.com/time/magazine/article/0,9171,1050626-1,00.html.
69 Alexander and Breese, xiii.

70 Beatriz Camargo, "Eart" (unpublished manuscript, 1991), 1.

71 Ibid., 19.

72 Ubo J. Hebel, "Towards a Descriptive Poetics of *Allusion*," in *Intertextuality*, ed. Heinrich F. Plett (Berlin: W. de Gruyter, 1991), 135, 139.

73 Ibid., 138.

74 Ibid., 154.

75 Domino Renee Perez, *There Was a Woman: La Llorona from Folklore to Popular Culture* (Austin: University of Texas Press, 2008), 137.

76 Irene Silverblatt, "The Evolution of Witchcraft and the Meaning of Healing in Colonial Andean Society," *Culture, Medicine and Psychiatry* 7, no. 4 (1983): 413–27. Silverblatt observes that since the time of the Conquest, herb healers were perceived and described by the Spanish *cronistas* as feared indigenous witches devoted to the adoration of celestial bodies, *huacas*, mountains, rivers, trees, and stones, with supernatural powers over life and death, a stereotype that spread rapidly in the Andean region. Although socially and legally marginalized, the so-called herb healers/witches used their talents and knowledge of the natural world to reposition themselves in their communities as vehicles to reestablish the balance of individuals and groups by ensuring the protection and help of unknown forces.

77 Anthony Stevens, *Ariadne's Clue: A Guide to the Symbols of Humankind* (Princeton: Princeton University Press, 1998), 275.

78 Silverblatt, "Evolution," 418–19.

79 These events have a metonymic value when examined in the Latin American context of the 1980s and 1990s. The inventory of ills affecting the region at that time is quite long: wars in Central America, assassinations (such as Archbishop Romero's in 1980), dictatorships and human rights violations in the Southern Cone, disappeared and displaced populations, narcotrafficking, the activity of guerrilla and paramilitary organizations, rampant corruption, and the devastation of the rainforest, among many others.

80 Fanny Mikey (1930, Buenos Aires, to 2008, Bogotá) played a key role in the development of theater as a cultural activity in Colombia. Mikey's vision, talent, and leadership as actress, producer, and director in Colombia and abroad, her roles as founder and director of the *Teatro Nacional de Bogotá* (1981), cofounder with Ramiro Osorio of the *Festival Iberoamericano de Teatro de Bogotá* (1988), founder of the *Casa del Teatro Nacional* (1994), and movie producer gave theater practitioners and audiences the opportunity to grow in their experience, understanding, and appreciation of the world of theater within a global perspective.

81 Humberto Dorado and Matías Maldonado, *El deber de Fenster* (unpublished manuscript, 2009). I would like to express my appreciation to Manuel José Álvarez for guiding me in the right direction to obtain a copy of this play and to Hernando Parra for his diligence in providing the text itself. Although I have seen the play performed, without their generous and timely help, it would have been impossible to include it in this study.

82 Paola Villamarín, "El deber de indignarse frente a las masacres," *El Tiempo*, September 26, 2010, www.eltiempo.com/archivo/documento/MAM-4159171.

83 Ibid.

84 Alexander, "Toward," 27.

85 Villamarín, "El deber de indignarse," www.celcit.org.ar/noticias_3668_el-deber-de-indignarse-frente-a-las-masacres.html.

86 Perpetrators of the massacre identified through Arcila's testimony and subsequent investigation are Mayor Alirio Antonio Urueña Jaramillo (Army Officer), Teniente Coronel Hernán Contreras Peña (Army), Teniente Wilfredo Ruiz (Army), Teniente José Fernando Berrío Velásquez (Police), and their accomplices and narcotrafficker Diego Montoya and his criminal group "Los Machos." Henry Loaiza and Iván Uridinola configured a paramilitary group associated with the Army and the National Police, sponsored with money from narcotrafficking. The criminal group Los Rastrojos and some regional political leaders were also involved.

87 Avery F. Gordon, *Ghostly Matters: Haunting and the Sociological Imagination* (Minneapolis: University of Minnesota Press, 1997), 125.

88 Ibid., 115.

89 Kathleen Brogan, *Cultural Haunting: Ghosts and Ethnicity in Recent American Literature* (Charlottesville: University Press of Virginia, 1998), 5–6.

90 Ibid., 26, 29.

91 Dorado and Maldonado, *El deber*, 39, 49, 70. The official psychiatric evaluations for Arcila are a collection of undesirable and dangerous traits that emphasize his capacity to deceive and his mental instability due to his family and upbringing. It was later revealed that the psychiatrist was paid to write such an evaluation. Arcila's character assassination preceded his actual torture and homicide.

92 Brogan, *Cultural*, 27.

93 Ibid., 92.

94 Gordon, *Ghostly*, 179, xvi.

95 Teatro La Candelaria, "*Golpe de suerte* (Lucky Strike)" in *Cinco obras de creación colectiva* (Bogotá: Ediciones Teatro La Candelaria, 1986), 366. Teatro La Candelaria, "*El Paso*" in *Tres obras de teatro: El Paso, Maravilla Estar y La Trifulca* (Bogotá: Ediicones Teatro La Candelaria, Bogotá, 1991), 58.

96 Tognato, "Extending Trauma," 193.

97 Myriam Jimeno, "Después de la masacre, la memoria como conocimiento histórico," in *Cuadernos de Antropología Social*, no. 33 (2011): 45.

98 The installation *Magdalenas por el Cauca* by Gabriel Posada with the collaboration of Yorlady Ruiz is an exhibit-procession inspired by the Massacre of Trujillo that visualizes the pain of women whose husbands, children, brothers, and friends have been assassinated and thrown into the Cauca River. A special homage to Father Tiberio is included.

99 Corporación Colombiana de Teatro, "Patricia Ariza recibe premio por su labor en favor de los Derechos Humanos en Colombia," www.corporacionco lombianadeteatro.com/noticias-home/249-patricia-ariza-recibe-premio-por-su-labor-en-favor-de-los-derechos-humanos-en-colombia.

100 Corporación Colombiana de Teatro, "La colombiana Patricia Ariza recibirá el Premio Internacional del Teatro de la Mujer," www.corporacioncolombia nadeteatro.com/eventos/260-la-colombiana-patricia-ariza-recibira-el-premio-internacional-del-teatro-de-la-mujer.

101 The Unión Patriótica political movement was the result of a negotiated agreement in 1984 between the Colombian government and the FARC to open the way for members of the opposition to participate legally in political life in the country. However, as early as 1984, its leaders, members, followers, and sympathizers began to be systematically assassinated. The CIDH is investigating this case as a genocide. See www.elcolombiano.com/historico/fiscalia_lleva_1800_falsos_positivos-KWEC_282932. A false positive refers to criminal activity on the part of some members of the Armed Forces to kidnap innocent young men or recruit them under false pretenses, kill them, dress them like guerrilla members or accomplices of narcotafficking, and then claim that they were killed in combat to gain recognition in their respective institutions. So far 4,262 members of the Armed Forces have been involved in this activity, and about 1,800 cases are being investigated. See Semana, "Las Madres de Soacha," www.semana.com/especiales/proyectovictimas/crimenes-de-la-guerra/ejecuciones-extrajudiciales/las-madres-de-soacha. The *Madres de Soacha* (Mothers from Soacha) is a group of seventeen women who received the bodies of their disappeared children looking like they had engaged in combat with the Army (2008). This incident opened the investigation into the false positives, a practice that was found to be spread nationwide.

102 Patricia Ariza, "Mujeres arte y parte en la paz de Colombia," www.corpor acioncolombianadeteatro.com/proyectos/performances.

103 Mapa Teatro, www.mapateatro.org/artememoria.html. Mapa Teatro, directed by Rolf Abderhalden and Heidi Abderhalden, deserves special recognition for decades of work devoted to the exploration of innovative theater practices. They have created a laboratory of theater activity open to experimentation and have developed a series of projects that imply critical reflection on the urbanistic transformation of the city of Bogotá and its impact on the inhabitants and their way of life. Their installations in connection with the disappearance of *El Cartucho* integrate testimony, memory, and reflections on social change and political power.

104 Ileana Diéguez, "Prácticas escénicas y políticas en Latinoamérica: Escenarios liminales peruanos," *Latin American Theatre Review* 41, no. 2 (2008): 30.

105 Examples of this trend are Patricia Ariza's play *Antígona* (2006) and the performance *Mujeres en la plaza* (2009). *Antígonas: Tribunal de Mujeres* (2013), with dramaturgy and direction by Carlos Satizábal (*Teatro Trama-luna*), tells the stories of the Madres de Soacha's lost relatives who are synechdotically present on the stage through objects related to them.

106 Lemus Obregón, "Teatro que se resiste a olvidar" (see note 11) mentions that researchers like Sandra Camacho López and Jorge Dubatti (among others) assign such labels to dramaturgical productions related to sociopolitical violence (17).

107 Kate Schick, "Acting Out and Working through: Trauma and (In)Security," *Review of International Studies*, 37, no. 4 (2011): 1837.

108 Ibid., 1848.

109 www.centrodememoriahistorica.gov.co/micrositios/informeGeneral/voxpo puli.html.

110 Schick, "Acting Out," 1840.

111 Lemus Obregón, "Teatro que se resiste," 17–23.

112 The internationally renowned installations by Doris Salcedo, the work of Erika Diettes, the *Magdalenas por el Cauca* (Magdalenas Down the Cauca) project by Gabriel Posada with the collaboration of Yorlady Ruiz, the quilts made by the *Tejedoras de Mampuján* (Weavers of Mampuján), the narratives of Juan Gabriel Vásquez, Evelio Rosero, Antonio Ungar, and Daniel Ferreira, films by Víctor Gaviria, William Vega, and Carlos César Arbeláez, the studies of academic researchers devoted to the exploration of "violentology" since the early 1960s, the photography work of Juan Manuel Echavarría and Oscar Muñoz, museum exhibits, the journalistic work of Hollman Morris to document and denounce human rights violations, the Proyecto Rosa (Rosa Project) by Silla Vacía, and the emergence of multiple NGOs to provide an effective legal and humanitarian framework to help a traumatized civilian population, to mention just some recent examples, speak of the many spaces open to the configuration of cultural trauma in Colombia.

113 Eyerman, "Slavery," 66.

CHAPTER 9

The Colombian essay

Héctor Hoyos

In Colombia, essays and essayism are the norm, rather than the exception.[1] Etymologically, an essay is an attempt or try at conveying something; essayism its accompanying exploratory ethos. There is a rich corpus of Colombian writing along those lines. Instead of understanding the essay as autonomous genre, it is by appreciating it within the fold of essayism – in its most unbridled, protean dimension – that one may begin to appreciate its relevance and sheer potency in the Colombian context. At the same time, because the essay is everywhere, it is also nowhere. Dispersion of cultural capital and repetition are constant risks in the literature, as authors appear to be more adept at generating essayism than at building upon the exploits of their forerunners. The present chapter, by no means exhaustive, offers an account of this process and some of the signposts necessary to navigate its sprawling terrain.[2]

Montaigne (1533–92), often credited as the father of the essay, puts forward an adaptive exercise in judgment. He compares himself to a man who tests the waters and sees where they make take him:

> I take the first subject that chance offers. ... Scattering a word here, there another, samples separated from their context, dispersed, without a plan and without a promise, I am not bound to make something of them or to adhere to them myself without varying when I please and giving myself up to doubt and uncertainty and my ruling quality, which is ignorance. (219, qtd. in Gómez-Martínez 18)

Colombian essayism often displays many of the same traits, namely: self-irony, ludic tone, false modesty, style-driven persuasiveness, and supple reasoning. Many of its proponents present a happy combination of improvisation and judgment that, as in their early modern counterparts, desacralize and question. Others get the worse of this combination, leading to idiosyncrasy and thinly argued ex cathedra pronouncements.

A counterpart to the treatise in a country where treatises are seldom written, the Colombian essay must play multiple roles. With the notable exception of Héctor Orjuela, most accounts of the form start with the nation itself. The critic traces its origins back to *Sumario de la natural historia de las Indias* (1526, Summary of the Natural History of the Indies) by Gonzalo Fernández de Oviedo (1478–1557) and to *El antijovio* (The Anti-Jovius) by Gonzalo Jiménez de Quesada (1506–79), founder of Bogotá. (The latter also dates from the sixteenth century, but remained unpublished until 1952.) Early modern texts often defy genre definition. While the first – a *crónica* (chronicle) of early Spanish settlement – is of a decidedly historical bent, the second combines narrative, political philosophy, autobiography, and invective. Roughly contemporary to Montaigne, and similar in its blending of anecdote and argument, Jiménez de Quesada contrasts starkly with the Frenchman's ideology. Animated by the Spanish Counter-Reformation, the *adelantado* defends the record of Charles V during the sack of Rome. It is not difficult to observe how, in so doing, this man of arms and letters is also defending the imperial project in his adopted home in the New World. His work inaugurates two recurrent themes: American specificity, in the continental sense of the term, and its relationship to the Old World, especially Spain.

Orjuela highlights other colonial essayists. These include Juan Espinosa Medrano (1629–88), whose *Apologético a favor de don Luis de Góngora* (1662, Treatise in Favor of Don Luis de Góngora) is reportedly the first literary essay written in the territory – in a broad sense, for this hints at the pre-1717 belonging of today's Colombia to the Viceroyalty of Perú (9). A salutary reminder of the threads that extend beyond modern national boundaries, this text illustrates center-periphery dynamics of enduring legacy. Readers in Bogotá, twice removed from the metropolis that was Madrid, would read belatedly about a debate – the defense of Góngora against Quevedo – that was well underway, if not overdue, by the time the book reached its readers in Lima. (Quevedo died in 1627.)[3] It took nearly two centuries for Colombian capitals to find their voice, among other figures, in Francisco José de Caldas (1768–1816). True to his epithet, *el Sabio* was a polymath who participated in the geographic expeditions of José Celestino Mutis (1732–1808) and Alexander von Humboldt (1769–1845). His scientific-cum-essayistic writings, while focused on flora and fauna, gave the subjects of the by-then Viceroyalty of New Granada a sense of ownership over their natural resources. His editorials for *Diario político* were grounds for his execution in 1816, a mere three years before the realization of his cause: independence from the Spanish Empire. Of no less importance to this cause were Antonio Nariño's writings for *La Bagatela* and Simón Bolívar's well-known "Ensayo sobre las diferencias sociales en América" (1815).

Independence, a dream that essayists and revolutionaries dreamt, was now a reality. Not surprisingly, the themes of Colombia's place in Hispanic culture and in Western civilization thrived throughout the nineteenth century. José María Samper (1828–88) exemplifies this in his *Ensayo sobre las revoluciones políticas* (1861). There he argues in favor of *mestizaje* (miscegenation), with a caveat: one where the goal is *blanqueamiento* – whitening. As Carl Langebaek shows, Samper defends criollo hegemony over the country, characterizing Colombians of a lighter complexion as industrious, while lambasting afros, mestizos, and indigenous for their alleged laziness. The crux of the essay is representing an "accurate" portrayal of the country as an emerging, civilized counterpart of European nations. Samper had not one, but several, periodical outlets for his writing, including, from 1849 to 1855 alone, *El suramericano, La reforma, El pasatiempo,* and *El neogranadino.* To this day, Colombian essayists, who often double as journalists and social commentators, are wedded to similar periodicals. Meanwhile, Soledad Acosta de Samper, José María's spouse, wrote brilliant essays for *La mujer* (1878–1881). In recent years, critics including Montserrat Ordóñez and Carolina Alzate have revisited Acosta's *La mujer en la sociedad moderna* (1895) as a milestone in the emancipation of Colombian women. By her conservative yet feminist account, women could extend their sphere of action beyond the household *without* questioning traditional Catholic bourgeois values. For a useful contrast, Alzate reports that José María Vergara y Vergara (1831–72), whose own pieces for the highly influential periodical *El mosaico* (1858–72) are worthy of note, advised women "always to obey, to never cease ruling" (henceforth my translation, 166).

Partisan struggles between liberals and conservatives affected every sphere of Colombian life through most of the country's republican history. Essayism is no exception. In a lucid reflection, Jaime Alberto Vélez laments that, because of such struggles, essayists were never able to configure a space for the pure exchange of ideas. Instead, claims the critic, their words were used to annihilate their enemies (50). His examples include Miguel Antonio Caro (1845–1909), the famous president grammarian, whose erudition and style served a reactionary political agenda – the very opposite of the spirit of openness that, per Vélez's account, characterizes the essay. Whether one agrees with the assumption that there is a baseline democratic impulse to the essay or not, Vélez makes the important point that writers at the other end of the political spectrum share similar zeal and intransigence. Those would include radical liberals like José María Vargas Vila (1860–1933) and Juan de Dios "El Indio" Uribe (1859–1900). The latter was expelled from the country for his writings in *El correo liberal*, deemed immoral by president poet Rafael Núñez (1825–94).[4] Núñez and Caro were responsible for the restitution of diplomatic relations with Spain and the Holy See. They regarded the essay, and literature in general, as a space of art for art's sake – but only because they relegated different views to an externality, reducing them to barbarism. Indeed, anything outside of Christian civilization was anathema to them. This resulted in a rarified climate for essayism and culture more broadly. For Vélez, *Idola fori* (1909), a defense of "intellectual tolerance" by influential essayist Carlos Arturo Torres (1867–1911) resists such sectarianism (51). Torres takes his cues from Francis Bacon to produce an underexamined and highly suggestive variant of *arielismo*. He agrees with his more sectarian colleagues that the populace is to be feared: "To think that the many can interpret a political concept, defend a sentiment, and comprehend public interest better than the few is a hallucination of democracy, as difficult to defeat as the most entrenched of religious prejudices" (88). Reading the terms of these debates, it comes as little wonder that, with the glaring exception of assassinated leader Jorge Eliécer Gaitán (1903–48), democracy and populism have mostly parted ways in Colombia.

From the mid–nineteenth to the mid–twentieth century, there are manifestations of the essay both as heteronomous and autonomous genre. On one end of the spectrum, essayism peppers the pages of novels such as *María* (1867), by Jorge Isaacs, and *De sobremesa* (1925, written in the 1890s, After dinner), by José Asunción Silva. In a nod to the naturalistic writings of earlier generations, their narrators digress on the geographic and human aspects of the Cauca Valley region and of the Plains region (*llanos*), respectively. *Cuatro años a bordo de mí mismo* (1934, Four Years Aboard Myself) by Eduardo Zalamea Borda (1907–63) does something similar with the Guajira region. On the other end of the spectrum of essayistic autonomy, there are two central figures: Baldomero Sanín Cano (1861–1957) and Germán Arciniegas (1900–1999). The most anthologized figures to date, they cultivate the genre as an end in itself, at least partially independent from narrative, journalism, or politics. Their works are a milestone in the professionalization of writers in the country; several reach a broad Latin American audience.

In the case of Sanín Cano, his international appeal has to do with his own experience abroad. A regular contributor to the Argentine newspaper

La nación (1870-), Sanín Cano published his first book of essays, *La civilización manual y otros ensayos* (Manual Civilization and Other Essays) in Buenos Aires in 1925. By that time, he had already gained a reputation in Colombia for his writings in *Revista gris* (1892–6) and *Revista contemporánea* (1904–5), where he opposed Núñez. Other than Argentina, he spent long stints in Spain and in the United Kingdom, ultimately to return to Colombia as a university rector. Other notable books, compilations of short texts rather than organic pieces, include *Divagaciones filológicas y apólogos literarios* (1934, Philological Digressions and Literary Essays), *Ensayos* (1942, Essays), *Letras colombianas* (1944, Colombian Letters), and *El humanismo y el progreso del hombre* (1955, Humanism and the Progress of Man).

Wit and sweeping views are some of his traits. In "La civilización manual," he argues that Western civilization, of which he considers himself part and parcel, has been overly "cerebral." It should, taking its cues from Eastern painting, become more "manual." For Sanín Cano, truly great works of art have been made under the aegis of the hand, not the mind; throughout history, women have been disempowered because they have literally had their hands busy with children and house chores; the free use of hands have given our species its prominence, even over primates with opposable thumbs, because their hands are reduced to utilitarian tasks like locomotion; consequently, Ford's aspiration of making everyone a driver is barbaric, regressive: with no chauffeurs, we will revert to yanking at our limbs for locomotion (Ruiz and Cobo Borda, 29). This slippery slope of an argument is every bit as suggestive as it is fallacious. Note the sensibility it reveals: male-centered, despite its feminist intention; cosmopolitan in aspiration; positivist, aestheticist, and bourgeois. At the same time, the hand is more than a mere heuristic device. Sanín Cano's rejection of symmetry and rationalism is consonant with avant-gardist tropes of its day and even anticipates some aspects of postmodernism. His emphasis on the haptic speaks to the concerns of today's affect and cultural studies.

Not one to shy away from entelechies, in a different essay Sanín Cano talks about the exotic as a category. There he distinguishes between exotism of form and of feeling, defends a discerning imitation of worthy foreign authors, and questions nationalism as an organizing principle for literature. For a fin-de-siècle piece, "De lo exótico" (1894) is radical, as it calls for nothing short of the abolition of originality. Though similar in spirit, its promiscuous, voracious account of reading predates the "Manifesto antropófago" (1928), by the Brazilian Oswald de Andrade (1890–1954), for thirty-some years. It also takes exception from the more reverential take on European culture in *Ariel* (1900), by the Uruguayan José Enrique Rodó (1872–1917). His purported dissolution of center-periphery relations appears more casual than justified when compared with the much later, well-known lecture "El escritor argentino y la tradición" (1951, The Argentine Writer and Tradition) by Jorge Luis Borges (1899–86), but it certainly can be read alongside it.[5] Writes Sanín Cano: "There is no fault of patriotism nor racial apostasy in trying to comprehend what is Russian, or in trying to assimilate oneself to what is Scandinavian" (23). He goes on to lambast Rubén Darío (1867–1916) not for trying to imitate the French, but for stopping there.

Sanín Cano's cultural brokerage went mostly in one direction: He succeeded, along with other writers, at bringing world literature to Colombians – less so, Colombian literature to the world. Given the volume and singularity of his oeuvre, why this is so invites further study. Two factors seem to be at work here, namely, his eccentricity and anti-institutionalism. Although literary tradition often enshrines authors who systematically question it, Sanín Cano is asystematic even in this questioning. In the cited essay, he refers to Cervantes's time as one in which "the universal endemic evil of criticism" had not yet "invaded with so much arrogance the space of other literary genres" (Torres Duque, 72). It is unclear how he regards his own work as *other than criticism*. Similarly, he closes the essay with a note of profound ambiguity. Commenting on the trend of representing "the indigenous past" in the arts of Argentina and Peru, Sanín Cano opines that if Colombia does not share that trend it is because it feels that past all too close. The insinuation is that Colombians are more genuinely national, "not yet exotic" (25). Regardless, a legacy of the conquest is that Colombians, and Latin Americans more broadly, cannot not self-exoticize.

The essayist formulates similar reflections in pieces such as "¿Qué cosa es la hispanidad? (What Is Being Hispanic), "Hacia un imperio hispanoamericano del espíritu" (Toward a Spanish-American Empire of the Spirit), and "El descubrimiento de América y la higiene" (The Discovery of America and Hygiene). In the last, he makes the mordant argument that, as Spanish conquerors lacked in hygiene, they brought along the diseases that would decimate the indigenous peoples. All of these essays could be described as being "on a Colombian subject," borrowing the term that Torres Duque proposes to distinguish those from "Colombian essays" (xxv). (Indeed, essayists from many national-ities have written about Colombia and Colombian essayists have written about many subjects.) Although a significant portion of Sanín Cano's work is devoted to the country and its inscription in Hispanic and European culture, an important body of essays is also devoted to authors such as Mark Twain, Goethe, André Gide, and T. S. Elliot.

German Arciniegas is a close second in acclaim and prestige. He lived through the entire twentieth century, almost to the minute, as he was born in 1900 and died in 1999. Having written an estimated 15,000 essays and newspaper articles, spread over forty essay collections, he is an indispensable reference for anyone who, seeing the century through his eyes, wants to understand a certain worldview: Call it Latin Americanism with a Colombian inflection. His most influential works include *El estudiante de la mesa redonda* (1932, The Student of the Round Table), a thematization of university politics at the time; *Biografía del Caribe* (1945, Biography of the Caribbean), a grand narrative of the region that combines novelistic and historiographical material; and *Entre la libertad y el miedo* (1952, Between Freedom and Fear), an early denunciation of Latin American dictatorships, published while in an exile teaching post at Columbia University in New York. Also of note is the later *América en Europa* (1975, America in Europe), which makes the counterintuitive argument that the New World exerted more of an influence on the Old than the other way around. Arciniegas's view is hemispheric in scope, from Alaska to Patagonia, but he privileges Spanish America and Colombia in particular as the axes of his transnationalism, and always in opposition to Spain, whose diplomatic overreach in the celebration of the 500 years of the "discovery" of the Americas he was prompt to criticize (*Semana*). (He was a nonagenarian at the time.) Throughout his prolific life, he held numerous university, ambassadorial, and governmental positions – but at a cost: These occupations made his oeuvre more impressionistic than scholarly, as it might have been otherwise.

In his anthology, Torres Duque plays the contrarian by omitting him, charging him with being a mere "popularizer" (*divulgador*, xxiii). There is truth to this accusation, although it remains polemical to attribute it exclusively or even primordially to Arciniegas, among many other essayists who could be described in such terms. Moreover, Arciniegas would vindicate his role of bringing history to a broader audience. The populace or *vulgus* at stake is not the masses, and neither is he writing for the elites. In the phrase by Juan Ramón Jiménez that Álvaro Mutis utters in the famous sound bite of the cultural radio station HJCK, he writes for *la inmensa minoría*: mutatis mutandis, the middlebrow. Disciplinary history has, by and large, left Arciniegas behind – as it has his mentor, Tomás Rueda Vargas (1879–1943), who sought to depict "Colombia's past through the window of the imagination" (4). Meanwhile, if focusing on the essay strictly as autonomous genre, Arciniegas is left out of the picture. And yet the sheer eloquence of his language and its obvious pedagogical value merit him a second look. The same could be said about his political views, which totter between social and liberal democracy, anchored on anti-authoritarianism.

An illustration of his style and idiosyncrasies is *Los alemanes en la conquista de América* (1941, The Germans in the Conquest of America). It is an erudite compilation of vignettes about Germans in the settlement of the New World, German scientific travelers, and the dissemination of German thought in Colombia. The whole is larger than the sum of its parts: From piecemeal storytelling emerges a rapprochement of two cultures that are not as distant as they may appear. Addressing his Colombian readership, Arciniegas insists that "we" were subject to the same crown, during Charles V, and so in a sense Germans are "our" countrymen. Further challenging us versus them dichotomies, the author cites material evidence of German settlement in Tunja ("a city made of wind and ice," he muses), reminds the reader of the role of German geographers, and provides numerous details that bring the past closer to the reader (Ruiz and Cobo-Borda, 88). Novelization of history and pedagogical intent go hand in hand. Problematically, stylistic flourishes assume the role of logical transitions, sources are rarely credited, and factual accuracy is limited. Opinion is characteristically difficult to parse out from authority, but point of view is unequivocal: Referring to Staden's encounter with *tupi-guaraní* resistance, we read that he "knew the boldness [*los atrevimientos*] of the savages (96)." Like others before and after him, Arciniegas speaks for the creole establishment. However, the hagiographic account of the conquest, a feature of conquest itself, wanes throughout his pages and across the many chapters of his life. There is also awareness about how modern technologies and ease of travel have profoundly modified the dissemination of ideas. Significantly, Arciniegas reminds us that Sanín Cano worked in Bogotá for an English mule-drawn tram company. The preeminent essayist was "the only person who could speak in English with the managers and in muleteer-speak [*lenguaje de arrieros*] with the people in charge of the mules (101)." Bitingly, Arciniegas invites a comparison with his forerunner's role in translating and disseminating the ideas of Friedrich Nietzsche. And yet, with modesty and nostalgia, he questions his own role as a go-between of Germans and Colombians. He is aware that, as increased cultural exchange triumphs over parochialism, his broad strokes accounts of complex historical matters lose their relative standing.[6] Still, a work like *Biografía del Caribe* remains essential. Halfway between fiction and history, it sits somewhere between Alejo Carpentier and disciplinary scholarship on the region – prescient, in more ways than one, of the work of Antonio Benítez Rojo.

The most significant recent study on the Colombian essay is Efrén Giraldo's *La poética del esbozo* (2014). There, next to Sanín Cano, Giraldo situates two other authors who, the critic argues, are essential to the essay as an autonomous genre in the country. This triad omits Arciniegas because that author's essayism does not conform to a narrow genre definition – the unit of analysis of Giraldo's monograph. Per his account, the other two figures are Hernando Téllez (1908–66) and Nicolás Gómez Dávila (1913–94).

Téllez is a crucial figure in mid–twentieth century Colombian culture. Along with Jorge Gaitán Durán, Hernando Valencia Goelkel, and several other writers, Téllez contributed to *Mito* (1955–62), a periodical whose essayistic output, by Colombians and distinguished international figures, could well deserve its own chapter. (Especially since part of its editorial board diverted into *Eco*, a major forum from 1960 to 1984.) The essayist had already consolidated his reputation at the time, with works such as *Inquietud del mundo* (1943, The Disturbance of the World), *Bagatelas* (1944, Trinkets), and *Luces en el bosque* (1946, Lights in the Forest). His *Literatura y sociedad* (1956, Literature and Society) is a compilation of writings, whereas those earlier works had more unity of purpose. There are two strands in Téllez's essayistic output. One is straightforward cultural commentary on a broad variety of topics. The other is subtler and harder to define – musings that fictionalize the author and narrate his experience as a reader. These often include the more mundane aspects of the act of reading, down to details such as the paperweight on the author's desk. In Giraldo's words, the first strand is more readily canonizable (*patrimonializable*, 327), while the second could be described as a "phenomenology of reading" (306).

One essay that sits at the crossroads of self-reflection and social critique is "Notes about Bourgeois Consciousness" (1956). True to its title, the piece presents a series of observations, loosely woven together, that seek to turn an orthodox Marxist account of class consciousness on its head. Its fragmentary and brief nature impedes a direct comparison with a study like *Moral burguesa y revolución* (1963, Bourgeoise Morality and Revolution), by the Argentine León Rozitchner, but it is certainly interesting to read the essay in conversation with that book and against the backdrop of the Cold War. Colombia's maritime borders extend far into the Caribbean, and yet its mainstream political discourse could not be farther apart from that of the island of Cuba. While Rozitchner examined the bourgeois morality that led exile Cubans to join the Bay of Pigs [Playa Girón] Invasion, speaking obviously from the vantage point of the revolutionary, Téllez questions bourgeois morality from within. The Colombian assumes a bourgeois identity and a self-declared "cynical," but far from revolutionary, position. After Téllez, the fate of the bourgeois writer would be discomfort and guilt. Nonetheless, critique would still be possible. Examples include Téllez's counterintuitive characterization of U.S. society as being "bourgeois collectivist," satisfied with the "fair share of mediocrity"; his reflections of the differing attitudes of petty and proper bourgeois women regarding love (a topic that has occupied many male authors, from Engels to folk singer Silvio Rodríguez); and the remarkable glosses of Montherlant and D. H. Lawrence that allow him to formulate his views on the bourgeois. The sophistication with which Téllez goes from cultural politics to bedroom politics, and from art to mores, invites further study. His cosmopolitanism would exert a long-lasting influence on nonfiction and fiction writers alike. Nobel laureate Gabriel García Márquez (1927–2014), whose early newspaper column "La jirafa" (1950–2) has its own essayistic interest, was among them.[7]

Nicolás Gómez Dávila represents a strong backlash against the modernizing ideals of *Mito* and its cohort. Although he published and was referred to in that journal, most of his work did not have wide circulation during his lifetime. A man of strong convictions, Gómez Dávila follows in the footsteps of nineteenth-century conservative ideologues like Núñez and Caro, conservative humanists like Gilberto Alzate Avendaño (1910–60), and even polarizing figures like the mid–twentieth-century Laureano Gómez (1889–1965), the master rhetorician and political leader. And yet Gómez Dávila embraces anachronism with sophistication, instead of simply bemoaning the loss of *ancien régime* values – which he does, too. The anti-treatise tendencies of Colombian essayism reach their apex in his oeuvre, as it favors the shortest of forms. There are some conventional-length essays as well, including the noteworthy, posthumous "The Authentic Reactionary" (1995). However, most of his writings are aphoristic in nature, reminiscent of Pascal or Gómez de la Serna, albeit with a different political sign.

For illustration, consider his reformulation of Spinozian *conatus*, or perseverance in being, as universal competition for resources among beings: "The feeblest of animals, left unrestricted to his own feverish means, would fill space and devour the stars" (El animal más miserable, entregado sin prohibiciones a su fiebre, coparía el espacio y devoraría las estrellas) (*Textos I*, quoted in Giraldo, 368). Why "ontological collaboration" is not possible, Gómez Dávila does not say. Radically individualistic, Ayn Rand–esque moments like these are not uncommon.[8] A devout Catholic, Gómez Dávila remarks, in Roberto Pinzón's translation: "Before God there is nothing but individuals" (*Scholia*, 27). At times, the essayist treats concepts as characters, creating jarring effects that bridge imaginative and philosophical prose. Perhaps perceiving such idiosyncrasies as lack of rigor, the renowned scholar Rafael Gutiérrez Girardot (1928–2005), whose own essayism was markedly academic, both dismissed and attacked him (as he did Octavio Paz). As of late, and because of diligent reprints and translations, the oddity of Gómez Dávila's work has garnered him interest in some European philosophical circles.

Among more recent generations, one figure that stands out is Germán Colmenares (1938–90). Colmenares was a disciplinary historian trained in the *Annales* school; he produced learned studies about the Cauca Valley and other regions. His historiographical essay *Las convenciones contra la cultura* (1987, Conventions against culture) is of interest to historians and nonhistorians alike. As one critic puts it, in that work Colmenares shows how nineteenth-century Spanish American historiographers, imbued in patrician tales of heroism, were still "colonial subjects" (Garrido, 52). Putting liberalism to task, he questions the new nations' *criollo* ideologues for masking social contradiction in the name of a purported egalitarianism that was valid mostly, if not exclusively, on paper. The core argument resembles the Brazilian critic Roberto Schwarz's claims about "misplaced ideas," imported from Europe only to yield different social functions in their new homes. It also accords with the tenets of postcolonialism, as displayed in the Colombian context by such thinkers as Santiago Castro-Gómez (1958). However, Colmenares's originality lies in the careful close reading of historical sources, coupled with an attention to how the object of the past changes through language. Despite an excellent, multivolume edition of his works, the task of divulgating and building upon Colmenares's thought remains largely undone.

One essayist who shares the thrust of Colmenares's historiography is Rogerio Velásquez (1908–65). Recently featured in the *Biblioteca de literatura afrocolombiana*, a state-funded series that reinscribes Afro-Colombian authors in the national canon, his collected essays offer a keen view of the Chocó region. Against elite, major capital-centered accounts, Velásquez recounts Independence from the ground up, documenting the role of the region's enslaved in the cause against the

Spaniards. He coins the term *negredumbre*, an original category for political ontology, to refer to disenfranchised, racialized masses. Thought-provokingly, he is also one of the first to read Isaac's *María* from the perspective of the black folk depicted there (relegated to a secondary narrative role but, nonetheless, given agency). Velásquez's work raises the broader question of regional essayistic traditions vis-à-vis national traditions. There is a lively debate on whether essayists from powerful cultural centers like Bogotá, Medellín, or Cartagena have an undue ascendancy over their peers. In his prologue to Velásquez, Germán Patiño finds it "inexplicable" that Chocó did not join Panama in gaining independence from Colombia when it had the chance (10). Voicing a related concern, Jaime Jaramillo Escobar edited a hefty volume, *El ensayo en Antioquia* (2003, The essay in Antioquia), which singularizes that region as a unit of analysis. Fernando Cruz Kronfly and César Valencia Solanilla could be read within a similar regional framework, respectively, for the Cauca Valley and for the Greater Caldas region.

Contemporary Colombian essayism includes Antonio Caballero (1967), Héctor Abad Faciolince (1958), Juan Gustavo Cobo Borda (1948), William Ospina (1954), and Juan Gabriel Vásquez (1973), among other writers who practice across fiction and nonfiction genres. Caballero is a regular contributor to *Semana*; his sardonic and insightful op-ed pieces have been edited as a highly readable collection of essays (1996). For his part, Abad's essays articulate a humanist critique of narco-culture, although he is mostly known as a memoirist and novelist (unlike Caballero, whose standing as a public intellectual eclipses his one novel). In addition to an anthologist, Cobo Borda is a ubiquitous cultural and literary commentator, as well as a poet. Meanwhile, Ospina's *¿Dónde está la franja amarilla?* (1997, Where Is the Yellow Fringe?), a popular choice for secondary school curricula, is a broad-ranging, consciousness-raising examination of national politics. Since that work, the prolific writer has published several book-length essays, as well as historical novels. For his part, Vásquez presents his reading notes on several authors, elaborated into short essays, in *El arte de la distorsión* (2009, The Art of Distortion). Implicitly, the book also serves as an ars poetica for the author as novelist. Taken together, these authors invite further study about the relations between multiple genres. As essayism disseminates through cultural magazines of considerable national circulation, including *El malpensante, Número,* and *Arcadia,* not to mention newspaper supplements, the question remains open as to whether this represents a triumph or a dissolution of the essay as genre.[9] Meanwhile, at long last and facing many hurdles, specialized, peer-review journals grow in number, international recognition, and overall quality – but also occupying some of the space that the multifarious essay used to have.

On this last point, symptomatically, Vélez claims the essay has a free spirit ("un carácter libre"), unlike academic publications, which ultimately serve "secret societies" (71).[10] The purported antagonism of institutions and freedom is, ostensibly, a highly problematic feature of this corpus. Truly democratic essayism can exist alongside specialized audiences; ideally, broad readership and learned societies build on each other. Academia is a space of freedom – consider the alternatives. In the name of openness, the principled defense of the essay can, paradoxically, verge on anti-intellectualism. Arguably, this impedes the articulation of a more robust public sphere in the country. Academicism may be just as undesirable a pole, but it seems the lesser evil in a context of insufficient institutions and educational opportunity. Teasing out the full extent of the interconnection between essayistic authority and forms of power and entitlement in Colombia belongs to a future study.

Another line for further research is the relationship between the essay and the novel: Do they provide a good climate for each other? Alternatively, one could examine essayism's role in nurturing *cultura general*, a relatively popularized awareness of humanistic traditions that is absent in other countries. Yet another possible topic is the evolution of nation building in the essay, from Colonial Americanity to contemporary affirmations of pan-regional identity. Finally, there is the problem of Colombian essayism being "in sync" or "out of touch" with other Latin American and Western traditions. The present chapter suggests the broader role that Colombian essayism should have in Latin Americanism. It also discusses some of the themes and authors that bind Colombians with their Latin American peers and with the world at large. Surpassing insularity and exceptionalism, more should be done to that effect.

SELECTED REFERENCES

Alzate, Carolina. "Aptitud de la mujer para ejercer todas las profesiones." *Revista de Estudios Sociales* 38 (2011): 166–8.
Beverley, John. *Essays on the Literary Baroque in Spain and Spanish America.* London: Boydell & Brewer, 2008.
Caballero, Antonio. *Quince Años de Mal Agüero.* Medellín: La Hoja, 1996.
Colmenares, Germán. *Las convenciones contra la cultura: Ensayos sobre la historiografía hispanoamericana del siglo XIX.* Cali: Universidad del Valle, 1997.
Espitia, David Leonardo. "Problemas para una historia del ensayo en Colombia." *Literatura: Teoría, historia, crítica* 2 (2000): 61–76.

García, José María Rodríguez. *The City of Translation: Poetry and Ideology in Nineteenth-Century Colombia*. New York: Palgrave Macmillan, 2010.

Garrido, Margarita. "Germán Colmenares: Sobre investigación y escritura." In *Germán Colmenares, ensayos sobre su obra*, ed. Jorge Orlando Melo, 41–54. Bogotá: Tercer Mundo Editores, 1999.

Giraldo, Efrén. *La poética del esbozo: Baldomero Sanín Cano, Hernando Téllez, Nicolás Gómez Dávila*. Bogotá. Universidad de los Andes, 2014.

Gómez-Martínez, José Luis. *Teoría del ensayo*. Salamanca: Ediciones Universidad de Salamanca, 1981.

González Echevarría, Roberto. *Celestina's Brood: Continuities of the Baroque in Spanish and Latin American Literatures*. Durham: Duke University Press, 1993.

Hoyos, Héctor. "García Márquez's Sublime Violence and the Eclipse of Colombian Literature." *Chasqui* 35, no. (2006): 3–20.

Jaramillo Escobar, Jaime. *El ensayo en Antioquia*. Medellín: Alcaldía de Medellín, Secretaría de Cultura Ciudadana, 2003.

Jiménez de Quesada, Gonzalo. *El Antijovio*. Bogotá: Instituto Caro y Cuervo, 1991.

Langebaek, Carl. "La Obra de José María Samper vista por Élisee Reclus." *Revista de Estudios Sociales* 27 (2007): 196–205.

"La pelea del quinto centenario." *Semana*, January 14, 1991.

Melo, Jorge Orlando. "Las revistas literarias en Colombia e Hispanoamérica: Una aproximación a su historia." N.p., October 31, 2008.

Montaigne, Michel de. "Of Democritus and Heraclitus." In *The Complete Essays of Montaigne*. Vol. 1. Stanford: Stanford University Press, 1958.

Orjuela, Héctor H. *Primicias del ensayo en Colombia: El discurso ensayístico colonial*. Bogotá: Editora Guadalupe, 2002.

Pabón Pérez, Hugo Leonardo. *Bibliografía de y sobre Germán Arciniegas*. Bogotá: Instituto Caro y Cuervo, 2001.

Rueda Vargas, Tomás. *Visiones de historia y La Sabana*. Bogotá: Instituto Colombiano de Cultura, 1975.

Torres, Carlos Arturo. *Idola fori y Escritos políticos*. Ed. Rubén Sierra Mejía. Bogotá: Instituto Caro y Cuervo, 2001.

Torres Duque, Óscar. *El mausoleo iluminado: antología del ensayo en Colombia*. Presidencia de la República, 1997.

Velásquez, Rogerio. *Ensayos escogidos*. Ed. Germán Patiño Ossa. Bogotá: Ministerio de Cultura, 2010.

Vélez, Jaime Alberto. *El Ensayo: Entre la aventura y el orden*. Bogotá: Taurus, 2000.

Notes

1 For providing relevant materials from their publication series, I am grateful to Professors David Mauricio Solodkow and Hugo Ramírez at Universidad de los Andes, Bogotá, as well as to Professors Camilo Hoyos and Juan Manuel Espinosa at Instituto Caro y Cuervo.

2 Short of a comprehensive bibliography, Giraldo provides one of the most complete ones to date. See also the special issue "El Siglo del ensayo," *Credencial historia* 207 (March 2007).

3 For diverging views on the modernity of Espinosa Medrano's writings, see González Echevarría and Beverley.

4 The bond between power and literary culture in Colombia is thoroughly documented in Rodríguez García.

5 For a suggestive reading of Sanín Cano as a precursor to world literature ideals in Latin America, see Siskind, 168–83.

6 "De prisa, de prisa, sacando notas de un cubilete, ha ido formándose este anecdotario, sin tropiezos ni problemas, porque hasta ayer todo era un poco provinciano, recogido, fácil de contar. El modernismo inicia un loco deseo de viajar, un afán casi desmesurado de comunicación, que ya no tiene hoy frenos, ni límites ... todo encuentra difusión en las revistas" (104).

7 While the essay was never García Márquez's favorite genre, he wrote two pieces that exerted a profound influence: "Dos o tres cosas sobre la 'novela de la Violencia'" (1959, Two or three things on the novel of La Violencia") and "La literatura colombiana, un fraude a la nación" (1960, "Colombian litera-ture, a fraud to the nation"). For a discussion of these texts and their framing of violence in fiction, see my article "García Márquez's Sublime Violence and the Eclipse of Colombian Literature." There are also important essayistic moments in *Noticia de un secuestro* (1996) and *Vivir para contarla* (2002).

8 Gómez Dávila's eloquent language conforms to what Alberto Moreiras would call "la inquietante lucidez del pensamiento reaccionario," the namesake of a special number he co-edited for *Archipiélago* 56 (2003).

9 For an overview of Colombian magazines, see Melo (2008).

10 The full quote reads: "Mientras un buen ensayo posee un carácter libre, la mayoría de los trabajos académicos se escriben por encargo, y con la manifiesta intención de cumplir un determinado objetivo. La reducción a un propósito, a una verdad y a un lenguaje, termina por convertir este género en una forma de pertenencia a una sociedad secreta, tal como se percibe en ciertas pub-licaciones especializadas, destinadas sólo a miembros del grupo" (71, "While the good essay possesses a free character, the majority of academic works are written upon request, and with the specific intention of fulfilling a determined objective. The reduction to a purpose, a truth and a language ends up converting this genre into a form of belonging to a secret society, as is evident in certain specialized publications, destined to only members of a group").

PART II

Colombian culture and society in regional contexts

CHAPTER 10

Literature, culture, and society of the Magdalena River

Rory O'Bryen

Long before its identification as Colombia's *río patria* in 1919 and prior to its colonial baptism as Río Grande de la Magdalena in April 1501, the Río Magdalena, modern Colombia's principal waterway, was central to diverse cosmologies and went by many names: Guaca-Hayo ("river of tombs"), Yuma ("river of the country of the friend"), Arlí or Arbí ("river of fish"), Karacalí ("river of caimans"), and Karihuana ("large water").[1] Indeed, as it wound its way from the high *páramos* in the south and between the central and eastern *cordilleras* of the Andes in its middle reaches, before spilling its waters over its swampy delta and into the Caribbean Sea, it facilitated contact and commerce between diverse pre-Hispanic cultures.[2] Now many of these have been erased in all but name because of war and disease in the Colonial Period, the colonization and redistribution of lands aimed at securing agricultural exports in the nineteenth century, and a constantly evolving set of political conflicts that date back at least as far as the *Violencia* of the 1940s and 1950s. Thus the Magdalena basin, which covers 23 percent of Colombia's surface area, now contains 80 percent of Colombia's predominantly *mestizo* population and is where 85 percent of its economic activity takes place. Although it has lost its historic role as the nation's principal axis of communication and gateway to the Atlantic world, it nonetheless continues to connect (albeit in a spectral fashion) the distinct regions of what in many accounts is a highly fragmented nation.[3]

In his *Elegías de ilustres varones* (158, the chronicler Juan de Castellanos wrote that "con innumerable tinta/No se podrá decir la parte quinta" of the horrors endured during Gonzalo Jiménez de Quesada's first expedition up the river.[4] Advancing slowly up its densely forested course, Jiménez's men find only "Montaña tenebrosa y asombrada."[5] Romantic scientists like Alexander von Humboldt, Francisco José Caldas, and José Celestino Mutis would later supplant the terms of this Spanish colonial "heart of darkness" with an emphasis on the sublime beauty and abundance of its shores – tropes forged and negotiated in the "planetary consciousness" of imperial science.[6] Yet even after the consolidation of steam travel in the mid–nineteenth century, travel on its waters remained arduous. Indeed, with their reliance on the Magdalena to connect the cities in the Andes to the political and economic life on both sides of the Atlantic, many nineteenth-century statesmen saw the fate of the republic depending heavily on the development of transport connections with and along the river's shores. In Eugenio Díaz Castro's *Manuela* (1858), Demóstenes, a Liberal *letrado*, prognosticates that Colombia would not escape tyranny until it had built roads capable of transporting tropical produce to the river's ports for shipment abroad.[7] For Díaz's contemporaries like Rufino José Cuervo, José María Samper, and Manuel María Madiedo, progress also involved "civilizing" seemingly "barbaric" ex-slaves, runaways, and *bogas* living freely along the river's banks.

By the end of the twentieth century, the pursuit of "civilization" and "progress" begun in the nineteenth century seemed to many writers and artists to have culminated in the devastation of the river's ecosystems and transformation of its course into a string of political no man's lands.[8] In Pedro Gómez Valderrama's *La otra raya del tigre* (1977, The Other Stripe of the Tiger), Demóstenes' dream is shown to have been realized by German entrepreneurs as early as the 1870s, but as a nightmare that leaves the region of Santander's artisanal sectors and indigenous cultures in ruins, and its landscape scarred and striped like the skin of a jaguar.[9] In García Márquez's *El amor en los tiempos del cólera* (1985, Love in the Time of Cholera), set shortly afterwards, one of its characters has the foreboding that so much timber is needed to fuel steam navigation on the river that before long one might see motorcars driving along its dusty bed.[10] Now, in the novels of Fernando Vallejo, in canvases by Alfonso Quijano, and in the multimedia art of Clemencia Echeverri, the river no longer has a name.[11] In these and many other works, the river not only teems with anonymous corpses – prominent in the mid-century *novela de Laa Violencia* and in accounts of political violence from García Márquez onwards – but also with the detritus of a throwaway consumer culture compounded by international drug trafficking. Their authors reiterate what ecological reports never cease to inform: that this river, which now has the largest sediment yield of any river on the South American Atlantic, is dying.[12]

A long historical overview of literary representations of the river's geographical, cultural, social, and political landscapes presents a similar reduction in density and diversity to that evinced by the river's unification under its singular Christian name, and one that mirrors other accounts of the nation's precarious unfolding as an "imagined community."[13] Yet many works in which the river is central (and with it, the multidirectional movements of people and goods on its waters) demand that we think against the grain of this eschatological narrative. Nineteenth-century works on the Magdalena share with other "foundational fictions" a fragile interplay between the articulation of the nation as unifying ideal and the documentation of that ideal's fragmentation by regional, political, and identitarian differences.[14] They also hint at a second, intersecting tension between the desire, on the one hand, to territorialize within the fictive entity of the nation the flows of people, capital, and ideas that the river supports, and the recognition, on the other, that these same flows deterritorialize the nation's dramas as they fuel ideological and economic processes beyond its shores. The second tension becomes progressively more pronounced in the twentieth century and displaces the first as global flows of people, capital, and information (altogether more dynamic than river transport ever was in the nineteenth century) relentlessly supplant the river's metaphorical power to index the nation's historical integration into broader world systems.

The fixing of difference and the flow of capital 1850–80

Raymond L. Williams notes in his detailed overview of Colombian literature between 1844 and 1987 that the novel was for a long time considered a minor national genre. In the first half of the nineteenth century, written cultural expression remained, with few exceptions, in the hands of former military leaders, the landed elites, and the colonial *ciudades letradas* in Bogotá, Cartagena, Popayán, and Tunja. Writing in this period was more programmatic and essayistic than literary per se, often serving as a means to express pre-partisan desires for a return to Hellenic/Catholic Arcadia or for a more distinctly liberal future.[15] These contrasting outlooks would form the bedrock of the Liberal and Conservative parties, formed in 1849 and 1850, respectively. After the presidential election of Liberal General José Hilario López in 1849, they crystallize into opposing ideological stances on Liberal democratic reforms such as the abolition of slavery, the granting of press freedoms, the redistribution of Church lands, and the curtailment of the Church's influence in public life and education, as well as the implementation, later, of a federalist system of governance. In the ensuing period of fragile Liberal hegemony that lasted until the 1880s, few writers dedicated themselves uniquely to the writing of poetry or novels. Yet creative writing in this period supplemented the work of statesmanship in important ways.

In 1850 the Comisión Corográfica set out to produce a comprehensive map of the nation's human and material resources. Its members included the cartographer Agustín Codazzi, the botanist José Jerónimo Triana, and the artists Carmelo Fernández, Manuel María Paz, and Henry Price, all of whom worked under the Liberal intellectual Manuel Ancízar. The project aimed not only to extend state power into the spheres of popular life,[16] but also to attract the foreign capital and labor needed to construct a competitive national economy. The Comisión left behind it a detailed, albeit incomplete, visual assemblage of the nation, which, in distributing its internal differences in discrete temporal and spatial arrangements, resembles (in the words of a recent study) "un registro fotográfico de retratos de escenas que estaban ocurriendo en un lugar y un momento específicos."[17] Writings about the river in the period share a commitment to this "corographic" task, producing similar *cuadros* of popular life along the river's banks. Yet by actualizing the narrative dynamism hinted at, but formally fixed and frozen, in the Comisión's works, they often destabilize the latter's static arrangements of difference. Indeed, the messiness of life on the river frequently overspilled such representational fixities, and writings about it evidenced deep ideological rifts between *letrados* over how to channel its flows into the construction of a modern state, how to manage the movement of people along its shores, and even how to turn these sometimes anarchic movements into the basis of a national literature.

For José María Vergara y Vergara, the Jesuit-educated Conservative ideologue and founder of *El Mosaico* (1858–72), one of the first journals to promote a national literature in Colombia, literary traditions were themselves like rivers. In his *Historia de la literatura en Nueva Granada* (1867) he followed the Romantic ethos of the period to affirm that such a literature would take root in popular traditions, but stressed that "El que se toma el trabajo de recoger romances llaneros y cantares de los negros, entraría con ellos en la literatura española como entra el Meta en el Orinoco; llevaría una grandeza a otra grandeza."[18] When stripped of their rough grammatical infelicities – *rudezas* that Vergara y Vergara insisted on purging from texts like *Manuela* (1858),[19] the first novel published by *El Mosaico* – these oral forms would give voice not to a Colombian *Gemeinschaft* originating in the depths of its subsoil, but to the durability and noble *grandeza* of historic Hispanic forms. It was the task of the grammarian-*letrado* to oversee the linguistic purification of these forms and to ensure that the wellspring of Hispanic values and traditions were maintained intact. As indicated by the racial overdetermination of the terms in which it was hedged, Vergara's project also envisaged a literary future that would be coterminous with a future whitening of its population and with a return to Hispanic cultural traditions on which to construct the republic. Writing specifically about the poetry of the Magdalena River, Vergara y Vergara was scornful about the songs of the *bogas* – Afro-Colombian or mixed-race Afro-Indian boatmen who dominated river travel between Honda, the lower Magdalena, and the Caribbean coast until the late 1870s. He slips shamelessly between the questionable view that the *bogas'* songs lacked an awareness of history and an appeal to erase the *boga* from history itself, thereby enacting a shift between literary criticism and proto-eugenicist polemic that was not uncommon at the time. This slippage is heightened as he lauds steam travel's imminent displacement of "la ruda embarcación llamada *champán*; y con ella el tipo más rudo aún del boga . . . un hombre de color, alto, fornido, salvaje en sus costumbres, rival del caimán."[20] Many writers shared this view of the *boga*. Indeed (anti-) *boga cuadros* were so common in these years that they seem to constitute almost the sine qua non of national letters. Such hostility in nearly all instances expressed lettered prejudice toward the orality that represented, in a largely illiterate society such as was Nueva Granada, a threat and an embarrassment to elite claims regarding the nation's position at the vanguard of a distinctly cosmopolitan republican political modernity.[21] Yet the motivations behind it encoded divergent political views on the future of the republic and on the management of those flows of capital, people, and ideas that would sustain it.

For Conservatives like Manuel María Madiedo from Cartagena – a mulatto writer who criticized racist prejudice in public discourse – the *boga* represented an obstacle to the formation of the nation because of his indifference to Christian spirituality. In *La maldición* (The Malediction) published in *El Mosaico* (1859–62), a young Carlos, who is burdened by a past trauma, returns from Paris to his native Mompox. There he wanders along the river's Edenic shores like Noah in search of a new "ark" with which to construct himself anew. Driven by the memory of a childhood tale, he enlists a fisherman and a group of *bogas* to take him to a mysterious tributary of the river known as "el arroyo de otro mundo." On approaching this space his *boga* companions, still enslaved by the "false beliefs" of Indigenous myth, desert him out of fear of encountering the mythical "Mohán."[22] The enlightened Carlos climbs its waterfalls where he meets a bearded white anchorite living in pastoral harmony with his former slaves. The anchorite had withdrawn from the world of material affairs after the death of his daughter, which he had accidentally caused, and which, we finally learn, is the tragic loss at the root of Carlos' own unshakeable melancholy. The revelation leads Carlos to suicide, but the aim of the novel is to charm the reader into the belief that genuine republican liberty and equality can be founded only on the spirit of Christian fraternity that the anchorite has arrived at only too late.[23]

In works by Liberal-identified authors of the period, the shared ritualized scorn of the *boga*, his anarchic orality, sexual lubricity, and materialism, contrasts in key ways with Madiedo's derision of *boga* superstition and attendant call for a republican politics guided by Christian spirituality. Indeed, for authors like Eugenio Díaz and José María Samper, if the *boga* represented an obstacle to progress it was because he hindered the free flow of capital on the river. The case of Díaz's *Manuela* is complex, partly because Vergara y Vergara's purging of popular speech from the novel would highlight a rift between a narratorial display of "correct" Spanish and instances of "improper" popular usage that was less visible in the original. Furthermore, the novel's critique of a Liberal *letrado*-statesman's failure to legitimize his enlightened outlook in the Magdalena valley between La Mesa and the river port of Ambalema led it to be read as an expression of authorial conservatism.[24] Yet undercutting *Manuela*'s ostensibly conservative defence of immutable popular customs – its portrayal, in Colmenares's words, of "un espesor en las costumbres que la prédica política no puede penetrar"[25] – is its complacency (also noted by Colmenares) with the Liberal reforms underway at the time. Thus while documenting the complications involved in contracting *bogas*, it shares a Liberal outlook on the freedom created by salaried labor, as witnessed in the tobacco-producing region of Ambalema during a boom in tobacco production that followed the 1850 abolition of the state's monopoly on the product.

The tobacco bonanza freed Colombia from its historic economic dependency on gold exports, producing internal and external migrations of people to the region and a spike in exports that, to many, seemed to offer a vindication of liberal economic policies of laissez-faire.[26] In *Manuela*, Díaz expresses Liberal optimism in such policies when his protagonist, Manuela, fleeing the political bossing of don Tadeo – a remnant of the *draconiano* wing of the Liberal party, which had clamored for greater economic state protection before being defeated in its failed coup led by General José María Melo in 1845 – marvels at the freedom of life in Ambalema. In her encounter with workers from around the country, she shares the excitement generated by the flow of capital up and down the river, even seeing in the febrile activity of Ambalema's *tabacaleras* the potential for women's emancipation from the patriarchal economy of the region's traditional sugar estates. At this point the novel interrupts its production of *cuadros de costumbres,* momentarily allowing the fantasy of flow to dissolve its mosaic-like fixing of difference.[27] This interplay between the fixing and dissolution of difference is more sustained in José María Samper's *Viajes de un colombiano en Europa* (1862), where it is transposed onto a more overtly racialized set of oppositions between orality and writing, the *champán* and the steamship.

Actualizing ideas only latent in Díaz, Samper uses his travels down the Magdalena to rehearse his then staunchly Liberal credentials. Unlike Vergara or Madiedo, for whom the river's cycles, when properly managed, seemed to promise the nation's future return to its Catholic, Spanish source, Samper's river flows into a distinctly cosmopolitan Atlantic that connects the nation's future to British economic liberalism and French political republicanism. In tune with the 1853 constitution's conflation of the freedom of labor with the freedom of industry, he champions steam as the harbinger of a kind of "progress" that would erode the *boga*'s historic monopoly over river transport.[28] Although the steamboat represents pure dynamism and provides the ideal conduit for an international "flujo y reflujo de las instituciones y de las costumbres, de la literatura, de la ciencia y de la industria,"[29] a *currulao* danced by *bogas* on the shores of river's lower reaches indexes the coexistence of contradictory temporal planes. In contrast to the teleological dynamism embodied by this "segunda providencia" – one that becomes, in a sense, the very motor of writing itself – the circular dance represents "la inmovilidad en el movimiento" and the immutability of animal life stagnating in "una vegetación, una manera de ser puramente mecánica."[30] Singing to the tune of *La Marseillaise* and *God Save the Queen*, his desire is to see the free flow of ideas and new capitals drown out the noise of the diabolical *currulao* and erase such embarrassing historical remainders.

While in the aforementioned texts the *boga*'s anarchic orality and defence of autonomous labor place him at the outer limits of the nation's political modernity, *Cantos populares de mi tierra* (1877, Popular Songs of My Land) by Candelario Obeso, a mulatto *letrado* from Mompox, challenges these prejudices in ways that shine light on the elite anxieties about popular political participation at their root. Obeso symbolically usurps the place of the white *letrado* who typically appropriates plebeian orality to ventriloquize and "color" political ideology. He also voices the spirit of a powerful counterculture of plebeian democratic bargaining with lettered discourse that has its roots in post-Independence ideologies of racial harmony and political equality.[31] In "Epresión re mi amitá," a *boga* expresses his fraternity with a Liberal *letrado* and promises to defend the party in an imminent civil war with the Conservatives. Yet he does so in a way that makes his friendship and his labor conditional on the recognition of his political liberty and equality as a citizen. In "Epropiación re uno córigo," an artisan tells another *letrado* that he has pawned some legal papers entrusted to him, in exchange for half a pound of cotton fabric that he has used to patch up the holes in his humble dwelling. Such an act of "expropriation" enacts, in Carlos Jáuregui's words, "una desautorización del culto a la ley," revealing behind those lettered codes "una materialidad y una lógica que los convierte en objetos sin más valor que el del papel que los soporta."[32]

Such symbolic "expropriations," however, do not only empty out the letter. They also underscore how republican lettered codes (*córigos*) have the potential to serve a range of conflicting social interests once they are taken outside the institutions that oversee their interpretation. They allow Obeso, in other words, to muddle the "proper" distribution of difference performed by geographical entities such as the *Comisión Corográfica* and literary-political organs like *El Mosaico*, and to turn the geographic mobility of the *boga*, in whose voice he speaks, into an aesthetic principle that dissolves racial distributions of speech and writing, order and disorder, manual and intellectual labor. Speaking from the symbolic locus of the Magdalena's Afro-Colombian coastal reaches he thus turns writing into an instrument for realizing republican racial equality. Hence, in "Lucha e conquijta" – a poem that preempts his later reflections on urban prejudice in *Lecturas para ti* (1878, Readings for You) and *Lucha de la vida* (1882, Battle for Life) – he asks: "¿Pocque me ve la cuti/Re la coló e la tinta/ Acaso cré que é negra/También er arma mía?"[33] This rhetorical question presents his female white interlocutor with a conundrum. Whichever way she responds, he must be considered an equal, for by linking his blackness with writing via the metonymy "tinta," he shows that difference is either an *effect* of writing or its *source*, and the source of the very substance, writing, out of which "white" claims to mastery are manufactured.

Transition: the Regeneración and the Conservative republic, 1886-1930

In his *Cantos*, Obeso not only critiqued lettered prejudice about the *boga charlatán*, but also bewailed the breakdown, at the end of the 1870s, of a republican culture of interclass bargaining that had opened up significant channels for plebeian participation in the politics of the Magdalena's coastal regions. Poems such as "Serenata" and "Parábola" express the poet's disillusionment with the end of such forms of participation at a time, after the religious war of 1876–77, when many Liberals began joining the Independent party led by the *costeño*, former Liberal, and future president Rafael Núñez. Together with the Catholic grammarian and jurist Miguel Antonio Caro – author of the 1886 constitution, which aligned state power with the ultramontane authority of the papacy and made the grammarians of the *ciudad letrada* sovereign arbiters of all access to the public sphere[34] – Núñez's Independents pursued a program of political "Regeneration" aimed at disciplining the nation's contentious subalterns and at reversing the liberties formally introduced by the Liberal republic in 1850. Obeso's famous "Canció der boga ausente" gives a sense of the ensuing exclusion of plebeian subjects, voicing a *boga*'s lament as he finds himself punting indeterminately up and down the river in a dark night devoid of guiding stars. In the years that followed, politics would be recalled to the hallowed precincts of Bogotá's *ciudad letrada*, now enshrined as the "Athens of South America," bringing about a very real authoritarian "dark night" for subjects who had once identified with the Liberal republic's democratic experiments.

During this period of "Regeneration," which lasted from 1886 to 1900 and cemented the Conservative party's hegemony until 1929, intellectual life was largely dominated by Núñez and Caro, as well as by authors like José Manuel Marroquín, Soledad Acosta de Samper, and Eustaquio Palacios.[35] Many of these sought to refound the nation in the Arcadian Hispanic values once defended by Conservatives like Vergara y Vergara and given romantic expression in now canonized novels such as *María* (1867) – which had disingenuously foreclosed the social and racial conflicts that threatened Colombia's landowning elite in its time. Soledad Acosta de Samper, for example – who throughout the 1860s and 1870s had sought to vindicate the rights of modern Colombian women – now lauded, in *Los piratas en Cartagena* (1886, the year of Caro's constitution, translation Pirates of Cartagena), the heroism of Spanish colonials who had rebutted attacks on "Colombian" sovereignty by perfidious British, French, and Dutch pirates. The work would receive the imprimatur of President Núñez himself and offered a thinly veiled endorsement of the *Regeneración*'s denunciation of the Liberal experiments of the previous years.[36] However, the hegemony of the "Regenerationist" Conservative project would not go unchallenged in literary texts in these years. Nor would it succeed in producing the kind of Catholic-Conservative Arcadia imagined by its proponents.

In works produced during the years that span the *Regeneración* and the Conservative republic, we thus see a tension between new kinds of aesthetic autonomy, on the one hand, and an incipient radicalization of the novel in the service of social critique on the other. This tension mirrors the accompanying tension between liberal economics and conservative politics that characterized these years[37] and is given its most memorable expression in José Asunción Silva's *De sobremesa* (written in 1896, published in 1925, After Dinner). Staging an after-dinner reading of a diary written in Europe by the intellectual, dandy, and aesthete José Fernández – a diary containing his thoughts on art, love, and his various nervous ailments – the novel seems to exemplify *modernismo*'s desire to provide an autonomous form of aesthetic resistance to the bourgeois revolutions underway in the economic sphere.[38] Yet Erica Beckman convincingly argues that Fernández's discourse is in fact shot through with the tropes of an emerging consumer culture, with his search for a "refined" aesthetic echoing both private and public reveries about the luxury imports to which the export of raw materials would give rise.[39] It also notably parodies liberal reveries about the civilizing impact of these economic transformations – reveries present in more or less explicit form in fantasies about the increase of traffic along the Magdalena in works by Díaz and Samper.

In one of the most memorable sections of *De sobremesa*, Fernández recalls his delirious ascent of the Swiss Alps, from whose high vantage point he concocts a plan for modernizing his own nation. This he will fund by selling his gold mines to private owners in the United States. Like Bolívar in his *Delirio sobre el Chimborazo* (1823) and Andrés Bello in his *Silva a la agricultura de la zona tórrida* (1826), both of whom Fernández cites, he deliriously fantasizes that modernity will transform and civilize Colombia's social, political, and geographic landscapes. Like Samper too he dreams of "colosales *steamers* de compañías subvencionadas por el gobierno" traveling up and down its rivers[40] and of the subsequent arrival of torrents of foreign workers: "un río de hombres [. . . que] poblará hasta los últimos desiertos, labrará el campo, explotará las minas, traerá industrias nuevas."[41] This labor, he imagines, "levantará al pueblo a una altura intelectual y moral superior a la de los más avanzados de Europa."[42] Yet his vision of "el porvenir glorioso de la tierra regenerada" also has its darker political side, requiring "una dictadura conservadora como la de García Moreno en el Ecuador o la de Cabrera en Guatemala," especially to free the nation from "peroratas demagógicas y falsas libertades escritas en carta constitucional."[43] The nods to Núñez and Caro are hard to miss, particularly to their fetishization of steam power as an instrument for a distinctly authoritarian "regeneration" of the Liberal republic's "degenerate" legacies.

Beyond parodying such "import reveries," as Beckman calls them, and in addition to highlighting the political authoritarianism on which they were predicated, Silva also underscores their impossibility by framing them within the manic, "neurasthenic" cycling between euphoria and dejection caused by Fernández's excessive consumption of foreign commodities. "Estaba loco cuando escribí eso,"[44] Fernández avows after reading the diary entry about his modernization plan. He then moves into an account of equally mad efforts to find his elusive muse, Helena. These cycles, for Beckman, point beyond *De sobremesa*'s closed aesthetic sodalities to index the nation's oscillation between *economic* boom and bust, euphoria and depression, in these years,[45] making Silva's investment in fin-de-siècle decadence into a Spanish American "poetics of bankruptcy on the periphery of global capitalism."[46] While in *De sobremesa* such a poetics is formally confined to the closed spaces of Fernández's sumptuous interior and intimate personal diary, in texts written about the lower Magdalena, by contrast, crisis and breakdown are externalized in more concrete social forms.[47] Indeed, in the following decades, dependency on foreign capital and loans led to the growth of Barranquilla as the coast's main economic center and to the growth of a cosmopolitan literary culture that would displace Cartagena's historic *ciudad letrada*.[48] It also opened the region to foreign exploitation, creating forms of proletarian dispute that would culminate in the 1928 massacre of United Fruit Company workers in Ciénaga in 1928.

The return of the *Río de las tumbas*: violence and the Río Magdalena

After the massacre of 1928, an emerging literature of social critique links capitalism to political violence, reframing the Magdalena River as a "tomb-river" and as Colombian capitalism's symbolic graveyard.[49] Here the image of the "tomb-river" is key to novelists' critique of the subservience of the nation's political class to the deterritorializing powers of global capital. Indeed, it inverts the nineteenth-century trope of the river as index of the nation's return to Edenic shores, or of the providential flow of previously dormant capital unleashed by connectivity with cosmopolitan Atlantic markets. In so doing it points to extreme instances of capital's own *inversion* of social relations under the precarious conditions of piecemeal wage labor such that those relations appear, in Marx's words, "as material [*dinglich*] relations between persons and social relations between things."[50] After the massacre in *Cien años de soledad* (1967, One Hundred Years of Solitude), José Arcadio Segundo wakes up in a steam train headed for the coast, surrounded by the corpses of fellow *bananeros*. Heaped up like the pickings of their labor, they will be dumped into the sea "como el banano de rechazo."[51] Seen from this perspective, steam (the once fetishized index of progress that would to bring all the trappings of modernity) becomes visibly instrumental in this deathly inversion of social relations. The task of "magical realism," so called, is to explore and destabilize the narrative forms that uphold and are fueled by such mystified social inversions.

Other *costeño* texts like Manuel Zapata Olivella's *Tierra mojada* (1947, Wet Land), García Márquez's earlier *La hojarasca* (1955, Leafstorm), and Álvaro Cepeda Samudio's *La casa grande* (1962, La Casa Grande) link the arrival of foreign capital to state violence and to the dissolution of familial and social bonds. They underscore, respectively, the hardships of plantation labor, the alienation of deracinated proletarian laborers – as dehumanized "leaf trash" swept into the *zona bananera* by the whirlwind of global capital in García Márquez – and parallels between traditional forms of incestuous patriarchal violence and the violence committed against Colombian workers by a paternalist state. In doing so they too strip away the layers of aesthetic mystification that veil exotic commodities in modernist works such as Silva's. Yet they also provide demystifying narrative solutions to the hypostasis of violence – prevalent in earlier works about social violence – as a quasi-natural or divine phenomenon. Such mystification is common in the mainly Andean *novela de La Violencia* in contradistinction to which many of these authors (García Márquez in particular) developed their experiments in form. In the *novela de La Violencia* the image of the river-turned-cemetery resonates powerfully with the torrent of dehumanized "leaf trash" washed up in Macondo at the outset of *La hojarasca*. Yet beyond providing localized accounts of the partisan cruelty that preceded these acts of disposal – torture, murder, and the desacralizing mutilation of the body after death[52] – these novels often failed to connect such horrors to broader socioeconomic processes.

In Daniel Caicedo's *Viento seco* (1953, Dry Wind) a Liberal peasant, Antonio Gallardo, is dumped in the river Cauca – the Magdalena's largest tributary – after a massacre carried out by Conservative *pájaros* (hit men) in Ceilán. He survives but recounts that others were not so lucky: "cogían el cauce central y recorrían la llanada inflados, boca arriba o boca abajo, cabeza adelante con algunos gallinazos encima."[53] Alfonso Hilarión

Sánchez's *Balas de la ley* (1953, Bullets of the Law) offers a similar image in his account of the violence he witnesses in the coastal region of Bolívar. He recalls (not without enjoyment) seeing fellow Conservatives hacked to pieces and then dynamited in the Magdalena River at Magangué. This *espantosa carnicería* (horrifying carnage) confirms to him that the coast's "black" Liberals were "hordas sin dios ni ley"[54] (masses without God or law) and leads him to invoke the Falangist-identified Laureano Gómez as the nation's true savior.[55] Other novels such as Ernesto León Ferreira's *Cristianismo sin alma* (1956) contain similar scenes,[56] and yet their titles say it all: If the rivers ran red with blood and the rural sphere lay in ruins, this could only be the work of a heartless god or of godless men driven by dark drives located beyond any known pleasure principle. Indeed, it was only in a later context in which *La Violencia* had morphed into a new set of struggles that a generation of writers writing after García Márquez could shed light on the meaning of Colombia's "tomb-river" and through broader national and global prisms.

In Gustavo Álvarez Gardeazábal's *Cóndores no entierran todos los días* (1971, Condors Are Not Buried Every Day), where rivers also swell with corpses, the author is hard pushed to explain the cruelty of *La Violencia's* key actors, but its aims and effects seem clear. Behind the transformation of a small-town cheesemonger into a local hero lay the power of the political classes who could instrumentalize his zealous Catholicism and hereditary loyalty to the Conservative party for the purposes of expropriating peasant lands that could then be bought at slashed prices by regional capitalists. Once León María Lozano's work is done, he too will die an anonymous death like so many other members of his class whom he had terrorized. Although such insights correct the blind spots in the "realism" of works like *Viento seco*,[57] they do remain mired in a purely regional set of outlooks. In the testimonies of *La Violencia* compiled by Alfredo Molano in the late 1960s (also in the Valle del Cauca region), the accumulation of stories like Lozano's empties out the flow of time itself such that history breaks down into tales of repeated displacements in which peasants move from place to place in flight from one massacre after another. Historical depth gives way to a kind of empty "now-time" suspended between imminent repetitions of the same and the faint hope of a redemptive subaltern political turn.[58]

In works by Fernando Vallejo and Laura Restrepo, by contrast, the "tomb-river" becomes a cipher for the wastage of human life created when flows of illicit global capital meet a nation whose modernization process has been distinctly uneven. In Vallejo's *El río del tiempo* (river of time) cycle of five quasi-autobiographical novels, the corpse-ridden river becomes a metaphor of time itself. Sometimes it indexes personal mortality, evoking Heraclitus's river in which one never bathes twice; at others it stands for the nation's tragic demise. In all cases it points to the ineluctability of death (the existential "sea" of Manrique's *Coplas*), the oblivion guaranteed by a culture of forgetting (*desmemoria*) and the devaluation of human life in a consumer culture that reproduces social exclusion. For the American ecological economist Herman E. Daly, "man transforms raw materials into commodities and commodities into garbage."[59] For Vallejo, it seems, man turns *himself* into garbage in the process. Only writing and remembrance can reverse this ubiquitous haemorrhaging of life into garbage and turn the "río del tiempo" into a "río de doble corriente" (double current river). Yet in his tendency to collapse distinctions between collective and personal experience, he wavers between lamenting the devaluation of life in general under such conditions and offering post-Malthusian lettered celebrations of the "ecological" benefits of the population's decimation.

In *La Virgen de los sicarios* (1994, The Virgin of the Assassins), Vallejo enters into a symbolic relationship with two hired assassins, Alexis and Wílmar – the latter the killer of the former. Through their eyes he testifies to the deathly inversions of a kind of commodity fetishism that not even Marx could have imagined, witnessing killings performed by young boys happy to do anything to pay for a new pair of sneakers or stereo set, and emboldened to do so by Pablo Escobar's previous legitimation of their deathly labor. Echoing the words of Alonso Salazar, compiler of *testimonios* by young gang members, Vallejo shows how "el sicario lleva el consumismo al extremo: convierte la vida, la propia y la de las víctimas, en objeto de transacción económica, en objeto desechable."[60] Their bodies are cast into Colombia's temporal-existential "tomb-river" like any other immediately obsolescent throwaway *electrodoméstico*.[61] Yet the narrator's complicity in, and escape from, this cycle of consumption and disposal – his sexual union with both killers, for example, and his final leave taking of Medellín – show that the collective *uno* into which he frequently slips is as divided and stratified as the city itself. For Vallejo, "vivir en Medellín" may mean living death in a short-lived "sueño de basuco,"[62] but what fuels this *sueño* is no longer the export of the nation's gold, as it was for Fernández, but the killing of the nation's most vulnerable subjects by narco-capital's war machine.

In *La novia oscura* (1999, The Dark Girlfriend), Laura Restrepo returns to an altogether less metaphorical "tomb-river" to recover memory in a way that contrasts strikingly with Vallejo's effort to swim against the tide of Colombian *desmemoria*. By reconstructing the *huelgas heroicas* (heroic strikes) of the 1940s in which oil workers struck over labor conditions at the Tropical Oil Company's oil refineries in Barrancabermeja – Tora, where the novel is set, is Barrancabermeja's pre-Hispanic name – Restrepo recovers elements of class struggle and anti-imperialism whose absence she bemoaned in the *novela de La Violencia*.[63] She also sets up a dialectical engagement with the past that seeks to shed light on Colombia's (then) present predicament.[64] Here the Magdalena is just as contaminated as Vallejo's metaphorical river, but such "contamination" is now stripped of the racist overtones that it acquires in Vallejo. The industrial effluvia clogging the Magdalena's waters, her narrator writes, "la convertían en una prolongación de la refinería," making "el otrora Gran Río de la Magdalena" "una larga ausencia": a photographic negative of its nineteenth-century grandeur.[65] Yet by reconstructing the story of Sayonara – a prostitute of which all that remains is, symbolically, a photograph – that narrator seeks to restore the memory of vulnerable subjects who, in contrast with Vallejo's novel, are now given a voice as the altogether more human victims of the river's metaphorical absences, erasures, and disposals.

Such a reconstruction takes the form of a symbolic immersion into the river's contaminated flows and one that superficially enacts a passage from amnesia to memory, trauma to renewal, as well as from the isolation of individual experiences to the interconnection of those individual experiences with broader collective suffering. Midway through the novel we learn that Sayonara had performed such an act of immersion herself, entering the corpse-laden river in an act of communion with the swollen corpses of other peasant workers flowing downstream in the night. This act allows her to connect her traumatic history with that of others. Although she cannot see their faces in the night,

> los sintió pasar inofensivos en su tránsito lento y blanco ... Metió los pies en el agua para estar cerca de ellos ... tuvo la seguridad de que la romería silenciosa arrastraba también a sus seres amados ... que corrían Magdalena abajo purificados por fin y convertidos en recuerdos mansos. ... Supo también: Yo soy yo y mis muertos, y se sintió menos sola, como si se hubieran acortado los millones de pasos de su distancia.[66] [she felt them pass by passively in their slow and white movement ... she put her feet in the water to be near them ... she felt the security that the silent movement also carried along their loved ones ... that flowed along the Magdalena Rivera below, puried finally and converted into weak memories ... she also

> understood: she also realized: I am myself and my deaths, and she felt less
> solitary, as if they had cut her off.

Although the identity and stories of those other bodies remain shadowy
and hard to make out,[67] what is striking is Sayonara's desire to communicate – here in a very tactile physical sense – with a broader collective body,
and to connect to a collective history of loss of which her own is necessarily
a part. As the central image of Restrepo's novel, it also indexes the writer's
desire to establish a new kind of contact with those others historically
flushed out of the nation's histories, and one that is as much physical and
affective as it is representational.

Counterflows?

In many nineteenth-century texts the Magdalena River seemed often to
flow from the nation's fallen present toward an ideal, becoming that
which was located somewhere elsewhere, beyond the nation's shores.
In Conservative texts it pointed to the moral restoration of a spiritually
bankrupt nation that would come about through a return to the grandeur
of its Hispanic, Catholic "source." In Liberal works it signaled the
potential of contact with cosmopolitan cultural, political, and economic
networks to erase the politically unenlightened vestiges of this same
Colonial past. To return to José María Samper's words, the river's "flujos
y contraflujos" seemed always to index the nation's becoming other to
itself. Restrepo's return to the turbulent history of Barrancabermeja in
the 1940s is one of many late twentieth-century returns not only to an
iconic national landscape whose ability to index this kind of ideal
transformation seems to have come to an end, but also to turbulent
episodes in the nation's history that shed light on the human tragedies
generated by this kind of thinking. However, it is neither the first nor the
last to do so. Indeed, one of the most famous (Magdalena) river novels of
the twentieth century, García Márquez's *El amor en los tiempos del cólera*
(1985), not only looked back with nostalgia at this iconic nineteenth-
century landscape, but also seemed to hint that a happier national future
would involve reversing the nation's nineteenth-century self-definition in
foreign terms.

A revision of the nineteenth-century romance, *El amor* opens by satirizing
the *letrado*'s self-definition in foreign terms when one of the characters of the
love triangle at the novel's core, doctor Juvenal Urbino, comically meets his
death as he tries to capture his escaped pet parrot. This death sets up Urbino

as the victim of his own "parroting" of enlightened metropolitan discourses.[68] As the latter's rival and nemesis, the working-class Florentio Ariza who finally gains Fermina Daza's love seems to embody the antidote to such colonial "mimicry." He offers Fermina romantic love where Urbino had provided her only with security and upward social mobility and allows her, in a final journey up the Magdalena, to discover parts of herself suppressed for many years and a part of her own nation long since unbeknown to her – due to her former husband's preference for vacations in Europe. This, it seems, is García Márquez's call to retrace Colombia's "lost steps," the initiation of a journey back to the source of national identity that will provide the antidote to the curse of solitude prognosticated at the end of *Cien años de soledad*. It also seems to enact a return to romanticism, pledging a renewed loyalty to the foundational task of nation building.[69] However, these readings soon break down, much as they had done in Carpentier's *Los pasos perdidos* (1956, The Lost Steps), and García Márquez hints at a dark future looming beyond this optimistic surface narrative.

As Jean Franco notes, García Márquez's evident nostalgia for the river – nostalgia further documented in his autobiographical account of the journeys he made along the Magdalena as a student –[70] is rapidly vanquished by the death of nature that he witnesses along its course. Such deathliness "also involves the death of romantic and positivistic visions that are as closely linked as the two protagonists by having nature (woman) as their object."[71] Ariza and Urbino are equally selfish and amoral in the treatment of their lovers. Both also abuse their positions of privilege to achieve individualistic aims. Urbino may parrot European scientific discourses, but Ariza's poetry is chock full of romantic clichés and shamelessly recycles others' words. Indeed, even the *Nueva Fidelidad* on which Florentino and Fermina finally travel upriver, while ostensibly indexing a newfound fidelity to the nation, is a copy of a copy of a copy – a reincarnation of the *Fidelidad* brought to the Magdalena by the German-born Juan Bernardo Elbers in 1824 after the latter had already grafted his pioneering experiments in steam travel along the Rhine onto the American Mississippi. The happy ending, by contrast, can only be secured once the lovers turn their backs on the swollen corpses that fill the river's abject stream and that are more numerous than they were in Florentino's first ascent of the river.

As Jean Franco argues, at the end of *El amor en los tiempos del cólera* all that remains is a spirit of "sedentary nostalgia" for a river that, as in Restrepo's novel, is a reflection of a mirage of past grandeur.[72] More recent texts, while undertaking similar such "returns" to the river, are not only a great deal less nostalgic but also more doubtful about the possibility of channeling such "counterflows" into a full-fledged national romance. In testimonies from the lower Magdalena compiled by Alfredo Molano and María Constanza Ramírez, for example, *costeño* subjects bewail the destruction of their livelihoods by political violence and by the contamination of the river's waters. They lament witnessing the "river" of migrants leaving the region on a daily basis to find work in the nation's cities, as well as the figurative and literal drying up of the Magdalena's waters. In one account, "Mompox, tierra de Dios" – the title subversively interrogates Daniel Lemaitre's 1950 novel about the town's opulent colonial past[73] – becomes an island abandoned in the middle of an abject stream. In others, inhabitants of towns like Sincerín, Soplaviento, and Malagana – formerly market towns along the train line that cut across from Calamar to Cartagena – now struggle to make ends meet as they sell snacks and cold drinks along the region's toll roads.[74] Nostalgia remains, but even the flows of capital seem to pass these characters by, leaving a string of dusty "nonplaces" in their wake.[75]

Finally, in Juan Gabriel Vásquez's *El ruido de las cosas al caer* (2011, The Noise of Things Falling), the army's killing of a hippopotamus that had escaped from the former zoo of notorious drug baron Pablo Escobar at Hacienda Nápoles in 2009 prompts a return not only to the violence of the 1970s and 1980s but also to a landscape that has been transformed beyond all recognition. In Vásquez's novel, the death of the hippo allows his narrator to seek narrative closure to a shameful period of traumas and erasures, resistances and complicities. For others at the time, including political commentators, cartoonists, animal rights protestors, and political activists, the act demonstrated once more the sovereign violence of the state. Desperate, and yet unable, to police the influx of capitals occasioned by drug trafficking – to act as a powerful "Leviathan" over the "Behemoth"-like multitude of social actors connected via formal and informal social and economic networks – the state too finds itself in the position of the hippo: a nomadic entity that, like the hippo, must fight for survival in the uncharted waters of flows that take it out of its traditional confines. More crucially, "Pepe" the hippopotamus murdered on the banks of the Magdalena seemed not only to embody *narcotráfico*'s residual "folklore" but also the swathes of anonymous victims trashed as "bare life" by the state's territorializing war machine.[76] The Magdalena River thus remains an important site in which the violent dramaturgies of nation formation are continually enacted, even today when so much nostalgia suggests that its glorious years are very much a thing of the past.

Notes

1 See José Alvear S., *Manual del Río Magdalena* (Bogotá: Cormagdalena, 2005); *Río Magdalena, Navegando por una nación* (Bogotá: Museo Nacional, 2010) [seg. ed.]; and Carlos Castaño Uribe, *Río Grande de la Magdalena, Colombia*, 2nd ed. (Cali: Banco de Occidente, 2003).

2 Frank Safford and Marco Palacios note that San Agustín, founded near the source of the river around 200 B.C., made it a natural point of exchange between the Amazon and the Magdalena basin (2002:18). They also cite evidence of trade in emeralds, salt, gold, cotton and coca among diverse groups as far south as Neiva and as far north as Santander. *Colombia: Fragmented Land, Divided Society* (New York: Oxford University Press, 2002), 24–5.

3 See Safford and Palacios, *Colombia Fragmented*, and David Bushnell, *The Making of Modern Colombia: A Nation in Spite of Itself* (Berkeley: University of California Press, 1993).

4 Juan de Castellanos, *Elegías de varones ilustres de Indias*, seg. parte, canto tercero (Bogotá: Gerardo Rivas Molina Editorial, 1997) [1585], 581.

5 Castellanos, *Elegías*, 587.

6 Mary-Louise Pratt, *Imperial Eyes: Travel Writing and Transculturation* (London: Routledge, 1992).

7 Eugenio Castro Díaz, *Manuel* (Bogotá: Círculo de lectores, 1985).

8 Margarita Serje, *El revés de la nación: territorios salvajes, fronteras y tierras de nadie* (Bogotá: Uniandes, 2005).

9 Pedro Gómez Valderrama, *La otra raya del tigre* (Madrid: Alianza Editorial, 1996).

10 Gabriel García Márquez, *El amor en los tiempos del cólera* (Bogotá: Mondadori, 1991).

11 See Fernando Vallejo, *La Virgen de los sicarios* (Bogotá: Alfaguara, 1994), and *El río del tiempo* (Bogotá: Alfaguara, 1998); Alfonso Quijano, "La cosecha de los violentos," in *Arte y Violencia en Colombia* (Bogotá: Museo de Arte Moderno, 1998); and Clemencia Echeverri, *Sin respuesta* (Bogotá: Villegas Editores, 2009).

12 Juan Darío Restrepo and James P. M. Syvitski, "Assessing the Effect of Natural Controls and Land Use Change on Sediment Yield in a Major Andean River: The Magdalena Drainage Basin, Colombia," *Ambio*, 35 2 (March 2006): 65–74.

13 Benedict Anderson, *Imagined Communities: Reflections on the Origin and Spread of Nationalism*, rev. ed. (London: Verso, 1991).

14 See Doris Sommer, *Foundational Fictions: The National Romances of Latin America* (Berkeley: University of California Press, 1991); Idelber Avelar, *The Letter of Violence: Essays on Narrative, Ethics and Politics* (New York: Palgrave, 2004), 107–54.

15 Raymond L. Williams, *The Colombian Novel 1844–1987* (Austin: University of Texas Press, 1991), 23–8.

16 Gilberto Loiza Cano, *Manuel Ancízar y su época: Biografía de un político hispanoamericano del siglo XIX* (Medellín: Eafit, 2003), 190–1.

17 Sebastián Díaz Ángel, Santiago Muñoz Arbeláez, and Mauricio Nieto Olarte, *Ensamblando la nación: cartografía y política en la historia de Colombia* (Bogotá: Uniandes, 2010), 51.

18 José María Vergara y Vergara, *Historia de la literatura en Nueva Granada* (Bogotá: Biblioteca de la Presidencia, 1957), tomo III, 84.

19 For a detailed account of the modifications of Díaz Castro's text see Flor María Rodríguez-Arenas, *Eugenio Díaz Castro: realismo y socialismo en Manuela* (Novela Bogotana, FL: Stockero, 2011).

20 Vergara, *Historia*, 86.

21 See Frédéric Martínez, *El nacionalismo cosmopolita: la referencia europea en la construcción nacional en Colombia 1845–1900* (Bogotá: Instituto Francés de Estudios Andinos, 2001).

22 Javier Ocampo gives an account of the enduring of this mythical river-creature, who terrorizes fishermen and seduces young women in *Mitos Colombianos* (Bogotá: El Áncora, 1988), 266–70.

23 Alfredo Gómez Muller explains Madiedo's amalgamation of republican and Christian conservative ideologies in a recent edition of *La maldición* (Bogotá: Diente de León, 2010), 95–108.

24 Williams and Colmenares underscore *Manuela*'s conservative outlook although note ambivalences. Flor María Rodríguez-Arenas notes that the glut of socialist ideas gleaned from his vast, varied, and oft-cited readings of Louis Blanc, Jean-Joseph Proudhon, and Henri Saint-Simon (essayists explicitly banned by the Church but fundamental to early Liberal ideologies) suggests the opposite was true; Rodríguez-Arenas, *Eugenio Díaz*, 247–66.

25 Germán Colmenares, *Partidos políticos y clases sociales* (Medellín: La Carreta, 2008), 158.

26 Safford and Palacios, *Colombia Fragmented*, 192–7; Bushnell, *The Making*, 105.

27 See also Rory O'Bryen, "Affect, Politics and the Production of The People: Meditations on the Río Magdalena," in *Latin American Popular Culture: Politics, Media, Affect*, ed. Geoffrey Kantaris and Rory O'Bryen (Woodbridge: Tamesis, 2013), 227–48.

28 Jason McGraw provides a detailed overview of how these constitutional reforms affected *boga* life, and of the repressive measures used against *bogas* after the *boga* strikes of 1857. *The Work of Recognition: Caribbean Colombia and the Postemancipation Struggle for Citizenship* (Chapel Hill: University of North Carolina Press, 2014), 73–98.

29 José María Samper, *Viajes de un colombiano en Europa* (Teddington: Echo Library, 2006), 10.

30 Samper, *Viajes*, 23, 24.

31 See Marixa Lasso, *Myths of Harmony: Race and Republicanism during the Age of Revolution* (Pittsburgh: University of Pittsburgh Press, 2007); Sanders, *Contentious Republicans: Popular Politics, Race, and Class in Nineteenth-Century Colombia* (Durham: Duke University Press, 2004).

32 Carlos Jáuregui, "Candelario Obeso: Entre la espada del romanticismo y la pared del proyecto nacional," *Revista Iberoamericana*, 65 188–9 (1999): 578.

33 Candelario Obeso, *Cantos populares de mi tierra* (Mompox: Pluma de Mompox, 2007), 101.

34 On the relationship between literature and politics in this period, see José María Rodríguez García. *The City of Translation: Poetry and Ideology in Nineteenth-Century Colombia* (New York: Palgrave Macmillan, 2010), and Malcom Deas, *Del poder y la gramática* (Bogotá: Tercer Mundo, 1993).

35 Williams, *The Colombian Novel*, 25–39.

36 See Nina Gerassi-Navarro, *Pirate Novels: Fictions of Nation Building in Spanish America* (Durham: Duke University Press, 1999), 69–107, and the essays by Julián Vergara and Gustamo Otero Muñoz in the 2009 edition of Soledad Acosta de Samper, *Los piratas en Cartagena* (Bogotá: Alfaguara, 2009), 221–30 and 231–42.

37 Marco Palacios, "La Regeneración ante el espejo liberal y su importancia en el siglo XX," in *La clase más ruidosa y otros ensayos sobre política e historia* (Bogotá: Norma, 2002), 133–54.

38 See Julio Ramos, *Divergent Modernities: Culture and Politics in Nineteenth-Century Latin America* (Durham: Duke University Press, 1989); Aníbal González, *A Companion to Spanish American* Modernismo (Woodbridge: Tamesis, 2007).

39 Erica Beckman, *Capital Fictions: The Literature Latin America's Export Age* (Minneapolis: University of Minnesota Press, 2013), 61–9.

40 José Asunción Silva, *De sobremesa* (Bogotá: Norma, 1996), 351.

41 Ibid., 351.

42 Ibid., 352

43 Ibid., 353.

44 Ibid., 356.

45 Beckman, *Capital Fictions*, 121–44.

46 Ibid., 129. See Héctor H. Orjuela *"De sobremesa" y otros estudios sobre José Asunción Silva* (Bogotá: Caro y Cuervo, 1976) on the differences between *De sobremesa* and Joris-Karl Huysmans's *À Rebours*, particularly on its combination of physical as well as mental travel and departure from the French text's exilic withdrawal to the "inner sanctum" or "reino interior." See also Fernando Vallejo's *Chapolas negras, almas en pena*, where Silva is presented not only as the "precursor del modernismo," but also as the "precursor de la deuda latinoamericana" (Bogotá: Alfaguara, 2002), 189.

47 José Eustasio Rivera's *La vorágine* (1929) had also denounced the pillaging of the nation's resources during the Amazon rubber boom at the beginning of the twentieth century. It had also narrated a poet's mental breakdown, this time that of Cova as he faces the dehumanizing social injustices committed in the plantations.

48 For an account of the emergence of the literary magazine, *Voces,* and of the Grupo de Barranquilla, see Williams, *Colombian Novel*, 101–14.

49 The more widely read José María Vargas Vila voices in *Ante los bárbaros: Los Estados Unidos y la guerra: El Yanqui: he ahí el enemigo* (1917) a more powerful, albeit flawed and contradictory, spirit of anti-imperialism to that which Beckman identifies in larval form in *De sobremesa*. See Carlos Jáuregui, *Canibalia: canibalismo, calibanismo, antropofagia cultural y consumo en América Latina* (Madrid: Iberooamericana, 2008), 347–55.

50 Karl Marx, *Selected Writings* (Indianapolis: Hackett, 1994), 233.

51 Gabriel García Márquez, *Cien años de soledad* (Madrid: Cátedra, 1996), 430.

52 See María Victoria Uribe, *Matar, rematar y contramatar: las massacres de la Violencia en el Tolima 1948–1964* (Bogotá: CINEP, 1990).

53 Daniel Caicedo, *Viento seco* (Bogotá: Artes Gráficas, 1954), 132.

54 Hilarión Sánchez, *Balas de la ley* (Bogotá: Editorial Santafé, 1953), 430, 433.

55 Ibid., 498–9.

56 Ernesto León Ferreira, *Cristianismo sin alma* (Bogotá: Editorial A.B.C., 1956), 114.

57 While noting *Viento seco*'s realism, Antonio García observes that "desde la ortodoxia revolucionaria y socialista, esta novela empieza y termina en los 'viejos caminos': está encerrada en ellos; remata en 'el día de la venganza,' no en el 'día de la justicia'; desencadena la rebeldía que cobra ojo por ojo, no la revolución que descubre nuevos horizontes." In Caicedo, *Viento seco*, 27.

58 Alfredo Molano, *Los años del tropel* (Bogotá: El Áncora, 1985).

59 Herman E. Daly, *Steady-State Economics* (Washington: Island Press, 1991), 7. My thanks go to Rosemary Randall for providing this quotation.

60 Alonso Salazar, *No nacimos pa' semilla* (Bogotá: CINEP, 2002), 157.

61 It is common to hear both throwaway gadgets and those living in abject conditions of extremely precarious urban poverty referred to as *desechables* in Colombia.

62 Fernando Vallejo, *La Virgen de los sicarios* (Bogotá: Alfaguara, 1994), 60.

63 Restrepo noted that in the *novela de La Violencia*, "La estrechez de miras, la carencia de distanciamiento histórico y las tergiversaciones ideológicas, nos presentan la 'Violencia' como movimiento surgido ex nihilo, que se fecunda a sí mismo y cuyo único motor es su propio dinamismo interno: . . . circunscrito a la anarquía de las 'vendettas' locales entre los partidos, al terrorismo policial o bandolero, al oportunismo que la utiliza como negocio, al desquebrajamiento de los cánones morales, a las venganzas de la ignorancia, a las motivaciones personales." "Niveles de realidad en la literatura de la 'Violencia' colombiana." *Ideología y Sociedad* (1976): 17–18.

64 Claire Lindsay, "'Clear and Present Danger'": Trauma, Memory and Laura Restrepo's *La novia oscura*', *Hispanic Research Journal*, 4 1 (2003): 41–58.

65 Laura Restrepo, *La novia oscura* (Bogotá: Norma, 1999), 137.

66 Restrepo, *Novia*, 363–4.

67 I have argued elsewhere that Sayonara's final identification with those other corpses remains problematic, particularly as the latters' stories remain emphatically shadowy and indecipherably. As the title of the novel suggests, as an "absent" or "dead bride" Sayonara is herself a deconstructive entity as she

cannot be *married* – either literally or symbolically – to anyone else (see Rory O'Bryen *Literature, Testimony and Cinema in Contemporary Colombian Culture: Spectres of* La Violencia [Woodbridge: Tamesis, 2008], 103–13). For the purposes of my argument here, it suffices to note the desire to move toward the other, and to contrast this with Vallejo's altogether more stark maintenance of the gap between self and other, writer and working-class subject.

68 See Jean Franco, "Dr. Urbino's Parrot," in *García Márquez's* Love in the Time of Cholera, ed. Harold Bloom (Philadelphia: Chelsea House, 2005), 99–112.

69 For readings that make this case see the essays by Gene H. Bell-Villada, Roberto González Echevarría, and David Bueher in ibid., 29–35, 37–48, and 69–81, respectively.

70 Gabriel García Márquez, *Vivir para contarla* (México: Grijalba, 2002).

71 Franco, "Urbino's Parrot," 104.

72 Ibid., 110.

73 Daniel Lemaitre, *Mompós, tierra de Dios* (Cartagena: Editora Bolívar, 1950).

74 Alfredo Molano and María Constanza Ramírez, *La tierra del caiman: historias orales del Bajo Magdalena* (Bogotá: Aguilar, 2006).

75 Marc Augé, *Non-places: Introduction to The Anthropology of Super-Modernity*, trans. J. Howe (London: Verso, 1995).

76 For more on the responses to the shooting of "Pepe," see my essay in *Latin American Popular Culture: Politics, Media, Affect* (Woodbridge: Tamesis, 2013), 247–8.

The highland region as seen by an outsider from the inside and an insider from the outside

Juan Carlos González Espitia

In *Literatura fósil* (Fossil Literature), published in 1866, the Colombian writer from Bogotá José María Samper (1828–88) bewailed the provincial and derivative qualities of literary production at his time:

> Es que vivimos en un aislamiento moral, acaso mas notable que nuestro aislamiento físico; que vejetamos por incomunicacion. Es que nuestra literatura, arrastrada en su curso por la fuerza dominante de la pasion política o personal, carece de fuerza propia i no ha sabido ni podido crearse una existencia libre i autónoma ni formas peculiares. Es que en Hispano-América no hai todavía *pueblos,* sino apénas *poblaciones;* i las poblaciones no leen ni meditan, sino que duermen o vejetan: solo los *pueblos* alimentan las letras. (116)

The author uses isolation, lack of autonomy, and imitation to describe Spanish America; however, his acrid criticism of Modesto Pichón, the fictitious name used for a thriving, yet simpleton writer and politician, makes it clear that Samper is referring to his own environment in the Andean *población* of Bogotá, capital of the then Estados Unidos de Colombia. The dearth of reflection criticized in this text, and the sleepy and stagnant qualities awakened by personal or political passion described by Samper, mimic the state of affairs in the Andean highland region of Colombia. During this period, political tensions between Conservative and Liberal ideologies marked the urban and the rural milieu with violence and unrest, and the lack of a balanced cosmopolitan and open connection squelched the autonomous production of ideas.

This kind of discouraged outlook, popular in the second half of the nineteenth century, produced a type of solipsistic rendering of the highland region, epitomized by texts akin to the *cuadros de costumbres*. These texts comment obliquely on issues related to politics, religion, and class, but are imbued with condescending, humorous, or, at best, ironic features. The image produced under this set of narrative features is distorted and tends to render members of society as unsophisticated, naïve, or contemptible, characterizations saimed both at persons of the lower classes as well as at individuals in the higher echelons.

The other possible assessment found in texts at the time is one that examines the region and its inhabitants as subjects of study. This approach also distorts the region's image as it exoticizes features and congeals reality into vignettes. It hinders the reader's potential to understand reality as complex and multifaceted. These kinds of roadblocks often occur in texts where nature or geography take over, much like in the work of European travelers Alexander von Humboldt (1769–1859) or Jean-Baptiste Boussingault (1802–87).

This distorted narrativization of the Colombian Andean region has already been studied at length from other perspectives, and only a cursory assessment of its features is presented here. The main goal, however, is to work in an alternative sort of narrativization of the Andes that is equally distorted, but less studied. It refers to a perspectivist type of literary work developed from *outside* of highland reality, but written *about* that reality. Works such as those of Humboldt and Boussingault share this viewpoint but are written from the perspective of an outsider writing from inside. In addition to exploring Humboldt's perspective, this chapter delves mainly into the kind of work epitomized by José María Vargas Vila (1860–1933), who was born in Bogotá and died in Barcelona after a long life spent in exile in Venezuela, the United States, and Europe. Different from Humboldt's perspective, Vargas Vila's is one of an insider who writes from outside, a position upon which much of his narrative power rests. The expected result of this approach is to show that contrasting narratives that are saturated with local color, such as those of foreign explorers and Samper, with narratives written in somber tones will produce a richer, stereoscopic – to use the image of a most nineteenth-century invention – understanding of the Colombian highland region represented in these literary works between the nineteenth and twentieth centuries.

One element that accentuates this warped vision of the Colombian highland in the nineteenth century is the contrast between urban and rural spaces. Bogotá's isolated centrality is ideal to represent desired modernization while simultaneously representing the provincial quality of the region. At this point in time, many of the literary renderings of the highland are written in Bogotá and about Bogotá. If other places in the region are described, it is because people from Bogotá or people imbued in the capital's cultural sphere are describing them. Bogotá, then, is the measuring rod of the size and shape of the region in particular, and the nation in general. In addition, the members of the lettered elite in Bogotá author the virtual totality of writings of the region at this point and time. As a result, the portrayal of social interactions – with the *campesinos* in the rural area, or with the lower strata of society in the urban milieu – tends to be done in terms of differentiation. The consequence of this set of warped views of the Andes is that these literary representations tend to be marked by exoticization or by romanticization of the subjects and the nature that are represented.

Although written well into the nineteenth century, María Josefa Acevedo de Gómez's (1803–61) short piece "Santafé" offers a romanticized, harmonious view of Bogotá before the emancipation of 1810: "en cuanto a las costumbres, eran cristianas, pacíficas y decorosas, salvo también las excepciones, que no dejan de ser abundantes en la grande población de una ciudad que es capital de un extenso y rico virreinato" (18). Life seems to go slowly and calmly from everyday mass to intimate family lunch, and from strolls on a tree-lined path to sharing dessert at home. "Las criadas de Bogotá" by José Caicedo Rojas (1816–98) is an example of the exoticized valuation of peasantry and laboring classes, this time permeated by the aesthetic form of the *cuadros de costumbres*. The text describes female house servants by using classification that is similar to differentiating between qualities of tobacco. Although humorous, this objectification is as condescending as it sounds. In discussing the maids of the "fourth class," Caicedo illustrates the distanced view of society described before: "las de 4a clase . . . salen de la ínfima del pueblo, con perdón de la igualdad de la democracia, y son el *non plus ultra* de la mugre, desaseo y estupidez. Visten de frisa oscura y lienzo del Socorro; la cabeza, semejante a la de Medusa, causa espanto y horror; tal es su desgreño" (62).

While Caicedo Rojas's text stresses social class through derisive humor, Juan Francisco Ortiz's (1808–75) "Bogotá y siempre Bogotá" offers staunch praise of the capital city as a cosmopolitan cultural beacon – clearly an exaggeration, even if the author dearly loves his city – whose rural surroundings offer an Arcadian space overlooking the social complexities enacted therein. Even when Ortiz uses a drop of irony to spice his text, the embellished representation of Bogotá and its environs as both part of and different from the rest of the Andean region shows his actual belief in the city's unblemished superiority:

> ¡Gloria, pues, a esta tierra bendita de las claras fuentes y de las risueñas praderías! ¡Gloria a la tierra de las rosas y de la belleza! ¡Gloria a la tierra engendradora de los poetas y de los generosos caballos, vaca de leche de las

otras provincias, cuna de la hidalguía, santuario de la hospitalidad, centro de la política, foco de la chismografía, refugio de los pecadores y cabeza de la República[!] (298)

The narrow social and physical descriptions of the Andean capital by these three authors contrast with the comments written by Alexander von Humboldt in his 1801 travel diary. Humboldt was first in Cartagena, then went up the Magdalena River, ascended to Bogotá, and then continued along the Andes on his way to Ecuador and Peru. His account of the region is imbued in romantic language that isolates the subject of study. Humboldt's discourse is developed through quantifying and comparing European facts, as well as through recalling previous experiences visiting other places. His reliance upon measurement produces an objective and distant view of the region. This dynamic of differentiation, in which the gaze of the foreign explorer is overtaken by nature or geography, becomes even more apparent as he constantly contrasts the region with European geography. In one of his excursions outside Bogotá, he describes the area:

> Es como si Suecia estuviera a dos pasos de los desiertos de Africa, pues por una parte el termómetro en Santa Fé nunca desciende por debajo de 0°, no nieva como en Suecia en donde hay la ventaja de gozar de 3 a 4 meses de verano y de larga permanencia del Sol sobre el horizonte; en tanto que Santa Fé (en la gran sabana de Bogotá) la vegetación se entume eternamente bajo un cielo nebuloso, ningún fruto madura por la falta de Sol, no se ve sino una llanura carente de árboles y de verdor, con un perpetuo aspecto otoñal. (87)

This view of the outsider who compartmentalizes the subject of study also appears when Humboldt describes social situations. In these cases, however, his commentaries tend to serve as mirrors that show the not-so-smooth complexion of the elite society to which José Caicedo Rojas belonged. While Caicedo Rojas reviles the women servants of the lower classes, Humboldt vilifies the unfair justice that protects criminals who belong to the rich families of the Andean region and accuses privileged minorities of dispossessing indigenous peoples of their own lands:

> En el camino de Buga a Popayán, al norte de Río Palo, vimos con estremecimiento la localidad de García, donde habita la asesina Lemus, una mujer de la distinguida familia Arboleda de Popayán quien asesinó, con su primer marido y con dos negros, a un enemigo, europeo de nombre Crespo, en Popayán, a quien odiaban. La audiencia de Quito los condenó a todos a la horca, pero la sentencia se aplicó solamente a los esclavos, cuyas cabezas se ven en Popayán en las rejas. La poderosa familia escondió a la señora, la colgaron en efigie; y tiene la frescura, creyendo que todo está

olvidado, de volverse a casar y de vivir abiertamente a dos días de viaje del lugar donde cometió el crimen. (145)

He also writes regarding the expropriation of the best lands of the indigenous groups by powerful families and prominent political actors of the region:

> Es así como las familias distinguidas de Popayán, y anteriormente los jesuitas, han arrebatado sus tierras a los indios, mediante mil subterfugios; tal es el caso de los indios de Puracé, Coconuco, Poblazón. Esos infelices indios, antiguos y auténticos dueños del país, fueron expulsados con rumbo al más alto y frío espinazo de la cordillera. ... Pero esto sucede en todas partes. Nuestros aristócratas alemanes son los bárbaros que penetraron durante la transmigración de los pueblos desde el Mar Negro. (163)

These critical social commentaries about justice and land ownership are not usually the ones translated to show the relevance of Humboldt's work. Although these views are not usually broadcast or broached in studies or commemorative editions on the European explorer, they are accepted as observations of an external, objective traveler.

Although Humboldt's commentaries are generally accepted as authoritative, when these comments are written and published by a pesky autochthonous observer who belongs to the criticized Andean society, the reception is not usually as tolerant. Vargas Vila's textual production, developed in its entirety while he was in exile, indeed, falls prey to this double standard. Nevertheless, he defends his position as one that illuminates the truth of the country's situation:

> ¿Quién si no lo hacemos los colombianos emigrados podrá cantar las glorias de nuestra causa y el nombre de nuestros héroes? ¿Quién, si no somos nosotros, podrá desmentir tanta calumnia que diariamente se arroja sobre la frente del partido vencido, y disipar tanta gloria usurpada con que quieren engalanarse los Jefes conservadores aprovechándose del silencio impuesto á los vencidos, haciendo de cada derrota una victoria? ... no hay pues manera de que los libres hablen en el país, es preciso entonces, que lo hagamos aquellos á quienes por ahora no puede alcanzar la mano de hierro de los inquisidores de Colombia. (1887:56)

In addition to having published all of his work outside Colombia, Vargas Vila often stages his texts in settings that reverberate with the Andean region. As if in tension with the views exemplified by Humboldt, Caicedo Rojas, and Ortiz, Vargas Vila places a positive, powerful impetus in Andean nature, while simultaneously condemning Andean society. One of his very first books, published in Maracaibo, Venezuela, in 1887, is a political panegyric of the recently vanquished Liberal party military forces, a group with whom he had recently fought. In this *Pinceladas sobre la última revolución de Colombia y siluetas políticas*, the author from Bogotá blends the movements, skirmishes and battles of the contending parts with the backdrop of the Andean mountains, the difficult geography, the crushing weather, and the painful defeat. Vargas Vila's description of the Liberal army's situation is developed as a comparison to the already cemented image of the 1819 campaign lead by Simón Bolívar over the Andes through the bitterly cold Páramo de Pisba, and then to the defining highland battles of Pantano de Vargas and Puente de Boyacá. By situating his retelling of the 1885 internal dispute in the same place and circumstances as the fight for the independence of Colombia, Vargas Vila intends to identify his political and military ascription with the military and political side that founded the nation after defeating the Spanish crown. The author describes how General Daniel Hernández led the campaign against the government in a process that galvanized many Andean provinces in the northern Santander region, beginning with Pamplona and Cúcuta. As people slowly joined the army, the campaign moved south toward the boundary with the state of Boyacá:

> Al frente de aquel pequeño Ejército llegó Hernández á la frontera de Boyacá. Allí se detuvo.
>
> Pasaría aquel Rubicón?
>
> No éra él, hombre que vacilaba y lo pasó! ... Boyacá abría sus brazos á la revolución prófuga ... después del paso de la cordillera de los Andes por Bolívar, nada registra la historia militar del país, tan audaz como ésta invasión a Boyacá. (16)

The opposition between Bogotá and the rural areas in the Andes is presented here as a conflict between progressive radical liberal ideas, fostered and defended in peripheral districts, and the backward, stagnant politics firmly fixed in the nation's capital. Still, in the case of Vargas Vila, this tension between backwardness and renovation is paradoxical and shifting. The rural highland environment is sometimes presented as having Arcadian natural elements related to innocence, beauty, and strength, while at other times it serves as a social geography of ignorance, lack of tolerance, and retardation. In this regard, instances of positive description in Vargas Vila's work are usually associated with farms, ranches, and other rural estates where domesticated nature has made visible the intervention of manly work in the pastures and feminine care in gardens and groves. On the other hand, the negative conformation that disrupts pastoral peace in Vargas Vila's work is usually in the form of a traditional masculine figure, who represents the lasciviousness and injustice connected to conservative ideologies, or lewd, venal, or repressive priests, who are metonyms for the Catholic Church. The synthesis of these negative and positive features is resolved within the Romantic mood, where the main characters aim at producing change through individual struggle and even through self-immolation.

This is the case of Vargas Vila's first novel, *Aura ó las violetas*, first published in Maracaibo, Venezuela, in 1888. This is a work that he later condemned, calling it "libro inexperto de un romanticismo deplorable" (xx) in a 1919 edition. The novel narrates the love between two young people living in neighboring farms. The boy's family has arrived at the old family property, the only place where he, his recently widowed mother, and his sisters can manage their dire economic situation. The girl's mother is also a widow, as well as the owner of the land, and is also going through economic distress. The budding love between the boy and Aura is interrupted because he is sent to study in Bogotá for several years. Upon his return to the countryside, and after many instances of postponed conversation between the two lovers, he finds out that Aura has been promised in marriage to a rich old man in the city. This marriage of convenience is the only way that her mother and siblings can assuage their financial troubles. After her wedding in the small town's church, Aura is taken to Bogotá, where she gets sick and dies. The story all takes place in the Andean rural region, and the relationship between the two main characters evolves around their common upbringing in this environment. Their relation is presented in romantic terms as a balance between a shared past and a promise for the future:

> Los viejos árboles que nos habían visto crecer cerca de ellos, parecían brindarnos el toldo de su anciana vestidura para cobijar nuestros amores ... juntos habíamos nacido, bajo ese cielo siempre primaveral de nuestra patria, habíamos crecido a la sombra de aquellos bosques gigantescos, y nos había servido de horizonte la inmensa esplendidez de aquellos valles. (7)

These instances of Vargas Vila's work emphasize and utilize Romantic themes and strategies; nature and politics clash to produce cathartic emotional resolutions that allow the nation to reflect. The Andean region is encased in a space that ensures refuge and hope in the form of basic economy but also allows disjunctive situations such as expulsion and despondency. The nation seems to be condensed in the sphere of the Andes highland, therefore relegating all other peripheral areas to the status of an untamed locus, beyond civilizing reach, and not encompassed in its imaginary of progress.

Vargas Vila stages a feudalist and salient scene in the Andean milieu to attack the conservative political status quo in his country. Many years before José Carlos Mariátegui (1894–1930) and his essayistic study *Seven Interpretive Essays of Peruvian Reality* (1928), Vargas Vila took note of *latifundismo* and *gamonalismo* as an economic and political – that is, cultural – state that stifled the possibilities of change in the country. He used literary discourse not framed within a Marxist approach, as was the case of the important Peruvian author. For him, this feudal backwardness is buttressed by the unfailing presence of the Catholic Church. Though the novel *Los parias* (1902) is one of the lesser-studied works of Vargas Vila's extensive production, it clearly summarizes his pertinacity in criticizing the politics of the region. Here Vargas Vila introduces the setting of the story by positively describing nature as free of the human element – "prados brillantes y bosques sombríos hacían arabescos glaucos y tiernos, bajo la transparencia suave de la cúpula azulada" (1). The tone, however, shifts when social elements intervene; Vargas Vila depicts the distinctive Andean town as a somber place that moves slowly under the sound of the chapel's bells as if in a funeral procession:

> se extinguía el clamor de las campanas, que habían tocado la oración, y cuyas voces de metal, subiendo al cielo claro, desde la torre fantasmal, pasando por sobre tanta cosa fundida en la sombra, ... los labradores, que en la calma religiosa de la hora, se diseñaban sobre la tierra negra, tenían gestos fijos de estatuas, ... acá y allá, viviendas miserables de campesinos, que en su inconsolable ruindad, hacían pensar, en chozas esquimales, en cabañas de pescadores salvajes, sobre una tierra polar. (2–4)

With this, Vargas Vila suggests that religious tradition is retrograde, consisting of a morose depiction of reality due to a lack of economic advancement. He disdainfully depicts religion as primitive and unsophisticated by comparing it with the improbable reality of the arctic cultures. In this paradoxical, removed view of the exiled author, the lack of education and narrow-minded course of action retain a motionless disposition in the periphery of the main urban centers: "un aire de miseria, de ruina, de estancamiento, desprendiéndose de todo aquel villorrio infecto y vegetativo, estercolero rural, donde se pudrían, en la misma disgustante promiscuidad, las almas y los cuerpos de los hombres" (83).

Religious institutions, initially depicted as solemn and gloomy, are later presented as clearly oppressive, even monstrous, and as almost literally feeding off the flesh of the uneducated masses:

> en la plaza principal, la vieja iglesia *barocco*, que llamaban Catedral, mostraba
> su estructura grotescamente presuntuosa, alzando al cielo sereno los dos
> crímenes arquitectónicos de sus torres, que con sus flechas enmohecidas,
> parecían desafiar la Belleza, el Arte y la Luz, con su aspecto de un crustáceo en
> furia que amenazase al espacio con sus dos cuernos deformes. (83)

In the author's view, however, the disharmony, obscurity, and clumsiness
that he relates to institutionalized and powerful religion does not function
alone. The pervasive influence of the church is presented in tandem with
the entrenched and unchallenged system of concentrated ownership of
land in the hands of a few families. The main character's villainous uncle is
presented as an antipathetic incarnation of greed and retrogression, and as
a stagnating institution that hinders democratic change by defending,
based on a spurious claim of nobility or aristocracy, an illegitimate possession of land:

> don Nepomuceno Vidal, residente en *Santa Bárbara*, propietario de todas
> las tierras que se extendían en ese valle, hasta perderse de vista, amo de vidas
> y haciendas. Señor feudal de esas comarcas, omnipotente y temido, caudillo
> ilustre de la causa del *Orden* y de la *Moral*, apóstol meritísimo de ideas
> conservadoras, el más poderoso sostén de la Religión y de la causa de la
> Autoridad, en aquella sociedad y aquel país. (5)

This attack of the social codes of the time contrasts the nephew, who
represents new ideals, with his uncle, who represents closed-mindedness. It
is radicalized by the narrator's negative depiction of the mother who,
although described as a loving, self-sacrificing paragon of virtue, is equally
portrayed as inheritor of illiberal and still oppressive colonial codes:

> última hija de una familia de campesinos millonarios, con ilusiones de
> nobleza ibera, pretensiosos, ignorantes, linajudos, espécimen escogido de
> esa *aristocracia* campestre, limo del coloniaje, quedado en asqueroso sedi-
> mento a las riberas de la República naciente;
>
> caballeros del arado, señores feudales, omnipotentes y crueles, tipos com-
> pletos de la más abyecta ignorancia, y de la más vil superstición;
>
> representantes de todos los odios anacrónicos contra la libertad, y de las más
> estrafalarias cruzadas contra el espíritu del siglo; ... de esa *aristocracia* de
> lacayos endomingados, a horcajadas en un escudo heráldico, apócrifo, y
> enredados en la partícula de *nobleza*, como un cerdo en su soga, eran los
> señores de Vidal y Vidaurrázar. (14–15)

Decades before what was called *La Violencia* in Colombia (1948–58),
Vargas Vila describes the pugnacious consequences of the mix between
political and religious ideology. Nepomuceno Vidal is not only a large

landowner and the incarnation of the relationship between church and politics, but he is also the sponsor of the private armies that enforce conservative political party ideology and control. These armed agents serve to protect his private ambitions to maintain control of the land. Although a staunch liberal, Vargas Vila takes care that his narrator blames this violence on the two contending parties of the time, signaling that latifundism and violent ideology in the Andean region belonged to both factions, and that the situation created a common negative outcome for the whole territory:

> guerrillas liberales y guerrillas conservadoras infestaban los campos y los pueblos adyacentes; todos los días se escuchaban crónicas terribles, de combates, saqueos, ataques en despoblado, asesinatos en las haciendas y cortijos cercanos; los dos partidos extremaban el odio hasta la ferocidad, y la ferocidad hasta el horror. (22)

It is amid this horror that the protagonist's father is decapitated in front of his children and wife. This violence and unlawfulness marks a persistent cycle whereby the son, Claudio Franco, leaves the rural Andean environment to obtain formal education in the urban Andean space of the capital. He returns to his place of origin with the goal of obtaining justice and producing progressive change by joining an opposing guerrilla group, only to meet, like his father, a horrific death. In this sense, the Andes, in Vargas Vila's work, are marked by and represent tragedy.

This form of tragedy, however, does not conform to the classic sense of the term, for there is no cathartic mimesis after which the public can leave, convinced that what has occurred is contained there, meant to serve as an example, but nothing else. Perhaps Vargas Vila hopes that representing this reality of the Andes will help the reader establish an emotional bond – some sort of disturbing mimesis that will produce some change in that society. The persistent reoccurrence of this type of shocking scene, however, suggests the idea that, for Vargas Vila, a project signaled by harmony does not even deserve hope. In Vargas Vila's work, catharsis may be found in the nature he describes, as seen in his almost bucolic rendering of mountains, rivers, forests, and homesteads. Once culture and politics intervene, however, hope is temporary and fatuous, and the future becomes just a synonym for disaster.

In this depiction of the Andean region as a microcosm of the Republic, there is a possibility for generational change within the social structure, change that stresses the idea of evolution and progress. However, it can be gathered that this envisioning of a possible future does not necessarily involve a clear change for the peasantry. Instead, changes are pushed by the new generations, much like the protagonist Claudio Franco, who have been educated in large urban centers, especially Bogotá, and trained under the influence of progressive ideas from Europe. In Enlightened fashion, Vargas Vila seems to defend a dynamic of change for the highland in which the learned elite does everything for the people, but without the people.

A second consideration of an external view of highland reality indicates that Bogotá's society does not fare better than the rural environment. The removed position, represented this time by an outsider on the inside, is embodied by Humboldt and opposes idealized and partial positionings, like those in Acevedo de Gómez or Caicedo Rojas. It also characterizes Bogotá as not necessarily a place that fosters useful knowledge and ideas for change. For Humboldt, as would be the case for Vargas Vila many years later, the realm of future possibility for the highland region resides in the lushness of its nature, in the promise of its plants and rivers, in the near sublimity of its peaks and waterfalls. It does not rely on its ruling class, which is the one Humboldt sees as a European aristocratic outsider, as the entity that should administer change. For the authors, Bogotá is not presented as a place that, in its seat of centralized power, would equally function as a center for propagation of progress or equality and justice, or as an example of a functioning high society that could rightly hold the homeland's future.

Humboldt's voyage diary has been consistently mined to show off the richness and lushness of Colombian nature to be represented in coffee table book editions. Such assortment of the presentable, the colourful, or the suitable from his observations precludes the poignant sociological criticism he makes of his subjects of study. Like his stern accusation of iniquity against the powerful highland Arboleda family in Popayán, his ironic representation of high society of the capital does not appear in full color glossy editions. Similarly, a passage in his diary about his arrival to Bogotá is rarely brought to mind. In it, however, he reveals in a harsh, ironic, and somewhat gossipy way what he sees as snobbism, pettiness, and insularity in the families who would rule the country for over the next 200 years:

> Esa llegada fue tratada con mucha importancia, por eso se hizo traer un carruaje atrozmente trepidante, bellamente adornado con guarniciones de plata. . . . En las colonias se está inclinado a tratar así las cosas más pequeñas, con intrigas y hostilidad. . . . de todos los lados hacían discursos sobre el

interés de la humanidad, sacrificios por las ciencias y cumplimientos en nombre del rey y del arzobispo. ... Todo se desarrolló muy estiradamente; ... Yo estaba con el eclesiástico Caicedo y los Lozanos, en el carruaje de 6 caballos de estos últimos (¡un carruaje fabricado en Londres con resortes, en la latitud 4° 30', a 1370 toesas de altura!). ... Todos aseguraban que en la muerta Santa Fé, desde hace 20 años no se ha visto semejante movilización y amotinamiento. En Caracas eso hubiese sido imposible. Allí están acostumbrados a ver extranjeros y no españoles; pero en el interior de América del Sur se cree ver maravillosos herejes que recorren el mundo para buscar plantas. (191–2)

In Humboldt's eyes, rumor, swagger, affectation, and appearance are the features of Bogotá's society. However, the unfitness of this high society is contradictorily accompanied by the great value of isolated individuals, such as Mutis or José Lozano, who are identified with positive ideas of change and progress. This contradictory tension is clearly seen in Humboldt's comment in *Del Orinoco al Amazonas* on the quality of Mutis's work and his exceptional library: "Desde hace quince años trabajan a sus órdenes treinta pintores; él tiene de 2.000 a 3.000 dibujos en folio, parecidos a miniaturas. Excepto la de Banks, de Londres, nunca he visto una biblioteca más nutrida que la de Mutis" (388).

A specular view – that is, one that is the same and different, the same and its opposite – of Humboldt's Bogotá is seen in Vargas Vila's *Los estetas de Teópolis* (1918), a text marked by aggressive sarcasm and poignant scorn. Once again, instead of being an outsider writing from the inside like Humboldt, Vargas Vila is an insider writing from the outside. In this experimental text, written and published in Europe, the narrator attacks the society of a city named Teópolis, easily identifiable as Bogotá. Wavering between new and old, between progress and backwardness, Teópolis is hindered by the social double bind between religious morality and pretentious venality:

Teópolis, es la Capital de un Reino de América;/¿que no hay reinos en América?/pero, los habrá;/por eso, Teópolis, es una Ciudad Futurista, perteneciente al vasto Imperio de Marinetti;/y, sin embargo, Teópolis es vetusta, más allá de toda vetustez;/su nombre mismo lo indica: Ciudad de Dios;/y, Dios, empieza a hacerse un poco vetusto. (5–6)

This qualification of the city as archaic and dying is a clear allusion to *La Regenta* (1884) by Spanish author Leopoldo Alas "Clarín" (1851–1901), a novel that takes place in the microcosms of Vetusta, "la muy noble y leal ciudad, corte en lejano siglo, hacía digestión del cocido y de la olla podrida, y descansaba oyendo entre sueños el monótono y familiar zumbido de la campana del coro, que retumbaba en lo alto de la esbelta torre en la Santa Basílica" (121–2).

Much as it happened before in the rural highland environment, the author here signals sanctimonious religiosity in urban highland society as the source of a cultural matrix of underhanded behavior; vice is disguised as external piety and ignorance is paired with violence. In the same fashion, in Vargas Vila's literary and sociological reflection, he denunciates the idea that political oppression is masked with a staunch defense of the purity of language. In this regard, in *Los césares de la decadencia* (1907), the author overtly attacks Colombian president Miguel Antonio Caro (1845–1909), stating that "hay dos cosas inseparables de él: la Tiranía y la Gramática; . . . sus actos, como sus rimas, son igualmente despóticos y áridos;/no ha tenido sino una voluptuosidad en su vida: violar las Musas;/y, las tiene ya domesticadas á su caricia brutal" (69). This acrid accusation against what he considers empty and impractical formal preoccupation is revisited literarily in *Los estetas de Teópolis,* which stresses the lack of practical value in quarreling tooth and nail about grammatical purity in a city and nation that are in dear need of structural reformation rather than formalistic stricture:

> ¿cuál es la desgracia sucedida al Duque de Loyola, y que usted anuncia?
>
> – Una desgracia gramatical.
>
> – Entonces, es muy grave, porque en Teópolis, la Gramática es el cuarto Dios, y es el único Talento del Noventa por Ciento de nuestros escritores;
>
> en Teópolis, respetamos la Gramática todos, hasta los cocheros. (20)

The emptiness of this double-bind matrix in Teópolis/Bogotá is further represented by the description of the anxiety regarding blood purity and provenance elevation revealed by the narrator. The self-attribution of power and the ownership of land based on a dubious aristocratic origin, which Vargas Vila illustrated through the Vidal family in *Los parias* and connected to an unfair and unproductive pseudo-feudal economy, is revisited in the capital. Here, beyond the negative features of a backward economic system, the need to craft or defend a distinguished origin in the form of a title of nobility or a notorious last name is a symptom of the fact that 100 years after independence from the Spanish metropoli, this society has not yet liberated itself mentally and continues to be bound to a colonial condition:

– En materia de títulos, aquí en Teópolis, somos de una esplendidez regia;/ derrochamos los adjetivos, como si fuera el Tesoro Nacional;/aquí, todo el mundo es Ilustre;/el Ilustre Escritor, el Ilustre Arquitecto, el Ilustre Cochero .../el otro día quedé sorprendida recibiendo una esquela mortuoria que decía: el Muy Ilustre Señor Don Empedocles de Lascivia y Mal Contento, del Gremio de Taberneros de esta Corte, ha muerto. (37)

This obsessive insistence on nobility is therefore a symptom of the lack of confidence in the radical changes occurring as a result of the implementation of a republican and democratic project that, in theory, proclaimed equality for all, separated the church and state, and guaranteed the opportunity for personal advancement. Instead, the equilibrium that was supposed to have been attained by renewed democratic processes remained subject to traditional practices that assessed social fitness by examining an individual's bloodline. In this sense, a woman who acquired wealth by exercising her skill as a textile trader was not measured by her professional success, but by the perpetuation of the church's moral grip upon her and by her linkage to the nobility from which this society had supposedly been liberated: "la Señora de Mestres Travieso y Tapajada de las Hinojosas, vieja mercera enriquecida en comercio de encajes, y ahora dada a caza de un título nobiliario por el camino ya muy trajinado de construcción de templos y represión de la trata de blancas" (15).

In consequence, this matrix of occultation and deferment encouraged a shady atmosphere with no space for the purity of art and the true pursuit of liberty. These two ideas, absolute individual liberty and art detached from morals, are the measurement of the viability, in the still-romantic perspective that Vargas Vila cherished, of the liberal project he defended to his death.

For Vargas Vila, such possibility and such hope are doomed because the society he portrays here as Teópolis is in fact the real society of Bogotá, and the contradictorily bucolic countryside he presents is in fact the real environment of the Colombian highland. For Vargas Vila, these two corresponding settings are not to be depicted with vivid colors – but only with the harshness of a gray spectrum.

BIBLIOGRAPHY

Acevedo de Gómez, María Josefa. 1976. "Santafé." In *Narradores colombianos del siglo XIX*, ed. Henry Luque Muñoz, 17–20. Bogotá: Colcultura (Instituto Colombiano de Cultura).

Alas, Leopoldo. 1984. *La Regenta*. Madrid: Cátedra.

Caicedo Rojas, José. 1976. "Las criadas de Bogotá." In *Narradores colombianos del siglo XIX*, ed. Henry Luque Muñoz, 57–64. Bogotá: Colcultura (Instituto Colombiano de Cultura).

Humboldt, Alexander von. 1970. *Alexander von Humboldt en Colombia: extractos de sus diarios*. Bogotá: Biblioteca Luis Angel Arango. www.comunidadandina.org/BDA/docs/CO-CA-0004.pdf.

———. 1982. *Del Orinoco al Amazonas*, trans. Adolf Meyer-Abich. Barcelona: Ed. Guadarrama.

Mariátegui, José Carlos. 1971. *Seven Interpretive Essays on Peruvian Reality*. Austin: University of Texas Press.

Ortiz, Juan Francisco. 1976. "Bogotá y siempre Bogotá." In *Narradores colombianos del siglo XIX*, ed. Henry Luque Muñoz, 293–303. Bogotá: Colcultura (Instituto Colombiano de Cultura).

Samper, José María. 1866. "Literatura Fósil." In *Museo de cuadros de costumbres i variedades*, vol. 2, 115–23. Bogotá: F. Mantilla.

Vargas Vila, José María. 1919. *Aura o las violetas*. Barcelona: R. Sopena.

———. 1907. *Los césares de la decadencia*. Paris: Librería Americana.

———. 1922. *Los estetas de Teópolis*. Barcelona: R. Sopena.

———. 1920. *Los parias*. Barcelona: R. Sopena.

———. 1887. *Pinceladas sobre la última revolución de Colombia y siluetas políticas*. Maracaibo, Venezuela: Imprenta Americana.

CHAPTER 12

Racial fictions: constructing whiteness in nineteenth-century Colombian literature

Mercedes López Rodríguez

This chapter addresses the prominent role of literature in the emergence of a racialized discourse affecting Andean populations of Colombia that marginalized and subordinated perceived "non-white" subjects inside the Andean highland region. I place specific emphasis on the representation of poor whites, mestizos, indigenous, and mulatto subjects in *costumbrista* articles, novels, and essays. In these narratives, the depiction of non-white characters was a device used by lettered elites to establish the definition and limits of "whiteness" in the Andean highlands. The elite's use of racial depiction of the region as whiter than others became a key element in the formation of a hierarchical nation-state in Colombia, making the symbolic power of the Andean highlands powerfully associated to its racial representation.[1]

This essay examines interracial unions, as depicted in literature, especially in the works produced under the influence of *costumbrismo*; these works reveal the nineteenth-century notion of *mestizaje*, the mix of populations of different racial backgrounds, as a progressive process of becoming white. Despite the relevance of the concept of *mestizaje* in the nation-building process, interracial subjects are not frequently represented in literary texts of the time. Yet, when they appear, they conform to specific patterns marked by the intersection of race and gender: Women are often represented as white, and men as mulattos. By focusing on the depiction of gendered unions in stories such as *Federico y Cintia* (1859) by Eugenio Díaz or *Mercedes* (1869) by Soledad Acosta de Samper, this study explores the limitations and possibilities of the concept of *mestizaje* in Colombia and the pivotal role of gender in the construction of racialized representations of identity and alterity. Texts such as *Peregrinación de Alpha* (1853, The Pilgrimage of Alpha) by Manuel Ancízar and *Ensayo sobre las revoluciones políticas* (1860, Essay about Political Revolutions) by José María Samper created powerful racial images of "white" and "light-skinned mestizo" Andean peasants. These racial representations have survived over centuries and are continuously being reproduced by intellectuals, politicians, and scholars and used as a tool of racial discourse. Their permanence suggests that they served as a racial pedagogy intended to convince regional, national, and transatlantic audiences of the "whiteness" of Colombian Andean populations. It also exposes a contrast to other Andean nations, specifically Peru, Bolivia, and Ecuador, where the concept of *"lo andino"* (the Andean) is strongly associated with an indigenous identity, often constructed on the basis of racial categories.

Racial fictions beyond foundational romances

In her seminal work *Foundational Fictions, the National Romances of Latin America*, published in 1993, Doris Sommer proposed a groundbreaking approach to reading Latin American literary romances as political objects and significant instruments in the creation of new independent republics. Nations, internally divided by regional, racial, and class tensions, expressed through literature their desire for unification. Patriarchal, heterosexual romances served as an allegorical device to unify, among many other differences, the racial divisions that have fractured recently formed nations. In some cases, romances between female indigenous subjects and male descendants of Europeans would produce, at least in fiction, the new mestizo citizen of these nations. In others, the romance between lovers represented the union of separated regions. Sommer's suggestive framework has provided literary critics with a powerful tool of interpretation, influencing two decades of scholarly production on Latin American nineteenth-century culture and literature. Her approach facilitated our understanding of the political nuances contained in romantic stories such as *Irasema* (1865), *El Zarco* (1869), *Sab* (1841), and *Enriquillo* (1879–82). Sommer's interpretation faces some difficulties when examining readings from nineteenth-century literary production of Andean nations. Whereas Bolivia and Peru are left behind in her analysis, she focuses on the Colombian case by examining *María* (1866) by Jorge Isaacs, probably the greatest Latin American best seller of the nineteenth century. Notwithstanding its early success, *María* is not a tale of national unification through the love of its protagonists; rather, it is a romantic tragedy in which the female protagonist dies as a consequence of a mysterious disease, leaving her lover in a permanent state of chastity, loneliness, and sadness. This is the first of the failures of *María*, if considered as a "national romance." Furthermore, the protagonists do not represent any antagonist sectors of the nation, as they are two members of the same class, race, and social group.

Even more relevant, it is hard to think of *María* as a national romance because it lacks the "national" sense. In fact, the story takes place in the bucolic landscape of the Cauca Valley, amid the cane plantations, far from the nation's metropolitan centers of political and economic power. Sommer is perfectly aware of these problems, and she points them out in her analysis of the Colombian classic. Despite being the most famous romance of nineteenth-century Latin American literature, *María* does not easily fit the profile of a "national romance." Sommer's explanation of the unusual nature of *María* hinges on the exceptionality of the Colombian nation-state in the nineteenth century and its inability to achieve any form of political, economic, or cultural unification throughout its republican history. She aptly suggests that *María* deals with the striking racial divisions that divide the nation, and, in that respect, the novel conveys the desire for unification that characterizes other Latin American *foundational romances*. According to her, the Jewishness of the main characters serves as an allegory to speak about the unspeakable racial difference between the black majority of the population and the minority of white plantation owners in the Cauca region.

Following the insightful analysis proposed in *Foundational Fictions*, this chapter deals with the representation of this "unspeakable" racial difference in literature, which fragmented the Colombian nation throughout the nineteenth century – and beyond. Why did Colombian nineteenth-century literary production not conform to the critical framework provided by the notion of "foundational fiction"? Unlike literature in other Latin American countries, why did Colombian novels rarely portray romances that cross the regional and racial boundaries dividing the nation? Indeed, interracial romances are very scarcely depicted in Colombian literature; this is especially true for literature from the Andean region. In contrast, a variety of writers from the late Colonial Period to the mid–nineteenth century, the onset of the republican period, commented on the advances in the process of *mestizaje* caused by interracial mixtures. How can one reconcile this emphasis on the Andean highlands as a fertile social space for *mestizaje* with the lack of representation of interracial unions in literature or arts? In other words, if *mestizaje* was so prevalent, why do the relationships that made it possible so rarely appear in the literature of the time?

To explore these questions, attention needs to be given to other materials less famous than *María*. Indeed, before *María's* appearance on the literary scene in 1862, many had claimed other novels to be the origin of the Colombian national novel. In fact, in these early republican years, every novel wanted to be considered as the first national novel, and publishers and commercial agents advertised the latest publications as being the truly first Colombian national novel. This desire to be "national" highlights the powerful interlinks that bound together literary and political power in what Ángel Rama has referred to as the Latin American "lettered city." Among these novels that predate *María, Manuela* (1859) by Eugenio Díaz was known and celebrated as a national Colombian novel.

Manuela, which takes place at the outskirts of the Andean region, is the story of Don Demóstenes, a young and idealistic liberal politician, who discovers the boundaries of his egalitarian ideology while visiting a rural town beyond the limits of the city. It was first printed in the literary magazine *El Mosaico* in 1859, almost thirty years before its first publication as a book, at a time when periodicals were the most common instruments to spread the rising national literature heavily influenced by *costumbrismo*. In spite of *Manuela's* early success, it was later forgotten and disregarded by audiences and critics, a fate shared by many other texts that had widely circulated among the readers of periodicals. Many of them became marginal works in the canon despite their initial success. A close reading of these materials reveals how literature became the arena for political and ideological debate during the mid–nineteenth century. It also shows a growing interest on the part of writers in characterizing the national population according to racial categories. In contrast to the allegorical devices studied by Sommer in *María*, the literature explored in this section openly deals with race.

A new racialized discourse about Andean populations that is marginalized and subordinated for being perceived as "non-white" emerges during the early republican period of 1830 to 1875. Characters in literature are represented not only as female or male, good or evil, poor or wealthy, but also embody racial categories such as white, indigenous, or black. In novels such as *María* or *Manuela*, the main protagonists are described as whites, a condition that is corroborated through the deployment of several non-white secondary characters that play the role of servants or subordinates. As the literary critic Walter Benn Michaels has argued regarding blacks characters in Faulkner's *Absalom Absalom:* "[B]lack men are only the technology through which the difference between white men is established."[2] The presence of black and indigenous servants around white family members provides the readers with information about the economic situation and status of the family, as well as the kind and benevolent nature of the masters. For instance, it is evident in *Manuela*, where the presence of José Fitatá, Don Demóstenes's indigenous servant helps the reader to understand the protagonist's prominent economic and social position, one which allows him to have a personal helper during his journey to the outskirts of the Andean region. Sometimes the presence of non-white characters helps the readers to recognize the racial position of the protagonist, such as in *El boga del Magdalena* (1866, The Magdalena River Rower) by M. M. Madiedo in which the black rowers refer to the protagonist as *branco* – a mispronunciation of *blanco*, white in Spanish.

Despite the growing interest in racial descriptions of non-white characters, the protagonists of these stories are dominantly white lettered men, such as Don Demóstenes in *Manuela*, or Efraín in *María*. In the margins of these novels' central plots, it is possible to see interactions between these protagonists and black, mestizo, or indigenous servants or town dwellers. These interactions, however, do not take the form of romances between individuals from different racial or social origins. In Colombian nineteenth-century fiction, white, lettered men were almost immune to the charms of any subaltern women. No matter how young, or beautiful, or desirable these women might be, the good, handsome, and correct white men were in love only with women of their own race and class. Even in the most daring novels, like *Manuela*, the flirtatious Don Demóstenes develops a pure friendship with the beautiful but humble Manuela, and their feelings never become romantic. Demóstenes almost forgets about his blond and wealthy girlfriend who was left behind in the city; however, he still only expresses interest in someone from his same social position: a local female member of the elite. This racial and class inbreeding challenges common assumptions of contemporary scholars interested in Colombia. Indeed, it diverges from the general consensus among these scholars that *mestizaje*, the mixing of different racial groups through marriage, cohabitation, and sexual relations, is central to the formation of a racially homogeneous Latin American society. In countries such as Brazil, this concept took the name of "racial democracy," and in twentieth-century Mexico it became a national ideology known as "the cosmic race," an ideological construction that proposes that because of the permanent racial mix, Latin America has been the cradle of a new unified race that combines all the previous ones.

If *mestizaje* is the pervasive racial discourse in Latin America, why is Colombian fiction so reluctant to represent stories of interracial romances? I suggest that in nineteenth-century Colombian fiction, interracial romances do not represent a desire for unification of the nation through the union of lovers of different races. Instead, interracial unions explore the elite's anxieties about the limits and the contents of the notion of whiteness, especially for individuals situated in liminal categories such as poor whites or light mestizos. More importantly, interracial unions, as presented in literature, seem to expose the perils posed by liberal policies that sought to spread "whiteness" along the Colombian Andean region through the promotion of mixed unions. Indeed, it is important to emphasize the particularities of the idea of *mestizaje* held by Colombian liberals such as Ancízar and Samper. They valued *mestizaje* as a progressive process of becoming white.[3] The product of a racial amalgamation would not be an individual from a new intermediate racial category; rather, this person would be classified as white, black, or indigenous, according to a combination of physical appearance and physiognomic traits. In contrast, liberal intellectuals throughout the other Andean countries considered *mestizaje* as a danger to the nation as Broke Larson has shown.[4]

In the Andean Colombian region, two writers, liberal intellectuals, politicians, and entrepreneurs were specially committed to praising *mestizaje* and its benefits to the nation: Manuel Ancízar and José María Samper. Samper's *Ensayo sobre las revoluciones políticas y la condicion social de las repúblicas colombianas* (1861) celebrated *mestizaje* as one of the most positive characteristics of Spanish American history, even linking democracy and *mestizaje* in the new nations. Ancízar was also member of the *Comisión Corográfica* (1850–9), the most relevant national project of exploring, describing, mapping, and documenting the geography and populations of the Colombian regions during the nineteenth century. In his *Peregrinación de Alpha* (1853), a textual by-product of the *Comisión Corográfica*, Ancízar depicts an Andean highland that is slowly turning white because of the advance of *mestizaje*. However, although Samper's analysis tends to understand *mestizaje* mainly as the result of mixing different bloods, Ancízar holds to a more heterodox view on the subject: In addition to the mix of the population, other factors such as education, hard work, and even wearing western clothes have an impact on the racial classifications of Andean populations. Instead of looking at the descendants of mixed ancestors as degenerate or impure, liberals saw in *mestizaje* a possibility to redeem the nation.

The dark side of this liberal racial optimism becomes evident when we examine the actions taken by liberals in power to contest centuries of indigenous isolation caused by the Spanish colonial rule. They promoted the parceling out of native communal lands, directly leading to a rise in the amount of destitute peasants along the Colombian Andes. Furthermore, liberal policies promoted the elimination of legal distinctions between individuals of socio-racial groups. Intellectuals such as Samper were confident of the benefits that integration of the former "Indians" would produce for them and the nation. Despite liberal attempts to undermine the social structure inherited from the colonial system, racial classifications continued to be the norm in social interactions informed by the confluence of social practices beyond phenotypes. During the early republican years, racial categories continued to be extremely flexible, shaped in the interaction with other social markers such us gender, social status, marriage, and even dress. Instead of being the straightforward product of fixed "pseudo-scientific" notions of race, throughout the nineteenth century, racial representations were negotiated, especially for those individuals situated at the borders of social groups, such as poor white women, rural light *mestizos*, or former Muisca Indians.[5] With the elimination of the legal framework provided by the colonial system, racial classifications practically disappeared from republican documentation. Because of the liberals' focus on avoiding legal distinctions among individuals, it is not in the archives but in literature where many of these negotiations took place. In this sense, literature – representing the milieu of educated citizens – served as a powerful tool in the formation of ideologies of race in the context of making the nation, which was a process of consistent adaptation and negotiation.

In part, liberal narratives concerning Andean populations, such as those of Samper and Ancízar, acknowledge a social process in existence since Colonial times. According to Spanish policies regarding separation of natives from other populations, whites, African descendants, and people of mixed parentage were not permitted to live in indigenous towns. However, neither Colonial nor conservative republican policies promoting racial separation were effective. Throughout the eighteenth century, Colonial authorities repeatedly denounced the proximity between indigenous, poor whites, and people of mixed parentage in the rural communities of the Andean region. Indeed, at the dawn of the republican era, the number of *mestizos* had overtaken the indigenous population, making it difficult to establish solid distinctions between them, as the Spanish administrator Francisco Moreno y Escandón stated in his report to the Spanish king in 1772.

The question about the status of people of mixed parentage also proved to be far from straightforward for republican society, in part because these categories were not entirely clear to anyone and because a strong bias carried over from Colonial times made people fearful of any classification except for "white." In the early republican Andean region, the increasing process of *mestizaje* and the decline of the indigenous population posed a dilemma reflected in literature. In his novel *Bruna, la Carbonera*

(1879, Bruna, the Coal Worker), writer Eugenio Díaz portrays the protagonist as a white impoverished Andean female peasant, who is often
mistaken for an Indian by the elite city dwellers. She works as a coal carrier
from the outskirts of Bogotá to the city's homes, a job that makes her look
dirty and dark. This situation, entangled with her cultural proximity to
the indigenous world, fueled constant misunderstandings about her racial
status. Eugenio Díaz had already explored the overlapping between race
and class in his most famous work, *Manuela*, in which he devoted a
chapter to depict the Andean estate of La Esmeralda. The narrator also
presents two other female peasants, one white and one indigenous, in
order to comment upon the tendency of members of the elite to wrongly
classify all Andean peasants as non-white. In contrast to liberal intellectuals, Díaz's narrative does not have a place for individuals of mixed
ancestry. It seeks to understand the diversity of the populations through
a set of fixed racial classifications, which avoids dealing with the liminal
status of interracial children. Intermediate categories, such as *mestizo* and
mulatto, convey a contradictory sense of racial ambiguity and social
fluidity that collide with the more solid categories that inform the
nineteenth-century highly politicized debates regarding the nature and
origins of the Andean populations. Despite republican efforts to erase
the remnants of Spanish rule, Colonial ideas were reassembled into republican notions of race disparity and classification of difference, and the
literature of the time mirrors this contradiction.

Interracial unions depicted in fiction constitute a vantage point to
explore these ambiguities because of the central role of *mestizaje* in the
ideological construction of a supposedly white Andean region as seen
in Ancízar and Samper. However, legitimate interracial unions do not
frequently appear in texts, and when they do, they conform to specific
patterns marked by the intersections of race and gender: Women are often
represented as white descendants of Spaniards and men as mulattos. In
Eugenio Díaz's *Federico y Cynthia* (1859, Federico and Cynthia), we meet a
literate, hardworking mulatto artisan who is in love with the daughter of
a liberal politician, descendant of the first Spanish conquerors of the city.
Cynthia loves Federico in return, but their union becomes impossible
because of the blatant opposition of her father, who despite being a liberal
and publicly defending equality for all races, privately declares that a
descendent of Spaniards will never consent to a marriage with a mulatto.
In this short piece, originally published in the literary magazine *El Mosaico*,
Díaz attempts to demonstrate the duplicity of liberals who extol equality
while enjoying the privileges they inherited from the old hierarchical

colonial system. Interestingly, Díaz follows here the same gender pattern that we will see in the novel *Mercedes* (Acosta de Samper, 1869), about a Spanish female descendant who marries a male mulatto. Both *Federico y Cynthia* and *Mercedes* explore interracial unions, but not with the intention of offering the foundation for a new society. Although these narratives hold different ideological places of enunciation, in both mixed ancestry's characters threaten the whiteness of the female protagonists.

Mercedes by Soledad Acosta de Samper was originally published in 1868 in *El Hogar*, a magazine specifically oriented to a female readership. In 1869 it was reprinted as part of the book *Novelas y Cuadros de la vida suramericana* (Novels and Sketches of South American Life).[6] The novel explores the interracial marriage of a white female protagonist to a mulatto, a descendant of parents of African ancestry. I suggest that the representation of an African descendant character in this story is a device to establish the limits to Mercedes's whiteness. Moreover, the depiction of an interracial union does not allegorize the process of *mestizaje* or the unification of a racially divided nation. Instead, it is presented as punishment of the female character who has rejected the emergence of the independent nation. The sympathy of Mercedes's family for the Spanish royal government is behind her fall from grace during the war of independence, which coincides with her own youth: "I had just turned seventeen when the war of Independence began and my father went into hiding, unable to hide his royalist feelings."[7]

Although Mercedes's story is not a foundational fiction for the new nation, Colombian national history provides the backdrop for the plot: Her early youth overlaps Colombia's initial period of independence (1810–16), and her final years coincide with the republican civil wars, thus emphasizing the connection between literature and nation making. To save her father's life, young Mercedes seeks help from Antonio, a former and often scorned suitor now converted into a revolutionary. Antonio's intervention saved the life of Mercedes's father, although she never learns about it, harboring a strong resentment toward her former suitor. When the Spaniards finally regain control over the revolutionaries, Mercedes's family comes out of hiding to claim its former power and privileges. While she returns to her shallow and egotistic lifestyle, the local society of Bogotá suffers the rigors of the Spanish reconquest. Nevertheless, Mercedes remains indifferent to the predicaments of her former friends. Under these circumstances, Antonio arrives to Mercedes's home seeking protection from Spanish persecution, confident that his participation as the savior of Mercedes's father will be rewarded. But Mercedes, unaware of Antonio's role in her father's salvation, sees opportunity for revenge. She betrays Antonio, giving him away to a group of Spanish soldiers who are guests at her home.

This arrogance and contempt for the patriots will bring personal tragedy into Mercedes's life. Once the colonial order is fully restored, Mercedes falls for Pablo, a young Spanish officer who promises to take her to Spain. She plans to elope with him once he receives orders to move to a regiment in another city. Unlike foundational romances, which deploy allegories to glorify the formation of the nation, in this story the protagonist betrays her country out of love for the opposition. When Mercedes rides off on her horse to elope with the Spaniard officer, she encounters Antonio and other prisoners sentenced to hard labor. In a final act of arrogance, she whips her horse while mocking them.[8] This pride and hate for Antonio triggers her tragedy. Mercedes loses control of her horse, falls, and loses her beauty: "a wide scar cut my forehead, white and smooth as it was before."[9] After the accident she becomes a new woman: humiliated, physically disfigured, missing some of her teeth and hair, she also loses the love of Pablo, who is unable to bear her condition; he flees to his death in the final battle that the revolutionaries win in 1819.[10]

After the war, Mercedes and her family are condemned to poverty and marginalization in the new republican society, since the rise of the independent nation means the fall of their old privileges. Socially excluded, the family leaves the city looking for shelter in the countryside. However, her the misfortune does not diminish the whims which had guided Mercedes's her destiny. A chance incident on the way leads her to meet her future husband:

> I insisted on changing the mule I was riding for a horse that a mulatto was leading. The mulatto was a native of Jamaica, who had joined us on the way. He was the butler of a foreigner who owned a small farm on the banks of the Black River. The mulatto Santiago wanted to be accepted in our company, proving himself to be very accommodating and kind to me.[11]

The first encounter between Mercedes and Santiago emphasizes the difference in status and social position between them: She rides a horse but he makes the journey on foot; she is capricious and he satisfies all her whims. More important, although he is a "mulatto," she still enjoys a privileged position within the socio-racial hierarchy. Despite her misfortunes, during their first meeting the distance separating Mercedes and Santiago remains unabated as they continue to act within established social limits of a racialized social system. The endurance of colonial classifications and their durability in republican society are evident in the narration when

Mercedes's family fails to integrate into the new post-independent society because of the pride that prevented them from mixing with the new citizens of the nation: "Our pride of race and family was noticeable even in the kindest words."[12] Although the family circumvents these difficulties, Mercedes faces her personal distress: Banished and deformed, she is no longer a member of the elite. Nevertheless, her social and racial origins make it impossible for her to become part of the working classes of the nation.

While Mercedes is facing this vulnerable state, Santiago has earned a much better position in the republican order. After the death of his former employer, he inherits his land near the town where Mercedes's family now modestly lives. As a landowner, Santiago, the mulatto, becomes a frequent visitor, bringing gifts from the city to the poor white family. Santiago brings bread, sweet fruits, and other commodities the family can't afford anymore, which enhances the irony, since the consumption of these goods is often associated with the elite;in this case these treats are available only through Santiago's mediation. Of course, all these nuances do not erase the racial distinction between them, as Mercedes remarks: "his attentions flattered my vanity, and I considered him, although dark, with better taste than the white youth who had looked at me with disdain."[13]

The separation between Mercedes's and Santiago's worlds, so far unquestioned, begins to display some cracks. Santiago takes a class position that does not resemble his position in the socio-racial hierarchy. Through Santiago, Mercedes's family reconnects with a world from which they have been excluded because of political and ideological reasons. When Santiago finally dares to ask for Mercedes's hand, her parents' reaction confirms that the old colonial privileges are still in place: "a mulatto, a former slave, a miserable man ... ask for the hand of my daughter!" exclaims her father while the mother is "distressed to see the humiliations to which we were exposed because of our poverty."[14]

While the family expresses a resounding rejection to the marriage proposal, Mercedes takes an ambiguous position on the matter: "He assured me that he only wanted to be my humble slave and that I would be the mistress and ruler of his property and person."[15] By using a female narrator, the text reflects on the reasons to justify an interracial marriage. Mercedes's motives combine the vanity of being admired with the desire to create a less pressing economic position. However, the figure of the Spanish father serves as a barrier preventing the interracial marriage, which will be possible only after his death.

Mercedes's and Santiago's interracial relationship is not motivated by love. Rather it is born out of a necessity created by social mobility and class rearrangements produced during independence. The story seeks to avoid any possible romantic motivation: A few hours before fleeing with Santiago, Mercedes recalls her ill-fated love for Pablo, which makes her reconsider her escape with Santiago; however, once she is back at home, witnessing her sister and mother's hunger, she marries Santiago in secret as a sacrifice to save her family: "When I returned home that evening I was the wife of a mulatto but I had all kinds of food and clothes for my mother and sister, that I told them I had bought with the proceeds of my work as a seamstress."[16]

The real issue underlying Mercedes's story is progressive social humiliation, which the female character must undergo as a punishment for her pride. The mulatto Santiago is not a fully developed character in this story. Rather, his function is secondary, serving to exemplify how far a white woman can be humiliated, even to the point of accepting a clearly unequal interracial marriage. The character of Santiago helps create a scenario in which class position manages to reverse the socio-racial hierarchy. There is no love. Rather, revenge motivates Santiago to marry a deformed woman as she quickly notices: "He wanted the satisfaction of showing everyone that a lady of one of the finest families in Bogotá was his wife. He wanted revenge from the same society which had so often despised him."[17] Here interracial marriage is represented in a negative light, motivated by revenge and despair. The only sign of intimacy between the couple is the birth of a son, baptized as Francisco, the name of Mercedes's Spanish father. By naming the fruit of the interracial union with the name of the Spanish grandfather, the story tries to align him within the social space that had once belonged to her mother at the top of the socio-racial hierarchy. However, the text does not offer other clues to identify Francisco's racial status. There are no physical descriptions nor racial markers in talking about him. The word "mestizo" is never used to describe him. In a world that understood *mestizaje* as a process of becoming white, this silence reveals an attempt to associate the products of interracial unions with their white heritage. Despite social conflicts that had led to his birth, Francisco is represented in a redemptive light, almost justifying Mercedes's and Santiago's marriage. Mercedes's old pride and selfishness are transformed by her son: "who daily earned intelligence and vigor, and whose loving little hands made me forget even the memory of my youth. I taught him myself how to read and then he was docile and studious."[18] Mercedes's son redeems her from her past sins, and we can even come to think that

Francisco is an allegory of the desire for unification in a nation deeply divided by racial and social fractures. Despite not being a product of a foundational romance, we might think of him as the ideal citizen: educated, docile, hard-working, and studious – an individual capable of unifying the tensions between his parents. But Francisco's birth has not relieved his parents' racial strains. Santiago continues humiliating his wife, reducing her to servitude in a bizarre attempt to reverse the earlier colonial racial discrimination.[19]

Mercedes's and Santiago's interracial marriage is based on the resignation of the white woman, her submission to a brutal mulatto husband, and her devotion to a nonracialized child. Can this scenario work as an allegory of national unification? On the contrary, in many senses this interracial union represents a failure of the national project. Their marriage is not the solid foundation of a new prosperous society that soon finds itself in another civil war. Mercedes has learned to work to survive, but her husband is a drunken gambler who hosts orgies with his friends at the same house where his wife and son live. A white friend who recognizes Mercedes comments: "But I met you rich, proud and beautiful ... how do I find you married to this despicable mulatto?"[20] Santiago's moral decadence forces her to flee with Francisco and to work as a maid in Bogotá. Mercedes' falling off in the social scale culminates with her marriage to a mulatto. It reveals that, even in fiction, legal interracial unions were almost unthinkable.

Could Francisco eventually offer himself as a vehicle of integration for the new nation? He is a good worker, a lettered carpenter, the model citizen that a new nation needs. Many years later, Santiago returns, bringing back violence and instability into Mercedes's life. Francisco does not recognize his father and tries to attack him when Santiago throws himself drunk on Mercedes's bed. At that point she has no choice but to admit with shame that Santiago is Francisco's father: "Do not come to pervert your son with your bad example," she begs.[21] While Francisco, the young national citizen, does not recognize his mulatto father, he must bear the burden of being his descendant. Mercedes fears Santiago's influence over her child and claims her right to keep them apart, seeking to associate him only with the fragments of her former white world. Finally, she seems to succeed after Santiago's death. But the nation's history will again twist Francisco's fate, with the outbreak of a new civil war in 1840. Francisco is forcibly recruited by one of the armies, and while returning sick and exhausted from the battle he dies in his mother's arms. Francisco's death represents the ultimately fruitless nature of interracial marriage. National history eliminates the fruit of interracial marriage, leaving the country as divided as it was a few decades earlier when it gained the independence that left the country in shambles. This negative example of the representation of interracial unions in literature through marriage is an illustration of a failure in the ideals of a new nation. Mercedes fails to accept the new republican values because of her stubborn commitment to the pro-Hispanic world of her father. Her marriage does not represent any positive national principles; rather, it exemplifies a moral critique of Santiago, who drinks and forces Mercedes to do things that are beyond the responsibilities of a good wife. She flees to the city to work as a maid, a form of reconciliation with the values of productive and liberal individualism. The abrupt return of her husband and her son's death prevent this interracial marriage from becoming a vehicle of reconciliation in the culturally, economically, and racially divided Colombia. At the end of the story Mercedes dies alone in a distant rural parish.

In this novel, the vilified mulatto Santiago is actually a supporting character that illustrates Mercedes' downgrading in the social republican scale. It reveals that interracial unions depicted in Colombian literature did not allegorize any desire of national integration. Rather, they exposed the attempts of the elite to distance themselves from non-white populations. It also reveals that fiction in Colombia was more interested in defining the limits of "whiteness" than in creating a national discourse of unification. The intention of fiction is to represent whites as supreme citizens while maintaining Afro descendants and indigenous peoples in a subaltern position. The depiction of these characters serves to express differences among whites, making poor whites closer to other non-white groups, as in the case of Mercedes and Santiago.

This exploration is possible only when we pay more attention to new materials and collections that are not necessarily part of the cannon. Many of these materials are of high quality, but they were forgotten for reasons beyond strictly literary considerations. They were placed at the margins of the canon because they couldn't survive the material conditions of a society devastated by constant civil wars, making nineteenth-century literature a vibrant field that is still ripe for discovery and exploration.

REFERENCES

Acosta de Samper, S. (2004). *Novelas y cuadros de costumbres de la vida suramericana.* Bogotá: Editorial Universidad de los Andes. (Originally published in 1869.)

Ancízar, M. (1942 [1853]). *Peregrinación de Alpha por las provincias del Norte.* Bogotá: Editorial ABC.

Appelbaum, N. (2003). *Muddied Waters; Race, Region, and Local History in Colombia 1846–1948*. Durham: Duke University Press.

Arias Vanegas, J. (2005). *Nación y diferencia en el siglo XIX colombiano: orden nacional, racialismo y taxonomías poblacionales*. Bogotá: Universidad de los Andes.

D'Allemand, P. (2007). "Quimeras, contradicciones y ambigüedades. El caso de José María Samper." *Historia y sociedad* 13, 45–63.

Dueñas, G. (1997). *Los hijos del pecado. Ilegitimidad y vida familiar en la Santafé de Bogotá colonial*. Bogotá: Universidad Nacional de Colombia.

Díaz, E. (1859). Federico y Cintia o la verdadera cuestión de las razas. *El Mosaico* 22.

(1889). *Manuela*. París: Librería Española de Garnier Hermanos.

(1985 [1879]) *Bruna la Carbonera*. Bogotá: Procultura; Editorial Printer Colombiana. Also published online as Biblioteca Virtual del Banco de la República: www.banrepcultural.org/blaavirtual/literatura/bruna/indice.htm.

Fisher, A., and M. O' Hara. (2009) *Imperial Subjects: Race and Identity in Colonial Latin America*. Durham: Duke University Press.

Isaács, J. (1983 [1866]). *María*. Madrid: Sociedad General Española de Librería.

Larson, B. (2004). *Trials of Nation Making. Liberalism, Race and Ethnicity in the Andes, 1810–1910*. Cambridge: Cambridge University Press.

López Rodríguez, M. (2012). *La invención de la blancura: la racialización del espacio andino colombiano a mediados del siglo XIX. Estar en el presente. Literatura y nación desde el Bicentenario*, ed. E. Cortez and G. Kirkpatrick, 79–98. Lima and Berkeley: Centro de Estudios Literarios Antonio Cornejo Polar–CELACP: Latinoamericana Editores.

Madiedo, M. M. (1866). "El boga del Magdalena." In *Museo de Cuadros de Costumbres*. Bogotá: Editorial El Mosaico.

Martínez-Pinzón, F. (2012). *La mirada invernocular: clima y cultura en Colombia (1808–1924)*. PhD dissertation. New York University.

Michaels, W. B. (2003). "Absalom, Absalom! The Difference between White Men and White Men" In *Faulkner in the Twenty-first Century*. Jackson: University Press of Mississippi.

Múnera, A. (2005). *Fronteras imaginadas. La construcción de las razas y de la geografía en el siglo XIX colombiano*. Bogotá: Planeta.

Rappaport, J. (2014). *The Disappearing Mestizo. Configuring Difference in the Colonial New Kingdom of Granada*. Durham: Duke University Press.

Safford, F. (1991). Race, Integration and Progress: Elite Attitudes and the Indian in Colombia. *Hispanic American Historical Review* 71, no. 1: 20–27.

Samper, J. M. (1945 [1860]). *Ensayo sobre las revoluciones políticas y la condición social de las repúblicas colombianas con un apéndice sobre la orografía y la población de la confederación granadina*. Bogotá: Biblioteca Popular de la Cultura Colombiana.

Sommer, D. (1993). *Foundational Fictions: The National Romances of Latin America*. Berkeley: University of California Press.

Wade, P. (1995). *Blackness and Race Mixture: The Dynamics of Racial Identity in Colombia*. Baltimore: John Hopkins University Press.

Notes

1 Nancy Appelbaun (2003) has studied the dynamics of race and the nation-building process in nineteenth-century Colombia, approaching regions as locus of racial representations. Peter Wade (1995) has successfully shown how regions in Colombia are depicted not only as geographical entities but rather as racial identities. In his work about the Colombian Caribbean region, Alfonso Múnera (2005) has explored how the Colombian Andean region was depicted as the core of the nation, in contrast to others represented as racially and politically marginal to the nation. A specific examination of how Colombian literary production engaged in the racial debates over whiteness can be found in López Rodríguez (2012). Recent studies on the interactions between region and nation in nineteenth-century Colombia include Arias Vanegas (2005) and Martínez Pinzón (2012).

2 See Michaels (2003).

3 See Safford (1991).

4 See Larson (2004).

5 Joanne Rappaport (2014) has studied a similar situation for the early Spanish American *mestizos* in the New Kingdom of Granada. Matthew O'Hara and Andrew B. Fisher (2009) have also explored the fluidity of race during the early years of Spanish rule in the Americas.

6 Acosta de Samper (2004).

7 Acosta de Samper (1869: 266).

8 Ibid., 272.

9 Ibid., 273.

10 Ibid., 272.

11 Ibid., 276.

12 Ibid., 277.

13 Ibid., 278.

14 Ibid.

15 Ibid.

16 Ibid., 281

17 Ibid., 281–2.

18 Ibid., 284.

19 Ibid., 283.

20 Ibid., 284.

21 Ibid., 286.

CHAPTER 13

Literature and culture in Antioquia: between stories and accounts

Juan Luis Mejía Arango

Colombia is a fragmented country, difficult to understand as a homogeneous whole. Each natural region into which it is divided has its own characteristics. One of these regions is Antioquia, where, for various reasons, a distinct group of people exist with marked differences from the rest of the population. Anthropologists, historians, sociologists, and economists have written countless interpretations of *El caso antioqueño* (The Antioquia Case). One of the pioneering works is by the American geographer James Parsons, who, in 1948, as part of his PhD written at the University of Berkeley, California, wrote the classic study *La colonización antioqueña en el occidente colombiano* (The Antioquian Colonization in Western Colombia). In the words of the researcher Alejandro Reyes, in this book the American geographer "se concentró en el problema de explicar cómo un grupo regional se distinguió y acumuló tantos recursos morales e intelectuales, cómo su cultura perfiló una ética basada en el trabajo familiar y el ahorro que permitieron hacer de Antioquia la región industrial y emprendedora que la distingue en Colombia" (focused on the problem of explaining how a regional group located and accumulated so many moral and intellectual resources, and how its culture outlined an ethic based on family labor and savings that led to the making of Antioquia as the industrial and entrepreneurial region that stands out in Colombia) (Reyes 1986:199). This chapter proposes to provide a description of the cultural evolution of this region's society during the second half of the nineteenth century and the early twentieth century.

Antioquia was different between the Colonial period and the years following independence from the Spanish crown in 1819. In fact, all written reports from the colonial officials in the late eighteenth century speak of an underdeveloped region, with a population immersed in poverty, isolated from the rest of the colonial territory by a lack of roads, as well as by a lack of entrepreneurial initiative. A century later, the perception of Antioquia was completely different, and in the collective imaginary the *antioqueño* became a synonym for strength, entrepreneurship, and economic prosperity.

One of the reasons for this profound transformation is connected to gold. Early Spanish settlers decided to establish themselves in this isolated territory as a result of the existence of precious metals, but throughout the Colonial period its exploitation was performed with artisanal and rudimentary methods in the alluvial beds of the insalubrious lowlands. A goal of the population at the end of the Colonial period was to bring in mining engineers to facilitate the extraction of minerals embedded in the veins of the mountains. However, the policy of isolation by the Spanish crown prevented a legitimate mining industry from being developed in the territory.

After independence from Spain, European miners equipped in knowledge and skills began arriving. Their arrival allowed for penetration into the mountains and for exploration of the veins of gold. In the first stage foreigners worked in the rich northern plateau, formerly known as *el Valle de los Osos* (the Valley of the Bears), where the first manufacturing establishments appeared. Alluvial mines could be exploited for only a few months of the year, depending on the rainy season, generating a constant displacement of miners; however, the establishments of veins could operate year 'round and, thus, people could settle stably.

For the proper operation of mines foreigners had to train the population in techniques to adequately reap the benefits of the mines, and so skilled carpenters, blacksmiths, smelters, and those with other vocations were required not only for their physical ability, but also for their professional training to solve technical problems. This specialized technical craftwork came to distinguish them from the rest of the incipient nation's workforce. It is revealing to track the families belonging to those first two or three generations, for the most important figures of the growing cultural life of Antioquia would later emerge from this core group of original specialized technicians.

It is no coincidence that all these individuals were from the northern towns of Antioquia. A brief history confirms their origin from the north: painter Francisco Antonio Cano and poet Epifanio Mejía came from Yarumal; sculptor Marco Tobón Mejía and poet Porfirio Barba Jacob came from Santa Rosa de Osos; novelists Tomás Carrasquilla and Francisco de Paula Rendón were from Santo Domingo; writer and pioneer of journalism Fidel Cano hailed from San Pedro de los Milagros; and muralist Pedro Nel Gómez was from Anorí.

However, the northern mining cycle would remain ephemeral, and for the second half of the nineteenth century the economic epicenter would move to the southwest, where the mines of Zancudo, located near the town of Titiribí, would would become the wealthiest territory in Colombia. Equidistant from the mining centers, and located in a bucolic and healthy valley, the until then small town of Medellín, (which in 1826 became the capital of the province by displacing stately Santa Fe of Antioquia) stands as the political and economic epicenter of the region and, over the years, has become an active cultural center.

According to the census conducted in 1870, Medellín had 29,765 inhabitants; the chronicler Lizandro Ochoa observes that during the era

> funcionaban tres bancos, cuatro malos hoteles, siete carpinterías, cinco sastrerías, seis boticas, cuatro peluquerías, seis cantinas, dos fotografías, tres imprentas, dos casas de baños públicos, siete zapaterías, y una litografía; cincuenta y dos casas de dos pisos y una de tres pisos, catorce consultorios médicos, un teatro, una notaría, dos librerías, tres fábricas de mala cerveza, una casa de locos, cuatro herrerías y un hospital de caridad (there were three functioning banks, four bad hotels, seven carpenter shops, five tailor shops, six pharmacies, four hairdressing salons, six bars, two photography studios, three printing houses, two public bathhouses, seven shoe shops, and a lithography; fifty two two-story houses and one three-story house, fourteen medical offices, a theater, a notary, two bookstores, three bad breweries, a madhouse, four blacksmith workshops and a charity hospital) (Ochoa 1984:8)

Of importance in the context of this essay was the existence of a theater and two bookstores. According to the chronicler Eladio Gónima (1909), it was the theatrical activities what would from time to time alter the monotonous life of the city. In 1830 the Drama Company was founded, and it promoted the construction of the theater. The numerous newspaper reviews of the time testify to the presence of theater companies that would make long trips to perform in Medellín. From the same press we know that the first opera company that presented in the city was that of Darío Acchiardi, which in 1864 performed *Lucía di Lammermoor*, and in 1871, the company of José Zafrané shared the first zarzuelas, a genre that henceforth would enjoy wide acceptance among the public. As for bookstores, with the limited data available to us, we can deduce that these were establishments of miscellaneous trade, and, among the books, the distribution of religious texts was prioritized.

It is important to highlight that in the middle of the federal system of a national government of Liberal tendencies, which enacted the constitution of 1863, Conservative leaders, among whom stands the figure of Pedro Justo Berrío, ruled the Sovereign State of Antioquia. While other states were subject to frequent changes of government and continuous wars,

Antioquia enjoyed, for almost three decades, greater political stability, which allowed economic growth and hence higher tax revenues, which lessened dependence on the federal government.

If during the years following independence the arrival of European miners had a major impact on the economic development of the region, during the second half of the nineteenth century it was the arrival in Europe of the sons of merchants and miners who had gone to study in Europe that began to exert a significant influence on society. These young men just arriving from Paris and London began incorporating the so-called *civilization project* represented in new institutions, fashions, sensitivities, and aesthetics. An early example is the founding, in 1865, of a Beautified Society and School of Arts by the engineer Vicente Restrepo, the architect Juan Lalinde, and doctors Ricardo Rodríguez Roldán and Manuel Uribe Ángel, who, after their studies in Europe, attempted to incorporate elements of modernity in the province of Medellín. In this fledgling society two establishments would later exert an indubitable influence on social life, economy, and culture in the city: the School of Arts and Crafts and the Society of Public Improvements. Other manifestations of the civilization project were the creation of literary circles and the foundation of social clubs to which only males had access; Photographs taken by Pastor Restrepo Ascarte de Visite illustrate this period in which these men appear with pretentious cosmopolitan airs.

During the Conservative period, two poets dominated literary life: Gregorio Gutiérrez and Epifanio Mejía. As scholars Dora Tamayo Ortiz and Hernán Botero Restrepo argue, they belong to

> lo que puede denominarse la segunda generación del romanticismo hispa-
> noamericano – caracterizado por un tono dolorido y con frecuencia lacri-
> moso – que alcanza en ellos la dignidad de la sencillez intensamente sentida
> de la vida cotidiana, en un marco campesino y en la exaltación de los
> sentimientos y emociones familiares de sus pobladores, con los cuales cada
> uno de los poetas se identifica a su manera, de tal modo que sus versos han
> llegado a formar parte de la memoria colectiva. (what may be called *the
> second generation of romanticism in Latin America* – characterized by a
> painful and often lachrymose tone – in which the dignity of simplicity
> intensely felt in everyday life marks their writing, within a rural context, and
> in the exaltation of feelings and emotions familiar to its residents, with
> which each one of these poets identifies in his own way, in such a manner
> that his verses have formed part of a collective memory.) (Tamayo Ortiz
> and Botero Restrepo 2005:24)

In the imaginary collective of Colombians the idea of an *antioqueño* dedicated exclusively to economic activities, completely removed completely from the labors of spirit and culture became to take shape. A phrase has been attributed to President Miguel Antonio Caro that in Antioquia the only letters that flourished were those of change. An example of this perception is a comment that appeared on August 20, 1871, in *La Revista científica e industrial* (Scientific and Industrial Journal) in Bogotá:

> El antioqueño es ante todo, productor de oro, que es un trabajador vigoroso y pertinaz puesto que lo persigue tanto en el lecho de los ríos como en los socavones abiertos a través del duro cuarzo, que forma un pueblo sin goces refinados, apto para descuajar bosques i soportar todo género de labores recias, i totalmente extraño a las bellas artes y a las letras. ¿Qué haría un artista o un literato en Antioquia? (The *antioqueño* is foremost, a producer of gold, which is a vigorous and pertinacious work since he is chased both by riverbeds and open tunnels through the stiff quartz, forming a village without refined enjoyments, capable of dissolving forests and resisting all types of demanding labors, and completely foreign to fine arts and letters. What would an artist or a writer do in Antioquia?) (5)

That *ideal of practicality*, as the historian Frank Safford calls it, is also supported by the idea of an elite *antioqueño*. In a letter written by Mariano Ospina Rodríguez to his sons, Tulio and Pedro Nel, he advises them:

> No se metan con lo más alambicado de la mecánica analítica y de las matemáticas trascendentales, consagrándose de preferencia a lo aplicable en la práctica, y procurando adquirir los conocimientos de los que llaman ingenieros mecánicos. ... Hay ciencias muy atractivas, pero poco provechosas, como la botánica, la zoología, la astronomía, que deben dejarse a los ricos, y en el mismo caso se halla la literatura. Religión y Moral, cuanto les quepa en el alma y en el cuerpo; ciencia aplicada y aplicable, muchísima; idiomas vivos, bastante; ciencia puramente especulativa, literatura e idiomas muertos, algo; novelas y versos, nada. (Do not get involved with the complexity of analytical mechanics and transcendental mathematics, devote yourself preferably to *the applicable in practice*, and seek to acquire the knowledge of the so-called mechanical engineers. ... There are very attractive sciences, but unprofitable, such as botany, zoology, astronomy, which must be left to the rich, literature finds itself in the same category. Religion and morality, how they fit into the soul and the body; applied and applicable science, many; living languages, a fair amount; purely speculative science, literature and dead languages, some; novels and poetry, none.) (Tamayo Ortiz and Botero Restreppo 2005:20)

In 1907 a group of young writers from Manizales wrote to the general and Liberal politician Rafael Uribe Uribe a collaborative effort to be published in the second number of the journal *Albores*. The general, a veteran of many wars, in a long diatribe against the petition of the young writers, writes to their mother the following:

Dejen la revista, dejen la literatura y tomen otro oficio. **¡No más versos!**
¡Y con qué pena, con qué alarma, contemplo desde lejos propagarse más,
cada día esa epidemia en mi tierra! Es un constante resonar de nombres
nuevos, adquiridos para la malhadada secta versificadora; es una viciosa
floración de publicaciones literarias por todas partes, como una especie de
maleza nacional. ... Los compadezco y les digo que antes debieron cortarse
con la izquierda la mano derecha, que emplearía en hacer frases: que lo
único propio del hombre son los hechos, y que para abrirles campo es
menester dar primero muerte a las palabras que sólo sean palabras. Pueden
ser perdonadas las palabras que sean hechos; pero la mera verborragia, sobre
todo si es rimada, "es el mayor flagelo" para un pueblo. (Leave the journal,
leave literature and find another profession. **No more verses!** With what
shame, with what alarm, do I contemplate the daily spread of such an
epidemic in my country! It is the constant resounding of new names,
acquired to serve the ill-fated versifier sect; it is the vicious bloom of literary
publications everywhere, like a kind of national weed. ... I pity them and
tell them that they should have cut their right hand with the left one, before
using it to make statements: that the only thing proper to human beings
are the facts, and to give them space it is necessary to kill the words that are
merely words. The words that are only facts can be forgiven; but pure
verbosity, especially if in rhymes, "is the biggest scourge" for the people.)
(Pensamiento Político de Rafael Uribe Uribe 1974:56)

Despite this stigma, from the beginning of the republican era there
have been people who have gone against this argument and have opted to
value writing, initially as a hobby and later devoting their lives to the
practice of literature. This process has been traced by the scholars Dora
Elena Tamayo Ortiz and Hernán Botero Restrepo in the seminal study
Inicios de una literatura regional (Early Study of Regional Literature),
published by the Editorial of the University of Antioquia in 2005, and
by Professor Jorge Alberto Naranjo in his *Antología del relato temprano en
Antioquia* (Anthology of Early Story in Antioquia), edited by the Collection of Authors *Antioqueños* in 1995.

In their book, Tamayo Ortiz and Botero Restrepo, from a selection of
texts collected in an exhaustive investigation of journal publications of
the time, sustain the thesis that "desde 1835 – fecha de aparición de la
Miscelánea de Antioquia – hasta los últimos años del siglo XIX, se puede
afirmar que durante ese lapso se origina y configura en Antioquia una
literatura regional con características propias" ((since 1835 – the date of
appearance of the *Miscellanea Antioquia/Miscelánea de Antioquia* – in the
latter years of the nineteenth century, it can be affirmed that during this
period in Antioquia a regional literature arose and configured itself with its
own specific characteristics) (Tamayo Ortiz and Botero Restrepo 2005:13).

Among the nearly one hundred recovered texts, the authors group into three tendencies the literary evolution of narratives in Antioquia: *costumbrismo*, romanticism, and realism.

This process also responds to an intellectual climate that slowly developed in the region, and not just in in Medellín, which took the initiative toward active literary productivity. Therefore, it is interesting to trace the cultural environment of the second half of the nineteenth century through three manifestations: the publication of books, newspapers, and magazines; bookstores and libraries; and literary circles.

With respect to newspaper and magazine publications, the scholar and journalist María Cristina Arango de Tobón, in her book *Publicaciones Periódicas en Antioquia 1814–1960: del chibalete a la rotativa* (Published Periodicals in Antioquia 1814–1860: From Woodblock Printing Press to Rotary Printing Press), successfully identified 210 publications among newspapers and magazines between 1835 and 1900. Almost all were of partisan or religious nature but they also, as Tamayo Ortiz and Botero Restrepo attest, served to publish the first writings of a literary nature. At the turn of the century strictly cultural publications appeared such as *Miscellany* (1894–1901), *Repertoire* (1896–7), *Highlander* (1897–9)/*La Miscelánea* (1894–1901), *El Repertorio* (1896–7), and *El Montañez* (1897–9).

Books and readers

Unlike the abundant production of magazines and newspapers, relatively few books were published during the nineteenth century in Antioquia. An incipient typography infrastructure, difficulty obtaining paper, and a narrow market did not allow for the development of a robust publishing industry. Therefore, the effort by Juan José Molina was laudable; he promoted a literary circle in his residence, and in 1878 he published *Antioquia Literaria* (Literary Antioquia), which was the first noteworthy publishing effort in the region. This book, with more than 400 pages, collects texts written between 1810, the year of the proclamation of independence, to 1878. It is a wide-ranging selection that includes stories, poems, and essays collected with the intention of "reclamar el rango que en justicia merezca Antioquia en la familia literaria de Colombia. . . . Con este libro se probará a la República que Antioquia ha tenido y tiene en la actualidad poetas, filósofos, moralistas, escritores de costumbres y novelistas que pueden brillar dignamente en el cielo literario" (reclaiming the status Antioquia justly deserves in the literary family of Colombia. . . . With this book it was proven to the nation that Antioquia indeed had poets, philosophers, moralists, custom writers and novelists that shined with dignity in the literary sky) (Molina 1998:19, 21). Since its publication it has had a great impact because it became a required text in schools and currently provides a depiction of life and the imaginary of the inhabitants of that region during much of the nineteenth century.

Despite the myth of isolation in which the region lived due to lack of roads, there is evidence of a relatively high level of circulation of books. Lizandro Ochoa's description of the existence of several libraries in Medellín in the late nineteenth century affirms a literary infrastructure. It is also most noteworthy that two of the most prominent political figures of the time pursued the profession of booksellers. Indeed, we know that Rafael Uribe Uribe, the Liberal leader, was a correspondent at the bookstore Camacho Roldán in Medellín, and that Carlos E. Restrepo, the future Conservative president, had an accredited library called the Librería Restrepo (Restrepo Bookstore), which he sold upon assuming the presidency, since ruling the nation was not compatible with private business. Abraham Moreno owned another important bookstore of the time dedicated to distribution of texts of Catholic doctrine. Tomás Carrasquilla writes: "Y puesto que se sostenían tales comercios era señal de que se vendían. Y vendían no sólo libros religiosos o textos escolares, sino también de todos los autores profanos que no estuvieran incluidos en el Gillabus" (And since such trade was sustained it was a sign that they were sold. And they sold not only religious books or school textbooks, but also all other secular authors that were not included in the Syllabus) (Carrasquilla 1964:00). This observation by the novelist from Santo Domingo reveals the strong ideological control exercised by the church through the famous index of authors that Catholics were forbidden to read under penalty of mortal sin. Nevertheless, despite this control, the forbidden books circulated underground and were read eagerly. Carrasquilla, in recounting his passion for reading, says, "Pues ahí me tenéis a mí, libro en mano a toda hora, en la quietud aldeana de mi casa. Seguí leyendo y creo que en el hoyo donde me entierren habré de leerme la biblioteca de la muerte, donde debe estar concentrada la esencia toda del saber hondo. He leído de cuanto hay, bueno y malo, sagrado y profano, lícito y prohibido, sin método, sin plan no objetivos determinados, por puro pasatiempo." (Well, there you have me, book in hand at all times, in the quiet of my home village. I keep reading and I think that in the hole where I shall be buried I will read the library of of the dead, where the essence of deep knowledge shall be concentrated. I've read everything there is, good and evil, sacred and profane, licit and forbidden, or at random, just as pure pastime) (ibid.).

As happened in other Latin American countries, the "civilizing project" promoted the creation of public libraries. We have no evidence that in those early days in Medellín there was knowledge of Domingo Faustino Sarmiento's writings on the civilizing role of public libraries. The fact is that in 1881 a group of professionals promoted the creation of the Museo y Biblioteca de Zea (Museum and Library Zea), in memory of Francisco Antonio Zea, a scientist and local hero of independence. In his inaugural speech as the first director, doctor Manuel Uribe Ángel concluded: "Un pueblo que no lee, es por lo mismo ignorante y sin educación" (A people that does not read, is therefore ignorant and uneducated). The Canadian scholar Kurt L. Levy, in his seminal book *Vida y obras de Tomás Carrasquilla* (1958, Life and Works of Tomás Carrasquilla), emphasizes the importance of the creation of the so-called Biblioteca del tercer piso (Library on the Third Floor) in the literary formation of the novelist, in his home town of Santo Domingo. The French traveler Pierre D 'Espagnat recounts his amazement in reaching this village before arriving in Medellín: "Caí en un ambiente intelectual atrayente, que, sin que se sepa cómo ni porqué, se desenvuelve aquí en algunos círculos ignorados de esta pequeña ciudad. Pasé algunas horas deliciosas en el silencio de la amplia biblioteca" (I landed in an attractive intellectual environment which, without knowing how and why, operates here in some ignored circles of this small town. I spent some delightful hours in the silence of the vast library) (Levy 1958:00). Another interesting modality was the existence of rent libraries. The French miner Jorge Brisson recounts his surprise at finding "en Medellín varias librerías en donde alquilan libros mediante una pequeña retribución. Contienen especialmente obras de escritores espa-ñoles, traducciones de novelas francesas y algunos escritos de autores nacionales. Me han parecido bastante concurridas, lo que demuestra el culto por la lectura, poco desarrollado en otras repúblicas del sur" (several bookstores in Medellín where books are rented for a small fee. They especially contain works by Spanish writers, translations of French novels and some writings by national authors. In my perspective they seem pretty busy, demonstrating a cult for reading, undeveloped in other republics of the south.) (Posada 1988:517).

After independence, relations with Spain were completely broken, and Latin American countries sought associations with the United States and various European nations, especially France and England. However, a Hispanist movement, very close to the conservative circles, promoted an approach to the "motherland" to which they owed, among other things, their spoken language. This movement created the Colombian Academy of

Language, the first of its kind on this side of the Atlantic. Also, from Madrid, Spanish publishers demanded the resumption of diplomatic relations with countries of Spanish America, a natural market for the expansion of their industry. With these new relationships established, Spanish publishers lobbied their government to subscribe to the treaties of the nations of the Americas that were aimed at protecting copyrights; as these were essential for the legal protection of the sector.

Juan Guillermo Gómez (0000) studied the impact that the collection *España Moderna* (Modern Spain)had in this region, published by the editor and antiquarian José Lázaro Galdeano; he also examined the relationships that bookseller Fernando de Fé began to establish in these regions. It is also relevant to emphasize the importance of the collection *Rivadeneira*, a main reference source for Rufino José Cuervo in the preparation of his monumental *Diccionario de Construcción y Régimen de la Lengua Castellana* (Dictionary of Construction and Rules of the Spanish Language).

Due to the new trade with Hispanic publishers, it was logical that in this intellectual milieu Spanish writers began to exert a great influence. Baldomero Sanín Cano narrates how "the literature of the city suffered the influence and spread of Spanish letters of the moment" with citizens intently reading Pérez Galdós, Valera, Clarín, Pereda, Palacio Valdés, and, of course, Pardo Bazán. In more liberal circles the preferred author was Victor Hugo, who was translated by figures such as Fidel Cano, founder of the newspaper *El Espectador* (The Spectator) (Sanín Cano 1949). In a setting strongly influenced by religion, it is interesting to find that in several private libraries books were found by authors included in the list of forbidden works, such as Allan Kardec, promoter of spiritualism who apparently had many followers in the emerging city. The role of the book market and the influence of spiritualism in intellectual life in Antioquia are two topics that await future research.

Literary casino

In the absence of academic institutions, literary gatherings became fundamental epicenters for the distribution of literature. As we discussed earlier the importance of initial gatherings run by the great cultural disseminator Juan José Molina. But without a doubt the *Casino Literario* (Literary Casino), founded in October 1887, constituted the most influential gatherings of the nineteenth century in Antioquia. The rigor governing the institution can be seen in its statutes on issues such as punctuality at meetings and fines for breaching any of its norms. The objective of the Casino, whose regulatory number for meetings was twelve members, was to "ejercitarnos en la composición, leer y procurarnos ratos de solaz y expansión por medios honestos" (practice composition, read and procure moments of solace and expansion by honest means) (Levy 1958:250). These individuals committed themselves to forming a library of history of the Americas and to developing a common catalog with the titles owned by each one of the members, in order to make them available to the entire group. As a prerequisite for admission, members were required to write and subsequently to read before all the members an unpublished text. To fulfill this obligation and to be admitted, Carrasquilla wrote the story "Simón el Mago" (The Magician Simon), which was read at the meeting of February 6, 1890, by his compatriot and intellectual accomplice Francisco de Paula Rendón.

In an ordinary meeting at the Casino, possibly the one on April 17, 1890, a discussion took place about the reasons for novels not flourishing in Antioquia. In his *Autobiography*, Carrasquilla recalls:

> Tratábase una noche, en dicho centro, de si había o no en Antioquia materia novelable. Todos opinaron que no, menos Carlosé y el suscrito. Con tanto calor sostuvimos el parecer, que todos se pasaron a nuestro partido y todos, a una, diputamos al propio presidente como el llamado para el asunto. Pero Carlosé, resolvió que no era él sino yo. Yo le obedecí, porque hay gentes que nacen para mandar. ... Una vez en la quietud arcádica de mi parroquia, mientras los aguaceros se desataban y la tormenta repercutía, escribí un mamotreto, allá en las reconditeces de mi cuartucho. No pensé tampoco en publicarlo: quería probar solamente, que puede hacerse novela sobre el tema más vulgar y cotidiano. (It was debated one night, in said center, whether or not there were noteworthy matters in Antioquia. All felt that there were none, except for Carlosé and the secretary. With such fervor we held our view that everyone switched to our side and all, at once, delegated the president himself to the subject matter. But Carlosé, decided it was not he but myself. I obeyed him, because there are people who are born to rule. ... Once in the stillness of my Arcadian parish, as the rains unleashed and the storm reverberated, I wrote a tome, back in my small recondite room. I did not think of publishing it: I only wanted to prove that a novel could be written about the most common and everyday themes.) (Carrasquilla 1964:00)

The "tome" had the original title *Solomos y Jamones* (*Solomos and Hams*), and Jorge Roa, in Bogota, published it in early 1896 with the title *Frutos de mi tierra* (Fruits of My Land).

After a long period of gestation and maturation, narrative reached maturity with the publication of the first Antioquian novel. As Tamayo

Ortiz and Botero Restrepo noted: "Con la obra de Carrasquilla, regional y Universal a la vez, se consolida la narrativa antioqueña, y una de las explicaciones de ello, además del genio del autor y su formación y conocimiento de las literaturas extranjeras, tiene que ver con la culminación de un proceso de búsqueda que desembocó en él y en los narradores más solventes de su generación" (Carrasquilla's work, simultaneously regional and universal, represents the consolidation of Antioquian narrative. In addition to the genius of the author and his training in and knowledge of foreign literatures, the main explanation for this resides in the fact that he and the other trustworthy narrators of his generation were considered the culmination of a search for consolidation (2005:12).

However, *Frutos de mi tierra* also sparked fury. In the following years a group of fiction writers erupted onto the novelistic and short story scene, stripping the story from its *costumbrismo* trappings and seeking an appropriate language close to realism. Among contemporary storytellers like Carrasquilla were Eduardo Zuleta, who published his novel *Tierra Virgen* (Virgin Land), in 1897 and Francisco Gómez Escobar, better known as Efe Gómez, who began publishing his stories in 1896. From the vitality of the narrative of those pre–Civil War days (the so-called thousand days, 1899–1901) a surprising fact is evident: the magazine *La Miscelánea* (Miscellany) announced in 1897 a novel contest that received fifty-eight works! The winner was *Madre* (Mother), by Samuel Velásquez, published the same year. Other important postwar novels were published, such as *Kundry*, by Gabriel Latorre in 1905; *Mercedes*, by Marco Antonio Jaramillo in 1907; and stories and tales by Jesús del Corral and Francisco de Paula Rendón.

It is noteworthy to observe the use of popular language in the works of these traditional writers. Not surprisingly, for example, Carrasquilla, always a dandy in fashion and behavior, translated his works in the language used by the people to express themselves. In defense of the novel *Tierra Virgen* by Eduardo Zuleta, Carrasquilla argued:

> Se ha dicho que nuestro lenguaje popular es áspero y feo, y que por eso no puede tener cabida en la novela; pero pocos habrá tan gráficos, tan expresivos tan pintorescos, como el que usa nuestro pueblo. Ese lenguaje esmaltado de imágenes, de frases hechas, riquísimo en léxico, en voces viejas que sólo usan los clásicos, lo consideramos lo suficientemente bello para verterlo en un libro, sin mayores componendas. (It has been said that our popular language is rough and ugly, and therefore cannot fit into the novel; but few languages are so graphic, so expressive so picturesque, as the one used by

our people. That language enameled with images and unique phrases, rich in vocabulary, communicated in ancient voices used by only the classics, we consider it beautiful enough to pour it into a book, without major compromises). (Carrasquilla 1964:629)

The use of popular language was taken to the extreme with the publication of the story "El machete" (The Machete), written and illustrated by the author, Julio Posada.

The awakening of narrative fiction was not an isolated cultural process. To use the categories established by Leopoldo Zea, although elite groups attempted to establish a civilizing project, aimed at implementing the canons of European culture, another group of intellectuals reached what the Mexican philosopher has called a *proyecto asuntivo* (project of transcendence). Indeed, from different angles, their own project was assumed and valued. For example, in 1895, doctor Manuel Uribe Ángel published in Paris the monumental *Geografía General y compendio histórico del Estado de Antioquia en Colombia* (General Geography and Historical Overview of the State of Antioquia in Colombia), a first and early attempt to describe the region of Antioquia. Around the same time, a group of botanists including Andrés Posada Arango and Joaquín Antonio Uribe carried out a systematic study of the flora of the region. In the field of visual arts, Francisco Antonio Cano painted the first known landscapes in the history of Colombian painting. Carrasquilla, locked in his room in Santo Domingo, gave names to nature and social reality in their native language, Cano, in his study of Medellín, departed from religious tradition and portrait painting and depicted the surrounding nature and landscape. To understand the tensions between "civilization" and "transcendence," one can turn to the archives of photographers Melitón Rodríguez and Benjamín de la Calle. The former portrays a commercial and mining elite that enjoys representing (masquerading in) latest in European fashion. By contrast, in the study of Benjamín de la Calle came the carriers, farmers, and craftsmen who posed unpretentiously in front of the photographer's camera.

Another manifestation of cultural vitality palpable in the last decade of the nineteenth century was the existence of various cultural and scientific journals that served as witness to the intense narrative activity that existed in the village attempting to become a city. Among the literary publications it is important to note *la Miscelánea* (Miscellany), edited by Carlos A. Molina, son of Juan José, promoter of the literary circle and book *Antioquia Literaria* (Literary Antioquia); *El Repertorio* (Repertoire), edited by Luis de Greiff and Horacio M. Rodríguez, the first illustrated journal in the area; and last, *El Montañés* (Highlander), directed by Gabriel Latorre, Efe Gómez, and Mariano Ospina V., heir to the *Repertoire.*

The end of the nineteenth century surprised the country in the last and bloodiest of its civil wars, known as the War of a Thousand Days, which suspended all economic and cultural activity. It is relevant that in an announcement in 1901, Henrique Gaviria, the director of the newspaper *El Cascabel,* formed a group of writers to write a story about the effects of war when it was still raging. The announcement reads: "Un pobre recluta que ha hecho campaña en la presente guerra civil y que a su regreso encuentra en su hogar ... lo que quisieran que encuentre los señores Tomás Carrasquilla, Efe Gómez, Eusebio Robledo, Julio Vives Guerra, Alfonso Castro, Armando Carrera y K Ombre a quienes suplicamos encarecidamente tengan la fineza de desarrollar dicho argumento" (A poor recruit has fought in this civil war and upon his return finds in his home ... what Tomás Carrasquilla, Efe Gómez, Eusebio Robledo, Julio Vives Guerra, Alfonso Castro, Armando Carrera and K Ombre want him to find; we urgently beg these gentlemen to have the delicacy to develop their argument) (*El Cascabel,* July 10, 1901, p. 8). The stories were collected in a small volume entitled *El Recluta* (The Recruit). Among the published texts Carrasquilla's *A la plata* (Silver) stands out.

After the war

With the conclusion of the war daily life resumed and the suspended projects came back to life. Francisco Antonio Cano, the painter who had to discontinue his studies in Paris and return to the country because of the war, decided to undertake the ambitious project of publishing a magazine of arts and letters in the company of the sculptor Marco Tobón Mejía, the musician Gonzalo Vidal, and the poet and bookseller Antonio J. Cano. *Lectura y Arte* (Reading and Art, 1903–5) is one of the most beautiful publications published in Medellín. In it we see the noticeable influence of the new decorative arts, especially the *art nouveau* introduced by Cano. It was also an organ of a new group that replaced the Literary Casino and that now called itself the *Centro Artístico* (Artistic Center) promoting diverse cultural activities among which stands out a call, in 1905, to the first *floral games* (*juegos florales*) held in the city. The scholars Camilo Escobar and Adolfo Maya have studied the significance of these literary contests.

Once the cycle of *Lectura y Arte* ended, it was replaced by *Alpha,* led by Mariano Ospina Vásquez, the bookseller and poet Antonio J. Cano, and Luis de Greiff Obregón (the father of Otto and León de Greiff). In its ten years of existence (1905–15) this journal became the organ of diffusion for intellectuals in Antioquia headed by the most representative figure, Carrasquilla, who published several of his works using the pseudonym Carlos Malaquita. The uninterrupted thirteen tomes of twelve volumes in *Alpha* concluded in 1915 when Archbishop Manuel José Cayzedo ordered its closure following the publication of an article on spiritualism.

When carefully observing the executive management of all cultural organizations of the early twentieth century, the figure of Antonio J. Cano is always present. Indeed, this self-taught intellectual owned a renowned bookstore in which, at sunset, intellectuals met to discuss the divine and the human and to promote cultural activity in the city. The poet Ciro Mendía (pseudonym of Carlos Mejía Ángel) immortalized those meetings in the poem *La tertulia del "Negro" Cano* (The Gathering of the "Black" Cano).

A few steps from the Negro Cano (Black Cano) bookstore was a café that also had a library of books for rent. It was called *El Globo* (The Globe) and was ironically located diagonal to the door of forgiveness in the Church of the Candelaria and adjacent to the offices of the newspaper *El Espectador* (The Spectator), owned by liberal writer Fidel Cano. In the bar-library a group of young intellectuals began to gather. Born in the agonizing nineteenth century, these writers scandalized the church with their bohemian lifestyle and defiant intellectual stands. The group, led by poet León de Greiff, philosopher Fernando González, artist Felix Mejía, and cartoonist Ricardo Rendón, began to publish a minor biweekly magazine that, according to tradition, was funded by Carrasquilla. The journal was called *Panida* in honor of the Greek god Pan; ten numbers were published between February 15 and June 20, 1915. Ephemeral in its circulation, the publication signified a rupture with the literary and pictorial tradition of the time and opened the paths of cultural modernity in the narrow intellectual sphere of the city. The pseudonyms speak to the writer's pretensions. The second number announces that "lo que aparece firmado en la revista con los nombres de: C. R. Pino, Fernando Villalva, Leo le Gris, Jean Genier, El Visir Gulliver, Cebrián de Amocete, Juan Cristóbal, M. Carré, Helena de Mai, Xavier de Lis, pertenece a la redacción" (what appears in the journal signed with the names of C. R. Pino, Fernando Villalva, Leo le Gris, Jean Genier, El Visir Gulliver, Cebrián de Amocete, Juan Cristóbal, M. Carré, Helena de Mai, Xavier de Lis, belongs to the editor) (*Panida* 1983:00):

"Músicos, rapsodas, prosistas,	Musicians, rhapsodists, prosodians,
poetas, poetas, poetas,	poets, poets, poets,
pintores, caricaturistas,	painters, cartoonists,
eruditos, nimios estetas,	erudites, aesthetes,
románticos o clásicos,	Romanticists or classicists,
y decadentes, si os parece;	and decadents, if you will;
pero eso sí, locos y artistas	but yes, madmen and artists
los panidas éramos trece."	we *panidas* were thirteen.

The small town had aspirations of becoming a city. After the War of a Thousand Days, a transformation began, a change from an economy based on gold and coffee to one of trade and craft production. Beginning in 1904, in the corners of the *Valle de Aburrá* (Aburrá Valley), locals began to take advantage of the waterfalls that generated electricity, and a manufacturing-based economy emerged, particularly with regards to textiles, food, and beverages. With this emergence of industrialization, a the working class also emerged, which, in Medellín, consisted overwhelmingly of women. The union leader Betsabé Espinoza promoted the first strike in an industrial establishment in Colombia in 1920.

Another woman, María Cano, became the symbol of the first socialist movement in the region. Cano published her first poems and Christmas chronicles in the journal *Cyrano* (1921–3), but during her election as *flor del trabajo* (flower of work), on the first of May 1925, her poetry became an incendiary speech, and she traveled the country promoting the organization of a working class. By the end of the 1920s, a victim of the purge of her own party by revisionist members, María Cano took refuge by taking on the humble occupation of a book cataloguer in the library of Medellín, where she spent the remainder of her life. When students rediscovered her in the agitated decade of the 1960s and asked if she was actually María Cano, she simply replied: "I *was* María Cano."

At the beginning of the 1930s the country had been transformed. The agrarian world gave way to urban life. More than forty years of hegemony by the Conservative Party ended, and the Liberal Party came to power, initiating a *"Revolución en marcha"* (Revolution in Progress). Art began to break the molds of the academy, and, as in other Latin American countries, indigenous peoples and peasants began to appear as subjects of sculpture and painting.

Medellín was also transformed. At the end of the 1920s, the city had about 150,000 inhabitants and its urban layout was perched on the eastern slopes, although it did not yet dare crossing the Medellín River in search of the "Otrabanda." Bohemian life had moved from the artisan neighborhood of Guanteros to the Guayaquil neighborhood that included the railway station and the marketplace. Fokloric popular music, *bambuco*, and *pasillo* (little step) gave way to a melody that came from the south and spoke to the heart of immigrant peasants transformed into workers: tango. Manuel Mejía Vallejo masterfully recounted these transition years later in his novel *Aire de Tango* (1973, Tango Air).

These were the last years of Tomás Carrasquilla, who, despite his blindness and disability, was able to dictate more than one thousand pages of his final work, *Hace tiempos* (Time Ago). In 1927 he made his last visit to the city of Porfirio Barba Jacob, when he shook the inhabitants of the city with his performance at the Bolívar Theater. Meanwhile León de Greiff went to work as a statistician at the Pacific Railroad, and there he would discover *Bolombolo, país nada utópico* (Bolombolo, Not a Utopian Country) in his *Libro de relatos* (Book of stories). Around the same time, in December 1928, Fernando González began his *Viaje a pie* (Trip on Foot) through the Central Andes in search of the heights of Ruiz and his sorrowful soul.

The solitary streets captured by photographers in the nineteenth century were now crammed with people. A new character had emerged: the crowd. The photographer for this period was, without doubt, Jorge Obando, who with his panoramic camera captured the large human concentrations, promoted by political parties and the church, in a strong push to demonstrate strength in streets and squares. Social life was imposed on paintings, and the walls of the City Hall were covered with frescoes painted by Pedro Nel Gómez in an open rebellion against the canons of academic art. During this time period the tango was adopted as a cultural expression, and the Argentine masterCarlos Gardel died in an airplane accident at the Las Playas airport of Medellín in 1935, perpetuating a myth.

Juan Luis Mejía Arango
Translated by Judith Cervantes

REFERENCES

Carrasquilla, Tomás. *Herejías.* Op. Cit. Volume II.
  Obras Completas. Autobiografía. Medellín: Editorial Bedout, 1964.
Gómez, Juan Guillermo. *Lectura, lectores y lectoras en la obra de Tomás Carrasquilla.* Inédito, Copia suministrada por el autor.
Gónima, Eladio. *Apuntes para la historia del teatro de Medellín y Vejeces.* Medellín: Tipografía San Antonio, 1909.
Levy, Kurt. *Vida y obra de Tomás Carrasquilla.* Medellín: Editorial Bedout, 1958.

Molina, Juan José. *Compilador. Antioquia Literaria. Colección Autores Antioqueños*. Bogotá: Colcultura Volume 117. Medellín, 1998.

Ochoa, Lizandro. *Cosas Viejas de la Villa de la Candelaria*. Volume 8. Medellín: Colección Autores Antioqueños, 1984.

Panida. Revista literaria. Edición Facsimilar. Bogotá: Instituto Colombiano de Cultura. Colcultura, 1983.

Pensamiento Político de Rafael Uribe Uribe. Antología. Bogotá: Instituto Colombiano de Cultura/Colcultura, 1974.

Posada, de Greiff, Luz. *Historia de las Bibliotecas, en Historia de Antioquia*. Jorge Orlando Melo, editor. Medellín: Suramericana de Seguros, 1988.

Revista Científica e Industrial. Bogotá, August 20, 1871.

Reyes, Alejandro. *Revista de Estudios Sociales*. Medellín: Fundación Antioqueña de Estudios Sociales/FAES, 1986.

Sanín Cano, Baldomero. *De mi vida y otras vidas*. Bogotá: Ediciones Revista de América, 1949.

Tamayo Ortiz, Dora Helena, and Hernán Botero Restrepo, compilers. *Inicios de una literatura regional. La narrativa antioqueña de la segunda mitad del siglo XIX. (1855–1899)*. Medellín: Editorial Universidad de Antioquia, 2005.

CHAPTER 14

Colombian marginalized literatures

Valentín González-Bohórquez and Diana Dodson Lee

With the signing of the new constitution in 1991, Colombia was recognized for the first time in its history as a multiethnic and multicultural nation. This step was the result of many years of organized struggle by minority groups in defense of their rights, cultures, and territories. The constitution expressly acknowledged minority groups present in the country before the formation of the Republic of Colombia; among these groups are indigenous peoples and Afro-Colombians (including the *raizales* [native peoples] of San Andrés and Providencia, and the Afro-Colombian community of San Basilio de Palenque). In 1999, the *rom* or gypsies were also added as a community that formed an integral part of Colombian nationality. Traditionally excluded or marginalized from the national dialogue, these groups began to emerge toward the end of the twentieth century with their distinctive voices, both in the political debate and in their cultural manifestations in the national panorama. In literary production, indigenous authors of diverse ethnicities have increasingly stood out in the past few decades, and to a lesser degree, so have the *raizal* authors from the Islands of San Andrés, Providencia, and Santa Catalina. This chapter briefly explores the historical contexts of the indigenous populations and the *raizal* groups from the Colombian Caribbean and summarizes some significant literary works from these two marginalized people groups, whose incorporation in mainland, dominant culture is becoming increasingly pertinent to literary studies.

Indigenous literatures in Colombia

When the first Spanish expeditions arrived in the sixteenth century to the territory known today as Colombia, the region was already inhabited by numerous indigenous groups in the Guajira Desert, the Andean mountains, and the Amazon jungle. The estimates regarding the number of indigenous inhabitants during this time period vary considerably between 800,000 and

6 million; distributed unevenly in dozens of ethnicities, many of these aboriginals belonged to the two most technologically advanced groups of the time, the *muiscas* and the *taironas* of the *chibcha* culture.[1] The challenges facing these natives during the Conquest and Colonial periods were no different than those that the majority of indigenous people suffered through-out the American continent. In a few decades, the Colombian native populations were decimated by war, hard labor conditions, and European diseases, such as typhus, measles, and smallpox, against which they had no built-up immune defenses. Despite the valiant resistance and uprisings of several indigenous groups, the conquistadores and colonizers ultimately usurped power from the indigenous populations and reduced them to a life of exploitation and servitude via a system of forced labor. The natives went from being the owners and lords of their land to living, as the Mayan *Popul Vuh* says, "una vida en la sombra" (a life in the shadows).

The majority of the Spanish who came to conquer America were males, and so it was not long before native women and the Spanish produced interracial offspring. Starting in the sixteenth century, slaves brought from the Caribbean or directly from Africa were added to these interracial relations. Colombian ethnography, then, is composed of indigenous, European, and African peoples. Toward the end of the nineteenth century and the beginning of the twentieth, migratory flows from other parts of the world, especially from the Middle East and Asia, continued to foster a complex variety of ethnicities and cultural traditions. The 2005 census by the National Administration of Statistics Department (Departamento Administrativo Nacional de Estadísticas or DANE), estimated that in 2005 there were close to 1.4 million indigenous tribes grouped into eighty-seven ethnicities, constituting 3.4 percent of the national population; many of these groups lived in their ancestral territories under native reservations.[2] In the country, indigenous people speak sixty-four Amerindian languages and a plethora of dialects that constitute thirteen linguistic families. The constitution of 1991 recognized, in addition to Spanish, indigenous lan-guages as official in their respective territories.

Before the European incursion into the territories, the natives had developed a system of pictographic writing and petrography. Andean populations of *quechua* origin at the south of the present-day Nariño Department used *quipus* (talking knots) through which they registered their individual and collective stories. During the conquest and colonial periods, Europeans focused on teaching Spanish and Catholicism in an effort to indoctrinate and convert indigenous groups to reading. However, these processes were slow and in general unsuccessful, either because of apathy by the dominant society in enforcing these policies or because of resistance by the natives to assimilation. However, the leaders of the indigenous populations found themselves needing to speak and write in Spanish to be able to fight more effectively for their rights. For this reason, it is not surprising that the first indigenous and *mestizo* writings in Spanish were letters of protest or lists of grievances directed to the Spanish authorities; these authors sought, through writing, to alleviate the suffering to which the natives were subjected.

One of the most prominent texts from the colonial period is the letter written by the *muisca* mestizo Chief of Turmequé, Diego Torres, who personally delivered the letter to Spanish King Phillip II in 1584. In this extensive list of grievances, Torres's goals are twofold. First, he presents a series of claims to support his argument that his chiefdom should be restored (his brother Pedro had taken it away by claiming that Diego was an illegitimate son). Second, he recounts abuses against indigenous and mestizo peoples to bring their situation to the attention of the Spanish royalty. Don Diego Torres, among other things, issues formal complaints about the excesses of tributes that the land bosses demanded – excesses that kept the people in poverty – as well as the humiliating servitude to which the Spanish subjected indigenous people. Stylistically, the letter reflects an affinity with the writings of Bartolomé de las Casas and is, ultimately, a demand for liberty from imperial subjugation. The Chief of Turmequé's letter constitutes a project to use testimony to speak for the subaltern indigenous people; Restrepo contends that this project, "no se ahogaba en la melancolía [sino que] superaba el sentido trágico de la historia para luchar por un futuro para la América indígena" (was not mired in melancholy but rather overcame its tragic sense of history to fight for a future for indigenous American groups).[3]

In the post-colonial era, the situation did not significantly change for indigenous groups in spite of the fact that on May 20, 1820, President Simón Bolívar signed several decrees, including one that ordered the return of all lands to the indigenous people as their rightful owners. These laws, like others during the post-colonial period, were not put into practice, and the relationship of the natives with the New Republic continued to be similar to the one during the colonial period. What did begin to develop during the second half of the nineteenth century was a growing interest in ethnographic, linguistic, and anthropological studies with the goal of understanding and classifying the multifaceted indigenous ethnicities in the country. One of these studies was undertaken by the renowned poet and novelist from the Cauca Valley, Jorge Isaacs, who participated at first as a member of a scientific expedition that sought to complete an ethnographic study of the natives of the northern part of Colombia. Isaacs ultimately separated from the group and finished the work on his own. As a result of his investigation, in 1864 he published "Estudio sobre las tribus indígenas del estado del Magdalena" (A Study Regarding the Indigenous Tribes in Magdalena State) in the *Anales de Instrucción Pública* (Annals of Public Instruction).[4] In this study he narrates his contact with the indigenous communities in the Departments of La Guajira and Magdalena, particularly in the Sierra Nevada de Santa Marta. Isaacs's text reflects more his poetic and literary style than his scientific rigor; however, it is a worthwhile register of the traditions, legends, and myths of these communities that were given to him first-hand by, among others, the *businka* priests of the Sierra Nevada.

The publication in Italian in 1890 of *Yurupary* (*Leggenda dell' Jurapary*) (Legend of the Yurupary), one of the foundational pre-Colombian myths of the linguistic families *arawah*, *tucano*, and *tupí-guaraní*, on the Colombian/Brazilian Amazon border, inaugurated a copious production of ethnoliterature that continued incessantly in Colombia during the twentieth century. Printed in the *Bolletino della Società Geografica Italiana* (Bulletin of the Italian Geographic Society), this first version of the myth is the product of transcriptions in the *ñe'engatú* language into Spanish. Maximiano José Roberto, an indigenous man, completed this project, and it was translated into Italian by Count Ermanno Stradelli. *Yurupary* is often considered the South American *Popul Vuh* because of its content, extension, and narrative structure.

In the first few decades of the twentieth century a slow presence of activist indigenous leaders emerged, including Manuel Quintín Lame, member of the *nasa* and the *guambianos misak* in the Cauca Department. Quintín Lame was a recognized organizer and mobilizer of the indigenous cause. In the tradition of the Chief of Turmequé, he also utilized the written word as the instrument of his activity. Throughout his long life (1860–1967), he wrote numerous lists of grievances to the regional and national authorities. His *Defensa de los resguardos* (In Defense of the Native Reservations) from January 17, 1922, is an elaborate reaction against the rents paid to land owners. These rents were part of a system of exploitation in which the natives were given a small plot of land in exchange for working most days of the week on a proprietor's ranch without receiving any salary. In 1939 he wrote, "En defensa de mi raza (los pensamientos del indio que se educó dentro de las selvas colombianas)" (In Defense of My Race [Reflections of a Native Educated in the Colombian Jungles]), in which he debates the present and future of the native peoples in the country and the problems they face under national laws. He also criticizes the leaders of the dominant society in the Tolima, Cauca, and Huila Departments. Only part of Quintín Lame's writings were edited and published posthumously. A considerable number of his manuscripts still remain unpublished, but a valuable selection of his texts was compiled in 1973 in *Las luchas del indio que bajó de la montaña al valle de la civilización* (The Struggles of an Indian Who Came Down from the Mountain to the Valley of Civilization). In his political work, Quintín Lame advocated for an autonomous indigenous government. His liberationist thought remained influential decades later when Colombia first recognized itself as a multiethnic and multicultural nation in its 1991 constitution, which created legal precedents for indigenous groups to possess territories, preserve their culture, create their own educational systems, ensure their participation in the national government, and exercise their own government on their reservations.

In the first part of the twentieth century, ethnologists undertook several ethnographic, ethnoliterary, and anthropological investigations. In 1926 German ethnologist Theodor Preus studied the Kogui people in the Sierra Nevada de Santa Marta and the Uitoto people in the Amazon. During the same period Miguel Ángel Asturias published *Las leyendas de Guatemala* (1930, Legends of Guatemala) and the novel *Hombres de maíz* (1949, Men of Maize), both of which present indigenous themes. These works were antecedents for *El Canto General*, by Chilean poet Pablo Neruda in 1950; Juan Rulfo's *Pedro Páramo*, published in 1955; and *Los ríos profundos* (Deep Rivers), by Peruvian José Carlos Mariátegui in 1958. These foundational works by prominent authors exemplified the attempt to reverse the predominant westernizing discourse in Latin American writing by calling attention to the ignored, but always present, voices of the original inhabitants of the continent. Contemporary to these texts is *Los dolores de una raza* (The Pains of My Race) by Antonio Joaquín López Briscol, a Colombian-Venezuelan author of *wayuu* indigenous roots. *Los dolores* is considered to be the first novel written by a an indigenous person born in Colombia. Published in 1956 in Maracaibo, Venezuela, this historical novel narrates the vicissitudes of the Guajira natives located between the Colombian and Venezuelan borders.

From 1962 to 2002, the linguistic and missionary activities of the Protestant North American SIL International in Colombia contributed to the production of numerous volumes of texts and grammar notebooks that used Spanish letters to translate parts of the Bible into native tongues.

The use of informants and native co-authors for the creation of these materials enabled some of these indigenous authors to appropriate these alphabets and the Spanish language to produce their own ethnoliterate texts. Alberto Juajibioy Chindoy, a *camëntsá* writer, was one of the instrumental native authors in the transition between the ethnoliterary studies produced by researchers and writers without indigenous roots and those belonging to the native groups. Starting in 1962 Juajibioy began to publish in the *Boletín del Instituto de Antropología* (Bulletin of the Anthropological Institute) at the Universidad de Antioquia. In his diverse studies, he transcribed traditions, myths, and legends utilizing a method of scientific analysis in his texts. Juajibioy continued publishing his ethnoliterary texts in the *Boletín* in the following decades and was an influential figure in contemporary indigenous narrative and poetry in Colombia.

The publication in 1975 of the story "Ni era vaca ni era caballo …" (It Was Neither a Cow nor a Horse …), by Miguel Ángel Jusayú, in *Jüküjaláirrua wayú* (*Relatos guajiros*) (Guajira Stories), represents one of the first written narratives by a native author (*wayuu*) in which the focus is not on ethnoliterary elements, but on contemporary indigenous elements. The indigenous authors in this generation have participated in diverse national and continental anthologies, in cultural and political forums, and they have received prizes that have contributed to the consolidation of the presence of indigenous literature in Colombia and other Latin American countries such as Chile, Mexico, Peru, Guatemala, and the United States.

These indigenous writers have continued the nineteenth- and twentieth-century Latin American tradition in which authors have simultaneously been public intellectuals and political actors; the indigenous literary and cultural movement has been in constant contact with the political struggles inspired by historical figures like the Chief of Turmequé and Manuel Quintín Lame, both of whom consistently used oral and written discourse to support their causes. This literary generation has also admired figures like La Gaitana (Guatipán), heroine of the *yalcón*, and Juan Tamana de la Estrella, a member of the *nasa* community, two leaders from the Andean Colombian region who waged military campaigns against the Spanish occupation in the first part of the sixteenth century. In the last decades of the twentieth century and the first part of the twenty-first century, members of native populations in Colombia were forced into joining various guerilla groups and have suffered massacres, displacements, and pillaging by narcotraffickers. This has pushed indigenous groups to intensify their political and social activism and spurred on the creation of groups such as the Organización Nacional Indígena (ONIC; National Organization of Indigenous People) in 1982. This organization seeks to continue efforts to make the dominant majority recognize indigenous rights and territories.

The quincentennial of the Spanish arrival in 1992 coincided with a decisive period of legal and social acknowledgment of indigenous cultures in Latin America. In 1992, the Nobel Peace Prize was awarded to *maya-quiché* activist Rigoberta Menchú, which was an explicit recognition of the centrality of indigenous peoples in the continent and their demand for justice and equal rights. Her autobiography, *Me llamo Rigoberta Menchú y así me nació la conciencia* (My Name Is Rigoberta Menchú and This Is How My Conscience Was Born, co-authored with Elizabeth Burgos), published in 1983, illuminated the inner workings of the *maya-quiché* culture from the perspective of one of its members, inspiring international solidarity with the struggles of a sector that constitutes more than half of the Guatemalan population.

During this active decade for indigenous rights, a number of indigenous Colombians published works associated with *oraliture,* a term adopted during a convention of writers in Latin American indigenous languages in Temuco, Chile, in May of 1997. This term designated the transition from indigenous oral expressions to written expressions. Among this wide and diverse group of ethnically native Colombians, a few authors and their works stand out, including Esperanza Aguablanca, whose native name is Berichá (*uwa*), Vicenta María Siosi Pino (*wayuu*), Fredy Chikangana (*yanakuna-mitmakuna*), Miguel Ángel López Hernández (*wayuu*), Hugo Jamioy Juagibioy (*camëntsá*), and Estercilia Simanca Pushaina (*wayuu*). Berichá became known in 1992 with *Tengo los pies en la cabeza* (I Have My Feet on My Head), a narration that intercalates autobiographical aspects and oral traditions of the *uwa* with political condemnation against the exploitation of oil in her ancestral territories. This was the first literary work by an indigenous woman to achieve attention from the press and literary critics. Transcribing from her personal diary, the author begins the book,

> Yo me llamo Berichá, soy una mujer indígena U'wa de la comunidad Barrosa que queda cerca a la misión de San Luis del Chuscal en la cabecera de Cubará, Boyacá. Mis padres tenían funciones religiosas dentro de la comunidad, desarrollaban ritos y ceremonias. Yo nací sin piernas, sin embargo tengo los pies en la cabeza porque he podido desarrollar mi inteligencia; eso me ha ayudado a salir adelante, a defenderme en la vida y a ayudar a mi comunidad. (My name is Berichá, I am an indigenous U'wa

woman from the Barrosa community which is close to the San Luis del Chuscal mission at the top of Cubará, Boyacá. My parents had religious roles in the community, they led rituals and ceremonies. I was born without legs; however, I have feet on my head because I have been able to develop my intellect; this has helped me to move forward, to defend myself in life and to help my community.)[5]

Having been born handicapped, Berichá's community's laws condemned her to abandonment and death in the forest; however, her father managed to save her life, and with the help of a Catholic mission, she received an education and returned later to her town as a teacher. Berichá has also been an indefatigable activist for her community.

Vicenta María Siosi Pino from the *wayuu* people is a fiction writer who wrote *Esa horrible costumbre de alejarme de ti* (That Horrible Habit of Distancing Myself from You), which was originally published in the *Woummainpa* journal at the Universidad de la Guajira in 1992, and later in the cultural supplement of the newspaper *El Tiempo*, in Bogotá in 1997, and finally in 2000 in the collection *Woumain, poesía indígena y gitana contemporánea de Colombia* (Woumain, Contemporary Indigenous and Gypsy Poetry of Colombia). This book deals with the problem of cultural alienation as its narrator and protagonist, a young girl from the *wayuu* community, is brought to the city to be educated by a family that treats her like a servant. The character finally becomes accustomed to life in the city, and, although she occasionally returns to her village, she no longer feels like she belongs there. In one of her soliloquies she says, "Tengo confusión de sentimientos. Creo mía esta casa ajena y de mi Guajira indomable ni recuerdos tengo ya" (I feel conflicting sentiments. I believe this foreign house to be mine, but of my indomitable Guajira I now have no memories).[6] Narrative techniques such as introspection and stream of consciousness, as well as the treatment of the problem of the contradictions of a population that faces the dilemmas of cultural assimilation, made this story an innovative approach in Colombian oraliture. Other stories by Siosi Pino such as "El honroso vericueto de mi linaje" (The Honorable Shortcut of My Lineaje) and "El dulce corazón de los piel cobriza" (The Sweet Heart of Copper Skin) have been widely disseminated in magazines and anthologies. In 2000 Siosi Pino won the first prize in the Concurso Nacional de Cuento Infantil (National Concourse of Children's Stories) with "La señora iguana" (Mrs. Iguana), a brief text advocating the protection of animal species, which also represents a metaphor of the environmental needs of the native people. This was the first time that an indigenous writing obtained a literary prize at the national level.

The writer of oralitor Fredy Chikangana, whose indigenous name is Wiñay Mallki, is a *yanakuna-mitmakuna* poet from the south of the Cauca Department and author of several collections of poems such as *Canto de amor para ahuyentar la muerte* (Song of Love to Scare Away Death) and *Yo Yanacoma, Palabra y memoria* (I, Yanacoma, Word and Memory). He is one of the most active poets in the dialogue about multiculturalism in Colombia and Latin America, and he is part of the growing network of native authors who are seeking to publish both in their own languages and in bilingual editions. His first compilation of poems in quechua and Spanish was *El colibrí de la noche desnuda y otros cantos del fuego* (The Hummingbird of the Bare Night and Other Songs of Fire). In 2008 Chinkangana won one of the three Nósside de Poesía Global prizes in Rome, the first time it had been given to an indigenous writer in Colombia. In January 2015 *Voces originarias de Abya Yala* (Original Voice of Abya Yala) was published, an anthology in which Chikangana partici- pated together with two other renowned native poets, Vito Apüshana and Hugo Jamioy. (Abya Yala is the original name that the *tule-kuna,* an ethnic group between Panama and the west side of Colombia, called the Ameri- can continent before the arrival of Columbus and whose name has been widely adopted by indigenous peoples today.) His poems are a constant evocation of the indigenous connection with nature, silence, and otherness in the face of the dominant culture. In an article in the *Manual intro- ductorio y guía de animación a la lectura* (Introductory Manual and Guide of Literary Animations) in the *Biblioteca Básica de los Pueblos Indígenas de Colombia* (Basic Library of the Indigenous Peoples of Colombia. 2010), Chikangana makes an appeal that the indigenous people should no longer be seen "con una mirada paternalista y folclorista" (with a paternalistic and folkoric gaze) while also asserting that "aquí estamos para ayudar a con- struir un puente que permita caminar por esas fuentes ariscas y bravas tratando de ver cómo podemos compartir para llegar como sociedades a un mismo destino" (we are here to help construct a bridge to walk above these fierce and wild rivers, trying to see how we can share with each other in order to become societies with the same destiny).[7]

In 2000, Miguel Ángel López Hernández (whose native name is Vito Apüshana), won the Premio Casa de las Américas (Casa de las Americas Prize) with his book of poetry *Encuentros en los senderos de Abya Yala* (Encounters on the Paths of Abya Yala), which was the first literary prize in the Spanish-speaking world awarded to a Colombian poet and writer of indigenous origin. The book relates his encounters with diverse native poets, including his own *wayuu* culture, the *kogui* of the Sierra Nevada, and other Latin Ameircan indigenous groups outside the borders of Colombia – the *mapuches,* the *quechuas,* and the *nahuatl* –within a cosmogony in which the entire continent is interrelated with one millennial culture, the "universo de la palabra-pintura de Abya Yala" (universe of the word-painting of Abya Yala).[8] Previously, in 1992, Apüshana had published an intimate view of *wayuu* cosmogony in his book of poems *Contrabandeo de sueños con alijunas cercanos* (Contraband of Dreams with Nearby Alijunas).

Hugo Jamioy Juagibioy (camëntsá) published *Danzantes del viento/ Bínÿbé oboyejuayëng* (2005, Dancers of the Wind), a book of foundational bilingual poetry – foundational for contemporary indigenous Colombian literature in that it explores, in constant tension, the cultural border between the tiny community of the *camëntsá,* with no more than 6,000 members, and the majority culture of the *squená* (foreigners or white people). Jamioy assumes the role of the voice of his generation with the urgent task of "entender, practicar y enseñar" (understanding, practicing, and teaching) the pillars of their ancestors "para preparar el lugar sagrado en donde vivirán nuestros hijos, y los hijos de ellos, como un solo cuerpo, como un solo pueblo" (in order to prepare the sacred space where our children and their children will live, as one body, as one people).[9] As part of a fusion between oraliture and the pictographic tradition of his ancestors, Juan Andrés Jamioy, the poet's brother, illustrates the cover of the book of poems. Jamioy also published other books before *Danzantes,* including *Mi fuego y mi humo, mi Tierra y mi sol* (My Fire and My Smoke, My Land and My Sun), in 1999, y *No somos gente* (We Are Not People) in 2001.

Another notable author from this first generation of oraliture writers is Estercilia Simanca Pushaina (wayuu), known for "Manifiesta no saber firmar: Nacida el 31 de diciembre" (It Seems They Can't Write: Born on December 31st) a short story in which she relates the fact that none of her relatives from the Pushaina clan know how to write and that everyone seems to have been born on December 31. Simanca Pushaina decides to celebrate the birthdays of everyone on that day as well as undertake the task of registering not only her family, but all the *wayuu* in the civil registry. This task was completed in November 2014 when, by way of a national decree, the government established the means for not only the *wayuus* but all indigenous people to access the national registry. Pushaina identifies herself as an "urban *wayuu*"; she is also a lawyer and maintains her own blog. She is the author of a 2002 book of poems, *Caminemos juntos por la sombra de la sabana* (Let Us Walk Together by the Shadow of the Sheet) and *El encierro de una pequeña doncella* (2006, The Confinement of a Young Lady), which includes three of her many stories.

In 2010 the Department of Literature of the Ministry of Culture published the Biblioteca Indígena y la Biblioteca Afrocolombiana (Indigenous Library and the Afrocolombian Library) with texts by Fredy Chikangana, Vito Apüshana, Hugo Jamioy, Fernando Urbina, Enrique Sánchez Gutiérrez, and Hernán Molina Echeverri as well as the anthologies *Antes el amanecer* (Before Dawn) and *El sol babea jugo de piña* (The Sun Drools Pineapple Juice), by Miguel Rocha Vivas. That same year two work groups, one from the Universidad de Zulia and the other from the Universidad de la Guajira, begin translating García Márquez's *Cien años de soledad* (1967, *One Hundred Years of Solitude*) into the indigenous language *wayuunaiki*.

The new generation of Colombian indigenous writers and poets from the first decade of the twentieth century is known for its growing urban narrative. Many authors have emigrated from their communities to the city to pursue their studies, while also maintaining contact with their hometowns. Among these authors are Francisca Muchavisoy, Juan Guillermo Sánchez, and Ana María Ferreira. These native writers continue to be intensely connected with themes about nature. Rivers, mountains, trees, fauna, and the universe are constant references. Additionally, as part of the tradition of their ancestors, the natural environment is related to the sense of fighting that the indigenous groups face from the foreign, dominant culture. Regarding this relationship and tension, Rocha Vivas says,

> Los escritores indígenas contemporáneos cumplen con roles importantísimos. Por ejemplo, al sensibilizar a un mayor número de personas sobre la realidad de sus lenguas, cuestionan las univocidades nacionales y los formatos identitarios anglocéntricos; al presentarnos sus formas de verse, nos permiten reconocernos. (Contemporary indigenous authors play very important roles. For example, to make a large number people aware about the reality of languages, they question national homogeneity and Eurocentric identity; by showing us the way they see themselves, they allow us to recognize ourselves.)[10]

There is no doubt that the indigenous peoples in Colombia and the rest of Latin America have much to do to recover from marginalization in the past and to benefit from democratic participation in the region. However, signs certainly indicate that the situation has changed considerably: The 1991 constitution and the enormous indigenous literary production in the last few decades give proof of progress. The threat of assimilation versus the preservation of indigenous cultural identities continues to remain an issue. What indigenous leaders, artists, and writers demand through their efforts is recognition and the right to live within their own norms, under their own laws, and to contribute positively as older children of the land. In 1884 the Cuban poet and independence leader José Martí offered a visionary assessment of territory and native cultures in the continent: "Se verá un espectáculo sublime el día que se sienta con fuerza y despierte" (The day that indigenous people feel strong and wake up, we will witness a sublime spectacle).[11] This awakening and emergence of marginalized voices clearly demonstrates that the indigenous people in Colombia have arisen from the world of shadows and continue toward what the *Popul Vuh* also describes as "la visión del alba de la vida" (the vision of the dawn of life).

Colombian Caribbean literatures

Although officially part of Colombia, the islands of San Andrés, Providencia, and Santa Catalina are actually closer to Central America. Part of an archipelago, the three islands measure about 57 square kilometers, and although only a little more than 200 kilometers east of Nicaragua, they lie over 700 kilometers northwest of their closest Colombian neighbor, Cartagena. The position of the islands in the southwestern Caribbean Sea underlines several historical factors that have fostered their multiethnic and multilingual climate: the archipelago's settlement and development reveal a tapestry of cultures woven together in a complex and oftentimes conflictive setting. Although the English/Creole (a dialect combining English and African elements) -speaking Afro-Caribbean population parallels that of other Caribbean nations, the influx of mainland Colombians and tourists underscores a problematic convergence of peoples that currently threatens the traditions, livelihood, and ecology of the "native" islanders. A brief history of the islands demonstrates the roots of the current crises that vex the Colombian territories.

No natives were living on the islands when European adventurers began their sojourns across the Atlantic Ocean in the sixteenth century; Dutch and English pirates first capitalized on the fortuitous location of the islands in the Caribbean by utilizing the islands as a launching point to raid Spanish galleons. The pirates' stay was fleeting; eventually Puritan settlers from the Massachusetts colony funded expeditions to the area to establish economic centers and religious freedom. Nevertheless, the English were unsuccessful in producing a profit off the land and eventually took to beleaguering Spanish vessels to recover part of their investment. This provoked Spanish retaliation, and during the next twenty years the Spanish and British fought over the islands. However, in 1655 the British deserted the archipelago in favor of the newly founded English base on Jamaica, and the Spanish lost interest in the territory. While the first colonization project was ultimately abandoned, the early history foreshadowed the confluence of English, Spanish, and African peoples and the tensions that would eventually plague several aspects of islandic culture.

British settlers returned with their slaves to San Andrés in the early eighteenth century, but agreements between the British and the Spanish in 1783 and 1786 gave formal control over the islands to Spain. The British inhabitants petitioned the Spanish government for permission to remain, and after some negotiations the Spanish acquiesced under the stipulations that the British convert to Catholicism, profess loyalty to Spain, and terminate trade relations with Jamaica. The islanders agreed to these terms, but many continued to speak English/Creole as their first language and self-identified as Protestants. Furthermore, the lack of tangible oversight meant that the trade demands were largely unenforced. After the Wars of Independence against Spain, the archipelago came to be under Colombian control.[12] However, Colombia was far more concerned with forming its own identity as a newly independent nation; this political milieu and the geographical distance between Colombia and the islands meant that although this territory ostensibly was Colombian, in practice the archipelago benefited from a great deal of autonomy.

During the nineteenth century the abolition of slavery greatly influenced the future cultural makeup of the island because the slaves took on the surnames of their British owners when they were freed, and the white and black peoples began to form a mixed race of people who spoke English and Creole. Furthermore, the arrival of the Baptist religion shaped the island culture, and many people were converted to Protestantism. Moreover, trade with the United States and Jamaica during this time became a focal point for economic stability, with the burgeoning coconut sales enabling the inhabitants to avoid poverty. June Marie Mow contends that during the ninety years after their inception as Colombian citizens, the "native islanders were virtually left alone; they were self-sufficient and organized, and had their own education, religious and justice systems."[13] Until the early twentieth century, island people had sufficient freedom and time to forge their own unique syncretic identity as the "native" group of people on the island in opposition to Colombian mainland immigrants.

The relationship between the islands and Colombia changed in the early twentieth century when Colombia first began to take definite stances regarding the control and governance of the island. In response to the

United States' maneuvering in Panama, Colombia decided to set up an Intendancy on the islands in 1912 that gave direct control of the region to Bogotá.[14] During this time Colombia also supported Catholic efforts to make inroads in Protestant areas. The first Catholic missionaries understood the importance of English as the traditional language of the islanders, but in 1925 Spanish Capuchins took over the mission and focused on the Colombianization of the islanders through the use of Spanish in schools. In the first half of the century the clash between mainland Colombian interests and the customs established on the island became more acute. As James Ross comments, "Conflicts, particularly over religion, language, education, and administration, arose and were never satisfactorily dealt with, but the fabric of the Islander community had remained relatively untouched."[15] The newer generations of islanders did begin to speak Spanish in schools, but the people maintained their simplistic lifestyles of farming and fishing, and Creole-English was still the primary language spoken in the home.

Colombian life was transformed dramatically in 1953 when military dictator Gustavo Rojas Pinilla once and for all changed the nature of the islands' economy by declaring them a tax-free port and by mandating the construction of an airport on the island of San Andrés. The several-day boat journey from the Colombian mainland to the islands was transformed overnight into a relatively accessible airplane flight. Furthermore, the new regulations mandated that only Catholic-sponsored churches and schools could provide resources to the islanders; subsequently, Protestant schools closed against the wishes of the English/Creole-speaking population. Ross contends that this policy instigated the "massive immigration of mainlanders, particularly from the Atlantic Coast [of Colombia] and Antioquia, who brought with them their own culture and customs. The agricultural and fishing community of English, Creole-speaking, Protestant peoples became physically displaced by Spanish-speaking, Catholic immigrants from the Colombian mainland."[16] Spanish fluency became a more important factor in economic success during this time period.[17]

The sudden incursion of mainland immigrants transformed daily life and the traditions of the island peoples. In the 1960s and 1970s the population exploded as did the tourism industry. However, the ownership of new business fell disproportionately into the hands of people with Colombian currency and capital, the new Spanish-speaking arrivals. The shifts in population had some advantages. For instance, between the opening of the Freeport in 1953 and the 1990s, the Creole-English speaking population strengthened its community ties. The group as a whole came to be known by the term *raizales*, a Spanish-derived concept meaning those with roots on the island; this term also celebrated the African lineage of the islanders, inspiring the native population to delineate their identity more explicitly in face of the population explosion of "foreigners." However, for the most part these decades saw a decline in the standards of living for the *raizales* who were largely marginalized by mainland policies and relegated to service industries since the changing economic practices privileged those with Catholic, Spanish backgrounds.

In 1991 Colombia ratified its new constitution, which, in theory, altered the dynamics operating between the Colombian mainland administration and the islands. The constitution advocated for marginalized groups in general, and in particular it gave the people of the archipelago more protection as ethnic minorities and recognized officially the use of the English language on the islands. However, as Ross notes, "In the over ten years since the new Constitution, *raizales* have made great advances on paper but conditions on the islands have not really improved."[18] Furthermore, the push to develop and industrialize on the islands has caused damage to the environment; these ecological challenges combined with overpopulation represent significant challenges to the identity of the native peoples. The English/Creole Protestants face the threat of losing their traditional lifestyles, and the cultural heritage of the *raizales* remains tenuous as the people seek to define themselves in the new context of twenty-first-century globalization and capitalism.

The historical negotiation of language between the English/Creole and Spanish communities and the islands' geographical isolation from Colombia are likely factors as to why relatively few literary pieces associated with the area have been circulated in Spanish. However, in the last few decades this trend has shifted, and some authors have begun to publish narratives in Spanish with connections to the archipelago. Four authors in particular have been recognized for their work, including two native islanders, Lenito Bent Robinson and Hazel Robinson Abrahams, and two Colombian authors from the mainland, Fanny Buitrago and Claudine Bancelin.

Lenito Bent Robinson was born on Providencia in 1956, and although he eventually left the island to study in Paris and live in the United States, the strong influence of island culture nevertheless permeates his work. His collection of short stories, *Sobre nupcias y ausencias*, (1986, About Marriages and Absences), was the first fiction published by a native of the archipelago. Bent Robinson reminds his readers of the challenges of living in a region in which so many travel the seas to earn a living and connect with the larger world. Themes such as death, the power of the sea, absence, and love characterize his accounts. In several stories the changes of culture of the twentieth century also emerge. Bent Robinson expresses the anxieties of the natives threatened by immigrants and the clash of their new technologies and economic systems. For example, in *El viernes del hidroavión* (The Friday of the Hydroplane) the narrator remembers the life of a Spanish-speaking politician who became powerful and rich by taking advantage of the naivety of the native islanders by dispossessing them of their land through unfair dealings. He dies off the island and his body is brought back by air. The procession of his funeral is quickly converted into a spectacle because the natives have never seen a seaplane. Yet their expectations end in a jumble of emotions as his dead body is carried off and the seaplane leaves expeditiously, covering them in a cloud of dust.

> Nos pusimos a mirar cómo se iba a elevar de nuevo el avión. ... Una vez despejada la nube de polvo, nos dimos cuenta de que por el otro lado el avión nos había bañado con furia infernal al despegar. Con todo, estábamos demasiado indignados para determinar si nos sentíamos ofendidos o vengados. (We positioned ourselves to see how the airplane would rise again. ... Once the cloud of dust cleared, we realized that on the other side the airplane had covered us with infernal fury on take-off. With that, we were too indignant to determine whether we felt offended or avenged.)[19]

In this story the islanders communicate doubt about a future infiltrated by mainland immigrants and the modern world while maintaining a common-sense approach to reality by holding to the knowledge that death is the great equalizer of all peoples. Bent Robinson's eloquent use of Spanish to convey the characteristics and concerns of life on the islands speaks to the process of Colombianization that enabled his fluency in both languages and cultures of the archipelago.

Since the islands have always been the site where several people groups inhabit the same space, it is hardly surprisingly that San Andrés native Hazel Robinson Abrahams addresses this convergence of races and language in her three novels, *No Give Up Maan!* (2002) *Sail Ahoy!!!* (2004), and *El príncipe de St. Katherine* (2009, The Prince of St. Katherine). Born in 1935, Robinson Abrahams's first language is English, but she was educated in Spanish and adeptly wields the language to portray life on the islands. Robinson Abrahams penned her first pieces for a column in the newspaper *El Espectador* from 1959 to 1960, articles in which she narrates the experience of being a native of the islands for mainland Colombian readers. Four decades later, her three novels were published in a series dedicated to rescuing the traditions of the archipelago's history. In her novels, Robinson

Abrahams converts island experiences into fictions by mapping the contours of the development of cultures through historical romances.

In her first published book, *No Give Up Maan!* the narrative harkens back to the mid–nineteenth century, right after the abolition of slavery on the islands. A white woman is shipwrecked on the archipelago, and a man of mixed black and white race saves her. Through their love story the novel explores issues of racism, passion, and religious hypocrisy while simultaneously offering a picture of the daily life of plantation workers during that time period. Robinson Abrahams's third novel, *El príncipe de St Katherine,* also relates a story of love, but this time the love is explicitly forbidden as the main character, a German doctor who settles on the island of Providencia, falls in love with a married midwife. The novel places the romance in the historical context of a problematic economic milieu in the early twentieth century; during this period the islands suffered a crisis due to receding coconut crop exports caused by diseased coconut trees and competition from newly seeded lands outside the archipelago. The novel, in a similar vein to *No Give Up Maan!,* outlines several features of the mixed-raced heritage that characterizes the islands.

Although *Sail Ahoy!!!* was published before *El príncipe de St. Katherine,* the action of the novel takes place during the latest chronological period of the three novels, the 1930s. Of the three novels, *Sail Ahoy!!!* offers the most complete picture of the oscillation between harmony and tension experienced by islanders throughout the various historical cultural and religious encounters. As Doris Sommer has explained, Latin American novels in the nineteenth century often employed the romance genre to solidify national plans of hegemony.[20] In a nod to this type of literature, Robinson Abrahams constructs a narrative focusing the action on a mainland Colombian nun who falls in love with a mestizo native of Providencia. However, the novel problematizes the idea of accomplishing long-term, amicable connections between the *raizales* and mainland immigrants without sacrificing the lifestyle and traditions of the native peoples. The decision to publish this type of novel at the beginning of the twenty-first century is indicative of a project that aims to highlight the relationship between the two cultures and express ambivalence about the long-term success of maintaining *raizal* traditions in the current political climate on the islands.

The novel begins when the protagonist, Sister María José, and two other nuns board a schooner in Cartagena on its way to San Andrés. During the journey María José falls in love with Henley, a native of Providencia, a Protestant, and a schooner captain. María José is an oddity in terms of cultural upbringing. Although Colombian, she grew up in Europe and the

United States, and so she speaks Spanish, English, and German fluently. Henley also speaks English and Spanish, and so the two easily navigate linguistic boundaries. However, this easy access to language is not shared by many of the islanders. The Catholic nuns and priests insist on speaking Spanish and even isolate María José when she arrives at San Andrés because of her ability to speak English, in spite of the fact that she was sent specifically for her facility to communicate in the native language of the land. The resistance to María Jose's presence underlines the conception of what being Colombian means to the Catholic missionaries; their resistance mirrors the historical tension between the linguistic groups.

At first it might seem that the romance between María José and Henley develops over the course of the novel as a prototype of how to bridge the two language groups, since they model fluid bilingualism. However, other impediments to their relationship exemplify the specific points of tension typical in the island, particularly religious affinities and cultural histories. Henley is an Adventist, and his family disapproves of the decision to convert to Catholicism, spurred on by his desire to be close to María José. Furthermore, María José's parents look down on Henley. Although he is described in the novel as a redhead with gray eyes and Scottish ancestry with U.S. citizenship, her family still sees him as "Un isleño, negro e inculto" (An islander, black and uneducated).[21] As upper-class Colombian citizens, María José's parents perpetuate the prejudices of the mainlanders who view the islander folk, regardless of their actual backgrounds, as uneducated and backward.

Much of the novel portrays María Jose's soul-searching related to her relationship with Henley. She desperately loves Henley but feels threatened by his deeply entrenched cultural roots and his family's idea that he should marry a native. Despite these differences, toward the end of the novel the two decide to forsake all ties that would keep them separate and María José renounces her monastic vocation to marry Henley. In some ways, the novel seems to suggest that the joining of the two represents a rapprochement between native English/Protestant and immigrant Spanish/Catholic interests. However, the end of the novel questions the positive nature of their union. After they get married, María José and Henley move to the Panama Canal area and have twin boys, but María José is unhappy living there because of the way in which the people treat Henley with disdain because of his race. The novel briefly suggests that the solution for this problem is for them to move back to Providencia, where María José found the most solace in life. However, the novel ends with a boat accident that kills Henley's parents and close friends, and the couple emigrate to the United States. The last sentence underlines the uncertainty that the novel ascribes to the future of the islands.

> Y ellos, como muchos otros isleños que vivieron en Colón, la zona y Panamá, que salieron a Norteamérica durante y después de la segunda guerra, sea por voluntad o por desprecio a los recuerdos del abandono de la nación a su lugar de origen, nunca más dieron señales de vida. (And like many other islanders who lived in Colón, the zone and Panama who left for North America during and after the Second World War, whether by choice or from disdain for their memories of abandoning the nation of their origin, they were never heard from again.)[22]

The disappearance of the characters into the vast obscurity of the United States is an unusual ending for a novel attempting to argue the merits of peaceful coexistence of race on the islands. Robinson Abrahams returns to the genre of romance fiction to subvert the idea that marriage of the two cultures is the necessary solution to the racial and cultural differences. Although their marriage might in some ways be a positive step, ultimately the two are unable to find a home on the islands. In this way *Sail Ahoy!!!* questions whether the confluence of cultures on the island is tenable for the foreseeable future.

Finally, two mainland authors have also contributed to the literature of the Colombian Caribbean islands. Fanny Buitrago, who is from Barranquilla, has published two works, *Bahía sonora* (1976, Sonorous Bay), a collection of short stories, and *Los pañamanes* (1979, The Panyamans), a full-length novel. In *Bahía Sonora*, Buitrago assembles oral traditions from the islands and coverts them into the written word; many stories highlight the preoccupations of older *raizales* as they seek to preserve their oral culture in new contexts that privilege Spanish and the written word. *Los pañamanes* repeats several leitmotifs from Buitrago's short stories. The title is a derivative of the word *panya*, which the *raizales* employ to describe native Spanish speakers, and the novel underscores the heteroglossia of the islands and the crosshatch of people and linguistic identifiers. *Los pañamanes*, written by a non-native islander, maintains a critical perspective toward the policies and trends that suppress *raizal* culture and favor immigrant cultures. Claudine Bancelin has also published a novel, *Entre ráfagas de viento* (2004, Between Gusts of Wind), which employs island culture and themes. The plot revolves around the love story of Micaela and Santiago, who meet on San Andrés while he is evading extradition for drug trafficking. The novel details the types of relationships that exist in such a small island as well highlights the problems with corruption and drug trafficking that have affected so many Caribbean islands.

As with marginalized groups throughout Latin America, Colombian indigenous groups and Colombian Caribbean *raizales* have suffered from historical discrimination and injustices. Unfortunately certain injustices continue to this day. However, these two groups have fought to obtain rights at the national level and be recognized as equal participants in Colombian society. The literature reviewed in this chapter has shown that the indigenous groups have always utilized writing to defend their rights. For the indigenous authors, the literature of the past few decades has focused on the creation of works that highlight and safeguard native traditions while also exploring the new trends in oraliture and urban indigenous literature. The literature from the Colombian Caribbean demonstrates the confluence of cultures that has always made the islands a unique, multi-cultural region. Although marginalized, both the Colombian indigenous and Colombian Caribbean authors are making important in-roads into the dominant writing culture centered in the Andean Highlands and Bogotá.

BIBLIOGRAPHY

Abrahams, Hazel Robinson. *El príncipe de St Katherine*. San Andrés, Colombia: Universidad Nacional de Colombia, Instituto de Estudios Caribeños, 2009.

No Give Up, Maan! San Andrés, Colombia: Universidad Nacional de Colombia, Instituto de Estudios Caribeños, 2002.

Sail Ahoy!!! Bogotá: Universidad Nacional de Colombia; Unibiblos, 2004.

Bancelin, Claudine. *Entre rafagas de viento*. Colombia: Maremagnum, 2004.

Berichá, E. *Tengo los pies en la cabeza*. Bogotá: Los cuatro elementos, 1992.

Buitrago, Fanny. *Bahía sonora: relatos de la isla*. Bogotá: Instituto Colombiano de Cultura, Subdirección de Comunicaciones Culturales, División de Publicaciones, 1976.

Los pañamanes. Barcelona: Plaza & Janés, 1979.

Forbes, Oakley. "Aproximaciones sociolingüísticas en torno a la realidad de las lenguas en contacto en las islas de San Andrés y Providencia: Bilingüismo y diglosia." In *San Andrés y Providencia: tradiciones culturales y coyuntura política*, ed. Isabel Clemente, 161–80. Bogotá: Ediciones Uniandes, 1989.

García, Daniel. "El Caribe se vuelve americano: la política de Estados Unidos en el siglo XIX." In *San Andrés y Providencia: tradiciones culturales y coyuntura política*, ed. Isabel Clemente, 83–110. Bogotá: Ediciones Uniandes, 1989.

Gómez Londoño, Ana María. In *Muiscas: representaciones, cartografías y etno-políticas de la memoria*, 76–7. Santa Fe de Bogotá: Pontificia Universidad Javeriana, 2005.

Hernández Romero, Astrid. *La visibilización estadística de los grupos étnicos colombianos*. Departamento Administrativo Nacional de Estadística, Bogotá: DANE, 2005.

Isaacs, Jorge. *Estudio sobre las Tribus Indígenas del Estado del Magdalena. Exploraciones. Obras completas, vol. VI.* Edición crítica de María Teresa Cristina. Universidad Externado de Colombia y Universidad del Valle. Bogotá: Ediciones Sol y Luna, 1967.

Jamioy Juagibioy, Hugo. *Danzantes del viento: poesía bilingüe. Bínÿbe Oboyejuayëng.* Bogotá: Ministerio de Cultura, 2010.

López Hernández, Miguel Ángel. *Encuentros en los senderos de Abya Yala.* Quito, Ecuador: Ediciones Abya Yala, 2004.

Martí, José. *Periodismo de 1881 a 1892.* La Habana, Cuba: Casa de las Américas, 2003.

Mow, June Marie. *The Native Islanders of San Andres, Old Providence and Santa Catalina: Dreaming between Two Worlds.* CORALINA Report. San Andres, San Andres Island: Providence Foundation, 2005.

Restrepo, Luis Fernando. "The Cacique of Turmequé or The Affronts of Memory." *Cuadernos de Literatura* 28 (July–December) (2010): 31.

Robinson, Lenito Bent. *Sobre nupcias y ausencias, y otros cuentos.* Reprint. Bogotá: Ministerio de Cultura de Colombia, 2010.

Rocha Vivas, Miguel, compiler. *El Sol babea jugo de piña. Antología de las literaturas indígenas del Atlántico, el Pacífico y la Serranía del Perijá.* Bogotá: Ministerio de Cultura, 2010.

Palabras mayores, palabras vivas. Tradiciones mítico-literarias y escritores indígenas en Colombia. Madrid: Taurus, 2013.

Ross, James. "Routes for Roots: Entering the 21st Century in San Andrés Island, Colombia." *Caribbean Studies* 35, no. 1 (January–June 2007): 3–36.

Sánchez, Enrique, Fredy Chikangana [Wiñay Mallky], et al., coords. *Manual introductorio: Biblioteca básica de los pueblos indígenas de Colombia. Nación desde las raíces.* Bogotá: Ministerio de Cultura, 2010.

Sommer, Doris. *Foundational Fictions: The National Romances of Latin America.* Berkeley: University of California Press, 1991.

Notes

1 See Gómez Londoño (2005:76–77).

2 See Hernández Romero (2005).

3 Restrepo (2010:31).

4 Jorge (1967).

5 Berichá (1992).

6 Rocha Vivas (2010).

7 Sánchez et al. (2010).

8 López Hernández (2004:129).

9 Jamioy Juagibioy (2010:24).

10 Rocha Vivas (2013:309).

11 Martí (2003:192).

12 According to James Ross, the written history proffers that adherence to Colombian sovereignty was voluntary. However, oral tradition holds that the

islanders were forced to become part of the Gran Colombia project implemented by Bolívar. Regardless of the history, Ross purports, "no doubt feeling the need for protection from somewhere, the British clearly having withdrawn from the islands, Gran Colombia was seen as a better bet than the Central American Federation and the islands came to be administered from Cartagena, the principal Colombian coastal city" (2007:1).

13 Mow (2005:5).

14 Daniel García argues that during this time period, because of its location, the Archipelago, "fue sin duda la parte del territorio colombiano más afectada por la política exterior estadounidense" (was, without a doubt, the part of Colombian territory most affected by U.S. foreign policy) (1989:3).

15 Ross (2007:21).

16 Ross (2007:22).

17 In his sociolinguistic study of the island, Oakley Forbes recognizes that the categories of linguistic registers are not limited to just English/Creole and Spanish speakers and that bilingualism is typical. Furthermore, he argues that there are at least eight types of bilingualism/diglossia on the island and because of this, "el fenómeno sociolingüístico de las islas de San Andrés y Providencia es el laboratorio lingüístico vivo más interesante del país" (the sociolinguistic phenomenon of the San Andrés and Providencia islands is the most interesting living linguistic laboratory in the country) (172:7).

18 Ross (2007:31).

19 Robinson (2010:77–8).

20 See Sommer (1991).

21 Robinson Abrahams (2004:170).

22 Ibid., 196.

PART III

Beyond the boundaries

CHAPTER 15

García Márquez as public intellectual

Gene H. Bell-Villada

The descriptive noun "intellectuals," as we know, first arose in late-nineteenth-century France, when Émile Zola and other literati took to writing polemics in defense of the falsely accused and unjustly imprisoned Captain Alfred Dreyfus. The word was initially deployed by the reactionary anti-Dreyfusard camp as their term of abuse against Dreyfus's lettered champions. As sometimes happens with attack words ("Gothic" and "Impressionists" are familiar enough instances), the epithet caught on and evolved into a neutral, common sort of currency.

The origin of the term "public intellectuals" is less precise or certain. The signifier enjoyed a sudden vogue in the United States, however, with the publication of Russell Jacoby's *The Last Intellectuals* (1987). The author, a historian at UCLA, lamented the academization of the American life of the mind as well as the emergence of a specialized clerisy that writes more for the professional guild than for a broader, general range of readers.[1] Jacoby's book sparked some lively discussion in the years that followed, giving the phrase considerable visibility. A casual Google search shows that the appellation, and the ideal it stands for, has remained part of the discourse of the scribbling classes (as is indeed shown by the title of this essay).

In the English-speaking world, public *literary* intellectuals have in our time constituted a relatively rare breed (Harold Pinter in England being an exception). Perhaps the only American imaginative writer to have earned such a distinction after 1945 was Norman Mailer, and his statements shaded more into those of a comedian and jester rather than of a serious spokesperson. The fields of politics and of science, on the other hand, can boast some prominent exemplars – Noam Chomsky and Paul Krugman in the former, Stephan Jay Gould and Richard Dawkins in the latter spring immediately to mind. In addition, a vast array of well-funded, right-wing think tanks have afforded a platform for an entire generation of conservative intellectuals (though, again, no literati worth mention).

Latin America, by contrast, has a long history of men of letters being engaged in the public arena. (Their role is roughly analogous to that of writers under Tsarism, men of conscience who, faced with Russia's backwardness, took active, passionate part in the debates over their homeland's present and future.) In this regard, some Latin American literati have become elected presidents of their republics – Argentina's Sarmiento in the nineteenth century, Venezuela's Rómulo Gallegos (briefly) in the twentieth. Some have struggled and even died for their causes, as did the great Cuban lyrist, essayist, and freedom fighter José Martí, killed in action against a Spanish expeditionary force; or the Chilean bard Pablo Neruda, who served a stint as Communist Party senator in the 1940s (and had to flee right-wing repression) and who, in his last days, suffered some abuse at the hands of the military during the onset of the Pinochet coup. Nicaragua's revolutionary Sandinista regime, for its part, could claim a roster of literary artists within its ranks, including novelist Sergio Ramírez, memoirist Omar Cabezas, and poet Ernesto Cardenal. In addition, the traditional Latin American practice of appointing writers to diplomatic posts necessarily involves the literati in the textures of public life.

Several of the leading lights of Latin America's fabled "Boom of the Novel" have hewed resolutely to the public intellectual path. In a prime instance, from early in his career, Mexican author Carlos Fuentes took on the job of representing internationally the history and the progressive elements of the Ibero-American continent and of his native country. Handsome and gracious, fluent and articulate in three languages, and thoroughly at ease as a public speaker, Fuentes was a frequent – and urbane and informative – presence on television (including a TV series of his own, *The Buried Mirror*, done in both Spanish and English) and in academia, as well as in the print media.

Peruvian Mario Vargas Llosa, by contrast, started out as a leftist in the 1960s, then began a slow but steady move to the right in the wake of the Padilla affair in 1971, and even ran for president of his country on a Conservative ticket in 1990, losing to Alberto Fujimori. Since the mid-1990s he has served as a biweekly op-ed columnist for the prestigious Madrid daily *El País*, where he vigorously defends the absolute free market; criticizes labor unions, state pensions, and government regulations as inimical to liberty; and frankly identifies himself as an American-style libertarian. Nevertheless, the shift has not harmed his literary gifts, as demonstrated by the stunning artistic success of *La fiesta del chivo* (2000, The Feast of the Goat), his powerful novel about the Trujillo dictatorship.

On the other hand, Cuban author Guillermo Cabrera Infante, creator of the comic masterpiece *Tres tristes tigres* (1967, Three Trapped Tigers) and of the unique film script for the Hollywood road movie *Vanishing Point* (1971), became a bitter, full-time anti-Castro publicist starting with his exile to London in 1966. As a result he ended up squandering his narrative talents, never producing a major literary opus again after *Infante's Inferno* (1979), a kind of spoof of the Don Juan memoir.

Throughout his creative lifetime, Gabriel García Márquez stood as a classic example of the free-standing public intellectual. During many of the years of his celebrity he was renowned as much as a spokesman for left-wing causes and for his ties with Fidel Castro as for his luminous and complex works of fiction. The very fact that in the Hispanic mass media and to his mass readers he was known simply as "Gabo" says a great deal about his standing as a grass-roots figure. (One scarcely imagines Fuentes, Vargas Llosa, or Cabrera Infante being alluded to in the press by their household nicknames.)

García Márquez, it goes without saying, could not have achieved such a popular profile were it not for the world-wide reach of *One Hundred Years of Solitude* and the superb novels that followed. The conscientious artist and meticulous craftsman who had made good also enabled the public figure, without either side of him losing its touch in the process. Of course, the barbs from the right – from, say, Cuban exiles, American neoconservatives, or Vargas Llosa himself – might take issue with his political associations, yet they could not dismiss his fictions as hack work or propaganda. Ironically, the Colombian never held a government post in his native land (even though presidents López Michelsen and Betancur offered him consulships and ambassadorships in Europe), and he summarily rejected any suggestions from his fellow left-wingers that he run for chief of state. A shy person, García Márquez seldom appeared on TV talk shows and always felt uncomfortable speaking in front of large audiences. To my knowledge, he never once delivered so many as a few words at a political rally.

From the outset, it bears noting, García Márquez was a public writer whose initial medium – and sole salaried occupation – was journalism. (Not for him the life of the isolated aesthete à la Mallarmé or Nabokov, standing outside and above it all in one's study while fashioning a purist art.) He began writing daily whimsical columns for his very first job in 1948, at age twenty-one, as a poorly paid stringer for *El Universal* in Cartagena, and assumed the same task for *El Heraldo* in Barranquilla in 1950–2. He later spent two years as a field reporter and sometime film critic for the staff of *El Espectador* in Bogotá, Colombia's oldest and at the time second-largest newspaper. The short, personal essay, in particular, was a genre that he would excel in and return to periodically, even producing in the 1980s a weekly column, syndicated in several newspapers and magazines across the Hispanic world.

What is distinctive about García Márquez's journalistic output is that it is all but exclusively narrative (or, at other times, personal and reflective). A press piece from him is seldom if ever a strictly ideological platform with some grand plan or agenda behind it. Whereas the later Mario Vargas Llosa will pepper his columns with programmatic statements and references to such authorities as von Hayek, von Mises, and Milton Friedman, in contrast, comparable allusions to Marx, Engels, or Lenin are seldom to be found in the Colombian's occasional articles. Even as a columnist he is less the commentator than the reporter, the amiable and articulate story-teller, a modern avatar of the town-crier in the square.

Still, all columnists and reporters have ipso facto a point of view; and García Márquez is no exception, even though the view is subtly embedded in his prose. In many respects he does qualify as an "advocacy journalist." This side of him already became clear when, in 1957, still barely known as a fiction writer, he penned a series of reports from the Eastern Bloc countries. The articles provided some genuinely balanced in depth accounts of both the positive and negative features of the Communist regimes, seen through a Latin American's optics (unlike the automatic, condemnatory stance of U.S. journalists at the time). The accounts at first had some difficulty finding a home and appeared only two years hence in *Cromos*, a Colombian glossy. They later rode in on the coattails of García Márquez's fame in a collection entitled *De viaje por los países socialistas* (1980, Traveling through the Socialist Nations).

In 1959, with the Fidelista revolution in full swing, through some left-wing friends the writer offered his skills to Prensa Latina, the official Cuban press agency. He thereby started a two-year stint for the organization as a writer-reporter, first from Bogotá, then moving on to Havana, and finally joining some staffers at its offices in downtown Manhattan. There García Márquez had to contend with threatening phone calls from Cuban exiles to him and his family. After just five months in New York he resigned in protest against the "sectarian" battles unfolding between the youthful regime and the old-guard, Moscow-oriented, Communist Party hard-liners back on the island.

Not all of the vast early output of García Márquez "the journalist" qualifies as "serious" work. He also was to be employed at various illustrated gossip glossies in Caracas and Mexico City, cranking out or editing fluff pieces on demand for a monthly check – the lot of many a salaried scrivener in today's commercial world. As we know, the astounding best-seller status of *Cien años de soledad* allowed the writer to put that sort of scribbling-for-hire behind him.

García Márquez went into a kind of literary seclusion during most of the writing (1968–74) of *El otoño del patriarca* (1975, The Autumn of the Patriarch). Presumably out of prudence he remained silent about political developments in Franco's Spain. And of course the process of crafting so complex and unique an artifact as *Patriarch* was surely an all-absorbing task. In September 1973, though, García Márquez opened up to the larger world once again when he fired off a telegram to the new military junta in Chile, dubbing them "a gang of criminals in the pay of North American imperialism."[2] In addition, with this latest "big" novel now completed, in 1975 he started to serve, as elected vice-president, on the Second Bertrand Russell Tribunal that investigated war crimes, an association he maintained until 1980.

These initiatives can be seen as García Márquez's first steps toward entry into his latter-day, prominent role as a now-renowned public intellectual. And this he did, once again, via journalism – independently and on his own terms. With the aid of Colombian sociologist Orlando Fals Borda and progressive businessman José Vicente Katараín, and investing his own funds, the writer launched a left-wing biweekly magazine, based in Bogotá, called *Alternativa*, the very name drawing attention to its dissenting stance within the larger press system.

García Márquez played a minimal role in the day-to-day operations of *Alternativa*, since administration was not and would never be his forte, but he served as a frequent contributor to its pages, writing on such timely topics as the last days of President Allende in Chile, the Portuguese revolution of 1974, the reformist military regime in Peru, postwar Vietnam, the Sandinista seizure of the National Palace in 1978, and assorted news and issues from Cuba. He also interviewed a thirty-something Felipe González, just emerging from clandestine status during Spain's transition to democracy. Several of these pieces were translated and ran in international venues like *Harper's*, *Rolling Stone*, and *New Left Review*. At its height, *Alternativa* commanded a paid circulation of 40,000.

Unfortunately, *Alternativa*'s frank opposition to the right-wing Liberal government of Julio César Turbay Ayala made for a tense atmosphere within the magazine's ranks. Over the years there were police confisca-tions, "court interventions, economic blockades and a sabotage of distribution."[3] In addition, a mysterious bomb went off at its offices in 1975; García Márquez blamed the Army, yet no legal proceedings followed. Such circumstances gave the publication a precarious existence, and the executive decision not to accept advertising further compounded its problems. In 1980 the magazine at last ceased operation. The history and the contents of *Alternativa* have been the subject of entire scholarly articles.[4]

The demise of *Alternativa* was not enough to deter García Márquez, whose journalistic mission continued to grow. Between 1980 and 1984 he worked as a weekly syndicated columnist, dashing off 173 personal essays for the international Hispanic press.[5] He dropped the routine only to bring the finishing touches to *El amor en los tiempos del cólera* (1985, Love in the Time of Cholera), then in progress, yet later kept up with his nonfiction production as a freelancer, for instance, condemning in Cuba's *Granma* the 1990 invasion of Panama (now largely forgotten) by U.S. President George H. W. Bush.

The author further expanded his journalistic range by starting, in Cartagena in 1996, with UNESCO backing, the Foundation for a New Ibero-American Journalism, a school designed to provide further training for younger news people from all over the continent. The novelist himself ran some of the practicums, the "workshops" (he avoided the term "classes"), deliberately focusing on the narrative aspect of news reporting. International figures from the field such as Ryszard Kapuscinski and Jon Lee Anderson (from Poland and the U.S., respectively) also participated. In yet another initiative, in 1998 García Márquez purchased *Cambio* magazine, the Colombian offshoot of Spain's prestigious *Cambio 16* and a competitor to the local heavyweight *Semana*. García Márquez, as expected, wrote regularly for *Cambio*, including an article on the 1999 inauguration of President Hugo Chávez in Venezuela.

In his 1983 *Playboy* interview García Márquez remarked, "a reporter is something I've never stopped being."[6] Nor did he ever stop. García Márquez "the journalist" constitutes a major facet of his professional profile. At least nine collections exist of his past articles, and there are book-length studies of the same, for instance, Robert L. Sims's *The First García Márquez*.[7] Naturally, little of this corpus would have been compiled or examined had it not been for his literary fame. Many an imaginative writer since 1800, one should note, has turned to journalism only half-heartedly, as a means of paying the food bills. In the case of García Márquez, doing journalism was an essential complement to his literary labors, a part of his personal vocation to tell as well as poeticize the truth – and of his lifelong role as public intellectual.

There exists a public side of García Márquez that is especially legend-ary: his amicable ties with heads of state. It has been quipped that these gentlemen needed him as much as he needed them. Or, as *New Yorker* writer Jon Lee Anderson puts it, quoting a source in Bogotá, "All of the presidents want to be his friend, but he wants to be their friend, too."[8] Over the years García Márquez would meet on occasion and be on friendly terms with presidents López Portillo of Mexico, Carlos Andrés Pérez of Venezuela, López Michelsen and Betancur of Colombia, and Spain's Felipe González. He was particularly close to Panama's Omar Torrijos and, along with Graham Greene, both of them being supplied with Panamanian passports, was included in the official entourage when the chief of state went to Washington in 1977 to negotiate the transfer of the Canal. In addition, when he was at the 1987 Moscow Film Festival as guest of honor, he met with Mikhail Gorbachev.

And then there was the famous extended 1994 meeting at Martha's Vineyard with Bill Clinton, where it is important also to note the attend-ance of Fuentes and William Styron, whose reportedly favorite novel was *One Hundred Years of Solitude.* The encounter led to Clinton's lifting the bothersome, absurd, McCarthyite, U.S. travel restrictions that had been imposed on the writer since 1961. Yet further, in 2002 the novelist delivered a copy of his memoirs, *Vivir para contarla* (2002, Living to Tell the Tale), to Mexico's President Vicente Fox at the Los Pinos national palace. President Hugo Chávez, for his part, publicly waved a copy of the autobiography before the cameras during his weekly TV broadcast, passionately recommending it as reading for his fellow Venezuelans.

By far the most visible of García Márquez's friendships in high places, however, was the one he sustained, beginning in the late 1970s and intensifying in the 1990s, with Fidel Castro. The author and his wife, Mercedes, frequently spent time on the island as personal guests of Fidel, staying in a house set aside for them in the Siboney area of Havana, near Miramar. The couple celebrated many a New Year's Eve in the Antillean capital. García Márquez actually received news of his Nobel Prize in October 1982 during a visit to Cuba, and that December he flew to the Stockholm ceremony from Havana airport. During his Cuban sojourns he often sat or travelled about with Castro and members of his inner circle. According to the author they scarcely talked "politics," the most common topics of conversation being rather literature, about which Fidel, he would assert, is quite knowledgeable, and – of all things – seafood.

In his ties with the Cuban leader García Márquez served as a kind of "ambassador without portfolio," defending the positive aspects of the regime before its detractors worldwide. Moreover, through his diplomatic efforts some major imprisoned oppositionists of the regime were released and given exit visas – notably Reynol González and Armando Valladares. In what may be a case of hyperbole, Plinio Apuleio Mendoza, journalist and longtime associate of the author, "cites a figure of 3,200 political prisoners freed on [García Márquez's] behalf."[9] The author also aided in the emigration of writers Heberto Padilla and Norberto Fuentes and helped the parents of novelist Severo Sarduy leave the island to visit their son in Paris.

García Márquez's record as Fidel's best-known supporter, interlocutor, and confidante is not a spotless one – the Heberto Padilla case being one of the major sore points. His refusal to sign the famous second letter to Castro in 1971, signed by sixty intellectuals from three continents, in protest against the imprisonment and forced "confession" of the dissident Cuban poet, was the complex and agonizing decision of a man conflicted in his equal loyalties to his fellow leftist writers and to the Revolutionary project on the island.[10] At the time, it should be said, García Márquez was not yet close to Castro. Ten years later, moreover, when their friendship was growing, he was instrumental in securing Padilla's emigration, as remarked earlier.

Looking at things more broadly, one could say that, even at the height of his relationship with Fidel, he did not and could not defend every possible dissenter. While he was certainly aware that torture existed in the island's prisons, or that unjust executions had taken place, presumably he also knew that there were limits to his influence with Castro, and that to push things too far could have led to a falling out between the two. On the other hand, many of García Márquez's harshest critics who enjoy good ties with and admire the United States have not seen fit to break with its leading circles over, say, the Iraq War, or over the persistent holding and torture of Muslim prisoners at the U.S. naval facility in Guantánamo. García Márquez's ideological adversaries thus at times hold him to a higher moral standard than they do to others, or to themselves. (Incidentally, in a glaring case of misconstruction, when, over Colombian radio in 2003, Vargas Llosa accused García Márquez of being a "cortesano de Fidel Castro," the English-speaking media inaccurately rendered "*cortesano*" as "courtesan – that is, "upper-class whore" – rather than as "courtier." As far as I know, this astoundingly obtuse translation gaffe has never been corrected, and to this day continues to circulate on the Internet and in print, including in Esteban and Panichelli.)[11]

Looking back at this later phase, just as García Márquez's life as a journalist is the topic of entire volumes, his history as an intimate to presidents could also serve as the subject of a strictly political biography. (There is in fact a whole book that focuses largely on the Fidel–García Márquez ties; see Esteban and Panichelli, passim.) Still, a volume that would deal exclusively with García Márquez's high-end friendships, to the exclusion of his literary prowess, might have its pitfalls. After all, a study consisting of little more than a famous author's encounters with men of power would mostly be lacking in narrative variety and suspense and thus become static and presumptuous, even shallow. The author's access to the powerful is nonetheless a phenomenon unique in literary history. Perhaps not since Molière wrote and directed his comedies for the French Sun King has there been such an instance of a major creative writer being so close to and on such good terms with a chief of state. The writer's presidential friendships, moreover, were not just one – but multiple, serial.

In the end, though, the area where he most stands out in his role as public intellectual can be located in what he's best known for: namely, his dazzling works of fiction. Many of his novels and stories deal with themes of social conflict and political power. Thus, *One Hundred Years of Solitude* in its central episodes depicts a civil war, an exploitative agribusiness firm, a workers' strike, and a military massacre. *The Autumn of the Patriarch* anatomizes two, or perhaps five, centuries of Latin American dictatorship, going back to Columbus, while *Crónica de una muerte anunciada* (1981, Chronicle of a Death Foretold) shows readers the ages-old, Iberian family honor-and-virginity code as the destructive force it can be – and not just for women. *El general en su laberinto* (1989, The General in His Labyrinth), in turn, paints an up-close, highly realistic portrait of Bolívar, the continent's most mythologized and sanctified political-military leader. And the otherwise beautiful *Del amor y otros demonios* (1994, Of Love and Other Demons) also evokes the ravages of Afro-Hispanic slavery and of the colonial Spanish Inquisition.

The trend, moreover, is already to be seen in García Márquez's earlier works. The Spanish title of his very first novel, *La hojarasca* (1955, Leaf Storm) alludes metaphorically to a massive human migration, brought about by a Yankee banana firm. His weakest, rather flawed book, *La mala hora* (1962, In Evil Hour), evokes grass-roots, underground resistance as well as government repression. Even many of the stories in García Márquez's first mature collection, *Los funerales de la mamá grande* (1962, Big Mama's Funeral), focus, in oblique and comic ways, on public issues – notably the local oligarchy (its visionary title piece), the violent nouveaux-riches elements ("La prodigiosa tarde de Baltazar" [Baltasar's Prodigious Afternoon], "La viuda de Montiel" [Montiel's Widow]), barracks dictatorship ("Un día de estos" [One of These Days]), and priestly authority (" La siesta del martes" [Tuesday Siesta], "Un día después del sábado" [One Day after Saturday]). The miracle of García Márquez's best works is that they give narrative shape to such public issues without lapsing into the heavy-handed preachiness and didacticism of socialist-realist or protest literature. He rather leavens the materials with poesy and humor, placing the characters and events within broader contexts that allot equal weight to things like family ties and romantic love, human emotions, and concerns quotidian.

García Márquez passed away on April 17, 2014, at age 87. In life as in death, he remained every inch the public intellectual. For the memorial service held on April 21 at Mexico City's Palacio de Bellas Artes, thousands of mourners queued up to attend the official farewell. Yellow flowers and butterflies decorated the stately, neoclassical edifice, in keeping with the favored color in his most famous work. The presidents of both Mexico and Colombia each delivered solemn eulogies in tribute to the literary master. In Aracataca, García Márquez's original hometown, 3,000 admirers of all ages participated in a funeral procession. The following day, readings of his works were announced at schools and libraries across the celebrated compatriot's native land.

Such an outpouring of collective grief served as a fitting last sign of García Márquez's standing as man of the people and as public intellectual. For massive acclaim and affection on a comparable scale one needs to go back to the nineteenth century, when loving mourners filled the streets of London and Paris to pay final respects to their dearly departed Charles Dickens and Victor Hugo.

People. Popular. Public. These three Latinate words are all etymo-logically interrelated. And Gabriel García Márquez in full represents all three.

BIBLIOGRAPHY

Benson, John. "García Márquez en Alternativa (1974–1979): Una bibliografía comentada." *Chasqui* 8, no. 3 (May 1979): 69–81.
    "García Márquez en Alternativa (1978–1980): Una bibliografía comentada." *Chasqui* 10, nos. 2–3 (February–May 1981): 41–6.
Dreifus, Claudia. "*Playboy* Interview: Gabriel García Márquez." In *Conversations with Gabriel García Márquez*, ed. Gene H. Bell-Villada, 93– 132. Jackson: University Press of Mississippi, 2006.

Esteban, Ángel, and Panichelli, Stéphanie. *Fidel and Gabo: A Portrait of the Legendary Friendship between Fidel Castro and Gabriel García Márquez.* Trans. Diane Stockwell. New York: Pegasus, 2009.

Jacoby, Russell. *The Last Intellectuals: American Culture in the Age of Academe.* New York: Basic Books, 1987.

Martin, Gerald. *Gabriel García Márquez: A Life.* Toronto: Viking Canada, 2008

Sims, Robert L. *The First García Márquez: A Study of the Journalistic Writings from 1948 to 1955.* Lanham, Md.: University Press of America, 1992.

Notes

1 Jacoby (1987:5–6).
2 Martin (2008:376).
3 Ibid., 379.
4 Benson (1979, 1981).
5 Martin (2008:413).
6 Dreifus (2006).
7 Martin (2008:630).
8 Esteban and Panichelli (2009).
9 Ibid., 221.
10 Ibid., 50–2.
11 Ibid., 47, 304.

CHAPTER 16

Women writers in Colombia

Claire Taylor

This chapter charts the development of women's writing within Colombia from independence up until the present day. Although women were writing in Colombia as early as the Colonial period, it was in the nineteenth century, with the rise to prominence of one of Colombia's most prolific writers, that women first made their mark on the national literary scene in a sustained fashion. Following on from this, the early twentieth century saw a significant number of women poets, short story writers, and writers of *crónicas*, followed, in the second half of the twentieth century, by the rise of the post-Boom generation and a significant number of women novelists. Toward the latter part of the century, a generation of new women writers emerged whose prose was heavily influenced by journalism, and since then and into the twenty-first century, we have seen the rise of urban, popular, and genre fiction among Colombian women writers.

The nineteenth century

In the nineteenth century in Colombia, as with most other Latin American countries, letters and politics were intimately entwined, with literature mostly dominated by male writers who were often at the same time statesmen and military leaders. Yet the nineteenth century also saw the emergence of published women writers, and in Colombia none was more prominent than Soledad Acosta (1833–1913). Widely recognized as Colombia's most significant woman writer in the nineteenth century, Acosta was a hugely prolific writer who turned her hand to a myriad of genres and styles, including short fiction, novels, drama, translations, essays, *crónicas*, and journalistic articles.

Daughter of the famous national hero of the War of Independence Joaquín Acosta and wife of the prominent Liberal politician and writer José María Samper, Acosta formed part of the Liberal elites of the time, yet her works also display a growing concern for women and their roles within the nation. Among her most famous works is the novel *Dolores: cuadros de la vida de una mujer* (Dolores: Portraits of the Life of a Woman), published originally as a serial in the newspaper *El Mensajero* in 1867 and subsequently republished in the book *Novelas y cuadros de la vida sur-americana* (Novels and Portraits of South American Life) in 1869. In *Dolores,* the eponymous heroine discovers she has leprosy and as a result must cancel her marriage plans subsequently withdrawing from the world. Three particularly interesting aspects come to the fore in this novel: first, the fact that it is a failed romance, and that the national conciliation as embodied by the lovers cannot take place; second, the fact that discourses of whiteness are thrown off course, with the whiteness of Dolores indicating not racial purity but instead sickness; and third, that the novel sets up writing as a form of self-expression for women, with Dolores usurping the narrative voice from her cousin Pedro and engaging in her own self-expression.[1]

While undoubtedly Acosta's most accomplished novel, some of her other novels share similar concerns with women's fate, such as *Teresa la limeña* (1869, Teresa the Woman from Lima), which details the life of Teresa, the protagonist, whose fiancé abandons her and who eventually retreats from society and resolves to write her memoires. As scholars have noted, this novel presents a denouncement of marriage as a commercial transaction that victimizes women and illustrates how, for the protagonist, writing provides "the path to self-knowledge and creates a kind of symbolic liberation."[2] Similarly her novel *Una holandesa en América* (1888, A Hollander in America), written in style of the *novela de costumbres*, not only engages in the civilization–barbarism debate that was at the heart of much nation-building discourse in Colombia and across Latin America, but also legitimizes traditionally feminine forms of writing, such as letters and diaries.[3] In these and many other works, Acosta revealed herself to be a writer in touch with Colombia's predominant national concerns, while also pointing forward to what were to become some of the key issues of women's writing in the twentieth century.

The twentieth century

Toward the early part of the twentieth century, women's writing in Colombia tended to fall within the genres of the short story, the chronicle, and poetry. One of the most prolific women writers of the early twentieth century, Sofía Ospina de Navarro (1893–1974) wrote journalistic pieces, short stories, poetry, drama, culinary tips, and advice. Her stories, *crónicas*, and commentaries on domestic life from the 1920s onward have been seen as significant for the way in which they offer an account of contemporary life in her home city of Medellín. Her collection of short stories published in 1926, *Cuentos y crónicas* (Stories and Chronicles), takes as its central theme the modernization of Medellín and provides, as Berg argues, "un retrato detalladísimo de una sociedad tradicional en transición" (a detailed portrait of a traditional society in transition).[4]

A significant number of women poets were writing in Colombia in the first half of the twentieth century, among whom the most renowned is Meira Delmar (1922–2009). Born Olga Isabel Chams Eljach, she started writing at a very young age and took up the penname "Meira Delmar" when she first decided to submit her poetry for publication. One of the most widely recognized poets in Colombia, Delmar was elected member of the Academia Colombiana de la Lengua (Colombian Language Academy) in 1989, and after her death, a poetry prize was created in her name, the *Premio Nacional de Poesía Meira Delmar*.

Delmar's first published poems appeared in the journal *Vanidades* in 1937, and five years later her first poetry collection was published, with the title *Alba del olvido* (1942; Dawn of Oblivion). Delmar went on to publish six further collections, bringing together more than 100 poems in total: *Sitio de amor* (1944, Place of Love), *Verdad del sueño* (1946, Truth of the Dream), *Secreta isla* (1951, Secret Island), *Huésped sin sombra* (1971, Guest without a Shadow), *Laúd memorioso* (1995, Memorious Lute), and *Alguien pasa* (1998, Somebody Passes). Her poems frequently include references to classical antiquity and to nature, and she employs, in the words of Jaramillo and Osorio, a "vocabulario simbólico que le permite recuperar vivencias que se conectan con el mundo sensorial" (a symbolic vocabulary that permits her to recover experiences connected to the sensorial world).[5] Recurrent themes in her poetic oeuvre include love, beauty, pain, and loss, and her later collections, particularly *Laúd memorioso* and *Alguien pasa*, focus on the passage of time, the persistence of memory, and the "fugacidad de la experiencia humana" (fleeting nature of human experience).[6]

Contemporaries of Delmar include Maruja Vieira (b. 1922), who has had one of the longest literary careers in poetry of her generation. Her first published poetry collection, *Campanario de lluvia*, came out in 1947, and, more than fifteen books later, Viera is still publishing today, in her nineties. Elected *miembro correspondiente* (corresponding member) of the Academia Colombiana de la Lengua in 1991, and awarded the Premio Nacional Vida y Obra by the Ministerio de Cultura in 2012, Viera's poetic oeuvre tends to focus on themes of love (and loss of love); on death; and also on poetic creation itself, with her poems often envisaging the writing of poetry as a challenge that the poet faces.[7]

Another contemporary of Delmar is Blanca Isaza (1898–1967). One of Colombia's most prominent women poets in the early to middle part of the century, Isaza published her first poetry collection, *Selva florida* (Florid Jungle) in 1917, and went on to publish fifteen volumes of poetry in her lifetime. Isaza's poems focus on daily life and frequently take as their themes family, nature, and death. A particularly notable feature of her poetry is the predominance of religious elements, with numerous poems dedicated to Christ or to saints, and numerous references to Catholicism and its rites within the poems themselves[8]

As the century progressed, notable women novelists began to emerge, with one of the most prominent in the middle decades of the century being Elisa Mujica (1918–2003). Born in Bucaramanga, but having moved to Bogotá at an early age, Mujica also spent a period in Ecuador as secretary of the Colombian Embassy in Quito from 1943 to 1945. Her first short story, "Tarde de visita," (An afternoon visit) was published in *El Liberal* in 1947, and her first published collection of short stories, *Ángela y el diablo* (Ángela and the Devil), was published six years later in 1953, during her time in Madrid (1952–9). Although Mujica published a relatively small number of novels – only three, with several years between each – she is nevertheless recognized as one of Colombia's foremost writers of the twentieth century. One of the most decorated women writers in her country, Mujica was elected *Miembro correspondiente* of the Academia Colombiana de la Lengua in 1982 and in 1984 promoted to *Miembro de número* (Numerary Member) of the same institution – the first woman to gain this position. In 1984, she was also voted *Miembro correspondiente hispanoamericano* (Corresponding Hispanic American Member) of the Real Academia Española.

Her first novel, *Los dos tiempos* (1949, The Two Times), was written while she was in Ecuador and is marked by her experiences there. The novel is a Bildungsroman that narrates two stages in the life of the protagonist, Celina, a middle-class Colombian woman, depicting, first, her childhood in a small town and subsequently in Bogotá and, second, her life as a grown woman in Quito.

Yet it was Mujica's second novel, *Catalina* (1963, Catalina), that broughther recognition, as it was shortlisted for the prestigious Esso National Novel award. The novel is told in the first person from the point of view of Catalina, the eponymous protagonist, and starts from the point at which, widowed and pregnant, she returns to Bogotá to meet up with her brother. The majority of the narrative is then told in retrospective, depicting Catalina's earlier life and her marriage. The novel is at once the personal story of Catalina and a detailed account of Colombia in the transition from the nineteenth to the twentieth century. As Ordóñez argues, one of the particular strengths of the novel lies in the way it sets up as one of its structural axes the tension between speech and silence, and that "vencer el silencio se convierte . . . en un claro objetivo que permitará la recuperación de la historia, propia y ajena" (overcoming silence becomes a clear objective that will enable the recovery of both one's own and other people's history).[9]

Mujica's third and final novel, *Bogotá de las nubes* (1984, Bogotá of the Clouds), depicts the experiences of the protagonist, Mirza, and her life in a gray, inhospitable Bogotá. As with her two earlier novels, Mujica here links the life of her protagonist to the wider shape of societal change in Colombia, with the particular focus in this novel being the urban development of Bogotá. In so doing, Mujica once again illustrates the links between the public and the private.[10]

A contemporary of Mujica's, but writing somewhat later in life, was María Helena Uribe (1929). Born in Medellín, although studying for some years first in Brussels and then in the United States, Uribe published a collection of short stories, *Polvo y ceniza* (Dust and Ashes), in 1963 and subsequently her only novel, *Reptil en el tiempo* (Reptile in Time), in 1986. With its highly experimental format, its play with the layout of the words across the printed page, and its disruption of narrative coherence itself, Uribe's novel displays the fragmentation of identity. As Borsò notes, the novel focuses on "la condición del encierro de la mujer" (woman's condition of confinement)[11] and sketches out possible ways of escaping this confinement.

Women writers of the post-Boom

Where Mujica led the way in the middle decades of the twentieth century, it was in the post-Boom period that Colombia witnessed a real flourishing of women novelists, among whom the most notable are Albalucía Ángel, Fanny Buitrago, and Marvel Moreno. Ángel was born in Pereira in 1939 and since 1964 has resided mostly outside Colombia in various European countries, including Italy, France, and England, as well as the United States, India, Australia, and Mexico. Her early work tends to reflect her experiences in Europe, with *Los girasoles en invierno* (1970, The

Sunflowers in the Winter) depicting the life of a young woman named Alejandra and her experiences as she travels around Europe, taking as its structure the memories of the protagonist.[12] *Dos veces Alicia* (Two Times Alicia) is set in London of the 1960s and intersperses interior scenes with scenes in the streets and parks of London, episodes that are often the catalyst for the protagonist's imaginings and refigurations of reality. Rather than a linear presentation and clear character development, the narrative constantly shifts from one diegetic level to another, and the narrator often projects herself into fictional characters who come to invade her own subjectivity[13]

Ángel's third novel, *Estaba la pájara pinta sentada en el verde limón* (1975, The Singing Bird Was on the Green Lemon Tree), is widely acknowledged as her most accomplished work, for which she won the *Vivencias* magazine prize for best Colombian novel, the first time the prize was awarded to a woman. This novel is much more historically rooted than her earlier work, set during the period of *La Violencia* from the late 1940s to the 1960s. Yet this novel is not a conventional *novela de la Violencia* in that it narrates the episodes from the point of view of a child growing up in Colombia and conveys its narrative through experimental formal structure that disrupts teleological movement. The novel's central focus is Ana, a young girl growing up in Colombia during the 1950s and 1960s, and is narrated from several points of view.

Ángel's subsequent novel, *Misiá Señora* (1982, The Missus), portrays the life of the protagonist, Mariana, a middle-class Colombian woman, and narrates, first, Mariana's childhood, subsequently her marriage and the birth of her children, and finally her descent into madness. The novel depicts, in the words of Keefe Ugalde, the "closed, suffocating space of a traditional existence"[14] and reveals how Mariana is unable to escape the traditional roles and value systems that are imposed upon her. Published some two years later, *Las andariegas* (The Travellers) is one of Ángel's most experimental novels to date and is composed of sixty-two episodes interspersed with line drawings, with the narrative loosely tracing the journey of groups of women through differing historical periods and geographical settings. The novel explicitly dialogues with Monique Wittig's *Les Guérillères*, one of the influential works of French feminist theory of the 1960s and 1970s, and reworks a series of foundational myths and tales, as the women protagonists refashion such stories in an act of mythopoesis.[15]

Ángel's most recent novel, *Tierra de nadie* (2002, No Man's Land), follows a dual structure, with two alternating narrative voices, geographical locations, temporal settings, and type faces. The first of these depicts a group of extraterrestrial women who descend to Earth and travel through various regions in their quest to redeem the Earth and its inhabitants, while the second narrates the experiences of a female protagonist who travels around the globe, experiencing different cultures. Although less accomplished than Ángel's earlier works, the novel is of interest in its deliberate intermingling of the discourses of science fiction and travel writing, with the codes of both genres coming under question.[16]

A contemporary of Ángel, Fanny Buitrago (1940) is one of Colombia's most prolific women writers. Her work is characterized by its narrative experimentation, often involving postmodern play and meta-literary commentary; as Montes argues, throughout her work Buitrago "emplea la novela como un medio para exponer y retar la autoridad de sus mecanismos de representación" (employs the novel as a medium to expose and challenge the authority of its mechanisms of representation).[17] At the same time, her work often delivers a biting commentary on contemporary Colombian society.

Buitrago's first novel, *El hostigante verano de los dioses* (1963, The Harassing Summer of the Gods), narrates the story of Marina, a journalist from Bogotá, who arrives in an unnamed tropical city (but that closely resembles Barranquilla) in order to discover the author of a famous novel that was published anonymously. The novel is structured into twenty chapters that alternate between four different narrators: Marina, the journalist, and three women – Hade, Isabel, and Inari – who appear within Marina's narration but who also come to narrate their own stories in their respective chapters. Buitrago's early work, and this novel in particular, are often associated with the *nadaísta* movement in Colombia, which aimed to critique the values, institutions, and social mores of the time; yet, as Montes argues, this novel is much more than a simple exposition of *nadaísta* ideas: instead, as Montes demonstrates, this novel "revela una profunda crítica a la manera como los nadaístas se desentendía totalmente de los problemas socioeconómicos y políticos en una sociedad en crisis" (reveals a profound criticism of the way in which the nadaists completely ignored the socioeconomic and political problems of a society in crisis).[18]

Buitrago's subsequent works continue with her dual preoccupations with narrative experimentation and social commentary. Her second novel, *Cola de zorro* (Fox Tail, shortlisted for the Seix Barral prize in 1968), again has multiple narrative voices and engages in literary play, while also undertakinga critique of patriarchal values and foundational myths.[19] Her novel *Los pañamanes* (1979, The Panamanians), set in the fictitious islands of San Gregorio and Fortuna – clearly representing San Andrés and Providencia – mixes historical fact with fiction and provides a critique of the racial discourses associated with Colombia's nationhood. *Los amores de Afrodita* (1983, Aphrodite's Lovers) has been analyzed as a postmodern novel, in its parodying of melodrama and serialized fiction.[20] More recently, her novel *Bello animal* (2002, Beautiful Animal), set in Bogotá, narrates the story of a supermodel, Gema Brunés. This time Buitrago's critique is aimed at the vacuities of contemporary society and the increasing mass-mediatization of Bogotá; as Celis Salgado argues, in this novel "los publicistas, los empresarios de la televisión y del Internet, se erigen como los dioses de un nuevo orden, dominado por las redes de comunicaciones y de información" (the publicists, the television and Internet business people are erected as the gods of the new order, dominated by communication and information networks).[21]

Marvel Moreno (1939–95) is, despite her relatively small published output in her lifetime, seen along with Buitrago and Ángel as one of the most important women writers of the post-Boom.[22] Her short story collection *Algo tan feo en la vida de una señora de bien* (1980, Something So Ugly in the Life of a Well-to-Do Lady) deals with the societal expectations and conventions placed upon women and their attempts to express themselves outside of these confines. Stories within the collection such as "Oriane, tía Oriane" (Oriane, Aunt Oriane), about the awakening of a young girl's sexuality, demonstrate the tensions between social mores and the desires that transgress these.[23]

Moreno's sole published novel in her lifetime, *En diciembre llegaban las brisas* (1987, In December the Breezes Came), is set during a thirty-year period from the early 1950s to the late 1970s and is told through the narrative voice of Lina. The novel has been described as postmodernist, with its features including "an obsessive world, built around temporal and geographical distance; voices that are woven through polyphonic relations derived from orality and from individual and collective memory."[24] Of particular interest in the novel is the character-narrator Lina, who turns out to be an elusive figure and who reveals herself in the first person only in the novel's epilogue.[25] Moreno's last published book was a collection of short stories in 1992, *El encuentro y otros relatos* (The Encounter and Other Stories). Containing twelve short stories, all of which have women as their protagonists, the collection explores themes such as female sexuality and relationships between the sexes and frequently portrays the attempts of the female protagonists to define themselves as active subjects and not passive objects of a male gaze.

A contemporary of Ángel, Buitrago and Moreno, Helena Araújo (b. 1939) is perhaps best known for her essays and volumes of literary criticism, in particular her ground-breaking *La Scherezada Criolla: ensayos sobre escritura femenina latinoamericana* (1989, The Creole Shahrazad: Essays on Feminie Latin American Writings), but has published a number of significant short stories and novels from the 1970s onwards, which deal with the social mores of upper-class Colombian society, women's position within it, and the decadence of the upper classes. Her first novel, *Fiesta en Teusaquillo* (1981, Party in Teusaquillo), is set in Teusaquillo, one of the central barrios of Bogotá, and narrates the goings-on at a party attended by the upper class *bogotanos*. Written in an experimental style, the novel is told through multiple narrative voices of the various dispersed guests at the party and provides a biting critique of the upper-class milieu, revealing "el ambiente social en toda su decadencia" (the social environment in all of its decadence).[26]

After a gap of almost twenty years, Araújo's second novel, *Las cuitas de Carlota* (The Troubles of Carlota), was published in 2003 and is a type of Bildungsroman, with the narrative told through a series of letters written by Carlota to her cousin. Through an intimate and confessional tone, the story tells of Carlota's life, detailing her pregnancies, the births of her children, and the breakdown of her marriage. As Pérez Sastre argues, while the protagonist initially appears weighed down by her responsibilities and by what life has thrown at her, she increasingly grows in self-awareness, with, at the end, the way out for the protagonist being language and self-expression itself.[27]

Born in the same decade as Araújo but coming somewhat later in life to writing was Helena Iriarte (1937), whose first novel, *¿Recuerdas Juana?* (Remember Juana?) was published in 1989. This novel is written in the second person and portrays the memories of the young protagonist, Juana, utilizing a form of interior dialogue as the narrative voice.[28] Iriarte's next novel, *Frente al mar que no te alcanza* (1998, In Front of the Ocean That Does Not Reach You), is narrated from the perspective of the protagonist, María, and takes the form of letters written by her to her sister Laura, again focusing on identity and memory. *La huella de una espera* (2004, The Trace of a Wait) tells of the life of Marian and her family in the changing landscape of Bogotá of the mid–twentieth century, while *Llegar hasta tu olvido* (2006, Until Arriving at Your Forgetfulness) is an emotional tale of a young woman whose mother has lost her memory and recounts the daughter's attempts to recover memories of the past. Iriarte's most recent novel, *El llamado del silencio* (2011, The Call of Silence), again focuses on memories and remembering, with the protagonist Adelaida deciding to undertake a journey as a form of remembering her past.

The late twentieth century

After the post-Boom generation, the last two decades of the twentieth century saw the rise to prominence of women writers who have combined their journalistic investigations with fictional narrative. One such writer is Silva Galvis (1945–2009), who was active in journalism for much of her life, contributing to and having regular columns in a variety of Colombian newspapers and magazines. Galvis's first published novel was ¡*Viva Cristo Rey!* (1991, Live Christ the King!), a historical fiction set in the 1930s and dealing with the political intrigues and conflicts of the times. What was innovative about Galvis's approach in this novel is that she narrated the events not through the more conventional approach of focusing on the male protagonists, but instead told the stories predominantly through the perspective of women. Her second novel, *Sabor a mí* (1994, A Taste of Me), is set in the time period from the fall of the Laureano Gómez–led administration in 1953 to the fall of Rojas Pinilla's military government in 1957. Galvis narrates her story through the perspective of the two adolescent protagonists, Ana and Elena, who relate their growing up against a backdrop of the political turbulence of their country.

Three years later, Galvis published a short play, *De la caída de un ángel puro por culpa de un beso apasionado* (The Fall of a Pure Angel because of a Passionate Kiss), and five years after that another historical novel, *Soledad, conspiraciones y suspiros* (2002, Loneliness, Conspiracies, and Sighs), based on the life of Soledad Ramón. In this latter work, Galvis attempts to rescue the historical figure of Ramón, oft-vilified lover and wife of nineteenth-century Colombian president Rafael Núñez (1825–94), and she aims to "subvertir la historia oficial para (re)descubrir la figura liberal y rebelde de esta mujer" (subvert the official history to (re)discover the liberal figure and rebel which this woman was).[29] In 2006 Galvis's *La mujer que sabía demasiado* (The Woman Who Knew Too Much) was published, taking the form of a detective novel, and engaging in deliberate intertextual play with G. K. Chesterton's famous book *The Man Who Knew Too Much* (1922).[30] After Galvis's death a further novel, *Un mal asunto* (A Bad Issue), was published posthumously in 2009; it is set in contemporary Colombia, portraying a tale of corruption, conspiracy, and fraud. Although covering different timeframes, Galvis's various novels share concerns with uncovering hidden voices behind official histories on the one hand, and narrating the links between personal stories and wider political scenarios on the other.

Born five years after Galvis, Laura Restrepo (1950) has become one of the most prominent of Colombia's contemporary novelists. One of the main characteristics of Restrepo's work is the mixing of factual information and a semijournalistic mode of writing with fiction. Indeed, a common conceit in many of her novels is the figure of the journalist who sets out to investigate a particular phenomenon or issue (but who then, often, goes on to discover something else).

Her first published book was *Historia de un entusiasmo* (1986, History of an Enthusiasm), a chronicle that detailed Restrepo's own experiences in the peace process in Colombia in 1982. Following this, *La isla de la pasión* (1989, The Island of Passion) was a novel set on the desert island of Clipperton, some 500 miles off the Mexican coast, and portrays the hardships of the small community of inhabitants who are condemned to scrape a living on the inhospitable island. The story is partly based on real-life events and, as Davies argues, this novel is "notable for its New Historical features such as its self-conscious preoccupation with the relationship between history and fiction."[31] Her subsequent novel, *El leopardo al sol* (1993, Leopard in the Sun), told the story of a feud between two familias, the Barragáns and their cousins, the Monsalves, and had an experimental narrative format, with contrasting narrative voices that often conveyed diverse points of view, described by Cardona López as a "forma dialogada." (dialogued form)[32] *Dulce compañía* (Sweet Company), which followed two years later, tells the tale of a journalist sent to a poor barrio in Bogotá to investigate rumors of the arrival of an angel within the midst of the residents.

La novia oscura (1999, The Dark Bride) is set in 1940s Colombia in a northeastern town in the midst of the oil boom, identified by Davies as Barrancabermeja,[33] and narrates the attempts by a female journalist to uncover the story of one of the most famous prostitutes of that era, Sayonara. Again, this text is made up of competing and divergent voices, and Lindsay has argued that in its constant oscillation between past and present this novel represents trauma – both the personal trauma of Sayonara and the trauma of the nation.[34] Restrepo's subsequent novel, *La multitud errante* (2001, A Tale of the Dispossessed), focused on the effects of violence and displacement on the population and intertwined the experiences of internally displaced peoples with a love story. Her next novel, *Delirio* (2004, Delirium), tells the story of Agustina and her sudden descent into madness and the attempts of her boyfriend, Aguilar, to discover the reasonsfor her delirium. Again, the novel has multiple narratives, and Agustina's madness has been widely interpreted as an allegory for Colombia, with her trauma representing the collective trauma of the nation. In *Demasiados heroes* (2009, Too Many Heroes) Restrepo narrates the story of a young man, Mateo, who attempts to discover the whereabouts of his father, a former militant during the Argentine *guerra sucia* of the 1970s.The novel also has several narrative levels and takes the form of a dialogue between a Colombian novelist, a political activist, and her son. Her most recent novel, *Hot sur* (2012, Hot South), is set in the United States and portrays the life of María Paz, a Colombian immigrant whose husband is murdered, and is again narrated through competing narrative voices.

In a similar fashion to Galvis and Restrepo, Patricia Lara (1951) has been active in journalism while also venturing into fictional genres. Her first book that crossed over to the literary was *Las mujeres en la guerra* (The Women in the War), which won the Planeta Prize for journalism in 2000. The book narrates the experiences of nine women who have in different ways been directly affected by the violence in Colombia and is based on interviews Lara held with them. Lara's 2005 novel, *Amor enemigo* (Enemy Love), continues with her interest in women's relationships and political violence, this time pitting a young *guerillera* against a paramilitary. *Hilo de sangre azul* (2009) (Thread of Blue Blood), her most recent novel, is a thriller set in an apartment block in the north of Bogotá.

Other writers of this period, although not influenced by journalistic style in the same way as Galvis, Restrepo, and Lara, include Carmen Cecilia Suárez (1946), who has become a leading writer of *microrrelato* fiction. Her published collections of short stories include *Un vestido rojo para bailar boleros* (1988, A Red Dress to Dance Boleros), which includes more than thirty-five short stories, each lasting no more than a couple of pages; *Cuento de amor en cinco actas* (1997, Love Stories in Five Acts), encompassing ten very short stories; and *La otra mitad de la vida* (2002, The Other Half of Life), comprising twelve short stories. Throughout all her short stories, Suárez focuses on the relationships between men and women, often related from unusual perspectives or including unexpected twists. Born a decade later than Suárez, Nana Rodríguez Romero (b. 1956) has also published numerous collections of poetry and *microrrelatos*, including *La casa ciega y otras ficciones* (2000, The Blind House and Other Fictions). Rodríguez Romero's stories take a much less realist stance than Suárez's and tend to be characterized by their surreal, oneiric qualities, with the fantastic often intermingling seamlessly with the quotidian.

Writing both short stories and novels, Consuelo Triviño (1956) was born in Bogotá in 1956 and moved to Madrid in 1983, where she has lived since, apart from a three-year period in Bogotá in the late 1980s. She published a collection of short stories in 1976 and subsequently her first novel in 1998, *Prohibido salir a la calle* (Prohibited to Go onto the Street), which was shortlisted for the Eduardo Caballero Calderón Prize. This novel is set in Bogotá and is narrated from the perspective of eleven-year-old Clara, the novel's protagonist; the novel takes the form of a Bildungsroman, depicting Clara's house, her family, and her growing up, and ending with the moment in which she is about to be sent away to boarding school. Yet the novel does not provide a reaffirmation of family life; as Bados Ciria argues, this novel in fact "cuestiona la imagen de la familia nuclear y feliz reafirmada por la clase burguesa colombiana, una imagen que ha servido para cohesionar una visión de nación homogénea" (questions the image of the nuclear, happy family reinforced by the Colombian bourgeoise class, an image which has served to draw together a vision of a homogenous nation)[35]

Triviño's next book was a collection of short stories, *La casa imposible* (2005, The Impossible House), which brought together nineteen stories that narrate tales of loss, frustration, and suffering. Her next novel, *La semilla de la ira* (2008) (The Seed of Anger), is a fictionalized account of the life of the turn-of-the-century Colombian author José María Vargas Vila (1860- 1933). Based loosely on fragments on Vargas Vila's diary, the novel is narrated in first person and conveys the life of the protagonist and the *belle époque* society of which he formed a part. Triviño's latest novel, *Una isla en la luna* (2009, An Island on the Moon), has an urban setting and narrates the lives of various characters and their attempts at self-definition and youthful rebellion.

Into the twenty-first century

At the turn of the century, new generations of women writers are coming to the fore, some combining journalism or academia with a writing career, and others turning to the fiction genre as an effective route to publication. Of the former, Margarita Posada (1978) has worked as a journalist for various magazines and newspapers in Colombia and in 2005 published her first novel, *De esta agua no beberé* (From This Water I Will Not Drink), a portrayal of the life of the upper classes of Colombia, painting a picture of drugs, decadence, and moral vacuity. Her second novel, *Sin título [1977]* (2008, Without Title [1977]) is about the experiences of Magdalena, an artist, and her attempts to combine her artistic dreams with the reality of marriage and children.

Her contemporary Carolina Sanín (b. 1973) has similarly combined an academic career and journalism with her career as a writer. Her first novel, *Todo en otra parte* (Everything in Another Part), was published in 2005 and narrates the experiences of Carlota, who decides to give up her job to travel the world. Five years later, Sanín published *Ponqué y otros cuentos* (2010, Ponqué and Other Stories), a collection of eight short stories that include a mixture of realist and fantastical elements. Her most recent novel, *Los niños* (2014, The Children), narrates the story of the protagonist Laura, who discovers an abandoned child on the street outside her apartment and the growing relationship between them. More recently, María Paz Ruiz Gil (1978) published a volume of *microrrelatos* in 2011, and her first novel in 2012, *Soledad, una colombiana en Madrid* (Soledad, a Colombian in Madrid), a semiautobiographical piece about a young Colombian woman trying to make a living in Madrid.

Of the authors who focus on genre fiction, undoubtedly the most commercially successful has been Ángela Becerra (b. 1957). After a collection of poems in 2001, entitled *Alma abierta* (Open Soul), Becerra published her first novel in 2003, *De los amores negados* (Of Denied Loves), and has subsequently become one of the best-selling women authors of Latin America. Her self-styled mode of "idealismo mágico" involves, in the words of the author herself, putting "la magia al servicio de las emociones,"[36] (the magic in the service of emotions) and her novels combine a mostly urban setting with passionate love stories, with her characters constantly in search of their soul mate. Her accessible style, focus on the emotions, and reliance on many of the stock devices of the popular romance story, such as unrequited love, plot twists, and love at first sight, have led her work to be frequently classified as *novela rosa*.[37]

As can be seen from this discussion, women's writing in Colombia cannot be subsumed into one genre, and the various writers discussed here have published in genres as diverse as the *crónica*, the novel, poetry, drama, the short story, and the *microrrelato*. Nor can these writers be grouped into one generation or movement, since their works span nearly two centuries, and each writer takes differing stances – sometimes oppositional – to the predominant literary movements of their times. Similarly, we cannot necessarily identify shared stylistic features across all these writers, with some engaging in deliberately difficult experimental writing, others opting for a direct, accessible writing style, and still others choosing to resurrect colloquial speech within their works.

That said, what this overview of women writers in Colombia allows us to do is to trace certain commonalities within and across generations. Thus, for the post-Boom generation, for instance, we can draw out a shared focus among the works of Ángel, Buitrago, and Moreno on the questioning of language and literary representation itself on the one hand, and the questioning of women's identity on the other. For those writers from the last decades of the twentieth century, we can observe a shift toward journalistic tropes and the new historical novel. There are even some formats that cross generations, such as the Bildungsroman, which has been put to effect (and called into question) by women writers across the generations. The richness and variety of the writing discussed in this chapter is a testament to the sustained contribution that women writers have made and continue to make to Colombia's literary heritage.

BIBLIOGRAPHY

Abdala Mesa, Yohainna. "El engranaje del tiempo en las novelas de Marvel Moreno." *Caravelle*, no. 84 (2005): 235–46.

Acosta, Soledad. *Una nueva lectura,* ed. Montserrat Ordóñez. Bogotá: Ediciones Fondo Cafetero, 1988.

Aguirre, Beatriz. "Soledad Acosta de Samper y su performance narrativo de la nación." *Estudios de Literatura Colombiana* 6 (2000). 18–43.

Ángel, Albalucía. *Los girasoles en invierno*. Bogotá: Linotipia Bolívar, 1970.

   Dos veces Alicia Barcelona: Seix Barral, 1972.

   Estaba la pájara pinta sentada en el verde limón. Bogotá: Instituto Colombiano de Cultura, 1975.

   ¡O Gloria inmarcesible! Bogotá: Instituto Colombiano de Cultura.

   Misiá Señora. Barcelona: Argos Vergara. 1982.

   Las andariegas. Barcelona: Argos Vergara. 1984.

   "Siete lunas y un espejo." In *Voces en escena: antología de dramaturgas latinoamericanas*, ed. Nora Eidelberg and María Mercedes Jaramillo. Medellín: Universidad de Antioquia, 1991. 13–79.

   Tierra de nadie. Bogotá: Proceditor, 2002.

Araújo, Helena. *La 'M' de las moscas*. Bogotá: Tercer Mundo, 1970.

   Fiesta en Teusaquillo. Bogotá: Plaza y Janés. 1981.

   La Scherezada criolla: ensayos sobre escritura feminina latinoamericana. Bogotá: Universidad Nacional de Colombia, Bogotá. 1989.

   Las cuitas de Carlota. Barcelona: March Editor. 2003.

   "Aída Martínez y Silvia Galvis: del documento al relato y de la ficción a la historia." *Literatura: Teoría, Historia, Crítica* 8 (2006): 143–63.

Arbaiza, Diana. "Spain as Archive: Constructing a Colombian Modernity in the Writings of Soledad Acosta de Samper." *Journal of Latin American Cultural Studies: Travesia* 21, no. 1 (2012): 123–44.

Bados Ciria, Concepción. "Consuelo Triviño: una narradora transatlántica." *Revista Hispanoamericana*, no. 3. http://revista.raha.es.

Becerra, Ángela. *Alma abierta*. Barcelona: Planeta, 2001.

De los amores negados. Bogotá: Villegas, 2003.

El penúltimo sueño. Bogotá: Villegas, 2005.

Lo que le falta al tiempo. Bogotá: Villegas, 2006.

Ella, que todo lo tuvo. Bogotá: Villegas, 2009.

Memorias de un sinvergüenza de siete suelas. Bogotá: Villegas, 2013.

Berg, Mary G. "Sofía Opsina de Navarro: la voz de la abuela que cuenta." In *Literatura y diferencia: escritoras colombianas del siglo XX*, vol. 1, ed. María Mercedes Jaramillo, Betty Osorio de Negret, and Ángela Inés Robledo. Bogotá: Ediciones Uniandes, 1995a. 56–75.

"Las novelas de Elisa Mújica." In *Literatura y diferencia: escritoras colombianas del siglo XX*, vol. 1, ed. María Mercedes Jaramillo, Betty Osorio de Negret, and Ángela Inés Robledo. Bogotá: Ediciones Uniandes, 1995b. 208–28.

Borsò, Vittoria. "La escritura femenina en Colombia en la década de los 80." In *La novela colombiana ante la crítica*, ed. Luz Mery Giraldo B. Cali: Universidad del Valle, 1994. 71–95.

Buitrago, Fanny. *El hostigante verano de los dioses*. Bogotá: Espiral, 1963.

El hombre de paja y Las distancias doradas. Bogotá: Espiral, 1964.

Cola de zorro. Bogotá: Monolito, 1970.

La otra gente: cuentos. Bogotá: Instituto Colombiano de Cultura, 1973.

Bahía sonora: relatos de la isla. Bogotá: Instituto Colombiano de Cultura, 1976.

Los pañamanes. Barcelona: Plaza y Janés, 1979.

Los amores de Afrodita. Barcelona: Plaza y Janés, 1983.

Los fusilados de ayer. Badajoz: Badajos Ayuntamiento, 1986.

¡Líbranos de todo mal! Bogotá: Carlos Valencia Editores, 1989.

Señora de la miel. Bogotá: Arango Editores, 1993.

Bello animal. Bogotá: Editorial Planeta, 2002.

Cardona López, José. "Literatura y narcotráfico: Laura Restrepo, Fernando Vallejo, Darío Jaramillo Agudelo." In *Literatura y cultura: narrativa colombiana del siglo XX*, vol. 2, ed. María Mercedes Jaramillo, Betty Osorio de Negret, and Ángela Inés Robledo. Bogotá: Ministerio de Cultura, 2000. 378–406.

Castellanos Llanos, Gabriela. "Maruja Vieira: la mujer en la poeta." In, *Literatura y diferencia: escritoras colombianas del siglo XX*, vol. 1, ed. María Mercedes Jaramillo, Betty Osorio de Negret, and Ángela Inés Robledo. Bogotá: Ediciones Uniandes, 1995. 150–66.

Celis Salgado, Nadia. "El imperio de las imágenes: la fotografía y el simulacro de la nación en Bello animal de Fanny Buitrago." *Cuadernos de literatura del Caribe e Hispanoamérica* 2 (2005), 43–56.

"La traición de la belleza: cuerpos, deseo y subjetividad femenina en Fanny Buitrago y Mayra Santos-Febres." *Chasqui* 37, no. 2 (2008), 88–105.

Davis, Lloyd Hughes. "Imperfect Portraits of a Postcolonial Heroine: Laura Restrepo's La novia oscura." *Modern Language Review* 102 (2007), 1035–52.

"Laura Restrepo (1950-)." In *A Companion to Latin American Women Writers*, ed. Brígida Pastor and Lloyd Hughes Davies. London: Tamesis, 2012. 197–211.

Delmar, Meira. *Alba del olvido*. Barranquilla: Editorial Mejoras, 1942.

Sitio de amor. Barranquilla: Editorial Mejoras, 1944.

Verdad del sueño. Barranquilla: Editorial Arte, 1946.

Secreta isla. Barranquilla: Editorial Arte, 1951.

Huésped sin sombra. Bogotá: Ediciones de la Revista Ximénez de Quesada, 1971.

Laúd memorioso. Bogotá: Carlos Valencia, 1995.

Alguien pasa. Bogotá: Carlos Valencia, 1998.

Díaz-Ortiz, Oscar A. "Dualidades femeninas en Soledad: conspiraciones y suspiros de Silva Galvis." *Estudios de Literatura Colombiana* 22 (2008), 47–61.

Flórez García, Mónica María. "La mujer que sabía demasiado, de Silvia Galvis: el móvil detrás de la historiografía metaficcional." *Estudios de Literatura Colombiana*, 31 (2012), 197–211.

Garavito, Carmen Lucía. "Ideología y estructuras narrativas en *Algo tan feo en la vida de una señora bien* de Marvel Moreno." In *Literatura y diferencia: escritoras colombianas del siglo XX*, vol. 1, ed. María Mercedes Jaramillo, Betty Osorio de Negret, and Ángela Inés Robledo. Bogotá: Ediciones Uniandes, 1995. 399–421.

Garzón, María Teresa. "'Pero en mi soledad estaré tranquila': blanquitud y resistencia en Dolores, de Soledad Acosta." *El Cotidiano* 184 (2014), 23–30.

Giraldo B., Luz Mery. "Fanny Buitrago: de relatos y retratos." In *La novela colombiana ante la crítica 1975–1990*, ed. Luz Mery Giraldo B. Bogotá: Centro Editorial Javeriano, 1994. 203–16.

Gómez Ocampo, Gilberto. "Soledad Acosta de Samper 1833–1913: Colombian Prose Writer." In *Encyclopedia of Latin American Literature*, ed. Verity Smith. London: Fitzroy Dearborn, 1997. 1–2.

Gutiérrez Mavesoy, Aleyda. "Cola de zorro: ¿otra hierba mala del Caribe?" *Cuadernos de Literatura del Caribe e Hispanoamérica* 2 (2005), 70–80.

Iriarte, Helena. *¿Recuerdas Juana?* Bogotá: Carlos Valencia, 1989.

Frente al mar que no te alcanza. Bogotá: I/M Editores, 1989.

La huella de una espera. Bucaramanga: Editorial, 2004.

Llegar hasta tu olvido. Bogotá: I/M Editores, 2006.

El llamado del silencio. Bogotá: Babel, 2011.

Isaza, Blanca. *Selva florida*. Manizales: Renacimiento, 1917.

Jaramillo, María Mercedes. "Albalucía Ángel: el discurso de la insubordinación." In *¿Y las mujeres? ensayos sobre literatura colombiana*, ed. María Mercedes Jaramillo, Ángela Inés Robledo, and Flor María Rodríguez-Arenas. Medellín: Universidad de Antioquia, 1991. 203–38.

La poética amorosa de Meira Delmar." In *Literatura y diferencia: escritoras colombianas del siglo XX*, vol. 1, María Mercedes Jaramillo, Betty Osorio de Negret and Ángela Inés Robledo. Bogotá: Ediciones Uniandes, 1995. 131–49.

"La influencia sufí en la obra de Meira Delmar." *Revista de Estudios Colombianos* 22 (2001), 41–6.

Jaramillo, María Mercedes, and Betty Osorio. "La poética de Meira Delmar: belleza y conocimiento." In *Meira Delmar: poesía y prosa*, ed. María Mercedes Jaramillo, Betty Osorio, and Ariel Castillo Meir. Barranquilla: Ediciones Uninorte, 2003. 15–40.

Keefe Ugalde, Sharon. "Between "In Longer" and "Not Yet": Women's Space in *Misiá señora.*" *Revista de Estudios Colombianos* 1 (1986), 23–8.

Lara, Patricia. *Las mujeres en la guerra* Bogotá: Planeta, 2000.

Amor enemigo. Barcelona: Seix Barral, 2005.

Hilo de sangre azul. Bogotá: Norma, 2009.

Lindsay, Claire. ""Clear and Present Danger": Trauma, Memory, and Laura Restrepo's La novia oscura." *Hispanic Research Journal* 4, no. 1 (2003), 41–58.

Luque de Peña, Myriam. "Helena Araújo: la búsqueda de un lenguaje femenino." In *Literatura y diferencia: escritoras colombianas del siglo XX*, vol. 1, María Mercedes Jaramillo, Betty Osorio de Negret, and Ángela Inés Robledo. Bogotá: Ediciones Uniandes, 1995. 342–71.

Montaña Cuellar, Jimena. "Su lectura es como visitar un salón de belleza seis veces en una semana: De los amores negados, Ángela Becerra." *Boletín Cultural y Biográfico* 42 (2005), 143–4.

Montes, Elizabeth. "El cuestionamiento de los mecanismos de representación en la novelística de Fanny Buitrago." In *Literatura y diferencia: escritoras colombianas del siglo XX*, vol. 1, María Mercedes Jaramillo, Betty Osorio de Negret, and Ángela Inés Robledo. Bogotá: Ediciones Uniandes, 1995. 322–41.

Moreno, Marvel. *Algo tan feo en la vida de una señora de bien.* Bogotá: Editorial Pluma, 1980.

En diciembre llegaban las brisas. Barcelona: Plaza y Janés, 1987.

El encuentro y otros relatos. Bogotá: Áncora, 1992.

Mujica, Elisa. *Los dos tiempos.* Bogotá: Iqueima, 1949.

Ángela y el diablo. Bogotá: Aguilar, 1953.

Catalina. Madrid: Aguilar, 1963.

Bogotá de las nubes. Bogotá: Tercer Mundo, 1984.

Ordóñez, Montserrat. "Elisa Mújica novelista: del silencio a la historia, por la palabra." *Revista de Crítica Literaria Latinoamericana* 13 (1987), 123–36.

"One Hundred Years of Unread Writing: Soledad Acosta, Elisa Mujica and Marvel Moreno." In *Knives and Angels: Women Writers in Latin America*, ed. Susan Bassnett. London: Zed Books, 1990. 132–44.

Osorio de Negret, Betty. "La narrativa de Albalucía Ángel, o la creación de una identidad femenina." In *Literatura y diferencia: escritoras colombianas del siglo XX*, vol. 1, ed. María Mercedes Jaramillo, Betty Osorio de Negret, and Inés Robledo Bogotá: Uniandes, 1995. 372–98.

"Bogotá de las nubes: el surgimiento de un sujeto femenino en Colombia." In *Elisa Mujica*, ed. Ana Cecilia Ojeda. Bucaramanga: Universidad Industrial de Santander, 2007. 157–70.

Ospina de Navarro, Sofía. *Cuentos y crónicas.* Medellín: Tipografía Industrial, 1926.

Pérez Sastre, Paloma, and Claudia Ivonne Giraldo G. "¿Cómo hallar esa palabra que soy yo misma? acerca de la obra de Helena Araújo." *Revista Universidad de Antioquia* 280 (2005), 68–83.

Posada, Margarita. *De esta agua no beberé.* Bogotá: Ediciones B., 1995.

Sin título [1977]. Bogotá: Alfaguara, 2008.

Restrepo, Laura. *Historia de una traición* (later republished as *Historia de un entusiasmo*). Bogotá: Plaza y Janés, 1986.

La isla de la pasión. Bogotá: Planeta, 1989.

El leopardo al sol. Bogotá: Norma, 1993.

Dulce compañía. Bogotá: Norma, 1995.

La novia oscura. Bogotá: Norma, 1999.

La multitud errante. Bogotá: Planeta, 2001.

Delirio. Madrid: Alfaguara, 2004.

Demasiados héroes. Madrid: Alfaguara, 2009.

Hot sur. Barcelona: Planeta, 2012.

Robledo, Ángela I. "El mercado como razón de ser de cierta escritura femenina: Ángela Becerra o el amor que vende." In *Independencia, independencias y espacios culturales: diálogos de historia y literatura,* ed. Carmen Elisa Acosta Peñalosa, César Augusto Ayala Diago , and Henry Alberto Cruz Villalobos. Bogotá: Universidad Nacional de Colombia, 2009. 389–401.

Rodríguez Romero, Nana. *Hojas en mutación.* Tunja: Instituto de Cultura de Boyacá, 1996.

La casa ciega y otras ficciones. Bogotá: Cooperativa Editorial Magisterio, 2000a.

El sabor del tiempo: minificciones. Tunja: Colibrí, 2000b.

Efecto mariposa: minificciones. Tunja: Colibrí, 2004.

Sanín, Carolina. *Todo en otra parte.* Bogotá: Planeta, 2005.

Ponqué y otros cuentos. Bogotá: Norma, 2010.

Los niños. Laguna, 2014.

Suárez, Carmen Cecilia. *Un vestido rojo para bailar boleros.* Bogotá: Pijao, 1988.

Cuento de amor en cinco actos. Bogotá: Arango, 1997.

La otra mitad de la vida. Bogotá: Serpiente Emplumada, 2002.

Taylor, Claire. *Bodies and Texts: Configurations of Identity in the Works of Griselda Gambaro, Albalucía Ángel, and Laura Esquivel.* Leeds: Modern Humanities Research Association, 2003.

"Wandering Texts and Theories in Albalucía Ángel's Las andariegas." *Tesserae/ Journal of Iberian and Latin American Studies* 12, no. 2 (2006), 247–59.

"Between Science Fiction and a Travelogue: Albalucía Ángel's Tierra de nadie." *La Manzana de la Discordia* 4, no. 2 (2009), 7–14.

Triviño, Consuelo. *Prohibido salir a la calle.* Bogotá: Planeta, 1998.

La casa imposible. Madrid: Verbum, 2005.

La semilla de la ira. Bogotá: Seix Barral, 2008.

Una isla en la luna. Murcia: Alfaqueque, 2009.

Vallejo, Catharina. "Dichotomy and Dialectic: Soledad Acosta de Samper's Una holandesa en América and the Canon." *Monographic Review/Revista Monográfica* 12 (1997), 273–85.

Velasco González, Gloria. "Blanca Isaza o la serena virtud de las palabras." In *Literatura y diferencia: escritoras colombianas del siglo XX*, vol. 1, María Mercedes Jaramillo, Betty Osorio de Negret, and Inés Robledo. Bogotá: Uniandes, 1995. 76–91.

Vieira, Maruja. *Campanario de lluvia*. Bogotá: Editorial Iqueima, 1947.

Notes

1 See Garzón (2009).
2 Gomez Ocampo (1997:2).
3 See Vallejo (1997).
4 Berg (1995b:59).
5 Jaramillo and Osorio (2003:18).
6 See Jaramillo (2001).
7 See Castellanos Llanos (1995).
8 See Velasco González (1995).
9 Ordóñez (1987:130).
10 See Osorio (2007:159).
11 Borsò (1994:197).
12 See Osorio (1995:375).
13 See Taylor (2003).
14 Keefe Ugalde (1986:26).
15 See Taylor (2006).
16 See Taylor (2009).
17 Montes (1995:324).
18 Montes (1995:327).
19 See Gutiérrez Mavesoy (2005).
20 See Giraldo B. (1994:206).
21 Celis Salgado (2005:45).
22 Abdala Mesa (2005:235).
23 Garavito (1995:407).
24 Ordóñez (1990).
25 See Abdala Mesa (2005).
26 Luque de Peña (1995:362).
27 Perez Sastre (2005:73).
28 Borsò (1994:194).
29 Díaz-Ortiz (2008:49).
30 See Flórez García (2012) for more on this.
31 Davies (2012:197).
32 Cardona López (2000:385).
33 Davies (2007:1038).
34 Lindsay (2003:48, 50).
35 Bados Ciria (2013).
36 Robledo (2009:394).
37 See Robledo (2009); Montaña Cuellar (2005).

CHAPTER 17

Colombian queer narrative

Gina Ponce de León

Introduction

I would like to begin with a quote from the scholar of Colombian literature J. Eduardo Jaramillo-Zuluaga (1957–2008), in which he states that the greatest pleasure in reviewing recent Colombian narrative is returning to previously known works; in doing so, we restore the certainty of our perplexity. He refers to the greatest pleasure of literature as the moment in which one revisits these past texts; in exploring a different meaning, they betray the interpretations attributed to them in previous readings. Needless to say, understanding the representation of contemporary queer narrative in Colombia continues to enlighten us today about issues that concerned the earliest Colombian queer writers.

The word "perplexity" is accurate in describing the extraordinary literary production and cultural work that queer writer Porfirio Barba Jacob produced in his poetry in the early twentieth century. He was an extraordinary poet and has been followed and never forgotten for his contributions to Colombian literature. Marta Elena Casaús Arzú appropriately describes some of his pursuits as follows:

> Participó con el pseudónimo de Ricardo Arenal, en varios diarios guatemaltecos entre ellos, el *Diario de Centroamérica, El Demócrata* y *Nuestro Diario.* Desde que inició su trabajo en Guatemala tenía la obsesión de crear una nueva revista *Ideas y Noticias,* bajo el amparo del director de *El Imparcial,* Alejandro Córdova.

> [Under the pseudonym of Ricardo Arenal, Porfirio Barba Jacob contributed to several Guatemalan newspapers including *Diario de Centroamérica, El Demócrata* and *Nuestro Diario.* From the start of his work in Guatemala, he was obsessed with creating a new magazine *Ideas y Noticias,* under the patronage of the director of *El Imparcial,* Alejandro Córdova. (2011:96)]

He was a gay writer at a time when being homosexual was considered a disgrace and reason enough to be alienated from mainline Colombian society. His great poems describe a deep anxiety that can be understood as a state of being "displaced," a feeling about which other Colombian queer writers have written in a variety of texts. Some queer writers have chosen exile to other countries as the solution. I define "exile" as a *condition* for queer authors, given that many queer Colombian writers have lived or are living in exile. Exile can be understood not only as leaving one's country, but also leaving small towns for large cities, or leaving the nuclear family for different groups that are more receptive. Exile can involve the need to leave the sociocultural environment that is the source of alienation. Exile is an act of what these writers' works are representing. This concept of "exile" is apparent in the last stanza of one of Barba Jacob's most famous poems, "Canción de la vida profunda":

> Mas hay también ¡Oh Tierra! un día ... un día ... un día ...
> en que levamos anclas para jamás volver ...
> Un día en que discurren vientos ineluctables
> ¡un día en que ya nadie nos puede retener!
> (But there is also, Oh Land! A day... a day... a day...
> in which shall weigh anchors to never return
> A day in which the inescapable winds will blow
> a day in which no one will be able to hold us as prisoners!)

This stanza illustrates how one day one has to leave, never to return; one day the inescapable winds arrive, and then, one does not need to hold on any more. These words express the feeling of exile and, more specifically, exile in Colombian queer writing of the twentieth century.

Queer topics in Colombian narrative represent a major breakthrough within a national cultural scenario that has been historically patriarchal and in which gender identity has been determined in accordance with what has been considered acceptable in mainline society. The topic of patriarchy has been mainly studied in association with feminist issues, but patriarchy marks the rules for gender performance in Colombian society. In her chapter "Feminist Criticism," Lois Tyson comments on how women have interiorized the gender role: "By *patriarchal woman* I mean, of course, a woman who has internalized the norms and values of patriarchy, which can be defined, in short, as any culture that privileges ... traditional gender roles" (2006:85). Queer topics can be approached from the standpoint of gender roles: the way in which one is expected to perform within a particular gender tradition.

Colombian society has adapted to this traditional gender "perform-ance," and, therefore, what does not fit the traditional definition of gender has been considered a deviation. This statement is foundational for the representation of queer issues in Colombian narrative. The representation of queer topics has had different approaches in different historical periods. For writers of the early twentieth century, there was no open declaration of their being gay; therefore, it was not the focus of their work. The result can be seen as a concealed representation of their sexual orientation. Consequently, there are relatively few known and widely recognized queer Colombian writers from the early twentieth century.

This silent attitude is related to a defiance concerning not only sexual orientation, but also the problems of Colombian society. In this context two of the most prominent queer Colombian writers are José María Vargas Vila, an early twentieth-century writer, and Fernando Vallejo, a late twentieth-century writer who began publishing in the late 1980s. Their defiant attitude can be considered part of queer narrative of the twentieth century.

Since the late twentieth century and well into the twenty-first, it is obvious that the globalization of Western civilization has allowed for the queer lifestyle to become less defiant in Colombian queer representation; these lifestyles have moved toward a level of increased "suitability" and many of these people have established a certain level of recognition inside their sociocultural contexts. One should recognize the contributions of Fernando Molano Vargas, a young writer who epitomized this change within Colombian society, but who passed away in 1998 at the age of thirty-six.

Colombian queer narrative has referred to specific Colombian authors that have been recognized as "gay" writers. In order to analyze Colombian queer representation, one should differentiate gay writers from queer representation. Gay writers have been categorized in Colombian literature. Nevertheless, queer representation in contemporary Colombian narrative involves a broader and more complex sociocultural scenario of Colombian society.

Understanding queer representation: the Colombian context

Analyzing queer representation brings forth the issue of using a term that is useful in the sociocultural context – deviance. Eve Kosofsky explains in her book *Tendencies*:

> Queer is a continuing moment, movement, motive – recurrent, eddying, *troublant*. The word "queer" itself means *across* – it comes from the Indo-European root -twerkw, which also yields the German quer (transverse),

Latin *torquere* (to twist), English *athwart*. . . . The immemorial current that *queer* represents is antiseparatist as it is anti-assimilationist. Keenly, it is relational, and strange. Besides acknowledging that the etymological roots of queer are relational and strange, the usage of 'queer' to define sexual deviance, especially that of male homosexuals, was first recorded in the late nineteenth century. (1994:xii)

Colombian queer narrative focuses on texts that represent this "deviance" within the sociocultural and traditional patriarchy of Colombian society. As mentioned above, in order to analyze queer representation in Colombian narrative it is necessary to understand patriarchy in Colombian society. Considering Maite Escudero-Alías's approach to the meaning of the term "queer," we can see how the use of the term already situates the texts in a marginal situation: "Since its appearance in the English language in the sixteenth century, the term 'queer' has generally meant 'strange' or 'unusual'. Despite these meanings, the trespassing character of queer is evident from its very origins" (2009:390).

These early definitions of the term "queer" can be applied to the contemporary Colombian patriarchal context in which queer issues are, as stated earlier, a "deviance" from the patriarchal order. The sociocultural environment in Colombia has profoundly marked its society, which has been delimited by social norms. The attitude of Colombian society toward queer issues is as repressive today as it has been historically. Today, the "acceptance" of homosexuality inside the sociocultural context is deceptive. In practice, laws and regulations delineate the unacceptability of homosexuality in Colombian society.

In a review of the Colombian legal history of Lesbian, Gay, Bisexual, and Transsexual (LGBT) persons, Diana Carolina Pinzón Mejía and Julián Eduardo Prada Uribe have carried out a thorough and in-depth study titled "Algunas consideraciones sobre la adopción homoparental en el ordenamiento jurídico colombiano" in which they assert the following:

La caracterización jurídica de los asuntos sexuales es reciente, de modo que su confrontación sorprende todavía. Los derechos de la comunidad LGBT han experimentado un progresivo respaldo legislativo y jurisprudencial en cuanto a la legalidad de la orientación homosexual, la no-discriminación por dicha preferencia, el reconocimiento de las uniones homosexuales y los efectos patrimoniales y extrapatrimoniales subsiguientes. No obstante, en materia de adopción homoparental ha prevalecido la evasión a cualquier razonamiento.

[The legal characterization of sexual matters [in Colombia] is recent, so that their confrontation is still surprising. The LGBT community has experienced a progressive legislative and jurisprudential support in terms of the legality of homosexual orientation, nondiscrimination for such preference, the recognition of homosexual unions and the equal economic rights that heterosexual couples have with regard to property rights. However, the legal system has been avoiding decisions with regard to LGBT adoptions. (130–1)]

This suggests a contradiction in terms of the rights that the LGBT community has gained, and the legal denial to recognize the parental rights of gays. The LGBT community has experienced progressive legislative and jurisprudential support, but with respect to LGBT adoption, evasion has prevailed.

The article asserts that since 1980, a series of decrees were issued that protected the existence of gay relations and warned against discrimination in matters such as heritage, prison visits, and health insurance for couples who demonstrated cohabitation for more than two years (131). In 2008, the right to equality and pension were recognized, and "en el 2009, la Corte Constitucional decidió la modificación de 42 normas con el fin de alcanzar la equidad entre parejas heterosexuales y homosexuales, pero no hizo referencia a la adopción" (in 2009, the Constitutional Court decided on the modification of 42 rules with the goal to achieve equality between heterosexual and gay couples, but made no reference to adoption"; ibid.).

Since 2001, Colombia has undergone a significant transformation in terms of the rights of homosexuals. However, the refusal of the law to talk about the right of paternity or "homopaternity" underlines a fundamental contradiction within the ideology of equality and equity, which requires further legislative change. The Colombian Congress has confirmed the contradictions of the legal system in terms of gay rights, and Pinzón Mejía and Prada Uribe conclude the following:

> No existen *razones científicas* para oponerse a la adopción por parte de familias homoparentales, sino *más bien argumentos suficientes para respaldar su institucionalización*. Es inminente sincerar la legislación y eliminar los alegatos discriminatorios radicados en la preferencia sexual de cada ser humano, para responder merecidamente al interés superior de los niños, las niñas y los adolescentes.

> [There are no *scientific reasons* to oppose the adoption by homosexual families, but *rather sufficient arguments to support its institutionalization*. It is necessary for the law to be honest and remove discriminatory allegations based on the sexual preference of each human being, to respond worthily to the best interests of children and adolescents. (140)]

In Colombia, the law has evolved to try to accommodate international law. Nevertheless, LGBT groups experience a sense of failure when they compare their situation with other LGBT groups in the West that have achieved recognition through their fight against discrimination.

According to David William Foster, in an interview with W. Daniel Holcombe: "queered is a matter of degree, not a yes/no [or a] (+/−) proposition. Queer is a way of seeing the world, not an element of identity" (2012:209). In his dialogue with Holcombe, Foster affirms that, in his book *Nuestro ambiente,* he does not intend to "identificar a los escritores de los textos como gay, sino ... identificar producciones culturales que son de interés desde el punto de vista de las investigaciones queer" (identify the writers of the texts as gay, but ... to identify cultural productions that are of interest from the point of view of queer research; 2012:204). Foster's approach to queer issues is valuable in the sense that it allows us to look for the meaning of "deviance" as a cultural production. It is important to emphasize that my approach involves the analysis of representations that contextualize the specific meaning of "deviating" from the Colombian patriarchal context. As Maite Escudero-Alías has stated:

> Despite the fact that 'queer' signalled degradation and an aberrant sexuality, the term also became subject to positive re-signification and claimed its space as a legitimate word to name non-heterosexual identities some decades later. Thus, in 1990, the New York pride parade witnessed how a group of queers distributed a leaflet entitled 'Queer Read This', with the purpose of contesting the widespread pejorative connotations of the term 'queer'. (2009:391)

Colombian society has been receptive to western queer movements, and it is in the light of these movements that we can also contextualize Colombian patriarchal society. As indicated, Colombia belongs to the colonized countries of Latin America, and therefore, it is possible to establish the study of queer topics in a postcolonial theoretical context.

Theoretical approaches to queer Colombian literature

In his article "(Post)colonial, Queer: *Lord Jim,*" William Lee Hughes asserts that some critics "attempt to use the tools provided by each of these theories [Post-colonial and Queer] to better understand and critique texts" (2012:71). Some specific aspects of each of these theories can be used to understand the representation of queer topics in Colombian narrative. As I stated in *Twenty-first Century Latin American Narrative and*

Postmodern Feminism, "Nothing is more appropriate to defining postcolonial theory than the term 'heterogeneous,' which is irrevocably linked to its description" (2014:16). In this book, I used Michael Chapman's definition of Postcolonialism:

> postcolonialism has come to describe heterogeneous, though linked, groupings of critical enterprises: a critique of Western totalizing narratives; a revision of the Marxian class project; utilization of both post-structural enquiry (the displaced linguistic subject) and postmodern pursuit (skepticism of the truth claims of Cartesian individualism); a marker of voices of pronouncement by non-resident, 'Third-World' intellectual cadres in 'First World' universities. (ibid.)

Postcolonial Colombia is still a country on the margins of Western civilization. Therefore, queer representations not only belong to an already marginal context but possess a double marginalization because their subjects belong to the deviations inside the patriarchy. The idea of a double marginalization comes from Leela Gandhi's theory of the "double colonization" of women (1998:83), from her book *Postcolonial Theory: A Critical Introduction.* In my book, I use José Antonio Figueroa's term *humanismo periférico.*[1] Peripheral humanism recognizes a period of "Europeanization," and creates awareness that this is based on the legacy of the colonial heritage that traditionally has undermined the idea of liberation and the search for recognition. In addition, I propose in my book that Figueroa sets forth the following:

> Certain postcolonial contributions allow searching for practices in which groups situated in the periphery are claiming for modernity based on the criticism of their own cultural traditions. These approaches are recognizing the right to dissent and to cultural criticism as an inheritance of the humanist tradition built simultaneously in the centre and the periphery of modernity. Some post-colonial authors validate criticism toward cultural traditionalism, since they recognize that own traditionalism is a creation of the colonial or neo-colonial experience (Guha 1997; Spivak 1988). In these cases, rather than cry out for a subject that take shelter in its own tradition, it is valid to recognize deliberation, doubt, scepticism and irony toward culture by itself, as conditions for relocating peripheral groups in the present context. (2014:19–20)

The term "peripheral humanism" sets forth a dilemma related to the postcolonial condition. Contemporary queer Colombian narrative certainly is situated on a periphery. On the basis of the term "peripheral humanism," we speak also of "peripheral patriarchy," and in this sense, queer representation is facing, as stated, a double marginalization and a double search for cultural suitability. The quest for suitability is one of the issues that appears in queer Colombian narrative of the twenty-first century, while in the last thirty years of the twentieth century queer Colombian narrative represents the right to dissent and to engage in cultural criticism. Three writers that articulate this right to dissent are Fernando Vallejo, Gustavo Álvarez Gardeazábal, and Jaime Manrique.

Nevertheless, the writers of contemporary queer Colombian narrative are the ones that, in their search for suitability inside the patriarchy, are opening a space to show the contradictions in which Colombian society is situated today.

Queer Colombian writers

The history of Colombian queer literature goes back to Porfirio Barba Jacob, whose real name was Miguel Ángel Osorio Benítez (1883–1942). Some of his works are *Parábola de la vida profunda* (1907, Parable of the Profound Life), *Canción innominada* (Nameless Song), *Elegía de septiembre* (September Elegy), *Lamentación de octubre* (October Lamentation), *Soberbia y Canción de la vida profunda* (1915, Arrogance and the Song of the Profound Life). After his death, his friends published *Rosas negras* (1932, Black Roses), *Canciones y elegías* (1933, Songs and Elegies), *La canción de la vida profunda y otros poemas* (1937, The Song of the Profound Life and Other Poems, and *Poemas intemporales* (1944, Timeless Poems).

As Daniel Balderston asserts in his article "Baladas de la loca alegría: Literatura Queer en Colombia":

> Se podría decir que la literatura *queer* colombiana comienza con la caricatura que un guatemalteco hace de un colombiano: nace de una amistad equívoca y de una especie de venganza homofóbica. Me refiero, claro está, a 'El hombre que parecía un caballo' (1914) de Rafael Arévalo Martínez, un cuento sobre Miguel Ángel Osorio, que en ese momento usaba el seudónimo de Ricardo Arenales, aunque pasaría a la historia de la literatura con un seudónimo posterior, Porfirio Barba Jacob.

> [It is possible to say that Colombian queer literature begins with the parody that a Guatemalan makes of a Colombian: born from a misleading friendship and a kind of homophobic revenge. I am obviously referring to 'The man who looked like a horse' (1914) by Rafael Arévalo Martínez, a tale about Miguel Ángel Osorio, who at the time used the pseudonym Ricardo Arenales, although he would pass into the history of literature with a subsequent pseudonym, Porfirio Barba Jacob. (2008:1059)]

Porfirio Barba Jacob represents a significant part of the history of Colombian literature and at the same time may be the first eminent Colombian queer writer. His literary production has been studied, and historically and literarily contextualized by another queer writer, Fernando Vallejo:

La importancia de lo homosexual en Barba Jacob es mucho más clara ... gracias a la labor importantísima que ha hecho Fernando Vallejo: su magnífica biografía *El mensajero* y sus cuidadas ediciones de las cartas y los poemas de Barba Jacob.

[The importance of the homosexual in Barba Jacob is much clearer... thanks to the very important work made by Fernando Vallejo: his magnificent biography *El mensajero* and his careful editions of Barba Jacob's letters and poems. (2008:1060)]

Barba Jacob has been internationally recognized by critics of Latin American literature. His many publications were organized by Rafael Heliodoro Valle and published, after Valle died, by Emilia Romero de Valle. In the *Bibliografía de Porfirio Barba Jacob*, she talks about Heliodoro Valle and his great admiration for the poet:

Y le interesaba especialmente la vida de Barba Jacob por todo lo que había en ella de peculiar, de original. 'Hay que asomarse a las vidas de los hombres de letras, a la intimidad de su espíritu, para poder explicarse su obra. ... Algunos necesitan ser interpretados no sólo por el crítico, sino por el psiquiatra. Todos han sido de carne y hueso y alma ...' Y a este interés humano se unía la admiración por el poeta, de quien consideraba que 'en sus versos revive la excelsitud que el idioma tuvo en los clásicos.'

[And he [Eliodoro Valle] was especially interested in the life of Barba Jacob because of all the peculiarity and originality that his life contained. 'You have to peer into the lives of men of letters, to the intimacy of their spirit, to be able to understand their work. ... Some need to be interpreted not only by the critic, but by the psychiatrist. All have been of flesh and bone and soul ...' Added to this human interest was his admiration for the poet, that he [Eliodoro Valle] considered to have 'in his verses, revived the majesty that the language had in the classics.' (Valle 72)]

Another notable queer writer of the early twentieth century is José María Vargas Vila (1860–1933). Among his works are *Aura o las violetas* (1887, Aura or the Violets), *Pasionarias, álbum para mi madre muerta* (1887, Passionflowers, Album for my Dead Mother), *Césares en la decadencia* (Caesars in Decadence), *La muerte del cóndor* (The Death of the Condor), *Los providenciales* (1892, The Providencial Ones), *Ibis* (1900, Ibis), *Rosas de la tarde* (1900, Afternoon Roses), *Rubén Darío* (1917, Rubén Darío), *El cisne blanco, novela psicológica* (1917, The White Swan, Psychological

Novel), and *Mis mejores* (1922, My Best). Some of his published works are compiled in *La conquista de Bizancio* (1919, The Conquest of Byzantium). According to Álvaro Pineda, Botero Vargas Vila is:

> presumiblemente el [escritor] más prolífico (su bibliografía sobrepasa los cien títulos) y también el más polémico de toda la historia literaria del país. Escribió en varios géneros literarios, en especial el panfleto, para atacar de manera virulenta a los gobiernos conservadores de la Regeneración y a las figuras sobresalientes de Rafael Núñez, Miguel Antonio Caro, Carlos Holguín, Manuel Antonio Sanclemente, José Manuel Marroquín.

> [presumably the most prolific [writer] (his bibliography exceeds one hundred titles) and also the most controversial in the entire literary history of the country. He wrote in several literary genres, notably the pamphlet, to virulently attack the Conservative governments of the Regeneración and the important figures of politics: Rafael Núñez, Manuel Antonio Sanclemente, Miguel Antonio Caro, Carlos Holguín, José Manuel Marroquín.]

Juan Carlos González Espitia draws a relevant parallel between Vargas Vila and Fernando Vallejo. In his attempt to define Latin American literature, González Espitia proposes that the concept of an "intellectual" must be connected with the creation of guidelines pertaining to everyday public affairs. That is precisely why González Espitia conceptualized these two writers as "incisivos e influyentes productores de juicio" (incisive and influential producers of judgement) (2015:193). He noted that they have articulated reality in aesthetic terms and that that articulation has been represented as a claim against the sociocultural system. González Espitia's notes the following:

> Aun en los muchos momentos en los que estos autores describen su entorno con detalles repulsivos o toscos, sus descripciones se mantienen dentro de los límites de una normatividad estéticamente mediada, es decir, informada por la idea de lo bello, aunque sea oponiéndose a ello.

> [Even in the many moments in which these authors describe their environment with repellent or rough details, their descriptions are kept within the limits of an aesthetically mediated normativity, i.e., informed by the idea of what is beautiful, although opposing it. (2015:192)]

I would like to call attention to what González Espitia calls "normatividad estéticamente mediada," given that it is precisely this mediated system that creates these two writers' need to be understood – not in order to be accepted, but for the (patriarchal) system to register their divergence. In other words, in order to reject, one must be placed within what is rejected. This resistance gives them the possibility of establishing an alternative to what they reject. In a way, moreover, they prepared the foundation of queer narrative for the literature that followed, specifically, twenty-first century queer literature. The work of José María Vargas Vila, much like Fernando Vallejo's writing, has been recognized within Colombian narrative precisely because of this iconoclastic desire. The work of these two writers, according to González Espitia, consists of the following:

> la manifestación del deseo de mostrar una puerta de escape para los muchos proyectos fallidos en la región ya desde el siglo XVIII. En este sentido, Vargas Vila y Vallejo deben entenderse como intelectuales. ... Su papel tiende a ser localizado, y en ese sentido obedece a necesidades temporales, ataca y al mismo tiempo adopta las idiosincrasias locales, y su lenguaje es capaz de registrar y adoptar los cambios resultantes de la discusión con un solo propósito fijo: la oposición.

> [the manifestation of the desire to open an escape hatch for many of the failed projects in the region since the eighteenth century. In this regard, Vargas Vila and Vallejo must be understood as intellectuals. ... Their role tends to be localized, and in this sense it is due to temporal needs and attacks; at the same time it adopts local idiosyncrasies, and their language is able to register and adopt the changes resulting from the discussion with a fixed purpose: opposition. (2015:192)]

The need for this "puerta de escape," or way out, has its origins in the extreme tension that is experienced by these iconoclastic intellectuals that results from the pressure of living in a patriarchal society without much hope of being able to open new concepts of gender. Their defiance could be translated as the need of having that "place" in which the "queer" coexist with other cultural denominations of gender.

In 1971 Fernando Vallejo left Colombia and moved to Mexico, where he became a Mexican citizen in 2007. He has published several works, including *El río del tiempo* (1999, The River of Time), which is composed of five novels – *Los días azules* (1958, The Blue Days), *El fuego secreto* (1987, The Secret Fire), *Los caminos a Roma* (1988, The Roads to Rome), *Años de indulgencia* (1989, Years of Indulgence), and *Entre Fantasmas* (1993, Among Ghosts)– *El Mensajero* (1991, The Messenger), *La Virgen de los sicarios* (1993, Our Lady of Assassins), *El desbarrancadero* (2001, The Precipice), *El don de la vida* (2010, The Gift of Life), *El cuervo* (2012, The Crow), *Casablanca la bella* (2013, Casablanca the Beautiful), and *Peroratas* (2013, Long-Winded Speeches). An important recognition within Colombia came relatively late in his life: in 2001 he was named *Doctor Honoris Causa* from a major public university in Colombia, the Universidad Nacional. *La Virgen de los sicarios* (1993, Our Lady of Assassins) is among the most recognized of Vallejo's works. The novel exposes the harsh reality of drug trafficking and assassins in Medellín. This novel places us in the context of gay adolescents, which is obscured by the reality of *sicariato* (paid assassins), drugs, death, and murder. The combination of these themes, and their contextualization in the environment of social tragedy, make the queer topic as equally problematic as the matter of paid assassins. Consequently, the narrator generates the reader's rejection and also draws attention to queer issues by emphasizing the evident loneliness of the main character. On the other hand, the combination of these themes represents how the *sicarios* are a sociocultural production, just as the *sicarios* among the queer characters are also a sociocultural production.

Gay literature had "come out of the closet" in Colombia by the mid-1980s, when Fernando Vallejo, along with Gustavo Álvarez Gardeazábal and Jaime Manrique, were recognized for their boldness addressing formerly unspeakable subjects in Colombian society. Three works that stood out in this period were Álvarez Gardeazábal's *El Divino* (1985, The Divine), Vallejo's *La Virgen de los sicarios* (1993), and Manrique's *Maricones eminentes* (1999, Eminent Maricones). *Maricones eminentes* is an autobiography of Manrique's own gay experience and his understanding of three famous queer Hispanic writers: Federico García Lorca, Manuel Puig, and Reinaldo Arenas. The book explains how, for many years, Manrique had to conceal his own homosexuality:

> En esos años ... no había hecho explicita mi homosexualidad ante mi familia ni ante la mayoría de mis amigos. Puesto que en la sociedad no había más que un tipo de homosexual – la loca – desde muy temprano decidí cultivar una apariencia muy masculina.
>
> [In those years ... I did not reveal my homosexuality to my family or my friends. Since in society there was no other type of gay than – la loca – I decided to cultivate a very masculine look. (1999:85)]

According to an author profile by the University of Wisconsin Press, Manrique was recognized by *Washington Post Book World* as the "The most accomplished gay Latino writer of his generation." His most prominent works include *Los adoradores de la luna* (1977, The Moon Worshippers), *Mi noche con Federico García Lorca* (1995, My Night with Federico García Lorca), *Sor Juana's Love Poems* (1997), *Twilight at the Equator* (1997), *Mi cuerpo y otros poemas* (1999, My Body and Other Poems), *El callejón de Cervantes* (2011, The Alleyway of Cervantes), and *Nuestras vidas son los ríos* (2006, Our Lives Are the Rivers).

Álvarez Gardeazábal's total fictional output consists of *Piedra Pintada* (1965, Painted Stone), *La novelística de la violencia en Colombia* (1970, The Narrative of Violence in Colombia), *El bazar de los idiotas* (1074, Bazaar of the Idiots), *Cóndores no entierran todos los días* (1976, Condors Don't Bury Everyday), *El divino* (1986, The Divine), *Cacique: El último gamonal* (1987, Cacique: The Final Chieftain), *Novela Colombiana entre verdad y la mentira* (2000, Colombian Novel between Truth and Lies) , *Manual de crítica literaria* (2000, Manual of Literary Criticism), and *La misa ha terminado* (2013, The Mass Has Finished). His work deals with a broad range of sociopolitical issues, as outlined by Gustavo Páez Escobar in the Colombian newspaper *El Espectador,* he:

> es el iconoclasta perfecto. . . utilizando un estilo agresivo y franco destapa las ollas podridas de la vida contemporánea. . . . y a través de sus bobos, . . . sus homosexuales, sus prostitutas, sus divinos y un conjunto heterogéneo de pintorescos títeres locales – o sea, la humanidad entera – describe la comedia humana.

> [is the perfect iconoclast ... using an aggressive and forthright style to uncover rotten pots of contemporary life ... and through his imbeciles, his homosexuals, his prostitutes, his 'divinos' a heterogeneous set of picturesque local puppets – that is, the whole of humanity – he describes the human comedy.]

His recent book *La misa ha terminado* (2013) is about the sexual abuse in the Catholic Church that has occurred in recent years. His criticism of Colombian society places Álvarez Gardeazábal's work in a noteworthy place in queer narrative during the second half of the twentieth century. One characteristic that differentiates him from other queer writers is that his narrative does not demonstrate the anxiety of *exilio* that appears in almost all twentieth-century Colombian queer narrative.

In addition to Vallejo, Manrique, and Álvarez Gardeazábal, another writer who has set forth an explicit representation of queer topics is Alonso Sánchez Baute (1964), who won the Premio Nacional de Novela Ciudad de Bogotá award in 2002 for his novel *Al diablo la maldita primavera* (2013, To the Devil with This Damned Spring). He has also published *Líbranos del Bien* (2011, Free Us from Good). *Al diablo la maldita primavera* deals with the extreme experience of solitude that can be a part of the isolation felt by gays in Colombian society. This novel is an attack on the empirical reality of Colombian society. It is also a metafictional reflection on the author's life. The novel is based on the popular 1980s American prime time television series *Dynasty*, shown on ABC from January 12, 1981, to May 11,

1989. The novel begins with this series that, at the same time, delineates the reality depicted within the narrative. The novel suggests that reality is a creation, as are TV series. The protagonist, Edwin Rodriguez Buelvas, lives an alternative reality that he creates for himself; the objective of this creation is to avoid the loneliness and rejection that he is suffering in his society. It is important to emphasize that the activities developed by the protagonist are "unreal." His life is a permanent search for ideal love and the pursuit of success within the fictional reality that he has created for himself. For example, he travels to New York City to attend the famous gay "Block Party," which garners status among his Colombian gay partners. The narrator speaks in the first person in order to astonish the reader with the description of the affairs being narrated. These series of events are included to avoid the loneliness that is attached to his being gay. It is worth noting that loneliness leads to the creation of this alternative reality, which is based on an active life of frequenting nightclubs and taking part in other activities that are restricted by social norms. For example, the character has a lover, an idealized creation, whom he's never met, but only communicated with through a "chat room" on the Web.

Vallejo, Manrique, Álvarez Gardeazábal, and Sánchez Baute are writers who represent the double marginalization of the queer writer within the patriarchy of the postcolonial era. Colombian queer literature provides us with this "deviation" that stands in opposition to the patriarchal system through the representation of extremes that are embedded in the creation of another "setting" which conveys various sociocultural and political shortcomings. These writers represent exile from the sociocultural system.

There are two main categories of queer Colombian literature: The first belongs generally to the twentieth century and is characterized by an absence from the sociocultural environment of Colombian society, with characters suffering a profound solitude. There is a lack of cultural identity for these writers inside the patriarchy. The second category belongs mainly to the twenty-first century, in which we can observe a desire for cultural "suitability," which translates into the search for acceptance or recognition. Contemporary queer writers are in a search for cultural suitability.

Within the most recent and what might called postcolonial Colombian queer narrative one should note the following queer writers: Fernando Molano Vargas (1961–98). Gonzalo García Valdivieso (b. 1943), Ignacio Zuleta Lleras (b. 1955), Efraím Medina Reyes (b. 1967), and César Alzate Vargas (b. 1967). Regarding issues of postcolonialism and queer identities in *Lord Jim*, William Lee Hughes sets forth the question in his article: "Where do we separate postcolonial from queer? Where do we separate the

homosocial from the imperial? It seems that they overlap to a great extent"
(2012:73). In this article, Hughes cites Padmini Mongia discussion about
Lord Jim and he argues that "For Mongia, Jim's desire for romantic
heroism is also a desire for imperialism" (72); for Hughes this can also
be a "homosocial," desire. This term, according to Hughes, is a "desire that
will always verge on the homosexual if it is not already homosexual to
begin with" (ibid.). The term "homosocial" corresponds to the concept of
colonization and the patriarchal empire. According to Hughes, "Jim's
desire to be a hero is a desire to be desired by other men and to control
colonial subjects" (73).

It is useful to use the term "homosocial" to discuss queer representation
in contemporary Colombian narrative. In the works of the twenty-first
century, there is a recurring desire to be accepted (recalling the term
"peripheral humanism") by the peripheral patriarchy. The main point of
what contemporary Colombian queer representation is facing is what I call
double marginalization, which means a double search for cultural suitability. Today we can argue that twenty-first century queer representation
demonstrates a consciousness of being located on the margins of patriarchal society, and that there is a need to create a space for the queer
representation inside it. In Colombian queer narrative, the characters'
desire to be recognized is a desire to be reconciled with the patriarchy or,
in other words, to fit in and to be accepted. In that sense, the queer
characters in this fiction are searching for a twofold acceptance: They want
to be accepted in the patriarchy, and they want to be accepted by men
inside the patriarchal context.

Using the concept of "homosocial" Diana Ireland Stanley makes the
following observation: "While homoeroticism expresses same-sex love and
desire in narrow, personal terms, homosociality extends beyond individuals into the social order. Homosociality reveals male relationships as an
unstable balance of power, rivalry, and non-sexual intimacy" (2008:115).
Once again, the "homosocial" concept is, for the queer Colombian narrative, a desire for acceptance by the patriarchy, and at the same time is a
wish to be desired by the patriarchy. This translates into a desire to be
accepted within the sociocultural context.

Wanting to belong is an important characteristic in queer Colombian
contemporary novels. The patriarchy is evident in family, friends, and the
desire to remain within social groups, namely, high school peers. The need
to be desired is a longing to be admitted into the patriarchal system, a
longing for reconciliation. Contemporary queer narrative is seeking an
identity that can be reconstructed within a cultural context that must also

be rebuilt. The novels and writers that we can place in this context include Manuel Valdivieso (1988), the author of *Los hombres no van juntos a cine* (2014, Men Don't Go to the Movies Together), a novel about a love affair between two teenagers who live in the city of Cúcuta. The protagonist, Arturo, is pressured by his sociocultural environment to have sex with his girlfriend. All the romantic elements of the narrative created by Arturo are meant for Emilio, his schoolmate, with whom he is in love. Unlike the narrative of the second half of the twentieth century, this novel illustrates the construction of a world that is unknown and that is yet to be created. In this narrative, harsh issues are meant to create an environment where being gay fits within a patriarchal society. The narrator is not against society, but is against himself for not being able to face his own contradiction. For him, his high school, a purely patriarchal context, is a place to which he and his companions belong.

This novel represents the issues that we have raised concerning contemporary queer representation. First, the protagonists do not seek moral or physical exile seen in the queer narrative of the 1980s and 1990s. Second, there is a desire to fit within the patriarchal context, and for acceptance within this patriarchal context, which we have called a "homosocial" relationship. This novel is optimistic, and its description is based on the acquisition of the identity that the sociocultural context denies. In queer Colombian narrative of the twenty-first century, the critique of the patriarchal system is less stereotyped compared with that of the twentieth century; however, there is a need to create an alternative "place," as shown in the novel:

> Había ingresado a una parte de la ciudad completamente desconocida para mí, un fragmento maravilloso e irreal, como sacado de una novelita de ciencia ficción. Un grupo de travestis armados hasta el pescuezo se encerraban a planear venganzas en el sótano de una discoteca gay en Cúcuta.
>
> [I had entered a part of the city completely unknown to me, a wonderful and unreal fragment, something out of a science fiction novel. A group transvestites armed to the teeth were hiding and planning revenge in the basement of a gay discotheque in Cúcuta. (2014:128)]

We can observe the description of the "place" as a part of town completely unknown to the narrator, wonderful and unreal; the "place" is a fragment of something belonging to science fiction, and symbolically the ideal place for the queer characters.

The author of *Narciso en vilo* (2010, Narcissus in Suspense), Ignacio Zuleta Lleras-Dharmadeva, wrote the book in the late 1980s, but it was not

published until 2010, when he was awarded the Literaturas del Bicentenario prize. The story of the two lovers Andrés and Bío, it takes place in
Bogotá in 1985 during the "Toma del Palacio de Justicia" (the Palace of
Justice Siege). During this period, members of the M-19 guerrilla group
took over the Palace of Justice, and after a military raid, the siege left
almost half of the twenty Supreme Court justices dead. In the novel, there
is a description of the sociocultural and political environment in which the
main characters live. This description demonstrates the awareness of
the characters' sociopolitical context. As the narrator states:

> Pero Bío ya dormía y no oyó su pregunta [de Andrés] ni las descargas de
> dinamita que hacían saltar, en medio de la noche de la Plaza, los últimos
> fragmentos de la justicia muerta. Andrés pasó sus dedos por el pelo
> abundante de su niño dormido y sintió que el corazón se le volvía un ovillo
> de plumas.
>
> [But Bío was already asleep and didn't hear his [Andrés's] question, nor the
> dynamite that exploded in the middle of the night in the main plaza. The
> destruction was also the proof of the death of the justice system. Andrés ran
> his fingers through the thick hair of his sleeping child [his gay partner] and
> felt that his heart was like a ball of feathers. (2010:178)]

The first chapter begins with the title "El espacio todavía le era ajeno"
(The space was still foreign to him): Without having read the novel, the
reader focuses on the word "still," *todavía,* which in the light of this analysis
marks the absence of something that will arrive sooner or later. In the same
chapter, the narrator takes us through the city of Bogotá, through streets
that mark past and present history, and an environment that is recognizable to any reader who has lived in that city. The readers are seduced by the
agile, talkative, and rich descriptions that prompt them to observe the
depiction of the fiction as if it were a drawing or a painting. The sensitivity,
understanding, and sense of belonging by the characters of their own
environment is comparable with other queer novels published during the
same period.

The characters of these novels can be compared to the characters of the
novels of the "exile" of the twentieth century. These characters are situated
in their own environment even though they are placed on the margins of
the patriarchy.

Gonzalo García Valdivieso (1943) is the author of the novel *Los Putos
Castos. Memorias inconfesables de un doble discurso* (2010, The Chaste Male
Whores. Shameful Memories of a Double Discourse). It begins with the
narrator's first-person account of why his family leaves Bucaramanga to

live in Bogotá. They travel first to Spain so that they might acquire a certain amount of status before moving to their new city. The narrator tells us about the discovery of his homosexuality while he was still a child. The novel extends from the Franco era in Spain to contemporary times. The narrator mentions famous international actors, which shows that queer narrative is immersed in a globalized Western world. This can be noted in the following passage: "No perdemos la cabeza por un apuesto como Matthew McConaughey, pero si por ese vecino chiquito" (We don't lose our heads over a good-looking boy like Matthew McConaughey, but over his short, fat neighbor; 2010:37). In this novel, we see a full acceptance of homosexuality, and the main objective points toward obtaining "suitable" space for the queer Colombian characters.

Fernando Molano Vargas (1961–98) has published *Un beso de Dick* (1992, A Kiss from Dick), a collection of his poems titled *Todas tus cosas en mis bolsillos* (1997, Your Things in My Pockets), and *Vista desde una acera* (2012, Seen from a Sidewalk). *Un beso de Dick* won the Concurso Nacional de Novela y Cuento de la Cámara de Comercio de Medellín award in 1992. Molano Vargas's narrative is one of the most recognized recent examples of queer Colombian writing. His use of language is noteworthy: The simplicity of the words, together with the depth of thought and feeling, make his narrative special. *Vista desde una acera* is quite likely Molano Vargas's best work. It relates his discovery of his homosexuality as a boy and growing up to adapt to the cruelty of the patriarchal world around him; at the same time he narrates this cruelty as a part of the human experience:

> En fin, creo que nunca dejarán de castigarme por ser un marica; y el látigo siempre golpeara donde sea más frágil mi piel. O donde la tenga herida como ahora. Y habrá de ser así hasta el fin, me digo. Tan solo no me acostumbro a la vulgaridad con que este mundo les manda a los perseguidos sus zarpazos de perro ciego.
>
> [Anyway, I think that they will never stop punishing me for being a fag; and the whip always hits where my skin is most fragile. Or where it is wounded, as it is now. And it will be so to the end, I say. Only I can't get used to the vulgarity with which this world slashes its persecuted, torturing them as if they were surrounded by hungry dogs. (2013:77)]

For Molano Vargas, the queer issue was his motivation for writing; his narrative depicts a complex world in which being queer is one of the many matters that one encounters in daily life. This writer situated queer narrative in a world that already has a place for it, an unjust place; but even so, life is worth living. In the "Postfacio" (epilogue) of the novel,

written by Hector Abad Faciolince, he cites Molano Vargas, from his book
Todas mis cosas en tus bolsillos:

> A veces temo que los hombres seamos solo una raza de náufragos perversos,
> y no exista en la isla el verdadero amor, como no sea el propio. . . . Aun así, a
> mí la vida me seduce, y siempre aguardo a que en cualquier esquina me
> asalte la bondad de algún extraño. Esto escribía Fernando Molano en la
> página 66 de su segundo libro publicado en vida, *Todas mis cosas en tus
> bolsillos*.

> [I sometimes fear that humans are just a race of shipwrecked people,
> trapped on an island where true love does not exist – only self-love. Even
> so, I'm still in love with life and hope that one day, in some corner of the
> world, I'll be struck by the kindness of a stranger. This was Fernando
> Molano, writing on page 66 of his second published book, *Todas mis cosas
> en tus bolsillos*. (2013:251)]

César Alzate Vargas is best known for his book *Mártires del deseo* (2007,
Martyrs of Desire), for which he received the Premio Nacional de Literatura award in 2001. In the same year he also received the V Concurso
Nacional de Novela y Cuento award from the Cámara de Comercio. *La
ciudad de todos los adioses* (The City of All the Goodbyes) presents an
atmosphere that defines his narrative: absence. And His only destiny is a
self imposed exile. Interestingly, however, this is the only novel that brings
back the anxiety of the exile notable in queer narrative of the twentieth
century.

Other queer narratives written by recognized contemporary Colombian
authors are *Melodrama* (2006, Melodrama) and *El mundo de afuera* (2014,
The World Outside) by Jorge Franco, as well as *Delirio* (Delirium) by
Laura Restrepo. Both writers won the prestigious Premio Alfaguara de
Novela prize for *El mundo de afuera and Delirio,* respectively.

In conclusion, when referring to the contextualization of queer topics
in Colombian narrative, it can be observed that contemporary queer
representation recognizes its marginalization inside the patriarchy, and
at the same time, queer representation navigates in a wave of uncertainty
because its models are following the patriarchal imagination and ideology. Contemporary queer characters look for acceptance inside patriarchal society, and their struggles seem to be following the model of
patriarchal heroes.

In terms of queer representation, the problem is mainly based on
cultural confrontation between the patriarchy imposed on the colonies
and the awareness of being marginalized, both of which establish a series of
relations and dynamics that unfold differently in each novel. The

confrontation is fueled by globalization, which recognizes that in the Western world an atmosphere of support for homosexual relationships has been generated. In postcolonial Colombia, gays are doubly marginalized, both from the impossibility of society to create a cultural understanding of queerness and from the inability of gays to fit into the patriarchy. Finding a cultural identity inside a colonized society involves a double stigma because it belongs to an "ideal Western cultural context" within a patriarchal society, and it also belongs to the rebel who accepts marginalization.

BIBLIOGRAPHY

Álvarez Gardeazábal, Gustavo. *La misa ha terminado.* Medellín: Ediciones UNAULA, 2014.

Alzate Vargas, César. *La ciudad de todos los adioses.* Medellín: Imprenta Universidad de Antioquia, 2001.

Balderston, Daniel. "Baladas de la loca alegría: Literatura Queer en Colombia." *Revista Iberoamericana* 74 (2008): 1059–73.

Barba Jacob, Porfirio. "Canción de la vida Profunda" *Poemas del Alma*.com. www.poemas-del-alma.com/porfirio-barba-jacob-cancion-de-la-vida-profunda.htm#ixzz3TA2qsp20.

Casaús Arzú, Marta Elena. "El vitalismo teosófico como discurso alternativo de las élites intelectuales centroamericanas en las décadas de 1920 y 1930. Principales difusores: Porfirio Barba Jacob, Carlos Wyld Ospina y Alberto Masferrer." *Revista de Estudios Históricos de la Masonería Latinoamericana y Caribeña* 3 (2011): 81–120.

Escudero-Alías, Maite. "Transatlantic Dialogues and Identity Politics: Theorising Bilateral Silences in the Genesis and Future of Queer Studies." *Journal of Transatlantic Studies* 7 (2009): 389–98.

Figueroa, José Antonio. *El realismo mágico, vallenato y violencia política en el Caribe colombiano.* Dissertation. Georgetown University, 2007.

Foster, David W. *Gay and Lesbian Themes in Latin American Writing.* Austin: University of Texas Press, 1991.

Sexual Textualities: Essays on Queering Latin American Writing. Austin: University of Texas Press, 1997.

Gandhi, Leela. *Postcolonial Theory: A Critical Introduction.* New York: Columbia University Press, 1998.

García Valdivieso, Gonzalo. *Los putos castos. Memorias inconfesables de un doble discurso.* Bogotá: Ediciones Banana Rosa, 2010.

González Espitia, Juan Carlos. "Vallejo, Vargas Vila. Oposición, redundancia" *Cuadernos de Literatura* 19 (2015): 185–203.

Holcombe, Daniel W. "Desarrollando una óptica queer: coloquio con David William Foster." *Studies in Latin American Popular Culture* 30 (2012): 194–214.

Hughes, William Lee. "(Post)colonial, Queer: *Lord Jim*" *Conradiana* 44 (2012): 73–83.

Jaramillo-Zuluaga, J. Eduardo. "Alta tra(d)ición de la narrativa colombiana de los ochenta." *Boletín Cultural y Bibliográfico del Banco de La Republica.* http://publicaciones.banrepcultural.org/index.php/boletin_cultural/article/view/2837/2919.

Kosofsky Sedgwick, Eve. *Tendencies.* London: Routledge, 1994.

Manrique, Jaime. *Maricones eminentes.* Bogotá: Alfaguara, 1999.

"My Night with Federico García Lorca, Jaime Manrique." http://uwpress.wisc.edu/books/2593.htm.

Molano Vargas, Fernando. *Vista desde una acera.* 2nd ed. Bogotá: Seix Barral Biblioteca Breve, 2013.

Páez Escobar, Gustavo. "El Divino" *Gustavo Páez Escobar Novelista, ensayista, cuentista, y biógrafo colombiano.* www.gustavopaezescobar.com/site/tag/novela/page/5/.

Pineda Botero, Álvaro. "La fábula y el desastre. Estudios críticos sobre la novela colombiana. (1605–1931)." www.javeriana.edu.co/narrativa_colombiana/contenido/bibliograf/pineda_fabula/aura.htm.

Pinzón Mejía, Diana Carolina, and Julián Eduardo Prada Uribe. "Algunas consideraciones sobre la adopción homoparental en el ordenamiento jurídico colombiano." http://www.leyex.info/magazines/TSVOL28N596.pdf.

Ponce de León, Gina. *Twenty-first Century Latin American Narrative and Postmodern Feminism.* Newcastle: Cambridge Scholars Publishing, 2014.

Sánchez Baute, Alonso. *Al diablo la maldita primavera.* Bogotá: Alfaguara., 2003.

Stanley, Diana Ireland. "*The Two Gentlemen of Verona:* The Homosocial World of Shakespeare's England." *Journal of the Wooden O Symposium* 8 (2008): 115–24.

Tyson, Lois. *Critical Theory Today a User-Friendly Guide.* 2nd ed. New York: Routledge, 2006.

Valdivieso, Manuel. *Los hombres no van juntos a cine.* Bogotá: CAMM Editores, 2014.

Valle, Rafael Heliodoro. *Bibliografía de Porfirio Barba Jacob.* Ordenada por Emilia Romero de Valle. http://cvc.cervantes.es/lengua/thesaurus/pdf/15/TH_15_123_079_0.pdf.

Vallejo, Fernando. *La Virgen de los sicarios.* Bogotá: Alfaguara, 1994.

Zuleta Lleras, Ignacio (Dharmadeva). *Narciso en vilo.* Bogotá: Taller de Edición Rocca, 2010.

Note

1 "Peripheral humanism" is a term that José Antonio Figueroa uses in his dissertation, *El realismo mágico, vallenato y violencia política en el Caribe colombiano.*

CHAPTER 18

Extracting nature: toward an ecology of Colombian narrative

Mark D. Anderson and Marcela Reales

From early *costumbrista* novels like Eugenio Díaz's *Manuela* (1858,- Manuela) and Jorge Isaacs's *María* (1867. *Maria, a South American Romance*) up through more recent narrative by authors such as Gabriel García Márquez, Laura Restrepo, and Alfredo Molano, much of Colombian literature deals explicitly with the relationships between human societies and the environments they inhabit. In the nineteenth century, literary depictions of Colombian ecosystems most often looked to assess their value and possibilities for integration into postcolonial nation-building projects. Many twentieth- and twenty-first century works take a more critical stance toward these projects, drawing attention to the gaps between the political discourse of development and Colombia's socio-economic realities and attesting to the effects of these modernizing projects for Colombia's diverse human populations and environments. Perhaps because of the nation's history of political conflict, however, critics have tended to focus almost exclusively on the representation of social relations in Colombian narrative, often discounting even the most detailed representations of local environments as the mere setting for social and political struggles. By singling out and privileging social representation, this style of criticism fosters a binary opposition that subordinates nature to the social in ways that are often not so clear in the works themselves, thus transforming what many authors present as complex, lived environments or "places" into abstract spaces for the elaboration of social theory.[1]

Recent critical work has revisited this problem, examining more closely the specificity of relations between local societies and their environments as well as the dynamics of exchange, transculturation, and environmental modification that emerge in the incorporation of local environments into larger economic and political systems.[2] In this chapter, representations of nature and social relations are revealed to be mutually constitutive rather than discrete categories. This ecocritical approach looks to disentangle the correspondences between aesthetics, social and political practices,

363

economic regimes, and specific environments, while eschewing the kind of nineteenth-century environmental determinism that justified European neocolonialism by classifying the tropics as pathological spaces that engendered inferior, unbalanced, and ill human inhabitants. These studies remind us that social relations never exist abstractly; rather, they arise through regimes of material and symbolic practices employed in concrete environments at particular historical junctures.

We follow this ecocritical work in reexamining how Colombian societies have been constructed in relation to nature; we also take a step back, however, emphasizing the distinction between "nature" as a symbolic or cultural category and "environments" as unique material systems located in specific geographies. We are thus interested in the processes by which lived experiences of local environments are transformed into a symbolic master image of environments called "nature" as part of particular political and economic projects. At the same time, we recognize that this abstract sign of nature manifests itself materially through cultural and economic practices that also inform and/or transform local environments, thereby creating circuits that bind together the material and the symbolic.

In this chapter, we examine the ways in which nature is institutionalized through literature in several moments of Colombian cultural and economic history. We argue that the trope of nature is used to draw into productive tension certain political models, modes of economic production, and cultural practices. In this sense, Colombian conceptualizations of nature emerge not solely through the empirical observation of distinct environments within the national borders, but also, even primarily, as a tool that allows for the national territorialization of diverse environments, largely through the implementation of liberal export capitalism. Our study of the relationships between literary representations of nature and social organization reveals that specific forms of nature writing correspond to particular modes of natural resource extraction.

The first part of our chapter analyzes several nineteenth-century works that portray the implementation of capitalism in the Colombian countryside, which, rather than being carried out by foreign exploiters, is undertaken by local landowners or travelers from Bogotá. This nationalistic literature representing the implementation of capitalism in Colombia as a home-grown, local process plays the postcolonial counterpart to the European and North American travel narratives that Mary Louise Pratt studies as the "capitalist vanguard" in *Imperial Eyes*.[3] We examine two distinct nineteenth-century modes of representing nature: romanticism and naturalism. Romanticism is often viewed as a reaction against

Enlightenment empiricism and its privileging of the rational over the emotions; we take a somewhat different approach, however, arguing that, in Colombian literature at least, romantic representations of nature play a complementary role to Enlightenment liberalism, sequestering "irrational" attachments to the environment to the realm of the literary in order to carry out purely pragmatic development projects. Similarly, more than objective knowledge about the natural world, naturalism's preoccupation with abstract classification frees its practitioners from affective attachments to their objects of study, while its "empiricism" is in reality a form of prospecting whose goal is to render the environment and its inhabitants productive in economic and (bio)political terms.

The second part deals more directly with commodities narratives that portray specific regimes of extraction. We take a close look at the representation of nature in two novels dealing with the rubber boom at the turn of the twentieth century, as well as several that mark key moments in the development of the energy industry. We argue that the massive, global scale of these extractive practices and the ways in which they transform environments into bodiless organs within economic circuits force the imaginary of nature to enter into contradiction with the reality of extraction. The ecological imagination emerges from this dialectical confrontation, giving rise to a generalized movement of literary ecology dedicated to decapitalizing environments and replacing the subject within them. The final portion of the chapter discusses several works that explore different procedures for reemplacement.

The nature of extraction in Colombia

Tellingly, much of Colombian nature writing is embedded within what Ericka Beckman, drawing on Karl Polanyi, has called "capital fictions," that is, the myths enabling and promoting liberal capitalism in the newly formed Latin American republics.[4] These capital fictions set the ideological framework that allowed for the commodification of labor and environments in ways that were inconceivable in prior worldviews.[5] For this paradigm shift to occur, people had to be convinced that their everyday experience of the local environment, which was based largely on hunting, ranching, and subsistence farming, was unproductive. For modern capitalism to take hold locally, these specific places, each with its unique environmental history and cultural practices, needed to be transformed into flexible spaces for the production of wealth, which would be garnered through the extraction and exportation of prime materials from local places to national and international centers of industrialized production and consumption. Nonetheless, even a liberal demagogue would not want to see the farm he grew up on converted into a pit mine or oil field; the affective bonds people had developed with the land through their personal experiences of the environment thus had to be disrupted by geographic displacement and/or fantasies of wealth and development as objects of desire that are detached from any specific materiality or, indeed, even temporality, since modernity always recedes into the future. Capital fictions played a key role in this process of detaching identities from lived environments or places that was necessary to create capitalist spaces of development.

Strangely enough, these same fictions promoting capitalist development in the liberal model, which include to some degree most Latin American literature from the nineteenth and early twentieth centuries, very frequently contain extensive, meticulous descriptions of natural landscapes. This apparent paradox corresponds in part to the influence of Enlightenment naturalism in nineteenth-century Latin America; empirical observation was seen as a key representational strategy for producing the appearance of objective pragmatism. Observations on nature played a mercantile function in upholding the foundational narrative of underutilized natural abundance at the heart of the discourse of wealth and development. The relations between capital fictions and nature writing are more complex, however, since most of these descriptive passages have little to do with exportable commodities. The nature they describe exists primarily as excess in relation to capitalist production, as something that exceeds commodification or as an extraneous nonhuman aesthetic that, regrettably, must be demolished (after being sequestered, humanized, and/ or commodified in art or artful tourist destinations) as a condition for intensive natural resource extraction to take place.

This dynamic is captured succinctly in Colombian author Medardo Rivas's travel/development narrative *Los trabajadores de tierra caliente* (1899, The Lowland Developers), which describes the transformation of lowland tropical forests into pastureland and monoculture plantations using a rhetoric of epic labor:

> Los que trabajamos en tierra caliente, talando el bosque y quemándolo, trabajamos como bárbaros, pues destruímos una inmensa riqueza de maderas que hoy hacen falta, de tal manera que si un propietario hubiese conservado intacto su bosque en el trayecto de La Mesa a Girardot, su propiedad sería diez veces más valiosa de lo que hoy pueda representar cubierta de pastos. No hay una viga para construir casas en las poblaciones

de La Mesa, Anapoima y Tocaima; y si hubiera de continuarse el ferrocarril, no se encontrarían durmientes en toda la extensión que debe recorrer.

Además se quitó la belleza y suntuosidad a estas regiones tropicales en otro tiempo tan hermosas, y hoy convertidas en inmensos pastales de triste y melancólico aspecto; y el viajero, agobiado por el sol, no tiene un árbol bajo cuya sombra pueda descansar.[6]

This passage is by no means an ecological manifesto; Rivas laments the loss not of biodiversity, but rather of use and surplus value in the apparently senseless burning of timber in swidden agriculture, which was being used to clear land for cattle ranches and sugar cane plantations. His appraisal of this process as inefficient and wasteful is closely tied to the two key tropes of progress or "civilization" in nineteenth-century Latin American liberal discourse: territorialization through population growth (thus the need to construct housing) and the expansion of infrastructure (extending the railroads) necessary for economic growth based on exportation. In this formulation, the forest is valuable only as a source for extracting a commodity: lumber. Tellingly, he does not invoke swidden's contributions to soil health (biochar's role in nitrogen fixation) in sustainable agriculture; the goal is extraction, not sustained production. On a similar note, the "*trabajadores*" in the title refer not to the actual laborers performing the work on the environment, but instead to the upper-class property owners, the "developers"; Rivas's epic of development thus falls squarely into Beckman's category of capital fictions, in which modernization implies the exploitation of both local environments and agricultural workers in the production of commodities destined for export.

Yet the second paragraph invokes an excess or supplementarity, that "additionally," that nature as a whole embodies with respect to the processes of the extraction and commodification of natural resources. "Beauty" and "sumptuousness" (that aspect of nature as a storehouse of limitless natural opulence that exceeds all modes of extraction) are aesthetic qualities frequently associated with tropical nature, but this paragraph makes it clear that they can appear only as categories through differential comparison with the "sadness" and "melancholy" evoked by the denuded landscape of the cattle pasture. The author seemingly uses these latter terms in a Freudian sense: He bemoans the depressing loss of the tropical forest, but more than the forest itself, he pines for its idealized image as nature, whole and sovereign from human intervention.[7] Nature thus comes to represent an aestheticized object of desire that can never be possessed since it may only be conceived as such when it has already been lost, when its integrity has been disrupted and it persists only as a ghostly or ruined presence. Indeed, the tropical biome persists, but always elsewhere: "En las Juntas de Apulo sí aparece la naturaleza tropical gigante y soberbia; y el horizonte que a los ojos del viajero se presenta al descender la cuesta, es el más hermoso que la imaginación pueda soñar."[8] This dream image of beautiful, whole, sovereign nature as exceeding place (the lived environment), lying just beyond the horizon of human industry, thus appears not as something preceding extraction and development, but rather as something that emerges during the process of extraction. Nature appears as the remnant of an affect that must be displaced from the environment to the symbolic realm of representation for extraction to occur.

At first glance, this constitutive relationship between extractive economic practices and the conceptualization of nature flies in the face of common sense. When one thinks of the two in relation, the initial truism that likely comes to mind is that the intensive extraction associated with global capitalism takes a terrible toll on nature. Resource extraction immediately conjures images of bulldozers, clear-cut forests, pit mines, mountaintop removal, oil slicks smothering birds and sea life, and the extraction of nutrients and labor in endless banana, coffee, corn, sugar cane, and palm oil monoculture plantations. From this point of view, extractivism represents the colonization of a pristine and timeless nature and its human inhabitants by the destructive forces of capitalist development.[9] Particularly in the context of a developing capitalist economy like Colombia, sites of extraction become centers of production and frontiers of accumulation as they supply raw materials that increase in value after being exported. This increase in exchange value is extracted directly from the environment and the objectified human worker, both of which are "continually devalued in the search for profit along an expanding frontier."[10] In this formulation, then, the process of industrialized extraction thrusts timeless, enduring nature into history as commodity, destroying its soul in the process, and it upends violently its human inhabitants' sustainable lifestyles, forcing them into modern forms of labor exploitation and capitalist consumption.

Upon looking more closely at representations of nature, however, one perceives that nature, as a trope, has traditionally appeared in Western cultural history not as an organic whole or totality, but rather as surplus and remnant, as what cannot be metabolized fully by culture at a given moment. Nature is not truly the totality of the physical world, but rather an image of wholeness that can appear only once extraction/abstraction has been implemented; what remains after extraction invokes an imagined whole that was inconceivable as such prior to the event of extraction because of its vast scale. Rather than infinite environment, the jagged contours of the pit mine or the opaqueness of the oil slick are what evoke that broken wholeness, a presence that can be conceived only negatively, in the vaguest of terms, reconstructed as it is from the outline or borders of disaster. The close relations between art and nature reveal that nature can be apprehended only as representation, as the image of something that is partially or wholly absent. Nature is a ghost, as Tim Morton calls it, or a specter in Derrida's language.[11]

In modernity, at least, nature always looks backward, to the past before human modification of the environment. Nature is static because it exists primarily as nostalgia. The timelessness of nature is only possible because it is unhitched from the forward march of both human history and geological time, whether defined by the biological succession of species or the physical processes of entropy that are currently used to measure time scientifically. In short, nature is not a material environment subject to physical laws, but rather a master image of environments that have been displaced in time and space from wherever the modern subject – the subject of progress and development – positions itself.

The role of the nature writer, then, becomes to monumentalize nature in her texts and to promote the conservation of what has not yet been lost, of what has still not entered history. Nature writing is thus fundamentally a genre of loss; even its more celebratory moments generally presage the impending expiration of a particular way of experiencing an environment, an experience that is no longer fully accessible due to environmental destruction or the dislocation of the experiencing subject to urbanized spaces. Paradoxically, the image of nature is timeless, but constantly changing in accordance with what is lost – that is, the experiential relationship to local environments. This capacity for absorption is what confers nature its polyvalence.[12]

Extractive subjectivities and nature affects in Colombia

If nature is not a standalone concept, what exactly is it standing on? If it is not rooted in a specific environment, it can be rooted only in a specific subject or mode of subjectivity. We argue that, in modern times at least, this mode of subjectivity is extractivism, which is characterized by the displacement of people from the lived experience of local environments and the capitalization of the economically valuable aspects of those environments as export commodities. Our examination of the relationships between representations of nature and specific economies of extraction throughout Colombian cultural history reveals that extractivism, as a mode of subjectivity, produces nature during the process of extraction of natural resources from distinct environments.

This relationship becomes particularly clear in two canonical Colombian narratives from the latter half of the nineteenth century: Jorge Isaacs's *María* (1867) and José Asunción Silva's *De sobremesa* (1896, After-Dinner Conversation; written before 1896, published in 1925). *María's* protagonist, Efraín, exemplifies the processes of subjectivation by which nature is created from the remnants of the affective experience of the environment following a series of displacements, while *De sobremesa's* José Fernández parodies this process, providing a powerful critique of the capitalization of environments through a satirical representation of the bourgeois life of luxury. José Fernández's diary reveals that the desserts served at the "banquet of civilization" are disaffect, unfettered consumerism, and endless *ennui*.

One of Latin America's most renowned romantic novels, *María* recounts the story of a doomed love affair between upper-class landowner Efraín and orphaned María, his father's ward. Tellingly, *María* deals quite transparently with the implementation of nineteenth-century liberal capitalism in Colombia; both Efraín and María are the children of cosmo politan Jewish businessmen who have migrated to the Americas in search of economic opportunities, and much of the plot centers on Efraín's father's business dealings.[13] The bulk of the novel takes place on Efraín's father's *hacienda* in the Valle del Cauca, from where he runs multiple international businesses involving cattle ranching, sugar production, mineral prospecting, and gold trading, many relying on slave labor. The action, however, is motivated almost entirely by Efraín's successive displacements to Bogotá and London and his ensuing attempts to reconcile the demands of global commerce (and his father's foreign creditors) with his affective ties to his place of origin.[14] Despite the centrality to the plot of Efraín's cosmopolitan education, which his father designs explicitly to stabilize his business dealings by diversifying the family holdings beyond volatile commodities to the service sector (Efraín studies medicine), the novel dedicates little space to his life as a student in Bogotá and almost none to his time in London, focusing instead on Efraín's "sentimental education," that is, his budding romance with María. In typically romantic fashion, María is closely tied to nature through a series of parallel descriptions and explicit commentary, thus conflating Efraín's two most salient relationships into a single affective landscape.[15] As proclaimed at the start of the novel, however, this is inevitably an education in loss: Efraín will be forced to confront the loss of his connection to his home due to his education abroad and, ultimately, the loss of María, who dies from a "nervous disorder" inherited from her mother two years into his studies in London.[16] Efraín arrives too late to say goodbye to María despite the epic journey home he undertakes after receiving a letter from his father urging him to return as quickly as possible. He is thus unable to achieve closure on his relationship with her, and since everything in and around his home, including the natural landscape, is imbued with her ghostly presence, he cannot bear to remain there after her death. The novel ends with Efraín riding off alone across the plains into the sunset.

María is clearly a masculine Bildungsroman tracing Efraín's transition from childhood to manhood through the experience of love and loss. This sentimental education is not limited to his love affair with María, however; it is also intimately related to his childhood experience of the Valle del Cauca environment, which is progressively transformed into symbolic Nature through Efraín's performance of masculinity.[17] In fact, his journey to manhood seems to follow a clear, predetermined progression that naturalizes a mode of subjectivation rooted in a series of affective losses that leads to a final estrangement and displacement of affect toward the symbolic.[18] This displacement toward the symbolic does not only occur in the realm of the emotional, however; it accompanies the capitalization of the environment, that is, Efraín's gradual coming into knowledge of its value as property, as the site of the extraction of wealth. In any case, by coordinating Efraín's experiences of loss with specific stages in the psychological development of the subject (infancy, adolescent, adult), these displacements appear inevitable, as part of growth itself:

> Aquellos momentos de olvido de mí mismo, en que mi pensamiento se cernía sobre regiones que casi me eran desconocidas, momentos en que las palomas que estaban a la sombra en los naranjos agobiados al peso de sus racimos de oro se arrullaban amorosas; en que la voz de María, arrullo más dulce aún, llegaba a mis oídos, tenían un encanto inefable. La infancia, que en su insaciable curiosidad se asombra de cuanto la Naturaleza ofrece de raro a sus miradas: la adolescencia, que adivinándolo todo se deleita involuntariamente con estas castas visiones de amor, presentimiento de una felicidad tantas veces esperada en vano: sólo ellas saben traer aquellas horas no medidas en que el alma parece esforzarse por volver al cielo, que aún no ha podido olvidar.
>
> No eran las ramas de los rosales, a los que las olas del arroyo robaban leves pétalos para engalanarse fugitivas; no el vuelo majestuoso de las águilas

negras sobre las cimas cercanas; no era eso lo que veían mis ojos; era lo que ya no veré más; lo que mi espíritu quebrantado por tristes realidades no busca, o admira únicamente en sus sueños: el mundo, como Adán pudo verlo en la primera mañana de su vida.[19]

Reading this passage backwards, one perceives a progression through the Lacanian stages of psychological development from the perception of the unfiltered Real ("the world, as Adam saw it on the first morning of his life") through the imaginary, associated with "Nature" (that magical infantile world), and its waning into adolescent dreams of love (in which only the object of desire, María, can be experienced imaginarily, not the entire world), a progression that also describes the displacement of affective bonds from experience to memory. Lacan's final stage, the full induction of the subject into the symbolic order of language, appears as the subject-ivity of the narrating I, which textualizes the memories in writing even as it laments the traumatic loss of these earlier stages in psychological devel-opment in which it was still possible to "forget myself" (that is, his subjectivity, now straightjacketed by the symbolic order) in affective experience.

In fact, this process of induction into the patriarchal symbolic order and the repression of these earlier "imaginary" stages is dramatized explicitly in the encounter in which Efraín's father imposes his will and worldview over his son's dreams, insisting that he conclude his education abroad despite his sympathy for his son's psychological distress at leaving María and his home: "no puedo dejar de conocer, a pesar de todo, que te dominan al hablar así nobles sentimientos. Pero debo advertirte que mi resolución es irrevocable."[20] The imposition of his father's authority, which appears pragmatic due to its coherence within the dominant symbolic order, forces Efraín to repress his affective responses: "Necesitaba disimular lo que sufría."[21] As we have already remarked, this final induction into manhood is concurrent with Efraín's displacement to London and his induction into the patriarchal economic order of liberal capitalism, which responds to the oedipal logic of capital inheritance: "Era preciso que yo me encontrase algún día en condiciones de poder mantener a la familia" and, even more evocatively, "Siempre que mi padre dejaba de ir a la mesa, yo ocupaba la cabecera."[22]

On the other hand, the role of institutional subjectivation in this process is equally apparent, even if it does not figure prominently in the plotline. A key component in this coming of age as capitalist subject, has involved synchronization with the institutionalized biopolitics of modern society during his six years of study at the preparatory school in Bogotá: the separation from family and home, the induction into the ordered school day, prelude to the industrial working day, and his investiture into abstract, theoretical knowledge, which soon becomes privileged over first-hand knowledge gained from the affective experience of the environment. The subordination of practical knowledge becomes evident when the narrator recounts a conversation with one of his father's tenants, José, in which "él quedó admirado de mis conocimientos teóricos sobre las siembras."[23] At this historical juncture, agricultural theory was dedicated primarily to industrializing production using natural sources of nitrogen such as guano as a way to end the reliance on slave labor; this theoretical knowledge is thus closely related to the transformation of land management practices and the transition from a colonial to a modern export economy.[24] Likewise, the melancholic meditation on time (those "unmeasured hours" of infancy and adolescence) in the passage cited earlier reveals the degree to which the narrating voice has assimilated the temporal logic of capitalist productivity, in which all time must be accounted for. This fixed, measured subjectivity no longer allows Efraín to lose himself in the affective experience of the environment, in the bodily experience of presence and ecological time.

Despite being exiled from direct experience, those affects nevertheless persist in memory as an excess that destabilizes the meticulously constructed capitalist subject, rendering it melancholic and unproductive. Even after María has been buried, Efraín is unable to assimilate them fully into his subjectivity; María's material remains (her braids) resist reduction to the narrative of her death: "Un grito, un grito mío, interrumpió aquel sueño; la realidad lo turbaba celosa, como si aquel instante hubiese sido un siglo de dicha. La lámpara se había consumido; por la ventana penetraba el viento frío de la madrugada; mis manos estaban yertas y oprimían aquellas trenzas, único despojo de su belleza, única verdad de mi sueño."[25] That excess of affect must thus be expended to do away with its toxic effects for productivity, and, in capital's logic of efficiency, it must be turned productive through writing.[26] Just as the narrating I brackets Efraín's affective relationship with María by transforming her into an idealized literary figure, nature emerges as the literary sequestering of his affective experience of the Valle del Cauca environment. Nature thus embodies those affects that linked the subject to the environment prior to abstraction, which is what gives rise to its patheticism: "La Naturaleza es la más amorosa de las madres cuando el dolor se ha posesionado de nuestra alma, y si la felicidad nos acaricia, ella nos sonríe."[27]

In this sense, we disagree with the stock critical dismissal of romantic landscapes as straightforward anthropomorphic projections of the writers' subjectivities over nature; instead, we view romantic nature as the complex remainder of the writers' affective experiences of the environment. As we have seen in *María*, nature emerges from the process of extraction (here the extraction of the capitalist subject, which enables that of gold, sugar cane monoculture, and nutrients in cattle ranching) as a constitutive remainder: It is what must be removed from environments to instrumentalize them for the purposes of systematic, industrial-scale production. Nature is thus not a monologic fabrication of the feverish romantic mind, but rather the disembodied soul of environment that is detached during the process of extraction. By soul, of course, we allude not to some metaphysical essence, but rather to the material and memory-based traces of those environments' abilities to affect people, the vestiges of lived experiences that haunt cultural artifacts as the memory of environments lost, but that nevertheless obligate the modern subject to respond to them, resulting in the generation of new subjectivities and modes of interacting with environments that are not strictly extractive (recreation being one of them).

Nature can thus be viewed as an excess of meaning that has been stripped from the material environment as part of the process of extraction, an excess that must be expended as nature writing. Writing about nature reincorporates that surplus of meaning into chains of production, whether those of the literary market, the circulation of ideologies, or the economy of identities. Postcolonial romanticism therefore seemingly consists in identifying unproductive affects in order to subject them to instrumentalist rationality – it is an acknowledgment of what must be suppressed, of sacrifices that must be made in the process of the subjectivation of the liberal, capitalist subject. Affective mechanisms are stimulated to control them through writing, through displacement to the bracketed space of nature.

In this panorama, María's death becomes an allegory of displacement that describes the breaking of affective bonds necessary to generate the idealized, self-sufficient capitalist entrepreneur, freed from the partiality of affect to make pragmatic business decisions governed solely by the logic of profit. María's death and Efraín's definitive departure from the Valle del Cauca enact the affective estrangement that is necessary for the capitalization of environment and also labor, if one considers the affective bonds that Efraín had developed with many of his father's workers and tenants, even serving as godfather to some of their children. As Efraín writes in one moment, "Ya no volveré a admirar aquellos cantos, a respirar aquellos aromas, a contemplar aquellos paisajes llenos de luz, como en los días alegres de mi infancia y en los hermosos de mi adolescencia: ¡extraños habitan hoy la casa de mis padres!"[28] The corollary of this state of exile is, of course, that wherever he may be narrating from, he himself has likewise become a stranger inhabiting someone else's home, a house that cannot be a place, but only a space for him, since he will doubtlessly not again allow himself to be affected in a way that caused him such pain.

Efraín repeats his father's experience as a Jewish exile, the displacement that never allowed his father to develop the same kind of affective bonds that Efraín feels toward the Valle del Cauca, since he had already undergone the experience of displacement from wherever his home had been and because, upon purchasing the property, he encoded it with the symbolic exchange value of capital. We do not know where Efraín goes at the end of the novel, but it seems unlikely that he has abandoned the social and economic capital he and his father have accrued. He has probably sold his father's estate, since he mentions that strangers now live there, but he surely has other business dealings, now dedicated solely to profit without the muddying ethical imperatives of affect. In all likelihood, if we collate this book with others from the time period, he has moved to the city – Bogotá, London, or Paris – to assuage his affective losses with material gain and a life of decadent luxury. Perhaps he has even changed his name to avoid drawing attention to his Jewish heritage and now goes by the more catholic pseudonym José Fernández.

The story José Fernández tells about his life in *De sobremesa* differs, of course, in many aspects from that of Efraín: orphaned of father and mother, raised largely by his grandmother in the capital, immensely rich, what we glimpse of his childhood experiences seemingly have little in common with Efraín's coming-of-age in the Valle del Cauca. Nevertheless, there is more continuity than might initially be evident. José Fernández reads almost like the sequel to Efraín's Bildungsroman, the larger-than-life culmination of the construction of the capitalist subject, the sovereign entrepreneur. If Efraín exemplifies the process by which nature is sublimated symbolically from the affective experiences of the environment for extraction to occur at the material level, José Fernández embodies the final stages in the extractive process, those related primarily to refinement and consumption. José Fernández is Efraín liberated from (almost) all affective ties, free to act on his every impulse with few if any ethical constraints. Yet, like Efraín, José Fernández is haunted by the ghosts of affects past, apparitions that must be bracketed through sublimation.

De sobremesa is the *modernista* narrative of an after-dinner conversation that Fernández holds with four of his friends, although the bulk of the novel is taken up by Fernández's reading of the diary of his travels in Europe. Written in an extravagant, hyperbolic style, the work's endless catalogue of the bourgeois consumption of luxury items satirizes mercilessly the logic linking labor productivity to elite accumulation and consumption. Fernández represents the "ends" of capitalist subjectivation; completely disconnected from any affective bonds to people, places, or things, he lives in a seemingly self-contained world of luxury in which his only goal is to exhaust, to consume completely, all that life has to offer. Despite his gargantuan appetites and powerful hoarding instincts, however, he ends up being entirely overwhelmed by his class imperative to collect and/or consume everything that is being produced. He is unable to exhaust his objects of consumption since they replicate serially with slight variations, rendering him unable to find a *telos* that would endow consumption with an ends beyond desire itself. In parodic fashion, José Fernández exemplifies the reality that elite consumption does not correspond to productivity in a meaningful way, especially in the postcolonial context in which such a minute proportion of the nation's inhabitants are charged with the social *telos* of generating internal markets.

Alejandro Mejías López reads this renunciation of the *telos* of consumption through the lens of Deleuze and Guattari's theorization of nomadic desire, in which desire itself becomes productive upon renouncing its oedipal pretensions to possess its objects fully.[29] Beckman seemingly coincides with this assessment, writing that "In the face of [Bogotá's] traditionalism, Silva's job as both decadent artist *and* luxury merchant became even more important: for what these two figures shared was a common desire to liberate material and sensual desire over and against moral prohibitions, to unshackle consumption from need, and attempt to free the sensual desire latent within objects."[30] For Beckman, this kind of anti-Oedipal consumption becomes possible because desire is displaced from the object to form in *modernismo*.[31] Despite José Fernández's anachronism with respect to current forms of global capitalism, however, he seemingly exemplifies Žižek's criticisms of Deleuze and Guattari's thought in *Organs without Bodies*; namely, that this kind of nomadic desire appears to be constitutive or at least complementary to neoliberal consumer society, in which "schizophrenic" desire generates the serial consumption of meaningless forms (disembodied, commodified object-images that affect the subject only in a fetishized way, never in a transformative way) that are possessed only momentarily before being relegated to the dump.[32] On the other hand, these objects persist in immaterial form beyond the moment of consumption in the inexhaustible lists in José Fernández's diary, which must be consumed in turn, like leftovers, by his fictionalized listeners and his real readers. The novel's title, *De sobremesa*, thus evokes the endless prolongation of the moment of consumption that has become the hallmark of capitalist society; when affects are abstracted from the material, there is no satisfaction (sense of satiation or well-being) possible, no end to the courses served at the banquet of civilization.

Despite the novel's overall focus on the dynamics of consumption in Colombian society as they relate to nineteenth-century globalization, a key passage in José Fernández's diary parodies the constitutive relationships between nature, extraction, and the production of the sovereign entrepreneur that we have examined in *María*. The oft-cited entry dated July 10 describes a scene in which Fernández hatches an elaborate, if absurd plan to transform single-handedly Colombia into a modern nation. In a clear satire of earlier nineteenth-century capital fictions, which rooted themselves in observations on Colombian nature to justify their development fantasies, Fernández conceives this entire scheme from atop a Swiss hilltop, a pastoral scene to which he has escaped from Paris after attempting to murder his lover in a fit of jealous rage. Loss is thus once again the condition for the production of this capitalistic subjectivity, but in Fernández's case, that loss is revealed to be narcissistic, the loss not of the woman (who it turns out has survived with only a scratch), but of an idealized image of himself and his intellectual powers of abstraction, which failed to neutralize the violent passions inspired by his lover. Like Efraín's María, José Fernández's María Legendre must be killed off, even if only symbolically, because of the affective pull she exercises on him, threatening his sovereignty: "Oh, la Circe que cambia a los hombres en cerdos!"[33] This misogyny repeats itself throughout the novel; José Fernández despises the women he desires because they detract from his self-sufficiency. And in a play off the enclosure of Efraín's affects for *María* through textual idealization, José Fernández ends up bracketing all women as "Ella," as Helena, an angelic fantasy that he constructs after a single encounter with a fifteen-year-old girl. Again, Helena dies from an unknown illness, thus liberating his constructed image of her from material reality – from the possibility of an affective relationship complete with ethical injunctions that would limit his sovereignty.[34] In an allegory that cannot fail to conjure the position of the postcolonial elite with respect to its political subalterns, the development fantasies that José

Fernández conceives in isolation from the Swiss mountaintop are aimed at compensating for this loss of sovereign power in which women – here María Legendre, who chose to cheat on him with a lesbian lover – cease to be mere objects of desire, acting autonomously, affecting him in ways that he cannot control. Desire is quarantined from affect through killing the object and preserving only its idealized image, thereby liberating the sovereign subject from any affective attachments.

The same procedure accounts for the representation of nature in this passage; it is instantly sequestered by removing it from Colombia to Switzerland and presenting it as a literary *locus amoenus*. Furthermore, Felipe Martínez Pinzón notes that this mountaintop location satirizes the postcolonial political elite's geographical hierarchy that located the highlands around Bogotá as the space of rational planning, while the tropical lowlands were viewed as mere sites of extraction that produced inferior humans whose only contribution to the nation could be their unskilled labor.[35] In this scene, then, nature appears not as a concrete place, but rather as an aesthetic space that is paradoxically or parodically beyond society (beyond human affect and social order) and outside of culture (the symbolic order and the restrictions that it imposes over the subject), from where it is possible to (re)constitute the sovereign subject:

> La naturaleza, ¡pero la naturaleza contemplada así, sin que una voz humana interrumpa el diálogo que con el alma pensativa que la escucha entabla ella, con las voces de sus aguas, de sus follajes, de sus vientos, con la eterna poesía de las luces y de las sombras. Cuando aislado así de todo vínculo humano, la oigo y la siento, me pierdo en ella como en una *nirvana* divina.[36]

The sensual interaction with gendered nature – that "dialogue" with a passive "ella" – displaces human affect ("all human ties"), freeing the "pensive soul" to imagine from beyond the ethical exigencies of affect and the tyrannical law of the symbolic order: "¡Instantes inolvidables cuya descripción se resiste a todo esfuerzo de la palabra!"[37] In fact, this "nature" does not speak at all – its voices are the white noise of wind and rushing water – nor does it affect the narrating subject in a way that would obligate it to respond to it. Here nature's only function is to liberate the subject from social ties; it has no content beyond the absence of the human, its formlessness serves only to disrupt established form and permit the sublime regression to the imaginary. There is no encounter between entities, only the limitless expansion of the subject: "olvidado de mí mismo, de la vida, de la muerte, el espectáculo sublime entró en mi ser, por decirlo así, y me dispersé en la bóveda constelada, en el océano tranquilo, como fundido en ellos en un éxtasis panteísta de adoración sublime."³⁸ What Fernández has forgotten in this passage is not his subjectivity (he is still a speaking I), but his body, subject to "life and death" – he has transcended the material to the immortal realm of thought. Godlike, beyond good and evil (in the Nietzschean sense), the transcendental subject is alone with itself in the universe. The sublime thus connotes a condition in which there are no limits to the sovereignty of the subject.

Nature provides a position of absolute sovereignty from which the entrepreneurial subject elaborates his grand plan for the total transformation of Colombia into a paragon of Western modernity: "El plan que reclamaba, el fin único a que consagrar la vida, me ha aparecido claro y preciso como una fórmula matemática. Para realizarlo necesito un esfuerzo de cada minuto por años enteros, una voluntad de hierro que no ceda un instante."³⁹ The scheme laid out in the following pages reads like an absurd (and clearly parodical) pastiche of nineteenth-century development fantasies.⁴⁰ Tellingly, all Fernández's plans rely on natural resource extraction as the base; he envisions doubling or tripling his fortune through gold and pearl extraction enterprises, then reinvesting that capital into the New York stock exchange while he studies U.S. civilization and culture. This accumulation of capital and knowledge of economic models will then be invested in development projects in the Colombian "provinces," for which he will hire foreign engineers and scientists to perform technical assessments. All Colombia's diverse climates and regions will be engaged in a massive development project designed for the total exploitation of natural resources. This vast extraction will be destined toward integration into international markets through marketing and distribution networks that he will establish by appointing judicious diplomatic agents to negotiate trade agreements and contracts with international consortiums. Parroting the liberal economic model down to the most minute details, Fernández envisions extraction and exportation leading to rapid economic growth, stimulating the immigration of specialized labor, which will in turn promote industrialization while simultaneously populating marginalized regions.⁴¹

All this development, of course, requires foreign investment; therefore political stability and fiscal reforms figure prominently in his plans. Achieving political stability will require the total political transformation of Colombia; he foresees putting an end to the history of strife between liberals and conservatives by creating political consensus rooted in economic pragmatism on the one hand, and, on the other, in sovereign power. After gaining experience and connections in the political sphere, he will attempt to create a single nationalistic party to carry out his plans: "un centro donde se recluten a los civilizados de todos los partidos para formar un partido nuevo, distante de todo fanatismo político o religioso, un partido de civilizados que crean en la ciencia y pongan su esfuerzo al servicio de la gran idea."[42] If this should fail, however, he will create a coalition between conservative landowners, warlike indigenous tribes, and the workforce involved in his development projects, and he will then use that force (especially the "*indios salvajes*") to defeat and repress through violence the corrupt liberals in power, installing himself as a kind of enlightened despot. Whether through persuasion or force, he will generate consensus between all sectors of Colombian society for the implementation of this massive modernization project under his tutelage.

An explicit satire of both the Nietzschean notion of the *Übermensch* and contemporary Colombian president Rafael Núñez's "*regeneracionismo*," Fernández's development plans reveal that political power is never achieved naturally, through social "leadership" or the Darwinistic mechanisms of natural selection that were in vogue when Silva was writing, but rather through the imposition of hegemony, through placing people in positions of voluntary tutelage or forced subjugation. Subalternity thus becomes the condition for amassing the political capital necessary to carry out this vast transformation, this "regeneration of the land."[43] In a post-political formulation (beyond liberalism or conservatism), power becomes its own ends and the only means to progress. Taking this discourse to its logical extremes, Silva represents development itself as a state of exception, a veritable war against poverty, corruption, inefficiency, and unproductivity. And, as Agamben points out via Schmitt, only the sovereign can declare the state of exception.[44] In this passage, then, Silva develops direct links between the renunciation of affective bonds with people and the environment, the constitution of the sovereign subject from the abstract space of nature, natural resource extraction as the base of all power, development planning, political hegemony, and the state of exception.

Indeed, it is the stripping of affects from the environment that renders it "bare" in a parallel way to the bare lives of the slaves and subaltern agricultural workers. This is why José Fernández must speak from abroad; nature resides in Switzerland because Colombia has become a site of extraction. Nature thus becomes the abstract space, beyond culture and affect, from where the sovereign subject can elaborate these semi-fascist development dreams, as Camacho Guizado labels them.[45] Nevertheless, the character himself recognizes the absurd contradictions within his plans when he reads them back to his friends: "Yo estaba loco cuando escribí esto, ¿no Sáenz?–exclamó Fernández, interrumpiendo la lectura, dirigiéndose al médico y sonriéndole amistosamente."[46] The real-life reader must agree with Fernández's self-assessment, particularly when he reveals that the whole point of this improbable project is to create a readership for his *modernista* poetry, to which he may finally return once the public has been modernized sufficiently to appreciate it fully.[47] The fictionalized listener, embedded within the discourse of bourgeois productivity, sees no irony, however: "Es la única vez que has estado en tu juicio – contestó Sáenz con frialdad."[48] In this way, Silva portrays this absurd development fantasy as normative within the Colombian postcolonial elite, thus bringing to light the genealogical continuity with colonial models of production that combined exploitative extraction with the antinomical discourse of civilization.

Regimes of extraction and the geopolitics of nature

When read together, Isaacs's *María* and Silva's *De Sobremesa* provide a cognitive map of the inner workings of extractivism in nineteenth-century Colombia. They reveal that nature, far from a wilderness that persists beyond the reach of capitalism, is actually a necessary component in its implementation, since its conceptualization generates the conditions by which environments and labor may be capitalized. Other Colombian works from the nineteenth century focus more concretely on the particular forms of extraction that were put into practice during this period. For example, Eugenio Díaz's novels *Manuela* (1858) and *Bruna la Carbonera* (written between 1858 and 1861, published in 1879–80) deal with the implementation of specific regimes of extraction in two contrasting, if geographically proximate, regions of Colombia: the central highlands surrounding Bogotá and the tropical lowlands along the Magdalena River. Both novels use iconic female characters to foreground social and racial issues that arose during postcolonial economic transformations in Colombia. *Manuela* concentrates primarily on the evolution of the semi-feudal sugarcane economy following the abolition of slavery in 1851 and the gradual shift toward a modern export economy, as well as the political conflicts that ensued from attempts to liberalize the economy and political structure.[49] The abject labor conditions and low productivity of the *trapicheros*, racialized workers in primitive sugar refineries, is contrasted with the comparative modernity of the newly inaugurated tobacco factories in nearby Ambalema, which generate a local wage economy in which lower-class women of all colors (as iconic subalterns) have access to capital, a higher standard of living, and political rights that are suppressed in the *trapiche* economy.[50] *Bruna la Carbonera*, on the other hand, deals with the expansion of the charcoal industry and the resulting deforestation in the environs of Bogotá. The charcoal industry is portrayed as sustainable when carried out by lower-class inhabitants of the area, but it becomes extractive when bourgeois speculators from Bogotá get involved in the business. Tellingly, the historical boom in charcoal consumption that attracts speculators in the novel occurred due to two modernizing developments: the rapid urbanization of the capital due to an influx of migrants from the countryside and the foundation of iron smelters in the area.[51] At the same time, the deforestation has as its complement the depopulation of the countryside: the deaths, disappearances, and displacement of the region's inhabitants due to political violence generated by the conflict between liberals, radicals, and conservatives over political power and economic resources.

In Díaz's novels, the *campo* (rural countryside) emerges as a distinctly national conceptual space that mediates as a buffer zone or frontier between the growing urbanization and industrialization of the capital and the undeveloped wilds of regions that have not yet been territorialized as part of the nation. Rather than these peripheral wilds, nature is explicitly associated with the *campo*, forming the constitutive counterpart of the cultured work environment of farms, ranches, and sugar plantations. Nature functions here as a conceptual machine for transforming partially territorialized internal spaces – spaces that still posed some risk to modernizing projects – into reserves, in the triple sense of future sources of national wealth, recreation areas for elite tourists, and storehouses of supplies for the destitute, thereby serving as a palliative for the lower classes' lack of access to consumer goods. Nature is actively preserved by the landowner classes as part of the *latifundio* system, in which upper-class landowners acquire enormous tracts of land, parts of which they then parcel out and rent to subsistence farmers in exchange for crops and labor in the cattle industry or sugar cane plantations. In Díaz's novels, these *latifundistas* exercise an iron control over the destitute peasants they allow to homestead plots of their land: despite the enormity of their holdings, they strictly limit the number of homesteaders to those necessary for their labor needs, while the unused land remains in reserve as nature. Furthermore, the landowners permit their tenants to engage only in very low levels of autonomous economic activity, purposefully maintaining them in poverty so that they cannot buy their own land and thus escape their rent and labor obligations in the *trapiches*.[52] As Germán Márquez argues, upon questioning why so much land produced comparatively so little: "la transformación [of old growth forest into pasture] se debe no sólo a razones de tipo económico directo, esto es, al propósito de obtener tierras para fines productivos, sino, y sobretodo, al propósito de controlar a la sociedad y la mano de obra a través del control de la naturaleza."[53]

In this inefficient, semifeudal mode of production, which is associated with the literary aesthetics of *costumbrismo*, nature appears alternately as a space of harmonious interrelations that revalidates the postcolonial social order, a Spencerian natural order in which the elite rule due to their cultural or biological (racial) superiority, and as a flexible reserve space that is capable of absorbing excess labor and social tensions. Nature thus functions as a seminomadic form of territorialization, a way of domesticating and occupying land that is always impermanent and peripheral due to the hegemonic centrality of the *casa grande* (master's house), the only permissible permanent structure. In turn, the spatiality of the *latifundio*, of the *casa grande/campo/*nature complex, reflects the national geographic order and the exclusionary centrality of the capital. In this sense, *costumbrista* nature is clearly constitutive to the neocolonial social order of the *latifundio* as well as the predominant notions of Colombian nationalism in the nineteenth century.

Díaz contrasts this romantic, *latifundista* nature with the emerging paradigm of liberal naturalism; the male protagonists of both novels are radical liberal demagogues – "*gólgotas*" – from Bogotá who make excursions into the countryside to undertake the naturalistic classification of social types and natural phenomena, educate the populace in their political rights, and recreate by hunting animals and flirting with adolescent peasant women. Despite the powerful ways in which lower-class Manuela and Bruna affect these liberal gentleman travelers, however, rigid class distinctions truncate the possibility of the nationalistic union of contraries in foundational romances. Both men return to Bogotá to marry women of their own social status, abandoning the lower-class peasant women in precarious situations amid rising political tensions, and both women die as direct or indirect victims of political violence. In these plot lines, the naturalistic classification of plants, animals, and minerals is thus shown to be bound up with the rigid drawing of internal geopolitical (capital/periphery) borders and class divisions; furthermore, these rigid classifications contribute to the deaths of the women and, in the case of *Bruna*, at least, environmental devastation due to deforestation.

Like its companion paradigm of romantic nature, then, naturalistic classification is revealed as a tool that sequesters the naturalist from material affects through creating exploitative hierarchies, enabling more efficiently the extractive subjectivities that we have already seen in *María* and *De sobremesa*. It is thus not surprising that don Demóstenes's and don Jorge Boscoso's naturalistic knowledge is primarily engaged in prospecting practices of different kinds, whether in the search for emeralds or gold or the fossils that would endow the nation with a national prehistory. Rather than an innocuous encyclopedia of objective knowledge about the natural world, then, naturalism transparently plays the role of capitalizing the land and implementing extractive industries. Furthermore, this prospecting activity is also at the root of the political conflict, as politics become a mode of extracting votes and accumulating wealth from the populace through taxation.

In nineteenth-century Colombian writing, nature is almost always tropical. Nature is a term applied to "*tierras calientes,*" geographies that resist conversion into forms compatible with Bogotá and its standards of living or, on a macro scale, integration into what Jason Moore has called the "capitalist world-ecology" in reference to (neo)liberal capitalism's massive terraforming project designed to make all environments productive and compatible with global commerce.[54] Despite the apparent marginality of tropical environments to these projects, however, tropical nature, as a representational mode, clearly forms part of this terraforming machinery. It identifies potentially threatening environments and transforms them into nature, subordinating their seemingly abject and dangerous elements to beauty, abundance, and adventure (national epic); mapping and stratifying their intricacies into the categories of natural history and economic production; unraveling their entanglements into discrete academic disciplines; and subordinating difference to science as the universal theory of knowledge. Nature and naturalism thus perform the initial work of ordering environments to make them available to extraction, while the naturalist, through his epic travels (whose narrative, like *María*, corresponds to the form of the Bildungsroman), constructs himself as the legitimate proprietor of that knowledge and thus places himself in a position to capitalize on it.

In contrast with the nineteenth-century *campo* and its natural/national reserves, the wilds, often called "*el monte*" or "*la selva*" in Spanish, denoted spaces beyond nature, and, therefore, beyond representation, although they did occasionally appear in travel literature either as abstract spaces of abjection or a kind of chaotic protonature. These are regions that existed in the national imaginary almost exclusively in the negative, as the "reverse of the nation" as Margarita Serje calls them, outside the scope of national politics or economy. They were characterized by a near total lack of communications and the absence of the state and its institutions, leading to representations in which "*la ley del monte*" (the rule of the strong) comprised a pre-political "constitutive violence," the most primitive form of territorialization.[55] On the other hand, these wilds also embodied zones of tolerance where illicit activities and bodies of all kinds found safe haven, including outlawed forms of subjectivity and economic activity. In Colombia, these unterritorialized wilds occupy the focal point of early twentieth-century literary *criollismo*, a movement that sought to integrate marginalized geographies and populations into autonomous national identities.[56]

During the first decades of the twentieth century, particularly after the great crash of 1929, many Latin American nations shifted from the nineteenth-century liberal model of export-driven modernization era to an "age of development."[57] Rejecting dependence on foreign investment, emerging nations turned inward to state-led economic policies designed to promote internal industrialized development and the creation of national markets. Literary *criollismo* followed this general trajectory, focusing on the representation of the internal political economy as it related to peripheral geographies of production. Although regionalism's "return" to local environments has traditionally been understood as detachment from the central, modern sites of progress that predominated in *modernismo* and the avant-garde writing of the 1920s and 1930s, we agree with Beckman's assessment that those apparently peripheral settings are at the center of export-driven modernization.[58] *Criollista* nature writing culminated Eugenio Díaz's shift from the perspective of urban, elite subjectivities and modes of production, refinement, and consumption to the extractive processes of natural resources themselves and the labor relations that emerged and were linked to them within marginal rural environments.

Tellingly, while *costumbrista* representations of distinct regions focused on the picturesque elements of local cultures and geographies, those that could be incorporated seamlessly into nation-building projects, twentieth-century *criollismo* reflects the difficulties in territorializing these areas. These texts depict the work of taming wilderness into a *campo*/nature complex and nationalizing abject or marginalized inhabitants as cultural, if not political citizens. This taming process is undertaken through the implementation of a kind of "savage capitalism" that is horrifying in its abuses, but whose violence is nevertheless represented as foundational, a taming of wild people and environments in preparation for their induction into the national civic and economic orders. Paradoxically, subjugation and subalternity are portrayed as the first steps toward citizenship. Likewise, seemingly marginal, preindustrial modes of extraction represent an initial nationalistic territorialization, capitalizing these marginal environments and linking them to distribution networks, even when there is no national regulation or taxation and those distribution networks ship materials and profits to foreign shores rather than national centers of production.[59]

Two Colombian *criollista* novels from the early twentieth century, José Eustasio Rivera's renowned *La vorágine* (1924, The Vortex) and César Uribe Piedrahita's *Toá: narraciones de caucherías* (1933, Toá: Stories of the Rubber Industry) explore the dynamics of the territorialization of wilds and their gradual conversion into the *campo*/nature complex through the capitalization of Colombia's quintessential marginal environment, Amazonia. These works span the peak and decline of the turn-of-the-twentieth-century Amazonian rubber boom, focusing on the migration of workers to the region and the industry's exploitative labor regime, as well as the nationalistic epic of taming a radically different environment.

The rubber boom resulted from the demand for a vital raw material during the era of rapid industrialization in western nations at the end of the nineteenth century. During this period, the North American automotive industry began the mass production of inexpensive family vehicles, leading to massive foreign investment in tropical lands because of the need for rubber and oil in various parts of their product.[60] The *caucherías* (sites of rubber extraction) of the upper Amazon region were subsidized by both local and international investors but were run mostly by local *capataces* (labor foremen), who established a system of debt bondage that *La vorágine* describes as "a new kind of slavery."[61] Employing technologies of control similar to those of the *trapiche* system that Eugenio Díaz critiqued in his novels, the *cauchería* engaged systematic, racialized violence and oppression to maintain the workers in a state of permanent dispossession. Because of the initial debts they incurred for foodstuffs and tools, the exploited men at the lower level of the hierarchy could generate no excess value by means of their labor; accumulation occurred only at the middle and top portions of the production chain. This value was thus obtained primarily through exporting the raw material, first from the jungle to shipping centers and from there to Europe and the United States. The international middle-men involved in the second phase of exportation profited the most from the business; the rubber industry is therefore depicted as a "mode of extraction" rather than a "mode of production." This model of systematic violence and oppressive extraction sustained the expansion of Western industrialization while leaving the vast majority of Amazonians in an impoverished state.[62] Little development occurred outside of the largest cities in the area; the Amazonian *caucherías* thus became semi-territorialized spaces that represented the frontiers of expansion of both the nation and global capitalism.

As in earlier nineteenth-century capital fictions, the main characters in *La vorágine* and *Toá* are upper-class, educated, urban men who enter the jungle as travelers. *La vorágine*'s protagonist and narrator, Arturo Cova, journeys to the jungle to exact revenge on his lover, Alicia, who has fled there with sinister labor contractor Narciso Barrera, while *Toá*'s Antonio Orrantia holds the governmental position of *visitador* (traveling inspector) of the *caucherías*. These characters' distant subjectivities are initially successful in insulating them from affective relationships with what they view as an alien environment. Nevertheless, as they travel deep within Amazonia, befriending *caucheros* (rubber workers) and building romantic relationships with women within the jungle, they undergo a process that is the inverse of that of *María* and *De sobremesa*: Their sequestering mechanisms disintegrate, and they end up being affected by the Amazonian environment in powerful ways that they are unable to control. In the inhuman Amazonian environment, romantic nature rapidly becomes unrecognizable and irrelevant. As Arturo Cova phrases it, "¿Cuál es aquí la poesía de los retiros, dónde están las mariposas que parecen flores traslúcidas, los pájaros mágicos, el arroyo cantor? ¡Pobre fantasía de los poetas que sólo conocen las soledades domesticadas!"[63] Orrantia's plans to write "bellos libros sobre los misterios de la selva" quickly fall apart as well.[64] Confronted with the materiality of life in Amazonia, symbolic nature loses its ability to account for environmental affects, and the natural sublime quickly degrades into the negative sublime. As Lesley Wylie points out, "The *novela de la selva* undermines not only the notion of 'landscape' as self-evident fact but also the existence of an autonomous subject capable of observing it."[65] The irreconcilable gap between the symbol and the material produces horror and abjection: "Por primera vez, en todo su horror, se ensanchó ante mí la selva inhumana."[66]

The characters initially react to this horror by treating the environment as enemy, as what must be combated to force it to conform to the nationalistic imaginary of nature. Tellingly, *Toá* is dedicated in part to "todos los hombres que en la Amazonía colombiana lucharon por esclavizar la Naturaleza y cayeron vencidos en la brega."[67] Stripped of humanist symbolism, the environment and its indigenous inhabitants are bared to the tactics of war, to the savage capitalism embodied in characters such as *La vorágine*'s Funes. The conceptual transformation of the Amazonian environment from nature into battlefield generates the representation of the jungle as the savage "heart of darkness." More than a space (even one of exception) for illicit or unethical human activities, the jungle conforms a kind of active, violent anti-Nature, a war-machine that produces the effect of endless aggression at every scale of life and economy:

> Por doquiera el bejuco de "matapalo" – rastrero pulpo de las florestas – pega sus tentáculos a los troncos, acogotándolos y retorciéndolos, para injertárselos y trasfundírselos en metempsicosis dolorosas. Vomitan los "bachaqueros" sus trillones de hormigas devastadoras, que recortan el manto de la montaña y por anchas veredas regresan al túnel, como abanderadas del exterminio, con sus gallardetes de hojas y de flores. El comején enferma los árboles cual galopante sífilis, que solapa su lepra supliciatoria mientras va carcomiéndoles los tejidos y pulverizándoles la corteza, hasta derrocarlos, súbitamente, con su pesadumbre de ramazones vivas.[68]

Human(ist)s have little hope of taming such systematic ferocity, a force that turns them against each other as it bestializes them, transforming them into predators of each other's bodies: "la selva trastorna a los hombres, desarrollándose los instintos más inhumanos; la crueldad invade las almas como intricado espino, y la codicia quema como fiebre."[69] At the end of the novels, both protagonists end up being "devoured by the jungle," seemingly victims of the war machine.

As much as the verb "devour" connotes violence, however, it also evokes metabolic processes of integration through digestive processes. Anything that is devoured in Amazonia is incorporated into an intricate web of nutrient recycling, of composting that sustains life in the porous, nutrient-poor Amazonian subsoil: "Entre tanto, la tierra cumple las sucesivas renovaciones: al pie del coloso que se derrumba, el germen que brota; en medio de las miasmas, el polen que vuela; y por todas partes el hálito del fermento, los vapores calientes de la penumbra, el sopor de la muerte, el marasmo de la procreación."[70] Or, as *Toá* frames it: "Allí estaba la vida en el umbral de la muerte. ¡La muerte transformándose en depósitos fertilizantes y creadores de nueva vida!"[71] The vast complexity of the Amazonian environmental cycles exceeds their representation as man-eating jungle. The disintegration of the sovereign, humanist subject and its sequestering mechanisms leads to an ecological perspective of the Amazonian environment in which humans are emplaced metabolically within their surroundings. Being "devoured" thus operates as a metaphor for the process of reincorporation into the affective experience of the environment; the transcendental symbol is destroyed, but the body persists in one form or another, even if dispersed as nutrients. In fact, there is no evidence at the end of either *La vorágine* or *Toá* that the characters have died; they have simply delinked from the exploitative rubber economy and disappeared from textual (symbolic) mediation. They may live on yet in the bowels of the Amazonian rainforest.[72]

The ecological turn in Colombian narrative

While extremely exploitative in terms of human labor, the rubber industry was relatively sustainable in environmental terms at the time that Rivera and Uribe Piedrahita were writing. As evidenced by the famous failure of Fordlândia, the rubber plantation founded by Henry Ford in 1928, the rubber industry had little success with creating monoculture plantations in Amazonia: the need to avoid the spread of pathogens forced the *caucherías* to maintain considerable distances between trees, leaving them in relatively natural configurations in the rainforest. Furthermore, the discovery during the 1930s and 1940s of techniques for mass-producing synthetic rubber polymers from petroleum made the *caucherías* nearly obsolete, while contributing to the vertiginous expansion of the oil industry. Widespread environmental devastation in Latin America has thus been more closely linked to monoculture and mineral and hydrocarbon extraction, while artisanal rubber harvesting is now viewed as a model of rainforest sustainability.

Due to the increased visibility of climate change induced by the massive, industrial release of carbon into the atmosphere, the extraction, production, and consumption of energy has become the privileged circuit for examining the intersections of local environments with larger economic systems, whether national or global. In the Colombian context, the ecological relationality between the economic regime of liberal capitalism, energy consumption, environmental transformations, and social crisis was established early on in Eugenio Díaz's *Bruna la Carbonera*, which focused on the political ecology of the charcoal industry. Similarly, deforestation due to the wood-burning nineteenth-century steamships that linked the Colombian interior to the network of global commerce figures prominently in García Márquez's *El amor en los tiempos del cólera* (1985, *Love in the Time of Cholera*, 1988). The Latin American oil narratives studied by Julia Elena Rial capture this ecology in higher resolution, however, because of the vast scale of the oil production and distribution networks that arose during the twentieth century following the shift from early industrial energy sources (charcoal and wood) to modern hydrocarbons (coal and oil).[73] The following passage from Uribe Piedrahita's *Mancha de aceite* (1935, Oil Slick) is exemplary:

> Lodo aceitoso barniza las escasas matas que se arrastran en el fango. Fuertes cercas de alambre aíslan el bosque de torres, de tanques y potentes motores que hacen circular la sangre negra desde las entrañas de la tierra y al través de las gruesas arterias de hierro, hasta la barriga de los buques. Ruido de martinetes, vahos hediondos de residuos asfálticos y gritos en mil lenguas saturan la atmósfera que hierve bajo el sol.

> En el pozo de 'La Flor' se arremolina sucia masa de hombres procedentes de todas las regiones del globo: yanquis y canadienses, armenios, griegos y judíos, antillanos y nativos del Continente que bañan el Caribe y el golfo de México.[74]

The local environment, transformed into oil camp, is enclosed (fenced off) as a discrete organ within a bodiless system, a territory without environment, in which steel oil derricks replace trees and the only "flower" is the oil well of that name. In turn, the oil is the "black blood" that links together the organs of the capitalist world-ecology in a single circulatory system, whose globality is emphasized in the novel's setting in Venezuela, the North American ownership of the oil corporation, the international provenance of the workers, and the ships waiting to transport the fuel abroad. The muscle of the laborers and the machinery pump it throughout this strange, decentralized global circuit consisting of transitorily connected, interchangeable "organs without bodies," to borrow Žižek's terminology once again. And, transformed into pure muscle, limited only to their functionality within the system, stripped down to their bare life, the bodies of laborers are strewn on Venezuelan shores like the greasy sediment of an oil slick.

In these commodity narratives, a dialectic emerges similar to that which we analyzed at the beginning of this essay in Medardo Rivas's *Los trabajadores de tierra caliente*; but here the global reach of extractive practices gives rise to new tensions within the conceptualization of nature. In the nineteenth-century capital fictions, nature served to bracket affects from local environments and thus permit their transformation into sites of extraction, while monumentalizing the affects themselves in art and memory. In the twentieth century, however, when the scale of extraction surpassed the wildest calculations of the nineteenth century, the natural imaginary rapidly entered into contradiction with the post-extractive landscape: There is no nature possible when one confronts the true dimensions of Uribe Piedrahita's oil slick. As one character in Laura Restrepo's oil narrative *La novia oscura* (1999, The Dark Bride) states when his coworker complains of the prison-like atmosphere of the Tropical Oil Company camp, which is shut off from the "insensatez de la selva" (senselessness of the jungle) by barbed-wire fences: "Alégrate en vez de lamentarte – contestó el Payanés –, porque ésta es la cara que tiene el progreso. Apréndetela bien, porque así va a quedar hasta el último rincón del mundo dentro de cincuenta años: puro desarrollo y goce para la humanidad."[75] Globalized industrial extraction quickly deflates the myth of the inexhaustibility of whole, untouched nature. And without nature, there is no place for environmental affects to go once they have been displaced by extraction: there is simply insufficient remnant to be fetishized as nature. The inescapable incommensurability of the ghost of environment and its material remains thus generates a critical perspective leading to ecological awareness of metabolic processes—the effects of capitalization on place.

Ecology, as a conceptual framework, emerges in response to extractivism as a set of procedures specifically designed for reemplacing subjects within the environment, of materializing subjectivity and bringing it down to earth. Whether through scientific methodologies or borrowing from premodern worldviews (as in "deep ecology"), ecology's project is the devaluation of modern Man as an absolute term, as the abstract position of sovereignty, with the explicit purpose of decapitalizing environment and restoring to it its ontological being, its right to exist as itself in all its heterogeneous complexity.[76] As *La vorágine* and *Toá* showed, literary ecologies often take the form of Bildungsromans in reverse, exemplifying the unwinding of the human, the dismantling or disarticulation of nature, and the material reintegration of the body into the environment. And in a world in which destructive modifications of the environment predominate due to intensive resource extraction, the environment often affects characters negatively, in toxic ways. The overbearing materiality of the environments produced by the capitalist world-ecology makes impossible the sequestering of affect to the symbolic realm; as much as pleasure and interconnectedness, affects are born indelibly on and in the body as mutilation and sickness.[77]

The problem of emplacement became increasingly urgent in twentieth-century Colombia with the massive displacements of local peoples during waves of political and economic violence. As Veltmeyer and Petras summarize, "in the current situation, 'accumulation by disposession' is taking the form of land-grabbing ("large-scale foreign investment in land acquisition," in the World Bank's lexicon), enclosure of what remains of the global commons, the privatization and commodification of land and water, the extraction and pillage of available natural resources, and the degradation of the habitats and ecosystems on which the communities affected by the operations of extractive capital depend for their livelihoods and way of life."[78] With fewer inhabitants left to stand up for them and scarce political standing of their own, environments have been increasingly laid bare to extractivist exploitation, whether that of local cattle barons, transnational oil and mining corporations, or paramilitary forces dedicated to coca monoculture. The project of literary ecology thus became finding a route back to emplacement, and through emplacement to sustainability, leading authors to experiment with a wide variety of tactics. La vorágine's metabolic reintegration of the body into the environment provided one route to reemplacement; however, the dissolution of the subject seems nihilistic, and it seemingly discounts any role for written or even spoken language in the material experience of environment. On the other hand, Enrique Leff argues that this dissolution of the subject can only ever be partial, a delinking from modern forms of subjectivity rather than the end of the subject itself; it is followed by an ecological recognition of the complex heterogeneity of our own identities in relationship to our ecosystem, which necessarily includes other people and forms of human and non-human communication.[79]

More recent Colombian literary works deal with this problem by addressing the materiality of language itself. In an interesting response to La vorágine, Héctor Abad Faciolince's Basura (2000, Garbage) resuscitates meaning from waste, from the remains of what is devoured. In this novel, a fictionalized reader reconstructs the life of a marginal author, who throws everything he writes down the trash chute of the apartment complex shared by the two characters. Writing becomes a process of literary composting, in which the narrator uses the waste left behind by another writer to cultivate his own story. Basura does not fully reconcile the material with the symbolic, however, despite its portrayal of writing as a form of physical waste or by-product of lived experience akin to the cheese wrappers and empty wine bottles that the author also tosses down the chute. Since what is reconstituted from the trash is already written – that is, encoded symbolically – the novel maintains the humanist position that life can only make sense when mediated by writing, even if that writing can be considered a form of waste. Symbolic abstraction may not be transcendental, but it still holds a privileged position in the construction of the subject.

Similarly, Juan Carlos Botero's *El arrecife* (2006, The Reef) takes a less than radical approach to the problem of bodily subjectivities, but it does provide an alternative to the modern sequestering of material affects through symbolic mediation. Rather than deconstructing the human subject, this novel develops an alternative masculine bildungsroman to those of *María* and *De sobremesa*; here the operative procedure is immersion rather than abstraction. This novel tells the story of a boy's coming into knowledge of the ocean through an extended education by his uncle, culminating in an epic rite of passage that consists in swimming through a dangerous, turbulent labyrinth of coral to the open sea. The boy comes into self-knowledge through his preparations for surviving this epic trial, thereby resuscitating pre-modern forms of subjectivity in which it was impossible to extricate oneself from the environment due to the threats it posed to the body. Despite its focus on the materiality of the bodily experience of the environment, however, the novel runs the risk of reintegration into the humanist paradigm and its nostalgic nature, since it takes place in an enclosed, insular environment, a Caribbean reserve to which the characters escape periodically from their normal, urban lives in Bogotá. No development plans are formulated in the novel, but its displacement of environmental affects to an island far removed from mainland Colombia has some similarities to *De sobremesa*'s Swiss nature.

Ecofeminist writing has gained the most traction in articulating the possibilities for material subjectivities due to its acknowledgment that, in patriarchal societies at least, the symbolic order inscribes bodies with hierarchical, gendered meanings that generate sovereign and subaltern subject positions. Ecofeminist writers seek to recover the meaningfulness of the body and the bodily experience of the environment as a way of resisting patriarchal biopolitics. Going beyond Abad Faciolince's recognition of the materiality of the written page or Botero's coming into subjectivity through an epic encounter with the environment, authors like Albalucía Ángel tend to portray writing as an ongoing bodily activity that, like any other bodily movement, interfaces with the environment, affecting it and being affected by it. In this framework, written expression becomes a muscular movement akin to the vocalization of sound or movement in dance rather than a machine for ex/abstracting the subject. Ángel's *Misiá Señora*, for example, transforms writing into an expression of the body in place:

> El río. Otros ríos. El tráfago del agua, el barbotear de la corriente que vibra
> como azogue, desciende en oleadas y te arrastra a la gruta donde se escucha
> el grito de las flores, malva, magnolia, madreselva, mandrágora, el llanto de

la muerte de tantos otros niños que buscan como tú la tumba errante, madrépora, mimosa, mirabel, danzan y cantan, malveloca, menjuí, dejas que esa babel se encienda en tu cerebro y te sumes también en el desate de los miembros, los brazos se abren para abrazar el aire dulce, la cabeza ondulea, salta, se ríe, Marianita, los oyes, las voces de los niños, aquel pedir de risa fresca, de olores nuevos llenando tu saliva, abriendo en tus entrañas compuertas olvidadas, porque era allí, en el centro de tu vientre donde todo latía, palpitaba.[80]

Written language provides no transcendental subject position beyond the environment; there is no narrating "I," only the "you," the body that palpitates in tandem with its surroundings. Language no longer generates mimetic representation, but rather becomes a kind of behavioral or affective display, a mechanism through which the body reacts to perception and makes itself perceived to other beings around it. In this sense, words do not function as discrete signs that objectify what they name; instead they morph seamlessly as sound and movement into a polyphonic soundscape that is no more than the material manifestation of heterogeneous environment. Even metaphors like the "cavern," which often symbolizes the subconscious in Western cultural representations, is rematerialized by tying it to the "womb." The subconscious, the imagination is subterranean, located within the material world, within the body. And like Rivera's *Vortex*, the "errant tomb" evokes the death of the transcendental subject, a dancing, singing death that is painless, even pleasurable, as it heralds the rupture with the patriarchal symbolic order and a coming into the full, material life of the body in flowing motion. Of course, there is danger as well, as Marianita's body is later subjected to sexual abuse.

Las andariegas (1984, The Wanderers), another novel by Ángel, takes a more systematic approach to the complicity between patriarchal subjectivities and destructive environmental practices. This work features extraterrestrial female travelers who descend to Earth only to bear witness to the atrocities committed by men throughout Western history, thereby revealing the historical subjugation of both women and diverse environments in the systematic production of Western Man. Influenced by Hélène Cixous's injunction that women create a new, gynocentric language to counter the phallocentric logic of the patriarchal symbolic order, the novel is written entirely without the use of capital letters (except in proper names), a structure that also serves to tie together the distinct mythohistorical moments in an ongoing narrative of oppression and resistance.[81] Women's voices appear primarily through song, underscoring once again the materiality of language as sound, while masculinity is represented not as a bodily property, but rather as the performance of unjust violence – usually the invasion of matriarchal societies that live in sustainable harmony with their environments. Feminized nature (associated with female goddesses and mythological characters) and women collaborate to defend this harmony from the masculine invaders. The end of the novel portrays a post-apocalyptic New York City that is inhabited only by horrific beasts and fungi; macho modernity appears to have culminated in a nuclear war in which it "rained fire and ash for seven days."[82] Some women survived this apocalypse, however, and will ostensibly repopulate the world in a more sustainable manner, recognizing the sacredness of the Earth, which is assigned agency through perspectival subjectivity in the final lines. Balance finally restored with the self-immolation of the patriarchal order, the wanderers ascend back into the heavens from whence they came.

A more obliquely ecofeminist text, Laura Restrepo's *La novia oscura* (The Obscure Girlfriend) delves into the relationships between extractivism and subalternity, with prostitution as the literal and metaphorical juncture between the two. The economy of extraction in Tora, a fictionalized version of real-life oil town Barrancabermeja, produces a situation in which male workers' bodies are objectified as mere tools for carrying out the extractive process, while women's bodies become the tools of masculine pleasure and recreation, thus maintaining productivity. Prostitution has no stigma attached to it in the novel, but it does denote a form of subalternity that is produced through inequality and exploitation, even when it can also become a way of garnering limited economic and political agency (both the male oil and the female sex workers participate in collective political action and strikes). In this sense, men, women, and the nation itself are all depicted as existing in a state of prostitution due to their economic and political subordination to the North American Tropical Oil Company, which exploits them all equally. The Tropical Oil Company is not solely responsible for all exploitation in the novel, however; the military, corrupt politicians, and governmental officials are also complicit. Unlike *La vorágine*, *La novia oscura*'s violence is not portrayed as the product of a jungle war-machine, but of human and environmental exploitation at multiple scales.

In this scenario, the body becomes the way back to the material and to a sense of collective belonging to place as well. On the one hand, sex and bodily contact in La Catunga, the red-light district of Tora, generate a kind of universal sociality that is capable of breaking through the concentric enclosures created by the oil company to divide and segregate distinct populations and territories. On the other, the extraction of oil, labor, and pleasure generates universal degradation; Tora's world slowly falls apart due to the pollution of the Magdalena River, a syphilis plague, and the toxic social environment caused by the military repression of the labor strike.[83] The mutual degradation of natural and human bodies in the oil industry reveals that the bracketing mechanisms have failed; humans' bodies are inevitably imbued with their environment, in this case, not a natural one, but the toxic one created by global, industrial capitalism.

Another response to the problem of displacement and the deterritorialization associated with globalization has been the vindication of local cultural and environmental differences, a project that works within the neoliberal paradigm of multiculturalism to make visible the contradictions between the rhetoric of development and the exclusionary practices associated with extractivism.[84] How can extractive practices that visibly marginalize entire ethnic groups or social sectors be consistent with the project of development if, as nationalistic proponents of neoliberal policies often claim, the goal of development is material and political democracy through inclusive, multicultural consensus? This is the question implicit in works of self-representation such as Afro-Colombian writers Gregorio Sánchez Gómez's *La bruja de las minas* (The Witch of the Mines, 1938) and Amália Lú Posso Figueroa's *Vean, vé mis nanas negras* (Look, See, My Black Mamas, 2006) as well as ethnographic travel writing by authors like Alfredo Molano, whose works refute homogenization and incorporation into the capitalist world-ecology by highlighting local cultural and environmental differences. These post-hegemonic, neoregionalist approaches to narrative are designed for the preservation of place in the conceptualization of the nation, portraying Colombia as a patchwork of interconnected places rather than a centralized, economic and political machine that produces homogenous space and uniform citizens. Furthermore, these works trace Colombia's history of violence to the forceful imposition of centralizing, homogenizing forms of territorialization, thereby postulating respect for cultural and environmental diversity as the only route to peaceful coexistence. Neoregionalist literature is often closely tied to local environmental and social activism as well, making local residents and the places they inhabit visible in a political sense and thereby validating their public dissent to extractive practices. In this way, they reveal that the neoliberal economic consensus is only a consensus among political elites, and that it is antidemocratic not only in the way in which it distributes power and wealth, but also exposure to violence and environmental toxicity.

Some of these neoregionalist works suggest radically different ways of conceiving collective identities. Such is the case in the Amazonian folktales compiled by Juan Carlos Galeano in *Cuentos amazónicos*, which fuse together indigenous Amazonian and Western worldviews to propose a radical, ecological cosmopolitanism in which people, plants, and animals all form a single, enmeshed society.[85] In this conceptualization, the human form depends on behavioral interactions with the environment rather than rationalistic abstraction, and forms can change along with behavior. Indeed, shape shifting is common: river dolphins and anacondas are able to assume human form, while shamans transform into jaguars and disobedient children turn into birds. In these interspecies entanglements, speech is not uniquely a human trait. Verbal communication becomes generalized to encompass all sound; as in Albalucía Ángel's ecofeminist writing, words, birdsong, wind, and rushing water all interact in a polyphonic soundscape in which every noise contains biosemiotic meaning. The ecosystem, rather than a collection of objects, is thus a communicative network in which humans are only one voice among uncountable others.[86] Furthermore, given that they are assumed to be capable of conscious perception, of responding to other presences, animals and plants are believed to see themselves as people, just as humans do. This horizontal conceptualization of the relationships between people and all other beings in their environment gives rise to a universal sociality or "multinaturalism" that supplements Western "multiculturalism" and its conceptualization of the cosmopolitan.[87]

In the introduction to *The Ecology of Others*, anthropologist Philippe Descola decries the generalized anthropocentrism of his discipline, searching for a reconciliation of the modern opposition between nature and culture:

> How to recompose nature and society, humans and non-humans, individuals and collectives, in a new assemblage in which they would no longer present themselves as distributed between substances, processes, and representations, but as the instituted expression of relationships between multiple entities whose ontological status and capacity for action vary according to the positions they occupy in relation to one another?[88]

These Colombian authors' exploration of strategies for reemplacing humans in their environments have gone a long way towards establishing this "ecology of relationships" to counter the displacement of the human subject, the extraction of the nature-image, and capitalization of environments. The acknowledgment of one's own materiality necessarily implies an openness to encounter, an acknowledgment that we constantly affect and are affected by the human and nonhuman entities that surround us, that form our environment. In this form of bodily subjectivity, the notion of self depends not on sovereign abstraction, but rather on recognition of the web of relationships that every living organism inevitably develops with the bodies around, on, and inside it, if one thinks of the microbes that inhabit our bodies, doing our digestive work and protecting us from pathogens. This ecological awareness of our material existence in relation to the places we inhabit precludes the abstraction of affect into a realm of pure symbolism, and with no nature to sequester those affects to, there can be no systematic capitalization of environments. This is not to say that an ecological perspective means the end of violence or development; but it does force recognition of the ways in which one's actions affect those around us, placing an ethical injunction on the individual that precludes the kind of systematic, conscienceless violence that is required in capitalist extractivism.

Notes

1 See Arturo Escobar, "El lugar de la naturaleza y la naturaleza del lugar: ¿globalización o postdesarrollo?" in Edgardo Lander (ed.), *La colonialidad del saber, eurocentrismo y ciencias sociales: perspectivas latinoamericanas* (Buenos Aires: Consejo Latinoamericano de Ciencias Sociales, 2000), 116.

2 Works exemplary of this tendency include Carlos Alonso's *The Spanish American Regional Novel: Modernity and Autochthony* (Cambridge: Cambridge University Press, 1990); Arturo Escobar's *Territories of Difference: Place, Movements, Life, Redes* (Durham: Duke University Press, 2008); Jennifer L. French's *Nature, Neocolonialism, and the Spanish American Regionalist Writers* (Hanover, NH: Dartmouth University Press, 2005); Germán Márquez's *Mapas de un fracaso: naturaleza y conflicto en Colombia* (Bogotá: Universidad Nacional de Colombia, 2004); Margarita Serje's *El revés de la nación: territorios salvajes, fronteras y tierras de nadie* (Bogotá: Universidad de Los Andes, 2005); and Lesley Wylie's *Colonial Tropes and Postcolonial Tricks: Rewriting the Tropics in the novela de la selva* (Liverpool: Liverpool University Press, 2009).

3 See chapter seven of Mary Louise Pratt, *Imperial Eyes: Travel Writing and Transculturation* (New York: Routledge, 1992).

4 See Ericka Beckman, *Capital Fictions: The Literature of Latin America's Export Age* (Minneapolis: University of Minnesota Press, 2013), xi–xii.

5 As a recent example of the progressive commodification of formerly inconceivable resources, Beckman cites the privatization of water resources in Cochabamba, Bolivia, which included "even the rain that falls from the sky" (*Capital Fictions,* viii). Spanish director Icíar Bollaín made a film on the topic with the same name.

6 "Those of us who work the lowlands, cutting down the forest and burning it, act like barbarians, because we are destroying an enormous wealth in lumber

that we desperately need, to the degree that if a property owner had conserved intact his forest along the route from La Mesa to Girardot, his property would be worth ten times as much as it is today as mere pastureland. There is not a single beam for building houses in the communities of La Mesa, Anapoima, or Tocaima; and if the railroad is to be extended, there are no ties to be found in the entire distance it must cover.

"Additionally, the beauty and sumptuousness of these tropical regions, so alluring in former times, disappeared and they are today converted into immense grasslands of a sad and melancholic aspect; and the traveler, exhausted by the sun, doesn't have a single tree under whose shade to rest." Medardo Rivas, *Los trabajadores de tierra caliente* (Bogotá: Universidad Nacional, 1946), 81. All translations are by Mark Anderson unless noted otherwise.

7 See Freud's "Mourning and Melancholy" in *The Standard Edition of the Complete Psychological Works of Sigmund Freud*, vol. 14, ed. and trans. James Strachey (London: Hogarth Press; Institute of Psychoanalysis, 1959), 243–58.

8 "In the Juntas de Apulo, tropical nature still appears, colossal and sovereign; and the horizon that presents itself to the traveler's eyes as he descends the slope is the most beautiful that one's imagination could possibly dream" (Rivas, *Trabajadores*, 82).

9 Luis Alfredo Bohórquez Caldera exemplifies this perspective in "Colonización de la naturaleza: una aproximación desde el extractivismo en Colombia" (*El Ágora-USB* 13.1 [2013)], 222).

10 Joel Kovel, *The Enemy of Nature: The End of Capitalism or the End of the World?* (New York: Zed Books, 2007), 121.

11 As Derrida writes about the "specter of communism," "the specter is a paradoxical incorporation, the becoming-body, a certain phenomenal and carnal form of the spirit"; *Specters of Marx: The State of the Debt, the Work of Mourning, and the New International*, trans. Peggy Kamuf, introduction by Bernd Magnus and Stephen Cullenberg (New York: Routledge, 1994), 5. See also Timothy Morton, *Ecology without Nature: Rethinking Environmental Aesthetics* (Cambridge, MA: Harvard University Press, 2007), 14.

12 For an overview of the polyvalence of nature taking as its point of departure Raymond Williams's assessment that "Any full history of the uses of nature would be a history of a large part of human thought," see the first chapter of Peter Coates's *Nature: Western Attitudes since Ancient Times* (Berkeley: University of California Press, 1998).

13 See Gustavo Mejía's in-depth analysis of *María*'s relationship to the expansion of industrial agriculture in the Cauca River Valley in "La novela de la decadencia de la clase latifundista: *María* de Jorge Isaacs," *Escritura* 2 (1976): 261–78. Jorge Isaacs was well known for his ties to the conservative political party in Colombia; nevertheless, Mejia points out that both liberals and conservatives were invested in the expansion of capitalism in Colombia, differing primarily with respect to the means of production, with conservatives defending slavery and monopolistic land management practices (267–71).

14 Regarding Efraín's father's business dealings, which mirror those of Jorge
   Isaacs and his own father, see pp. 15 ("an expensive and beautiful" modern
   sugar refinery, extensive cattle herds, and slave labor), 120 (his father's foreign
   creditors), and 170 (gold mining, slaver labor, and international commerce in
   the Chocó) of *María* (Madrid: Espasa-Calpe, 1976).

15 See Enrique Pupo Walker "Observaciones sobre las categorías artísticas del
   paisaje en *María* de Jorge Isaacs," *Kentucky Romance Quarterly* 15, no. 3
   (1968), 274. Taking an ecofeminist approach, Lee Joan Skinner notes that
   Efraín's way of seeing both María and the landscape involve writing about
   them, thus transforming them simultaneously into verbal objects of the
   speaking I in "The Functions of Landscape in Jorge Isaacs and Soledad
   Acosta de Samper," *Symposium* 68, no. 1 (2014), 14–15. We examine this
   dynamic in closer detail, particularly regarding the process by which affective
   relations are transformed into symbolic ones as the capitalist subject
   emerges.

16 "This prolepsis of personal disaster organizes the entire narrative," as Doris
   Sommer phrases it in *Foundational Fictions: The National Romances of Latin
   America* (Berkeley: University of California Press, 1991), 176.

17 Raymond L. Williams, "An Eco-critical Reading of *One Hundred Years of
   Solitude*," in *The Cambridge Companion to Gabriel García Márquez*, ed. Philip
   Swanson (Cambridge: Cambridge University Press, 2010), 67.

18 As Sommer points out, "Before loss, the boy cannot experience the absence
   that will require the supplement of writing, an absence that this text has to
   respect in order to continue writing itself" (*Foundational Fictions*, 173).

19 "Those moments in which I forgot myself, in which my thoughts drifted over
   regions that were unknown to me, moments in which the doves murmured
   lovingly in the shade of orange trees, exhausted under the weight of their
   golden clusters; in which María's voice, sweeter murmur still, reached my ears,
   had an ineffable charm. Infancy, which in its insatiable curiosity is amazed by
   anything new that Nature presents to its gaze; adolescence, which, guessing at
   everything, takes pleasure in chaste visions of love, premonition of a happiness
   so often waited for in vain; only they know how to convoke those unmeasured
   hours in which the soul seems to attempt to return to heaven, which it still
   hasn't been able to forget.
   "It wasn't the branches of the rosebushes from which the stream's currents
   pilfered delicate leaves to adorn themselves fleetingly; nor the majestic flight of
   the black eagles over the nearby summits; they were not what my eyes
   contemplated; it was what I will no longer see, what my spirit broken by sad
   realities no longer searches for, or admires only in dreams: the world, as Adam
   saw it on the first morning of his life" (Isaacs, *María*, 110).

20 "I can't help but recognize, despite myself, that you are overcome with noble
   sentiments upon speaking this way. But I must warn you that my determin-
   ation is irrevocable" (Isaacs, *María*, p150).

21 "I had to conceal my suffering" (Isaacs, *María*, 148).

22 "It was necessary that I find myself someday in conditions to be able to support the family" (Isaacs, *María*, 151); "Whenever my father did not appear at the dinner table, I occupied the head seat" (152).

23 "He was dazzled by my knowledge of agronomic theory" (Isaacs, *María*, 25).

24 See Edward D. Melillo, "The First Green Revolution: Debt Peonage and the Making of the Nitrogen Fertilizer Trade, 1840–1930," *American Historical Review* 117, no. 4 (2012): 1028–60.

25 "A scream, my own scream, interrupted that dream; reality disturbed it jealously, as if that instant had been a century of happiness. The lamp had burned out; the cold winds of the early morning seeped in through the window; my hands were stiff and they squeezed those braids, sole remnant of her beauty, sole reality of my dream" (Isaacs, *María*, 257).

26 We are building from Georges Bataille's notion of expenditure in *The Accursed Share: An Essay on General Economy, Volume 1: Consumption* (New York: Zone Books, 1988), 22. Nature writing is far from an "accursed share," or profitless expenditure, however, since it generates cultural capital through identity politics and economic capital in the literary market.

27 "Nature is the most loving of mothers when pain has taken possession of our soul, and should happiness caress us, she smiles" (Isaacs, *María*, 70).

28 "I will no longer admire those songs, breathe in those aromas, contemplate those light-filled landscapes, as I did in the happy days of my childhood and the beautiful ones of my adolescence: today, strangers inhabit my parents' home!" (Isaacs, *María*, 121).

29 See Alejandro Mejías López, "El perpetuo deseo: esquizofrenia y nomadismo narrativo en *De sobremesa* de José Asunción Silva," *Revista Canadiense de Estudios Hispánicos* 31, no. 2 (2007), 339.

30 Beckman, *Capital Fictions*, 65.

31 Beckman, *Capital Fictions*, 73.

32 See Slavoj Žižek, *Organs without Bodies: On Deleuze and Consequences* (New York: Routledge), 23–7 and pp. 163–73. Indeed, on p. 65 of *Capital Fictions*, Beckman finds that Silva's literary aestheticization of luxury objects seeks to suppress their commodity character, and thereby revalidate him as an artist rather than a merchant.

33 José Asunción Silva, *De sobremesa. Obras completas* (Caracas: Biblioteca Ayacucho, 1976), 137. "Oh the Circe, who changes men into swine . . . !" José Asunción Silva, *After-Dinner Conversation: The Diary of a Decadent*, trans. Kelly Washbourne (Austin: University of Texas Press, 2005), 85.

34 This is the only way he can escape his English psychiatrist's recommendation that he destroy his idealized image of the woman by getting to know her and marrying her, if he finds their personalities and interests to be compatible (Silva, *De sobremesa*, 170).

35 Felipe Martínez Pinzón, "Leer a Silva a contrapelo: *De sobremesa* como novela tropical," *Antípoda* 15 (2012): 92–5.

36 Silva, *De sobremesa*, 140. "Nature, but nature viewed thus, without a human voice interrupting the dialogue that it carries on with the pensive soul, with the voices of its waters, of its foliage, of its winds, with the eternal poetry of the lights and of the shadows! When isolated thus from all human ties, I hear it and feel it, I am lost in it as in a divine nirvana" (Silva, *After-Dinner Conversation*, 89).

37 Silva, *De sobremesa*, 141. "Unforgettable instants whose description resists the words' every effort to capture them!" (Silva, *After-Dinner Conversation*, 90).

38 Silva, *De sobremesa*, 141. "Lost to myself, to life, to death, the sublime spectacle entered my being, and I scattered into the starry firmament, into the peaceful sea, as if fused in them in a pantheistic ecstasy of sublime worship" (Silva, *After-Dinner Conversation*, 90).

39 Silva, *De sobremesa*, 141. "The plan that [I] called for, the only purpose to which to devote my life has appeared to me as clear and precise as a mathematical formula. To reach it I need to make an effort every minute for years, and to have an iron will that does not relent for an instant" (Silva, *After-Dinner Conversation*, 90).

40 See Martínez Pinzón's extensive discussion of Silva's parody of nineteenth-century Colombian geopolitical discourse in "Leer a Silva."

41 Silva, *De sobremesa*, 144.

42 Silva, *De sobremesa*, 142. "A center where the civilized from all parties are recruited to form a new party, removed from all political or religious fanaticism, a party of civilized men who believe in science and place their efforts in the service of the great Idea" (Silva, *After-Dinner Conversation*, 91).

43 Alejandro Quin discusses in depth the question of sovereignty and the "regeneration of the land" in this novel in a soon-to-be-published manuscript entitled "Negación sin oposición: el dandi como soberano en *De sobremesa*."

44 Giorgio Agamben, *Homo Sacer: Sovereign Power and Bare Life*, trans. Daniel Heller-Roazen (Stanford: Stanford University Press, 1998), 15–21.

45 See Eduardo Camacho Guizado's prologue to José Asunción Silva's *Obra Completa* (Caracas: Biblioteca Ayacucho, 1978), 1.

46 Silva, *De sobremesa*, 148. "'I was mad when I wrote this, wasn't I, Sáenz?' Fernández exclaimed, interrupting the reading, speaking to the doctor and smiling at him amiably" (Silva, *After-Dinner Conversation*, 98).

47 Silva, *De sobremesa*, 147.

48 Silva, *De sobremesa*, 148. "'It's the only time you've been in your right mind,' replied Sáenz coolly" (Silva, *After-Dinner Conversation*, 98).

49 Regarding the complementary changes in forms of labor, land management practices, and political regimes in the shift from *hacienda* and *trapiche* modes of production to industrial sugar plantations or *ingenios* toward the end of the nineteenth century and the beginning of the twentieth, see Irene Vélez Torres, Daniel Varela Corredor, Sandra Rátiva Gaona, and Andrés Salcedo Fidalgo, "Agroindustria y extractivismo en el Alto Cauca: impactos sobre los sistemas de subsistencia afrocampesinos y resistencias, 1950–2011," *Revista CS* 12 (2013), 165. These authors focus specifically on the transformations in

extractive practices in the Valle del Cauca, but similar processes occurred throughout Colombia.

50 For a characteristic passage describing the racialized abjection of the *trapiche* labor regime, which would "break a radical (liberal)'s heart," see Eugenio Díaz, *Manuela* (Medellín: Bedout, 1965), 42.

51 In the late nineteenth century, Colombia produced 300–350 tons of iron a year at iron foundries such as the Ferretería de Pacho, approximately 90 kilometers to the north of Bogotá, according to Alberto Corradine Ángulo and Helga Mora de Corradine in *Historia de la arquitectura colombiana: siglo XIX* (Bogotá: Universidad Nacional de Colombia, 2001), 20.

52 Eugenio Díaz, *Manuela*, 78–9.

53 "The transformation is due not only to economic reasons, that is, to obtaining land for productive ends, but also, even primarily, for the purpose of controlling society and labor by controlling nature" (Márquez, *Mapas*, 9).

54 See Jason W. Moore, "Ecology, Capital, and the Nature of Our Times: Accumulation & Crisis in the Capitalist World-Ecology," *Journal of World-Systems Research* 17, no. (2011): 107–46.

55 Serje, *El revés de la nación*, 5.

56 *Criollismo* is also known as *telurismo* or regionalism, the term favored by most North American critics. Regionalism does not function well to designate a distinctive literary movement in the Colombian context, however, due to the long history of federalism in Colombian politics. Regionalism was the predominant mode of representation throughout Colombia until at least the mid–twentieth century, with four main regionalist traditions, each characterized by its own aesthetic, as Raymond L. Williams shows in the introduction to *The Colombian Novel: 1844–1987* (Austin: University of Texas Press, 1991).

57 Beckman, *Capital Fictions*, x–xi.

58 Beckman, *Capital Fictions*, 158–9.

59 As Germán Márquez argues on p. 11 of *Mapas de un fracaso*, the contradictions in this development strategy inevitable led to its abject failure.

60 Michael Edward Stanfield, *Red Rubber, Bleeding Trees: Violence, Slavery, and Empire in Northwest Amazonia, 1850–1933* (Albuquerque: University of New Mexico Press, 1998), 21 and 116.

61 José Eustasio Rivera, *La vorágine* (Buenos Aires: Losada; Madrid: Alianza, 1987), 155.

62 Stanfield, *Red Rubber*, 41.

63 "Where is the pastoral poetry here, where are the butterflies like translucent flowers, the magic birds, the singing brook? Impoverished fantasies of poets who know only domesticated wilds!" Rivera, *La Vorágine*, 197.

64 "Beautiful books about the mysteries of the jungle," Cesar Uribe Piedrahita, *Toá: narraciones de caucherías* (Medellín: Editorial Bedout, 1933), 27.

65 Wylie, *Colonial Tropes*, 46.

66 "For the first time, the inhuman jungle rose up before me in all its horror" (Rivera, *La vorágine*, 196).

67 "All the men who fought to enslave Nature in the Colombian Amazon, and fell, defeated, in the battle" (Uribe Piedrahita, *Toá*, 7).

68 "Everywhere the "treekiller" liana – creeping octopus of the forests – grips the trunks with its suckers, collaring them and twisting them, grafting and transmigrating into them in painful metempsychosis. The ant hills vomit their trillions of devastating *bachaco* ants that cut the greenery from the hillsides and return to their tunnel in wide paths, like the heralds of destruction, holding aloft leaves and flowers as battle flags. Dry rot infects trees like raging syphilis, covering them with torturous sores as it riddles their tissues and pulverizes their bark until it brings them down, suddenly, with their grief of shattered but still living branches" (Rivera, *La vorágine*, 196–7).

69 "The jungle deranges man, making him develop the most inhuman instincts: cruelty invades the soul like an intricate thorn, and greed burns like a fever" (Rivera, *La vorágine*, 150).

70 "Meanwhile, the land fulfills its successive renovations: at the foot of the fallen giant, the seed that germinates; in the midst of the tropical miasma floats pollen; and everywhere the breath of fermentation, warm vapors in the dusk, death's lethargy, the torpor of procreation" (Rivera, *La vorágine*, 197).

71 "There was life, right at the threshold of death. Death transforming itself into fertilizing sediment, creating new life!" (Uribe Piedrahita, *Toá*, 61).

72 See Mark Anderson, "The Natural Baroque: Opacity, Impenetrability, and Folding in Writing on Amazonia," in Lesley Wylie (ed.), *Amazonian Literatures, Hispanic Issues On-Line* 16 (2014): 74–7.

73 See Julia Elena Rial, "Petronarrativas latinoamericanas," *Hispanísta* 4, no. 13 (2003), n.p.

74 "Oily mud coats the few plants that still drag themselves through the mire. Imposing barbed-wire fences isolate the forest of towers, of tanks and powerful motors that make the black blood circulate from the bowels of the earth, through the thick steel arteries, to the ship's bellies. The sounds of sledge-hammers, steam reeking of asphalt residue, yells in a thousand languages saturate the atmosphere, boiling under the sun.
"A dirty mass of men from every region of the globe mills around 'The Flower' oil well: Yankees and Canadians, Armenians, Greeks and Jews, Antilleans and natives of the continent bathed by the Caribbean Sea and the Gulf of Mexico"; César Uribe Piedrahita, *Mancha de aceite* (Bogotá: Editorial Oveja Negra, 1935), 26.

75 "Instead of worrying, be glad – replied the Payanés – because this is the face of progress. Learn it well, because this is how even the most remote corner of the world will look in fifty years: pure development and human pleasure"; Laura Restrepo, *La novia oscura* (Barcelona: Anagrama, 1999), 126.

76 See Enrique Leff, "El desvanecimiento del sujeto y la reinvención de las identidades colectivas en la era de la complejidad ambiental," *Polis* 27 (2010): 1–32.

77 See Stacy Alaimo, *Bodily Natures: Science, Environment, and the Material Self* (Bloomington: University of Indiana Press, 2010), 9–10.

78 Henry Veltmeyer and James Petras (eds.), introduction to *The New Extractivism: A Post-Neoliberal Development Model or Imperialism of the Twenty-First Century* (New York: Zed Books, 2014), 6.

79 Leff, "El desvanecimiento," 20.

80 "The river. Other rivers. The transit of water, the mumbling of the current that vibrates like mercury, it descends in waves and draws you to the cavern where you can hear the flowers' screams, the mallow, magnolia, honeysuckle, mandrake, the death-cry of so many other children who look, like you, for the errant tomb, madrepore, mimosa, sunflower, they sing and dance, malveloca, benzoin, you let that babel catch fire in your brain and you also sink into the looseness of your members, your arms open to embrace the sweet air, your head undulates, it jumps, it laughs, Marianita, you hear them, the voices of the children, that imploring with a fresh laugh, of new odors filling your saliva, opening in your insides forgotten hatches, because it was there, in the center of your womb, where everything beat, palpitated"; Albalucía Ángel, *Misiá Señora* (Barcelona: Argos Vergara, 1982), 17–18.

81 See Claire Taylor, "Wandering Text and Theories in Albalucía Ángel's *Las andariegas*," *Journal of Iberian and Latin American Studies* 12, nos. 2–3 (2006), 255.

82 Albalucía Ángel, *Las andariegas* (Barcelona: Argos Vergara, 1984), 137.

83 See Isabel Vergara, "*La novia oscura* o la historia en combustión." *Inti* 63–4 (2006), 31.

84 Arturo Escobar studies the dynamic between this form of neoregionalist activism and neoliberal multiculturalism in the Colombian Pacific in *Territories of Difference*.

85 This project was already present to a degree in Uribe Piedrahita's *Toá*, which comprises a "frontier fiction" bridging indigenous Amazonian and Western identities and revalidating indigenous identities within the national order, as Lesley Wylie argues in "Frontier Fictions: The Place of Amazonia in César Uribe Piedrahita's *Toá*," *Bulletin of Spanish Studies* 87, no. 7 (2010), 969–70.

86 See Kalevi Kull, "Ecosystems are Made of Semiosic Bonds: Consortia, *Umwelten*, Biophony, and Ecological Codes," *Biosemiotics* 3 (2010): 347–57.

87 See Eduardo Viveiros de Castro, "Cosmological Deixis and Amerindian Perspectivism," *Journal of the Royal Anthropological Institute* 4, no. 3 (1998), 470.

88 Philippe Descola, *The Ecology of Others*, trans. Geneviéve Godbout and Benjamin P. Luley (Chicago: Prickly Paradigm, 2013), 5.

CHAPTER 19

Visions of nature: Colombian literature and the environment from the colonial period to the nineteenth century

Ana María Mutis and Elizabeth Pettinaroli

Nature's challenges to humankind have not been limited to the struggle to wrest survival out of its often difficult conditions, develop culture, and build enduring civilizations. Humanity has struggled, too, to make sense of nature. To apprehend its vastness, its complex and ever-elusive quality, beggars the imagination and frustrates the intellect. For Heraclitus, ceaseless transformation, interconnectedness, and the joining of opposites make nature endlessly elusive, as one of his most oracular sentences has it: *"Phusis kruptesthai philei"* (Nature loves to hide).

For the writers who set about describing the natural environment of what is now Colombia (part of the colonial Nuevo Reino de Granada [New Kingdom of Granada] and the early-national Nueva Granada [New Granada]), the region – with its stunning multiplicity of landscapes, its fauna and flora, and the humanity it sustained – embodies the dense layers of meaning latent in the philosopher's aphorism. At times nature hides as an object to be revealed; at times nature conceals the complexity of the world itself. Their descriptions reveal a series of concerns that reflect shifting modes of reasoning used to put forward particular visions of the region. In the late sixteenth century, literary works of the Nuevo Reino de Granada reveal changing views of the cosmos and preoccupations about the relationship between man and world through their descriptions of nature and space. Illuminated by intellectual projects that reconceived how to think about nature, these views furnish us a key with which to unlock the shaping power these representations exercised on the debates over the nature of the human, the image of the Earth as object, and the critique of intervention. Later the deployment of a new, scientific discourse and the delineation of new territorial entities in the eighteenth century, aligned with Spain's desire of commercial expansion, lay the groundwork for a novel envisioning of New Granada that would ultimately influence the rhetorical discourse of independence. The subsequent engagement of the scientific language of the nineteenth century shaped Colombia's foundational literature by forging diverging natural images of national identity.

These shifting visions of nature also reveal a set of concerns shared with certain strands of modern ecological criticism. Authors turn to nature to interrogate the complexities of the world as known and to discover how the production of such knowledge came about. They expose ideological projects founded on unilateral narratives that, as Enrique Leff notes, negate the contingent nature of notions of space, time, diversity, and otherness. An examination of the ways in which authors engaged representations of nature reveals the use of nature writing as a forum in which to voice critiques of the imperatives of global expansion, the ambitions for scientific enlightenment, and unidirectional visions of national consolidation.

Landscapes of experience and abstraction, and the critique of intervention

The descriptions of the natural world in Juan de Castellanos's first pan-egyric to the Kingdom of New Granada, the late sixteenth-century *Elegías de varones ilustres de Indias* (Elegies of Illustrious Men of the Indies), reveals an ontological shift in the imagining of the relationship between nature and humanity within the European worldview. The revival of descriptive geography in Humanism, the renewal of Ptolemaic carto-graphy, and the challenge the Copernican revolution posed to the inherited geocentric model fostered new theorizations that served as a foundation for novel philosophical, empirical, and political interpretations of nature. Spanish and Portuguese encounters with New World lands confirmed the inhabitation of the tropics. They also provided further evidence of the need to reassess Ptolemy's tripartite division of the sphere (a torrid uninhabitable belt in the equinoctial region, surrounded by two temperate regions extending to the respective poles) as determinant for the natural constitution of all matter in the cosmos and, consequently, for the definition of the nature of humans. In a fervor to supersede the knowledge inherited from the ancients, many intellectuals abandoned the idea of reducing the study of nature solely to Aristotle's abstract ideas about matter and privation and sought to identify more concrete explanations for natural phenomena. With the mission of mastering the world's com-plexity and revealing its mechanisms, they upheld human power as a force to interpret the *secretum* associated with the discoveries unfolding from conquest. As Alfonso Ingegno notes, within this animist-organic perspec-tive, nature came to be a deliberate activity perceptible to men.

Embracing this intellectual ferment, Castellanos joins the clinamen or swerve of the tradition in early modern epic initiated by Alonso de Ercilla's *La Araucana* (1569,The Araucaniad) and Luis de Camões's *Os Lusíadas* (1572,The Lusiads) to describe new discoveries and sing the praises of Portuguese and Castilian global ambitions, re-centering the narration and the history on the New Kingdom of Granada. Critics initially relegated the text to the status of a genealogical reference on the New Granadan elites (Juan Flores de Ocáriz's *Libro primero de las genealogías del Nuevo Reyno de Granada* [1674, First Book of the Genealogies of the New Kingdom of Granada]); a foundational work to a purported colonial corpus that buttressed the first national literary canon (José María Vergara y Vergara's *Historia de la literatura en Nueva Granada* [1867, History of the Literature in New Granada]); and as an example of early *criollismo* in the region (Francisco Elías de Tejada's *El pensamiento político de los fundadores de Nueva Granada* [1955, The Political Thoughts of the Founders of New Granada]). More recently, Luis Fernando Restrepo recovers the text's spatial mandate in his study *Un nuevo reino imaginado: las* Elegías de varones ilustres de Indias *de Juan de Castellanos* and observes the intersection of the textual and visual realms in the depiction of Nueva Granada. An approach from the perspective of postcolonial theory afforded the critic an appreciation of a variegated collection of literary forms in the poem's verses (elegy, epic, peregrination, sonnets, and *romanceros*) as well as what he has termed extraliterary resources (*probanzas de hidalguía, rituales fundacionales, requerimiento,* and topographic description). As Restrepo argues, these forms contribute to a semantic re-codification of indigenous territoriality that attempts to "naturalize" the ambition of colonizers over the New World by inscribing it in European terms. Their vivid descriptions bring those remote, trans-Atlantic lands alive in readers' imaginations.

Rooted in the new theorization of the Indies, and the impulse to unveil nature's *secretum,* Castellanos's poem presents two types of descriptions of the region that both advance an a priori notion of the New Kingdom of Granada, at times as a regular and ordered cosmos, at times as a chaotic proliferation variously integrated. The first type of description is present in the periegetic description of the Indies and the New Kingdom of Granada through the mode of representation of perambulation, a figure from medieval pilgrimage. This sort of narrative privileges the representation of space as experiential landscapes through the praxis of chorography (description of particular places) and literary and mythopoeic evocations. The narrative framework of a peregrination noted by Restrepo makes use of chorographic description to reveal a heroic topography in which readers can traverse the particular places of the Kingdom and learn about the great deeds of European conquerors. Castellanos draws the characterization of nature closer to the matrix of a human experience that oscillates wildly between extremes. Imagining the territory from an experiential center, the poet responds explicitly to the call Peter Apian issued in his *Libro de la cosmographia* (1548) to engage vivid depiction so as to make nature present to the reader's eyes and ears. This projection echoes topographies of marvel in Gonzalo Fernández de Oviedo's his *Sumario de la Natural Historia de las Indias* (1526, Summary of the Natural History of the Indies). Castellanos abandons the specific purpose that Oviedo assigns to nature as an aid in furthering Man's understanding of his place in the creation, opening his eyes to enlightenment, and illuminating his path to salvation. At times a generous, benevolent force, the natural world of the New Kingdom as envisioned by the poet facilitates the discoveries and foundations that Spaniards make in the course of their perambulations. Locals reveal to them their secrets for survival, sanctioning their mission with a natural authority and transforming the object of desire into a landscape of endless possibilities. Beatriz Pastor Bodmer identifies a utopian impulse in narratives of geographic exploration and conquest that conceived nature as a force that opened the doors of an Edenic garden to an imagined providential pilgrimage. This impulse would long remain central to the production of knowledge, the legitimization of conquest, the answers to social and moral dilemmas, and ultimately, the appeal to narratives of the vanquished. Seizing that power to interpret the *secretum* in new discoveries, Castellanos traverses nature in quest of no less than the orbs of the Indies, of an America that gently offers herself and her wonders to Europeans.

At other times, nature in *Elegías* transmutes into a terrifying foe ready to thwart the revelation of nature's secrets to men, encumbering the heroic expeditions of Europeans into the land, and transforming the mountains and rivers of the New Kingdom into landscapes of impossibility. In the passages that sing the history of Cartagena, Castellanos departs from the utilitarian characterizations of the region's navigational and commercial potential advanced by the "Cuestionarios de Indias," as well as by the descriptions in Juan López de Velasco's *Geografía y descripción universal de las Indias* (1574, Universal Geography and Description of the Indies) and Antonio de Herrera's *Historia general de los hechos de los castellanos* (1601, General History about the Acts of the Castellanos). Instead, the poet aligns his description of nature with the earliest depiction of the region in the *Epítome de las conquistas del Nuevo Reino de Granada* (1538, Epitomy of the Conquests of the New Kingdom of Granada), a text penned by Alonso de

Santa Cruz, the influential cosmographer, cartographer, chronicler, and astronomer to Charles V and Philip II. In these depictions, nature's former transparency to Europeans often gets lost in the linguistic gulf between Spanish and indigenous toponyms. Diego de Ordáz's excursion up the Uyaparí River exposes an episode of misreading of the natural world due to his mistaking the Muisca word meaning "cascade" for "foundry." The error disappoints Europeans feverish to discover not the magnificent waterfall revealed by locals but rather deposits of mineral wealth. Western aspirations betray the exegesis of nature of the New Kingdom "[p]ues allí cada cual interpretaba/segun aquel deseo que llevaba" (For there each one interpreted/according to the desire that he nursed).[1] The true nature of European desire makes it impossible to seize the powers of interpretation promised by projections of experiential landscapes. Thus, the New World's promise is condemned to remain unfulfilled.

The second type of projection to represent the natural world of the New Kingdom is offered by the author through direct allusions to, and discussion of, two maps, one (now missing) depicting the Gulf of Venezuela, the second the Great River of the Magdalena. Castellanos expands the spatial mandate with the intention of providing better "illustration" [muestra] for his verses in dialogical relation with the second map, containing what is today the earliest extant cartographical representation of Nueva Granada, the Carta Corographica de lo contenido en los tres brazos que cerca de la equinoxial hace la cordillera de las sierras que se continua desde el estrecho de Magallanes (Chorographic Letter of the Content on the Three Arms near the Equinoxial toward the Ridge of the Sierras That Is Continued from the Strait of Magellan). Evidence of the intersection of visual chorographic depiction, on the one hand, and abstraction in the use of coordinates and scales in the map, on the other, leads Eduardo Acevedo Latorre to conjecture about the mapmaker's knowledge of the local topography and familiarity with cosmography (the map is reproduced in his Atlas de Mapas Antiguos de Colombia [Atlas of the Antique Maps of Colombia]). Numerous chorographic details of the landscape naturalize an imposed European territoriality that coexists with a totalizing view that lays out an abstract space. As Restrepo notes, a combination of this sort generates a cumulative exercise of spatial interpretation. The geometric view evinces a new mode of reasoning about the region's space and yields a panoptic, omniscient envisioning in dialogue with epic. Early Modern European monarchies adopted global narratives, images, and myths from the Classical world as symbolic legitimation for their aspirations of expansion. The Greek and Roman myth of Phoebus Apollo best embodied the abstraction over the terrestrial sphere and the imaginative, synoptic capture of the globe. This speculist assumption diverges from the perception of world as an array of centrifugal spheres to be traversed from an experiential center. Such a perspective also invites contemplation of the ethical import of human intervention, a literary turn that, as Denis Cosgrove reminds us, educed a poetics of global space. Instead, the geometric form of a globe promoted the visualization of theoretical structures (fixed compass points, lines, and coordinates) that gave shape to symbolic power, and reified nature (formerly traversed and experienced) as an object separate from human experience, as a world apart from life.

These types of abstraction distance man from earth and nature as a concept and image. Tim Ingold identifies in this cognitive schism a global ontology of detachment that, at times, prevails over a local ontology of engagement, and he points to contradictions between the two. Envisioned now as globe and surface, world and nature lie beneath the observer awaiting human intervention. In a teleological paradox, this renewed ontological approach assumes the process of fashioning its object as an immanent force inherent to nature itself. It is at this crossroads where Ingold identifies links between the image of the world as a globe and the modern conception of the notion of environment as object of intervention rather than a dwelling, and of nature as an inheritance to be managed by humans. Notwithstanding their totalizing efforts, these global perspectives rest on partial and deliberate selections of parts of the natural world in order to gain explicative power and authority. They remain illusory and incomplete. The porous character of these purviews, in turn, opens up the possibility of questioning the role of man on earth and interrogating the relationship between them. In an intersection between cosmography and poetics, the world and the description of nature in all its contingencies served as form and forum to debate multiple views of dominion and humanity.

Castellanos's insistence on charging readers with the hermeneutical mission of seeing what nature painted for them through an experiential periegesis, along with a quasi-Apollonian view that transforms the space of the New Kingdom into planar representation (latitude, longitude, and scale), in both verses and maps, evinces an interplay of ontologies to apprehend the region. The exercise of deciphering nature's *secretum* through experiential and planar landscapes reveals the limitations in representing universal humanity. Furthermore, the poet's alignment with Alonso de Santa Cruz's *Epítome* and its narrative of impossibility rather than with other descriptions of the region opens up possibilities for dialogue between the poem and his predecessor's contemplations about the paradoxical (and unethical) nature of global expansion.

Scrutiny of the consequences of this ontological distancing and intervention of humans in the natural world is present in one of the early histories of the New Kingdom, Juan Rodriguez Freyle's *El carnero* (The Sheep) – a work also known as *Conquista i descubrimiento del nuevo reino de Granada de las Indias Occidentales del mar oceano, i fundacion de la ciudad de Santa Fe de Bogota* (1639, Conquest and Discovery of the New Kingdom of Granada of the Occidental Indies of the Ocean, and Founding of the City of Santa Fe of Bogota). Behind a picaresque gesture, a critical move identified by Roberto González Echevarría, Freyle makes a veiled critique of the ethical consequences of separating man and nature, and of the excesses of intervention in the landscape. In his fifth chapter, the author promises to fill in the gaps that Pedro Simón left in his *Noticias historiales* (1626, Historical News) as well as Castellanos's omissions in his "Historia del Reino de Nueva Granada" (fourth part of *Elegías*) and to offer a new history without poetic fiction in which "solo se hallará en ella desnuda la verdad" (nothing will be found there but the naked truth).[2] Freyle establishes a chain of typologies expanding from the stories of Adam and Eve to Don Rodrigo and Florinda as the key to the hermeneutics for his opus. In these stories, desire is the force that disrupts the course of history and imposes a new order. What is disturbed in this episode of *El carnero* is the immemorial ritual of "correr la tierra" (running the land), a religious festival involving a race through the sanctuaries in the territory, and entailed the depositing of offerings to their gods at the bottom of sacred lakes. In a descriptive passage, Freyle offers a mental map of the pre-colonial landscape of the Muisca world. Transforming the landscape into a geometric picture of such perambulation, he describes five altars and sites of worship by the side of the Guatavita, Guasca, Siecha, Teusacá, and Ubaque lakes, all different and distant from one another. The description relates an emplacement of the religious world in the topography, conveying a connection between cosmology and the natural world unique to the pre-Hispanic past. While ambiguous in its referent, the notion of quadrant by reference to "*cuadrar*" adopted by the author in the description invites readers to abstraction in gazing the sacred natural world of the Muisca.

The spiritual character that Freyle bestows upon the local landscape in the mental map is disturbed by Spaniards in the rupturing of an immemorial link between nature and man through drainage of these sacred bodies of water. This disruption, as William Ospina reminds us, entails a loss of any memory of origins and an abandonment of senses of the sacred and the divine. The technologies of management of indigenous hydraulic systems used by Europeans exacted a transformation of the landscape that in Freyle's eyes it is to proceed without end. This neglect of good environmental stewardship of God's world often proved futile and obviated the logics of local practices, both scientific and spiritual. Critique of the hydraulic project, which was brought about on the basis of capitulations between Philip II and Antonio de Sepúlveda in 1572 and by successive efforts by the Audiencia de Santa Fe, provides the author a framework for the imbricated story of the deception and thievery of the cleric Francisco Lorenzo. Rather than bringing a new spiritual order to a pagan world, this ambassador of the Catholic Church simulates the speech of a pagan god, deludes a cacique, and makes off with the sacred treasures that locals had hidden from Europeans. The intervention and extraction carried out on the environment were motivated by the myth of "El Dorado" (The golden man). As Pastor Bodmer reminds us, this legend lent symbolic power to the European imaginary, promoted geographic exploration in the region, and delineated new categories of perception in the cognitive realm. Appropriation of the topic of the Golden Age allows Freyle to challenge its original meaning and, as Julie Greer Johnson and Ivette Hernández Torres have noted, to expose the utopian fantasy behind the dismal failure. The embedding of the imbricated story in the controversial hydraulic project signals readers toward a historical depth that connects intervention and extraction – by the practice of drainage and the logic of desecration – as disruptions of the original, pre-Hispanic linking of natural and human worlds. Confronting the ontological distancing between man and nature caused by Europeans in the story problematizes the epistemological imperatives behind the cosmographic project and the technologies of intervention driving conquest. Moreover, the new history that Freyle presents in *El Carnero* exposes the ecological and ethical dimension of the intersection between an ascendant empire's politics of expansion with a universalizing science's politics of progress.

Nature as knowledge: New Granada as a geo-botanical unit

The view of the New Kingdom of Granada was transformed once more in the Jesuit Joseph Gumilla's natural, civil, and geographic history of the largest river traversing the region, *El Orinoco ilustrado* (1741, The Orinico Illustrated). In this case, the author reshapes the landscape into a new geographic and ecological entity. The pursuit of natural knowledge in order to assimilate the Indies into the European worldview and to further an Iberian world empire in the sixteenth century promoted eclectic methodologies that informed, and progressively were challenged by, the onset of experimentalism, mechanistic rationalism, and abstraction of natural phenomena in the "new philosophy" over the following centuries. As Edmundo O'Gorman observes, these eclectic methodologies were already present in Father Joseph de Acosta's *Historia natural y moral de las Indias* (1590), the earliest modern writer to reconsider some of the inherited knowledge of the ancients and Catholic dogma in the light of personal experience and observation of the New World. Catholic intellectuals in the late seventeenth and eighteenth centuries mediated the knowledge of scholastics and moderns with religious teachings in Spain and Spanish America, charting a middle course that Ruth Hill has cogently identified as a uniquely Hispanic approach to natural philosophy within the context of the European Enlightenment. Like his counterparts, Gumilla engages empirical methods that transcend knowledge through description and cataloging, and applies them analytically and experimentally to local cultural, racial, natural, and geographic data. In her *Peripheral Wonders: Nature, Knowledge, and Enlightenment in the Eighteenth-Century Orinoco*, Margaret Ewalt finds that through the textual construction of a cabinet of curiosities, the Jesuit applies categories of modern science to display the natural wonders of the region and reveal its evangelical, scientific, and commercial potential. Through the intermediation that Jerónimo Feijoo and other Spaniards exerted on Francis Bacon's natural philosophy and that of other European thinkers, he brings religion and science together as a pathway to modernity for Spain and its colonies.

Gumilla's view of the relationship between man and nature goes beyond the extolling of God through the discovery and appreciation of the natural paradise that predecessors like León Pinelo had described in the Indies. Embracing a philosophical and scientific middle path, he proposes that the Creator himself entrusted the whole *orbis terrarum* to man with the renewed purpose of scrutiny of its natural tenets. Now committed to a global mission of inquiry in Gumilla's view, man's role is to become acquainted with the natural truths ensuing from the great variety of assorted things, the characteristics of animals, the virtues of plants, and a certain knowledge of the Provinces and Nations that comprise the earthly Orb. Moreover, the implied leap from the isolated paradise of early exploration present in Pinelo's *El paraíso en el Nuevo Mundo* (1656, Paradise in the New World) to a particular province constitutive of the *orbis terrarum* realigns the inherited meta-geography of the region. Buttressed by the map accompanying the introduction, *Mapa de la Provincia y Missiones de la Compañia de HIS del Nuevo Reino de Granada* (Map of the Province and Missions of the Society of Jesus in the New Kingdom of Granada, available in electronic form through the John Carter Brown Library), Gumilla emplaces the river for the first time as the visual center of the area. The new projection obliterates the auriferous lands of riches purported in earlier maps of the New Kingdom and renders the river as a dilated chain of waterways that lends its connective properties to form a coherent Orinoquia, an Orinoco basin. Mountain chains accompany the length of its course in an orderly manner, reinforcing its westward orientation beyond the frame of the map. The scale of longitude on the left corner is betrayed as the projection compresses the distances between eastern and western edges of the continent and cuts off its territorial expanse by prematurely announcing the "Mar del Sur" (South Seas) on the topography.

This new geometric structure assembles an unprecedented metageography of Orinoquia that signals a reorientation and links the New Kingdom to Asian lands. This connection is also echoed by the author in his comparison of his mission with that of his Jesuit counterparts in the Philippines and repeated comparisons of local indigenous customs with those of Chinese peoples. As Ricardo Padrón reminds us, the "invention of America" went hand-in-hand with what we might call the invention of the Pacific Ocean. The territoriality of empire relied on the stitching together of its heterogeneous, scattered component spaces by the work of official literature, cartography, and historiography. To accomplish cohesiveness, apologists for imperial absolutism belonging to all the various factions set about rearranging the existing meta-geographies that supported the claims of their sponsors, in order to achieve a re-delineation of regions and continents into political entities. Transformed into a basin, the region is no longer a marginal annotation on the map of the Kingdom but rather part of a larger naturalized argument: now Orinoquia is conceived as a laboratory for scientific study and a geo-botanical microcosm constitutive of a larger globe endowed by Providence with its own natural laws. Gumilla's local knowledge of the Orinocco revamps European theories of knowledge, as Ewalt observes. Moreover, its contextualization within the larger global meta-geographies of the Hispanic world recenters Orinoquia as the new axis of scientific knowledge.

The rendition of the region as geo-botanical unit advanced by Gumilla is fundamental to how later botanical expeditions conceive of the regions of the New World in the years that followed. One of them, the Royal

Botanical Expedition of the New Kingdom of Granada, led by José Celestino Mutis, is launched in 1783 and continues for some thirty years. Arising out of the Bourbon Reforms that, following the Spanish defeat at the hands of England in the Seven Years War, sought to restore Spain's geopolitical preeminence, the expedition sought to catalogue New Granadan nature and make known its commercial benefits, to help Spain compete in global agricultural and botanical markets. As Jorge Cañizares-Esguerra aptly notes, the vision of New Granadan nature promulgated by Mutis and his young disciples conceives of New Granada as a microcosm in which all of the natural products of both New World and Old could be cultivated, due to the diversity of altitudes and climates offered by the Andes and the agricultural benefits of the equatorial climate. Francisco José de Caldas spearheads the charting of the geographical distribution of plants in the northern Andes and, subsequently, benefits from the notion of cross-sectional mapping advanced by Alexander von Humboldt to develop his biogeographical maps of the region. In the *Semanario Del Nuevo Reyno de Granada* the Spanish American naturalist claims that New Granada's geographical position makes it a privileged place for global trade, and its numerous rivers facilitate the transport of goods from interior to coast. Echoing Gumilla's notion of Orinoquia as a microcosmos constitutive of a greater globe, the scientists of the Botanical Expedition present the New Kingdom of Granada as a microcosm whose destiny was that of leadership on a world scale.

Although Mutis's expedition does not lead to the economic growth hoped for by the Spanish Crown, paradoxically its cultural influence in the movement for independence is notable. The exaltation of the natural riches of the New Granadan territory, riches verified by scientific means, and the insistence on the region's enormous economic potential strengthen *criollo* consciousness and permeate a pro-independence rhetoric that sought to inspire patriotic fervor. Undoubtedly, the writings of Caldas and the other scientists on the Botanical Expedition align with the interests of the Spanish Crown; yet the exaltation of the natural superiority of New Granada, its privileged geographical position, and its climatic diversity, together with the emphasis placed on the importance of creating programs to foster geographical knowledge of the region, combine a message of praise with one of self-sufficiency and autonomy. Moreover, these texts frame descriptions of New Granada's natural endowment, resources, and versatility within a rhetoric of difference that lends itself well to the elaboration of a unique national identity. In this fashion, the Botanical Expedition underscores the symbolic import of the country's natural exuberance and contributes, in manifold ways, to the bending of nature to ideological ends – not only during the struggle for independence but also during the consolidation of the nation-state in the nineteenth century.

The notion of the region as geo-botanical unit advanced by Gumilla and upheld by scientists of the botanical expeditions in New Granada is also central to the writings of the quintessential scientific intellectual of the European Enlightenment, Alexander von Humboldt, who adopted the Andes as a microcosmic space within which to essay theories of biodistribution following local scientists. Cañizares-Esguerra has placed the scientist's ecological sensibilities within the larger context of Spanish American scientific inquiry to which he arrived in the late eighteenth century. Like Gumilla, Humboldt conceives of nature as a forum for scientific study, and man's role in it as the examiner of its inherent characteristics – a task that his predecessor linked to the wonder of God's work on earth. In her recent study of the Jesuit's influences on the German naturalist, "Legacy of Joseph Gumilla's Orinoco Enlightened," Ewalt illuminates how what has been considered a "new literary genre" in Humboldt's approach to nature, namely, a scientific inquisition that effects an original amalgamation between literature and science, echoes the literary strategies engaged by Gumilla in his poetic prose. Through rhetorically constructed natural cabinets, Humboldt borrows and expands depictions of the Orinoco from Gumilla and duplicates their *dispositio* to illuminate some of the practices and methods that buttress his own scientific project. Infused by a Romantic spirit and a reliance on Kantian philosophy, and informed by Gumilla's conception of the Orinoquia basin, the German naturalist essays in his "The Nocturnal Life of Animals in the Primeval Forest" a theory of equilibrium between aesthetic experience and scientific observation. His quest for "truth to nature" is for an epistemology that will unveil human meaning that antecedes scientific inquiry of nature and traces relationships to other objects and projects. Refashioning that spirit of recovery of a hidden *secretum* present in early modern humanists like his admired Joseph Acosta, the Orinoco basin reified in Gumilla's new metageography serves Humboldt's effort to establish a link between the perception of nature and writing. It is in this discourse of unity of nature and knowledge that Jorge Marcone finds the emergence of a subjectivity that amalgamates disciplined scientific observation and a scrutiny of phenomenological perception in its speculation on the landscape's historical and natural secrets. Rather than escapism, the critic finds in this intersection an embodiment of the complexities and paradoxes of early-nineteenth-century

Romantic ecology as well as a preoccupation that prefigures diverse preoccupations of today's environmental humanities.

Humboldt himself had further foundational plans for his refashioning of Spanish America in general, and Orinoquia in particular, as an aesthetic, primal, natural geopolitical entity. In his *Personal Narratives of Travels to the Equinoctial Regions of the New World* (1805–38), he ponders the revolutions in the Spanish colonies and asserts that internal dissention, and the lightly rooted character of the civilization in the landscape, prevents the region from enjoying the benefits of constitutional liberty achieved by the inhabitants of the United States. The rescue of his works from oblivion, he hopes, will help the peoples of the banks of the Orinocco or Atabapo to behold with ecstasy "cities enriched by commerce and fertile fields cultivated by free men on the very spot where during my travels I saw impenetrable jungle and flooded lands." The unearthing of his epistemology of "truth to nature" was to transcend the individual's experience and to contribute to nothing less than a new social order. Such a project, entrenched in nature, entailed a foundational ambition that helped reify fictional narratives of collective universals. These narratives would deeply influence the region's intellectuals in New Granada and served to buttress ethical and political principles advancing the early projects of national consolidation.

Humboldt's Romantic approach to nature and his holistic way of envisioning it would enjoy enormous popularity in the foundational literature of Colombia throughout the later nineteenth century. That literature would inherit from the scientific expeditions an interest in depicting the region's natural specificity and would exploit its capacity to exalt patriotic fervor. The symbolic potential of nature would be placed at the service of new ideologies and new visions of the nation, from the pens of men who, like their predecessors, found in scientific discourse "the authoritative language of knowledge, self-knowledge, and legitimation."[3]

The Ideologies of nature in foundational narratives

During the nation-building period in the nineteenth century, Colombian authors find in nature an appropriate metaphor for national and regional identity. The land and its lush nature become sign and symbol of what made Colombia unique. To highlight this "uniqueness," authors frequently include listings of local flowers, plants, and animals in their descriptions of nature, most of which were unknown to the foreign reader. In a way that reminds us of the cabinets of curiosities or the natural history cabinets of the previous century, these listings of regional natural species are meant to emphasize the natural specificity of the region and link nature with national and cultural identity.

In this and other ways, the rhetorical conventions of scientific discourse permeated the foundational literature of the nineteenth century but were reformulated so as to favor political and literary genres central to projects of national consolidation. As Daniela Bleichmar explains, in the Royal Botanical Expedition, as in others at the time, images of plants provided a way of visualizing the Spanish empire through an "appropriation of nature" that decontextualized and uprooted specimens from their lands and their cultural contexts. The listings of regional specimens in the foundational narratives of the nineteenth century re-appropriate and re-locate these natural images in their native soil, thus re-claiming their natural resources through a symbolic gesture that, manifestly, is ideologically charged.

Perhaps the most revealing example of the use of natural sciences to allegorize an ideological debate is provided by *Manuela* (1858) by Eugenio Díaz Castro. The novel narrates the vicissitudes of Demóstenes Bermúdez, a liberal intellectual from the capital, during his sojourn in a small provincial town in the lowlands of Cundinamarca. The frustrated dialogues between Demóstenes and the villagers expose the ideological conflicts between various liberal and conservative factions which plunged the country into numerous civil wars, while at the same time exemplifying the battle between learned and popular cultures, as has been demonstrated by Raymond L. Williams, María Mercedes Ortiz, and, most recently, Sergio Escobar. In a revealing episode, Demóstenes Bermúdez returns to the rooming house where he is staying and finds that Manuela, a young country girl who lives there, has rearranged his room. Demóstenes, a collector of fossils and dissected flowers, had organized his collection on scientific principles; Manuela, with no inkling of the damage she was causing, establishes "un nuevo orden de cosas" (a new order of things), following her own system of classification and even discarding some samples that she regarded as rubbish.[4] The scientific principle on which Demóstenes arranged and classified his preserved birds, insects, fossils, and flowers means nothing to Manuela, who cannot comprehend Demóstenes's fury at her generous gesture. Besides pointing to the chasm between Demóstenes' scientific perspective and Manuela's pragmatic vision, this episode harks back to the scientific revolution of the eighteenth and nineteenth centuries to articulate the confrontation between the center of learned, elite power and the popular classes. Demóstenes embodies the naturalist-scientist that Mary Louise Pratt describes as the "bourgeois subject simultaneously innocent and imperial, asserting a harmless hegemonic vision that installs no apparatus of domination" while Manuela represents an innocent form of subversion toward Demóstenes's neocolonial impulse.[5]

The clash of these two attitudes, mediated by nature and by scientific knowledge of her, reveals the power of the naturalists' legacy in the cultural imaginary of the nineteenth century. As Roberto González Echevarría has so cogently noted, the taxonomic discourse of the natural sciences makes manifest the equation between knowledge and power, and Eugenio Díaz Castro is well aware of this, as the above episode makes clear. He is also aware, along with other writers of his era, of the traditional identification of the nation with its natural environment, which is why he uses nature as a means to point out the stumbles that face a project of national unification in a country marked by such deep social, cultural, and ideological differences.

This he achieves through a multifaceted representation of nature, a kind of representation that reflects the differing visions of a country in permanent tension. While it's true that in some cases these visions coexist harmoniously, as can be observed in the counterpoint between the external paradigm and the national expressed in descriptions of nature that conjugate and contrast European and American models of representing the natural (Pineda Botero), other debates are articulated through conflicting depictions of nature. In *Manuela*, as was the case in Juan de Castellanos's *Elegías*, nature, wise and benevolent, is also wild and destructive. Demóstenes exalts nature's wisdom, invokes its benevolence, and praises the richness of the local landscape. At the same time, the destructive and intractably wild side of nature, manifest in the combat the peasants must wage against the ferocious attacks of birds, squirrels, and monkeys to protect their crops, makes it clear that nature is more than an arena for contemplation – that it must be subjugated and forced into the service of man. This is how Demóstenes sees the matter, as he argues that poverty is inadmissible when there are "tierras fértiles y exuberantes" (fertile and exuberant lands).[6]

However, *Manuela*'s seeming endorsement of agricultural modernization is not so evident when we look at Demóstenes, who is portrayed as the main proponent of economic development but also as an inconsistent and unrestrained individual. His ideas about the animal kingdom, among others, are redolent of hypocrisy, and not a few times this character is depicted as an out-of-control hunter, firing his shotgun at any and every animal that crosses his path. His defense of monkeys on account of their resemblance to human beings, and his speech during the hunt about protecting them from extermination, ring hollow when he hands the shotgun to Pía so that she could be the one to annihilate them. In this fashion, though the novel tends to show humans as dominant over nature and the fundamental role of natural resources in the country's economic development, Demóstenes's self-contradictions present as misguided the imposition of an unfettered modernization, much like the efforts of the enlightened liberals represented by this character.

This debate is connected to Díaz's contrasting descriptions of the human and natural landscapes of agrarian economy in two distinct Colombian regions: the Sabana de Bogotá and the lowland regions of Cundinamarca. As Jennifer French explains, in the late nineteenth century Spanish American elites were hopeful that the export boom of raw materials would transform lands into modern agricultural landscapes, which in turn would lead to rapid growth and increased income. Rather than making the case for or against monocrop agriculture, Díaz chooses to present both sides of the same coin, by rendering two drastically different landscapes of industrialized agriculture. The hacienda of La Esmeralda, belonging to Don Alfonso Jiménez, in the Sabana de Bogotá, is a symbol of organization and progress; the meadows and wheat fields are verdant, the fences well kept, the animals young and well fed, and even the farmhands work with pleasure and skill. In marked contrast to this is the hellish depiction of the sugar mills. The El Retiro mill, located on rocky and forbidding terrain, full of mud-filled trenches, gives off a smoke that throws a coat of soot across the landscape and the downcast faces of the exploited workers alike, and the mill of don Matías Urquijo is marked by sulphur-ridden lagoons that generate a pestilent atmosphere.

The dramatic juxtaposition of these two images places in stark relief the differences in labor regime that obtained on the haciendas of the highlands near Bogotá, on the one hand, and on those of the lowland regions of Cundinamarca. For, even though the monopolization of land in the hands of a few estate owners was found in both areas, as Salomón Kalmanovitz explains the exploitation practiced by the landowners of the lowlands against their tenants was far more brutal than that of the *hacendados* (the landowners) of the Sabana de Bogotá. But, in addition to contrasting the two regions, Díaz proclaims the benefits of agrarian industrialization while at the same time warning against the perils of an uncontrolled quest for economic growth, with all the dismal consequences it may portend for society and the environment.

In this fashion, the ideological and cultural plurality that the novel succeeds in depicting takes shape not only through the fruitless dialogues between the protagonists, but also in multiple visions of the natural environment, some of them in blatant opposition to one another, others in apparent harmony, but always within an unstable equilibrium. Nature, in *Manuela,* takes no sides in these debates; rather, it's much more the case that it is molded to illustrate the varying visions of this country in gestation. The ideological wavering present in the representations of nature in the novel lend support to the cultural and ideological heterogeneity that the novel puts forward and that critics such as Pineda Botero and Escobar, among others, have identified and linked with the issue of nation building. Pineda Botero argues that the binary oppositions upon which the novel is erected – civilization and barbarism, countryside and city, the external and the national, high culture and popular culture – reflect a quest for identity. Escobar finds, moreover, that Díaz approaches this ideological and cultural pluralism as a sort of "balance sheet," avoiding at all costs the novel's transformation into a monological affirmation, or a master fable dispensing civilizing solutions to the obstacles facing national unity. The manifold perspectives from which nature is approached in *Manuela* provide another balance sheet, or perhaps an archive, of the cultural and ideological heterogeneity that thwarted national unity, here visible and embodied in the national territory, its landscapes and natural resources. In the end, the death of Manuela stands for the failure of a plural nation that vainly attempts to ignore its internal divergences. Nature, besides being the stage on which the attempt to negotiate these divisions unfolds, offers a gallery of images that reflect an unstable, divided, and plural society, one whose unification proves difficult if not impossible.

In marked contrast, just a few years after the publication of *Manuela,* there appears a novel that will manage to erect a myth of national unity – *María* (1867) by Jorge Isaacs. Unlike *Manuela, María* omits any reference to the tumultuous years that characterized this period of Colombian history and opts instead to present a harmonious, ideal world, anchored in a feudal past that, at that point, was on the path to extinction. As David Musselwhite explains, the years leading up to the publication of *María* were crucial in Colombian nineteenth-century history, as they marked a change from a conservative creole plantocracy to a liberal market-based economy. These changes, together with the abolition of slavery (1851) and the numerous rebellions and civil wars, affected wealthy landowners like Isaacs's family, who were deeply in debt and had to sell their haciendas or face financial ruin.

In its idealization of the past, *María* affords us a glimpse into a conservative worldview that, as a number of critics have joined in observing, laments the disappearance of the *latifundista* social order of which the Isaacs family was part. Nostalgia, understood as a temporal longing, is doubtless capable of a reactionary modulation, an exaltation of the past that elides its injustices. This is clearly the case in *María*, where the depiction of social and racial harmony glosses over the sins of slavery and the injustices of a patriarchal society. However, *María's* nostalgia has a quality that merits closer scrutiny: it is grounded in nature and the land. As Jennifer Ladino points out, critics have largely considered nostalgia as a temporal longing, when in fact, it was first conceived by Johannes Hoffer in 1678 as a condition caused by the "desire for return to one's native land."[7] Re-situating nostalgia, as Ladino proposes, opens up *María* to a new analysis of nature's presence in the text, as well as a better understanding of the ideological underpinnings of the representation of nature in Isaacs's novel.

The tragic love story of María and Efraín, is narrated by Efraín after María's death. It is revealing that there is no aspect of Efraín's yearning for the past and for his beloved María, untouched by a feeling of loss toward his native land and its natural environment. Efraín's childhood memories, particularly, are imbued with the sounds and smells of nature, as when, thinking of his early years, he remembers the peculiar scent of freshly felled forests and the sounds made by the parrots on the nearby trees. Later he laments that "Ya no volveré a admirar aquellos cantos, a respirar aquellos aromas, a contemplar aquellos paisajes llenos de luz, como en los días alegres de mi infancia y en los hermosos de mi adolescencia: ¡extraños habitan hoy la casa de mis padres!" (No more shall I revel in those songs, breathe in those fragrances, admire those landscapes full of light as I did in the joyous days of my childhood or the beautiful days of my adolescence – today, strangers live in my parents' house!).[8] By intertwining childhood with nature, Isaacs advances an aesthetic of belonging to one's native land infused with regional patriotic feeling. These descriptions emphasize the idea of origin, of the home, of the roots that bind the human being to the place where he was born and grew up. Even the comparison of nature with mother – "La naturaleza es la más amorosa de las madres" (Nature is the most loving of mothers) – reaffirms the idea of the natural environment as a home, as a space to which one is tied by the indissoluble bonds of kinship.[9]

In like manner, the amalgamation of María with the natural environment, the hacienda, and the Cauca Valley region, which critics have noted and accredited to the novel's Romanticism, is also a way to endow birthplace and local environment with a central role, exalting the sentiment of attachment to native land. There are even occasions when the longing for birthplace relegates the beloved woman to a secondary place. In London, when Efraín receives a letter from María, the first images he calls forth are not those of the woman he loves but rather the New World landscape, suggesting that the pain of exile is as great, or greater, than the longing to recover a lost love.

In the fusion of María with the natural environment of the region, and the accompanying merging of romantic love with love of country, there is doubtless an extrapolation of the personal and intimate to the collective and national. Doris Sommer perceives an opposition between these categories when she observes that "[t]he sense of loss in this novel seems always personal, rather than the regional or national loss felt in other canonical novels of nineteenth-century Latin America."[10] Yet, in fact, loss both regional and national is central to *María,* even if addressed in the framework of the personal. The powerful association of nature with childhood, too, foregrounds a feeling of belonging that runs counter to the novel's theme of exile; not only in Efraín's travel abroad is exile present, but also in other characters who have lost their native land, such as María, Efraín's father, and the slave Nay. Exile is the specter that feeds the nostalgia rooted in the natural space of the Cauca Valley, a nostalgia that, articulated through an aesthetic of belonging and of the conflation of local nature with the beloved woman, and expressed in personal and intimate terms, nurtures love of country and attachment to birthplace.

Nature and land as objects of longing in *María* also suggest a nascent ecological preoccupation, whether consciously intended by Isaacs or not. It is important to keep in mind that *María* was written in an era of tremendous economic and industrial development, and that in that period a number of massive transport construction projects were underway, such as the Cali-Buenaventura highway running the length of the Dagua Valley, on which Isaacs himself worked for a time, as well as the introduction of steamboat travel on the Magdalena River, among many other projects. It is possible that preoccupation with the environmental impact of these projects underlay the nostalgic vision of nature in *María.* Pineda Botero has pointed to the mention of burned forests in the novel and to the anxiety of the narrator over the arrival of the settlers assigned to cut down the natural forests in the cause of "progress" and "civilization" as illustrations of this concern. The same anxiety can be seen in the nostalgic tone with which Efraín recalls the intact natural world of his childhood, particularly if we take into account that, on occasion, Efraín's sadness is due less to losses of natural environment than to the loss of his ties of affection and admiration toward nature. When he looks out the window of his room, grieving over the landscape, Efraín admits that it was not nature that he beheld but rather "lo que ya no veré más; lo que mi espíritu quebrantado por tristes realidades no busca, o admira únicamente en sus sueños: el mundo que extasiado contemplé a los primeros albores de la vida" ([all] that which I will no longer see; what my soul, crushed by grim realities, can only seek out and admire in my dreams: the world that, ecstatically, I beheld in the first dawn of life).[11] In this passage Efraín's nostalgia for nature is in fact a nostalgia for the connection he had to nature in his early years: it is not the native landscape he misses, so much as his attachment to it. There is an implicit warning in this nostalgia, the sounding of an alarm about the changes ahead and the "grim realities" that modify the relationship between human beings and their environment. The novel may not put forward an explicit critique of industrialization, but its expression of the persistent threat of loss of our intimate bond with nature attests to an incipient ecological consciousness. Jonathan Bate's study of the influence of Romanticism on the environmental tradition has received scant critical attention within Latin American literary criticism. Bate refutes the traditional view of Romanticism's return to nature as a form of escapism and argues that the respect for nature and a skepticism toward economic growth and material production is central to the ecological import of the Romantic tradition. In *María*, the strong bond between humans and nature, and the fear of losing this connection, lend support to Bate's argument.

Nostalgia for nature is nuanced and complex, and, as Jennifer Ladino suggests, it serves a variety of political agendas. It is true that in *María*, the Edenic landscape accompanies the idealization of the great slaveholding plantation (Escobar) and the nostalgia for that landscape conceals a lament for the disappearance of patriarchal society. At the same time, however, this nostalgia exalts patriotic feeling and encompasses a budding environmental awareness that beholds with trepidation the particular dangers that modernization brings with it. These varying operations of nostalgia complement the vision of the desired nation that Isaacs advances in his novel. The plurality of voices and ideologies given voice in *Manuela* is left very much behind, for in *María* the fragmented nation achieves unity in the quest for a love of country that, rooted in the local natural environment, seeks to hold the past up as a model for the future. The representations of nature in *Manuela* and in *María* express two opposing ideological agendas, yet the novels coincide in embracing the symbolic potential of nature and its latent connection to national conciousness. These seminal texts of Colombian national literature draw on nature in order to elaborate their vision of the newly independent nation, of the ideological debates that were taking place, and of their hopes and fears of what the future would bring.

The visions of nature in the region of New Granada emerge from a flux of scientific, political, and cultural preocupations that, through continuities and breaks with inherited models, advance new perspectives that transform the natural world into historical objects that illuminate particular predicaments. They interrogate the complexities of the world as known, generate new knowledge about it, and mediate the experience of perception, knowledge, and representation of nature as new historical entities. The vision of the New Kingdom of Granada through landscapes of experience and abstraction in Castellanos's epic poem opens up new territory through which to perceive and know the region. These visions of nature renew, in paradoxical ways, the reader's place and relationship to nature observed through the evocative power of maps and verses and offer new vistas for the inspection of the imperatives of global expansion. Freyle's picture of the region capitalizes on the hermeneutical character of the natural world to critique intervention and expose the ecological and ethical implications of the alignment of the politics of imperial expansion with the imperative of scientific progress. These visions help us begin to lay bare the universalizing narratives that sustain these projects, as we unveil their contingent nature. The ambitions for scientific enlightenment in the works of Gumilla, Humboldt, and the scientists of the Royal Botanical Expedition led by Mutis adopt scientific knowledge as a new mode of representation. Now nature was placed at the center of a renewed project of imperial expansion that would eventually inform new visions for an independent nation. Later, Díaz Castro and Isaacs, through their diverging natural representation of the Colombian territory, elaborate two opposing images of the new nation, questioning the presence of a unidirectional vision of national consolidation. In these ways, the images of the natural world articulated by authors of New Granada and Colombia embody the capacity of transformation that Heraclitus identified as essential to nature itself.

BIBLIOGRAPHY

Acevedo Latorre, Eduardo. *Atlas de mapas antiguos de Colombia: Siglos XVI a XIX.* Bogotá, Colombia: Litografía Arco, 1971.
Acosta, José de. *Historia natural y moral de las Indias,* edited by Edmundo O'Gorman. México: Fondo de Cultura Económica, 2006.

Apian, Peter, and Frisius. *Libro de la cosmographia.* Anveres: Gregorio Bontio, 1548.

Bate, Jonathan. *Romantic Ecology: Wordsworth and the Environmental Tradition.* London: Routledge, 1991.

Bleichmar, Daniela. "Visible Empire: Scientific Expeditions and Visual Culture in the Hispanic Enlightenment" *Postcolonial Studies* 12, no. 4 (2009): 441–66.

Boym, Svetlana. *The Future of Nostalgia.* New York: Basic Books, 2001.

Caldas, Francisco José de. "Estado de la Geografía del Vireynato de Santafé de Bogotá con relación a la economía y el comercio." *Semanario Del Nuevo Reyno de Granada* 2 (1808): 10–13. www.banrepcultural.org/sites/default/files/lablaa/historia/semanario/senr02.pdf.

Camões, Luís de. *Los Lusiadas.* 2nd ed. Madrid: Catédra, 2009.

Cañizares-Esguerra, Jorge. *Nature, Empire, and Nation: Explorations of the History of Science in the Iberian World.* Stanford: Stanford University Press, 2006.

Castellanos, Juan de. *Elegías de Varones Ilustres de Indias.* Madrid: Imprenta de los Sucesores de Hernando, 1914.

Cosgrove, Denis. *Apollo's Eye: A Cartographic Genealogy of the Earth in the Western Imagination.* Baltimore: Johns Hopkins University Press, 2003.

Díaz Castro, Eugenio. *Manuela.* Bogotá: Editorial Kelly, 1942.

Elías de Tejada, Francisco. *El Pensamiento Político de Los Fundadores de Nueva Granada.* Sevilla: Publicaciones de la Escuela de Estudios Hispano-Americanos de la Universidad de Sevilla, 1955.

Ephesus, Heraclitus of. *The Art and Thought of Heraclitus: A New Arrangement and Translation of the Fragments with Literary and Philosophical Commentary.* Translated by Charles H. Kahn. Cambridge: Cambridge University Press, 1981.

Ercilla y Zúñiga, Alonso de. *La Araucana,* edited by Isaías Lerner. Madrid: Cátedra, 2002.

Escobar, Sergio. "*Manuela, by Eugenio Díaz Castro, The Novel About the Colombian Foundational Impasse.*" Ph.D. thesis, University of Michigan, 2009.

Ewalt, Margaret R. *Peripheral Wonders: Nature, Knowledge, and Enlightenment in the Eighteenth-Century Orinoco.* Lewisburg, Va.: Bucknell University Press, 2008.

"The Legacy of Joseph Gumilla's Orinoco Enlightened." In *Jesuit Accounts of the Colonial Americas: Intercultural Transfers, Intellectual Disputes, and Textualities,* edited by Clorinda Donato et al., 344–73. Toronto: University of Toronto Press, 2014.

Fernández de Oviedo, Gonzalo. *Sumario de la natural historia de las Indias.* Madrid: Universidad de Navarra/Iberoamericana/Vervuert, 2010.

Flórez de Ocáriz, Juan. *Libro primero [y segundo] de las genealogías del Nuevo Reyno de Granada.* Madrid: I. F. de Buendía, 1674.

French, Jennifer L. "Voices in the Wilderness: Environment, Colonialism, and Coloniality in Latin American Literature." *Review: Literature and Arts of the Americas* 45, no. 2 (2012): 157–66.

González Echevarría, Roberto. *Myth and Archive: A Theory of Latin American Narrative*. Cambridge: Cambridge University Press, 1990.

Gumilla, José. *El Orinoco ilustrado: Historia natural, civil y geographica de este gran rio*. Madrid: Manuel Fernandez, 1741.

Hernández-Torres, Ivette N. *El contrabando de lo secreto: la escritura de la historia en El Carnero*. Santiago de Chile: Editorial Cuarto Propio, 2004.

Herrera y Tordesillas, Antonio de. *Historia general de los hechos de los castellanos en las islas y tierra firme del mar oceano*. Madrid: Imprenta Real, 1601.

Hill, Ruth. *Sceptres and Sciences in the Spains: Four Humanists and the New Philosophy (ca. 1680–1740)*. Liverpool: Liverpool University Press, 2000.

Humboldt, Alexander von. *"The Nocturnal Life of Animals in the Primeval Forest." Aspects of Nature, in Different Lands and Different Climates: With Scientific Elucidations*. Philadelphia: Lea and Blanchard. 169–201, 203–16, 1850.

——— *Personal Narrative of a Journey to the Equinoctial Regions of the New Continent, 1805–1838*. Translated by Jason Wilson. London: Henry G. Bohn, 1995.

Ingegno, Alfonso. "The New Philosophy of Nature." In *The Cambridge History of Renaissance Philosophy*, 236–63. Cambridge: Cambridge University Press, 1988.

Ingold, Timothy. "Globes and Spheres: The Topology of Environmentalism." In *The Perception of the Environment*, 209–18. London: Routledge, 2000.

Isaacs, Jorge. *María*, edited by Donald McGrady. Madrid: Cátedra, 2012.

Kalmanovitz, Salomón. *Economía y nación: una breve historia de Colombia*. Bogotá: Editorial Norma, 2003.

Ladino, Jennifer K. *Reclaiming Nostalgia: Longing for Nature in American Literature*. Charlottesville: University of Virginia Press, 2012.

Leff, Enrique. "Pensar en la complejidad ambiental." In *La complejidad ambiental*, 7–53. Mexico: Siglo XXI, UNAM, PNUMA, 2000.

León Pinelo, Antonio de. *El paraíso en el Nuevo Mundo; comentario apologético, historia natural y peregrina de las Indias Occidentales islas de tierra firme del mar occeano*, edited by Raúl Porras Barrenechea. Lima: Imprenta Torres Aguirre, 1943.

López de Velasco, Juan. *Geografía y descripción universal de las Indias*. Madrid: Ediciones Atlas, 1971.

Marcone, Jorge. "Humboldt in the Orinoco and the Environmental Humanities." In *Troubled Waters. Rivers in Latin American Imagination*, edited by Elizabeth Pettinaroli and Ana Maria Mutis, 12: 75–91. Hispanic Issues Online, 2013.

Minguet, Paulus. "Mapa de la provincia y misiones de la Compañía de HIS del Nuevo Reino de Granada." Madrid: Manuel Fernandez. John Carter Brown Library, 1741.

Musselwhite, David. "The Colombia of María: 'Un país de cafres.'" *Romance Studies* 24, no. 1 (March 2006): 41–54.

Ortiz, María Mercedes. "De patrias chicas y grandes: La representación de la nación en *María* de Jorge Isaacs y Manuela de Eugenio Díaz Castro."

In *Literatura y otras artes en América Latina*, 141–9. Iowa City: University of Iowa, 2004.

Padrón, Ricardo. "A Sea of Denial: The Early Modern Spanish Invention of the Pacific Rim." *Hispanic Review* (Winter 2009): 1–27.

Pastor Bodmer, Beatriz. *El jardín y el peregrino: El pensamiento utópico en América Latina (1492–1695)*. México: Coordinación de Difusión Cultural, Dirección de Literatura/UNAM, 1999.

Pineda Botero, Álvaro. *La fábula y el desastre: estudios críticos sobre la novela colombiana, 1650–1931*. Medellín: Fondo Editorial Universidad EAFIT, 1999.

Pratt, Mary Louise. *Imperial Eyes: Travel Writing and Transculturation*. London: Routledge, 2010.

Ospina, William. "Poesía indígena." In *Historia de la poesía en Colombia*, edited by María Mercedes Carranza and Pedro Alejo Gómez Vila, 19–34. Bogotá: Casa de Poesía Silva, 1991.

Restrepo, Luis Fernando. *Un nuevo reino imaginado: Las elegías de varones ilustres de Indias de Juan de Castellanos*. Bogotá: Instituto Colombiano de Cultura Hispánica, 1999.

Rodríguez Freyle, Juan. *El Carnero*. Biblioteca Ayacucho 66. Caracas, Venezuela: Biblioteca Ayacucho, 1979.

Santa Cruz, Alonso de. "Epítome de La Conquista Del Nuevo Reino de Granada." In *Epítome de la conquista del Nuevo Reino de Granada: La cosmografía española del siglo XVI y el conocimiento por cuestionario*, edited by Carmen Millán de Benavides, 103–20. Bogotá: Pontificia Universidad Javeriana, Instituto de Estudios Sociales y Culturales Pensar, 2001.

Simón, Pedro. *Noticias Historiales de las conquistas de Tierra Firme en las Indias Occidentales*. Bogotá: Casa Editorial de Medardo Rivas, 1891.

Sommer, Doris. *Foundational Fictions: The National Romances of Latin America*. Berkeley: University of California Press, 2007.

Vergara y Vergara, José María. *Historia de la literatura en Nueva Granada*. Bogota: Impr. de Echeverría hermanos, 1867.

Williams, Raymond L. *The Colombian Novel. 1844–1987*. Austin: University of Texas Press, 1991.

Notes

1 Juan de Castellanos, *Elegías de Varones Ilustres de Indias* (Madrid: Imprenta de los Sucesores de Hernando, 1914), 85.
2 Juan Rodríguez Freyle, *El Carnero* (Biblioteca Ayacucho 66. Caracas, Venezuela, 1979), 6.
3 Roberto González Echevarría, *Myth and Archive: A Theory of Latin American Narrative* (Cambridge: Cambridge University Press, 1990), 103.
4 Eugenio Díaz Castro, *Manuela* (Bogotá: Editorial Kelly, 1942), 118.
5 Mary Louise Pratt, *Imperial Eyes: Travel Writing and Transculturation* (London: Routledge, 2010), 33.
6 Díaz Castro, *Manuela*, 75.

7 Quoted in Svetlana Boym's, *The Future of Nostalgia* (New York: Basic Books, 2001), 9.
8 Jorge Isaacs, *María*, edited by Donald McGrady (Madrid: Cátedra, 2012), 178.
9 Ibid., 121.
10 Doris Sommer, *Foundational Fictions. The National Romances of Latin America* (Berkeley: University of California Press, 2007), 176.
11 Isaacs, *María*, 166.

CHAPTER 20

The intersections between poetry and fiction in two Colombian writers of the twentieth century: Álvaro Mutis and Darío Jaramillo Agudelo

Enrique Salas-Durazo

The exploration of the poetic qualities of a novel is a task that necessarily acknowledges a considerable number of variants. The genre of the novel offers an open space for literary and nonliterary discourses in which lyric development may be intertwined with plot development and narrative devices. Moreover, a "poetic novel" tends to relate the physical world of objects with symbolic imagery to give the writer the opportunity to explore concepts such as memory, destiny, or the human condition. Moving beyond these matters, in this chapter I explore how poet-novelists not only encase passages of lyrical beauty or create allegory in their prose, but also how they consciously reflect on the act of writing and document those spontaneous strategies that occur as they go through the process of writing a novel. Consequently, a poet-novelist constantly makes use of a "mask" portrayed as a central narrative voice, which meditates on the process of finding the hidden meanings in a story not by telling but by writing and editing the text we are reading. Through the extensive use of metafiction, intertextuality (on occasions, self-referential), and procedures that connect symbolic images to plot and character development, a poet uses a novel as "a laboratory in which he develops narrative strategies, elaborates on personal sets of symbols, and refines themes that are employed in later novels."[1]

Colombian literature in the twentieth century offers a fertile ground to explore the labor of poet-novelists, and, in fact, there is extensive critical commentary on the works of most of them. Seminal works in Colombian literature such as Jorge Isaac's *María* (1867) and José Eustasio Rivera's *La vorágine* (1924; The Vortex, 1928) are early examples of novels written by aspiring poets.[2] Throughout the twentieth century, many Colombian poets tackled the genre of the novel with different degrees of success. A few noteworthy examples of novels written by Colombian poets are José Asunción Silva's *De sobremesa* (After Dinner Conversation, finished in 1896 but first published in 1925), Eduardo Zalamea Borda's *Cuatro años a bordo de mí mismo* (1934, Four Years Aboard Myself) and *La cuarta batería* (The Fourth Battery, the manuscript was found in 1952), Jorge Zalamea's *El gran Burundú Burundá ha muerto* (1952, Big Burundun-Burunda Has Died), and Héctor Rojas Herazo's later epic trilogy of novels *Respirando el verano* (1962, Breathing the Summer), *En noviembre llega el arzobispo* (1967, In November the Archbishop Arrives), and *Celia se pudre* (1985, Celia Rots). All of these works were influential according to some writers and scholars.[3] In the second half of the twentieth century, however, two writers who began their careers exclusively as poets in two influential Colombian literary circles (Los Nuevos and La Generación Desencantada, respectively) embarked on the writing of important narrative cycles: the recently deceased Álvaro Mutis (1923–2013) and Darío Jaramillo Agudelo (1947). Both writers, I would suggest, are among the most significant cases of poet-novelists in Colombia, not only because of the inherent aesthetic quality and coherence of their projects, but also because of their total novelistic production. In this chapter, I begin by explaining relevant aspects of the two writers' respective poetics, their conception of literature, some of the specific motives they had to write novels, and the connections with their previous poetry. Then I focus on the lyric qualities and rhetorical figures that have become crucial in their narrative strategies and delve specifically into the position of the narrator/writer in relation to the act of literary creation. My intention is to present an interpretation of the texts from the point of view of poetic creation intertwined with novelistic discourse.

Álvaro Mutis always considered himself primarily a poet even after he became widely recognized as a novelist in the 1980s and 1990s. Although Mutis jokingly claimed that there was a tendency to recognize his novels instead of his lyric poetry, the author constantly stated in his interviews and articles that he did not see a distinction between his poetry and narrative and that there was not a moment in which one ends and the other begins.[4] Moreover, Mutis explained that the argument of some of his novels directly came from the revision of his poetry. An example of this is the novel *La nieve del almirante* (1986; The Snow of the Admiral, 1995), which is considered by the author as a natural extension of a prose poem of the same title published in the book of poems *Caravansary*.[5] Considering this, Mutis's earlier poetic work, and his later statements about the intimate connection of his works (along with his reticence to strictly classify them altogether in particular genres) makes him an ideal example for the study and exploration of the strategies and techniques employed by a poet-novelist. In fact, many critics have specifically studied the relationship between Mutis's poetry and narrative and have provided numerous examples of the manner in which themes and figures from earlier poetry infiltrate his narrative. Some of them explain the way in which the language "tries to become the story it is telling" and comment on the meaning of character-archetypes who constantly reappear throughout his work.[6] In addition to this, Mutis's first attempts of writing narrative and poetic prose also had influence in the development of a key fictional character, Maqroll el Gaviero.[7] Maqroll is the core of what can be considered Mutis's highest literary achievement: the saga of seven novels reunited and entitled *Empresas y tribulaciones de Maqroll el Gaviero* (1993, The Adventures and Misadventures of Maqroll, 2002).

One of the features of a poetic novel is the lyric treatment of passages that break with the referentiality of the novelistic discourse related to plot development. Therefore, Mutis's poetic intuition is constantly perceived in many sections of his novels where everyday events are carefully treated with a lyric development of language and use of specific rhetorical figures. The literal inclusion of poetic language in the novel not only displays the vocabulary and themes of the poet but also emphasizes the meaning of poetry as a search of knowledge. Indeed, the fact that every novel in the Maqroll's saga contains a myriad of meanings in apparently trivial details entails a system of codes the reader must decipher; more importantly, as Hernando Valencia explains, the alignment of those signs are "organized in a poetic construction to which we lack the key" within an "open-ended construction which every reader can build as he/she pleases."[8]

Taking this as a starting point, in this section I go beyond the poetic images in the novels to explore how this intricate web of relationships work, in order to determine which aspects may help define the poetic aspect of his narratives. Indeed, a complete study of Mutis's poetic procedures in his narrative need to consider each one of the carefully crafted novels of the saga, a project beyond the scope of this study. Therefore, I exclusively focus on the fourth novel in the saga of Maqroll, *La última escala del Tramp Steamer* (1989; The Tramp Steamer's Last Port of Call, 1992), Mutis's own personal favorite and "his most literary novel."[9] This is a characteristic work in which a poetic structure firmly based on parallelism and moments of intense lyricism are very effectively joined with a complex use of narration, metafiction, and intertextuality. As is the case of many other works by poet-novelists, the narrator is a poet and a writer who not only tells a story but looks for the perfect manner of writing it: "there are many ways to tell this story, just as there are many ways to recount the most insignificant episode of any of our lives."[10] The narrator constantly establishes a connection between literature and life events and reflects on the hidden meaning behind common objects or situations. Therefore, the poetic of the novel comes mostly from the narrator's conscious intent of discovering the hidden associations between the tramp steamer's story of decadence and a passionate (and ultimately failed) love story and the structure of the narration.

Mutis explains that his first attempts of writing short stories and first novels was to give a broader life, "a destiny, an order, a logic, a character, a conduct" to the fictional characters "who suddenly appeared" in his earlier poetry.[11] In order to achieve this, Mutis decided to create a fictional editor capable of distancing himself from these characters to evaluate and organize their adventures. Each of Maqroll's novels follows the classic structure of the "editor-at-work," compiling "discovered texts" and oral transcriptions of the stories he has heard in order to create a coherent narrative. This strategy allows Mutis to add direct references to his own poetry by incorporating appendixes including the original prose-poems that inspired the novel (as in the case of *The Snow of the Admiral*) or the books of poetry the reader may want to consult to understand the story better (*Un bel morir*). More importantly, the figure of the editor encapsulates many of the methods Mutis utilizes to create his novels.

Besides metafiction, another crucial aspect in Mutis's writing is the use of intertextuality. The Colombian author was not only an avid reader of poetry but also a great admirer of classic travel novels, memories, and narratives in which the main Proustian themes appeared such as "memory and its traps, the paths where the past gets lost, and the constant and painful transformation of those who have been our great loves."[12] His experience as a reader of literature is closely related to a conscious search of elements from his own childhood that deeply affected his vision of the world: "One of the highest tasks for a poet or prose writer is transferring to the realm of language that thin matter weaved in the memory of our first living years."[13] As a perfect example of a writer relating life experiences with literature, Mutis constructs a solid body of works in poetry and prose in which themes such as the journey, the recovery of the intimate world of his memories (specifically, those linked with his childhood), and the metamorphosis and decadence of things in this world are all pivotal. Again, Mutis's literary creation is deeply moved by his readings and his search for a style in a novel that simultaneously encases poetic and narrative development. The author's project is to find "an efficient and flawless prose able to flow with the simplicity of a creek while roaming on the deepest and most essential human territories. A miracle always achieved and sustained with words and power of invocation ... a secret alchemy, a prose not imposed by current fashions."[14] One specific and significant example of Mutis's afterthoughts about his readings is his following observation on Faulkner's style:

> Faulkner's novels are written with the same rhythm of the rhythm in the south of the United States, monotonous, even lazy. From this sad tone, a strange and exotic lifestyle suddenly emerges. ... The key of Faulkner's method is based on presenting facts and moments as instantly perceived by the main character, that is, conditioned by a thousand of external factors that distort reality. ... In addition to his style, similar to that of Shakespeare, Faulkner sprinkles his writing with inimitable metaphors of great lyricism and evocative power.[15]

What is relevant about these intuitions is the fact that they are not truly developed in Mutis's articles or reviews, but more precisely, in his novels. Consequently, intertextuality and metafiction become the main strategies employed by the narrator in Maqroll's saga. But far from being a simple nod or homage to the works that Mutis adores, these references to literature and the act of creation are an indispensable part of the construction of the novelistic structure. In his study about the strategies poets make use of when writing novels, Ian Rae states that novels written by poets "stand in serial relation to their earlier long poems. Occasionally an author will acknowledge that a long poem establishes the template for his or her novel ... but more commonly the long poem serves as a laboratory in which the author develops narrative strategies, elaborates on personal sets of symbols, and refines themes that are employed in later novels."[16] Therefore, by blending his earlier poetics and the necessity to expand on his most cherished topics, Mutis's gradual development of his rhetorical methods began with prose poems that became fertile ground for his later novels. Taking these ideas as the base of this study, a more detailed analysis of one of Mutis's novels provides an explanation for the manner in which poetic figures and procedures infiltrate the novel and how these compliment plot and character development.

The structure of *The Tramp Steamer's Last Port of Call* is based on two independent but ultimately interrelated sections. The scheme followed is that of a long preface that eventually leads to the main conflict of the novel (a failed love story) creating an effective structure through the use of parallelism. Nevertheless, I argue here that the existence of the plot in the second part is explicitly forced by a narrator that constantly reminds us that he is *writing* (and not just "telling") the story in the text. Not coincidentally, the narrator is a poet and a novelist whose friendly relationship with Maqroll the Gaviero has produced many of his texts.[17] As suggested earlier, this narrative and editorial voice, which constantly interrupts the action in the novel and explains some of his aesthetic choices and strategies, is a "mask" of Álvaro Mutis reflecting on the act of writing. Rae explains that "rather than abandoning the lyric, many poets explore latent possibilities within the lyric voice ... a 'doubleness of voice' permeates the lyric so that the speaker's anomalous voice functions as something like a symbol of the author's voice. The poet-novelists accentuates this tension through a play of masks and narrative levels."[18] On the one hand, Mutis's exploration of "the latent possibilities of the lyric voice" is displayed in the carefully crafted structure of the work, the inclusion of passages of lyrical beauty, and a subtle but crucial use of metaphors and allegory. On the other hand, in order to face the development of plot and characters associated with a novel, Mutis employs multiple narrative levels and second-degree narratives – usually involving the written transcription and edition of an oral story told by one of the characters – to establish the sequence of actions and events.[19] Finally, as in the work of other novelists, Mutis's own voice filters in the narrator's discourse and inserts brief glances of his biography or his opinions. In regard to the poet at work, the narrative space also serves as a medium to provide commentary about his own poetics, the sources of his novels, and other aspects of his aesthetic search. In *The Tramp Steamer's Last Port of Call*, Mutis directly addresses the project of Maqroll's saga: "I intend one day to tell the story of those journeys, although there are traces of that time, that gift of the gods, in most of the poems I've been scattering in ephemeral magazines and no less forgettable volumes of poetry."[20] Taking this into account, an analysis of the literary mechanisms in *The Tramp Steamer's Last Port of Call* (both those addressed or not addressed by the narrator) provides insight into some of the procedures followed by a poet-novelist like Mutis.

The first half of the novel introduces the narrator and his random encounters in different parts of the world with the *Halcyon* (originally, *el Alción*), a very old and beaten tramp steamer. From the first time this boat crosses his path, the narrator feels a deep emotional impact. By meticulously writing about this, the narrator not only introduces the main plot but also explicitly (and intrinsically) sets in motion some of the narrative and poetic procedures used in the book. The narrator's first unexpected encounter with the tramp steamer is in Helsinki. In this city, he is able to glimpse St. Petersburg from the distance of Helsinki's port. This vision is an event that can be accessed only for brief amounts of time a year due to the changing weather; the narrator describes his reaction to this sight: " [This] brought me back to a present whose unmitigated folly was inconceivable at that moment and in that awe-inspiring setting with its perfect proportions and translucent, otherworldly air ... [I] became absorbed in contemplating a miracle I was sure would never be repeated."[21] In sharp contrast to this enlightening experience, the narrator immediately witnesses for the first time the slow-moving *Halcyon* and immediately perceives a connection between the object and the human condition: "the color of misery, of irreparable decadence, of desperate, incessant use ... a kind of witness to our destiny on earth, a *pulvis eris*, that seemed truer and more eloquent in these polished metal waters with the gold and white vision of the capital of the last czars behind them."[22] An emotional connection now has been created with the Halcyon since, in spite of its ruinous appearance, returns the narrator to his past, to the center of his "most essential memories" (302). In addition, the narrator explains that "the lovely Botticellian figure" of St Petersburg and "the crumbling ghost" of the Tramp Steamer "complement each other in my dreams, communicating their will to survive along the same channels where poetry also occurs" (307). In his last encounter with the tramp steamer in Venezuela, the narrator is enraged when he listens to the condescending comments of a captain and other people observing the damaged condition of the *Halcyon*. The narrator immediately likens the situation with that of a fallen hero: "What could this officer, this dandy, know about the hopeless, secret exploits of the venerable tramp steamer, my beloved *Halcyon*, patriarch of the seas, conqueror of typhoons and tempests ... and now it had a slight tremor that ran the length of the ship, like a hidden fever or a supreme weakness that could no longer be disguised" (314). These examples show how, at the hands of the narrator/poet, the tramp steamer functions primarily as a symbolic figure that adapts some of Mutis's interests found in his previous poetry. In fact, he will make use of this figure of the boat in another of his novels, *Abdul Bashur, Dreamer of Ships*.[23]

Moreover, this image also establishes a parallelism with the story of Jon Iturri, the true central character of *The Tramp Steamer's Last Port of Call*. As mentioned before, the first section is in reality a preface that sets in motion the pieces of the main plot involving Jon Iturri. In contrast to the relevance of the lyric and reflective passages, the plot development in the first half seems relatively unimportant. The events and description of the different spaces visited by the narrator are full of details and have entertaining anecdotes, but they do not appear to fully develop a story as expected in a novel. Nevertheless, it is by connecting the second section where we can clearly perceive how this poetic strategy is linked with plot development and the deep meaning of the first part begins to emerge. The second part of the novel begins with the narrator's encounter with Jon Iturri, a melancholic sailor who coincidentally used to work as a sailor on the tramp steamer. Both men eventually realize that they share a very personal and secret relationship with the *Halcyon*: "every one of your encounters with the *Halcyon* coincided with a decisive, critical moment in my love affair with Warda" (345). During a period of ten days both men travel together down a river. During a period of several nights, in an episode structurally reminiscent to the collection of stories *One Thousand and One Nights*, the introspective Jon tells of his passionate and ultimately failed love affair with a woman named Warda. Incidentally, Warda is the sister of Abdul Bashur, Maqroll's best friend and a recurring character in the narrator's books.

A very important aspect to consider in order to understand how the poetic voice infiltrates the plot development is the fact that the narrator writes and consciously edits Jon's oral discourse to connect it to his own vision of ineffable beauty and his conception of fatality as an inseparable part of life. Often throughout the narration, Jon's monologues are interrupted by "interminable silences" and a lack of crucial details that make it difficult for the narrator to put the story into writing (352). In addition, the narrator also indicates that transcribing Jon's failed love story entails the risk of making it a "a stale and inconsequential cheap romance," even though "nothing could falsify the story more than casting it in that light, stripping it of fatal impossibility" (328). Consequently, the colloquial voice of Jon is subject to poetic elaboration in order to understand the deeper meanings of his story. The narrator comments how he "was moved by his struggle with words, which are always so inadequate, so remote from a phenomenon like a person's beauty when it verges on what is essentially ineffable . . . a simple description of her face and body left little more than a confused, insubstantial image" (337). Very significantly, through the use of intertextuality the narrator connects his meditation about the transitory nature of joy and the search for "the ineffable beauty." One example of this is the manner in which he connects readings – "Dante says that there is no greater sorrow than recalling happy times when we are sad" (311) – with the story of Jon: "[Jon's] gray eyes had the characteristic look of a man who has spent most of his life at sea. They gaze directly at you but seem never to lose sight of something distant, a supposed horizon that is indeterminate but always present . . . he gave the impression of having been in a place like Dante's circles of Hell" (317). Jon's conception of Warda as "a vision of absolute beauty" as well as "a perfect face with features almost Hellenic" lead the narrator to warn the reader and consciously incorporate "museo-logical connections" in his writing (330). In addition to this strategy, the narrator also writes about a few aspects related to his perception of things and his poetics at the very beginning of the second section that are helpful to understand his motivations as a writer (315–16). Thus, the narrator emphasizes the links between the story of the rise and fall of the elusive tramp steamer; the breakdown of Jon's relationship is directly related to the concept of fatalism and human limits when accessing ultimate beauty: "[Abdul Bashur] uttered the words that would have such profound reper-cussions on our destiny, on Warda's and mine: 'What you two have will last as long as the *Halcyon*' ... this unappealable sentence had been hanging over our heads for a long time" (349). These passages already communicate some of the most cherished and recurring themes in Mutis's previous poetry: the idea of a paradise lost, the delicate and fragile structure of things and people, condemned from the beginning to slow physical decadence, and the presence of an unfathomable force that grants few moments of extreme joy to the human being. Siemens effectively summar-izes Mutis's creative vein in the following excerpt: "Mutis' universal vision of life and man is an absolute constant: nothing is permanent in this world. As he observed in the tropics, everything in life disintegrates, decays, and rusts. The joyful moments are transitory and we need to savor them."[24]

As can be seen, the literary game in this novel consists in having a narrative voice that expresses an intention to maintain fidelity and object-ivity to the original story while adapting it to the treatment of his interests. As a poet-novelist, Mutis develops here a relatively simple anecdote of an isolated individual by adding symbolic elements that connect characters with larger concepts that had been present in his poetry. By explicitly reflecting on the manner in which these are related through the narrator's interruptions, we have access to the process of creation of a fiction that employs a common story to explore the unnameable and the hidden threads that move human actions.[25] It is not difficult to understand why Mutis did not perceive a great difference in his poetry and the novels of Maqroll's saga. Besides the selective use of vocabulary and the inclusion of passages of lyrical beauty, plot development, embedded narratives, and metafictional procedures are intimately interrelated with poetic explor-ation. Not coincidentally, *The Tramp Steamer's Last Port of Call* ends with an afterthought about the need to tell a story and to explore its hidden connections to understand a little bit more about the human condition: "Before falling into the sleep I needed desperately, I pondered the story I had heard. Human beings, I thought, change so little, and are so much what they are, that there has been only one love story since the beginning of time, endlessly repeated, never losing its terrible simplicity or its irremediable sorrow."[26]

Darío Jaramillo Agudelo is another ideal example of a twentieth-century Colombian poet who has embarked on the task of writing a substantial body of novels in the latter part of his career.[27] It is worth mentioning that Jaramillo began writing novels simply as the consequence of an injury to his leg that prevented him from moving for long periods. Consequently, after writing poetry for a period, he needed to rest his mind and he began writing letters that eventually became the seed of his earlier novels.[28] In fact, in Jaramillo's second novel, *Cartas cruzadas* (1995, Crossed Letters), one of the main characters writes in his diary: "I clearly know that in order to write prose it is better to be seated. With regards to poetry, which is what interests me more, I have no clue. Maybe memory, the little piece of paper in my pocket, a notebook next to the bed. . . . In order to register the perfect verse I need to be walking, absorbed."[29] Very similarly to Mutis's case, critics of Jaramillo's work have highlighted the manner in which the recurrent procedures and themes in his poetry are an integral part of the novels he writes. With respect to this matter, Mexican writer Sergio Pitol explains: "Darío Jaramillo applies his lyric expertise to his novels. For him, any notable experience is poetry and any serious intent of writing is a poetic derivation. He makes use of letters since he has always considered that genre as one of the most perfect forms of poem."[30] Once again, defining the "poetic" in the novel requires a careful examination of the writer's own poetics and an analysis of the manner in which this precept permeates his narrative writings.

Jaramillo's *Historia de una pasión*, (History of a Passion) a literary autobiography that contains the deep roots of the author's aesthetic vision, contains some of the clues which allow for an understanding of his conception of poetry in a novel. First of all, Jaramillo evaluates the relationship between literary genres by considering that any serious writing is a poetic derivation: "I have to confess that I do not fully understand the difference among genres. Virginia Woolf used to say that the only genre was poetry. Poetry transforms a novel, a biography, or a chronicle into literature."[31] He adds: "in the uncertainty of genres, the obsessive and comforting poetry is always present."[32] Very similarly to Mutis's conception of poetry as a vehicle of inner knowledge, many other passages in *Historia de una pasión* show Jaramillo as a conscious writer who conceives the act of writing, regardless of the genre, as a way "to stop time, to hallucinate, to obtain revelations and magical moments, to get to know yourself, to sing with a pen on a paper, to recover the effect and rhythm of words."[33] In spite of this intimate relation among poetry and narrative, some passages in *Historia de una pasión* also address Jaramillo's awareness of the particular challenges of writing a novel. Specifically, he likens the novel to "a toy," that is, a ludic puzzle or machinery that always requires a creative approach to make it work.[34] This particular aspect is of great importance in understanding his labor as a poet-novelist since many of his books are in fact a playful cogitation on the inner workings of a novel.

To achieve this, Jaramillo's first two attempts at writing novels made use of the epistolary genre. The tone of intimacy found within this specific genre perfectly suited the tone of confidence coupled with the telling of a longer story. In fact, *La muerte de Alec* (1983, The Death of Alec) has been defined by the author as "a letter disguised as a novel" while the previously mentioned *Cartas cruzadas* expands the idea by having a complex net of communication among different characters who write letters to each other during the time span of a decade.[35] After these incursions in the epistolary genre, Jaramillo felt more confident as a narrator and tackled a third person narrative for the first time in *Historia con fantasma* (1996, A Story with a Ghost). However, after that novel, Jaramillo returned to first person narration in his following novels, now resorting to metafiction, intertextuality, and the "unfolding narrator" as the base of his fictions. For example, his fifth novel, *El juego del alfiler* (2002, The Game of the Pin), is a postmodern metanarrative that includes a character aware of the "ink in his veins" and his dependence to the "owner of a pen" (the narrator who gives him life and decides when his existence can be ended) and "a narrator and a character who calls himself Darío Jaramillo, who is fictitious, an imagined being who belongs to an imaginary story, a subject within a plausible reality, not reality."[36] The title of the novel comes from the idea that any fiction is "a bubble" inflated by a writer who decides when to burst it with his "pin." The prevalent frisky tone of the book not only displays the poet at work in the territory of a long narrative, but also adds a few elements that are constant in Jaramillo's books that are very useful to define the "poetic" in his novels.[37] Even though every novel incorporates Jaramillo's poetics thematically and structurally, in this section I will focus on the author's penultimate novel, *La voz interior* (2006, The Inner Voice) since it not only contains the unconscious inclusion of passages of lyrical beauty reminiscent of the topics of his previous poetry love lost, friendship) but also integrates the process of the unfolding" or "splitting" of the self (in Spanish, "*desdoblamiento*" and "*enmascaramiento*") as well as a complex use of intertextuality and metafiction.[38] This novel, I argue, can be considered as a formally ideal summary of Jaramillo's interests and procedures, and it demonstrates many of his strategies as a poet-novelist.[39]

La voz interior is the longest and more ambitious novel written by Jaramillo to date. As the author himself explains, *La voz interior* was an extensive project that took him many years until he ultimately decided to publish it after realizing that it was becoming endless.[40] I would argue that the mere content of the novel gives the reader a solid background of Jaramillo's own life as a writer and serves as an unofficial compendium of his most cherished and recurring interests, themes, and aesthetic discoveries. More importantly, it is also a celebration of intimate writing and a thoughtful reflection about the act of poetic and prose writing. Within the interest of this study, it is also a text that allows understanding of the steps that a poet-novelist follows in his writing. As in the previous poetic novels commented here, *La voz interior* also experiments with the hybridity of the novelistic form by incorporating the cleverly disguised author's poetics and many fictional texts of different genres (diaries, notebooks, letters, books of poems and aphorisms, semblances of fictitious writers, lives of imaginary saints, etc.) as part of a coherent whole. Moreover, it is constructed entirely through a play of masks and "unfoldings" of the narrator – an aspect that creates in a few instances very complex narrative levels – and employs a discourse that puts more emphasis on embedded narratives. Finally, through the use of metafiction, self-referential quotes, and intertextuality, many passages explicitly elaborate on the meaning of the procedures used throughout the text.

La voz interior begins with the first-person narration of Bernabé, a writer who finds out about the death of Sebastián – his best friend from his youth – that occurred ten years previously. Bernabé explains that Sebastián's family hired him to review a bundle of papers he left to find if there was something valuable or publishable. By meticulously reading these documents and writing about them afterwards, Bernabé recovers some of his own lost memories, understands the motivations and habits of his friend, and reflects on events of the past they shared. It is worth mentioning that Sebastián's life, partially referred to in unpublished books, is not "novelistic," and neither particularly interesting nor exciting. Tackling a narrative of this kind, according to Bernabé, is undoubtedly risky because it prevents the text from being appealing to all readers and critics.[41] Nevertheless, according to Bernabé, what justifies writing about this unconventional character is the possibility of revealing the intense inner life of an individual far from public life and to reveal the "spiritual biography" of a writer dissenting with the concept of public life and recognition."[42] This reflection comes directly from Jaramillo's perception of writing as a solitary and delectable act that leads to contemplation and inner knowledge. In contrast, the task of publishing a book is a public act that requires a careful selection and editing of the basic ideas and requires a different approach.[43] Taking this into account, it can be argued that Jaramillo uses Sebastián as a metaphor for the intimate workings of a writer during those singular moments of loneliness when, briefly distanced from the world, he is able to encounter his "inner voice." If Sebastián is always writing for himself, Jaramillo purposely employs Bernabé's distanced and analytic voice as a symbol of the act of publishing, that is, to bring the texts to the public. Hence, a recurrent technical procedure found in *La voz interior* is the inclusion of "quotations" of Sebastián's writings preceded and/or followed by a brief commentary of Bernabé, the editor: "In one of his notes, Sebastián wrote: *I write to find the words dictated by my inner voice, a voice without words.*"[44] Moreover, throughout this procedure, Jaramillo reflects and gives insight related to his procedures. This exercise is another example in which the author inserts his own poetics into the narrative he is creating.

All in all, the premise of the novel demands the use of an unorthodox structure: the first half of the novel is a critical study and biography presented by the editorial voice, Bernabé; the second half contains Sebastián's full texts in chronological order. On the surface, as in the case of Mutis's work, the novel follows the classic structure of the "editor-at-work," compiling recently discovered texts in order to create a coherent narrative. From this point of view, the resulting book is nothing more than the careful edition of Bernabé, a distanced editorial voice. In fact, the first half of the book is dedicated to commenting on the process of selection of the included texts, to add personal commentaries and to point out errors or inconsistencies in Sebastián's texts. On a deeper level, the written discourse of Bernabé is an inner dialogue with the lost-self and a remembrance of the many ideals of their youth and the destinies of his "broken generation, sometimes tragic, sometimes pathetic, always involved, intertwined in the strange spike of the years."[45] Incidentally, this is one of the subtle nods to the poetic group "La Generación sin nombre." Although the story and the names in the novel are entirely fictitious, Jaramillo explained that one of the projects of *La voz interior* is to recover the atmosphere of this group in the 1970's and to reflect on "the failure" of his generation and the publishing of books of poetry and literary magazines during that time.[46] In the novel, Bernabé explains: "During that time, we used to write to each other frequently with projects that were going to revolutionize the world. ... We were teenagers and during that time the meaning of poetry transcended the nature of the dispensable, becoming as essential in life as breathing. In our adolescence, this brotherhood was strengthened by searching for the vital meaning of poetry. It became a search for the words for a period marked with inner confusion."[47] Through the act of reading and writing, the biography of both characters converges and becomes one common voice: "We were the same person and a sum of different issues ... even with the mask of the biographer I cannot but feel affection for my character ... a common past united us and the awareness that the other was there, that eternal accomplice, transformed by time who would remain faithful, available,and constant in the distance."[48] This discourse is also a vehicle in which Jaramillo subtly expresses his opinions on many general subjects such as the state of Colombian literature and the failure of educational institutions particularly with regard to literature and poetry.

The final strategy in *La voz interior* is the constant use of the "mask," which results in *desdoblamiento* (doubling) and *"desyoización"* (a neologism that can be translated "to lose the self"). The fictionalization of a double, that is, the creation of an "imaginary brother" as an oblique reflection of the author himself, "is alternatively a narcissistic and a mocking gesture which hides a deep concern in relation to the act of creation inside the poem."[49] Jaramillo later explained: "My verses are about me, about those things I am and those I have been, about my masks."[50] In fact, this procedure has its origins in Jaramillo's earlier poetic production when Jaramillo collaborated with the group *La Generación sin Nombre*.

Alstrum argues that Jaramillo and his contemporaries found in the poetic semblance and the self-portrait in verse an effective poetic form at the service of self-conscious inquiry and a way to subject the status quo to harsh criticism. ... Almost all poets of Cobo Borda's generation resorted to poetic self-portrait to participate in the cosmopolitism that the magazine *Mito* glorified,as a special manner of allusion and intertextuality in which they could collate and evaluate their own poetry in order to unmask the empty values of their time.[51] Indeed, some sections of Jaramillo's earlier books of poetry pay direct homage to different world writers and historical figures in a series of "Imaginary Biographies" (*Historias*, 1974) or in a "Collection of Masks" (*Poemas de amor*, 1986). In *La voz interior*, Bernabé himself explains the procedures: "It is important to highlight a particular element that I consider essential in the literary writing of the notebooks and clearly enunciated by Sebastián: *el desdoblamiento*. This is the key of his later texts: Sebastián stops being himself, his creative work is then based on creating imaginary authors that are not mere pseudonyms because the mental universe of each one is another layer of the creation."[52] More importantly, this literary creation of a "mask" (based either on a real or an imaginary character) becomes an essential part of the creative machinery of *La voz interior.*

It can be argued that every novelist takes upon himself the task of creating "another self" when crafting a novel. However, as it was explained in the previous section of this essay, poet-novelists like Jaramillo utilize these masks to explore the possibilities of the lyric voice and to evaluate their own writing by creating a distanced commenter. Considering this specific idea, a poet writing a novel usually searches for a particular use of a narration and a vocabulary that may faithfully convey the content of the passage and may display its message in a more meaningful way. Therefore, as the narrator in *La voz interior* explains, Sebastián's style is defined by the particular search he embarks upon: "the verbal rhythm is dictated by a drug user in trance, or by the prose of someone writing about his child-hood, or by that individual who tries to transform musical pieces by Bach or Beethoven into words. Then, Sebastián unfolds and puts on the disguise of another in order to bare himself."[53] This opens many creative possibil-ities of experimenting with different styles. At the same time, in *La voz interior* the creation of "doubles" and the inclusion of distanced narrators not only allows Sebastián to evaluate aspects like the historical past, lost love, friendship, or literature, by observing characters in other narrative levels the novel truly becomes a self-exploration of the hidden doors a writer unconsciously opens through the act of writing. *La voz interior* provides many passages in which Bernabé comments and reflects upon Sebastián's necessity of creating "others." In some instances, a mask is a useful tool to confront pain and spiritual scars, "as if unfolding the self, one could see himself from the outside in such a way that the more intimate wounds are inflicted to the created character. As reading oneself in front of a broken mirror."[54]

A noteworthy example of this experimentation in *La voz interior* is Sebastian's intent of writing borderline experiences. Among Sebastián's notebooks there is *El cuaderno sucio,* "the dirty notebook" a series of texts written during a period of intense crisis that break the cleanliness and order of the previous papers.[55]. By "avoiding any rule of literary hygiene" – that is, disregarding norms of punctuation, rhythm and calligraphy – this diary explores in depth the acts of "searching for words that may liberate me" and "exploring myself and letting poetry pierce me."[56] In this case, through the character's voice, Jaramillo explores the possibilities of a discourse of "desperate writing" by selecting a style intimately related to the content and by distancing himself from the character. There are many "texts inside the text" that are relevant in the context of this essay. The first book written by Sebastián, "Liturgia de los bosques,"[57] is poetry aspiring "to create a vegetal book, a book with the fragrance of grass, an attempt to put words to the plants ... to allow the reader to perceive with his senses – sight, smell, hearing, lighting, tact – and to perceive in present time what the words are saying."[58] The recovery the poetry of "an unknown author" is a procedure previously used in *Cartas cruzadas*.[59] This provides insightful commentary related to Jaramillo's masks and enables understanding of some hidden aspects from the text. However, the apparent egocentrism of the writer includes a very subtle degree of sarcasm directed to the figure of a young poet who is always changing his perception of writing. In many ways, Jaramillo does not write the books in order to prove a point but to explore the developmental growth of a writer's journey.

A final example that is particularly noteworthy about *La voz interior* is the manner in which the narrative discourses of both Bernabé and Sebastián (which are only two of the masks Jaramillo puts on) directly comment and explain the tactic itself and apply it in their own fictions. Therefore, within the confined space of the novel, a great part of the plot development comes from embedded narratives originating from masks created by the characters themselves. Sebastián disguises himself in a series of alter-egos who write in different genres and routinely create other characters. The section entitled "El país de los poetas" ("The country of the poets," one of the books written by Sebastián and an imaginary literary space) takes this to the limit, since Sebastián "transforms" himself into many others who simultaneously create other identities by using masks. One example of this is the case of Segismundo Noble, a character who playfully emulates the style of Leon de Grieff by "becoming him" and using his characteristic language in his texts.[60] In fact, Segismundo Noble is the mask of another character named Margarita Peláez, an aspiring writer who imitates the style of other writers "as a way to attenuate my primary emotions by filtering them through a familiar style. By installing myself into Leon de Grieff's language ... my emotions become purified of the sentimental trash my own writings usually have. I am Segismundo Noble."[61] Needleless to say, Margarita is nothing more than a mask of Sebastián, and consequently, of Jaramillo himself. This example shows the manner in which literary expression is marked by a specific use of language and entails the workings of a writer looking for the perfect manner to express his message.[62]

This chapter has explored the strategies followed by Mutis and Jaramillo as poets writing novels. By adopting the novelistic genre as a space in

which storytelling becomes an open ground to elaborate a poetic conception of writing, both authors have created a series of novels that continue
the tradition of poet-novelists in Colombia. Maqroll the Gaviero's saga and
Jaramillo's novelistic portrayal of the projects of Colombian poets in the
1970s are poetic in the sense that they develop the expressiveness of
language as a medium for grasping the hidden layers of reality; as novels,
in addition to the anecdote itself, they also narrate the process behind the
act of writing and the position of the author behind the fiction. The result
is a fictional universe replete with nostalgia and many failed attempts to
grasp ultimate beauty, but also a re-encounter with the author's "self," that
character who believes in literature and attempts to narrate his frustrations
and loneliness in order to rediscover his inner world. The legacy of Mutis
and Jaramillo is undoubtedly reflected in the very promising work of
other contemporary poets writing novels such as Piedad Bonett, William
Ospina, Jaime Manrique, and Juan Manuel Roca.[63] The aesthetic search
of the poetic in the contemporary Colombian novel continues and it
undoubtedly opens a path that is worth studying as an integral part of
the history of contemporary Colombian literature.

BIBLIOGRAPHY

Alstrum, J. J. 2000. *La generación desencantada de Golpe de Dados: los poetas
colombianos de los años 70*. Bogotá: Ediciones Fundación Universidad
Central.
Ardila Ariza, J. 2013. *Vanguardia y antivanguardia en la crítica y en las publicaciones
culturales colombianas de los años veinte*. Bogotá: Universidad Nacional de
Colombia.
Cobo Borda, J. G. 1998. *Para leer a Álvaro Mutis*. Bogotá: Espasa.
    2003. *Historia de la poesía colombiana: de José Asunción Silva a Raúl Gómez
Jattin*. Bogotá: Villegas Editores.
Jaramillo Agudelo, D. 1999. *Cartas cruzadas*. México: Ediciones ERA.
    2001. *Nosotros los solitarios*. Valencia: Pre-Textos.
    2002. *El juego del alfiler*. Valencia: Pre-Textos.
    2003. *Libros de poemas (1974–2001)*. Bogotá: Fondo de Cultura Económica.
    2006a. *Historia de una pasión*. Valencia: Pre-Textos/Poéticas.
    2006b. *La voz interior*. Valencia: Pre-Textos.
    Personal interview. July 3, 2014.
Mercedes Carranza, M., et al. 1991. *Historia de la poesía colombiana*. Bogotá: Casa
de Poesía Silva.
Mutis, A. 1985. *La muerte del estratega: narraciones, prosas y ensayos*. México: Fondo
de Cultura Económica.
    1999. *De lecturas y algo del mundo (1943–1998)*. Ed. D. Santiago Mutis Bogotá:
Planeta.

2002. *The Adventures and Misadventures of Maqroll.* Trans. Edith Grossman. New York: New York Review of Books.

Ospina, W. 2011. *Por los países de Colombia: ensayos sobre poetas colombianos.* Bogotá: Fondo de Cultura Económica.

Rae, I. 2008. *From Cohen to Carson: The Poet's Novel in Canada.* Montreal: McGill-Queen's University Press.

Roca, J. M. 2012. *Galería de espejos: una mirada a la poesía colombiana del siglo XX.* Bogotá: Alfaguara.

Siemens, W. L. 2002. *Las huellas de lo trascendental: la obra de Álvaro Mutis.* México: Fondo de Cultura Económica.

Todorov, T. 1990. *Genres in Discourse.* Cambridge: Cambridge University Press.

Williams, R. L. 1991. *The Colombian Novel 1844–1987.* Austin: Texas University Press.

Notes

1 The aspects that define poetic prose have been thoroughly discussed in texts of literary theory since Aristotle's *On the Art of Poetry*. Specifically referring to the manner in which poetic writing is incorporated as part of the structure of a novel, I limit the scope by using a few seminal works of the twentieth century that are devoted to explain the mutual interaction of literary genres and the manner in which novelistic discourse is a representation of the author. Texts such as Bakhtin's *The Dialogic Imagination* and *Speech Genres* and Todorov's *Teoría de los formalistas rusos* (Theory of the Russian Formalists) and *Genres in Discourse* are a fundamental background for this study. In addition to this, a study I find particularly useful for the examination of poet-novelists is Ian Rae's book *From Cohen to Carson: The Poet's Novel in Canada*. By analyzing the manner in which five Canadian poets of the twentieth century made the transition from lyric to the novel, Rae provides very insightful notions of the methods a poet uses to overcome the limitations of the lyric when tackling a larger narrative structure. I elaborate more on the main procedures of poet-novelists in the introduction of my doctoral dissertation *Poetic Gestures in Narrative: Prose Poetics in Selected Works of Roberto Bolaño, Cristina Rivera Garza and Darío Jaramillo Agudelo* (Riverside, CA: University of California, Riverside, 2012, available at https://escholarship.org/uc/item/5km7q228). The quotation is from Rae, *From Cohen to Carson*.

2 On his study on the Colombian novel, Raymond L. Williams has pointed out that in spite of some significant individual novels, in Colombia "the novel has always been considered a relatively minor genre. The cultivation of poetry and the essay has been a historic ideal for its dominant elite of gentlemen-scholars. ... In a century, three novels of national and international import have been produced: Jorge Isaac's *María* (1867), José Eustasio Rivera's *La vorágine* (1924), and Gabriel García Márquez's *Cien años de soledad* (1967). *María* and *La vorágine* were written by writers who aspired to be poets and, in fact, had established credentials as poets prior to their celebrity as novelists"

(Williams, *The Colombian Novel 1844–1987*, 20). Williams gives a few examples of other novels written by poets – like José Joaquín Ortiz's *María Dolores o la historia de mi casamiento* (1841). Williams considers that Issacs's *María* has "[a] 'poetic' language compensated for the fact that it was written in the less dignified and still undefined genre of the novel" (30). In a similar fashion, the influential novel by José Eustasio Rivera "exploited the public image of himself as a poet and aesthete, a self-characterization he further promoted in his depiction of the protagonist Arturo Cova in *La vorágine*" (41). In my opinion, the case of Rivera is notable since the protagonist (Arturo Cova) is a writer whose poetic sensibility radically changes when encountering the sordid heart of the jungle; this representsthe evolution of a writer through experience. From the abstract realities derived from Romanticism (the search for the ideal, the soaring to the transcendental, the emotional and cordial relation between man and nature) the poet discovers the necessity of finding a new type of discourse that relates to this situation. *La Vorágine* is a perfect example of the "life changing journey of a poet" whose own style is contested and who looks for an alternative. For an analysis of Rivera's poetic vocabulary in his novel, see the introduction to the critical edition of *Tierra de promisión* by Luis Carlos Herrera (31–71). Other critics tend to compare the value of both texts in different manners. For example, De Onís argues that "*La vorágine*, "vigorosa pintura, a la vez realista y romántica, de la selva tropical. Los sonetos de su único libro de poesías tienen el mismo tema en forma más perfecta gracias a su mayor concentración" (Ardila Ariza, Vanguardia y antivanguardia, 24), while William Ospina considers that *La vorágine* is superior to the sonnets (*Por los países de Colombia*, 131–6).

3 One significant example of this influence is Gabriel García Márquez's commentary of *De sobremesa* in his brief essay "En busca del Silva perdido," in *José Asunción Silva: obra completa.* ed. Héctor H. Orjuela (Bogotá: FCE, 1996), 22–32. Silvas's work and the relationship between his poetry and his prose are thoroughly discussed in the many essays included in this book. On the other hand, the complex poetic novel *El gran Burundú Burundá ha muerto* (1952) by Jorge Zalamea, was translated into many languages and generated some cult following due to its treatment of the topic of dictatorship and absolute power. Among the studies of the poetic qualities of this unorthodox work, see the prologues by Alfredo Iriarte in both editions of Zalamea's work (*El gran Burundú Burundá ha muerto y La Metamorfosis de su excelencia* [Bogotá: Editorial Colombia Nueva, 1966 and Bogotá: Arango Editores, 1989]). Héctor Rojas Herazo wrote a noteworthy trilogy of poetically developed novels. In spite of its recognition and some prizes it received, the extremely complex use of language (following the experimental avant-garde emphasis on the search for astonishing metaphors) and the elaborate nonlinear structure prevented this work from successfully grabbing the attention of a wider audience. Additionally, there are a few examples of novels written by poets of the *Nadaísta* group such as Germán Pinzón's *El terremoto* (1966) and Humberto Navarro's *Los días más felices del año* (1966). During my interview with Darío Jaramillo, he explained that

only a few of the poets in poetic groups (*Piedra y Cielo,* "La Generación sin Nombre") claimed to have written at least a novel, but none of them have published any.

4 Siemens, *Las huellas de lo trascendental,* 59 and 100.

5 Ibid., 185.

6 In addition to Mutis's *De lecturas y de algo del mundo* – a compilation of his articles and reflections on different topics – two books that address the relationship between Mutis's poetry and prose have proved indispensable in the writing of this essay: *Para leer a Álvaro Mutis* by Juan Gustavo Cobo Borda and *Las huellas de lo transcendental: la obra de Álvaro Mutis,* by Siemens. Other more recent articles and short essays that I considered in this study are Ospina, "Un agua persistente y vastísima," in *Por los países de Colombia,* and Roca, *Galería de espejos.* Additionally, a large bibliography of articles and essays is also available in Siemens's book. It is very important to mention that since these all these books and articles are originally in Spanish, all the quotes in this essay are my own translations.

7 All of Mutis's short stories and novels before the Maqroll's saga (*La mansión de Araucaíma: relato gótico de tierra caliente, La muerte del estratega, El último rostro, antes de que cante el gallo,* and *Sharaya*) are included the compilation *La muerte del estratega* (1985). Many of the topics covered on them foreshadow themes and strategies in his cycle of novels. Moreover, Mutis's personal recollection of his poetry from 1947 to 2003 is entitled *Summa de Maqroll el Gaviero: poesía reunida.*

8 Cobo Borda, *Para leer a Álvaro Mutis,* 119.

9 Siemens, *Las huellas de lo transcendental,* 252.

10 Mutis, *The Adventures and Misadventures of Maqroll,* trans. Edith Grossman (New York: New York Review of Books, 2002), 297.

11 Siemens, *Las huellas de lo transcendental,* 91–4.

12 Mutis, *De lecturas y algo del mundo (1943–1997),* 108.

13 Ibid., 54.

14 Ibid., 59.

15 See the articles "*Luz de Agosto* (William Faulkner)" and "*Santuario* (William Faulkner)," in *De lecturas y algo del mundo,* 13–15 and 19–21, my translation. Similar reflections on European and American writers are found in the following sections of the same text: "Nostalgias de lector" (47–8), "Juan José Arreola recuerda" (54–6), "Testimonio de un poeta" (57–8), "El milagro constante" (59–60). On Siemens's study, see "Los años en Bruselas y Colombia," 7–39.

16 Rae, *From Cohen to Carson,* 6.

17 Mutis, *The Adventures and Misadventures of Maqroll,* 305.

18 Rae, *From Cohen to Carson,* 11.

19 In "A Poetic Novel" (*Genres in Discourse,* 50–9), Todorov proposes four types of phenomena found in a novel whose details are not "particularly novelistic:" the nature of the actions, the narrative embeddings, or the second-degree narratives; the parallelisms; the use of allegory" (53). Todorov adds that the

combination of these four procedures (among others) can create "a poetic impression, if at all, only through what unites them" (58).

20 Mutis, *The Adventures and Misadventures of Maqroll*, 313.

21 Ibid., 300.

22 Ibid., 301.

23 In *Abdul Bashur, Dreamer of Ships*, "the ideal" for what is characterized as a freighter is, "a constant in his destiny, more tenacious than any other and, for his friends, the most moving, it was his endless search, in every port on earth, for the ideal freighter . . . he is pursuing an impossibility. His ideal ship always slips between his fingers" (*The Adventures*, 5067).

24 Siemens, *Las huellas de lo transcendental*, 58.

25 Rae explains that the novel becomes a space in which a poet can explore the mythic within the quotidian by creating fictional worlds out of symbolic details: "The poet-novelists retain the emphasis on the perceptions and cogitations of the individuals through the lyric voice; however, the poet-novelists tell stories about isolated individuals finding and building a community outside the one into which they are born, and this social transformation is mirrored on the formal level by the process through which the novel's poetic fragments cohere into narrative" (*From Cohen to Carson*, 32).

26 Mutis, *The Adventures and Misadventures of Maqroll*, 359.

27 Darío Jaramillo began his career publishing poems in different literary magazines and newspapers and it was in the 1970s when he published his first books of poetry: *Historias* (1974) (Stories) and *Tratado de retórica o de la necesidad de la poesía* (1978) (Treatise on Rhetoric or, The Necessity of Poetry). These poems already experiment with narrative techniques, and are marked with the use of intertextuality and "*intrahistorias*" (that is, the depiction of the quotidian events of marginal characters). On this, see Sergio Pitol, "El té de las cinco y la poesía," in Alstrum, *La generación desencantada de Golpe de Dados*, 287–9. After these books, Jaramillo's lyric vein consolidated into a refreshing poetic vision on the topic of love in his celebrated book *Poemas de amor* (1986) (Poems of Love). As a poet, Jaramillo has pursued different objectives, including the "translation" of other art expressions to poetry – painting in *Del ojo a la lengua* (1995) (The Eye to The Tongue) and music in *Cuadernos de música* (2008) (Notebooks of Music) – and a book of poetic prose (*Guía para viajeros*, 1991) (Guide for Travelers). Although he published his first novel in 1983 (*La muerte de Alec*) (The Death of Alec), it was with *Cartas cruzadas* (1995) (Crossed Letters) – his second novel nominated as a finalist in the Romulo Gallegos competition – when Jaramillo gained more critical attention as a novelist. In total, he has published seven novels. Incidentally, in my recent interview with the writer, he commented that he is currently working on another book of poetry (tentatively titled *Conversaciones con Dios*) (Conversations with God) and a trilogy of novels based on the premise "you are going to die in six months."

28 Interview in Bogotá, July 3, 2014. This is also referred to in *Historia de una pasión*, 56.

29 Jaramillo, *Cartas cruzadas*, 21.
30 Jaramillo, *Libros de poemas*, 30.
31 Jaramillo, *Historia de una pasión*, 17.
32 Ibid., 64.
33 Ibid., 72–4.
34 Ibid., 80, 86, 90.
35 Ibid., 26.
36 Jaramillo, *El juego del alfiler*, 15.
37 It is worth mentioning that behind the reflection on literary procedures of a narrative, *El juego del alfiler* is also a commentary on the consequences of the violence in Colombia, the "pure evil" that lead to many assassinations, and the bloodshed derived from the drug trafficking in of the 1980s. Jaramillo explained to me that he originally had written out seven alternative endings to the novel but following his editor's suggestion, he had to choose only one. In the final version (one of the multiple possible endings of the story) every character violently dies in "circumstances that encircle the author, circumstances that overflow themselves and do not resist to invadethe invasion of the written text. There will be blood" (Jaramillo, *El juego del alfiler*, 147).
38 Interview in Bogotá, July 3, 2014. When I was pointing out a few excerpts in some novels that I perceived as an extension or reelaboration of poems in *Poemas de amor* and *Cantar por cantar*, Jaramillo explained that he was not consciously quoting himself but he later realized he was coming back to his beloved topics and interests. This commentary supports the idea of writing as an act of discovery and revelation and intrinsically leads an author to navigate a set of conceived thoughts.
39 As a complement to this essay related to the workings of a poet-novelist, James Alstrum has written an analysis of the poetic development of images in *La muerte de Alec* in Alstrum, "La escritura alusiva y reflexiva de Darío Jaramillo Agudelo," in *Ensayos de literatura colombiana Quirama, 1984*, 197–204. I have also incorporated a lengthy analysis of the poetic development of Jaramillos's fifth novel –*Memorias de un hombre feliz* (2000) – in the second chapter of my dissertation, *Poetic Gestures in Narrative*.
40 Interview in Bogotá, July 3, 2014. Incidentally, after the long effort of writing and publishing *La voz interior* – a novel defined as "intellectual" Darío Jaramillo felt the need to create a lighter fiction, *Historia de Simona* (2011) (History of Simona). Paying homage to the literary tradition of recovering characters from previous fictions, this novel expands the universe of *La voz interior* from a brief passage about the passionate love story between Sebastián and Simona, Bernabé's sister (*La voz interior*, 105–12). Nevertheless, José Hilario López, a new character that resorts to the strategy of "a writer inventing writers," narrates *Historia de Simona*. This novel also contains many passages with a poetic prose reminiscent of Jaramillo's love poetry.
41 Bernabé explains this in the following manner: "Sebastián's life is not particularly thrilling, and this is a warning for the reader . . . what justifies writing it then? Nothing, at least initially: it is possible the world does not need to know

the story and writings of Sebastian, a story without a story, the story of a man enclosed in a meticulous inventory of authors he imagines who populate an imaginary country of poets" (*La voz interior,* 34). Ironically, a real-life critic like Francisco Solano has harshly commented on the novel mentioning Jaramillo's "egotism of publishing unpolished writings in the form of a novel," many of them of questionable literary value, and lacking an interesting story, resulting in a book that is "unnecessary and monotonous." See Solano, review of *La voz interior, Revista de libros de la Fundación Caja Madrid* 125 (May 2007), 58. Solano's misinterpretation comes from the fact that every text included in the novel was intentionally created for it and does not comes from previous unpublished works, as Jaramillo himself explained to me during our interview. Also, the texts were not "polished texts" precisely with the intention of displaying the many stages of the act of writing.

42 Jaramillo, *La voz interior,* 41 and 53.
43 On this topic see *Historia de una pasión,* 30–1, 66–7, and 74–5.
44 Jaramillo, *La voz interior,* 50.
45 Ibid., 64.
46 Interview in Bogotá, July 3, 2014.
47 Jaramillo, *La voz interior,* 14–16.
48 Ibid., 169.
49 Alstrum, *La generación desencantada de Golpe de Dados,* 30.
50 Jaramillo, *Nosotros los solitarios,* 15.
51 Alstrum *La generación desencantada de Golpe de Dados,* 32–3.
52 Jaramillo, *La voz interior,* 201.
53 Ibid., 271.
54 Ibid.
55 Ibid., 234.
56 Ibid., 242.
57 Ibid., 387–409.
58 Ibid., 131 and 197.
59 The short book of poetry *Los poemas de Esteban* (1995, included in the antology *Libros de poemas: 1974–2001*) was written as a complement for *Cartas cruzadas.* According to Jaramillo, these are "recovered poems" penned by Juan Esteban, one of the main characters of this novel. Jaramillo clarifies that his role here is only that of a copyist, since Juan Esteban, in spite of being a fictional character, has the right of being considered as the real author. "Esteban is an unpublished, and not very prolific poet. The unquestionable fact that I transcribed his poems does not mean that I am the author of them. The actual writer is this character. In spite of being a fiction, during his precarious existence in the novel he wrote poetry. I have little to do with this, I am simply a copyist." (Jaramillo *Libros de poemas,* 107). This playful vision of the relationship between fictional characters and their author and the manner in which the former becomes independent after publishing a book, is one of the most recurrent topics in Jaramillo's books. About this, also see *Historia de una pasión,* 31, 56, 60, 80, 90, and 92.

60 Jaramillo, *La voz interior*, 497–510.

61 Ibid., 496.

62 Other similar examples in the same section include Marta María Medina Medina, a writer who imagines and writes biographies of saints (451–73); Servando Arroyabe, a writer published in Sebastián's literary magazines (475–7); and Juan Esteban, a sports commenter and an aspiring writer who emulates the poetry of José Asunción Silva under the name of Juan Amasilva (511–19). The most important example of Sebastián's masks is Walter Steiggel, whose books of epigrams and spiritual reflections ("Visiones en un espejo roto" and "Los motivos de Dios," respectively) are by far the longest texts in the second half of the novel and show the reflective side of Sebastián. Incidentally, following the literary game within the novel, Bernabé expresses that Steiggel may be an invention: "I believe that Steiggel is another fiction, another mask of Sebastian, a lifelong and definitive one, glued to his face, a witness of his deep crises" (267).

63 These four authors are a good example of the continuing tradition of the novel written by poets in Colombia. Piedad Bonnett published five books of poems between 1989 and 1998 before publishing her first novel, *Después de todo* (2001). Since then, she has published three more novels and a narrative testimony about the loss of her son, *Lo que no tiene nombre* (2013). Similarly, William Ospina published poetry and essays (specifically, during the years 1974–2007) before publishing his trilogy of historical novels *Ursúa* (2005), *El país de la canela* (2008, winner of the Romulo Gallegos Prize), and *La serpiente sin ojos* (2012). Jaime Manrique is a poet but is mostly celebrated as a novelist (mainly publishing in English) while Juan Manuel Roca is mostly a poet who has published a novel, *Esa maldita costumbre de morir* (2003).

Afterwords

CHAPTER 21

Colombian literature: national treasure or fraud?

Darío Jaramillo Agudelo[1]

Introduction

Often, and for a variety of purposes, the nineteenth century in the Americas is considered to be the period of the rise and consolidation of nations. To a large extent, after the wars of independence, each country developed a slow process of formation of legal and social mechanisms that constituted nations and national consciousness. In this packet of shaping issues were national literatures, which had national authors and their areas of influence, but each of these national literatures was a fragment of a larger corpus governed by the fact that they were written in the same language, Spanish, regardless of their geographic origin.

If we were to look at the path taken by literature written in Spanish, each can be seen as a group of local literatures that created its own tradition as a result of particularities in its local production, dissemination, and circulation in each country, alongside a production that was common to all because of those most renowned authors. If we were to imagine a pyramid as national literature, each renowned writer in each country would be living at the cusp.

From above, from an aerial perspective, we can see literature in Spanish as a set of pyramids of different sizes, each with its own production and cusps of most prominent writers who can be seen from the neighboring pyramids. No pyramid is the same size as the other, but three have played a greater role than the rest. During the first half of the twentieth century, the leading publishers of books in Spanish were located in Spain (Madrid and Barcelona), Mexico, and Buenos Aires. Therefore, what mainly came to Bogotá, Caracas, or Lima, for example, were books written by Spanish, Mexican, and Argentine authors.

An assessment can be made of each set in two different contexts: The first refers to the way in which each country's own literary production is judged, and the second, how others see them. With regard to Colombia,

Colombian evaluations of their own literature have fluctuated sharply over time. Among them, there is a prominent assessment – an article published in 1960 by Gabriel García Márquez titled "La literatura colombiana, un fraude a la nación" (Colombian Literature: A Fraud to the Nation). In this chapter, I review the evaluations that have been published in Colombia when reflecting on our own literature.

Exaggerating the image of the set of pyramids, I can add that each national space reproduces, in turn, a set of regional literatures that value local production and have created hierarchies in which some local authors do not transcend national borders. Extrapolating this image, it turns out that each national literature and pyramid is a metaphor containing smaller pyramids that represent regional literatures. I come from Antioquia where, historically, poets such as Epifanio Mejía or Carlos Castro Saavedra were considered important, but, according to literary histories being written today nationwide, they simply do not exist. Moreover, given that reflectors are placed on the legends that enshrine every era while the others are simply extras that can go upwards or downwards, that scenario is changing, so that each generation invents its own past. In Colombia, the first instances of independence began in 1810 and can be made into a list of presidents since 1819. From then forward, the slow formation of nationality begins. Thirty years after the Battle of Boyacá in 1848, the same year that slavery ended in Colombia, the first comprehensive anthology of Colombian poetry appeared in print, compiled by José Joaquín Ortiz.[2] The first history of Colombian literature had to wait another twenty years, until 1867, thanks to José María Vergara y Vergara.[3]

The purpose of José Joaquín Ortiz's publishing of *El parnaso granadino* in 1848 was addressed in the book itself: "It is a common opinion in the American republics where the language of Castile is spoken that New Granada ... lacks a literature and should therefore be considered using lower standards because of this fact. We can only blame ourselves for providing an impetus and wings to those who have excelled, by staring indifferently and neglecting our work." In other words, Ortiz believes that other parts of the world have a low opinion of Colombian literature and that itself is a mistake.

In 1860, a new anthology prepared by José Joaquín Borda and José María Vergara y Vergara appeared under the title *La lira granadina*. The most interesting part is the thesis found in the prologue: "Whether by providential arrangement, or because the pride of becoming independent awoke in the soul the most noble of feelings – this is why our literature does not begin in this century." In résumé, this means that before independence there was nothing, and Colombian literature was born the minute it gained independence from Spain.

2

Isidoro Laverde Amaya inaugurated dithyrambics and excesses at the same time in a very useful book, *Apuntes sobre bibliografía colombiana* (1882, Notes toward a bibliography of Colombian literature). A stroking of the ego with respect to national literary self-esteem took place with judgments such as "the name of José Eusebio Caro figures among the first-rate poets in the Americas" or when Rafael Pombo is widely referred to as the "first lyric poet of South America." As far as I been able to trace back, this is the first hyperbolic evaluative statement on our literature to have been written by a Colombian. It was the century of poetry, according to Carlos Monsivais, referring to the nineteenth century, and the national boasting tended to be about the poets.

Indeed, taking the authors sampled from Laverde Amaya, the appearance of our poets in a Latin American context was rare – practically nonexistent – and the most notable figure of Colombian literature in the world was Jorge Isaacs with his the novel *María*, published in 1867. Fifteen years later, when Laverde Amaya published his *Apuntes*, *Maria* became well known throughout the Americas, although its recognition in Colombia as part of the literary canon had to wait several more years.

In any case, at the time of Laverde Amaya's *Apuntes*, shares of Colombian literature were trading higher in the stock market of prestige and praise: both locally, as expressed by Laverde Amaya, and in similar commentary from abroad. In 1884, *En viaje* appeared in print – a delicious and informed chronicle by the Argentine writer Miguel Cané. This Argentine traveled to Bogotá, where he got to know the local authors intimately and wrote about them and the country.

The quality that Cané most praised became a defect, a danger to the Colombian poet, although Cané recognized this problem He exclaims: "Easy ... Behold the intellectual characteristics of Colombians! You cannot imagine such spontaneity. It stuns and confuses. In a table where desserts, wine, and common joy invigorate intelligence in the brain, it sparks a burst of quartets, tenths, and limericks!" He recounts the time when they sat at a coffee table and played a game of finishing each other's stanzas: "By the end of the night, we are all speaking in verse, with such ease of rhyme that I've heard Carlos Sáenz writing poetry for a quarter of an hour, without stopping. Mostly nonsense, the majority of the time, but never a poor poem or rhyme. In general, the spirit flows freely; a word, a phrase, gives rise to admirable improvisation." This ability to improvise, the practice of wit, Cané illustrated further with another example: "Mr. Soffia, the minister of Chile, who is a very distinguished poet, invented a mosaic, in the form of a complex sonnet, a very difficult one, indeed. The next day, upon invitation, were forty sonnets, with the same rhymes."

If you were to keep this fluency of incontinence of speech, eloquence being the profession, you would have the following, according to Cané:

> The Colombian is a true orator; his phrases are elegant, filled with life, movement, and grace. In larger theaters, Esguerra, Becerra, Galindo, and Arosemena enjoyed a universal reputation. The fluidity and abundance, was inimitable; it arose, hovered on the heights of eloquence and moved with ease like an eagle in the clouds ... for these men, intellectual conversation was a delight and the free right to express their ideas. More than once I have attended sessions of the Senate of plenipotentiaries, I heard for three hours a citizen who had the word and who carried on until it was time for adjournment– unable to deal with the matter under discussion. Each speaker had the right, if it suited him, to relate the campaigns of Alexander, concerning the establishment of a blacksmith in Boyacá. Many carry on like this, but some deplore the time lost for dealing with matters of real general interest.

Intending to extend praise, the Argentine Cané refers to the Colombian intellectual José María Samper as someone who has written six or eight volumes of history, three or four verses, ten or twelve novels, many travels, speeches, political studies, reports, polemics. ... What do I know! It's one of those facilities that astonish for their tireless activity. Never a moment of rest for the spirit; when the pen is not in motion, the tongue is. After Congress, where he has spoken for three hours, he continues to rant until nightfall, and once at home, he writes until dawn. And that was every day, years ago.

En viaje by Miguel Cané, besides being a delightful book, represents the most positive evaluation of Colombian literature in the nineteenth century. He dedicates an entire chapter to Colombian letters, a chapter that begins:

> I've already mentioned that the intellectual development of Colombian society in Bogotá is an incontestable superiority. It is certainly not my intention here to draw a historical sketch of Colombian literature, well known in America and highly appreciated by the most enlightened critics of the motherland. Colombia has produced, since the early days of its independent life until today, great poets, prose writers, thinkers, and scientists, all of which it is justly proud.

It is very possible that the label of "Colombia, a country of poets" is due to Cané: "It is the land of poetry; from the man of the world, political, military, to the humble peasant, all of them have a verse on their lips, everyone knows by heart the poetic compositions of popular poets." After this appetizer, he refers to one of the writers whom he knew – Gregorio Gutiérrez González – as the most popular poet in those days: "His verses are read today and will always be read with pleasure; . . . he sees the beauty of nature with unparalleled clarity and reflects it in happy, easy, and harmonious verses."

The already mentioned Rafael Pombo refers to books that in Appleton, his home in New York, adults had placed in the hands of children in all the Americas. Before going to Bogotá, Pombo did not know the funny and naive little story about an old woman without anything to eat that his four-year-old daughter would recite to him; it was by none other than the immortal author of the song "Niagara." For Mr. Cané, Pombo is "one of the greatest poets to have written in Spanish."

After referring to the fact that Pombo had not published a book (in fact, like Silva, he never saw a tome with his poems while he lived), Cané relates that Diego Fallon had just published a volume with only two poems – to which he says: "I prefer the two compositions of Fallon to the thick tomes of verses that have made the Spanish American and Spain presses moan." Of the work of José Manuel Marroquín, he highlights "a rhymed gloss of the first books of Tito Livio, that I do not hesitate to consider as one of the most perfect works of this genre that are written in our language. Purity, correct, seems to look for the most difficult moments of syntax, to prove that the treasures of the Spanish language are inexhaustible." He also commends the festive poems of Marroquín and Carrasquilla. He apologizes for not transcribing his poems, "but if you were to reproduce all of the good that contemporary Colombian literature has produced, a volume alone would certainly not be enough."

Cané ends his lengthy praise stating: "Colombia can rightly be proud of two men, still young but whose reputation for wisdom and profound literacy have sailed the seas and extended themselves in the Spanish peninsula. The first is Miguel Antonio Caro, son of the inspired poet José E. Caro, whose noble verses in *En boca del último Inca* are known to all Americans." Caro praises his translation of Virgil and his prose and adds, "Mr. Caro has read everything you can in the span of thirty years of his intellectual life." He then refers to the other young man, Rufino José Cuervo, and reports that "currently, Cuervo is located in Paris, in his Carthusian niche, lifting, stone after stone, the vast monument of all time that has been undertaken to honor the language of Castile."

The overview of Cané is explicit:

> In short, an educated, intelligent, and special society. I've said before that Colombia has taken refuge in the heights, avoiding the painful life of the coasts, whose compensation was an unparalleled intellectual culture, with a complete lack of material progress. It is certainly curious to arrive by mule, on primitive paths in the mountains, sleeping in inns out of the Middle Ages, a city of refined literary taste, where we talk about the latest developments in science as if it were the heart of a European academia. They certainly do not figure in Spain, when their most distinguished men of letters unreservedly applaud the great works of a Caro or a Cuervo, whose authors live in the region of the condor, in the bowels of America; at times, and for prolonged days, without communication with the civilized world.

Arcadia, the South American Athens, a cliché that more than a hundred years later would be dubbed, with the typical wit of the Bogotá intellectual, as "barely South American."

3

The Colombians, specifically the citizens of Bogota, were so convinced by Cané's reflections – a preexisting reflection of themselves – that in 1886, in the preliminary study of the Colombian Parnassus by Julio Añez, the writer José María Rivas Groot believes that local production is most worthy of export and predicts in the preface that the book "will be a book widely read in other [countries] in Latin America and in Spain, as well as consulted by scholars." Some eighty years later, however, this attitude would be interpreted by García Márquez as a "national megalomania," similar to "a sterile form of artistic conformity."

Two years after the Colombian Parnassus of Añez, in 1888, the Spanish novelist Juan Valera unveiled his *Cartas americanas* (Letters of the Americas) in which he widely discusses Añez's book, recognizing that "it is a double fault by Spain for its general ignorance (and I do not deny that there are exceptions and people here that know what there is to know) of the intellectual movement of that Republic. You read us, know us, study us; but Spain knows very little of Colombian authors." Varela praises some authors included in Añez's book – Rafael Pombo, Joaquín González Camargo, Rafael Núñez, Mercedes Flórez, Agripina Montes, José Joaquín Ortiz, Manuel María Madiedo, Rufino José Cuervo, Diego Fallon, and Miguel Antonio – as "the best known among us." But he notes that "it is not fair to stay quiet for there are many compositions in the Colombian Parnassus that show not only the general culture of Colombia, but also an extreme fondness for poetry with the citizens of that republic. There are quite a number of insignificant, colorless, but correct compositions that anyone, whether young or old of any discipline, can do, if he insists on it." However, he admits that Colombian poetry is "good and original."

Juan Varela's fondness for Colombian literature would be turned years later into boundless enthusiasm. Colombia would become the country of poets, only to be confirmed by Marcelino Menéndez y Pelayo, who wrote in his *Antología de poetas hispanoamericanos*, tomo III (1894) that "no offense is made to state a truth as noticeable as the Colombian Parnassus which now surpasses in quality, if not in quantity, any region of the new world." This praise would be reaffirmed by a follower of Menéndez y Pelayo, Rabió y Llunch: "among all the South American republics, the former New Granada is the one that ranks first for its literary importance."

In the markets of literary value, the end of the nineteenth century found Colombia, surprisingly, at its zenith. Writers and citizens embraced and assimilated the praise that had been given to their writers. As a relatively young country, its behavior in this regard was perhaps a little adolescent: It gave importance to these evaluations, it trusted them, and it even believed that they were immutable and true.

4

The most notorious of judgments that were pronounced in the nineteenth century regarding Columbian literature as a whole, both among Colombian intellectuals and in the writings of Cané and Menéndez y Pelayo, is that they are valid only with respect to poetry. Only with poetry do they offer concrete examples and references. Prose doesn't seem to exist. The first novels are not mentioned, nor do they seem to be given any importance, even regarding such widely read works as *Manuela* by Eugenio Díaz. And that's not all. The main issue is that no one mentions the work that has more historical importance, from our perspective, today – *María* by Isaacs. Nobody remembers it, despite the fact that it had been circulating throughout the Americas, and, in 1890, Martí highlighted how its translation into English was even marketable.

As always, the problem was much more complex and hidden. For these writers in the latter half of the nineteenth century, it was even questionable that everyday Colombian reality was a suitable subject to be represented in fiction. The turn-of-the-century writer Tomás Carrasquilla recounts,

Every day I would write but with no intention of publishing; and there, surround by my pages, similar to now; I think that instead of advancing I am taking a step back due to such literary delusion. No one knew about my drafts. Not even my family. But as usual people sniff around and the devil picks up on everything, on a day where it was least expected I received a note that appointed me as a member of a literary center in Medellin directed by Carlos E. Restrepo himself.

Carrasquilla added later that

one night at the literary center, the topic came up as to whether or not there was any novel-worthy material in Antioquia. Everyone there didn't think so except for Carlos and myself. Due to the heat of the matter; we all tried to convince the other side to see our view, and we debated so much that the president himself was called to the matter. But Carlos decided it was not he but I. I obeyed him, because there are people who are born to lead. Once in the utopian stillness of my home, while the rain was unleashed and the storm was in full splendor, I sat quietly at home and wrote a tome, back in the recesses of my little room. I did not plan to publish it: I wanted to try and see if it was possible to create a novel about the most ordinary, everyday subjects of life in Antioquia.

The novel was published in 1896 under the title *Frutos de mi tierra*, although the author had first titled it *Jamones y solomos*. Indeed, Carrasquilla found it to be entirely possible to fictionalize a story about everyday reality in Antioquia. Not only was it possible, but the final result was good.

It was not until the twentieth century that Roberto Cortázar, the first literary historian to specialize in the genre of the novel, wrote in *La novela en Colombia* (1908) that the Colombian nation begins to configure and set up the necessary space for the literary glories of the nation. However, throughout his analysis he assumes that Isaacs and his novel *María* are a paradigm of narrative in the Americas.[4]

The Colombian critic Carlos Rincón ascribes the following importance to the enthronement of *María* at the altar of Colombian literature:

It is because of this set of circumstances [the Constitution of 1886, the War of a Thousand Days, the separation of Panama] that a literary historical fact, cultural and socio-political as the explicit transformation of *María* as the centerpiece of a national canon that is in training, constitutes an event of such significance. Specific and decisive moments of action and communication within the incipient process of national literary communication were able to contribute decisively to provide that status. This process extended from 1905 when in Medellin *La gran apoteosis* by Isaacs was published on the eve of the centenary of the independence of Colombia; in 1909, they decreed that a bust should be erected in honor of the writer in the park that was then under construction to celebrate the anniversary. In 1926 Cali itself celebrated Isaacs, and in 1928 the national senate passed a law to restore the house of El Paraíso, the setting of *María*. Known critics of the time, such as Ignacio Altamirano, Guillermo Prieto and Justo Sierra in Mexico, wrote articles that fueled his reputation as the great "novel of the Americas," while the legend of *María* spread across Latin America. So between those dates *María* became a basic part of a Latin American canon, and with three translations into English (1890, 1900, 1918), it was placed next to *Uncle Tom's Cabin* (1852) by Harriet Beecher Stone, the "American novel" best known in Europe. By 1890, the circulation of *María* had exceeded the numbers achieved by any other Latin American novel. This mass circulation during the early twentieth century explains the reception of film adaptations of Rafael Zatorain in Mexico (1918) and the Spaniards Alfredo de Diestro and Mario Calvo in Colombia (1921). At the same time in comparison to a more elite literature like the French Charles Baudelaire had to wait another two decades to be considered a "canonical author." Isaacs, as the "original romantic genius," and with him *María* became the canonical core of a minor literature, with broad reading across Latin America. Isaacs's bust in the Centennial park confirmed his status as truly important national author so that the celebrations of 1926 confirmed Isaacs as a great novelist, the greatest national poet, the glory of the nation. At the same time *María* had already separated from the author and became a national myth to the nation of Colombia.[5]

María's presence continued into the twentieth century, reinforced by an article by Jorge Luis Borges in 1937 along with a fissure, the first notable one, caused by Eduardo Caballero Calderón's article that appeared in *El Tiempo* on December 18, 1938, *A propósito de Isaacs: por qué ya no amamos a María*, which says the following about Isaacs's novel: "its disjointed and slow episodes, the author failed to sew with the needle the psychological interpretations; his long descriptions of the landscape; his characters as absent and so distant from my spirit, whose concerns are moving at a faster pace and stains with a deeper color; and brings me to great boredom."[6]

5

For the centenary of independence in 1910, Colombians considered themselves to have a consolidated national literature, with Isaacs as the central figure. Until then, everyone agreed, for lack of anything better, that the founder of the nation, the Spanish conquistador who was the first European to set foot in this land, Gonzalo Jiménez de Quesada, was also the founder of the national literature. We lacked the most legitimate birth certificate of any literary corpus, we had no foundational epic, as we should have. As told by Nelson González Ortega:

> For Vergara the absence of a poet and an epic colonial poem with a Colombian theme was only a concern for the bibliophile and Colombian poet José Franco Quijano, because the lack of an epic poem that is to be considered "noble" to the supposed "last barbarian" of Colombia was a completely unacceptable fact. In order to overcome this cultural gap, Franco Quijano turned to poetic adulteration, writing a romance in the twentieth century himself and publishing it as if it had been written in the sixteenth century by a Catholic priest who accompanied Jiménez de Quesada in 1538 in the discovery of the New Kingdom of Granada or the current Colombia. In an article published in 1919 in the journal of the Colegio Mayor del Rosario, Franco Quijano fraudulently reported the discovery of the first Colombian romance, which was eighty-eight syllables and whose title was, according to him: "Romance de Ximénez de Quesada, dated Sancta Fe and third of September in fifteen hundred and thirty-eight by Don Antón de Lescanes."[7]

Everyone was happy; at first no one discovered the trick and initially abided by that mythical principle, until, first Otero Muñoz and then Gisela Butler upset everything with "el romance de Ximénez de Quesada' ¿primer poema colombiano?" Gisela Butler has demonstrated that the so-called "Romance" was written in the early twentieth century – in the margins of an old medicine manual, owned by the priest known as Lescámez or Lescánez – by J. Franco Quijano, archivist at the library of the Colegio Mayor de Nuestra Señora del Rosario. Butler states that "the Romance of Ximénez de Quesada, with the alleged year of which it was written, 1538, work of Antón de Lescámez, is not an authentic document from the early sixteenth century of the New Kingdom of Granada, but a literary hoax, from – due to the absence of other indications – its editor, Mr. J. Franco Quijano." The documented evidence of this literary fraud was published by Butler in the *Deutsche Forschungsgemeinschaft und Deutsche IberoAmerica Stiftung* and later published in the form of an article in *Thesavrvs. Bulletin of the Instituto Caro y Cuervo* 17 (1962).

6

The year 1924 is significant in this story. In November of that year José Eustacio Rivera's *La vorágine* appeared, and it joined the canon of Colombian literature almost immediately. Its phenomenon of internationalization was also swift, allowing Colombia, from that moment on, to rely not only on the great novel of the Spanish American

Romanticism – *María* – but also *La vorágine*, a work that was both the great novel of *modernismo* and the great novel of the jungle out of all those that had been written on the continent.

The process by which it quickly became a phenomenon across the continent is astonishing. The English translation, spearheaded by Rivera himself, appeared in New York in 1928. In 1930 it was already published in French. The book having just appeared, the Argentine Manuel Ugarte exalted it from Paris; and from Buenos Aires, the Uruguayan Horacio Quiroga put it atop all South American literature: "the most transcendental book that has ever been published on the continent."

By rethinking the evaluation of Colombian literature since the publication of *La vorágine*, we find that, at the time, the most known and respected outside the borders were the novels by Isaacs and Rivera, while opinion on Colombian poetry was diffused, without the recognition of other poets. Public opinion maintained the popular literary myths, as well as the dominant lies and apologies. I don't know exactly why Colombia was supposedly a country of poets.

7

The domestic opinion of our own literature has been outrageously benevolent. Beyond the widely accepted value of *María* and *La vorágine*, opinion on the poets was so exceptionally exaggerated that it was obvious. In 1930 the *Antología de poetas colombianos* (1800–1930) was published. Here Guillermo Valencia occupied the center stage of Colombian poetry, in addition to his political role as two-time presidential candidate of the republic. As a poet, the scholars who repeated his verses admired him, and as an intellectual authority he was as untouchable as was Miguel Antonio Caro in the second half of the twentieth century.

For the author of the biographical notes of poets, "as a poet, it took [José Eusebio] Caro to one of the highest peaks of the Latin American poetry"; and Miguel Antonio Caro is "the most remarkable writer of Spanish America after Bello." But that is relatively little, for he considered Guillermo Valencia to be a "world famous speaker, writer and poet." Period.

Inevitably, the building had been raised to such a height that it was time for it to collapse. And in 1942 came the first toppling, launched by Eduardo Carranza toward the end of Valencia's life in a famous text *Un caso de bardolatría* (A Case of Idolatry of Storytellers) He notes that the poetry of Valencia "over forty years has fallen upon a flood of praise . . . the prince of Spanish poetry, the best poet of the language, the greatest among those who now sing in America" and warns that "establishing a reserve fence around Valencia's work is not devoid of danger: it seems that in the country there is no room for reasonable admirers of Valencia. This is a case of 'bardolatry'" (or idolatry of storytellers).

His attack begins as follows:

> It's exhausting to hear that Valencia is a great poet ... For me – a blasphemy of mine – Valencia is barely a good poet! A good poet at the use of Parnassus. His work lacks transcendence, vitality, and human pulse. His poetry is burdened with ideological-verbal eloquence. An impassive architect of idiomatic material who sings behind his time and his people. Great rhetoric, if you will, at the service of a minor poet.

And yet the commonplace form of mockery circulating around the world, "Colombia country of poets," remained until in 1947 came another devastating attack from Cuba. José Rodríguez Feo, at the magazine *Origenes,* says in a letter to José Lezama Lima: "I was reading the modern Colombian poets: Valencia, De Greiff, Llanos, Carranza, and so on, how boring, archaic, and so little that they tell us in 1947." To this, José Lezama Lima responds: "I think it is very true what you say of Colombian poetry. Chewing too many gerunds and passive participles, and their poetry becomes formulaic and thin."[9]

8

The decade that began in 1960 was a time of reevaluations, demolitions, and revisions, along with the collapse of commonplaces of social life that concealed prejudices, lies, and discrimination. There was a sexual revolution, humankind reached the moon, there were revolution on campuses and desertions in the fields of war; it was the decade of the Beatles and the Rolling Stones; the Boom in Latin American literature took place and the counterculture appeared.

In that atmosphere it is understandable that the foundations of writing and its history would be shaken. In a controversy that occurred in the temple of official history, Colombia's Academy of History, Juan Friede questioned the historical work: "The historian Friede said that Colombian historiography suffered from improvisation and cultivated within a small group of intellectuals dealing with the discipline at times by family traditions and others for political or ideological convenience." Álvaro Tirado Mejía relates in *Los años sesenta, una revolución en la cultura,* quoting Germán Colmenares: "History had not been conceived in Colombia as knowledge constituted around the explicit formulation of problems, which should be resolved according to an appropriate methodology. The exercise of history was vaguely a literary activity that was practiced as a moral duty and as a proof of love of country."[9]

The writing of history was a matter of professionals dominating certain methodologies, and its purpose was not to form national consciousness, or good conscience, or anything that has to do with the word conscience. In short, so began a time when everything was in question and criticism of what was already established was a need for survival, an imperative to oxygenate the intellectual debate. And it was in that spirit, and as one of its strongest manifestations, that García Márquez's "La literatura colombiana, un fraude a la nación" appeared.

It is not easy to summarize the 1960 article. Perhaps the title is the best summary. Let's hear what García Márquez had to say:

> Definitely, one of the factors of our literary delay was that national megalomania – the most sterile form of conformism – that threw us to sleep on a bed of laurels that we ourselves continue inventing. ... We keep nourishing the feeling of superiority that we inherited from our ancestors thanks to *María* in five different languages, written 109 years ago and *La Vorágine* into eight languages, including Chinese, written thirty-five years ago. I think it's time to admit that it is absolutely false that the world is aware of our literature.

For García Márquez a national literature does not exist, "the story of Colombian literature, from colonial times, is reduced to three or four individual successes through a tangle of false prestige. ... Generally speaking, in three centuries of Colombian literature it has not yet begun to lay the foundations of a tradition." What happened instead was

> a whole literature of entertainment, jokes and parlor games [that] flourished in the country, while the nation made a painful transition into the twentieth century. Traditionalists were not interested in the man but to the most picturesque landscape element. In the golden age of Colombian poetry, some of the best European poems of Latin America were written. But no national literature was made.

Without a literature, several attempts were made to write its history:

> The history of Colombian literature has been written many times. We have also tried numerous critical essays by national, living and dead authors, multiple times. But in the majority of cases this work has been interfered with by outside interests, from complacency in friendships to political bias, and almost always by a distorted and misguided patriotic pride. Furthermore, the clerical intervention in various fronts of the culture is also a factor

in misrepresenting the religious moral aesthetic. . . . The Colombian critique has been a wasteful task of classification, historical order, and in exceptional cases a work of valuation.

For García Márquez, the problem stems from three things: the lack of serious literary criticism; in that "our writers have lacked a true sense of nationhood, it was definitely the safest condition so their works would have a universal projection"; and that they have not been given "the conditions to produce the phenomenon of a professional writer among us."

So what's left? Diligent and accusatory, the future Nobel Laureate clarifies:

> Six large benchmarks could serve as support to establish the colossal gaps of Colombian literature. From *El Carnero* by Rodriguez Freyle, until *María* by Jorge Isaacs, it took 260 years more until the appearance of the *La Vorágine* by José Eustasio Rivera. Since the death of Hernando Domínguez Camargo in 1669, we had to wait 200 years for the emergence of Rafael Pombo and José Asunción Silva and another sixty years for the appearance of Porfirio Barba Jacob.

As we can see, the six benchmarks are seven: *El Carnero, María, La Vorágine*, Domínguez Camargo, Pombo, Silva, and Barba Jacob.

9

I'm always interested in the way García Marquez deals with numerical data. They fascinate him. The best example, starting with the title, is *One Hundred Years of Solitude*. There are two memorable numerical citations. The first: "Colonel Aureliano Buendía promoted thirty-two armed uprisings and lost all of them. He had seventeen sons from seventeen different women, who were all killed one after another in one night, before the oldest turned thirty-five. He survived fourteen bombings, seventy-three ambushes, and a firing squad." Everything is precise. It's thirty-two, seventeen, thirty-five, fourteen, and seventy-three. Nothing more, nothing less. Someone did the math and offered precision to the lie that we call fiction. The use of figures makes the author more than plausible. He makes it believable – much more than if they were just countless uprisings, many children, several bombings and ambushes. The second: "It rained four years, eleven months and two days." That's a much better thing to say than simply it rained forever.

The issue of numbers is mine. Suffice to say that the first chapter of *One Hundred Years of Solitude* ends with the scene of José Arcadio and his two children paying ten reales each to see the ice and then later five more to touch it. A chapter that's fourteen pages long in the original edition contains sixteen precise amounts, all confirming my hypothesis that it is meant to give validity to the facts presented as an exact amount, similar to the galleon that the first Buendía found twelve kilometers from the seashore. Of course, sometimes that precision leads to conclusions as delusional as this: In the fourth line of the novel we learn that Macondo had twenty houses and five pages later three hundred inhabitants – more delusional than the magic carpet in Macondo, where fifteen people lived in each home. Maybe it's best we get back to our subject.

On one occasion García Márquez said that to express oneself very thoroughly and, somewhat precisely, numerical measure gives the impression of truth: someone did the math, weighed: quantified, one, two, three – and therefore it is true. In "La literatura colombiana, un fraude a la nación" García Márquez expresses a thesis that is hard not to share: We have lied to ourselves for a century and a half, for Colombian literature is not known worldwide and is not as wonderful as they claimed with supposed celebrities such as Miguel Antonio Caro and Guillermo Valencia.

What can be considered imprecise about García Márquez's text, beyond the success of his central thesis, is the wealth of numerical tests of their approaches, which belong to the very particular numerical universe of García Márquez, where the accuracy of a figure can be as diffused as any other word. Not lacking in these trials are substantiating arguments of the period that can qualify something as an erroneous vision, imposed by the times in which we live. I set forth some examples of these numerical tests and opinions that we suffer from today with certain anachronism.

10

"La literatura colombiana, un fraude a la nación" stems from a conjunction with the first Colombian book fair. The author in the first sentence makes reference to "in June 1959 it was sold in two cities of Colombia, and in just five days, three hundred volumes of national authors"; he also mentions this in several paragraphs below. These "book fairs" were an idea by the Peruvian editor Manuel Scorza, with a series of ten books sold in a set at very low prices. The first of these festivals was held in Peru in 1956 and then three times thereafter. It was also held in Venezuela, also three times in Cuba, and two times in Ecuador and Central America. The model of the book fair series was very similar: these "fairs" sold volumes of first two or three local "classics," anthologies of short stories and poetry, and the most representative essayist. That was the first Colombian festival in 1959;

García Márquez describes it with these words: "Of the volumes that were marketed for the Colombian book fairs, none were unprecedented and not even the most recent of which were written in the last five years. . . . Those volumes included an anthology of short stories and poetry, and adding *María* and *La Vorágine*, could be broadly accepted as an acceptable synthesis of a century of Colombian literature."

Specifically, the titles in these kits sold at book festivals were the following: (1) José María Cordovez Moure, *Reminiscencias de Santafé y Bogotá;* (2) Tomás Carrasquilla, *Sus mejores cuentos;* (3) Eduardo Zalamea, *Cuatro años a bordo de mí mismo;* (4) Eduardo Caballero Calderón, *El Cristo de espaldas;* (5) Hernando Téllez, *Sus mejores páginas;* (6) *Los mejores cuentos colombianos;* (7) *Las mejores poesías colombianas;* (8) Gabriel García Márquez, *La hojarasca;* (9) Germán Arciniegas, *El Caballero de El Dorado;* and (10) Jorge Zalamea, *El gran Burundún-Burundá ha muerto.* With a pessimism refuted by the facts, García Márquez said: "The volumes marketed at these book fairs, which restored the prestige of the Colombian buyer, cracked in less than a year the false prestige of the national literature. It is likely that the next event of this kind be postponed indefinitely, while the next Colombian books are found to be integrated into the new collection." Indeed, a year after the first, the second festival of books was held. And instead of the 250,000 copies that were made (not 300,000 as reported by the hyperbolic mathematics practices of García Márquez), at the second festival there were 500,000 printed books. Ah, another clarification that downgrades by 90 percent García Márquez's optimism with buyers: it was not 250,000 buyers but rather 25,000, because the books were sold as a collection, not as individual titles.[10]

In his attack based on statistical information, García Márquez ends with Colombian narrative. His judgment regarding the novel lies between the comic and the disheartened: "The conclusion may seem superficial, but it is perfectly displayable: only bad Colombian novelists have written more than one novel" citing Isaacs, Eustaquio Palacios, and Eduardo Zalamea as examples, while "Arturo Suarez wrote six novels and JM Vargas Vila wrote twenty-seven."

And in the short story we did not do any better: García Márquez refers to a short story contest organized by *El Tiempo* with 315 participants; the complaint of our Nobel Laureate is that "the three stories awarded after a painstaking process of elimination did not reveal the unpublished short story writer who supposedly was in the remote province, suffocated by intellectual centralism." Now, half a century later, when there are many short story contests, that "unpublished short story writer" has not appeared. It serves me as a consolation that other countries that also hold many competitions agree and rarely believe that's the best way to find the great "unpublished short story writer."

The numerologist García Márquez refers to "Antonio Curcio Altamar, the most honest accountant of the Colombian novel, [who] read nearly 800 novels that appeared between 1670 and 1953." For in the year in which García Márquez wrote, 956 novels had been published in Colombia, or an average of 3.29 novels per year for 290 years. Between 1960 and 2014, a period of 54 years, 1,834 novels by Colombian authors were published, meaning 33.94, or thirty-four novels published annually – an average that was ten times greater than the period mentioned by García Márquez.[11]

The same García Márquez, who uses many numbers and knows how to use them as poetic material, states that "the problem is not about quantity but about quality"; perhaps achieving this – following the same approaches of García Márquez – will contribute to the professionalization of fiction writers, who are now few.

II

The motive is now evident as to why this text is a redressing of the essay written by our Nobel Laureate. I only wanted to frame it in time, recounting some chapters of the foreign perceptions about Colombian literature along with the self-complacent and shortsighted apologetic view of our men of letters, a dish of only domestic consumption, since Colombian literature was mostly written with the intention of creating a national literary tradition.

The most important element of García Márquez's essay, whose conclusions are quite abstract, is the manner in which he denounces the poverty of our literary creation and the sentimentality of the history and criticism related to that creativity. In addition, he states the irrefutable fact that no one in the world was particularly interested in Colombian fiction and poetry.

Reading "La literatura colombiana, un fraude a la nación" with the criteria to see how certain his thesis is holding up now, after fifty-four years, is paradoxical because it was the author of those pages who refuted the previous canon with the very books he would write. There were no truly universal writers – he became the first one. Soon after, it was Gabriel García Márquez himself who made Colombian literature universal, but also as a world-class writer, as well as a nation that reads him with pleasure and fervor as well.

The specific weight of his narratives automatically became the center axis, the center for all those who have written before García Márquez in Colombia, those that were writing while he wrote, and this can now be told because he is at the center of that history. Soon you will be told the history of what was written after what he wrote. In any case, mainly thanks to him, literature is not a tool, whatever that tool may be, to form national consciousness, to form good citizens, for practicing religious piety, for anything other than the joy of imagination, or the inalienable freedom of knowledge and hallucination with words. To speak with the voice of García Márquez, "I know of no good literature that serves to exalt established values. In all good literature, I always find the tendency to destroy the established, the already imposed, and the desire to contribute to the creation of new life, new partnerships; in order to improve the lives of men."[12]

I imagine the ghostly reappearance of the thirty-something-year-old that wrote "La literatura colombiana, un fraude a la nación" to write a new version in 2014. That ghost would be required to recognize the existence of someone whom he does not know is himself a poor ghost, someone who today is a dazzling figure of our literature and language, an absolute milestone. Then the ghost would have to recognize that our literature is not a fraud given the mere fact of what our Nobel Laureate wrote what he did. It could confirm that, in all literatures, there are clumsy storytellers and bad poets. But, as he himself states, the question is not about quantity but quality. A single name transforms the dimensions of a literary universe. Just for a moment, let's make the analogy with great literature, for example, of Nicaragua, which is great just for the mere fact that the leading poet of *modernismo*, Rubén Darío, is a part of it. It almost does not matter, although it does matter to some exactly who else there is.

Notes

1 Translated by Juan Pablo Bustos.
2 José Joaquín Ortiz, *El parnaso granadino, colección escogida de poesías nacionales* (Bogotá: Imprenta de Ancízar, 1848).
3 José María Vergara y Vergara, *Historia de la literatura en Nueva Granada,* ed. Antonio Gómez Restrepo and Gustavo Otero Muñoz, 3 vols. (Bogotá: Biblioteca de la Presidencia de Colombia, 1958).
4 Diana Carolina Toro and Olga Vallejo Murcia, "Jorge Isaacs en la historiografía colombiana o de cómo se hace un canon," in *Jorge Isaacs en todas sus facetas, Memoria del primer seminario internacional,* ed. Darío Henao Restrepo (Universidad del Valle), p. 115 ff.

5 Carlos Rincón, "Sobre la recepción de *María* en Colombia, crisis de la lectura repetida y pérdidas de autoridad del canon (1938–1968)," in Henao Restrepo, *Jorge Isaacs en todas sus facetas,* p. 87 ff.

6 Ibid., p. 92.

7 Nelson González Ortega, "(Sub)versión del Nacionalismo oficial en literatura: el caso de Colombia," *Literatura: teoría, historia y crítica. Revista Universidad Nacional de Colombia* 1 (1997), 9–32.

8 José Rodríguez Feo, *Mi correspondencia con Lezama Lima* (Havana: Ediciones Unión, 1989), p. 68.

9 Álvaro Tirado Mejía. *Los años sesenta, una revolución en la cultura* (Bogotá: Debate, 2014), p. 259 ff.

10 All of the information about the festival of books is derived from Tomás G. Escajadillo, *Manuel Scorza, editor de libros de nuestra América, nota indispensable,* available at http://sisbib.unmsm.edu.pe/bibvirtualdata/publica ciones/san_marcos/n24_2006/a18.pdf.

11 Information provided by the Biblioteca Luis Ángel Arango based on their own funds and in the bibliographies elaborated by the Universidad Eafit.

12 The quote comes from Gabriel García Márquez and Mario Vargas Llosa, *La novela en América Latina: Diálogo* (Lima: Universidad Nacional de Ingeniería and Carlos Milla Batres/Ediciones, 1967) p. 88. I owe it to Nelson González Ortega in his essay "(Sub)version del nacionalismo oficial en literatura: el caso de Colombia," published online. His book *Colombia. Una nación en formación en su historia y literatura (siglos XVI al XXI)* (Madrid and Frankfurt: Iberoamericana and Vervuert, 2013) was also useful.

CHAPTER 22

Colonial legacies and Colombian literature: postcolonial considerations

Elzbieta Sklodowska

Over the course of the last three decades, the field of postcolonial studies – with its ample lexicon of derivatives (postcoloniality, postcolonial, post-colonial) and keywords (alterity, the Black Atlantic, borderlands, bricolage, cannibal, Créole/creolization, diaspora, frontier, heteroglossia, hybridity, in-betweenness, liminality, *mestizaje*, magical realism, mimicry, orality, resistance, subaltern, syncretism, third space, transculturation, trauma, among others) – has left an indelible mark across a range of disciplines in the humanities and social sciences (Fabian; Mason; Shohat and Stam; Taussig), including Latin American Studies (Durix, Faith, Mahoney, Moraña, Thurner, and Guerrero, Castro Klarén). From Central America, throughout the Caribbean, and all the way to the Southern Cono, the decolonizing desire for the unadulterated presence – and the voice – of the marginalized and oppressed "other" has found its expression in the surge and subsequent canonization of *testimonio*, a discursive mode purporting to combine truth, justice, and redress with "(para)literary" craftsmanship.[1] As Ella Shohat and Robert Stam point out, the wide adoption of postcolonial theories, insofar as they attempt to address multilayered identities, has had as its corollary a proliferation of "terms having to do with cultural mixing: religious (syncretism); biological (hybridity); human-genetic (*mestizaje*); and linguistic (creolization). . . . And while the themes are old . . . the historical moment is new."[2] Once again, many of these concepts resonate with the Americas and, in particular, with the Caribbean. In fact, it has become commonplace within literary criticism to assume and assert that Caribbean cultures in particular lend themselves almost by default to postcolonial interpretations, and such approaches have resonated with great force among the scholars from/of the region (Hofman, Balutansky, and Sourieau; Martínez San-Miguel).

Beginning in the late 1990s, postcolonial studies – launched by theorists such as Edward Said, Homi Bhabha, and Gayatri Spivak – became the target of unsparing criticism coming from some Latin American and Latin

Americanist quarters (Klor de Alva; Mignolo; Vidal; Torres-Saillant). In his introduction to *Histories/Global Designs*, Walter Mignolo attests to – and shares – the ongoing "suspicion" about "coloniality and postcoloniality,"[3] identifying the Southern Cone and Colombia as the epicenters of such skepticism. As Bill Ashcroft has aptly put it, "resistance to the idea of Latin American postcoloniality," verging at times on "an obsessive fear of the word 'postcolonial'" ("Modernity's" 7), had to do with the "skewed" and "rather eccentric view of postcolonialism, largely resting on the assumption of its emergence from poststructuralism, which has led to an understandable resistance to its neo-hegemonic discursive character" ("Modernity's" 8). Whether Latin America and Latin Americanists have been sidelined or self-marginalized from postcolonial studies remains open to debate, but the following summary offered by Jens Andermann foregrounds the most contentious aspects of this issue: "the *longue durée* of Latin American experiences of colonialism, independence, and neocolonialism (including the centuries-long legacy of anticolonial resistance and insurgency) sits uncomfortably alongside postcolonial theorizations modeled on eighteenth- and nineteenth-century European imperial expansion into Africa and Asia."[4]

Among prominent Latin Americanists who have voiced and echoed concerns about adopting and adapting postcolonial perspectives generated outside of Latin America to the study of Latin America, Fernando Coronil and Sylvia Molloy have been especially nuanced in providing careful articulations of the intricate tensions between postcolonial and Latin American studies. Citing the works of Hugo Achúgar, Mabel Moraña, Jorge Klor de Alva, and George Yúdice, among others, Coronil believes that "[m]any thinkers have doubted the appropriateness of postcolonial studies to Latin America, claiming that postcolonial studies respond to the academic concerns of metropolitan universities, to the specific realities of Asia and Africa, or to the position of academics who write about, not from Latin America, and disregard its own cultural traditions."[5] When addressing "the discomfort of many Latin American intellectuals when faced with a postcolonial 'model' into which they feel they are expected to fit," Molloy argues that this model feels out of place for Latin America and Latin Americans, "necessitating multiple reformulations and translations."[6] In addition to this tense interplay between various colonial pasts/locations and equally diverse post- or neocolonial presents/situations, the field of postcolonial studies is haunted by the alleged lack of methodological and terminological rigor, which, in turn, is held responsible for all sorts of pitfalls in critical practice.

As we turned the corner on the twenty-first century, "the postcolonial-theory-has-lost-its-groove" argument [7]has been eclipsed by the rapid growth of radical, anti-Eurocentric, action-oriented positions that have coalesced around the so-called "decolonial turn."[8] All along, the detractors of postcoloniality have accused it of (re)producing critical knowledge about/on behalf of the subaltern instead of creating new "decolonized" discourses alongside – and from the perspective of – the subaltern. The issue of drawing the theoretical tools (Gramsci, Foucault, Derrida) from the centers of former colonial powers (West, North) while the "objects" of study remained in former colonies (East, South) has been at the heart of many such critiques and polemics. Meanwhile, the "decolonial turn" has boldly shifted these concerns in the direction of the epistemology and agency forged by colonized people, and not on their behalf.

In spite of all the critiques of postcoloniality as a deficient methodo-logical tool, it would be unfair to overlook the fact that postcolonial theories have rendered a substantial body of critically productive contribu-tions to the study of literary and cultural practice of the Americas. Some theoretical concepts in particular appear to have an uncanny ability to travel, morph, and retain their illuminating power, as evidenced, for example, by Henry Louis Gates Jr.'s pioneering exploration of the con-testatory potential of Bakhtinian "double voiced" strategies within African American discourses. For Gates, it is the Yoruba trickster Eshu-Elegbara who embodies the deconstructive strategy of "signifying" in African-derived art forms. In his landmark book *The Signifying Monkey* (1988), Gates posits "a theory of the ironizing double-voiced 'trickster' discourse of the Black literary tradition in which one point of view is self-consciously layered palimpsestically on – and against – another."[9] In Latin America these critical possibilities inspired by Bakhtin merge into a potentially productive metaphor of cannibalization. Even though the intersection of cannibalism and the avant garde was first highlighted by European writers – from Alfred Jarry's "Anthropophagie" (1902) to Francis Picabia's lesser-known "Manifeste Cannibale Dada" (1920) – the trope of cannibalism became a true focus for Brazilian modernists of the 1920s. Oswald de Andrade's iconoclast "Manifesto Antropofágico" (1928, The Cannibalist Manifesto) stressed the "digestive" aspect of Brazilian culture in relation to the European, echoing the autochthonous tradition of the Tupinamba Indians who devoured their enemies in order to gain strength and vitality (Emery; Kilgour; Jáuregui, *Canibalia)*. In Roberto Fernández Retamar's *Calibán* (1971; trans. 1989, *Calibán and Other Essays*) it was precisely Calibán/cannibal who emerged as a metaphor of Latin American subaltern identity, a powerful symbol of the inverted relationship between the colonial center and the colonized periphery.

Faced with the vexing problem of postcolonial methodologies unraveling at a rapid pace – some of which are deemed obsolete as soon as they gain widespread acceptance in the intellectual marketplace – a Latin Americanist may be tempted to dispose of the postcolonial toolkit once and for all. I would argue, however, that the contentious nature of Latin American postcoloniality notwithstanding its imprint on the region's literary and cultural production has been of vast and enduring significance, including the legacy of Latin American Subaltern Studies Group (active during the 1990s). In fact, the previously mentioned "decolonial turn"[10] has firm Latin American/Latin Americanist roots, going back to Enrique Dussel's "transmodernity" and "geopolitics of knowledge," Aníbal Quijano's "coloniality of power," and Nelson Maldonado-Torres's "agency of the wretched of the earth."[11] What is even more significant for the purpose of this essay is the fact that postcolonial and decolonial approaches owe a great deal to Colombian intellectuals, most notably Santiago Castro Gómez. In an important tribute to Colombian critical thought, Mignolo also credits artist, activist, and scholar Adolfo Albán Achinte with forging the conceptual and pragmatic path from resistance to "re-existence" ("Decolonial Aesthetics"). And it is not a coincidence perhaps that an exhibit on "Decolonial Aesthetics" opened in Bogotá in 2010.[12]

Despite their disparate genealogies, "decolonial gestures," as conceived by Mignolo, continue to breathe new life into the broadly delineated realm of post/anticoloniality:

> "Decolonial gestures" would be any and every gesture that directly or indirectly engages in disobeying the dictates of the colonial matrix and contributes to building of the human species on the planet in harmony with the life in/of the planet of which the human species is only a minimal part and of which it depends." These gestures require radical "delinking" from the foundational paradigms of colonial legacy, including "delinking from democracy and development toward a vision of life that embrace harmony and plenitude, as many of us have been learning from *pueblos originarios*, Native Americans and First Nations; delinking from religion to liberate spirituality; delinking from science and Western philosophy to liberate wisdom, knowing, and sensing; and delinking from aesthetics to liberate aesthesis.[13]

While postcoloniality as a concept may not be at the foreground of the essays that comprise the present volume, its methodological imprint informs the overall design of the project and underlies many of the individual contributions. Given its inherently transdisciplinary approach, postcolonial studies allow for multifaceted inquiries into gender and race relations, along with the explorations of nation-building, transnationality, religion, geopolitics, and environmental issues, to name just the most obvious.[14] Even though these key features of postcoloniality are not always seen overtly throughout this volume, they conjure up radical reconceptualizations of postcolonial rewriting and delinking while tackling issues of gender and sexuality ("Women writers in Colombia," "Queer writing in Colombia"), ethnic identities ("*Costumbrismo* as a racial pedagogy: learning to perceive racial difference in the Andean highland," "Racial fictions: constructing whiteness in nineteenth-century Colombian literature"), canonicity ("La literatura colombiana, ¿fraude o tesoro?" "In the margins: indigenous writing and the literature of the Caribbean islands"), and the complex encoding and decoding of the environment that goes beyond the traditional usage of "scenery" ("Visions of nature: Colombian literature and the environment from the Colonial period to the nineteenth century," "Extracting nature: toward an ecology of Colombian narrative"). The importance of "situating" knowledge as a product of the location from which one sees, speaks, and writes – first championed by Enrique Dussel as "geopolitics of knowledge" (*Philosophy of Liberation*, 1977) – resonates with the broader rubrics that organize the volume, such as the many internal and regional frontiers that transverse the cartography of the national "body" of Colombian literature. Clearly, this project does not go in the direction of dismantling the notion of "national" literature as colonialist fiction, but it does, nonetheless, highlight the undercurrents and the fissures in the edifice – and the artifice – of "Colombian literature."

It is also the lasting legacy of subaltern and postcolonial studies that allows us to bring into focus forms of expression previously excluded from the canon (oral accounts, travel writings, confessions, testimonial narrative) by authors "from the periphery," marginalized because of their gender, class, race, or sexual orientation. Where we used to see only the superficial mirroring of the Eurocentric episteme, with the application of the postcolonial lens we can now detect the transgressive power of mimicry, mockingly defying the oppressive code of the "masters." Colombia's past and present are criss-crossed with tropes, tensions, and categories that connect it to the lexicon and the archive of the postcolonial in a quasi-organic way. At the same time, the historical coordinates that might align Colombian literature with a broader paradigm of Latin American and Caribbean cultural production – such as the coloniality of knowledge, the legacy of the "plantation machine," or the violent processes of nation-building – should not let us deemphasize regional differences, often so dramatic that they render problematic the very notion of national literature. Nor should the theoretical emphasis on the postcolonial obfuscate creative expressions of indigenous and Afro-descendant populations whose ancestral cultures have undergone the most violent forms of "hybridization" imaginable in the crucible of colonization and modernization. To provide a critically productive use of postcolonial wisdom in the context of Colombian literature means not only to recognize its "pluriversality"[15] but also to acknowledge the need for transdisciplinary approaches.

Lesley Wylie's recent book *Forgotten Frontier: A Literary Geography of the Putumayo* (2013) offers a great example of such an approach. Wylie draws on archival sources and interpretive tools ranging from visual studies to ethnography in order to delve into fictional and nonfictional writings (novels, diaries, oral poetry, travel accounts, journalism, war reporting, popular novels) by Colombian and foreign authors whose words had configured the vast region of Putumayo into an archetype of pervasive violence and horror ("savage frontier," "devil's paradise," "green hell," "no man's land"). At the crux of Wylie's project, however, we find a powerful decolonial gesture of delinking these fossilized images of Putumayo from their essentially Eurocentric roots. When Wylie turns her attention to "alternative" or noncanonical texts (testimonies from the 1933 war, accounts of the experiences with hallucinogenic *yagé*) she also foregrounds the ways in which these discourses undermine the colonial construction of Putumayo as a *locus terribilis* relegated to the sociopolitical margins of the nation aspiring to be modern.

Interestingly enough, *Forgotten Frontier: A Literary Geography of the Putumayo* incorporates – or at least alludes to – three major paradigms associated with Latin American literary postcoloniality: *la novela de la selva*, magical realism, and *testimonio*. Colombian literary production of the twentieth century revolves quite conspicuously around these three narrative modes, if only to transcend them through myriad "postmodern" transgressions (Williams, *The Postmodern Novel in Latin America: Politics, Culture, and the Crisis of Truth,* and *Posmodernidades latinoamericanas: la novela posmoderna en Colombia, Venezuela, Ecuador, Perú y Bolivia*). *Testimonio* and magical realism – arguably Latin America's most "autochthonous" discursive paradigms that emerged in the twentieth century – are frequently seen in synergy with postcolonial politics and poetics of anti-Western resistance (Upstone, "Magical Realism and Postcolonial Studies"; Faith and McCallum, *Linked Histories: Postcolonial Studies in a Globalized World*). For Ashcroft, one of the leading theoreticians of postcolonialty,

Latin American *testimonio* offers "a rich site for a postcolonial analysis, because it demonstrates the way in which individual lives are affected by a global system of capital initiated as the economy of the empire of modernity."[16] In what can be considered a gesture of symbolic consecration, Robert P. Marzec's opens his comprehensive anthology of postcoloniality with John Beverley's article "The Margin at the Center: On *Testimonio* (Testimonial Narrative)." These interpretations are clearly in tune with Román de la Campa's linking of the postcolonialist turn within Latinamericanism with the "subalternist" interpretation of *testimonio* "as a counter-postmodern genre."[17]

Whereas for some Latin Americanists *testimonio's* "culturalist matrix" represented a radical move away from the "textuality" of magical realism.[18] Homi Bhabha, one of the founders of postcolonial theory, did not hesitate to anoint magical realism as "the literary language of the emergent postcolonial world.[19] Wendy Faris, in turn, situates the "widespread popularity" of magical realism in the context of its recognition as "a significant decolonizing style, permitting new voices and traditions to be heard within the mainstream."[20] Nonetheless, as a literary comparatist working on Latin America she also acknowledges the position of those critics and writers who perceive magical realism as "a commodifying kind of primitivism."[21] With its Latin American/Caribbean pedigree duly noted, magical realism features prominently alongside *testimonio* – in the foundational compendium *Key Concepts in Post-Colonial Studies* (1998) only to become a member of the perfect *ménage-à-trois* and move on to claim "a paradoxical space at the center of the relation between Latin America and the discourse of world literature."[22] Canonized through myriad anthologies, "companions," and "readers" (Zamora and Faris, *Magical Realism: Theory, History, Community;* Hart and Ouyang, *A Companion to Magical Realism*), magical realism also keeps defying the intermittent announcements of its "death foretold" (Durix, *Mimesis, Genres, and Post-Colonial Discourse: Deconstructing Magic Realism;* Bowers, *Magic (al) Realism;* Schroeder, *Rediscovering Magical Realism in the Americas*).

It should be noted that it is outside of the Latin American literary and critical realm that magical realism appears to retain its "strange seductiveness"[23] well into the twenty-first century and continues to reinvent itself by expanding geographically "outward from Latin America and the Caribbean"[24] morphing into a "Cosmopolitan Form in the Era of Late Globalization" (Sasser, *Magical Realism and Cosmopolitanism;* Siskind, *Cosmopolitan Desires: Global Modernity and World Literature in Latin America*). Some critics suggest that magical realism's global projection and uncanny resilience as a "world literary genre par excellence" has to do with its all-encompassing scope.[25] According to Siskind, the "liberating poetics" of magical realism functions as a handy medium to reconcile the postmodern aesthetics of ex-centricity with the postcolonial agenda of political activism.[26] Colombia's literary contributions to the narrative modes of *testimonio* and magical realism are, of course, beyond dispute. At the same time, their individual trajectories appear to be quite idiosyncratic and, for the most part, divergent from global trends. Whereas Colombian writers – similarly to their counterparts throughout Latin America (Fuguet, Gómez, *McOndo*) – have unequivocally distanced themselves from the aesthetics of magical realism (Giraldo, *Más allá de Macondo*), testimonial or pseudo-testimonial writing has continued to flourish in Colombia long after John Beverly proclaimed in 1996 that "the moment of the *testimonio*" was over.[27]

The past two decades have brought both proliferation and diversification of testimonial narratives in Colombia, perhaps as an offshoot of a broader phenomenon, which Louise Detwiler and Janis Breckenridge have traced in their comprehensive book *Pushing the Boundaries of Latin American Testimony: Metamorphoses and Migrations* (2012) and which Stef Craps has situated within the larger postcolonial frame (*Postcolonial Witnessing: Trauma Out of Bounds*, 2013). And, as many of the chapters in this book remind us, texts written on behalf of the "other" had been at the heart of Colombian literature well before the official birth of the *testimonio* genre and prior to the ascent of postcolonial epistemology, ranging from harrowing depictions of the exploitation of the rubber gatherers in the Amazon in José Eustasio Rivera's (1889–1928) classic *La vorágine* (1924; tran. 1935, *The Vortex*) to countless narratives denouncing Colombia's pervasive phenomenon of *La Violencia*, and projects in oral history, such as what David Sánchez Juliao (1945–2011) called "cassette literature." The prodigious quantity of Colombian testimonial writings in the late twentieth and early twenty-first centuries makes any attempt at synthesis extremely difficult. We can rely, however, on an impressive critical bibliography that encompasses various strands of testimonial literature, from the narratives of *La Violencia,* through the *sicaresca* novels, to the parodic transfigurations of the "classic" *testimonio* genre (Jácome, Muñoz Morales, Ortiz, Ospina, Serra, Suárez Gómez, Vélez Rendón). If testimonial writing has not withered entirely under the weight of postmodern skepticism or has not been wiped out by the exponential growth of electronic media, it is because there is still some residual faith in its ability to summon truth, denounce, exorcise, and set aright official history. The routinization of oppression, the tragic plight of entire communities displaced from their homes in the wake of endemic violence, the ongoing silencing of the voices of the victims – each and all of these experiences indicate that there is plenty to denounce, exorcise, and set aright in today's Colombia.

At first glance, then, the evidence of the presence of postcoloniality – in its various guises and disguises – in Colombian literature and literary criticism seems beyond doubt. Given Colombia's geographical expanse, sociocultural stratifications, and multiracial diversity, we might also expect that everything and anything "Colombian" could be made "postcolonial." As it turns out, not so. While researching the topic a bit further, it becomes apparent that scholars of Colombian literature have been shying away from the explicit use of postcolonial terminology. On one hand, even a cursory search (Google Scholar, JSTOR, MLA, WorldCat, Project Muse) of keywords such as Colombian literature, *novela de la selva, testimonio,* and magical realism renders a bibliography of unmanageable proportions. On the other, refining the search by adding terms such as "postcoloniality" or "postcolonial" (either in English and in Spanish) reduces the relevant entries to a scant handful (Von der Walde's, "Realismo mágico y poscolonialismo: construcciones del otro desde la otredad"; Wylie, *The Putumayo: Colombia's Forgotten Frontier;* Davies, "Imperfect Portraits of a Postcolonial Heroine: Laura Restrepo's *La novia oscura*; Allemand, "Batallas de la critica postcolonial criolla en Colombia"), with several results only tangentially germane to the topic (Pineda Botero, "Albores y postcolonialismo en la novela colombiana: *Manuela* [1858] de Eugenio Díaz"). Unlike the label of "postmodernity" – which appears to be ubiquitous among Colombianists (Williams; Pineda Botero, *Del mito*) – postcoloniality might be tacitly assumed, but it is not explicitly embraced.

My initial impression about the relative paucity of postcolonial criticism pertaining to Colombian literature was further reinforced by Wylie's observation that the term "postcolonial" has not been applied to the *novela de la selva,* a literary subgenre almost coterminous with Rivera's *La vorágine.* As Wylie grapples with the issue of this peculiar "critical oversight" she attributes it to "the Anglocentric bias of much postcolonial criticism":

> Indeed, given the recent emergence of the "postcolonial" as a critical discipline, it may seem somewhat anachronistic to apply the term to the cultural production of Latin American intellectuals in the late nineteenth and early twentieth centuries, and even more so to intimate that these writers may have been aware that their anti-colonial postures would adumbrate the ideological strategies employed much later by writers as distant as New Delhi or Ireland. The precocity of Latin America's postcolonial stirrings, however, can be ascribed to the fact that much of the continent had achieved independence in the early nineteenth century. [28]

In her book *Colonial Tropes and Postcolonial Tricks*, Wylie herself over-comes this reticence to deploy postcoloniality as a critical tool and proceeds to develop a compelling argument that the Spanish-American "Jungle Novel," *novela de la selva*, was much more than "a minor offshoot of the *novela de la tierra*" as it "turned to the rainforest, and the indigenous communities who lived there, in order to construct a distinctively American literature."[29] By means of an organic interweaving of the postcolonial methodology with in-depth textual analysis, Wylie links the foundational thrust of *novela de la selva* to the decolonizing power of parodic reinscription:

> Through parodic reworkings of European perceptions of the tropics in literature and anthropology the *novela de la selva* transformed the burden-some texts of the colonial era into enabling stories of cultural and narrative self-determination. ... Adumbrating a now longstanding tradition of post-colonial nature writing, the authors of *novela de la selva* founded this new tradition not by turning their backs on the ever-growing body of European writing on the tropics, but by rewriting it.[30]

In another recent work, Diana Arbaiza follows a somewhat similar argu-ment regarding the inverted reinscription of European models in nineteenth-century Colombian literature. Arbaiza argues that Soledad Acosta de Samper's "instrumentalization of Spain revealed an inverted postcolonial paradigm in which the Spanish American Creole viewed their former metropole as a less developed nation, and furthermore, as a museum of their own traditions."[31] Studies such as those of Arbaiza and Wylie clearly benefit from the heightened awareness that coloniality and modernity are two, equally dark, sides of the same coin.

Inversion, parody, irony, mimicry (Bhabha), carnavalization (Bakhtin), and cannibalization are, of course, omnipresent in the lexicon of postco-lonial *and* postmodern discourses, charged with transgressive, contentious, defiant, and often playful rewriting and reinventing of the hegemonic epistemology. However, for many radical scholars – including decolonial critics – the problem with such postmodern/postolonial approaches is that they attempt to undertake the critique of Eurocentrism from a Eurocentric stance. For these critics, Audre Lorde's well-known statement that "the master's tools will never dismantle the master's house" reverberates as painfully and as powerfully today as it did in in 1984. But in spite of the bold turn taken by "decolonial" thinkers, their goals, as spelled out by Mignolo, do not seamlessly translate into critical practice: "The decolonial turn is the opening and the freedom from the thinking and the forms of living (economies-other, political theories-other), the cleansing of the coloniality of being and of knowledge: the de-linking from the spell of the rhetoric of modernity, from its imperial imaginary articulated in the rhetoric of democracy."[32] For example, decolonial publications such as *Trans-Modernity: Journal of Peripheral Cultural Production of the Luso-Hispanic World* would not be able to engage in their mission as effectively as they do without availing themselves of the channels of distribution that belong to the Western "order of discourse" (the Internet, the academic institutional base, the use of English).

Joanna Rappaport's fascinating exploration of indigenous Colombian intellectuals who, in her words, function as "inappropriate Others" in multicultural and transnational political spaces further illustrates both the limitations of postcolonial epistemology and the difficulties in transcending it through decolonial gestures. First, Rappaport argues that concepts associated with the postcolonialist lexicon, such as hybridity, heterogeneity, syncretism, or transculturation, fail as interpretive tools in the context of global displacements and complex forms of performativity assumed by these subjects:

> Exemplifying the "inappropriate Other" is the indigenous intellectual who works in the offices of the indigenous organization, traveling to New York, Paris or Mexico City to attend international conferences and returning to observe community assemblies in Toribío or Guambía; who is fluent in Nasa Yuwe (the Nasa language) or Guambiano, but writes in Spanish; and who is responsible for directing a process of cultural revitalization by creating educational policy for rural groups, but lives in the city. While all Others are in a sense inappropriate, ethnic activists consciously deploy their inappropriateness in the political arena ... the Caucan "inappropriate Other" forces other Colombians to rethink what "indigenous" means, insisting that they engage the cultural pluralism to which they have paid lipservice over the past decade. [33]

Rappaport's analysis then delves into the ways in which the Nasa conceptualization of *cosmovisión* reaches into the depths of Eurocentric episteme in order to "reinscribe Western ethnographic methodology with specifically Nasa conceptual agendas."[34] She proceeds to discuss the pitfalls of the decolonial efforts [35]illustrating the challenges of implementing what Mignolo has famously defined as "epistemic disobedience." Through her deft use of transdisciplinary approaches, Rappaport brings forth the nuances of the decolonial predicament of "learning to unlearn" as she analyzes the publications of the Guambiano History Committee, which "attempt to engage in dialogue with metropolitan readers and researchers, as well as with the

Guambiano community, through the adoption of a new language for interpreting the past."[36] Rappaport's conclusion about the nature of the projects fits more neatly within the postcolonial rhetoric of hybridity than within the radical "de-linking" proposed by decolonial critics: "what emerges is a hybrid type of writing, not strictly metropolitan academic discourse but certainly not 'typical' Guambiano orality, either ... while [the project] is indeed innovative, it does not depart substantially enough from academic genres of writing, however experimental its form."[37] Even though Rappaport's study revolves around concepts and methodologies honed by social scientists, it offers valuable insights for literary and cultural critics about the importance of recognizing the distinctiveness of Colombian reality and the unique challenges of its "undisciplined" diversity.

To be sure, postcolonial attempts at reinventing, recapturing, and decolonizing "inappropriate Others" most powerfully manifest themselves in the domain of ethnic identities, along with the emphasis on the constructed nature of racial categories and their intersections with the rubrics of class, gender and sexuality. Postcolonial perspectives also suggest shedding Eurocentric biases when approaching Latin American literary movements built around the notion of racial difference, such as *indigenismo* and *negrismo*. In the case of Colombia, the rise of postcolonial awareness coincides with the country's 1991 constitution, which is considered as a "watershed moment" for indigenous people because it heralded a more inclusive era in Colombian politics by espousing "the cultural and territorial rights of indigenous groups."[38] Paradoxically, during the process of constitutional reform the Afro-Colombians faced considerable resistance to receiving the same collective landholding and cultural rights as indigenous communities. Eventually, the intense process of negotiations and debates culminated in the passing of Law Seventy (*Ley de Comunidades Negras,* 1993), which recognized Afro-Colombians as a distinct ethnic group with collective territorial rights. The rise of Afro-Colombian and indigenous resistance in the wake of massive displacement of these communities from the ancestral lands – due to guerilla, paramilitary, and drug-trafficking related violence – has been receiving a lot of attention and finding its reflection in testimonial accounts and social advocacy initiatives (see, for example, *In Territories of Difference,* Arturo Escobar's study of Afro-Colombian activist movement known as Proceso de Comunidades Negras). While these complex socioeconomic and political issues go beyond the confines of my essay, the link between the constitutional reform and the recent developments in the areas of Afro-Colombian literary production and related criticism is certainly worthy of exploration.

Christopher Dennis provides an excellent point of departure for such an inquiry. His comprehensive analysis of the historical scarcity of Afro-Colombian writings brings up a variety of issues, ranging from the constraints embedded in the publishing industry and readership patterns to regional differences and topographical barriers not conducive to the formation of ethnic identity on a national scale.[39] In addition, as Dennis argues, ambiguous notions of "blackness" and downplaying of racial discrimination in the hegemonic rhetoric of *mestizaje* encouraged the identification "with local culture, region, class, and political affiliation more so than with their ethnic group on a national scale."[40] Dennis situates the literary production of such Afro-Colombian fiction writers as Arnoldo Palacios, Carlos Arturo Truque, and Manuel Zapata Olivella within the larger context of Colombia's "rediscovery" and official recognition of multiculturalism following the constitutional reform and *Ley de Comunidades Negras*, which "recognized Afro-Colombians as a distinct ethnic group."[41] It is worth noting that the ensuing "Afro-Colombian Renaissance" in various spheres of cultural production has been significantly belated in relation to areas such as the Caribbean or Brazil, where the process of reclaiming Afrodescendant traditions had taken place as early as in the 1920s and 1930s, often at a price of woeful folclorization.

The extent to which postcolonial critical thought has laid the groundwork for the recasting of Afro-Colombian heritage becomes evident as we survey the abundant corpus of critical works published in the past two decades (Camacho; Friedmann; Hurtado; Lawo-Sukam; Lewis; Maglia; Mosquera Mosquera; Ortiz; Pérez de Samper; Reales; Restrepo; Restrepo and Rojas; Restrepo and Salazar; Valero; Wade; Walsh; Zapata Pérez) along with such initiatives as launching of *La Biblioteca de Literatura Afrocolombiana*, which under the auspices of Colombia's Ministry of Culture has distributed through public libraries and made electronically available numerous novels, essays, poetry, and short stories by the nation's most renowned Afro-descendant writers (Manuel Zapata Olivella, Oscar Collazos, Helcías Martán Góngora, Arnoldo Palacios, Rogerio Velásquez, Candelario Obeso, among others).[42]

At the same time, postcolonial approaches continue to shape the gradual unraveling of the repositories of collective memory, an endeavor that has become the order of the day for social scientists, artists, writers, and literary critics interested in drawing a firm distinction between exoticized versions of African-descendant cultures and representations better attuned to decolonial conceptualizations. The complex inscriptions of Afro-descendant cultures in the works of Zapata Olivella in particular have benefited from the postcolonial studies' unique combination of sociocultural awareness with a deconstructive imprint.

As Silvia Valero has argued, hyphenated doubles, such as Afro-Colombian or Afro-descendant, are as deeply problematic as they are important in the emerging discourses that tackle Colombia's multiculturality ("Los complejos caminos de las políticas de identidad "afrodescendiente"; "¿De qué hablamos cuando hablamos de "literatura afrocolombiana"? o los riesgos de las categorizaciones"). Valero's concerns echo Nasser Hussein's more general take on hyphenation as a space of ambivalence and liminality: "Hyphens are radically ambivalent signifiers, for they simultaneously connect and set apart; they simultaneously represent both belonging and not belonging. What is even more curious about a hyphenated pair of words is that meaning cannot reside in one word or the other, but can only be understood in movement."[43] This metaphor of hyphenation could be further expanded through the Caribbean-based notion of *cimarronaje cultural* (cultural maroonization) forged by René Depestre and Kamau Brathwaite. Unlike "transculturation" – which lends itself to highlighting assimilation and integration – the trope of *cimarronaje* conveys both resistance and a heterogeneous layering of influences, with numerous codes and messages, some of them partly camouflaged, some completely erased. In *Contradictory Omens* Brathwaite also introduced the notion of "psychic maroonage" as "a syncretic vision of African patterns, symbols and communicative canons ... which the subordinate maintains in everyday life even in the course of submitting to large scale socio-economic pressures of dominance."[44] In art and literature, these subversive appropriations of master codes may come under different rhetorical guises, but they tend to retain an aesthetic that rejects formal harmony in favor of asymmetry, "strategic inflections," and "reaccentuations" (Lavie and Swedenburg 9). And in Colombian literature, the many postcolonial inflections of the concept of hyphenation might prove useful in critical (re) readings of such prodigiously complex writers as Zapata Olivella.

By way of conclusion, nothing is there to suggest that the postcolonial thought is a relic of the past or a scholarly artifact that has been fossilized and is now in its death throes. To the contrary, postcoloniality resurfaces in such unexpected spaces as the fairly recent area of postcommunist studies in Central and Eastern Europe (Kołodziejczyk et al.; Sandru; Tlostanova). I would argue that postcolonial critical perspectives continue to draw their resilience from the wisdom of reading against the grain and from the belief in disciplinary self-questioning, both of which might also help explain the variegated diversity of the field and its ability to keep reinventing itself. I believe that the "decolonization" of postcolonial studies undertaken as a critique of Eurocentrism through the lens of the subaltern episteme (Grosfoguel) is – or could be – aligned with the anticolonial thrust of such approaches as those famously outlined in *Teorías sin disciplina* (1998) under the auspices of two Colombian-born scholars, Santiago Castro-Gómez and Eduardo Mendieta. Thoughtful (re)articulations of postcolonial theories in response to local specificity and in conjunction with diverse textualities can only enrich and reinvigorate our understanding of the diverse constellation of texts known as Colombian literature.

BIBLIOGRAPHY

Agudelo, Carlos E. *Multiculturalismo en Colombia: Política, inclusión y exclusión de poblaciones negras*. Medellín: Carreta Editores, 2005.

Alaix de Valencia, Hortensia. "Prácticas ancestrales en la narrativa colombiana." In *Estudios afrocolombianos. Aportes para un estado del arte*, edited by Axel Rojas. Popayán: Editorial Universidad del Cauca, 2004. 303–16.

Albán Achinte, Adolfo. "Artistas indígenas y afrocolombianos: entre las memorias y las cosmovisiones. Estéticas de la re-existencia." In *Arte y estética*, ed. Zulma Palermo, 83–111.

Ali, Maurizio, and David Miguel Amórtegui. "Savage Mind and Postcolonial Representation in Colombian Journalism." *Cuadernos de Información* 29 (2011): 151–60.

Allemand, Patricia. "Batallas de la crítica postcolonial criolla en Colombia." *Journal of Iberian and Latin American Research* 8, no. 12 (2012): 119–34.

Andermann, Jens. "Placing Latin American Memory: Sites and the Politics of Mourning." *Memory Studies* 8 (January 2015): 3–8.

Arbaiza, Diana. "Spain as Archive: Constructing a Colombian Modernity in the Writings of Soledad Acosta de Samper." *Journal of Latin American Cultural Studies* 21, no. 1 (2012): 123–44.

Arocha, Jaime. "Afro-Colombia denied." *NACLA Report on the Americas* 25, no. 4 (1992): 28–47.

Ashcroft, Bill, Gareth Griffiths, and Helen Tiffin. *Key Concepts in Post-Colonial Studies*. London: Routledge, 1998.

"Modernity's First Born: Latin America and Postcolonial Transformation." *ARIEL* 29, no. 2 (April 1998): 7–29.

Asher, Kiran. *Black and Green: Afro-Colombians, Development, and Nature in the Pacific Lowlands*. Durham: Duke University Press, 2009.

Balutansky, Kathleen M., and Marie-Agnès Sourieau, eds. *Caribbean Creolization: Reflection on the Cultural Dynamics of Language, Literature, and Identity*. Gainesville: University Press of Florida, 1998.

Beardsell, Peter. "When the Gods Arrived: Wilderness in Latin America." *Romance Studies* 29, no. 2 (2011): 108–19.

Beasley-Murray, Jon. "Thinking Solidarity: Latinamericanist Intellectuals and testimonio." *Journal of Latin American Cultural Studies* 7, no. 1 (1998): 121–29.

Beverley, John. "The Real Thing." In *The Real Thing: Testimonial Discourse in Latin America*, ed. G. M. Gugelberger. Durham, NC: Duke University Press, 1996. 266–86.

Bhabha, Homi K. "Introduction: Narrating the Nation." In *Nation and Narration*, ed. Homi K. Bhabha. London: Routledge, 1990. 1–7.

Biblioteca de literatura afrocolombiana. Ministerio de Cultura de Colombia. www.banrepcultural.org/blaavirtual/biblioteca-afrocolombiana.

Bowers, Maggie Ann. *Magic(al) Realism*. London: Routledge, 2004.

Camacho, Juana. "Silencios elocuentes, voces emergentes: reseña bibliográfica de los estudios sobre la mujer afro-colombiana." In *Panorámica afrocolombiana. Estudios sociales en el Pacífico. Bogotá: Instituto Colombiano de Antropología e Historia ICANH-Universidad Nacional de Colombia*. Bogotá: Universidad Nacional de Colombia, 2004. 167–211.

Castro-Gómez Santiago, and Ramón Grosfoguel. *El giro decolonial: Reflexiones para una diversidad epistémica más allá del capitalismo global*. Bogotá, D.C: Siglo del Hombre Editores, 2007.

and Eduardo Mendieta. *Teorías sin disciplina: Latinoamericanismo, poscolonialidad y globalización en debate*. México, D.F.: Porrúa, 1998.

Castro-Klarén, Sara. *The Narrow Pass of Our Nerves: Writing, Coloniality and Postcolonial Theory*. Madrid: Iberoamericana Vervuert, 2011.

Cornejo-Polar, Antonio. "Mestizaje e hibridez: los riesgos de las metáforas. Apuntes." *Revista Iberoamericana* 180 (July–September 1997): 341–44.

Coronil, Fernando. "Elephants in the Americas? Latin American Postcolonial Studies and Global Decolonization." In *Coloniality at Large. Latin America and the Postcolonial Debate*, ed. Mabel Moraña, Enrique Dussel, and Carlos A. Jáuregui. Durham, NC: Duke University Press, 2008. 396–416.

"Latin American Postcolonial Studies and Global Decolonization." In *The Cambridge Companion to Postcolonial Literary Studies*, ed. Neil Lazarus. Cambridge: Cambridge University Press, 2004. 221–40.

Craps, Stef. *Postcolonial Witnessing: Trauma Out of Bounds*. New York: Palgrave Macmillan, 2013.

Davies, Lloyd H. "Imperfect Portraits of a Postcolonial Heroine: Laura Restrepo's La novia oscura." *Modern Language Review* 102, no. 4 (2007): 1035–52.

De la Campa, Román. "Latin American Studies: Literary, Cultural, and Comparative Theory." *CLCWeb: Comparative Literature and Culture* 4, no. 2 (2002): http://docs.lib.purdue.edu/clcweb/vol4/iss2/5.

Latin Americanism. Minneapolis: University of Minnesota Press, 1999.

Dennis, Christopher. *Afro-Colombian Hip-Hop: Globalization, Transcultural Music, and Ethnic Identities*. Lanham, Md.: Lexington Books, 2012.

Detwiler, Louise, and Janis Breckenridge. *Pushing the Boundaries of Latin American Testimony: Metamorphoses and Migrations*. New York: Palgrave Macmillan, 2012

Durix, Jean-Pierre. *Mimesis, Genres and Post-Colonial Discourse: Deconstructing Magic Realism.* Basingstoke: Palgrave, 1998.

Dussel, Enrique. *1492: El encubrimiento del Otro: Hacia el origen del "mito de la modernidad."* La Paz, Bolivia: Plural Editores, 1994.

Emery, Amy Fass. *The Anthropological Imagination in Latin American Literature.* Columbia: University of Missouri Press, 1996.

Escobar, Arturo. *Territories of Difference: Place, Movements, Life, Redes.* Durham, NC: Duke University Press, 2008.

Fabian, Johannes. *Time and the Other: How Anthropology Makes Its Object.* New York: Columbia University Press, 1983.

Faith, Wendy, and Pamela McCallum. *Linked Histories: Postcolonial Studies in a Globalized World.* Calgary: University of Calgary Press, 2005.

Faris, Wendy B. "The Question of the Other: Cultural Critiques of Magical Realism." *Janus Head* 5 (2002): 101–19.

Félicité-Maurice, Evelina. *La novela afro-colombiana: Palacios, Rojas Herazo, Zapata Olivella, mito, mestizaje cultural y afrocentismo costeno.* Ph.D. thesis, University of Colorado, 1994.

Fernández Olmos, Margarita, and Lizabeth Paravisini-Gebert. *Sacred Possessions: Vodou, Santería, Obeah, and the Caribbean.* New Brunswick, NJ.: Rutgers University Press, 2000.

Fernández Retamar, Roberto. *Calibán and Other Essays.* Minneapolis: University of Minnesota Press, 1989.

Fiddian, Robin W. *Postcolonial Perspectives on the Cultures of Latin America and Lusophone Africa.* Liverpool: Liverpool University Press, 2000.

French, Jennifer L. "Voices in the Wilderness: Environment, Colonialism, and Coloniality in Latin American Literature." *Review: Literature and Arts of the Americas* 45, no. 2 (2012): 157–66.

Friedemann, Nina. "La saga del negro: presencia africana en Colombia." www.banrepcultural.org/blaavirtual/antropologia/la-saga-del-negro.

Fuguet, Alberto, and Sergio Gómez. *Introduction: McOndo.* Barcelona: Mondadori, 1996.

Gates, Henry Louis, Jr. *The Signifying Monkey: A Theory of African-American Literary Criticism.* New York: Oxford University Press, 1988.

Giraldo, Luz Mary. *Más allá de Macondo: Tradición y rupturas literarias.* Bogotá: Universidad Externado de Colombia, 2006.

——— *Narrativa colombiana: búsqueda de un nuevo canon, 1975–1995.* Bogotá: Pontificia Universidad Javeriana, 2000.

Grosfoguel, Ramón. "From Postcolonial Studies to Decolonial Studies: Decolonizing Postcolonial Studies: A Preface." *Transmodernity.* www.dialogoglobal.com/granada/documents/Grosfoguel-Decolonizing-Pol-Econ-and-Postcolonial.pdf.

Gugelberger, Georg M. *The Real Thing: Testimonial Discourse and Latin America.* Durham: Duke University Press, 1996.

Hart, Stephen, and Wen-chin Ouyang, eds. *A Companion to Magical Realism.* Woodbridge: Tamesis, 2005.

Hofman S. "Transculturation and Creolization: Concepts of Caribbean Cultural Theory." In *Latin American Postmodernisms*, ed. Richard A. Young. Amsterdam: Rodopi, 1997.

Hooker, Juliet. "Indigenous Inclusion/Black Exclusion: Race, Ethnicity, and Multicultural Citizenship in Latin America." *Journal of Latin American Studies* 37 (2005): 285–310

Hurtado Saa, Teodoro. "Los estudios contemporáneos sobre población afrocolombiana." www.urosario.edu.co/urosario_files/b9/b9be0223-6669-411f-9853-1bda70a57749.pdf.

Hussein, Nasser. "Hyphenated Identity: Nationality, Discourse, History, and the Anxiety of Criticism in Salman Rushdie's *Shame*." *Qui Parle?* (summer 1990): 8–11.

Jácome, Margarita. *La novela sicaresca: testimonio, sensacionalismo y ficción*. Fondo Editorial Universidad EAFIT, 2009.

Jameson, Fredric. "On Magic Realism in Film." *Critical Inquiry* 12, no. 2 (1986): 301–25.

Jáuregui, Canibalia. *Canibalismo, calinbalismo, antropofagia cultural y consumo en América Latina*. Madrid: Vervuert, 2008

Kilgour, Maggie. *From Communion to Cannibalism: An Anatomy of Metaphors of Incorporation*. Princeton: Princeton University Press, 1990.

Klor de Alva, Jorge. "The Postcolonization of the (Latin) American Experience: A Reconsideration of 'Colonialism', 'Postcolonialism' and 'Mestizajes.'" In *After Colonialism, Imperial Histories and Postcolonial Displacements*, ed. Gyan Prakash. Princeton: Princeton University Press, 1995. 241–75.

"Colonialism and Postcolonialism as (Latin) American Mirages." *Colonial Latin American Review* 1, no. 1–2 (1992): 3–23.

Lewis, Marvin A. "Violencia y resistencia: una perspectiva literaria afrocolombiana." *Revista de estudios colombianos* 6 (1989): 15–20.

Treading the Ebony Path: Ideology and Violence in Contemporary Afro-Colombian Prose Fiction. Columbia: University of Missouri Press, 1987.

Treading the Ebony Path: Ideology and Violence in Contemporary Afro-Colombian Prose Fiction. Columbia: University of Missouri Press, 1987.

"Manuel Zapata Olivella y la condición postcolonial afrocolombiana." *Revista América negra* 10 (1978): 243–53.

Lorde, Audre. "The Master's Tools Will Never Dismantle the Master's House." *Sister Outsider: Essays and Speeches*. Berkeley, CA: Crossing Press, 2007. 110–14.

Maglia, Graciela. "Identidad afrocaribeña vs.conciencia nacional en la poesía poscolonial del Caribe hispánico." www.colombianistas.org/Portals/0/Revista/REC27-28/8.REC_27-28_GracielaMaglia.pdf.

Mahoney, James. *Colonialism and Postcolonial Development: Spanish America in Comparative Perspective*. Cambridge: Cambridge University Press, 2010.

Maldonado, Torres N. *Against War: Views from the Underside of Modernity*. Durham: Duke University Press, 2008.

Mallon, Florencia E. "The Promise and Dilemma of Subaltern Studies: Perspectives from Latin American History." *American Historical Review* (December 1994): 1491–1515.

Martínez-San, Miguel Yolanda. *Coloniality of Diasporas: Rethinking Intra-Colonial Migrations in a Pan-Caribbean Context.* New York: Palgrave, 2014.

Marzec, Robert P. *Postcolonial Literary Studies: The First 30 Years.* Baltimore: Johns Hopkins University Press, 2011.

McLaren, Peter. "The Ethnographer as Postmodern Flâneur: Critical Reflexivity and Posthybridity as Narrative Engagement." In *Representation and the Text: Re-framing the Narrative Voice,* ed. William G. Tierney and Yvonna S. Lincoln. Albany: SUNY Press, 1997. 143–78.

Mignolo, Walter. *"Looking for the Meaning of 'Decolonial Gesture.'"* 2014. http://hemisphericinstitute.org/hemi/en/emisferica-111-decolonial-gesture/mignolo.

———. *Local Histories/Global Designs: Coloniality, Subaltern Knowledges, and Border Thinking.* Princeton: Princeton University Press, 2012.

———. "Epistemic Disobedience and the Decolonial Option: A Manifesto." *Transmodernity* 1, no. 2 (2011): 45–66. http://escholarship.org/uc/item/62j3w283.

——— and Arturo Escobar. *Globalization and the Decolonial Option.* London: Routledge, 2010.

——— and Rolando Vázquez. "Decolonial AestheSis: Colonial Wounds/Decolonial Healings." http://socialtextjournal.org/periscope_article/decolonial-aesthesis colonial-woundsdecolonial-healings/.

———. "Epistemic Disobedience, Independent Thought and De-Colonial Freedom." *Theory, Culture & Society* 26, no. 7–8 (2009): 1–23 http://waltermignolo.com/wp-content/uploads/2013/03/epistemicdisobedience-2.pdf.

Molloy, Sylvia. "Postcolonial Latin America and the Magic Realist Imperative: A Report to an Academy." In *Nation, Language, and the Ethics of Translation,* ed. Sandra Bermann and Michael Wood. Princeton: Princeton University Press, 2005. 370–9.

Moraña, Mabel, Enrique D. Dussel, and Carlos A. Jáuregui. *Coloniality at Large: Latin America and the Postcolonial Debate.* Durham: Duke University Press, 2008.

Mosquera Mosquera, Juan de Dios. *Las comunidades negras de Colombia hacia el siglo XXI: historia, realidad y organización.* http://www.banrepcultural.org/blaavirtual/sociologia/comunida/indice.

Muñoz Morales, Sandra. "Literatura testimonial en Colombia y *El olvido que seremos* de Héctor Abad Faciolince." http://repo.komazawa-u.ac.jp/opac/repository/all/33769/rgs016-13-Morales_Munoz.pdf.

Orrego Arismendi, Juan Carlos. "La crítica de la novela indigenista colombiana: objeto y problemas." *Estudios de literatura colombiana* 30 (January–June 2012): 31–54.

Ortiz, Lucía. "Chambacú, la historia la escribes tú." In *Ensayos sobre cultura afrocolombiana.* Madrid: Iberoamericana, 2007.

———. "Narrativa testimonial en Colombia: Alfredo Molano, Alfonso Salazar, Sandra Afanador." *Literatura y cultura narrativa colombiana del siglo* 20 (2000): 339–77.

———. "Voces de la violencia: narrativa testimonial en Colombia." *Latin America Studies Association.* http://lasa.international.pitt.edu/LASA97/ortiz.pdf.

Ospina, María. *Evocar y convocar: Violencia y representación en la narrativa colombiana de fines de siglo XX (1994–2008).* Dissertation. Harvard University, 2009.

Palermo, Zulma, ed. *Arte y estética en la encrucijada descolonial.* Buenos Aires: Ediciones del Signo, 2009.

Pérez de Samper, Rocío. *Estudios afrocolombianos. Sistematización bibliográfica.* Ed. Alvaro Oviedo, 2001.

Pineda Botero, Álvaro. "Albores y poscolonialismo en la novela colombiana: Manuela (1858) de Eugenio Díaz." In *Actas del XIII Congreso de la Asociación Internacional de Hispanistas, Madrid 6–11 de julio de 1998.* Madrid: Castalia, 2000.

Álvaro. *Del mito a la posmodernidad. La novela colombiana de finales del siglo XX.* Bogotá: Tercer Mundo Editores, 1990.

Quijano, Aníbal. "Colonialidad y Modernidad/Racionalidad," *Perú Indígena* 29 (1991): 11–21.

"La colonialidad del poder y la experiencia cultural latinoamericana." In *Pueblo, época y desarrollo: la sociología de América Latina,* ed. Roberto Briceño-León and Heinz R. Sonntag. Caracas: Nueva Sociedad, 1998. 139–55.

Rappaport, Joanne, and Tom Cummins. *Beyond the Lettered City: Indigenous Literacies in the Andes.* Durham, NC: Duke University Press, 2012.

Utopías interculturales: Intelectuales públicos, experimentos con la cultura y pluralismo étnico en Colombia. Bogotá: Editorial Universidad del Rosario, 2008.

Intercultural Utopias: Public Intellectuals, Cultural Experimentation, and Ethnic Pluralism in Colombia. Durham, NC: Duke University Press, 2005.

"Redrawing the Nation. Indigenous Intellectuals and Ethnic Pluralism in Contemporary Colombia." In Thurner, *Mark and Andrés Guerrero. After Spanish Rule: Postcolonial Predicaments of the Americas.* Durham, NC: Duke University Press, 2003. 310–46.

Reales, Leonardo. "El aporte afrocolombiano a la literatura nacional. Entre la represión y la libertad." In *Memorias ciclo de conferencias Encuentros en la diversidad Tomo 1* Bogotá: Ministerio de Cultura, Imprenta Nacional, 2002.

Restrepo, Eduardo, and Axel Rojas. *Afrodescendienetes en Colombia.* Compilación bibliográfica. Universidad del Cauca Colección Políticas de la Alteridad, 2008.

and Jorge Salazar, eds. *Políticas de la teoría y dilemas en los estudios de las colombias negras.* www.banrepcultural.org/sites/default/files/lablaa/antropologia/politicas_teoria/politicas_teoria.pdf.

"Notas sobre algunos aportes de los estudios culturales al campo de los estudios afrocolombianos." *SIGMA Revista de Estudiantes en Sociología, Universidad Nacional* (2004).

"Afrocolombianos, antropología y proyecto de modernidad en Colombia." *Antropología en la modernidad* (1997): 279–320.

Rodríguez, Cabral C. *La narrativa postmoderna y postcolonial de Manuel Zapata Olivella.* Dissertation. University of Missouri, Columbia. 2004.

Sandru, Cristina. *Worlds Apart? A Postcolonial Reading of Post-1945 East-Central European Culture.* Cambridge: Cambridge Scholars Publishing, 2012.

Santamaría, Ángela, Bastien Bosa, and Eric Wittersheim. *Luchas indígenas, Trayectorias poscoloniales: Américas Y Pacífico.* Bogotá, D.C.: Editorial Universidad del Rosario, 2008.

Sasser, Kim Anderson. *Magical Realism and Cosmopolitanism.* New York: Palgrave Macmillan, 2014.

Schroeder, Shannin. *Rediscovering Magical Realism in the Americas.* Westport, Ct.: Praeger, 2004.

Serra, Ana. "La Escritura de la Violencia. La Virgen de Los Sicarios, de Fernando Vallejo, Testimonio paródico y discurso nietzscheano." *Chasqui* (2003): 65–75.

Shohat, Ella. "Notes on the 'Post-Colonial'." *Social Text* 31–2 (1992): 99–113.

and Robert Stam. *Unthinking Eurocentrism: Multiculturalism and the Media.* New York: Routledge, 1994.

Siskind, Mariano. *Cosmopolitan Desires: Global Modernity and World Literature in Latin America.* Evanston: Northwestern University Press, 2014.

Slemon, Stephen. "Magic Realism as Post-Colonial Discourse." In *Magical Realism: Theory and History,* ed. Lois Parkinson Zamora and Wendy B. Faris. Durham, NC: Duke University Press, 1995. 407–26.

Stam, Robert, and Ella Shohat. "Whence and Whither Postcolonial Theory?" *New Literary History* 43, no. 2 (2012): 371–90.

Suárez Gómez, and Jorge Eduardo. "War in Colombia Testimonial Literature: Between Memory, Culture, Violence and Literature." *Universitas Humanística* 72 (2011): 275–96.

"La literatura testimonial de las guerras en Colombia: entre la memoria, la cultura, las violencias y la literatura." *Universitas Humanística* 72, no. 72 (2009): 276–96.

Taussig, Michael T. *Shamanism, Colonialism, and the Wild Man: A Study in Terror and Healing.* Chicago: University of Chicago Press, 1986.

Mimesis and Alterity: A Particular History of the Senses. New York: Routledge, 1993.

Terao, Ryukichi. "¿Ficción o testimonio, novela o reportaje? la novelística de la violencia en Colombia." *Contexto: Revista anual de estudios literarios* 9 (2003): 37–59.

Thurner, Mark, and Andrés Guerrero. *After Spanish Rule: Postcolonial Predicaments of the Americas.* Durham, NC: Duke University Press, 2003.

Tillis, Antonio D. "Changó, el gran putas de Manuel Zapata Olivella: un volver a imaginar y localizar Haití y su revolución mediante una alegoría postcolonial." *Afro-Hispanic Review* 25, no. 1 (2006): 105–14.

Tlostanova, M. V., and Walter Mignolo. *Learning to Unlearn: Decolonial Reflections from Eurasia and the Americas.* Columbus: Ohio State University Press, 2012.

"Postsocialist ≠ Postcolonial? On Post-Soviet Imaginary and Global Coloniality." *Journal of Postcolonial Writing* 48, no. 2 (2012): 130–42.

Toro, Alfonso, and Fernando Toro. *El debate de la postcolonialidad en Latinoamérica: Una postmodernidad periférica o cambio de paradigma en el pensamiento latinoamericano.* Madrid: Iberoamericana, 1999.

Torres-Saillant, Silvio. *An Intellectual History of the Caribbean.* New York: Palgrave Macmillan, 2006.

Troyan, Brett. "Re-imagining the 'Indian' and the State. Indigenismo in Colombia, 1926–1947." *Canadian Journal of Latin American and Caribbean Studies* 33, no. 65 (2008): 81–106.

Upstone, Sara. "Magical Realism and Postcolonial Studies: Twenty-First Century Perspectives." *Journal of Commonwealth and Postcolonial Studies* 17, no. 1 (2011): 153–63.

Valero, Silvia M. "Los complejos caminos de las políticas de identidad "afrodescendiente."" www.visitasalpatio.com.co/pdf/No6/02_los_complejos_caminos.pdf.

"¿De qué hablamos cuando hablamos de "literatura afrocolombiana"? o los riesgos de las categorizaciones." *Estudios de Literatura Colombiana* 32 (2013): 15–37.

"El poder de definir identidades y (des)proveer de agencia literaria: el caso de los afrodescendientes en Colombia." *Estudios de literatura colombiana* 20 (January–June 2007): 103–20. http://aprendeenlinea.udea.edu.co/revistas/index.php/elc/article/view/16410/14253.

Vélez Rendón, Juan Carlos. "Violencia, memoria y literatura testimonial en Colombia. Entre las memorias literales y las memorias ejemplares." *Estudios Políticos* 22, no. 1 (2003): 31–57. Universidad de Antioquia, Medellín. http://bibliotecavirtual.clacso.org.ar/ar/libros/colombia/iep/22/03-velez-rendon.pdf.

Vidal, Hernán. "The Concept of Colonial and Postcolonial Discourse: A Perspective from Literary Criticism." *Latin American Research Review* 28, no. 3 (1993): 113–19.

Von der Walde, Erna. "Realismo mágico y poscolonialismo: construcciones del otro desde la otredad." www.ensayistas.org/critica/teoria/castro/walde.htm.

Wade, Peter. "Identidad y etnicidad." In *Escobar, Arturo and Álvaro Pedrosa. Pacífico ¿desarrollo o diversidad? Estado, capital y movimientos sociales en el Pacífico colombiano.* Bogotá: Ecofondo-CEREC, 1996. 283–98.

Blackness and Race Mixture: The Dynamics of Racial Identity in Colombia. Baltimore: Johns Hopkins University Press, 1993.

Gente negra, nación mestiza. Dinámicas de las identidades raciales en Colombia. Bogotá: Universidad de Antioquia, Centro Colombiano de Antropología, 1997.

Walsh, Catherine, coord. Pueblos de descendencia africana en Colombia y Ecuador. Compilación bibliográfica. www.uasb.edu.ec/tallerint/Compilacion_bibliografica_Ecuador-Colombia.pdf.

Weldt-Basson, Helene C. *Redefining Latin American Historical Fiction: The Impact of Feminism and Postcolonialism.* New York: Palgrave Macmillan, 2013.

Williams, Raymond L. *Posmodernidades latinoamericanas: la novela posmoderna en Colombia, Venezuela, Ecuador, Perú y Bolivia.* Bogotá: Fundación Universal Central, 1998.

The Postmodern Novel in Latin America: Politics, Culture, and the Crisis of Truth. New York: St. Martin's Press, 1995.

Wylie, Lesley. *Colonial Tropes and Postcolonial Tricks.* Liverpool: Liverpool University Press, 2009.

"Colonial Tropes and Postcolonial Tricks." *Modern Language Review* 101, no. 3 (2006): 728–42.

Young, Robert J. C. *Colonial Desire: Hybridity in Theory, Culture and Race.* London: Routledge, 1995.

Zamora, Lois Parkinson, and Wendy Faris, eds. *Magical Realism: Theory, History, Community.* Durham: Duke University Press, 1995.

Zapata Olivella, Manuel. *El árbol brujo de la libertad. África en Colombia: orígenes, transculturación, presencia, ensayo histórico-mítico.* Buenaventura: Universidad del Pacífico, 2002.

Zapata Pérez, Edelma. "Toma de conciencia de una escritora afroindomulata en la sociedad multiétnica de Colombia." *América negra* 11 (1996): 175–85.

Notes

1 Gugelberger (1996); Beasley Murray (1998).
2 Shohat and Stam (1984:41).
3 Mignolo (2015:xxx).
4 Anderman (2015:4).
5 Coronil (2008:229).
6 Molloy (2005:370).
7 Stam and Shohat (2012).
8 Castro-Gómez and Grosfoguel (2007); Mignolo and Escobar (2010).
9 Young (1995:24).
10 Mignolo and Escobar (2010); Castro-Gómez (0000); Palermo (2009).
11 Mignolo (2011).
12 https://transnationaldecolonialinstitute.wordpress.com/decolonial-aesthetics/.
13 Mignolo (2014).
14 Marzec (2011:1).
15 Mignolo (2011:63).
16 Ashcroft (1998:16).
17 de la Campa (2002:3).
18 Ibid.
19 Bhaba (1990:7).
20 Faris (2002:101).
21 Ibid.
22 Siskind (2014:56, 61).
23 Jameson (1986).
24 Slemon (1995:407).
25 Siskind (2014:56).
26 Ibid., 85.
27 Beverly (1996:280).
28 Wylie (2006:729).
29 Ibid., 1.
30 Ibid., 1, 7–8.
31 Arbaiza (2012:132).
32 Mignolo (2011:48).
33 Rappaport (2003:318).

34 Ibid., 318–19.
35 Ibid., 329–30.
36 Ibid., 324–5.
37 Ibid., 325.
38 Troyan (2008:86).
39 Dennis (2012:82).
40 Ibid.
41 Ibid., 81.
42 Ibid., 93.
43 Valero, "Los complejos caminos de las políticas de identidad 'afrodescendiente,'" 10.
44 Quoted in Fernández Olmos and Paravisini-Gebert (2000:2).

Index

CPSIA information can be obtained
at www.ICGtesting.com
Printed in the USA
BVHW082052070223
658071BV00004B/11